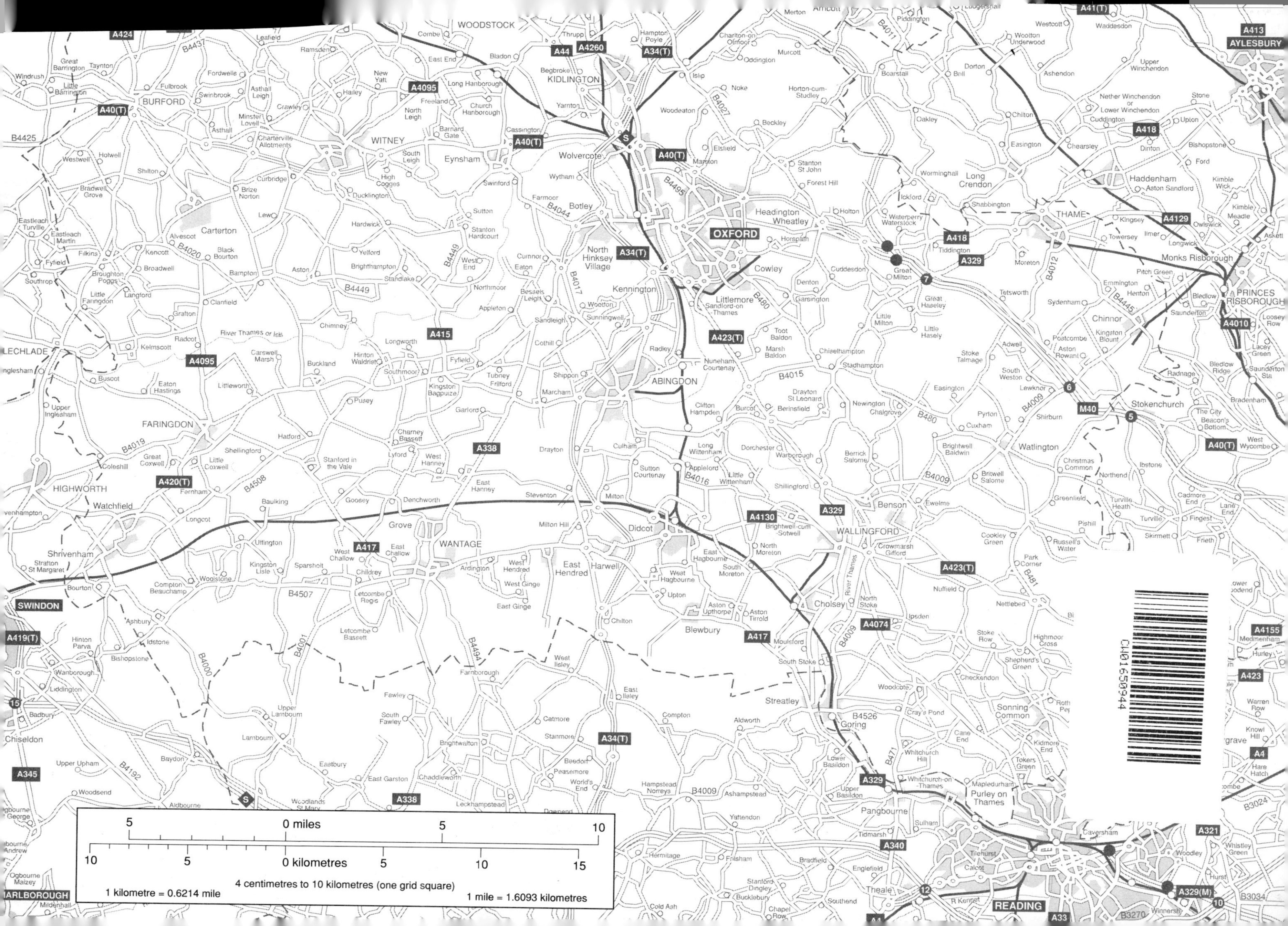
WOODSTOCK
KIDLINGTON
AYLESBURY
BURFORD
WITNEY
Eynsham
Wolvercote
OXFORD
Headington
Wheatley
Cowley
Littlemore
Long Crendon
Haddenham
THAME
Monks Risborough
PRINCES RISBOROUGH
Chinnor
Stokenchurch
Watlington
Benson
WALLINGFORD
ABINGDON
Kennington
North Hinksey Village
Botley
Carterton
LECHLADE
FARINGDON
HIGHWORTH
Watchfield
Shrivenham
SWINDON
Grove
WANTAGE
Didcot
Harwell
East Hendred
Cholsey
Blewbury
Streatley
Goring
Pangbourne
Purley on Thames
Sonning Common
READING
Theale
ARLBOROUGH
River Thames or Isis
River Thames
A40(T)
A34(T)
A4260
A44
A4095
A415
A338
A417
A420(T)
A329
A418
A4129
A4010
A423(T)
A4130
A4074
A340
A345
A419(T)
A413
A41(T)
A424
A423
A4155
A4
A321
A329(M)
A33
M40
B4015
B4009
B4449
B4507
B4000
B4494
B4001
B4016
B4017
B4480
B4020
B4508
B4019
B4192
B4526
B4481
B4027
B4011
B4012
B4445
B4425
B4437
B4044
B4495
B3270
B3034
B3024
0 miles
5
10
0 kilometres
15
4 centimetres to 10 kilometres (one grid square)
1 kilometre = 0.6214 mile
1 mile = 1.6093 kilometres

COUNTY
STREET ATLAS

OXFORDSHIRE

[redacted]

Ordnance Survey

COUNTY STREET ATLAS

PHILIP'S

OXFORDSHIRE

3½ INCHES TO 1 MILE

1st edition

COUNTY STREET ATLAS
OXFORDSHIRE

First Edition published 1992 by

Ordnance Survey and George Philip Ltd

Ordnance Survey
Romsey Road
Maybush
Southampton SO9 4DH

George Philip Ltd
59 Grosvenor Street
London W1X 9DA

ISBN 0 540 05665 0 [George Philip]
ISBN 0 319 00302 7 [Ordnance Survey]

Printed in Great Britain by
Butler & Tanner Ltd, Frome and London

CONTENTS

Key to map pages	vi-vii
Administrative boundaries	viii
Street maps	1-260
Index explanation and abbreviations	262
Index of towns, villages and rural localities	263
Index of street names	264-279

KEY TO MAP SYMBOLS

British Rail Station

London Transport Station

Private Railway Station

Bus or Coach Station

Heliport

Police Station (may not be open 24hrs)

Hospital with Casualty Facilities (may not be open 24hrs)

Post Office

Place of Worship

Important Building

P Parking

120 Adjoining Page Indicator

Motorway and Dual Carriageway

Main or through road

A27(T) Road numbers (Dept of Transport)

Gate or obstruction to traffic (restrictions may not apply at all times and to all vehicles)

Footpath

Bridleway

Path

Track

The representation in this atlas of a road, track or path is no evidence of the existence of a right of way.

Amb Sta	Ambulance Station	LC	Level Crossing
Coll	College	Liby	Library
FB	Foot Bridge	Mus	Museum
F Sta	Fire Station	Sch	School
Hospl	Hospital	TH	Town Hall

The large letters and numbers around the edge of the maps are the referencing system. An explanation of how to use the system for locating the position of street names appears on page **262**. The small numbers identify the 1 kilometre National Grid lines.

Scale of Maps is 3½ inches to 1 mile (1 : 18103)

0 ¼ ½ ¾ 1 Mile

0 250m 500m 750m 1 Kilometre

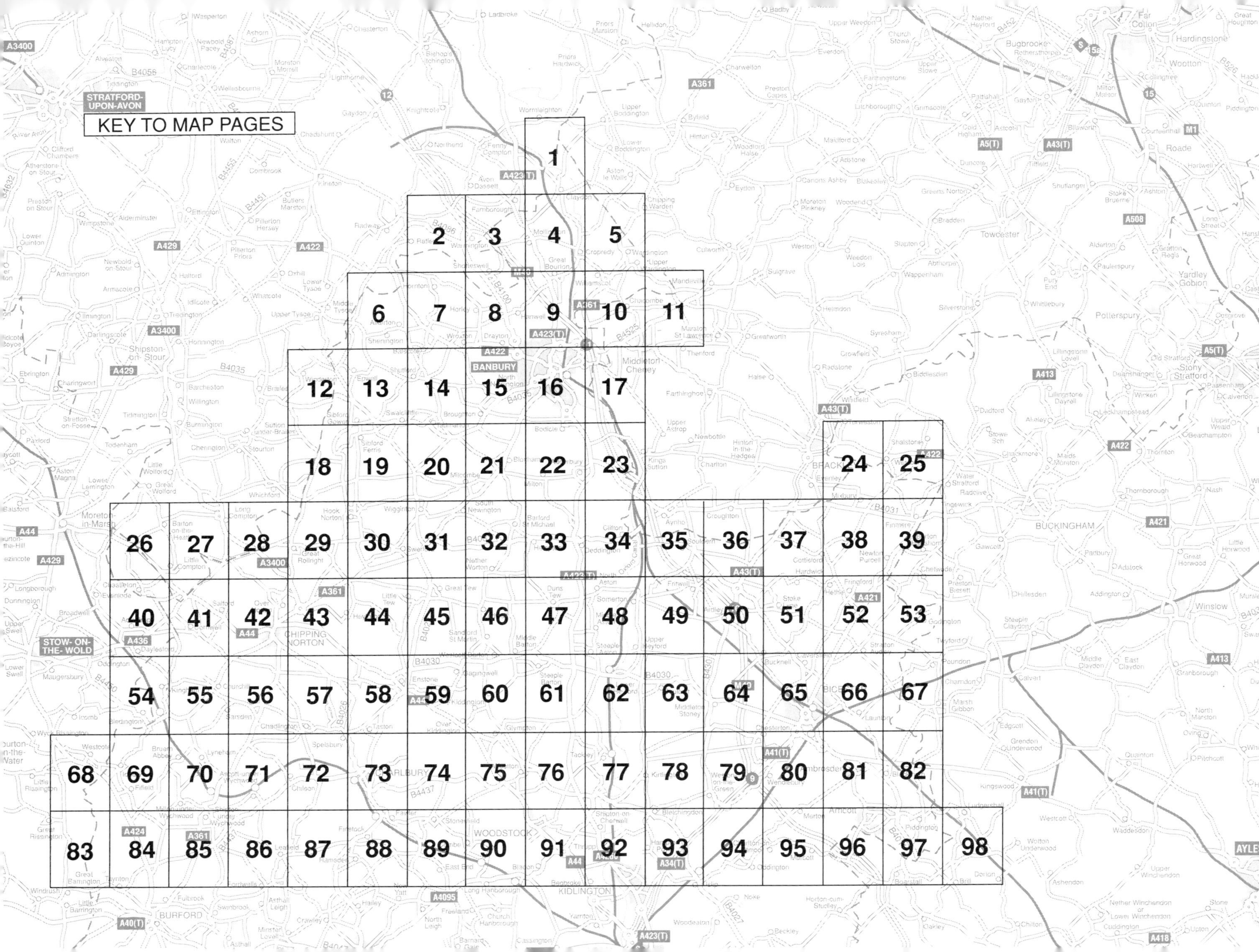
KEY TO MAP PAGES
STRATFORD-UPON-AVON
1
2 3 4 5
6 7 8 9 10 11
12 13 14 15 16 17
18 19 20 21 22 23 24 25
26 27 28 29 30 31 32 33 34 35 36 37 38 39
40 41 42 43 44 45 46 47 48 49 50 51 52 53
54 55 56 57 58 59 60 61 62 63 64 65 66 67
68 69 70 71 72 73 74 75 76 77 78 79 80 81 82
83 84 85 86 87 88 89 90 91 92 93 94 95 96 97 98
BANBURY
BUCKINGHAM
Towcester
STOW-ON-THE-WOLD
CHIPPING NORTON
WOODSTOCK
KIDLINGTON
BURFORD
AYLESBURY
Winslow
Middleton Cheney
Moreton-in-Marsh
Shipston-on-Stour
Potterspury
Stony Stratford
Wolverton

AYLESBURY
PRINCES RISBOROUGH
THAME
WOODSTOCK
KIDLINGTON
WITNEY
OXFORD
ABINGDON
WALLINGFORD
WANTAGE
FARINGDON
LECHLADE
SWINDON
READING
MARLBOROUGH
0 miles
5
10
0 kilometres
5
10
15
4 centimetres to 10 kilometres (one grid square)
1 kilometre = 0.6214 mile
1 mile = 1.6093 kilometres

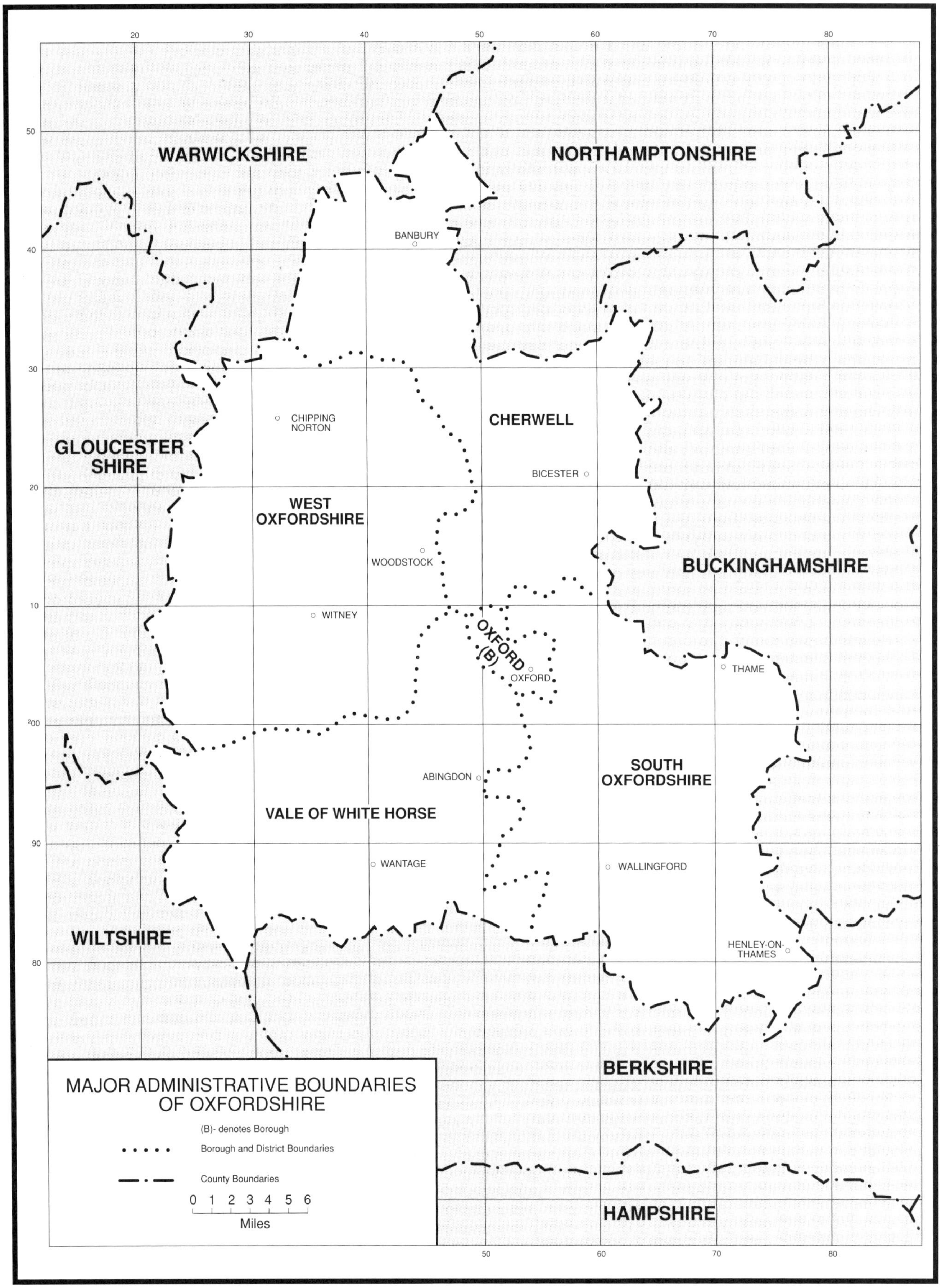
MAJOR ADMINISTRATIVE BOUNDARIES OF OXFORDSHIRE
(B)- denotes Borough
Borough and District Boundaries
County Boundaries
0 1 2 3 4 5 6
Miles
WARWICKSHIRE
NORTHAMPTONSHIRE
GLOUCESTER SHIRE
BUCKINGHAMSHIRE
WILTSHIRE
BERKSHIRE
HAMPSHIRE
CHERWELL
WEST OXFORDSHIRE
OXFORD (B)
SOUTH OXFORDSHIRE
VALE OF WHITE HORSE
BANBURY
CHIPPING NORTON
BICESTER
WOODSTOCK
WITNEY
OXFORD
THAME
ABINGDON
WANTAGE
WALLINGFORD
HENLEY-ON-THAMES
20
30
40
50
60
70
80
90
200

not continued, see key diagram

not continued, see key diagram

not continued, see key diagram

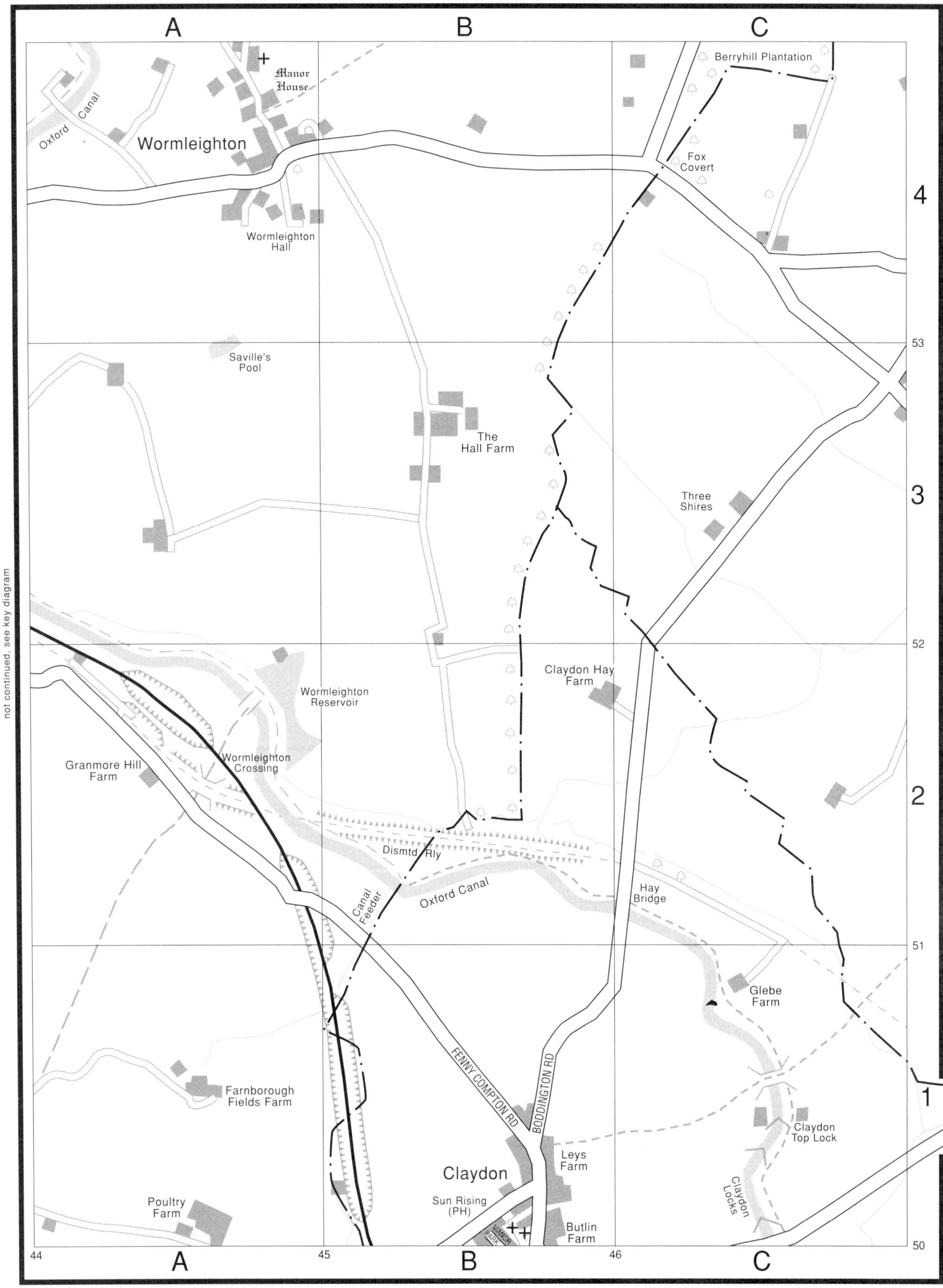

4

not continued, see key diagram

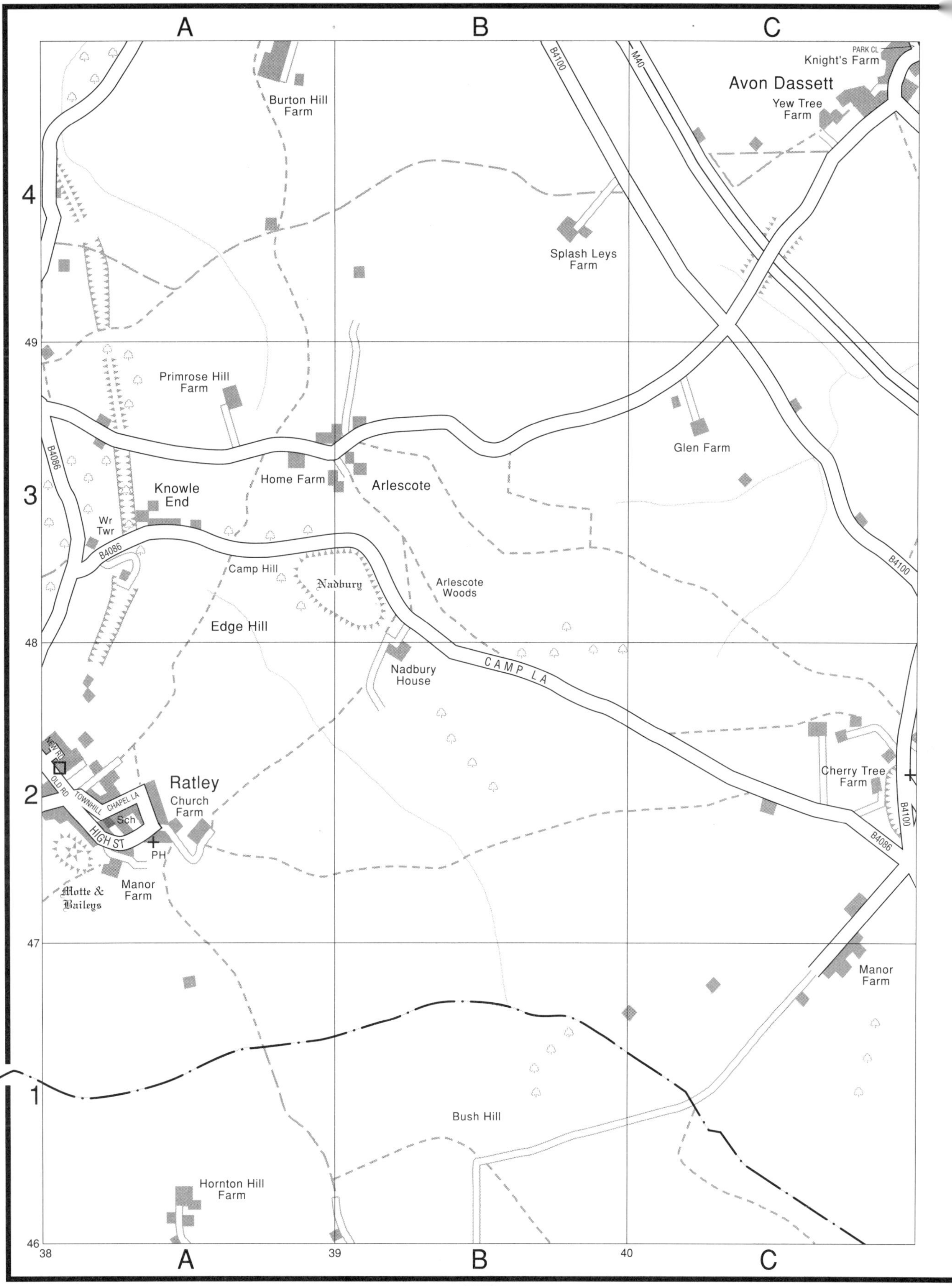

not continued, see key diagram

7

not continued, see key diagram

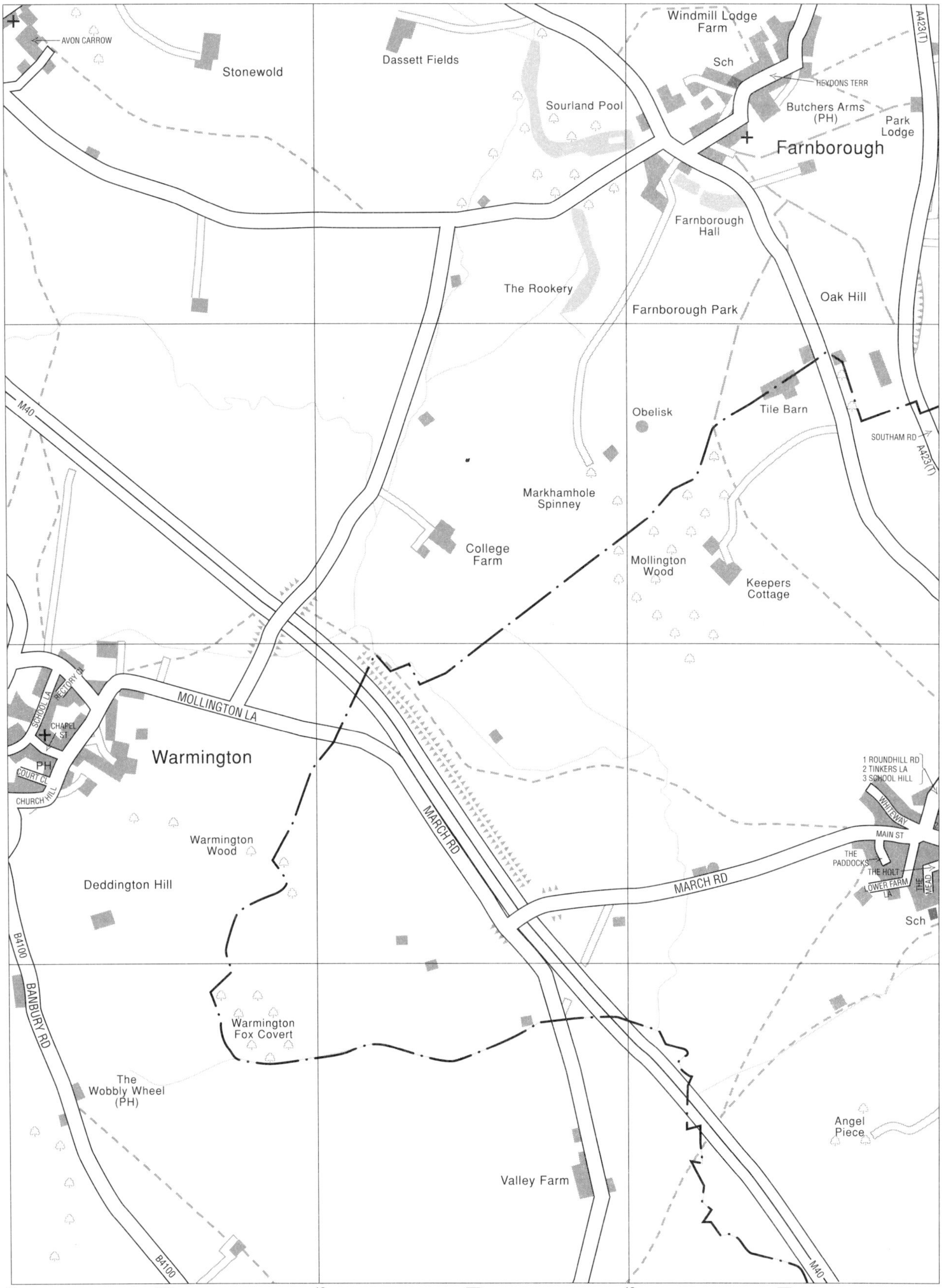

4

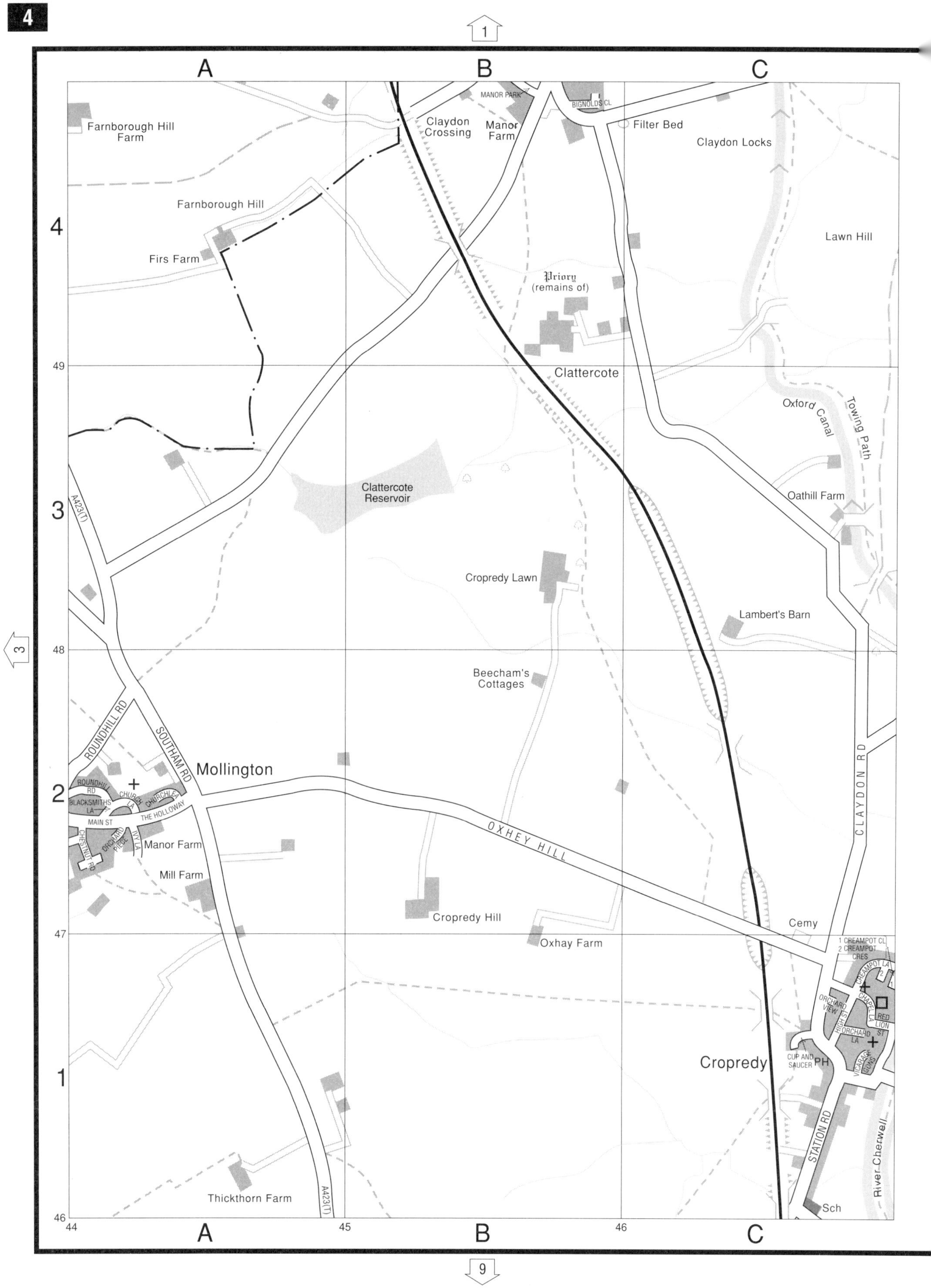
1
A
B
C
Farnborough Hill Farm
Claydon Crossing
MANOR PARK
Manor Farm
BIGNOLDS CL
Filter Bed
Claydon Locks
Farnborough Hill
4
Firs Farm
Lawn Hill
Priory (remains of)
49
Clattercote
Oxford Canal
Towing Path
Clattercote Reservoir
Oathill Farm
3
A423(T)
Cropredy Lawn
Lambert's Barn
3
48
Beecham's Cottages
ROUNDHILL RD
SOUTHAM RD
Mollington
CLAYDON RD
2
ROUNDHILL RD
CHURCH LA
CHURCH LA
BLACKSMITHS LA
THE HOLLOWAY
MAIN ST
CHESTNUT RD
ORCHARD PIECE
IVY LA
Manor Farm
OXHEY HILL
Mill Farm
Cropredy Hill
Cemy
47
Oxhay Farm
1 CREAMPOT CL
2 CREAMPOT CRES
CREAMPOT LA
CHAPEL LA
ORCHARD VIEW
HIGH ST
RED LION ST
ORCHARD LA
VICARAGE GDNS
CUP AND SAUCER
PH
Cropredy
1
STATION RD
River Cherwell
Thickthorn Farm
A423(T)
Sch
46
44
45
46
A
B
C
9

not continued, see key diagram

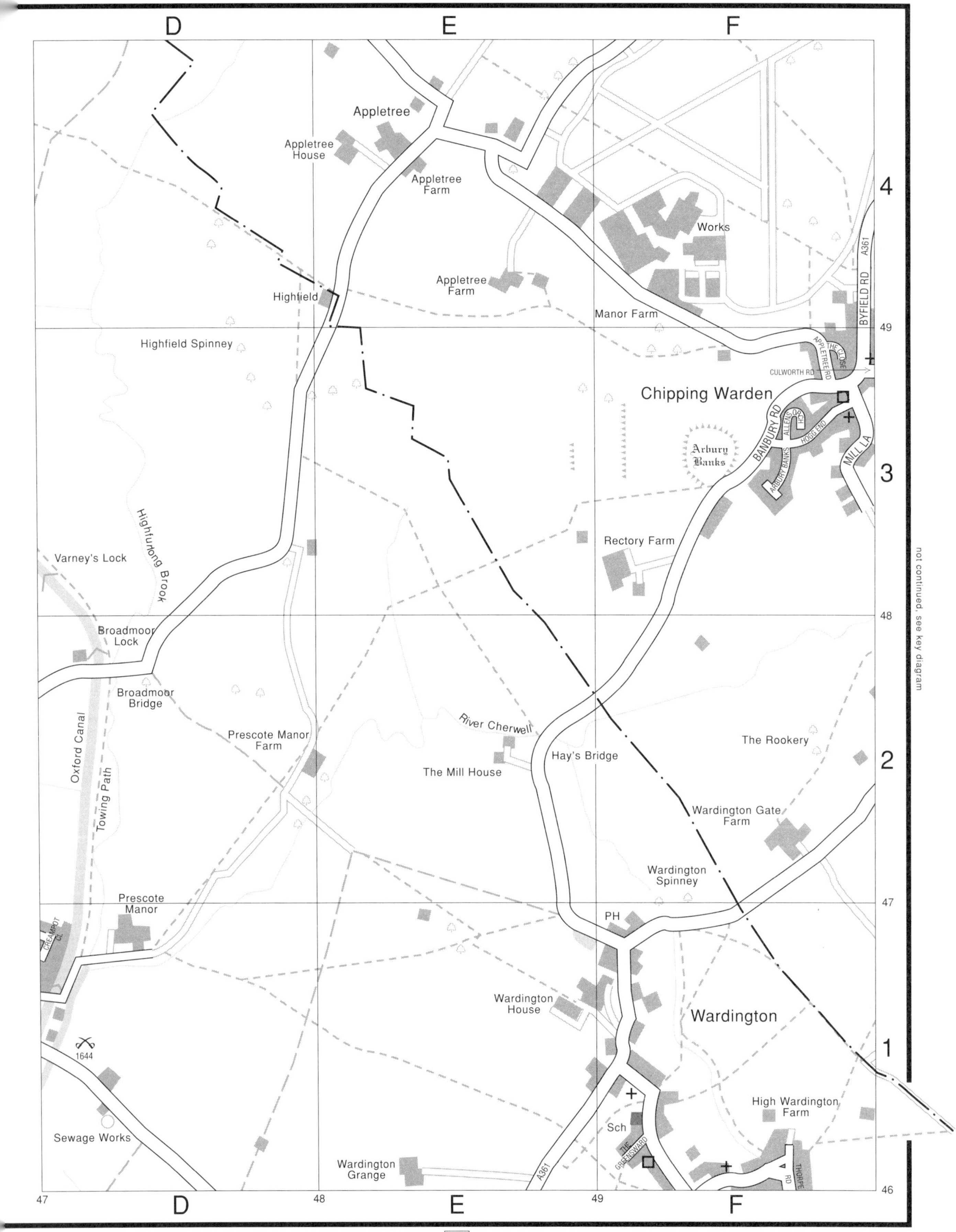

not continued, see key diagram

10

not continued, see key diagram

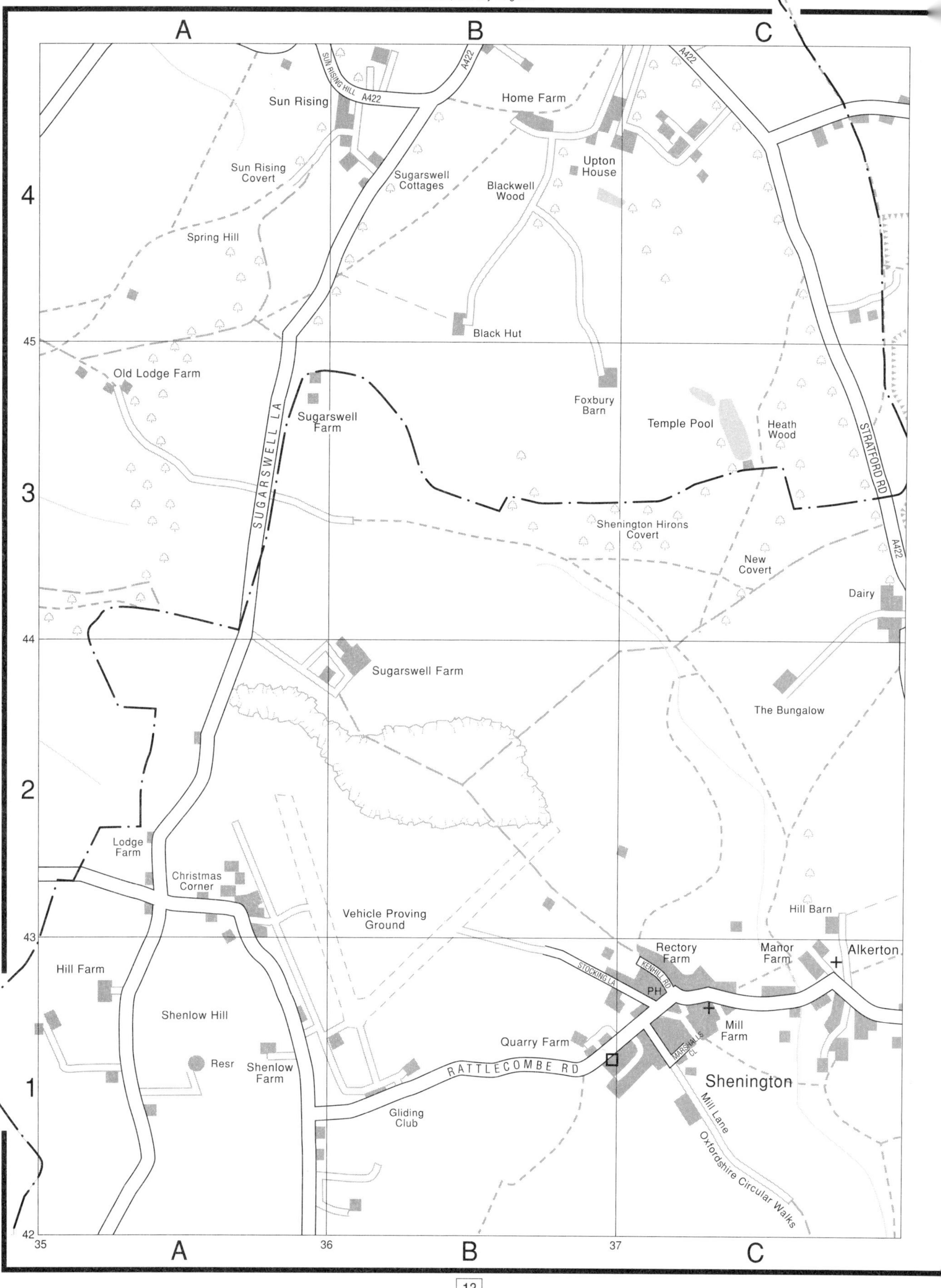

not continued, see key diagram

13

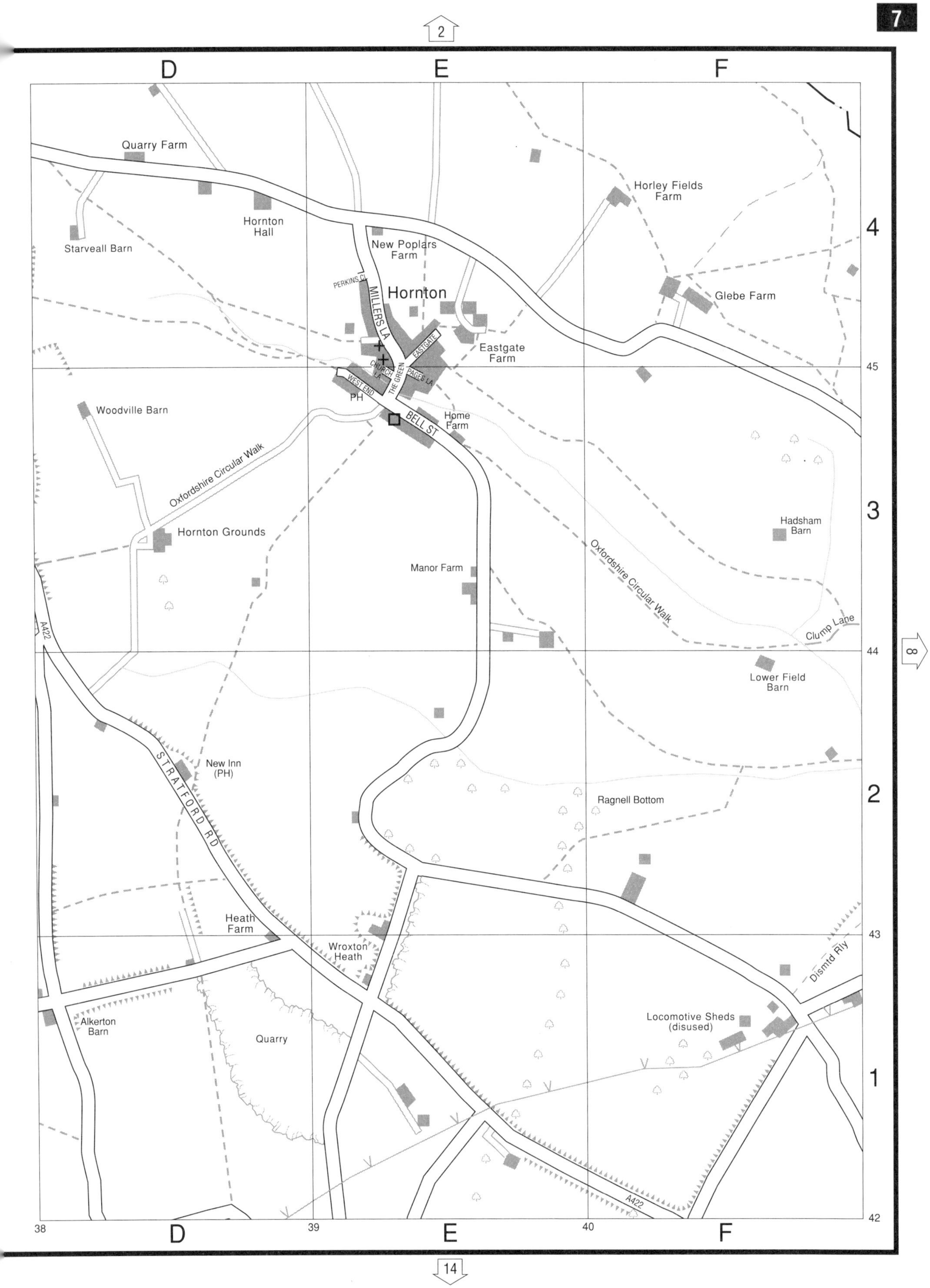
2
D
E
F
Quarry Farm
Hornton Hall
Starveall Barn
New Poplars Farm
Horley Fields Farm
Hornton
PERKINS CL
MILLERS LA
EASTGATE
CHURCH LA
THE GREEN
PAGES LA
WEST END
PH
BELL ST
Glebe Farm
Eastgate Farm
Woodville Barn
Home Farm
Oxfordshire Circular Walk
Hornton Grounds
Manor Farm
Oxfordshire Circular Walk
Hadsham Barn
Clump Lane
A422
Lower Field Barn
STRATFORD RD
New Inn (PH)
Ragnell Bottom
Heath Farm
Wroxton Heath
Dismtd Rly
Alkerton Barn
Quarry
Locomotive Sheds (disused)
A422
4
3
2
1
45
44
43
42
38
39
40
8
14

3

7

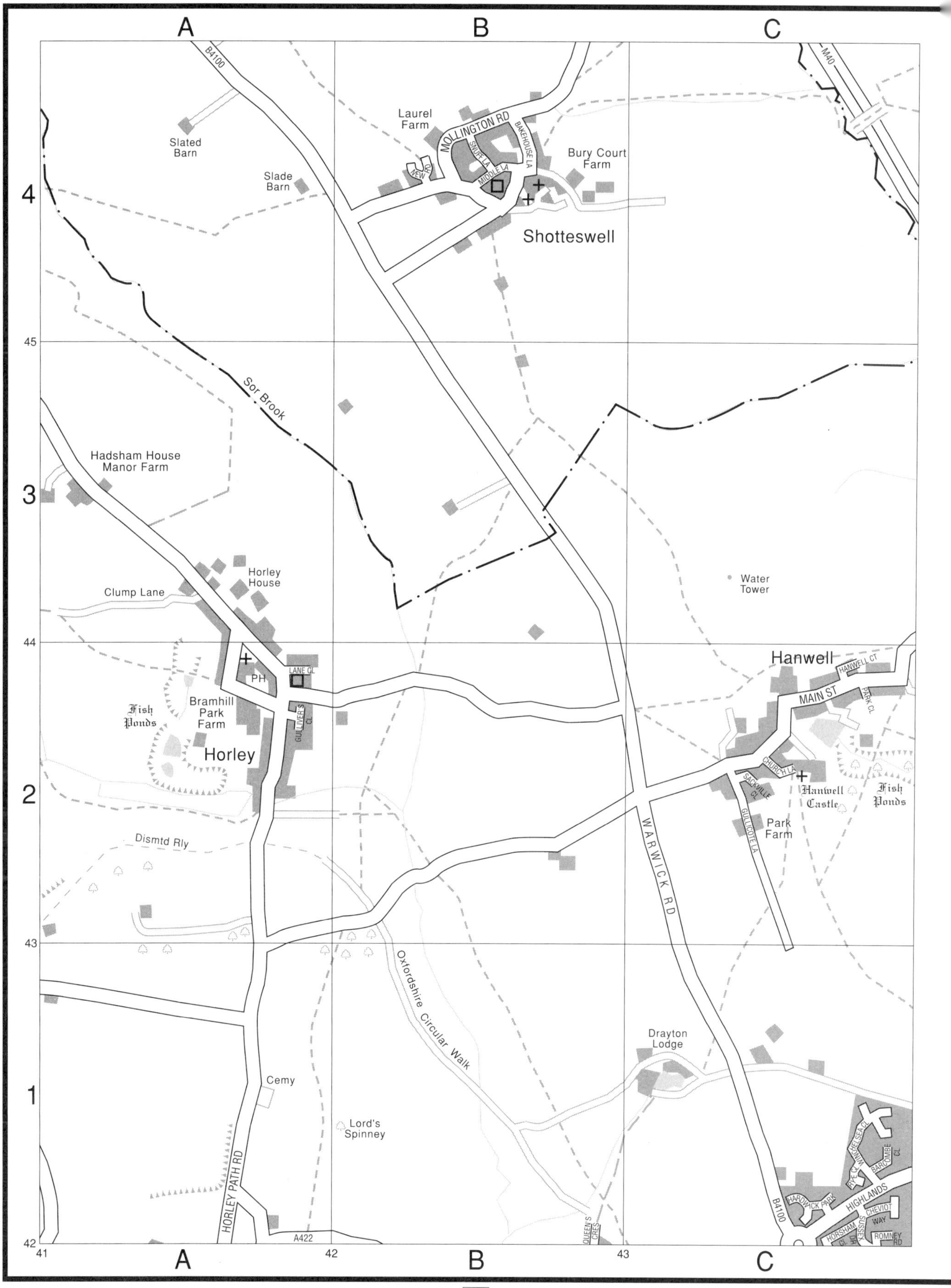

A
B
C
B4100
M40
Laurel Farm
MOLLINGTON RD
BAKEHOUSE LA
SNUFF LA
MIDDLE LA
NEW RD
Slated Barn
Slade Barn
Bury Court Farm
Shotteswell
Sor Brook
Hadsham House Manor Farm
Horley House
Clump Lane
Water Tower
PH
LANE CL
GULLIVER'S CL
Fish Ponds
Bramhill Park Farm
Horley
Hanwell
HANWELL CT
MAIN ST
PARK CL
CHURCH LA
SACKVILLE CL
GULLICOTE LA
Hanwell Castle
Fish Ponds
Park Farm
WARWICK RD
Dismtd Rly
Oxfordshire Circular Walk
Drayton Lodge
Cemy
Lord's Spinney
HORLEY PATH RD
A422
QUEEN'S CRES
B4100
HARDWICK PARK
WINCHELSEA CL
RYE CL
BARCOMBE CL
HIGHLANDS
CHEVIOT WAY
HORSHAM CL
SUSSEX DR
ROMNEY RD
4
45
3
44
2
43
1
42
41
42
43

15

4

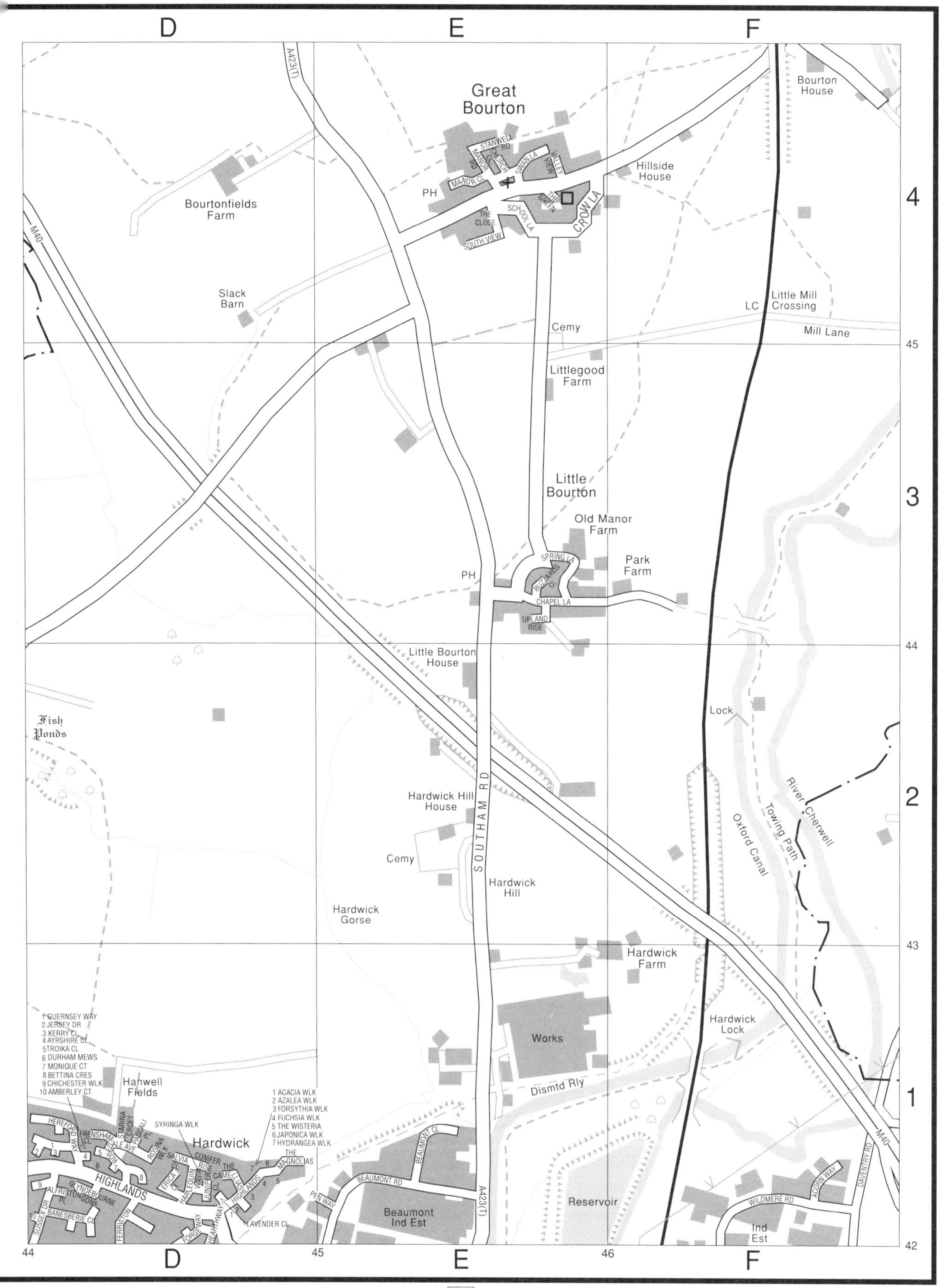
D
E
F
Great Bourton
Bourton House
Bourtonfields Farm
Hillside House
PH
STANWELL RD
MANOR RD
CHURCH CL
SWAN LA
VALLEY VIEW
MANOR CL
THE GREEN
SCHOOL LA
THE CLOSE
SOUTH VIEW
CROW LA
A423(T)
M40
Slack Barn
LC
Little Mill Crossing
Mill Lane
Cemy
Littlegood Farm
Little Bourton
Old Manor Farm
Park Farm
SPRING LA
BUZZARDS CL
CHAPEL LA
UPLAND RISE
Little Bourton House
Fish Ponds
Lock
River Cherwell
Towing Path
Oxford Canal
Hardwick Hill House
SOUTHAM RD
Hardwick Hill
Hardwick Gorse
Hardwick Farm
Works
Hardwick Lock
Dismtd Rly
Hanwell Fields
Hardwick
1 GUERNSEY WAY
2 JERSEY DR
3 KERRY CL
4 AYRSHIRE CL
5 TROIKA CL
6 DURHAM MEWS
7 MONIQUE CT
8 BETTINA CRES
9 CHICHESTER WLK
10 AMBERLEY CT
1 ACACIA WLK
2 AZALEA WLK
3 FORSYTHIA WLK
4 FUCHSIA WLK
5 THE WISTERIA
6 JAPONICA WLK
7 HYDRANGEA WLK
SYRINGA WLK
HEREFORD WAY
FRENSHAM CL
STARINA CROFT
PASCALI PL
ROSINA WLK
SALVIA CL
CONIFER RISE
THE CAMELLIAS
THE MAGNOLIAS
HIGHLANDS
GLYNDEBOURNE
ALFRISTON GDNS
BANESBERIE CL
SUSSEX DR
FERRISTON
ERICA CL
HARLEQUIN WAY
JUNIPER CL
FORGE WAY
HEARTHWAY
LAVENDER CL
PEN WAY
BEAUMONT CL
BEAUMONT RD
Beaumont Ind Est
Reservoir
WILDMERE RD
ACORN WAY
DAVENTRY RD
Ind Est
4
3
2
1
45
44
43
42
46

10

16

5

9

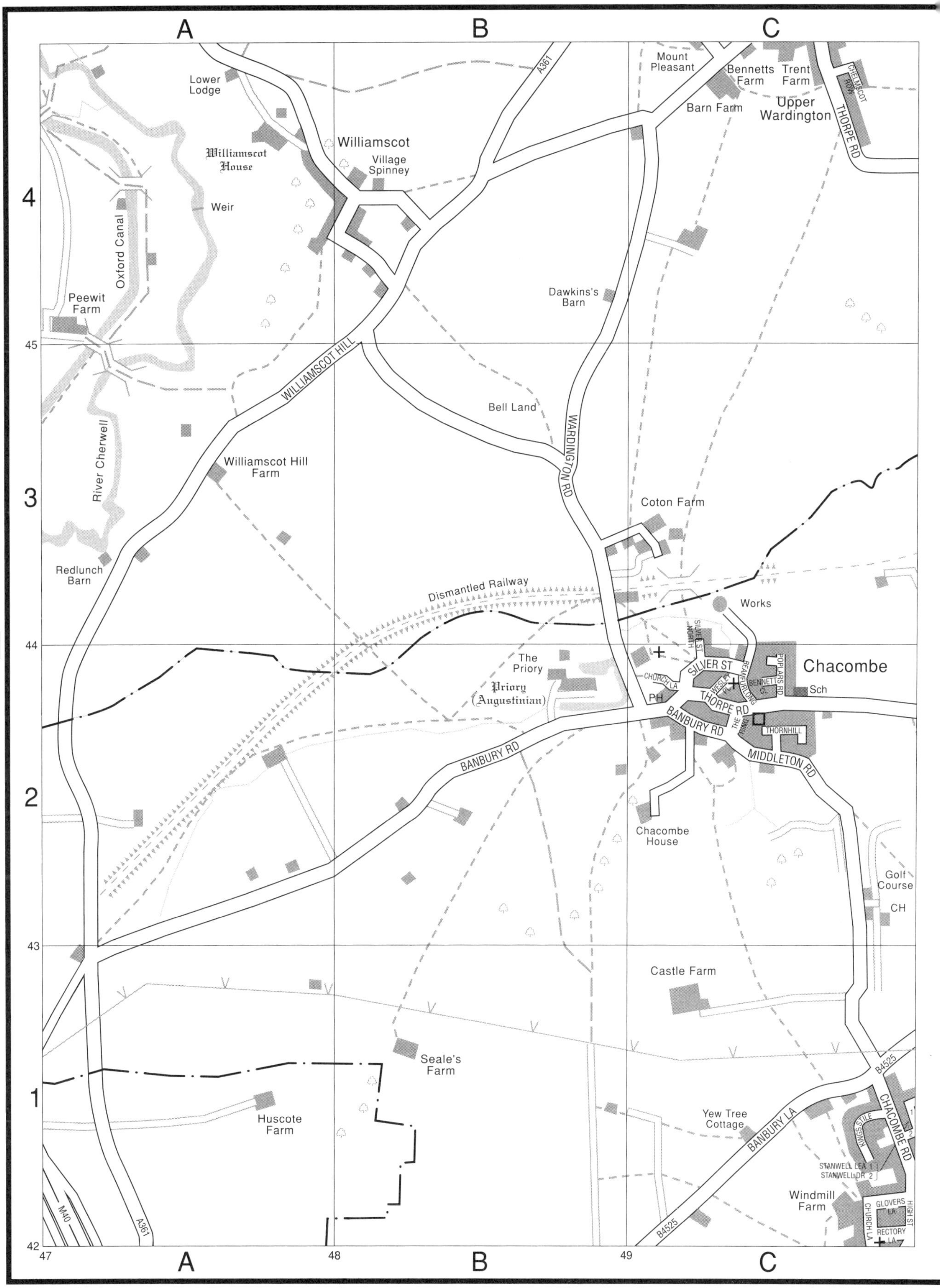
A
B
C
4
3
2
1
45
44
43
42
47
48
49
Lower Lodge
Williamscot
Williamscot House
Village Spinney
A361
Mount Pleasant
Bennetts Farm
Trent Farm
Upper Wardington
Barn Farm
CHELMSCOT ROW
THORPE RD
Weir
Oxford Canal
Peewit Farm
Dawkins's Barn
WILLIAMSCOT HILL
River Cherwell
Bell Land
WARDINGTON RD
Williamscot Hill Farm
Coton Farm
Redlunch Barn
Dismantled Railway
Works
NORTH
SILVER ST
Chacombe
The Priory
CHURCH LA
SILVER ST
WESLEY PL
BEANFURLONG
BENNETT CL
POPLARS RD
Sch
Priory (Augustinian)
PH
THORPE RD
BANBURY RD
THE RING
THORNHILL
BANBURY RD
MIDDLETON RD
Chacombe House
Golf Course
CH
Castle Farm
Seale's Farm
B4525
Huscote Farm
Yew Tree Cottage
BANBURY LA
KING'S STILE
CHACOMBE RD
STANWELL LEA
STANWELL DR
Windmill Farm
GLOVERS LA
HIGH ST
CHURCH LA
RECTORY LA
M40
A361
B4525

17

not continued, see key diagram

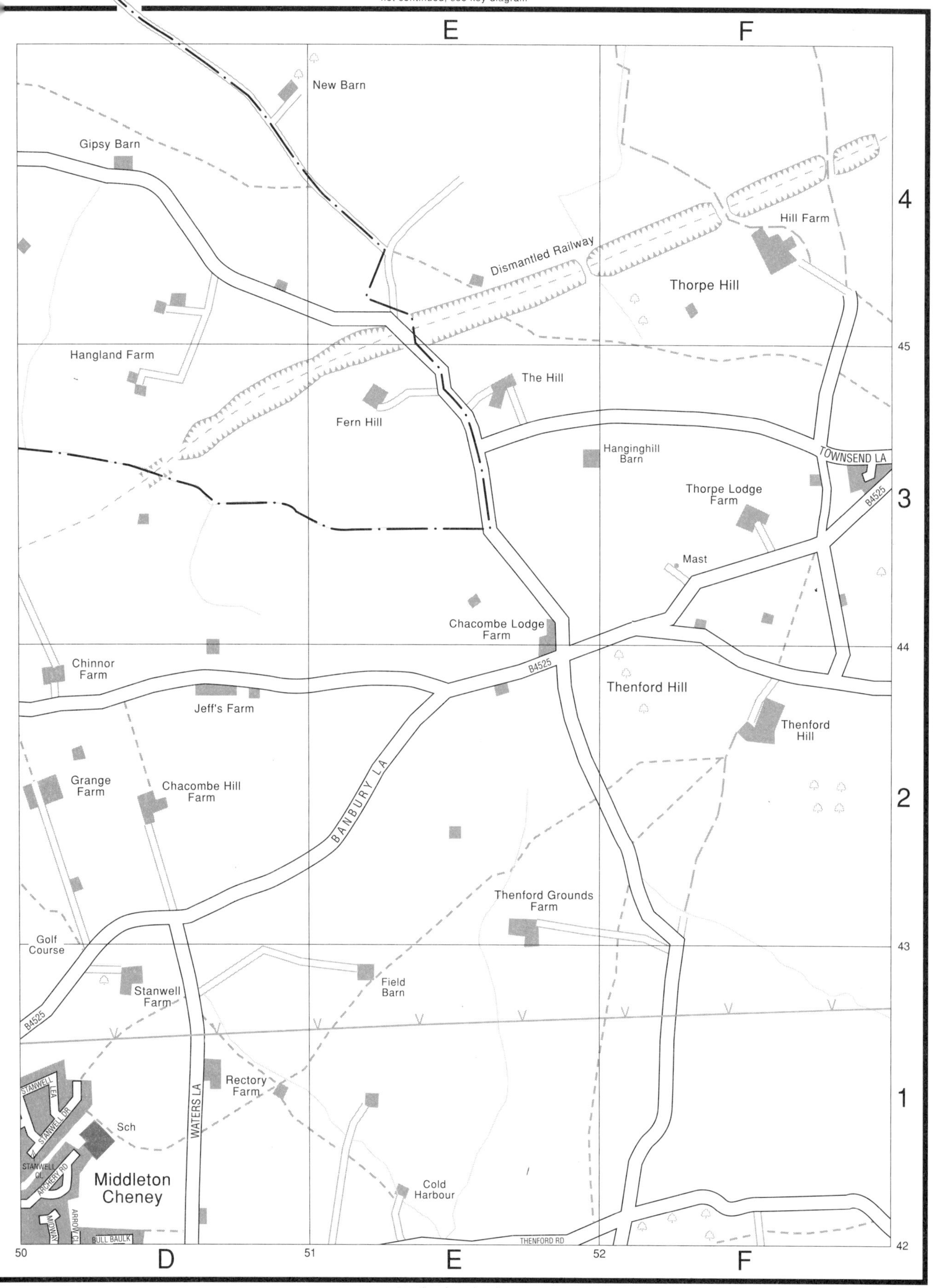

not continued, see key diagram

not continued, see key diagram

not continued, see key diagram

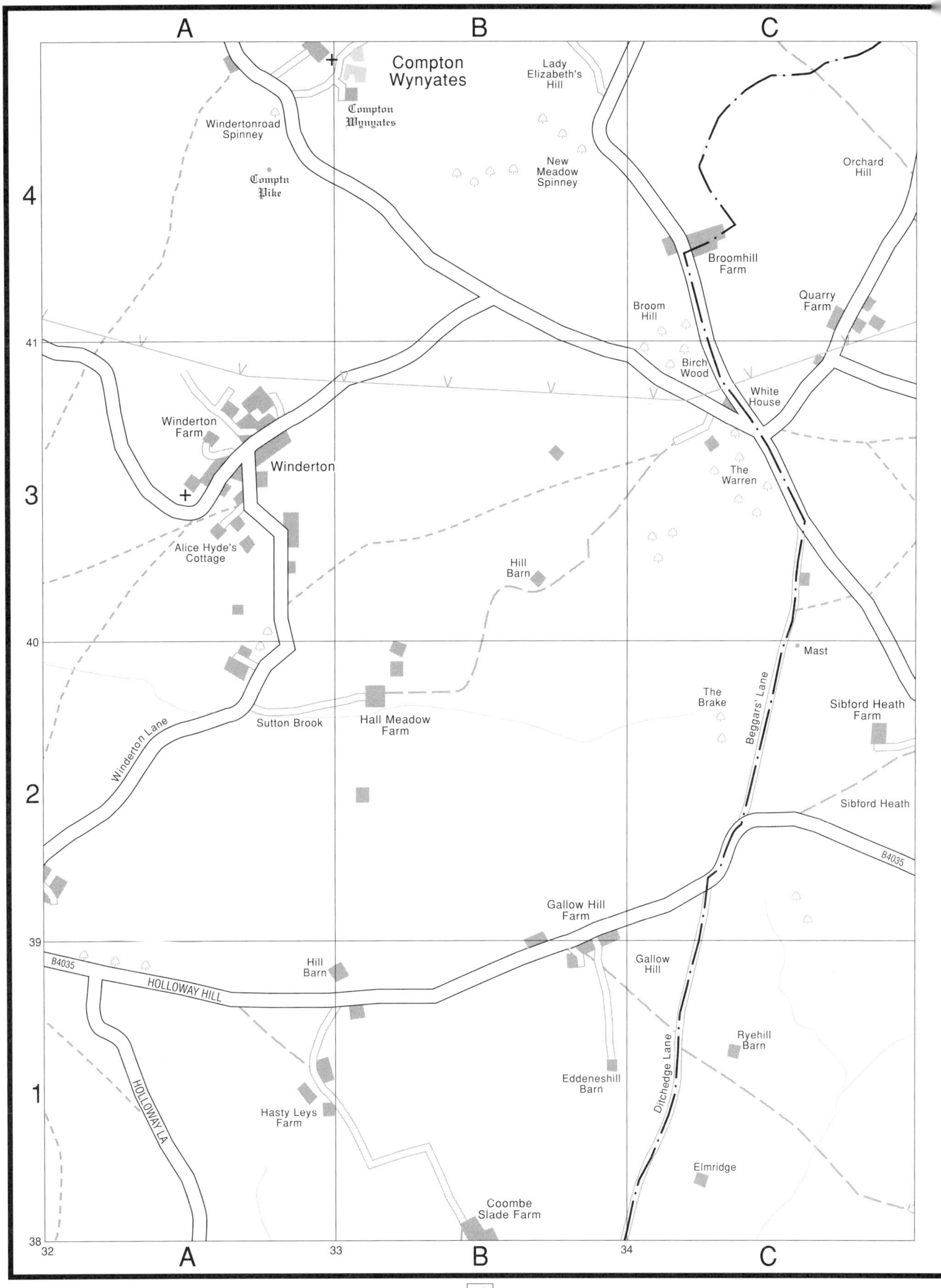

not continued, see key diagram

18

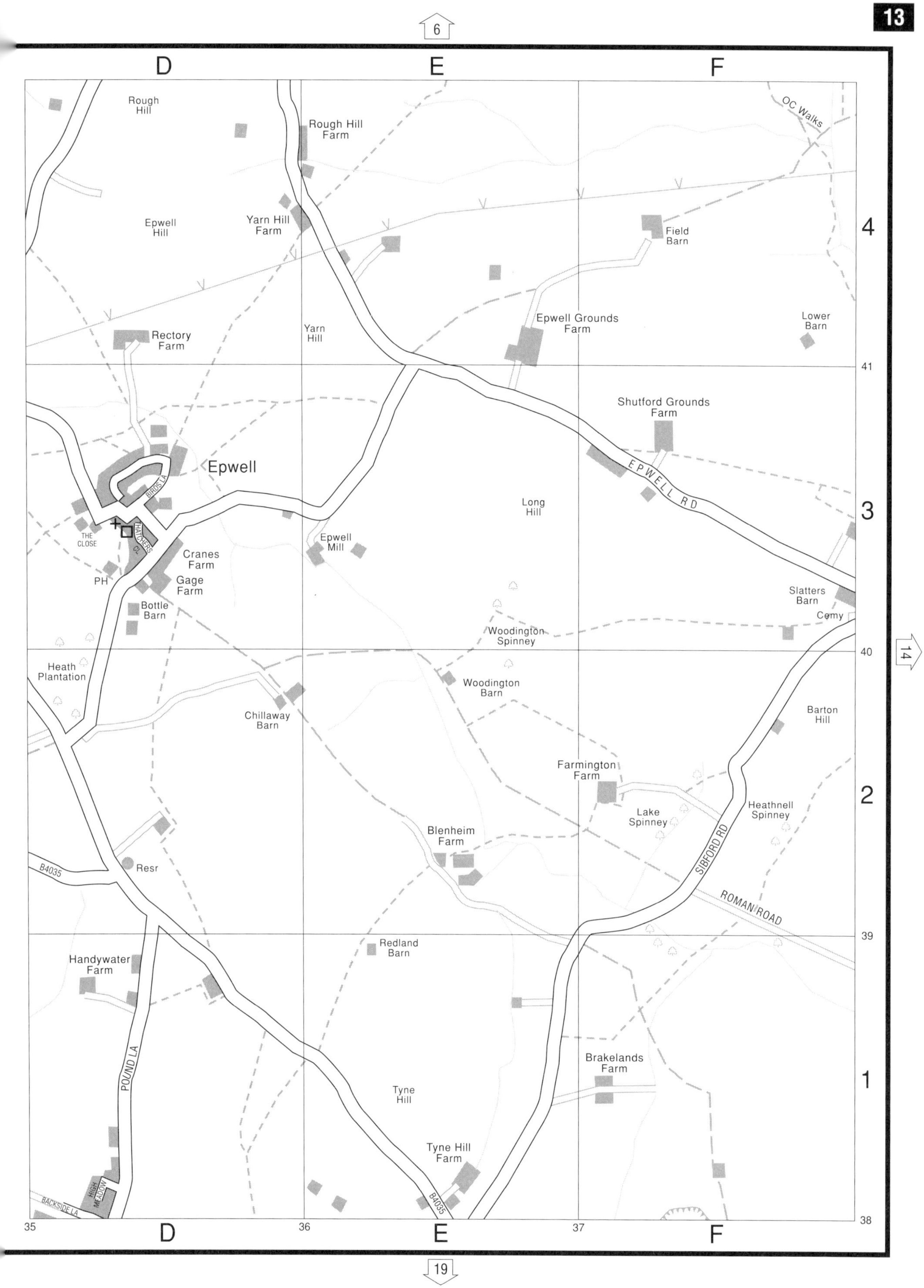
6
D
E
F
Rough Hill
Rough Hill Farm
OC Walks
Epwell Hill
Yarn Hill Farm
Field Barn
4
Rectory Farm
Yarn Hill
Epwell Grounds Farm
Lower Barn
41
Shutford Grounds Farm
Epwell
BIRDS LA
EPWELL RD
Long Hill
3
THE CLOSE
HATCHERS CL
Cranes Farm
Epwell Mill
PH
Gage Farm
Slatters Barn
Bottle Barn
Cemy
Woodington Spinney
14
Heath Plantation
40
Woodington Barn
Chillaway Barn
Barton Hill
Farmington Farm
2
Lake Spinney
Heathnell Spinney
Blenheim Farm
SIBFORD RD
B4035
Resr
ROMAN ROAD
Redland Barn
39
Handywater Farm
Brakelands Farm
1
POUND LA
Tyne Hill
Tyne Hill Farm
HIGH MEADOW
BACKSIDE LA
B4035
35
36
37
38
19

7

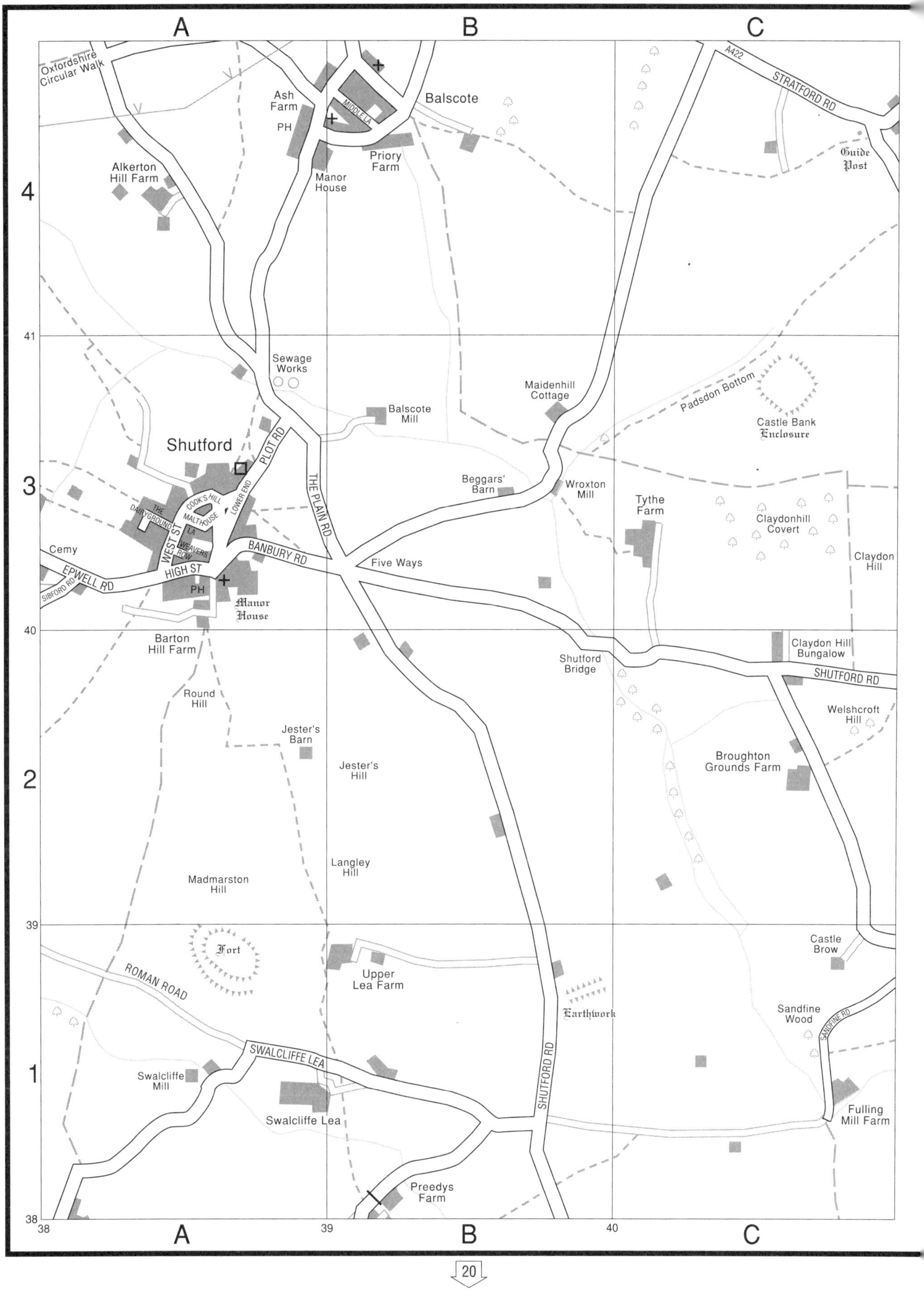

A
B
C
4
41
3
40
2
39
1
38
38
39
40
Oxfordshire Circular Walk
Ash Farm
PH
MIDDLE LA
Balscote
Priory Farm
Manor House
A422
STRATFORD RD
Guide Post
Alkerton Hill Farm
Sewage Works
Maidenhill Cottage
Padsdon Bottom
Castle Bank Enclosure
Balscote Mill
Shutford
PLOT RD
Beggars' Barn
Wroxton Mill
Tythe Farm
THE PLAIN RD
COOK'S HILL
LOWER END
THE DAIRYGROUND
MALTHOUSE LA
WEST ST
WEAVERS ROW
Claydonhill Covert
Cemy
BANBURY RD
Five Ways
Claydon Hill
EPWELL RD
HIGH ST
SIBFORD RD
PH
Manor House
Barton Hill Farm
Shutford Bridge
Claydon Hill Bungalow
SHUTFORD RD
Round Hill
Welshcroft Hill
Jester's Barn
Jester's Hill
Broughton Grounds Farm
Langley Hill
Madmarston Hill
Castle Brow
Fort
ROMAN ROAD
Upper Lea Farm
Earthwork
Sandfine Wood
SANDFINE RD
SWALCLIFFE LEA
Swalcliffe Mill
SHUTFORD RD
Swalcliffe Lea
Fulling Mill Farm
Preedys Farm

13

20

8

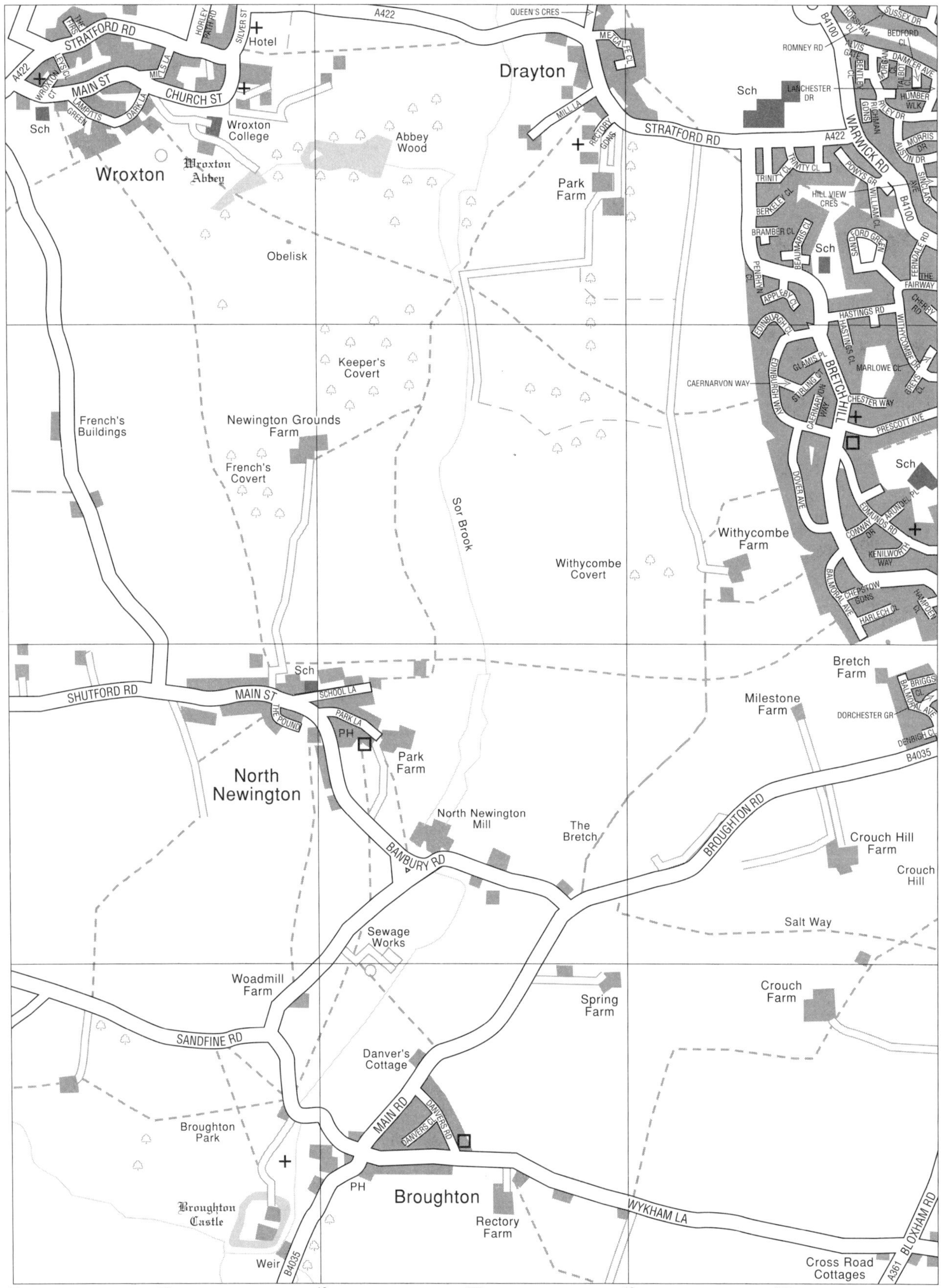

D
E
F
Wroxton
Drayton
Hotel
Sch
Wroxton College
Wroxton Abbey
Abbey Wood
Park Farm
Obelisk
Keeper's Covert
French's Buildings
Newington Grounds Farm
French's Covert
Sor Brook
Withycombe Farm
Withycombe Covert
STRATFORD RD
A422
MAIN ST
CHURCH ST
QUEEN'S CRES
MILL LA
RECTORY GDNS
METCALFE CL
WARWICK RD
B4100
BRETCH HILL
CAERNARVON WAY
MARLOWE CL
PRESCOTT AVE
CHESTER WAY
HASTINGS RD
TRINITY CL
HILL VIEW CRES
BRAMBER CL
BEAUMARIS CT
PENRHYN CL
APPLEBY CL
EDINBURGH CL
EDINBURGH WAY
GLAMIS PL
STIRLING CT
DOVER AVE
BALMORAL AVE
CHEPSTOW GDNS
HARLECH CL
KENILWORTH WAY
CONWAY DR
EDMUNDS RD
ARUNDEL PL
LARCHESTER DR
ROMNEY RD
THE FAIRWAY
FERNDALE RD
CHERRY RD
WITHYCOMBE DR
SANDFORD GREEN
POWYS GR
WILLIAM CL
4
3
2
1
41
40
39
38
North Newington
SHUTFORD RD
SCHOOL LA
PARK LA
THE POUND
PH
Park Farm
North Newington Mill
The Bretch
Bretch Farm
Milestone Farm
DORCHESTER GR
BRIGGS CL
DENBIGH CL
B4035
BROUGHTON RD
BANBURY RD
Crouch Hill Farm
Crouch Hill
Salt Way
Sewage Works
Woadmill Farm
Crouch Farm
Spring Farm
SANDFINE RD
Danver's Cottage
MAIN RD
DANVERS CL
DANVERS RD
Broughton Park
Broughton
Broughton Castle
Weir
Rectory Farm
WYKHAM LA
BLOXHAM RD
A361
Cross Road Cottages
42
43

16

21

9

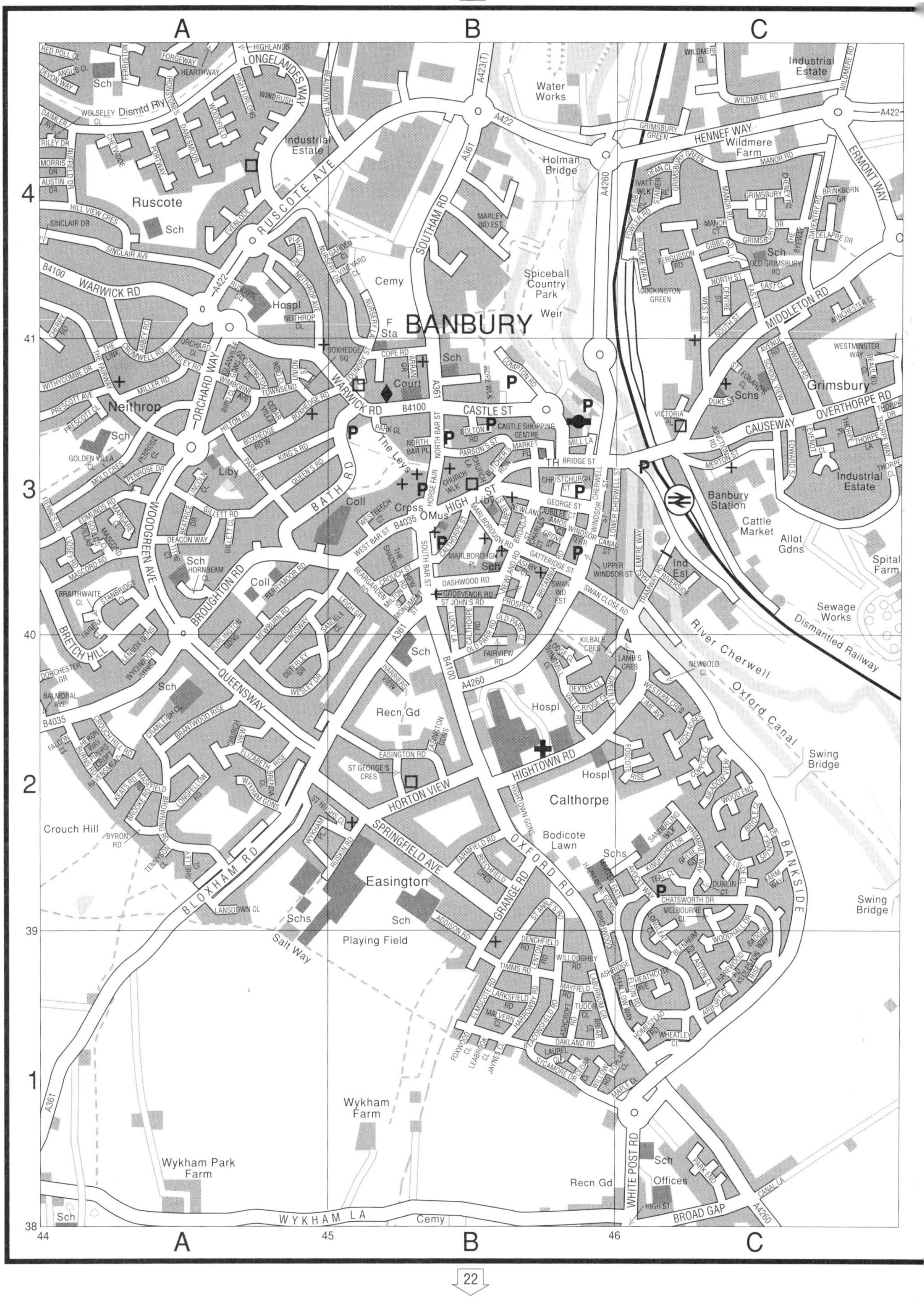
A
B
C
4
3
2
1
41
40
39
38
44
45
46
BANBURY
Ruscote
Neithrop
Grimsbury
Calthorpe
Easington
Crouch Hill
Bodicote Lawn
Industrial Estate
Water Works
Holman Bridge
Spiceball Country Park
Weir
Wildmere Farm
Banbury Station
Cattle Market
Allot Gdns
Spital Farm
Sewage Works
River Cherwell
Oxford Canal
Dismantled Railway
Dismtd Rly
Swing Bridge
Hospl
Cemy
Court
Liby
Coll
Cross
Mus
Sch
Schs
Recn Gd
Playing Field
Salt Way
Wykham Farm
Wykham Park Farm
Offices
Ind Est
WARWICK RD
RUSCOTE AVE
LONGELANDES WAY
SOUTHAM RD
HENNEF WAY
MIDDLETON RD
CAUSEWAY
OVERTHORPE RD
CASTLE ST
HIGH ST
BRIDGE ST
WOODGREEN AVE
ORCHARD WAY
BROUGHTON RD
QUEENSWAY
BRETCH HILL
BATH RD
HORTON VIEW
HIGHTOWN RD
SPRINGFIELD AVE
OXFORD RD
BLOXHAM RD
BANKSIDE
WHITE POST RD
BROAD GAP
WYKHAM LA
GRANGE RD
A422
A423(T)
A361
A4260
B4100
B4035

15

10

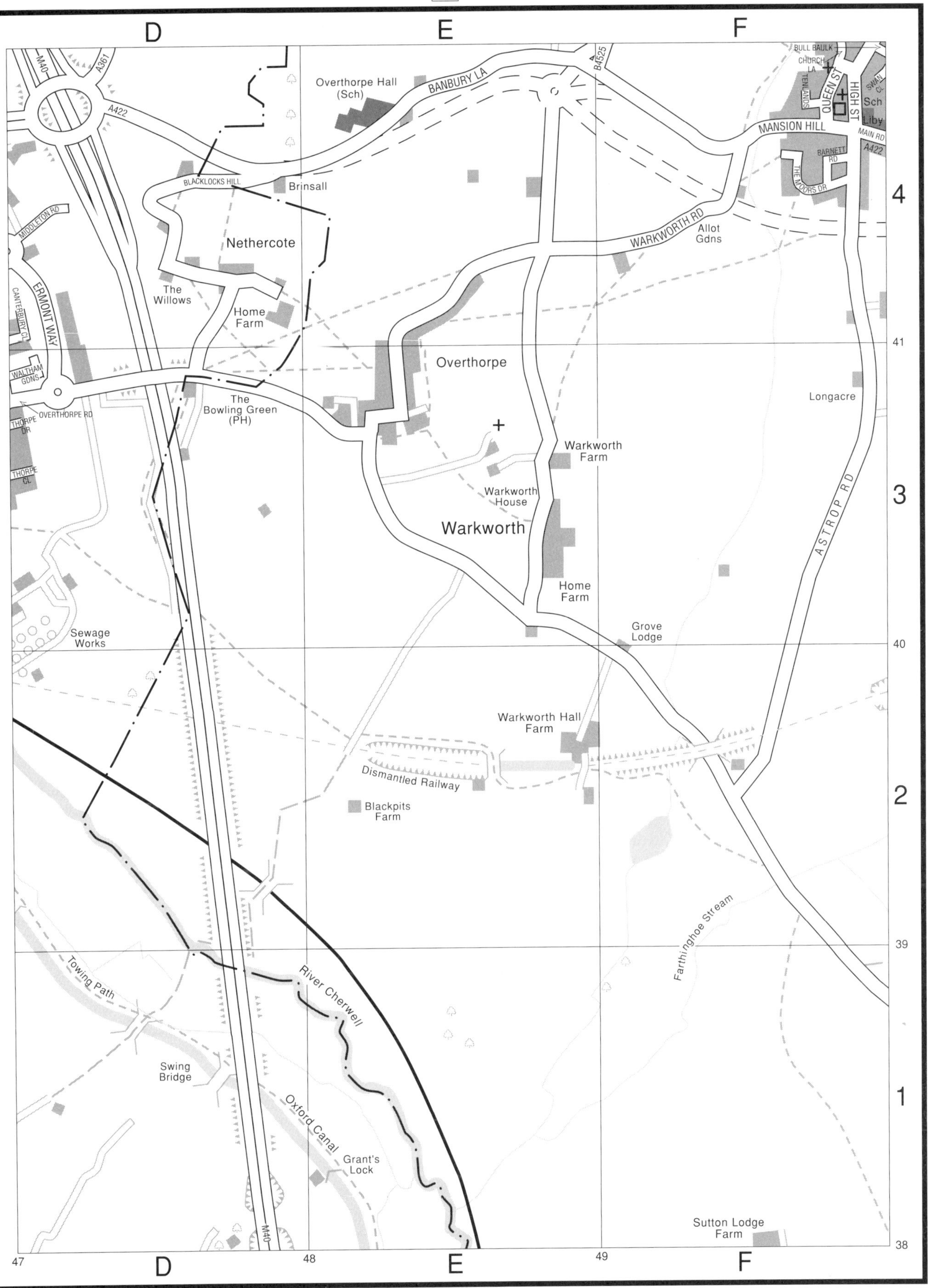

not continued, see key diagram

23

12

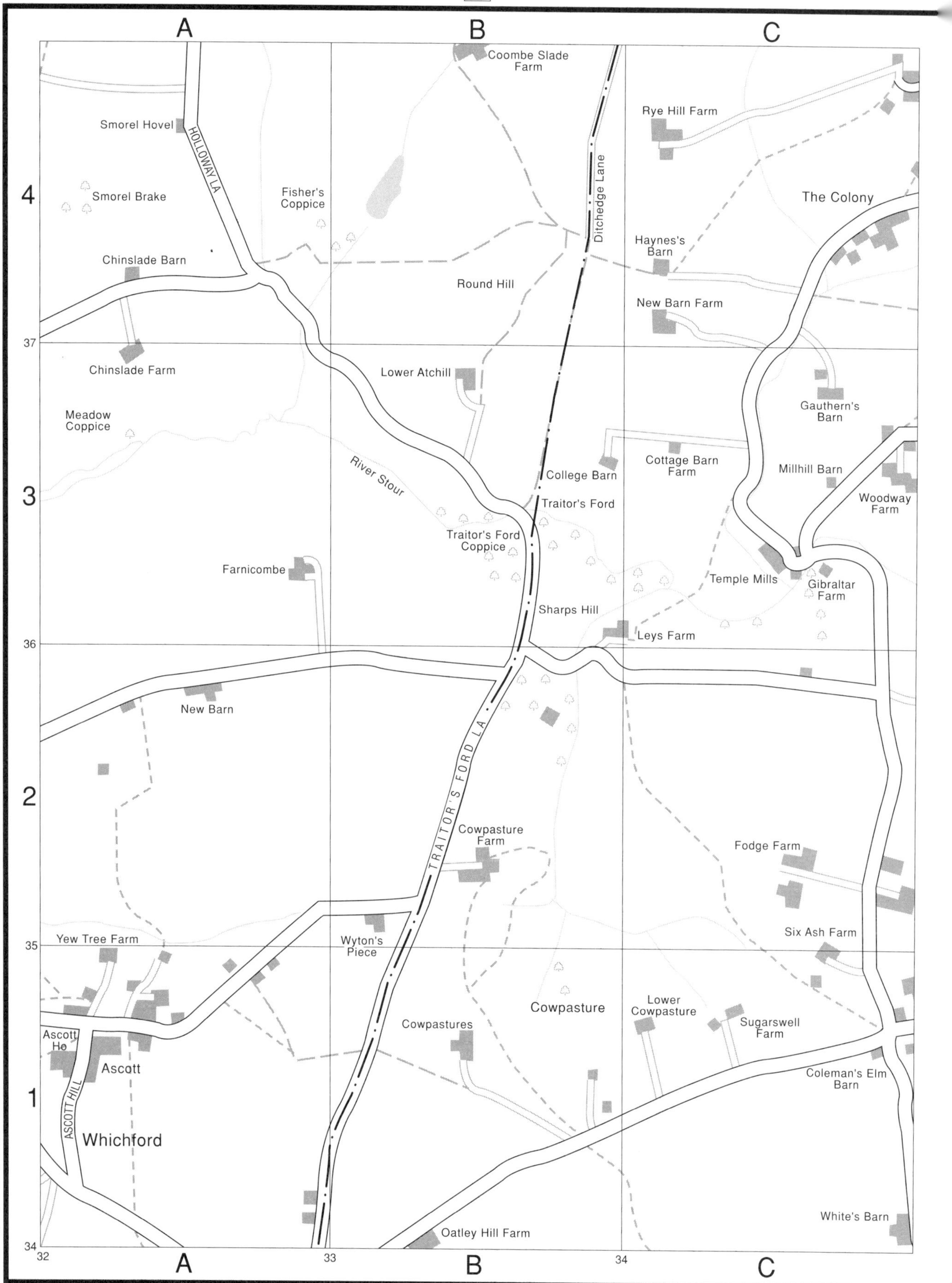

not continued, see key diagram

29

13

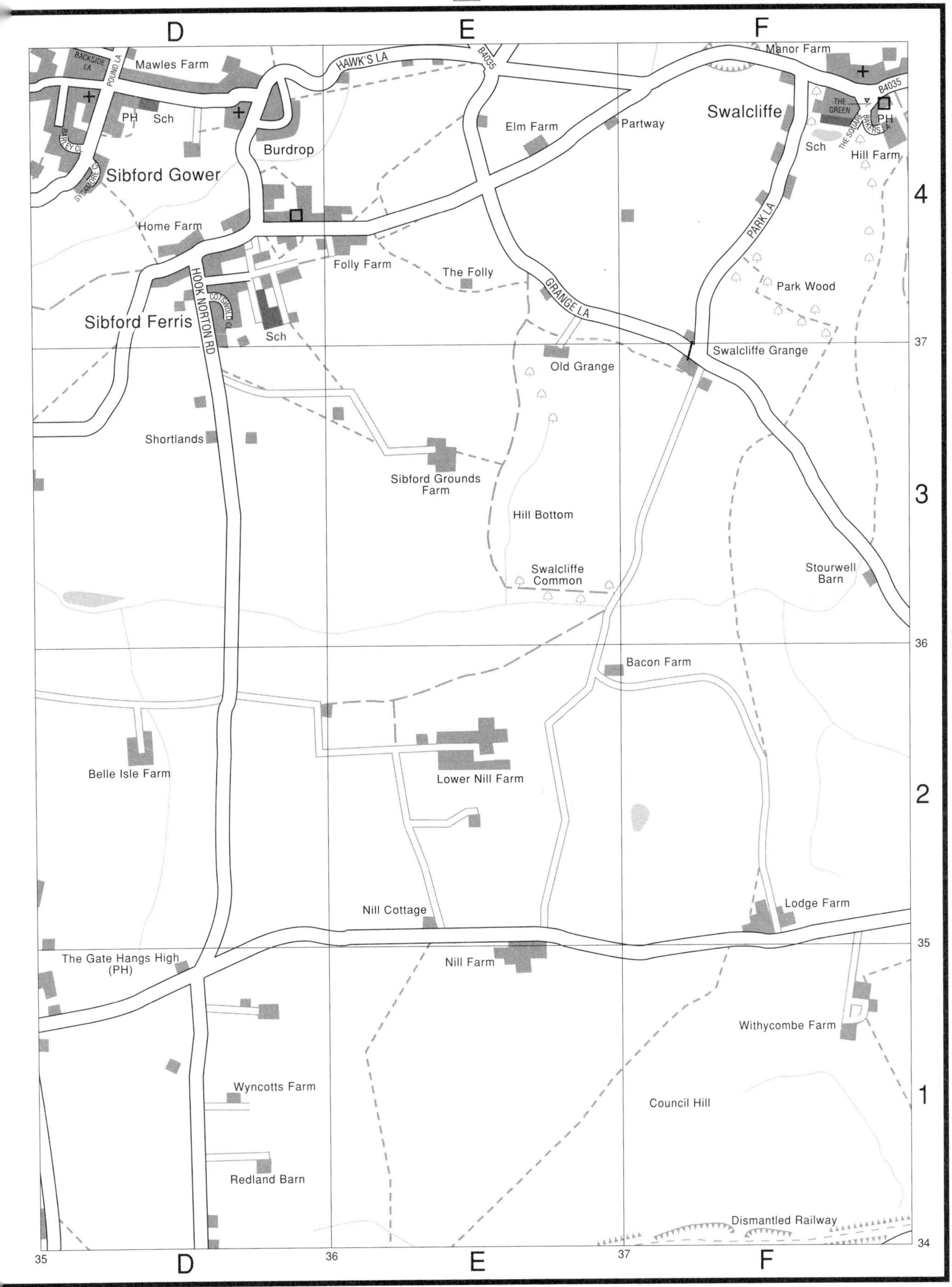
D
E
F
Mawles Farm
BACKSIDE LA
POUND LA
HAWK'S LA
B4035
Manor Farm
THE GREEN
THE SQUARE
BAKERS LA
PH
Sch
Swalcliffe
Hill Farm
Elm Farm
Partway
Burdrop
Sibford Gower
BARLEY CL
SYCAMORE CL
Home Farm
Folly Farm
The Folly
PARK LA
Park Wood
GRANGE LA
HOOK NORTON RD
COTSWOLD CL
Sibford Ferris
Sch
Swalcliffe Grange
Old Grange
Shortlands
Sibford Grounds Farm
Hill Bottom
Swalcliffe Common
Stourwell Barn
Bacon Farm
Belle Isle Farm
Lower Nill Farm
Nill Cottage
Lodge Farm
The Gate Hangs High (PH)
Nill Farm
Withycombe Farm
Wyncotts Farm
Council Hill
Redland Barn
Dismantled Railway
4
3
2
1
37
36
35
34
35
36
37
D
E
F

20

30

14

19

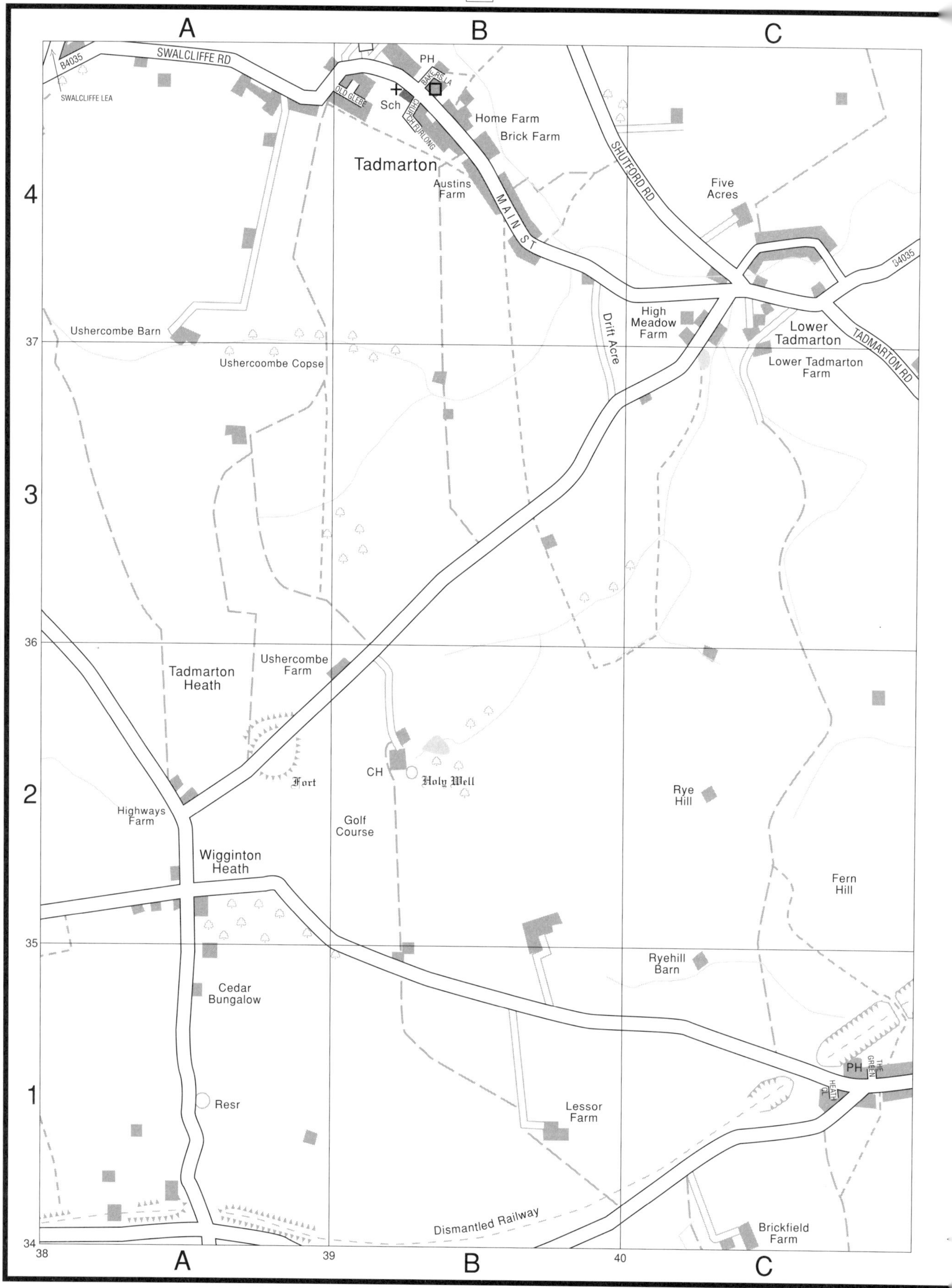
A
B
C
SWALCLIFFE RD
B4035
SWALCLIFFE LEA
PH
OLD GLEBE
Sch
BAKERS LA
CHURCH FURLONG
Home Farm
Brick Farm
Tadmarton
Austins Farm
MAIN ST
SHUTFORD RD
Five Acres
B4035
High Meadow Farm
Drift Acre
Lower Tadmarton
TADMARTON RD
Lower Tadmarton Farm
Ushercombe Barn
Ushercoombe Copse
Tadmarton Heath
Ushercombe Farm
Fort
CH
Holy Well
Highways Farm
Golf Course
Rye Hill
Wigginton Heath
Fern Hill
Ryehill Barn
Cedar Bungalow
PH
THE GREEN
HEATH CL
Resr
Lessor Farm
Dismantled Railway
Brickfield Farm
4
3
2
1
37
36
35
34
38
39
40

31

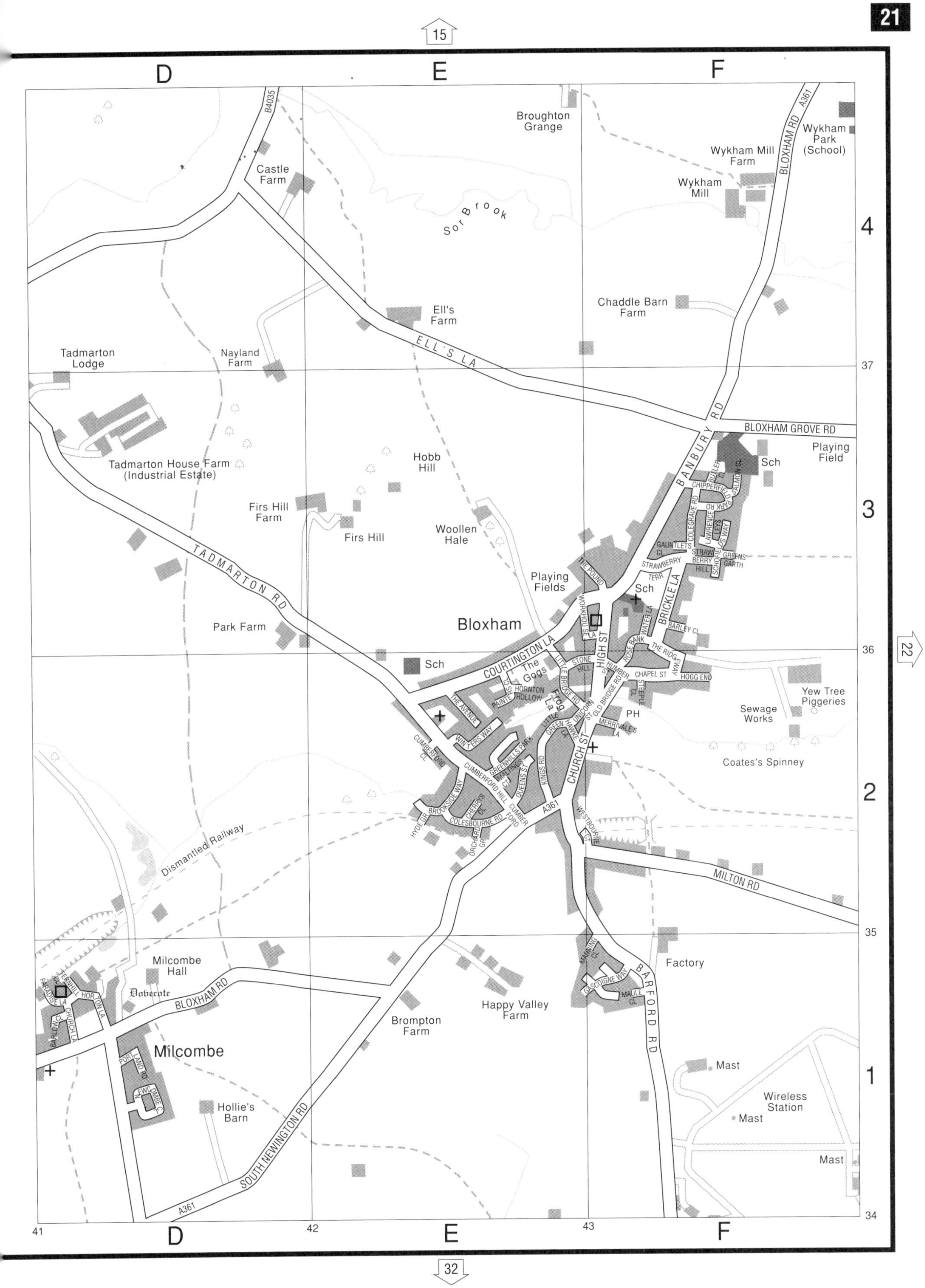
15
D
E
F
Broughton Grange
Wykham Mill Farm
Wykham Mill
Wykham Park (School)
BLOXHAM RD
A361
B4035
Castle Farm
Sor Brook
4
Chaddle Barn Farm
Ell's Farm
ELL'S LA
Tadmarton Lodge
Nayland Farm
37
BANBURY RD
BLOXHAM GROVE RD
Playing Field
Sch
Tadmarton House Farm (Industrial Estate)
Hobb Hill
Firs Hill Farm
Firs Hill
Woollen Hale
3
TADMARTON RD
Playing Fields
Bloxham
Park Farm
BRICKLE LA
HIGH ST
COURTINGTON LA
36
22
Sch
The Gogs
Frog La
CHAPEL ST
HOGG END
Yew Tree Piggeries
Sewage Works
PH
CHURCH ST
Coates's Spinney
2
Dismantled Railway
A361
MILTON RD
35
Factory
BARFORD RD
Milcombe Hall
Dovecote
BLOXHAM RD
Happy Valley Farm
Brompton Farm
Milcombe
1
Mast
Wireless Station
Mast
Hollie's Barn
SOUTH NEWINGTON RD
Mast
A361
34
41
42
43
D
E
F
32

16

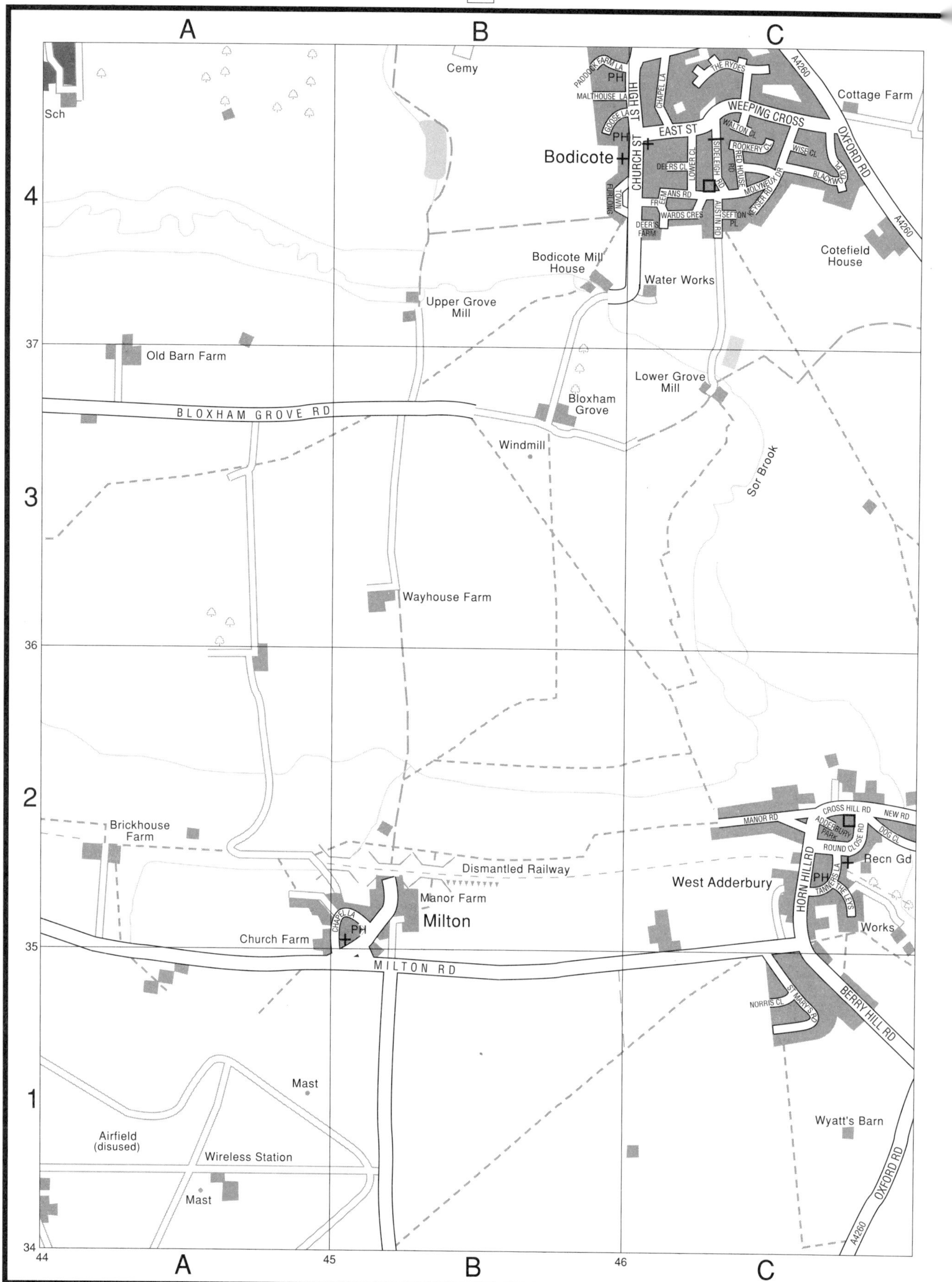

A
B
C
4
3
2
1
37
36
35
34
44
45
46
Sch
Cemy
Cottage Farm
PADDOCK FARM LA
PH
MALTHOUSE LA
GOOSE LA
HIGH ST
CHAPEL LA
THE RYDES
A4260
WEEPING CROSS
EAST ST
WALTON CL
OXFORD RD
Bodicote
CHURCH ST
DEERS CL
LOWER CL
SIDELEIGH RD
RED HOUSE RD
ROOKERY CL
WISE CL
BLACKWOOD PL
MOLYNEUX DR
KEYSER RD
TOWN FURLONG
FREEMANS RD
WARDS CRES
AUSTIN RD
SEFTON PL
DEER'S FARM
Cotefield House
Bodicote Mill House
Water Works
Upper Grove Mill
Old Barn Farm
Lower Grove Mill
Bloxham Grove
BLOXHAM GROVE RD
Windmill
Sor Brook
Wayhouse Farm
Brickhouse Farm
MANOR RD
CROSS HILL RD
NEW RD
ADDERBURY PARK
DOG CL
ROUND CLOSE RD
Becn Gd
Dismantled Railway
West Adderbury
HORN HILL RD
TANNERS LA
THE LEYS
Manor Farm
CHAPEL LA
Milton
Church Farm
Works
MILTON RD
NORRIS CL
ST MARY'S RD
BERRY HILL RD
Mast
Airfield (disused)
Wireless Station
Wyatt's Barn
OXFORD RD

21

33

17

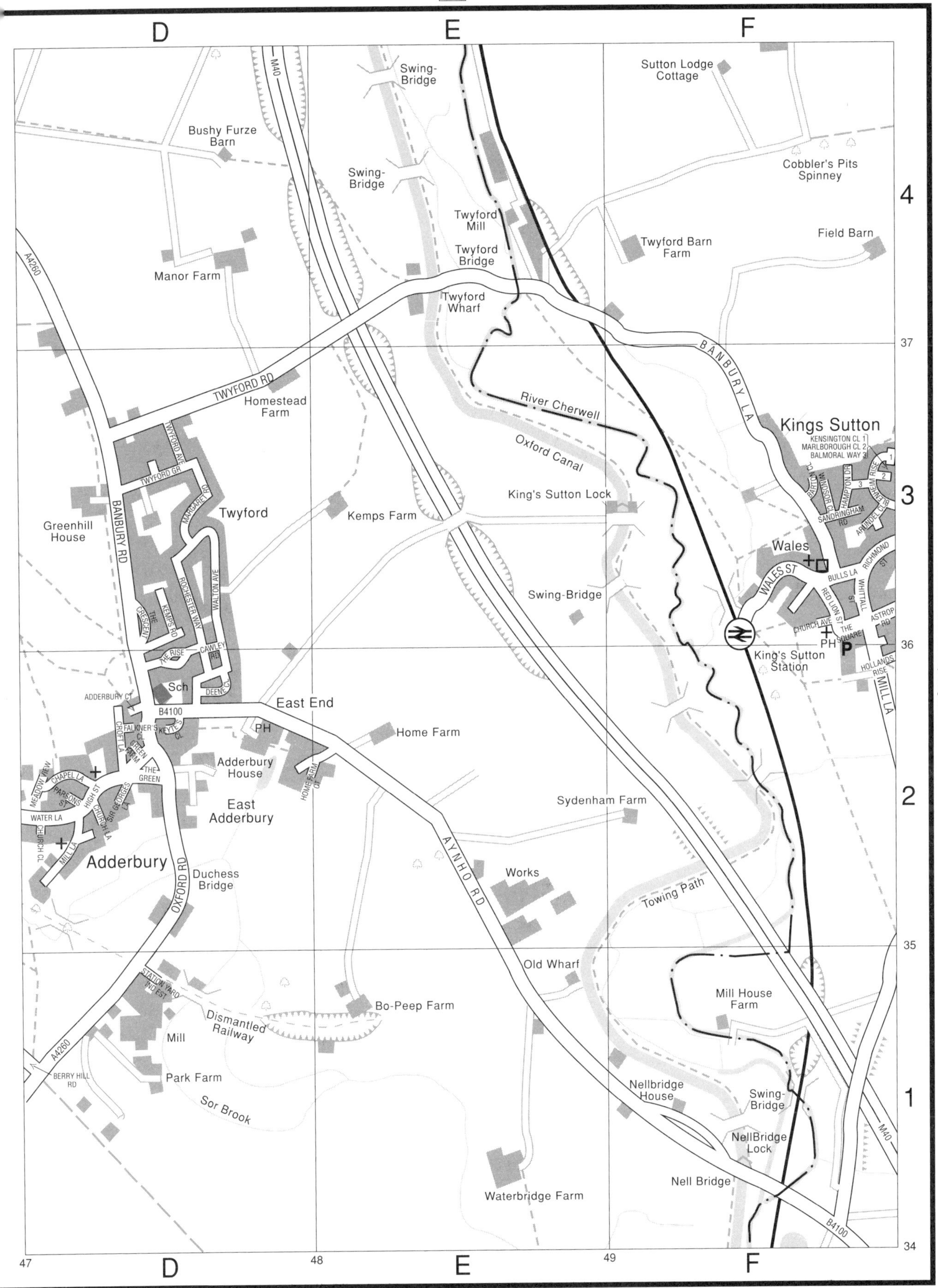

not continued, see key diagram

34

not continued, see key diagram

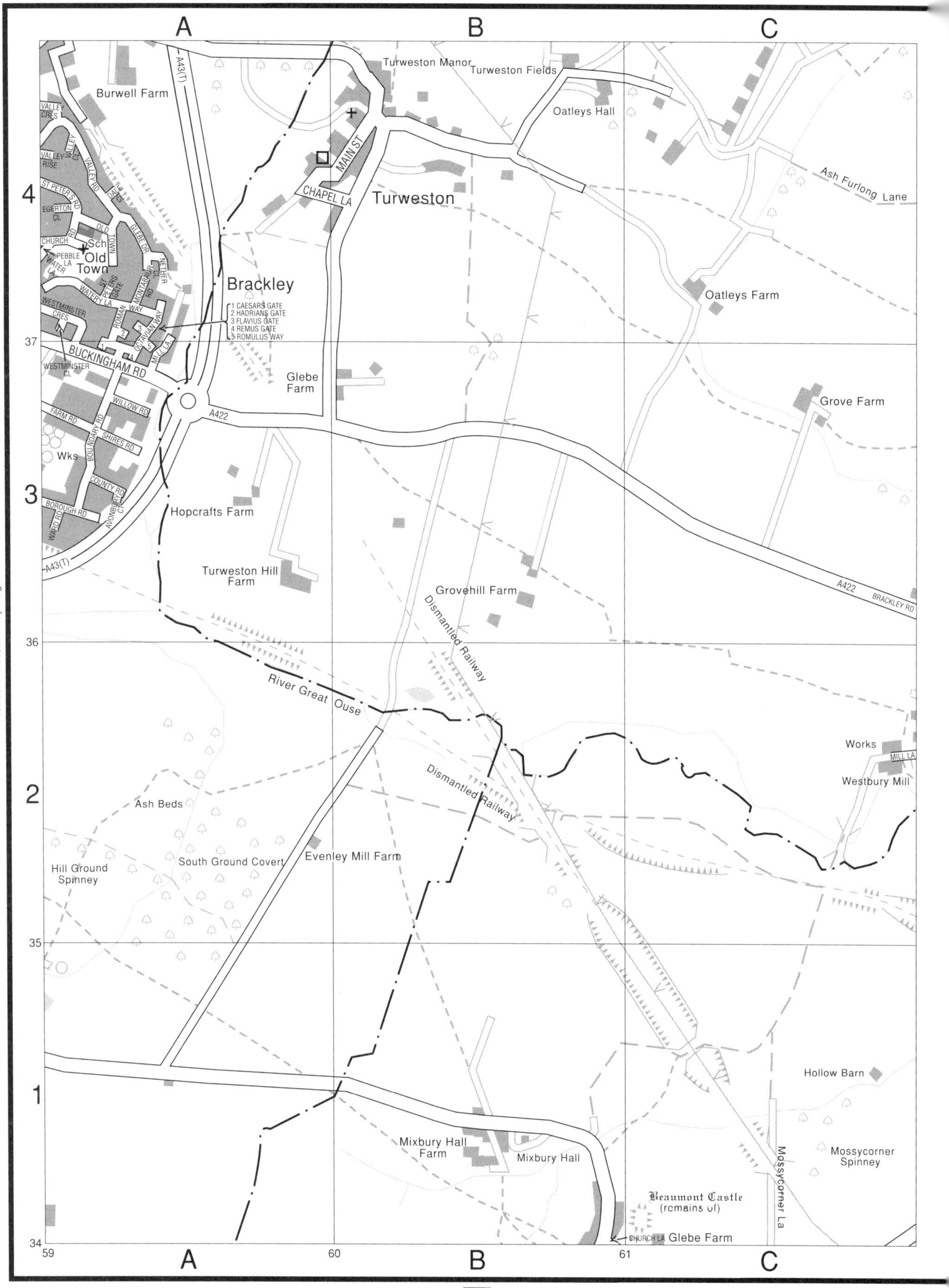

not continued, see key diagram

not continued, see key diagram

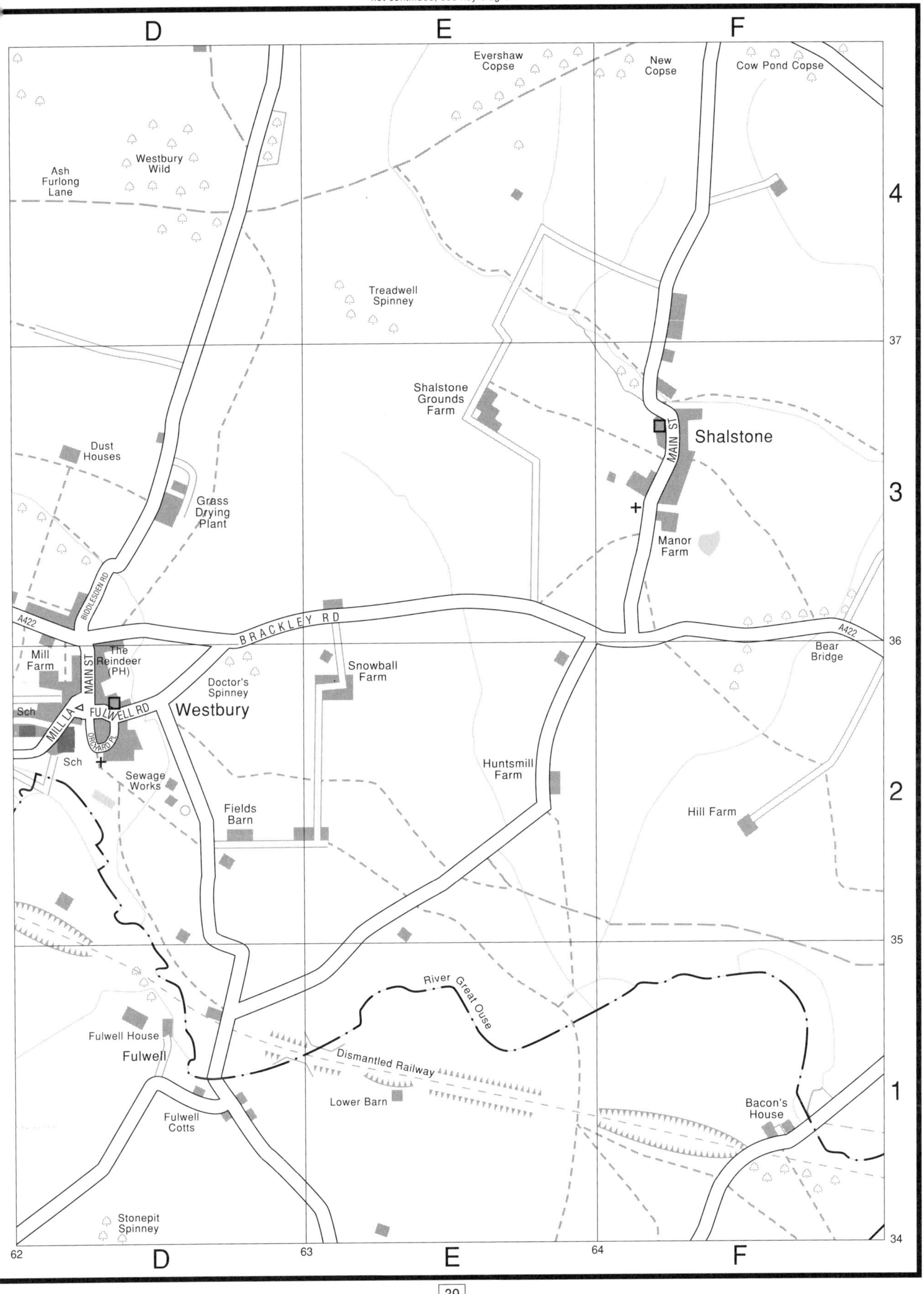

not continued, see key diagram

39

not continued, see key diagram

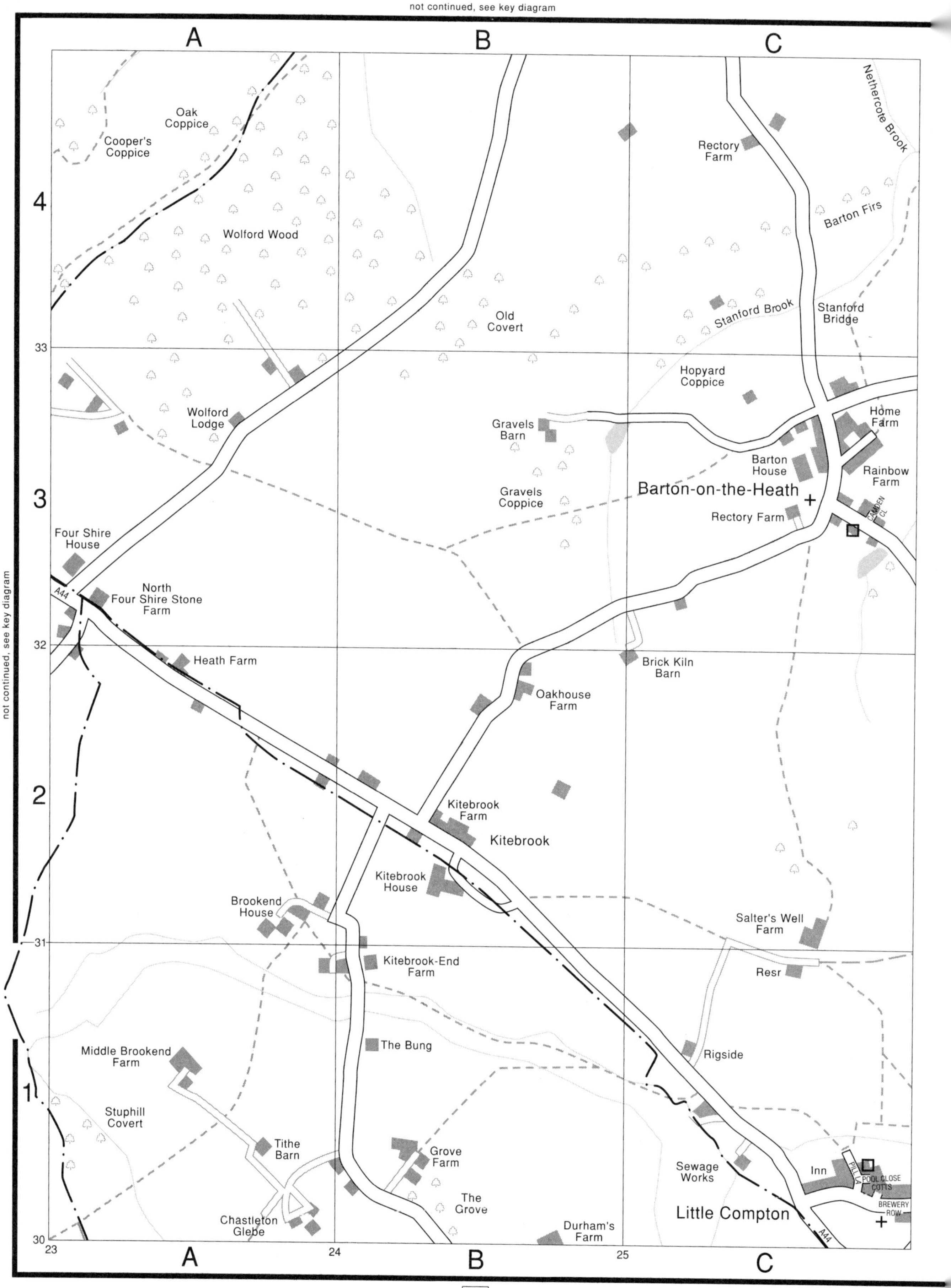

not continued, see key diagram

40

not continued, see key diagram

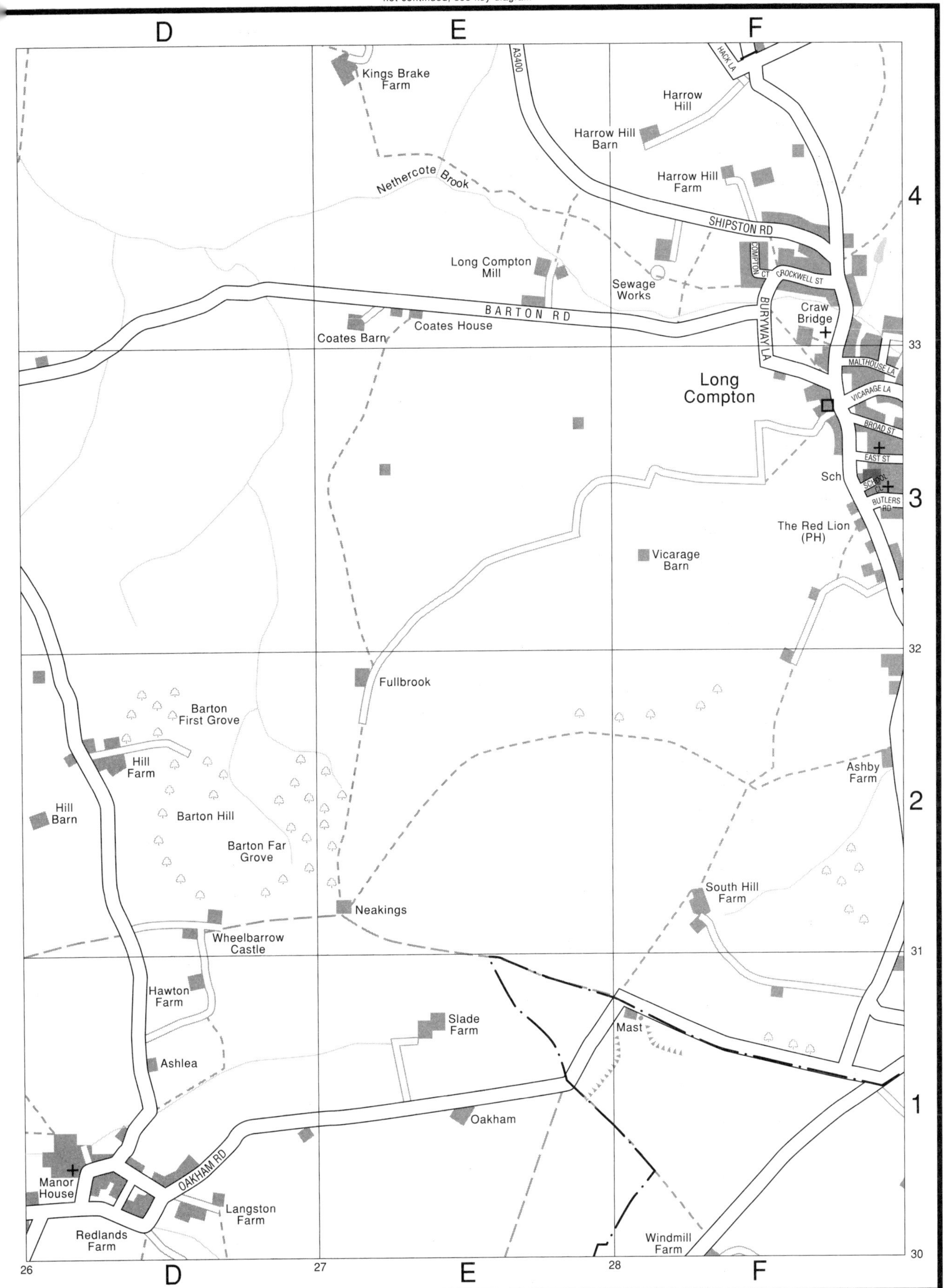

41

not continued, see key diagram

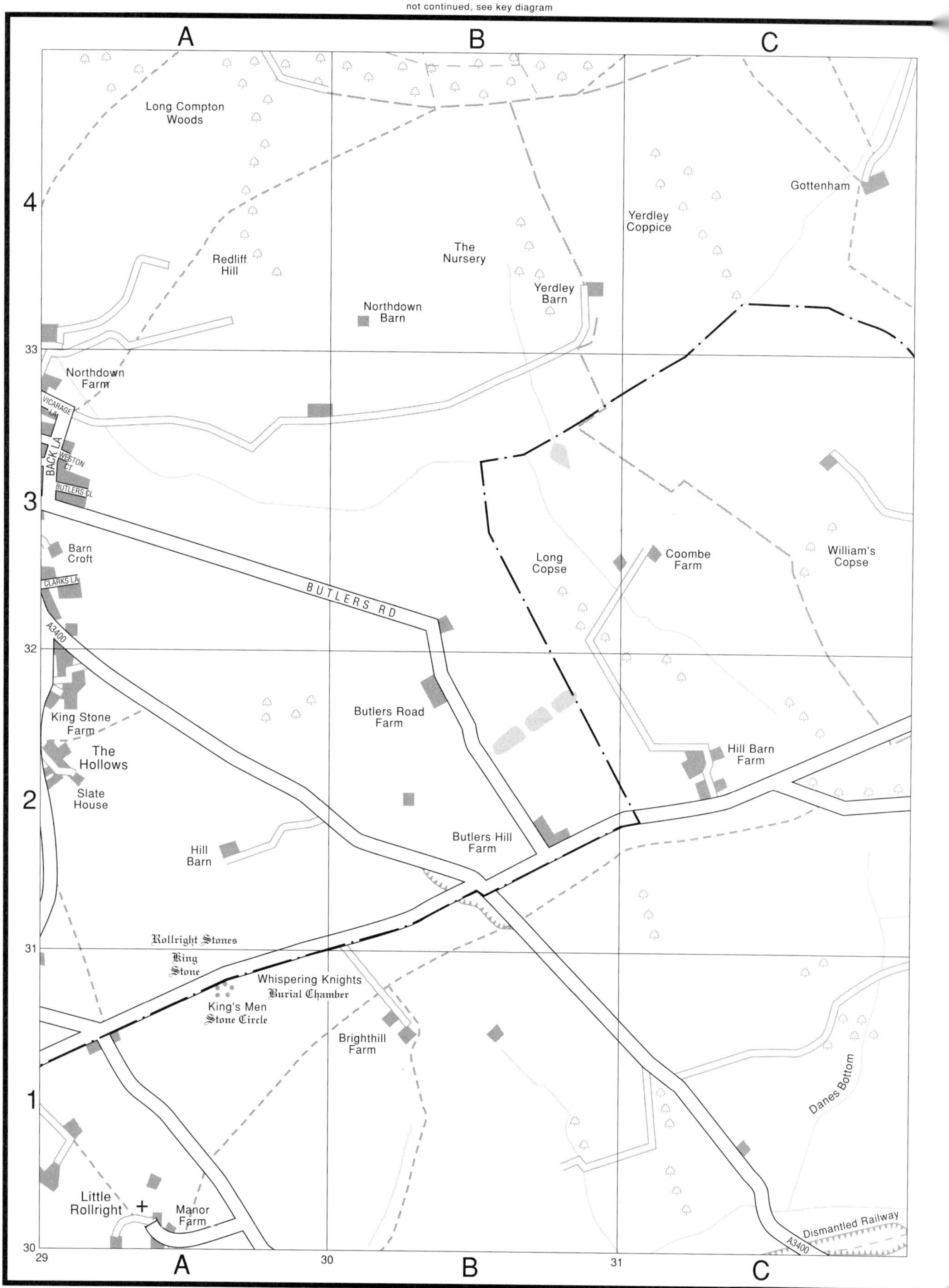

27

42

18

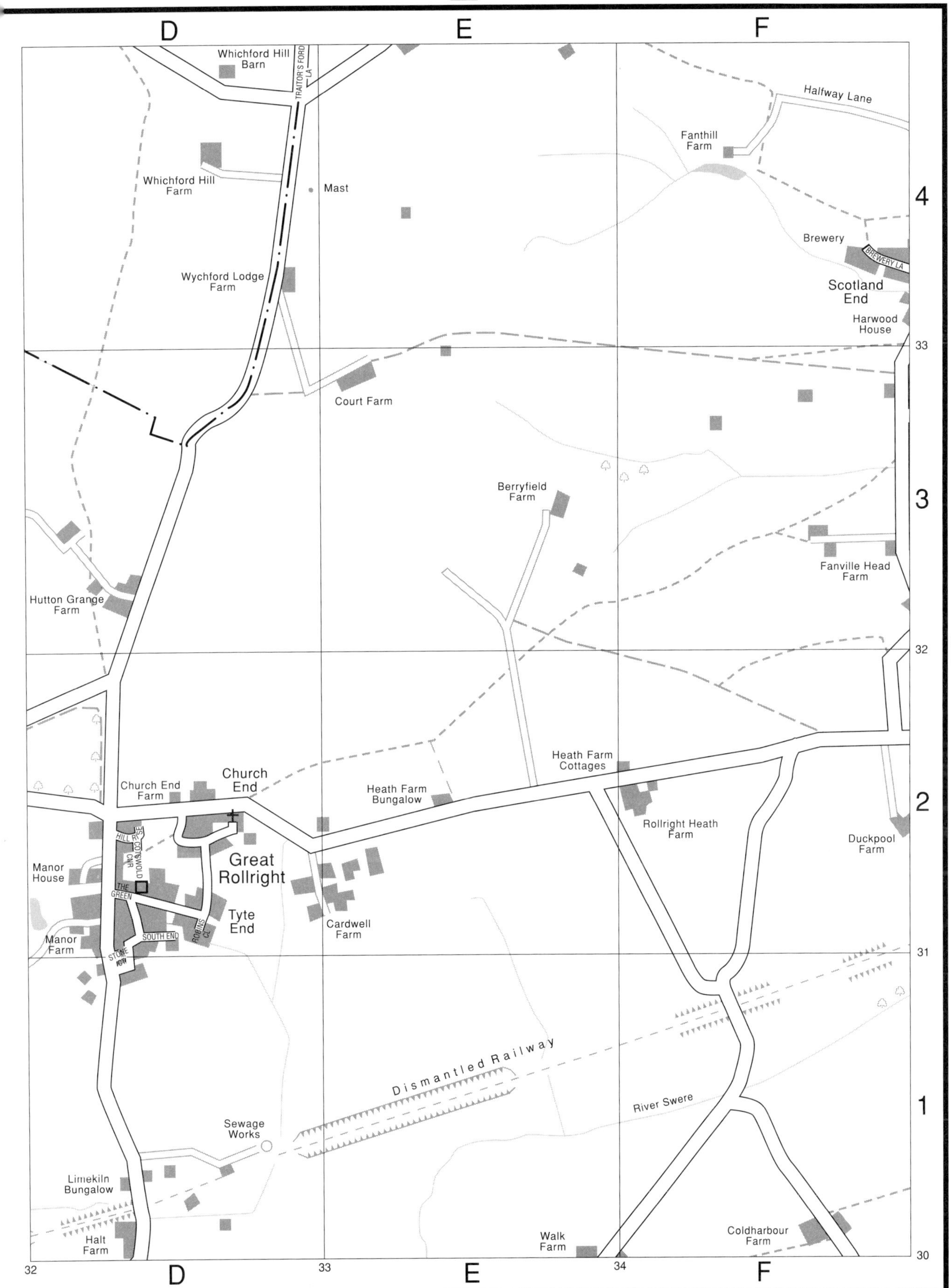

D
E
F
Whichford Hill Barn
TRAITOR'S FORD LA
Halfway Lane
Fanthill Farm
Whichford Hill Farm
Mast
4
Brewery
BREWERY LA
Wychford Lodge Farm
Scotland End
Harwood House
33
Court Farm
Berryfield Farm
3
Fanville Head Farm
Hutton Grange Farm
32
Heath Farm Cottages
Church End
Church End Farm
Heath Farm Bungalow
2
Rollright Heath Farm
Duckpool Farm
HILL RISE
COTSWOLD CNR
Manor House
Great Rollright
THE GREEN
Tyte End
ROBINS CL
Cardwell Farm
Manor Farm
SOUTH END
STONE ROW
31
Dismantled Railway
River Swere
1
Sewage Works
Limekiln Bungalow
Halt Farm
Walk Farm
Coldharbour Farm
30
32
D
33
E
34
F

30

43

19

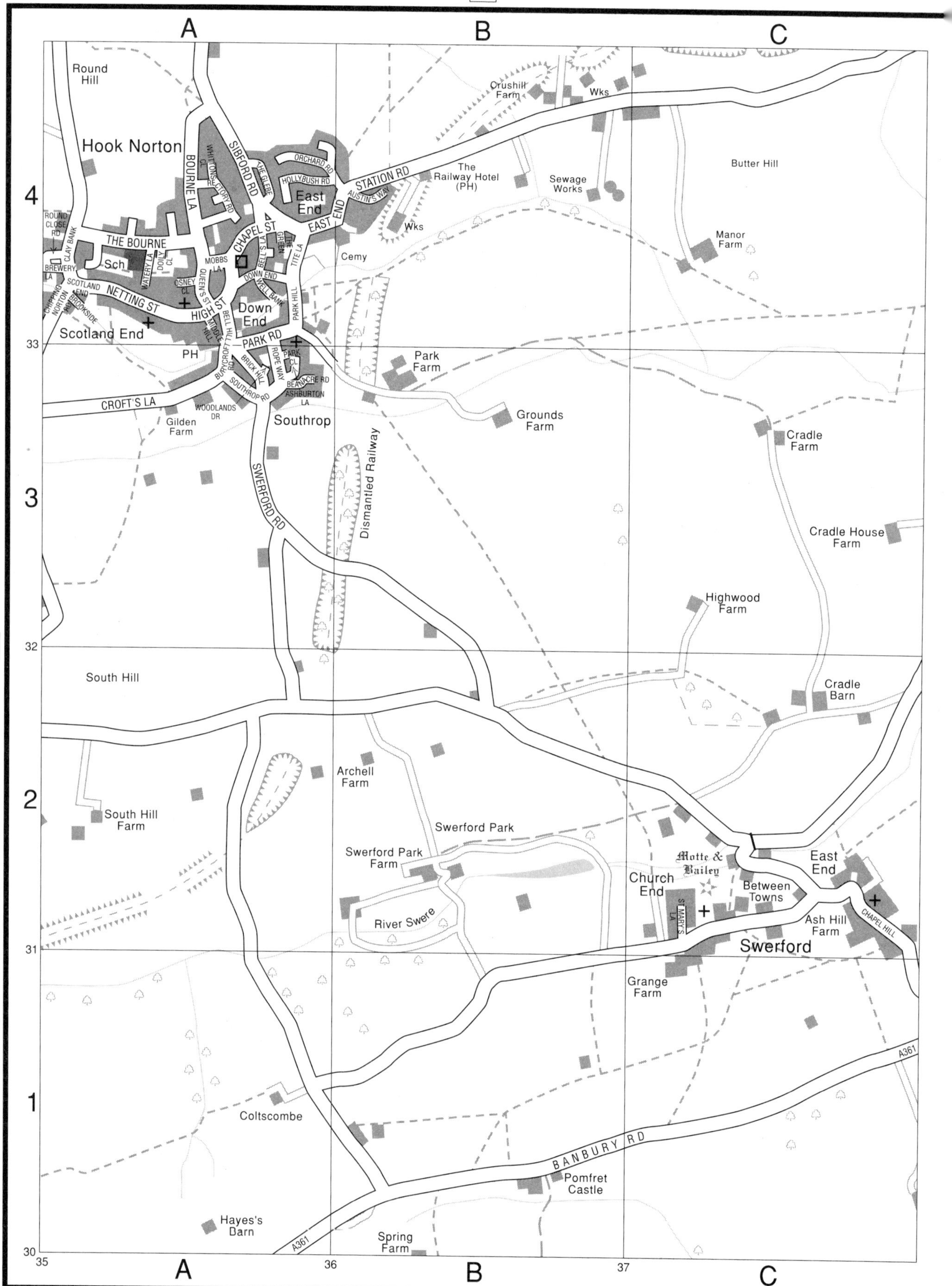

A
B
C
Round Hill
Crushill Farm
Wks
Hook Norton
BOURNE LA
WHITTONS CL
RECTORY RD
SIBFORD RD
THE GLEBE
ORCHARD RD
HOLLYBUSH RD
East End
STATION RD
AUSTIN'S WAY
The Railway Hotel (PH)
Sewage Works
Butter Hill
4
ROUND CLOSE RD
CLAY BANK
THE BOURNE
CHAPEL ST
EAST END
Wks
Manor Farm
BREWERY LA
Sch
WATERY LA
DOILY CL
MOBBS LA
BELL'S LA
THE GREEN
TITE LA
Cemy
CHIPPING NORTON RD
SCOTLAND END
BROOKSIDE
NETTING ST
OSNEY CL
QUEEN'S ST
DOWN END
WELL BANK
HIGH ST
Down End
PARK HILL
Scotland End
MIDDLE HILL
BELL HILL
PARK RD
33
PH
BURYCROFT RD
PARK CL
Park Farm
BRICK HILL
ROPE WAY
BEANACRE RD
SOUTHROP RD
ASHBURTON LA
CROFT'S LA
WOODLANDS DR
Gilden Farm
Southrop
Grounds Farm
Cradle Farm
Dismantled Railway
3
SWERFORD RD
Cradle House Farm
Highwood Farm
32
South Hill
Cradle Barn
Archell Farm
2
South Hill Farm
Swerford Park
Swerford Park Farm
Motte & Bailey
East End
Church End
Between Towns
ST MARY'S LA
River Swere
Ash Hill Farm
CHAPEL HILL
Swerford
31
Grange Farm
A361
1
Coltscombe
BANBURY RD
Pomfret Castle
Hayes's Barn
Spring Farm
A361
30
35
36
37
A
B
C

29

44

20

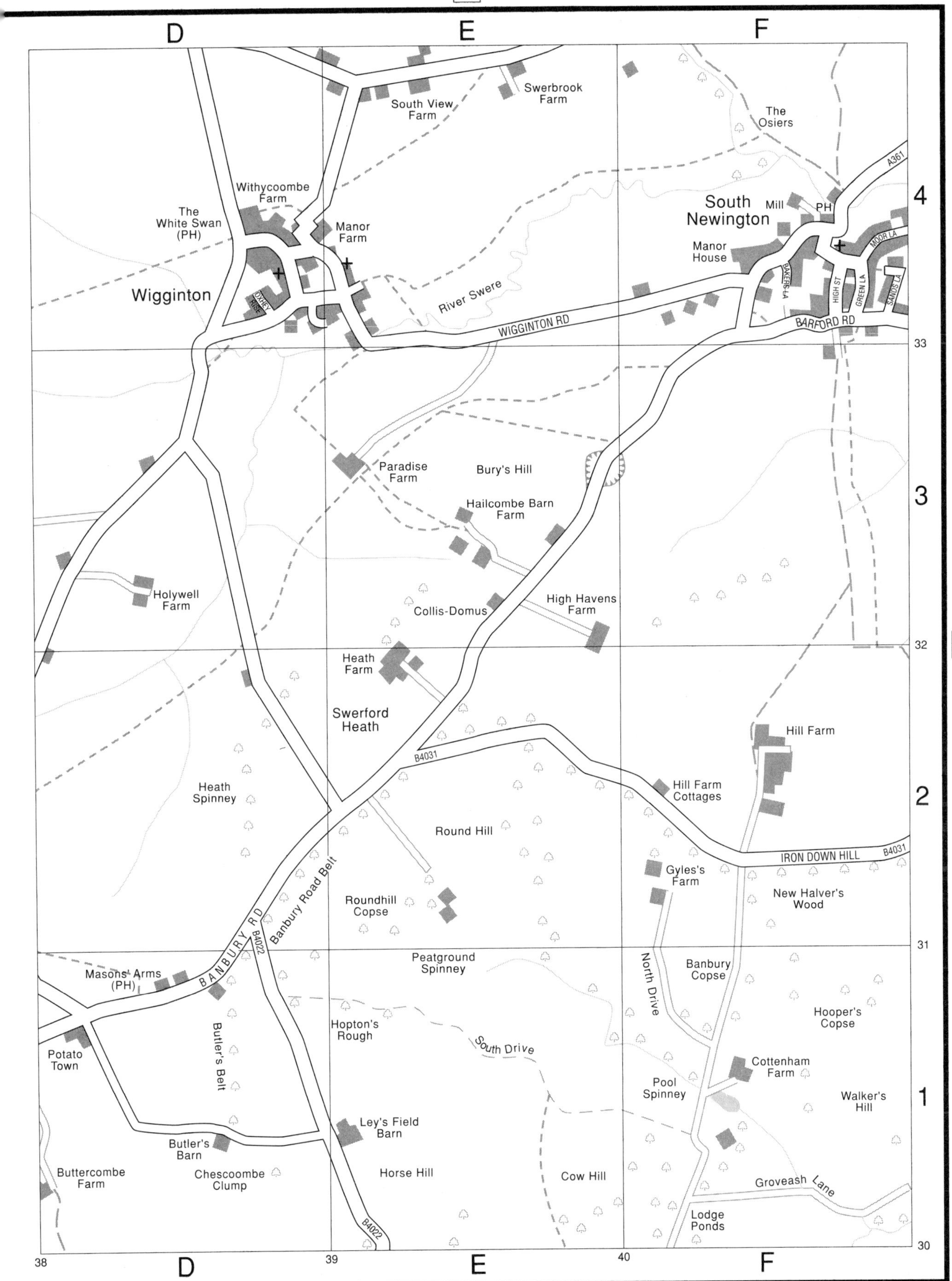
D
E
F
South View Farm
Swerbrook Farm
The Osiers
A361
Withycoombe Farm
The White Swan (PH)
Manor Farm
Wigginton
OXHEY RISE
South Newington
Mill
PH
Manor House
MOOR LA
BAKERS LA
HIGH ST
GREEN LA
SANDS LA
River Swere
WIGGINTON RD
BARFORD RD
4
33
Paradise Farm
Bury's Hill
Hailcombe Barn Farm
3
Holywell Farm
Collis-Domus
High Havens Farm
32
Heath Farm
Swerford Heath
Hill Farm
B4031
Hill Farm Cottages
Heath Spinney
2
Round Hill
IRON DOWN HILL
B4031
Gyles's Farm
Banbury Road Belt
New Halver's Wood
Roundhill Copse
BANBURY RD
B4022
31
Peatground Spinney
North Drive
Banbury Copse
Masons' Arms (PH)
Hooper's Copse
Hopton's Rough
South Drive
Butler's Belt
Potato Town
Cottenham Farm
Pool Spinney
1
Walker's Hill
Ley's Field Barn
Butler's Barn
Buttercombe Farm
Chescoombe Clump
Horse Hill
Cow Hill
Groveash Lane
B4022
Lodge Ponds
30
38
39
40

32

45

21

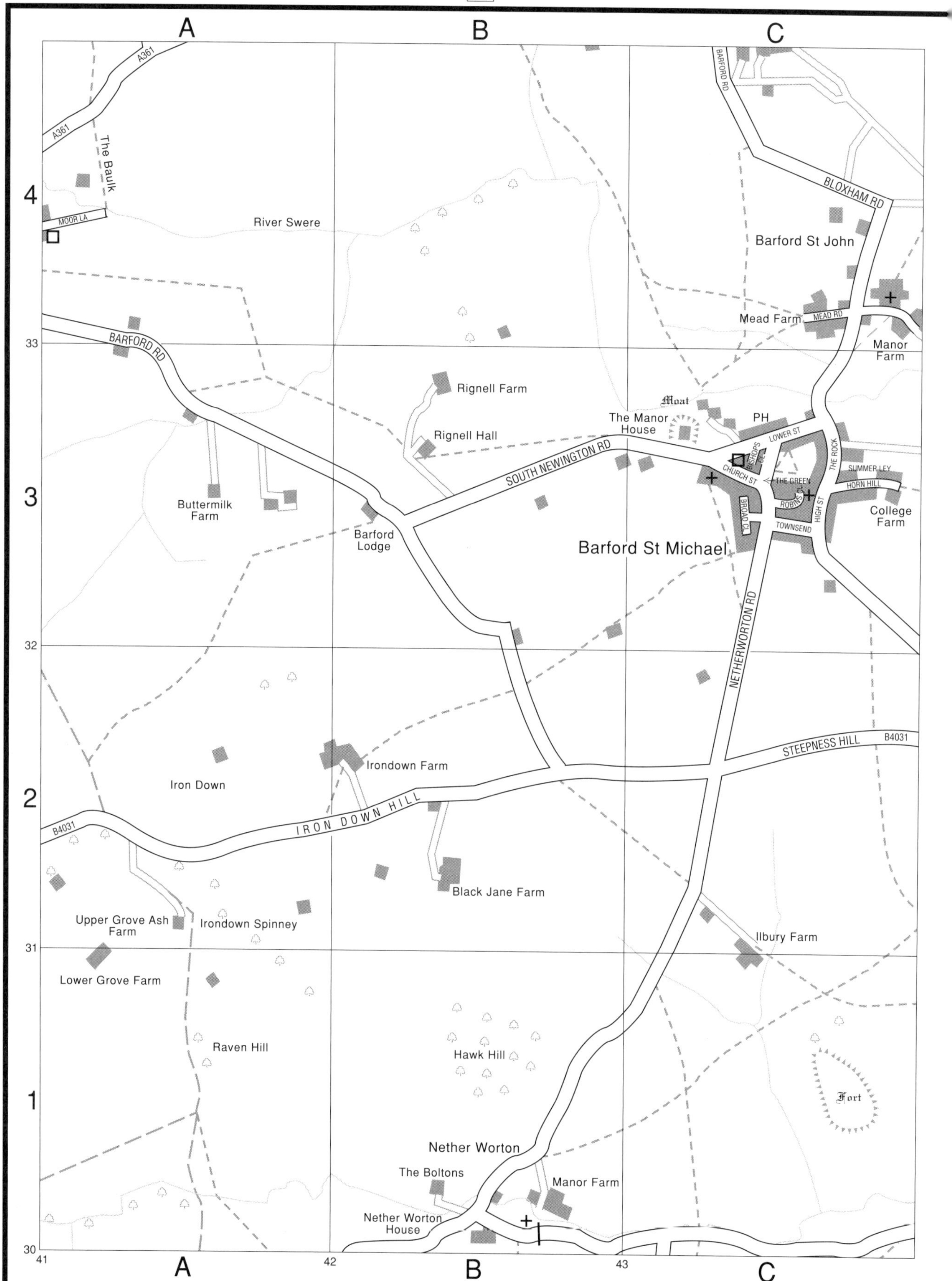
A
B
C
A361
The Baulk
MOOR LA
River Swere
BARFORD RD
BLOXHAM RD
Barford St John
Mead Farm
MEAD RD
Manor Farm
Rignell Farm
Rignell Hall
Moat
The Manor House
PH
LOWER ST
BISHOPS
CHURCH ST
THE GREEN
THE ROCK
SUMMER LEY
HORN HILL
ROBINS CL
BROAD CL
HIGH ST
TOWNSEND
College Farm
SOUTH NEWINGTON RD
Buttermilk Farm
Barford Lodge
Barford St Michael
NETHERWORTON RD
STEEPNESS HILL
B4031
Irondown Farm
Iron Down
IRON DOWN HILL
Black Jane Farm
Upper Grove Ash Farm
Irondown Spinney
Ilbury Farm
Lower Grove Farm
Raven Hill
Hawk Hill
Fort
Nether Worton
The Boltons
Manor Farm
Nether Worton House
4
3
2
1
33
32
31
30
41
42
43

31

46

22

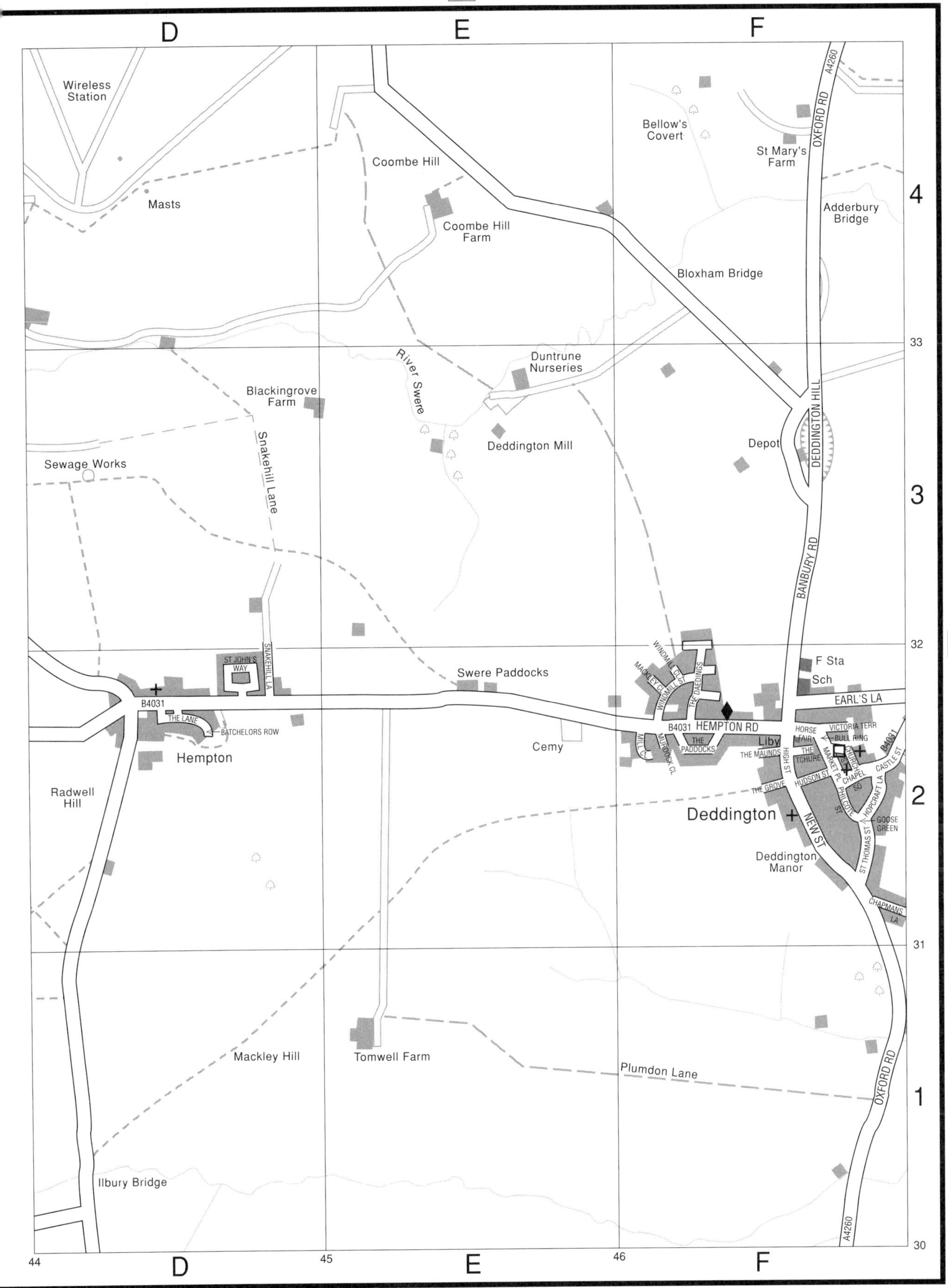

D
E
F
Wireless Station
Masts
Coombe Hill
Coombe Hill Farm
Bellow's Covert
St Mary's Farm
OXFORD RD
A4260
Adderbury Bridge
Bloxham Bridge
4
33
Duntrune Nurseries
River Swere
Blackingrove Farm
Snakehill Lane
Deddington Mill
Depot
DEDDINGTON HILL
Sewage Works
3
BANBURY RD
32
F Sta
Sch
EARL'S LA
Swere Paddocks
ST JOHN'S WAY
SNAKEHILL LA
B4031
THE LANE
BATCHELORS ROW
Hempton
Radwell Hill
Cemy
WINDMILL CL
MACKLEY CL
WINDMILL ST
THE DAEDINGS
B4031 HEMPTON RD
THE PADDOCKS
MILL CL
MURDOCK CL
Liby
THE MAUNDS
HIGH ST
HORSE FAIR
VICTORIA TERR
BULL RING
THE TCHURE
MARKET PL
CHURCH ST
CHAPEL SQ
CASTLE ST
HUDSON ST
THE GROVE
PHILCOTE ST
HOPCRAFT LA
GOOSE GREEN
Deddington
NEW ST
ST THOMAS ST
Deddington Manor
CHAPMANS LA
2
31
Mackley Hill
Tomwell Farm
Plumdon Lane
OXFORD RD
1
Ilbury Bridge
A4260
30
44
45
46
D
E
F

34

47

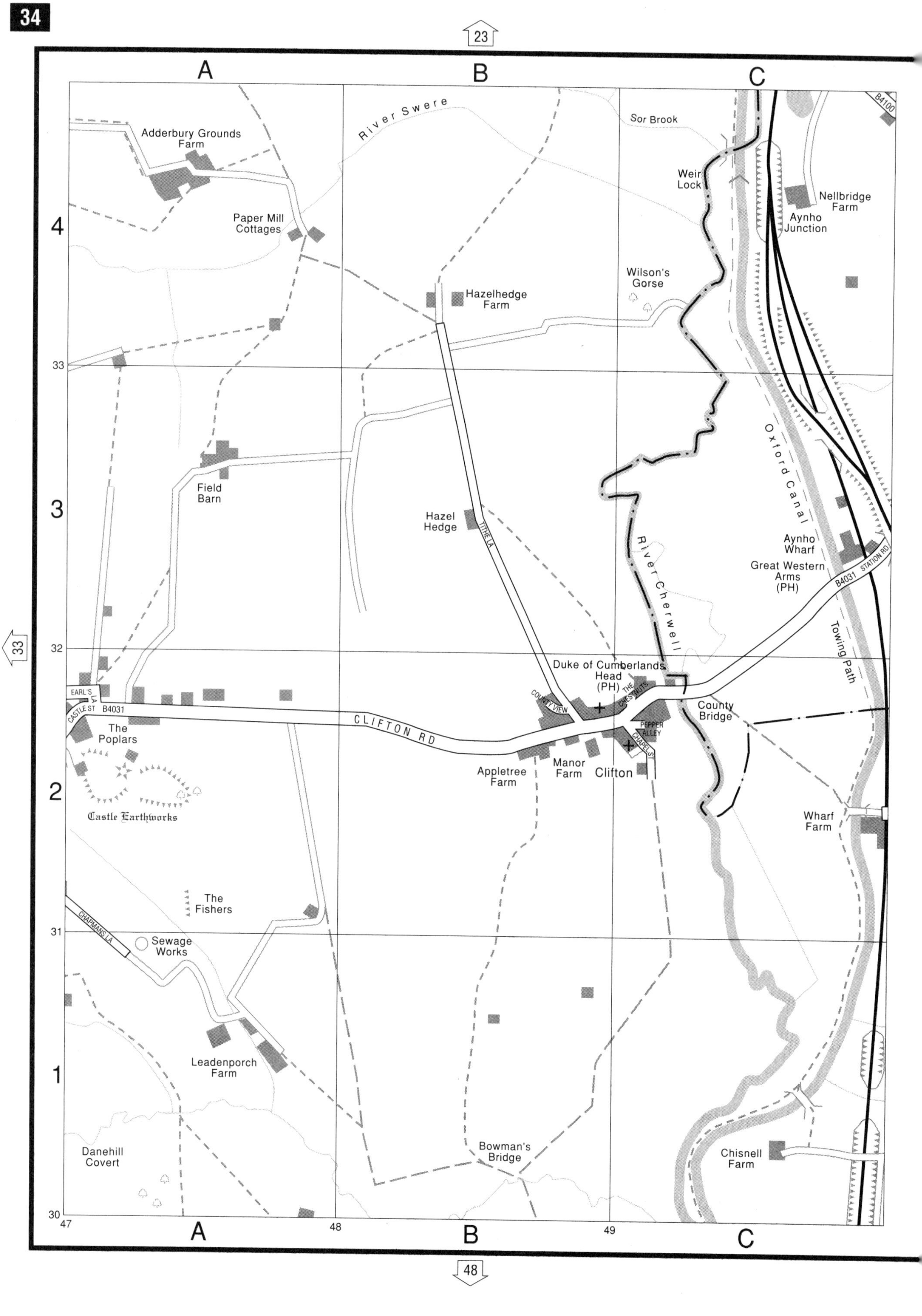
23
A
B
C
Sor Brook
River Swere
Adderbury Grounds Farm
Paper Mill Cottages
Weir Lock
Nellbridge Farm
Aynho Junction
B4100
4
Wilson's Gorse
Hazelhedge Farm
33
Oxford Canal
Field Barn
3
Hazel Hedge
TITHE LA
River Cherwell
Aynho Wharf
Great Western Arms (PH)
B4031
STATION RD
Towing Path
33
32
Duke of Cumberlands Head (PH)
THE CHESTNUTS
EARL'S LA
CASTLE ST
B4031
COUNTY VIEW
CLIFTON RD
PEPPER ALLEY
CHAPEL ST
County Bridge
The Poplars
Appletree Farm
Manor Farm
Clifton
2
Castle Earthworks
Wharf Farm
The Fishers
31
CHAPMANS LA
Sewage Works
Leadenporch Farm
1
Danehill Covert
Bowman's Bridge
Chisnell Farm
30
47
48
49
A
B
C
48

not continued, see key diagram

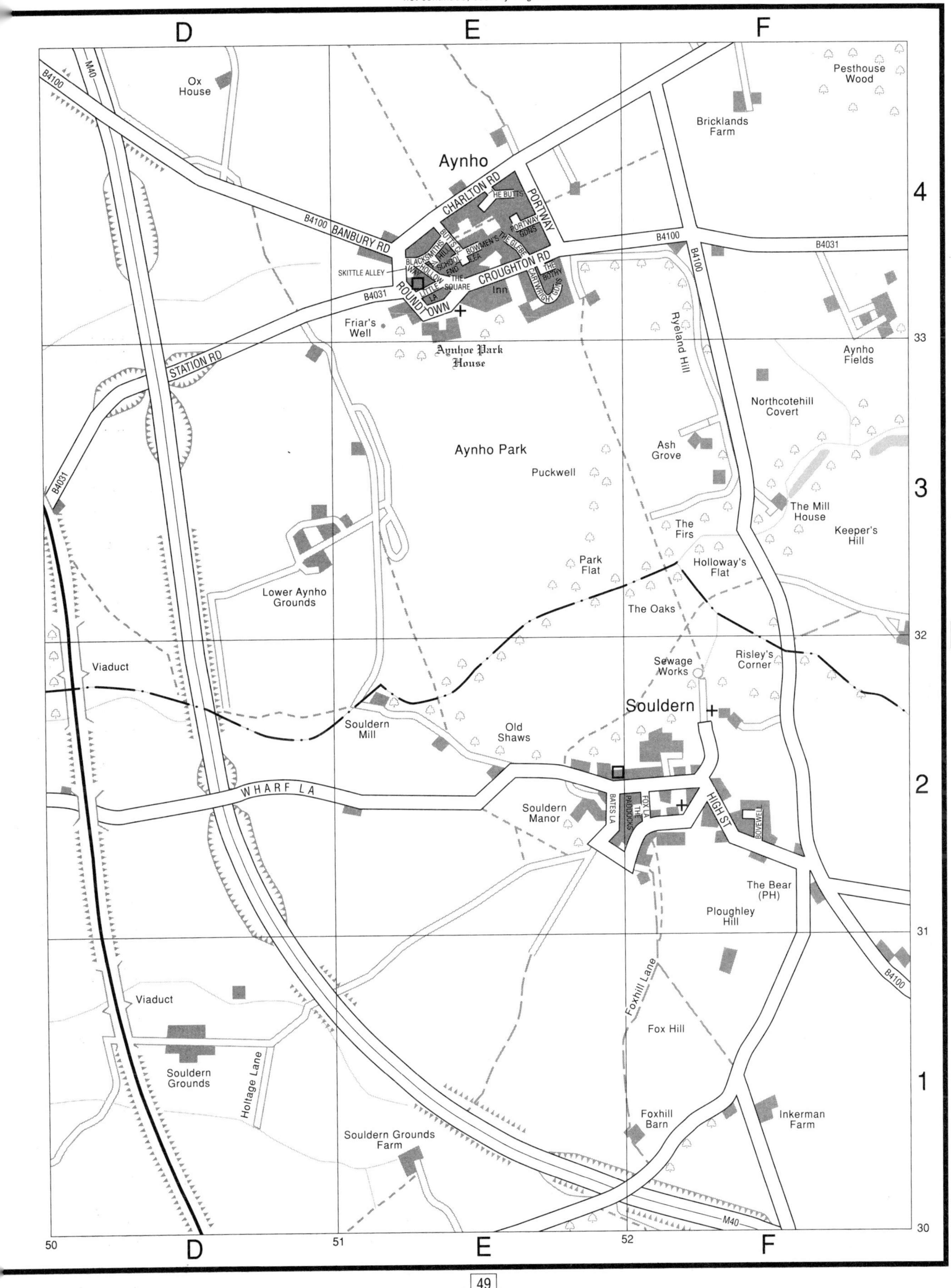

49

not continued, see key diagram

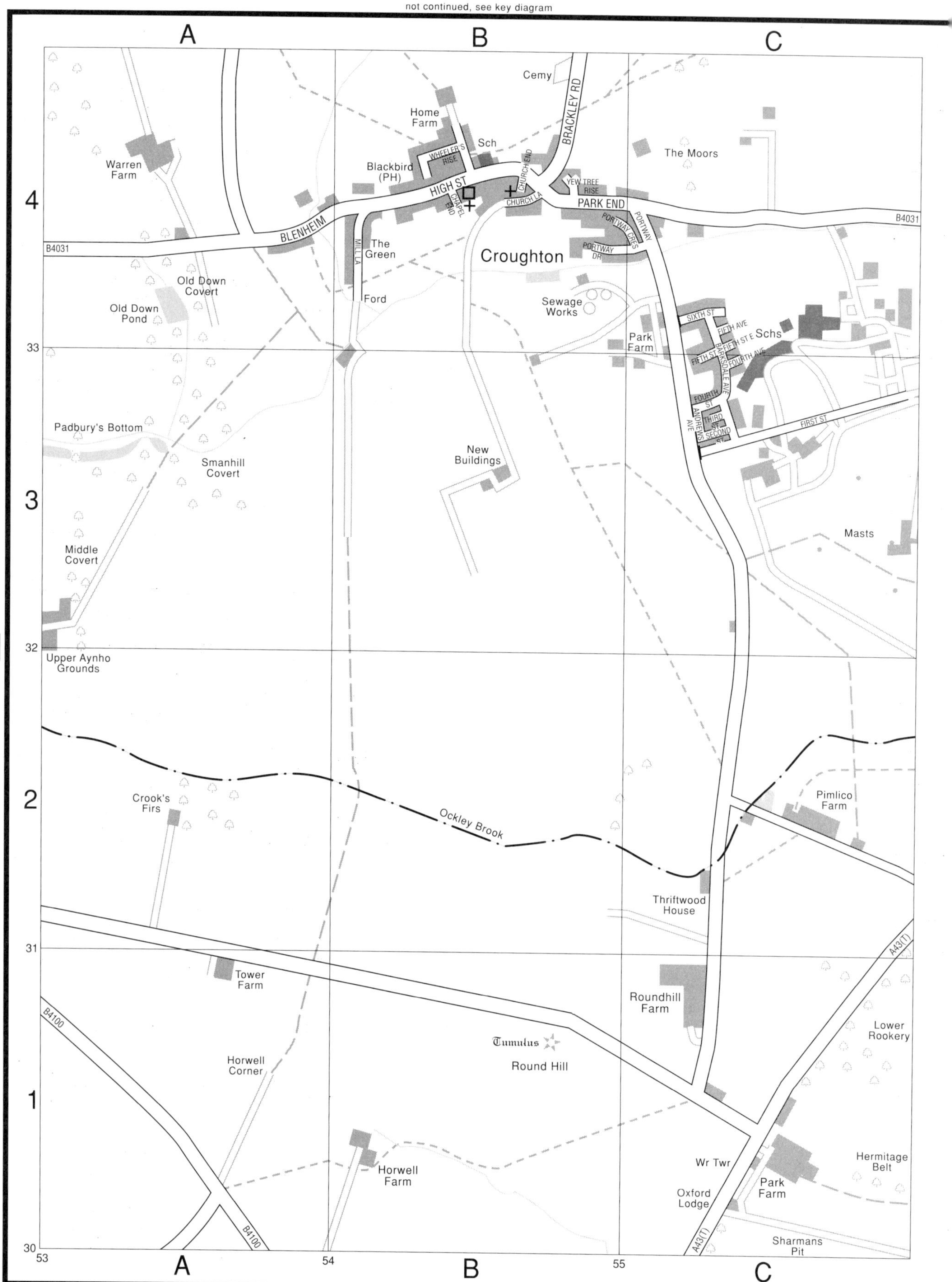

35

50

not continued, see key diagram

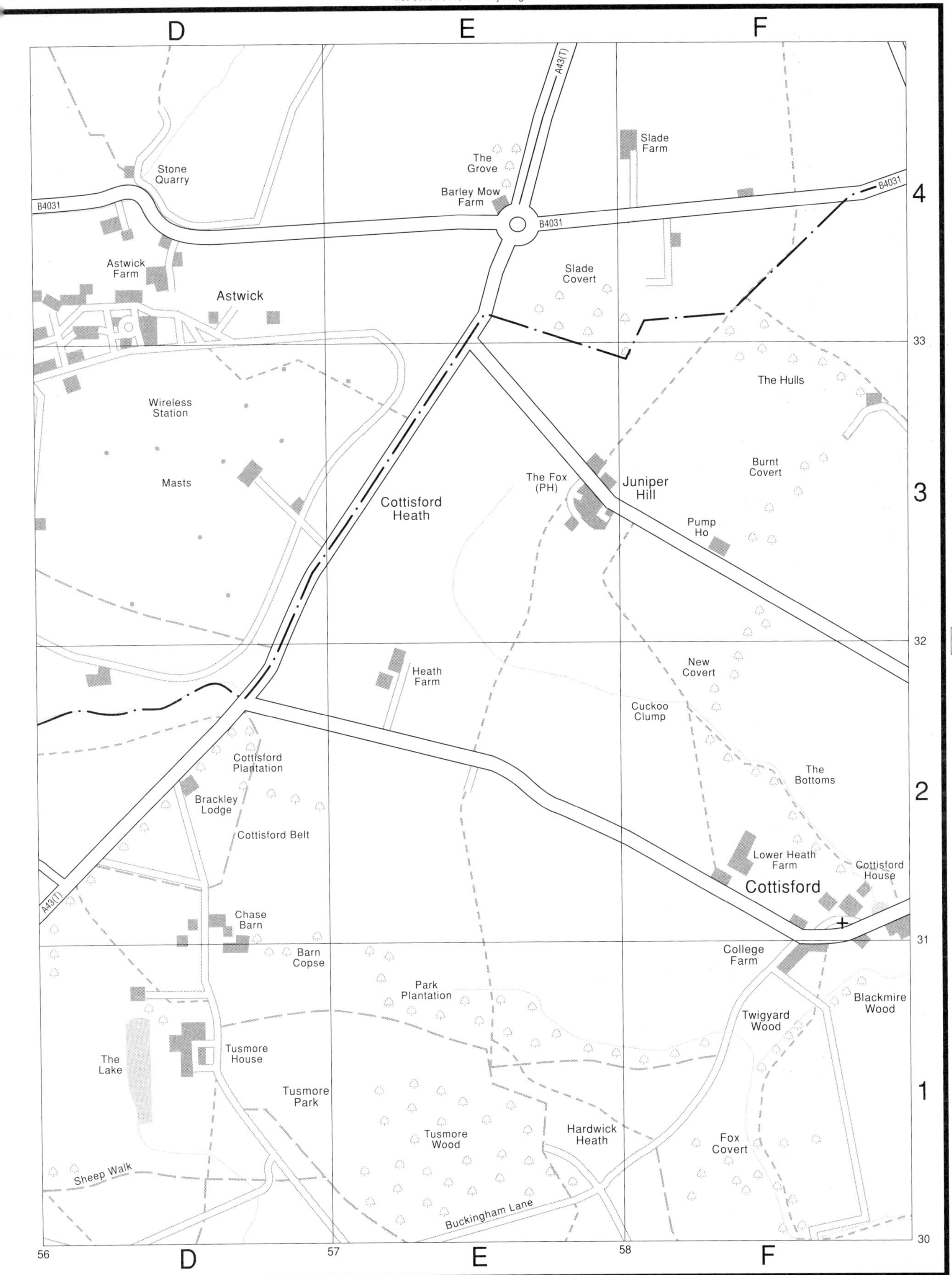

38

51

24

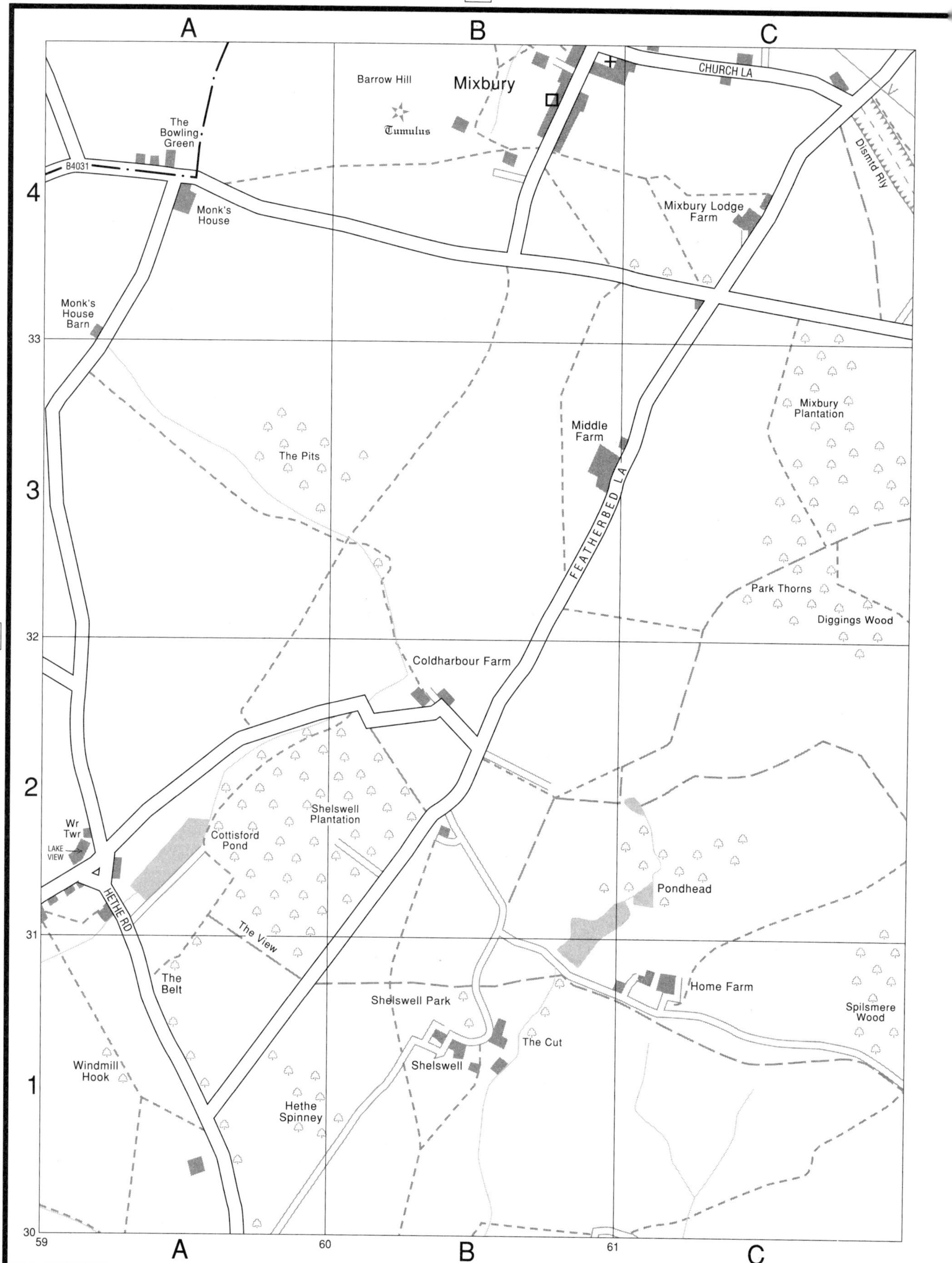

A
B
C
Barrow Hill
Mixbury
Tumulus
CHURCH LA
The Bowling Green
B4031
Monk's House
Mixbury Lodge Farm
Dismtd Rly
Monk's House Barn
Middle Farm
Mixbury Plantation
The Pits
FEATHERBED LA
Park Thorns
Diggings Wood
Coldharbour Farm
Shelswell Plantation
Wr Twr
LAKE VIEW
Cottisford Pond
HETHE RD
Pondhead
The View
The Belt
Home Farm
Shelswell Park
Spilsmere Wood
The Cut
Windmill Hook
Shelswell
Hethe Spinney
4
3
2
1
33
32
31
30
59
60
61

37

52

25

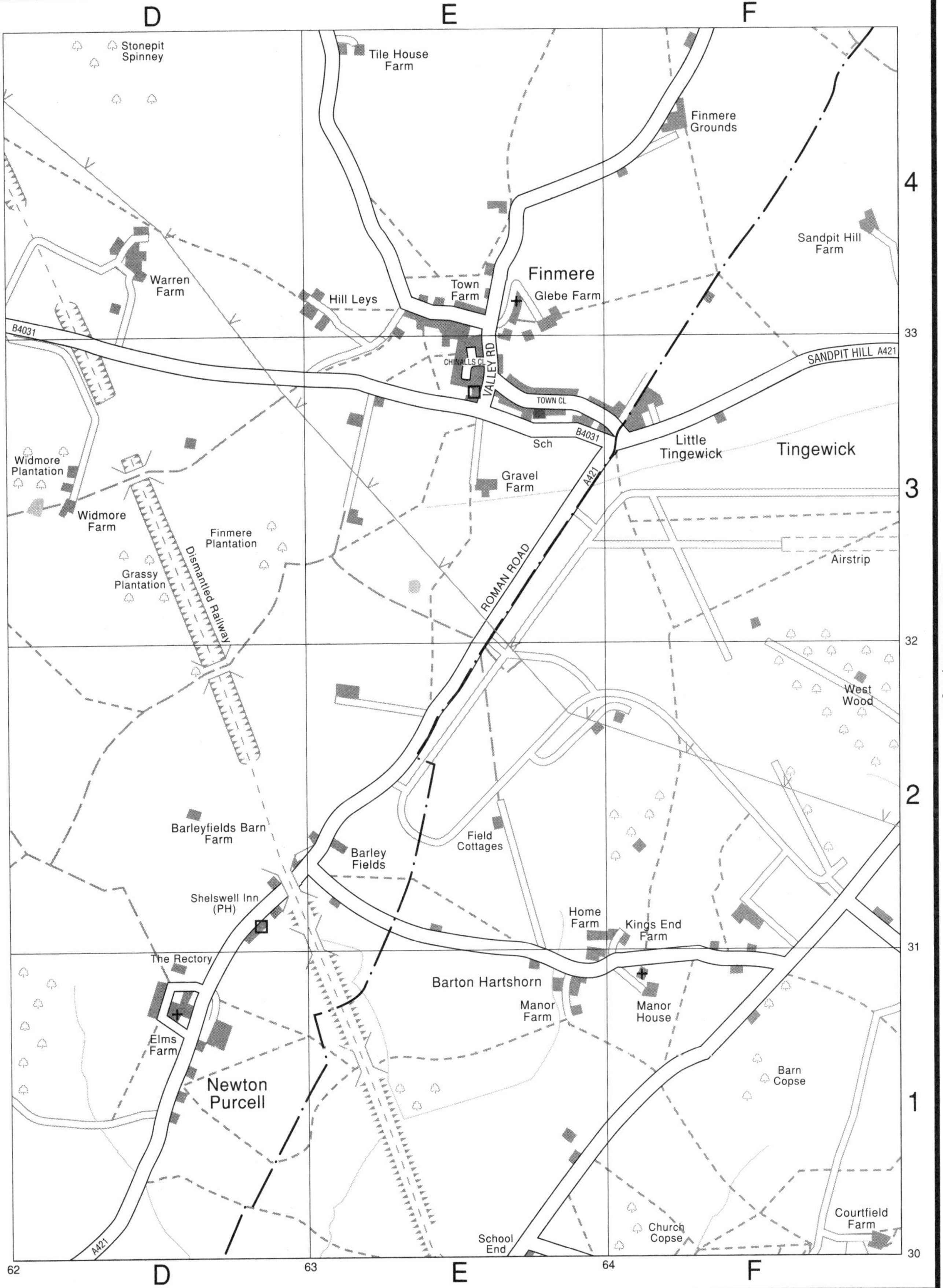
D
E
F
Stonepit Spinney
Tile House Farm
Finmere Grounds
Sandpit Hill Farm
Warren Farm
Finmere
Town Farm
Glebe Farm
Hill Leys
B4031
CHINALLS CL
VALLEY RD
TOWN CL
SANDPIT HILL A421
Sch
Little Tingewick
Tingewick
Widmore Plantation
Widmore Farm
Gravel Farm
A421
Finmere Plantation
Grassy Plantation
Dismantled Railway
ROMAN ROAD
Airstrip
West Wood
Barleyfields Barn Farm
Field Cottages
Barley Fields
Shelswell Inn (PH)
Home Farm
Kings End Farm
The Rectory
Barton Hartshorn
Manor Farm
Manor House
Elms Farm
Newton Purcell
Barn Copse
Courtfield Farm
Church Copse
School End
4
3
2
1
33
32
31
30
62
63
64
not continued, see key diagram

53

26

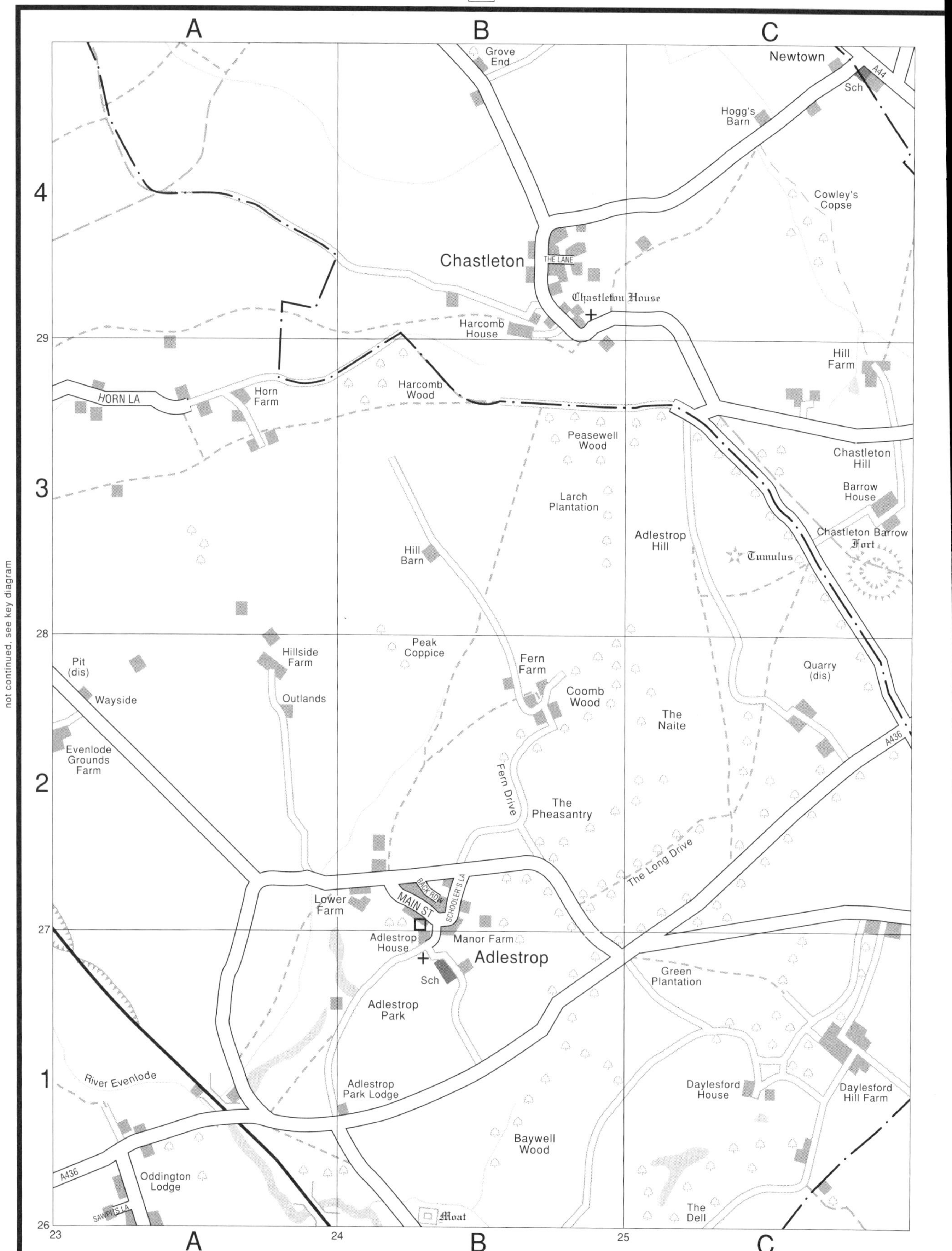
A
B
C
Grove End
Newtown
A44
Sch
Hogg's Barn
Cowley's Copse
4
Chastleton
THE LANE
Chastleton House
Harcomb House
29
Hill Farm
HORN LA
Horn Farm
Harcomb Wood
Peasewell Wood
Chastleton Hill
3
Larch Plantation
Barrow House
Chastleton Barrow Fort
Hill Barn
Adlestrop Hill
Tumulus
28
Pit (dis)
Hillside Farm
Peak Coppice
Fern Farm
Quarry (dis)
Wayside
Outlands
Coomb Wood
The Naite
Evenlode Grounds Farm
A436
2
Fern Drive
The Pheasantry
The Long Drive
BACK ROW
SCHOOLER'S LA
Lower Farm
MAIN ST
27
Adlestrop House
Manor Farm
Adlestrop
Sch
Green Plantation
Adlestrop Park
1
River Evenlode
Adlestrop Park Lodge
Daylesford House
Daylesford Hill Farm
Baywell Wood
A436
Oddington Lodge
SAWPITS LA
Moat
The Dell
26
23
24
25
not continued, see key diagram

54

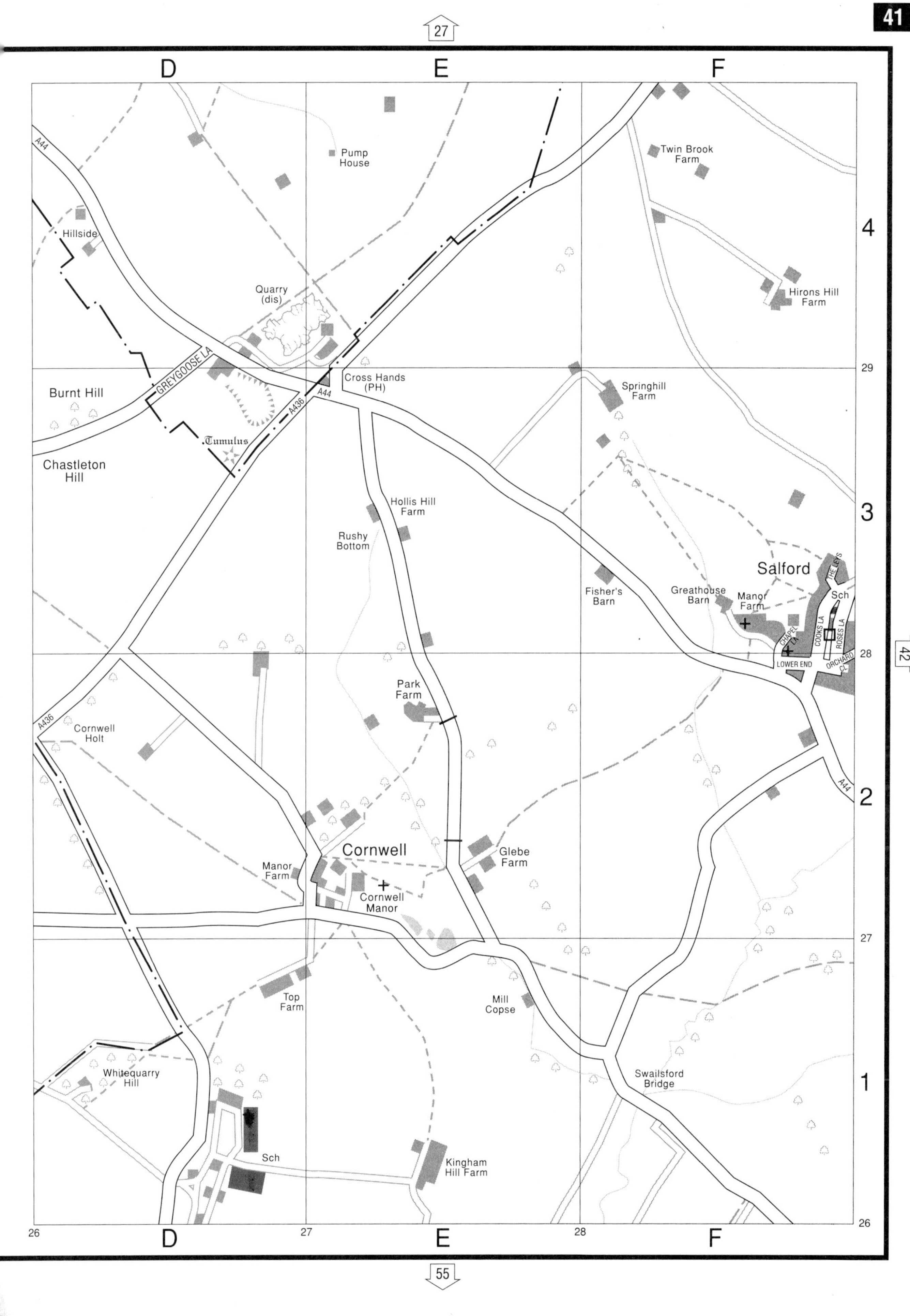
27
D
E
F
A44
Pump
House
Twin Brook
Farm
Hillside
4
Hirons Hill
Farm
Quarry
(dis)
29
Burnt Hill
GREYGOOSE LA
Cross Hands
(PH)
Springhill
Farm
A44
A436
Tumulus
Chastleton
Hill
Hollis Hill
Farm
3
Rushy
Bottom
Salford
THE LEYS
Fisher's
Barn
Greathouse
Barn
Manor
Farm
Sch
CHAPEL LA
COOKS LA
ROSES LA
LOWER END
ORCHARD CL
28
42
Park
Farm
A436
Cornwell
Holt
A44
2
Cornwell
Glebe
Farm
Manor
Farm
Cornwell
Manor
27
Top
Farm
Mill
Copse
Swailsford
Bridge
Whitequarry
Hill
1
Sch
Kingham
Hill Farm
26
26
27
28
D
E
F
55

28

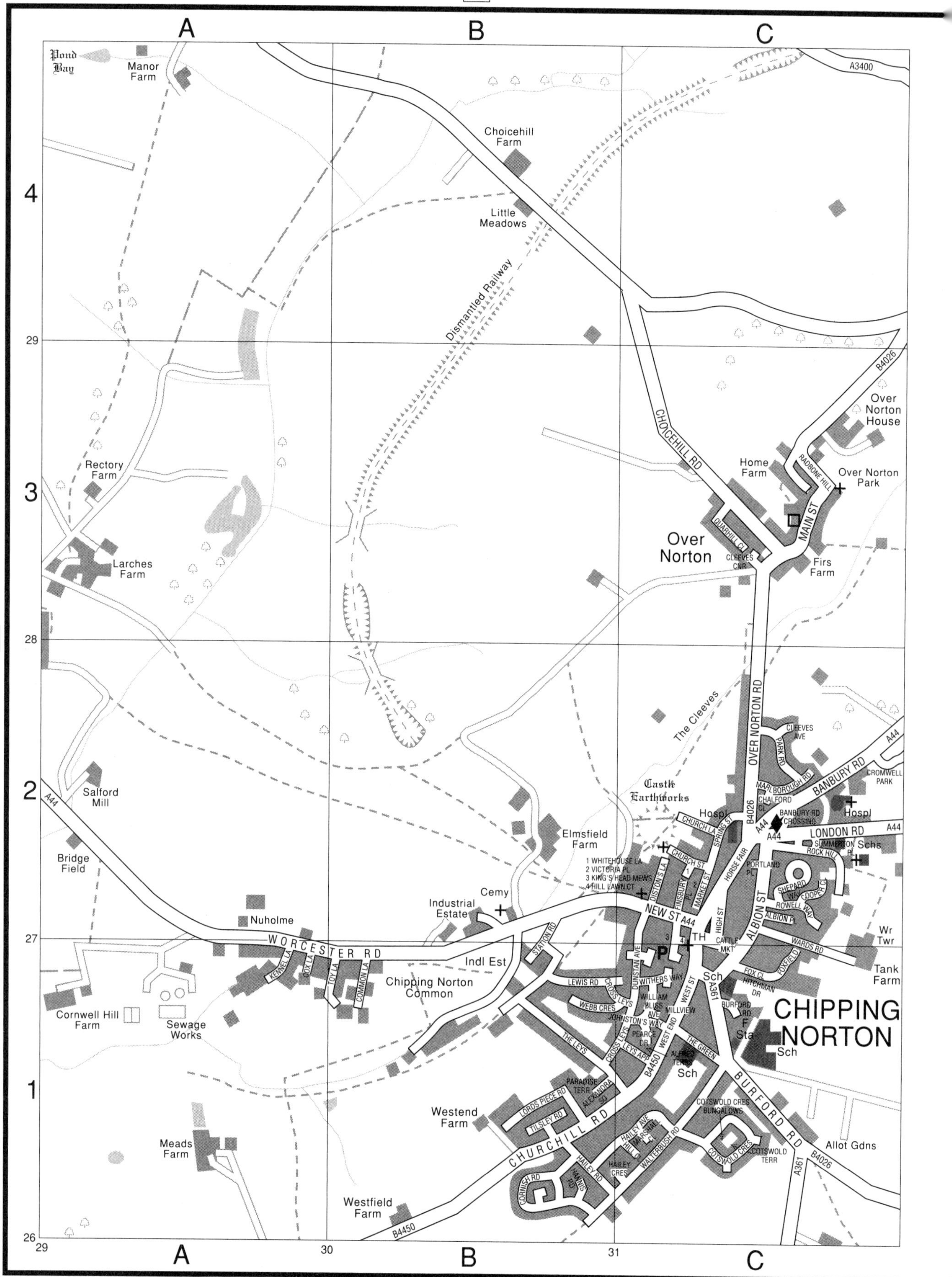
A
B
C
Pond Bay
Manor Farm
A3400
Choicehill Farm
4
Little Meadows
Dismantled Railway
29
Rectory Farm
3
Larches Farm
CHOICEHILL RD
B4026
Over Norton House
Home Farm
RADBONE HILL
Over Norton Park
MAIN ST
Over Norton
QUARHILL CL
CLEEVES CNR
Firs Farm
28
The Cleeves
OVER NORTON RD
CLEEVES AVE
PARK RD
A44
CROMWELL PARK
BANBURY RD
MARLBOROUGH RD
CHALFORD CL
2
A44
Salford Mill
Castle Earthworks
Hospl
CHURCH LA
SPRING ST
B4026
BANBURY RD CROSSING
Hospl
LONDON RD
A44
Elmsfield Farm
Bridge Field
CHURCH ST
SUMMERTON PL
ROCK HILL
Schs
1 WHITEHOUSE LA
2 VICTORIA PL
3 KING'S HEAD MEWS
4 HILL LAWN CT
HORSE FAIR
PORTLAND PL
DISTONS LA
FINSBURY PL
MARKET ST
SHEPARD WAY
COOPER CL
ROWELL WAY
Cemy
Industrial Estate
NEW ST
HIGH ST
ALBION ST
ALBION PL
Nuholme
27
WORCESTER RD
STATION RD
TH
CATTLE MKT
WARDS RD
Wr Twr
KENNEL LA
COX LA
TOY LA
COMMON LA
Indl Est
DUNSTAN AVE
P
WITHERS WAY
Sch
A361
FOX CL
HITCHMAN DR
FOXFIELD
Tank Farm
Chipping Norton Common
LEWIS RD
CROSS LEYS
WEBB CRES
WILLIAM BLISS AVE
WEST ST
BURFORD RD
F
Sta
CHIPPING NORTON
Cornwell Hill Farm
Sewage Works
JOHNSTON'S WAY
MILLVIEW
PEARCE DR
THE LEYS
CROSS LEYS
LEYS APP
WEST END
ALFRED TERR
THE GREEN
Sch
Sch
1
PARADISE TERR
ALEXANDRA SQ
B4450
BURFORD RD
LORDS PIECE RD
TILSLEY RD
Westend Farm
COTSWOLD CRES BUNGALOWS
HAILEY AVE
MARSHALL
WALTERBUSH RD
Meads Farm
CHURCHILL RD
COTSWOLD CRES
COTSWOLD TERR
Allot Gdns
HAILEY RD
HANNIS RD
HAILEY CRES
CORNISH RD
A361
B4026
Westfield Farm
B4450
26
29
30
31
A
B
C

41

56

29

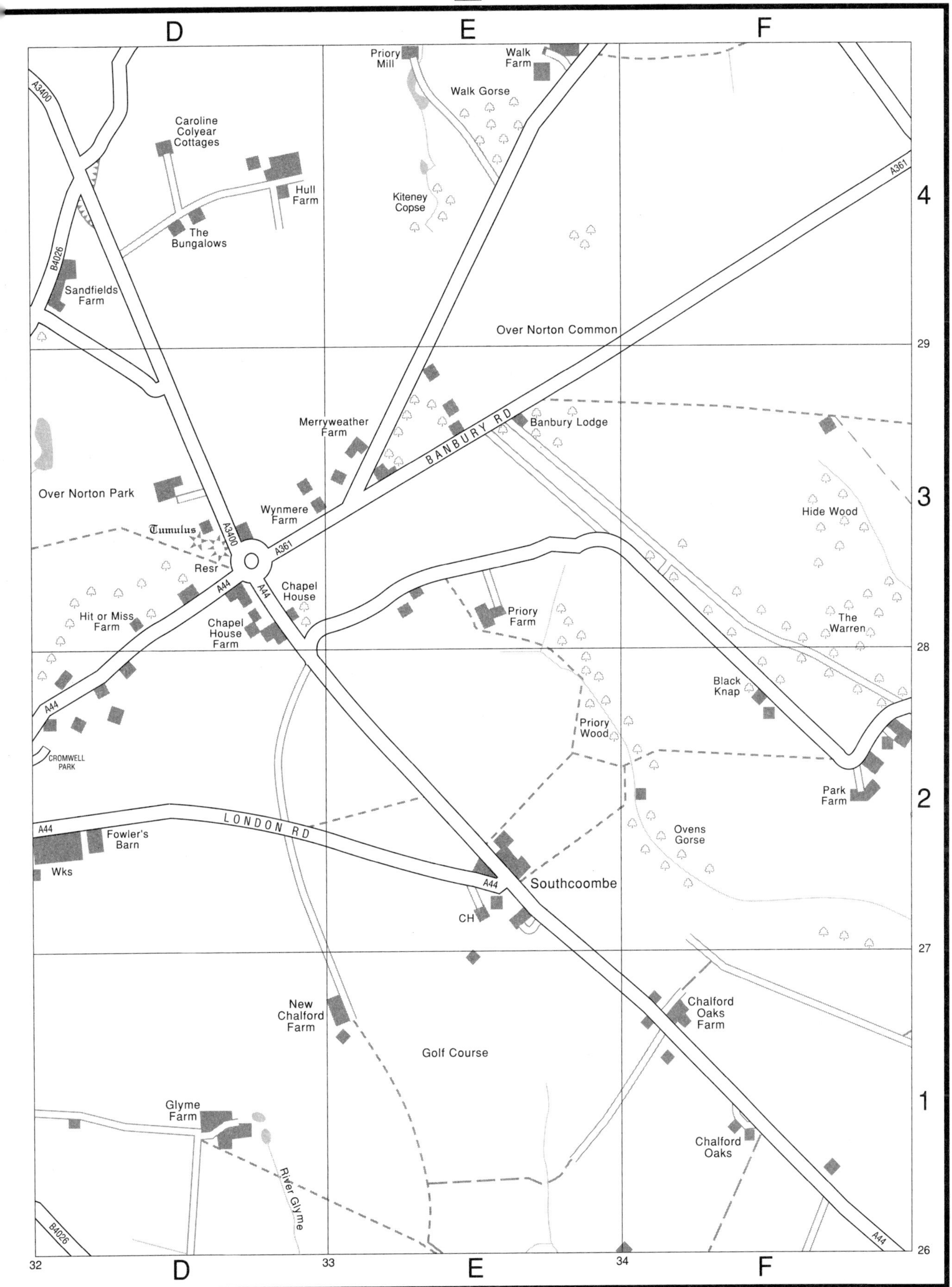

D
E
F
Priory Mill
Walk Farm
Walk Gorse
A3400
Caroline Colyear Cottages
Hull Farm
Kiteney Copse
The Bungalows
B4026
Sandfields Farm
A361
Over Norton Common
29
4
Merryweather Farm
BANBURY RD
Banbury Lodge
Over Norton Park
Wynmere Farm
Tumulus
Resr
A361
A3400
A44
A44
Chapel House
Hit or Miss Farm
Chapel House Farm
Priory Farm
Hide Wood
3
The Warren
28
Black Knap
Priory Wood
A44
CROMWELL PARK
Park Farm
2
A44
Fowler's Barn
LONDON RD
Wks
Ovens Gorse
A44
Southcoombe
CH
27
New Chalford Farm
Chalford Oaks Farm
Golf Course
1
Glyme Farm
River Glyme
Chalford Oaks
B4026
A44
26
32
33
34
D
E
F

44

57

30

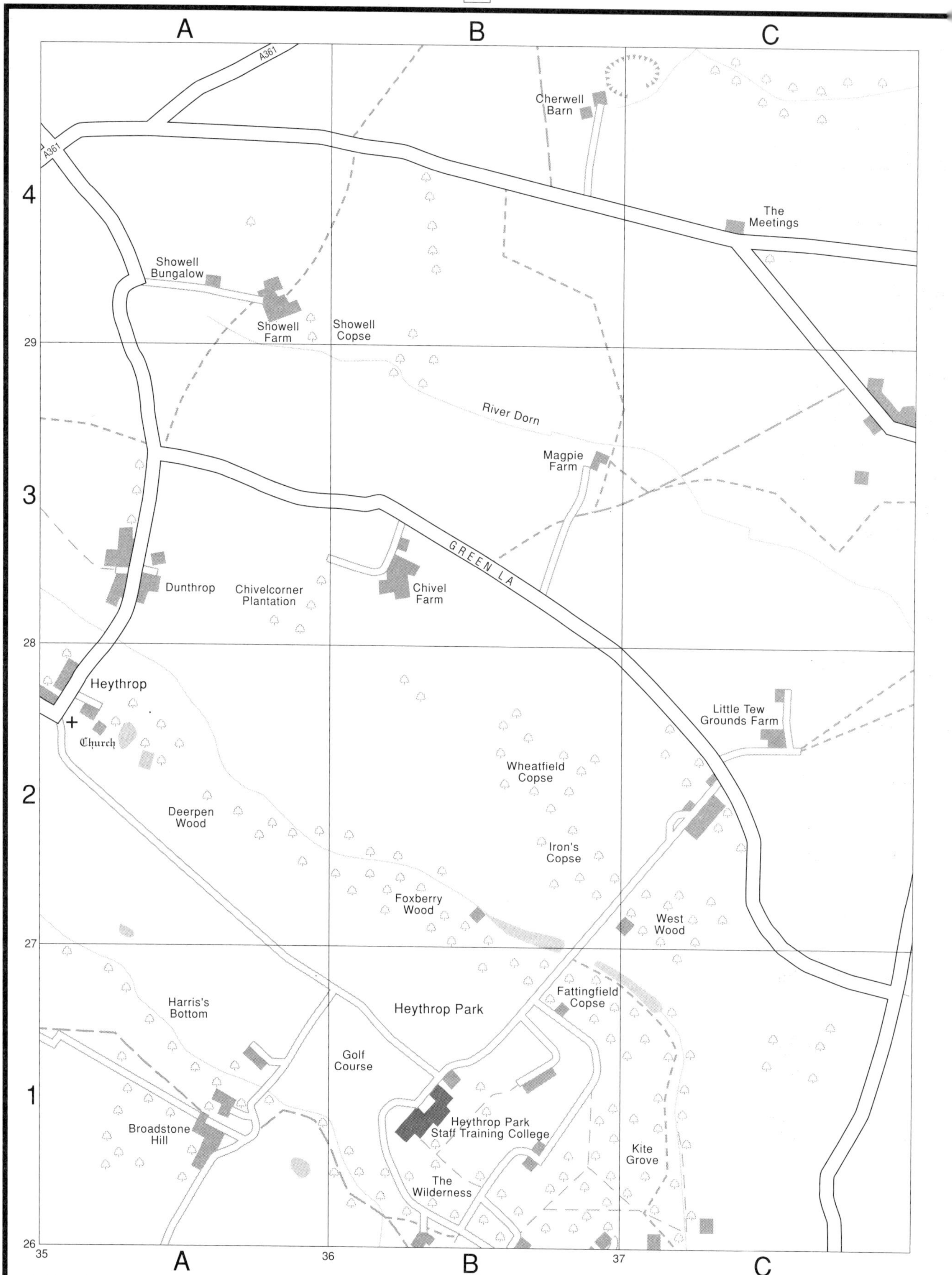
A
B
C
A361
A361
Cherwell
Barn
4
The
Meetings
Showell
Bungalow
Showell
Farm
Showell
Copse
29
River Dorn
Magpie
Farm
3
GREEN LA
Dunthrop
Chivelcorner
Plantation
Chivel
Farm
28
Heythrop
Church
Little Tew
Grounds Farm
Wheatfield
Copse
2
Deerpen
Wood
Iron's
Copse
Foxberry
Wood
West
Wood
27
Harris's
Bottom
Fattingfield
Copse
Heythrop Park
Golf
Course
1
Heythrop Park
Staff Training College
Broadstone
Hill
Kite
Grove
The
Wilderness
26
35
36
37
A
B
C

43

58

31

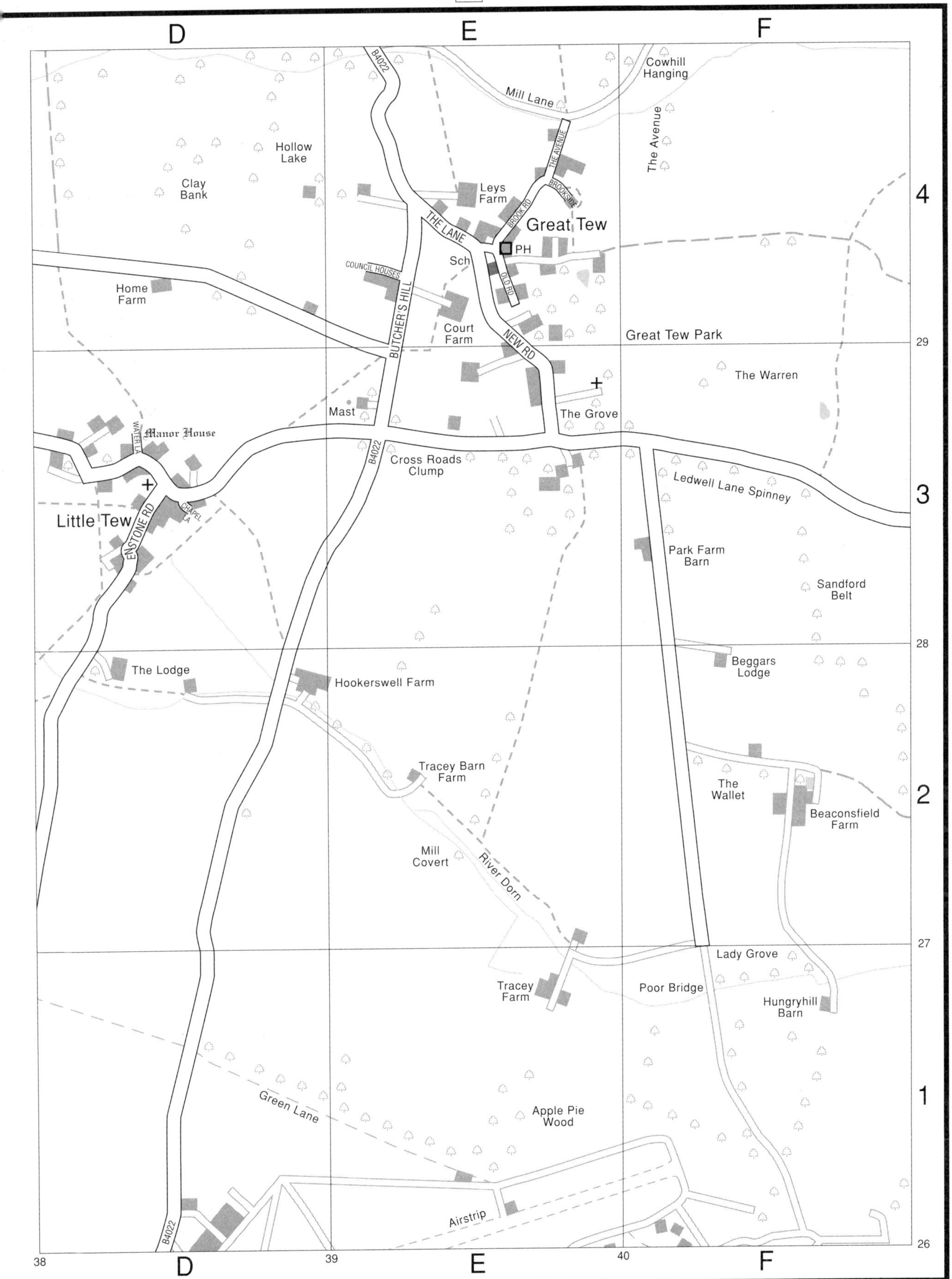

D
E
F
Cowhill Hanging
Mill Lane
The Avenue
THE AVENUE
BROOKSIDE
BROOK RD
Hollow Lake
Clay Bank
Leys Farm
Great Tew
THE LANE
PH
Sch
COUNCIL HOUSES
OLD RD
Home Farm
BUTCHER'S HILL
Court Farm
NEW RD
Great Tew Park
The Warren
Mast
The Grove
Manor House
WATER LA
B4022
Cross Roads Clump
Ledwell Lane Spinney
Little Tew
ENSTONE RD
CHAPEL LA
Park Farm Barn
Sandford Belt
The Lodge
Hookerswell Farm
Beggars Lodge
Tracey Barn Farm
The Wallet
Beaconsfield Farm
Mill Covert
River Dorn
Lady Grove
Tracey Farm
Poor Bridge
Hungryhill Barn
Green Lane
Apple Pie Wood
Airstrip
B4022
4
3
2
1
29
28
27
26
38
39
40

46

59

32

45

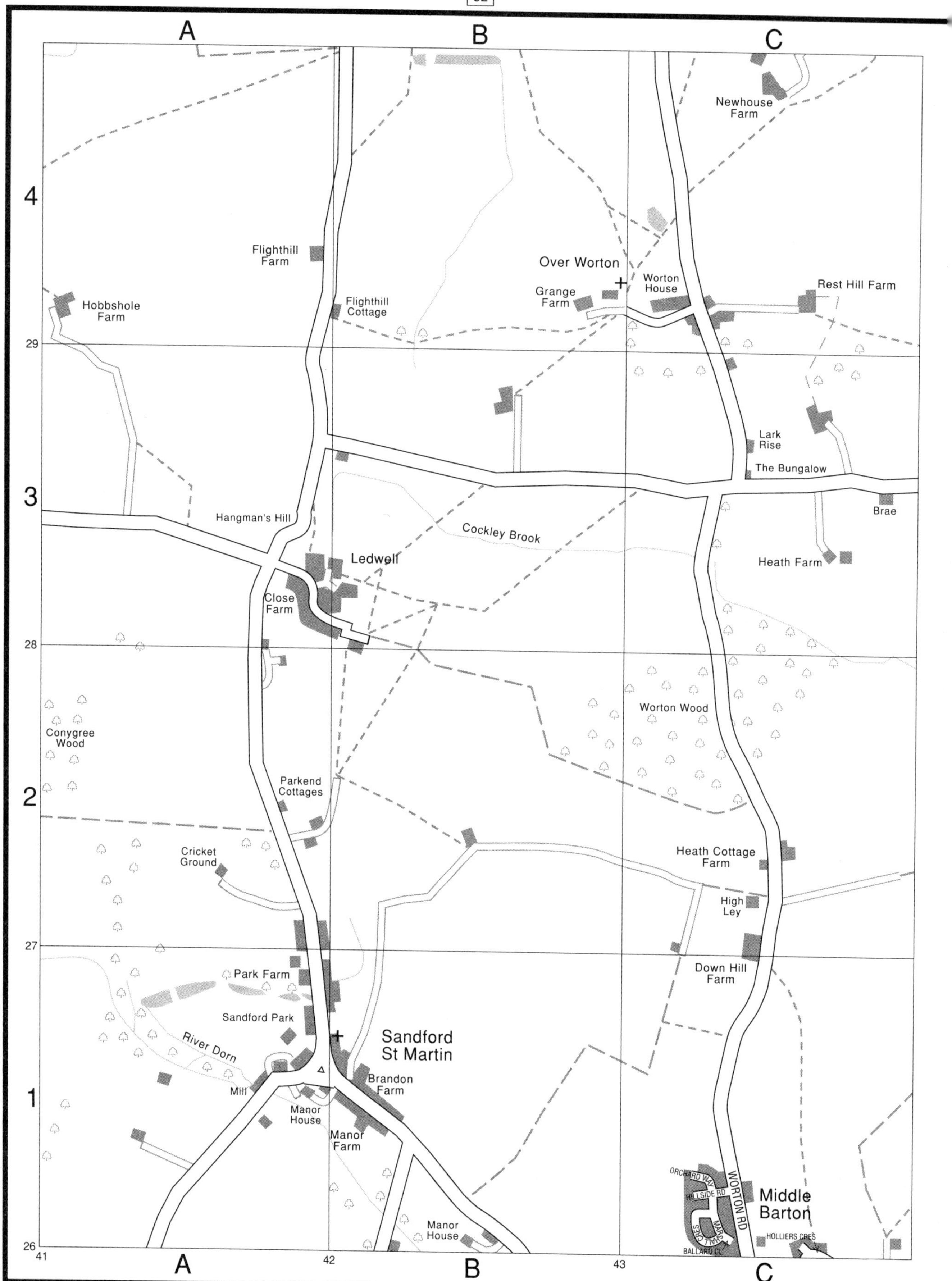
A
B
C
4
3
2
1
29
28
27
26
41
42
43
Newhouse Farm
Flighthill Farm
Over Worton
Worton House
Rest Hill Farm
Grange Farm
Hobbshole Farm
Flighthill Cottage
Lark Rise
The Bungalow
Brae
Hangman's Hill
Cockley Brook
Ledwell
Heath Farm
Close Farm
Worton Wood
Conygree Wood
Parkend Cottages
Cricket Ground
Heath Cottage Farm
High Ley
Down Hill Farm
Park Farm
Sandford Park
Sandford St Martin
River Dorn
Brandon Farm
Mill
Manor House
Manor Farm
Manor House
ORCHARD WAY
HILLSIDE RD
WORTON RD
Middle Barton
HOLLIERS CRES
BALLARD CL

60

33

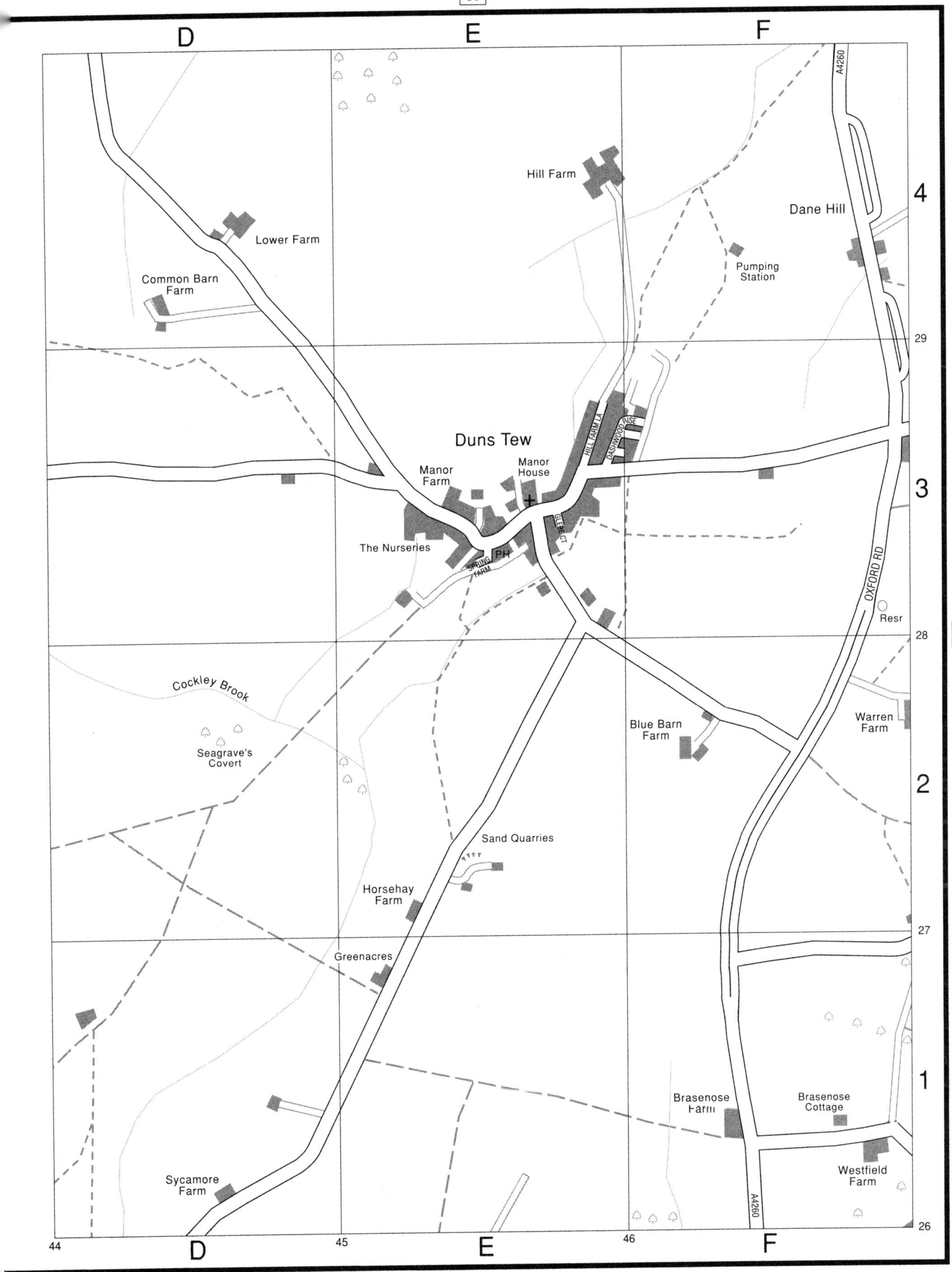

D
E
F
Hill Farm
Lower Farm
Common Barn Farm
Dane Hill
Pumping Station
A4260
4
29
Duns Tew
Manor Farm
Manor House
The Nurseries
HILL FARM LA
DASHWOOD RISE
GLEBE CT
SPRING FARM
PH
3
OXFORD RD
Resr
28
Cockley Brook
Seagrave's Covert
Blue Barn Farm
Warren Farm
2
Sand Quarries
Horsehay Farm
27
Greenacres
1
Brasenose Farm
Brasenose Cottage
Westfield Farm
Sycamore Farm
A4260
26
44
45
46
D
E
F

48

61

34

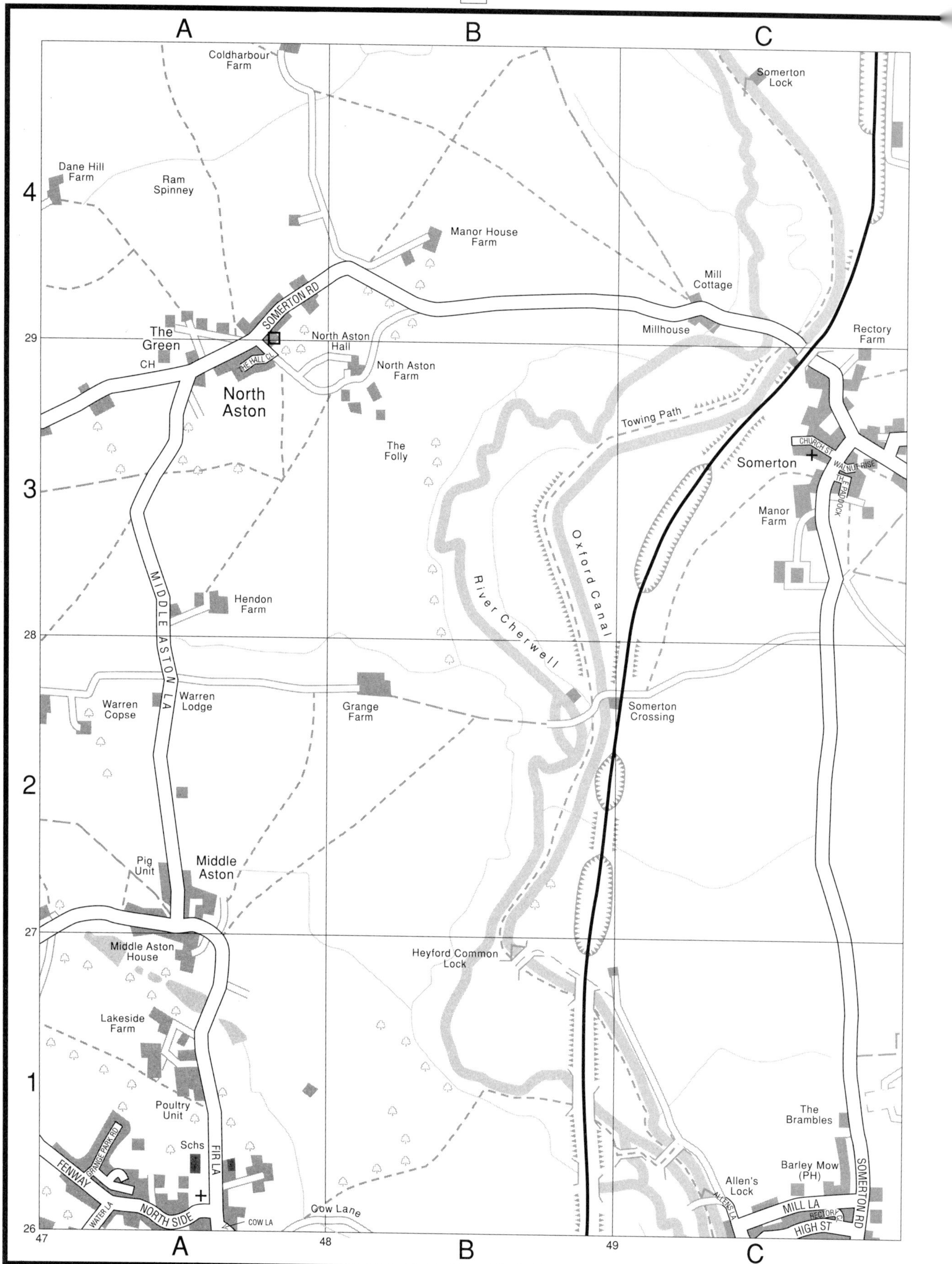
A
B
C
Coldharbour Farm
Somerton Lock
Dane Hill Farm
Ram Spinney
4
Manor House Farm
Mill Cottage
SOMERTON RD
The Green
29
North Aston Hall
Millhouse
Rectory Farm
CH
THE HALL CL
North Aston Farm
North Aston
Towing Path
The Folly
CHURCH ST
Somerton
WALNUT RISE
THE PADDOCK
3
Manor Farm
Oxford Canal
River Cherwell
MIDDLE ASTON LA
Hendon Farm
28
Warren Copse
Warren Lodge
Grange Farm
Somerton Crossing
2
Pig Unit
Middle Aston
27
Middle Aston House
Heyford Common Lock
Lakeside Farm
1
Poultry Unit
The Brambles
Schs
GRANGE PARK RD
FENWAY
FIR LA
Barley Mow (PH)
SOMERTON RD
Allen's Lock
ALLENS LA
MILL LA
RECTORY CL
HIGH ST
WATER LA
NORTH SIDE
COW LA
Cow Lane
26
47
48
49

47

62

35

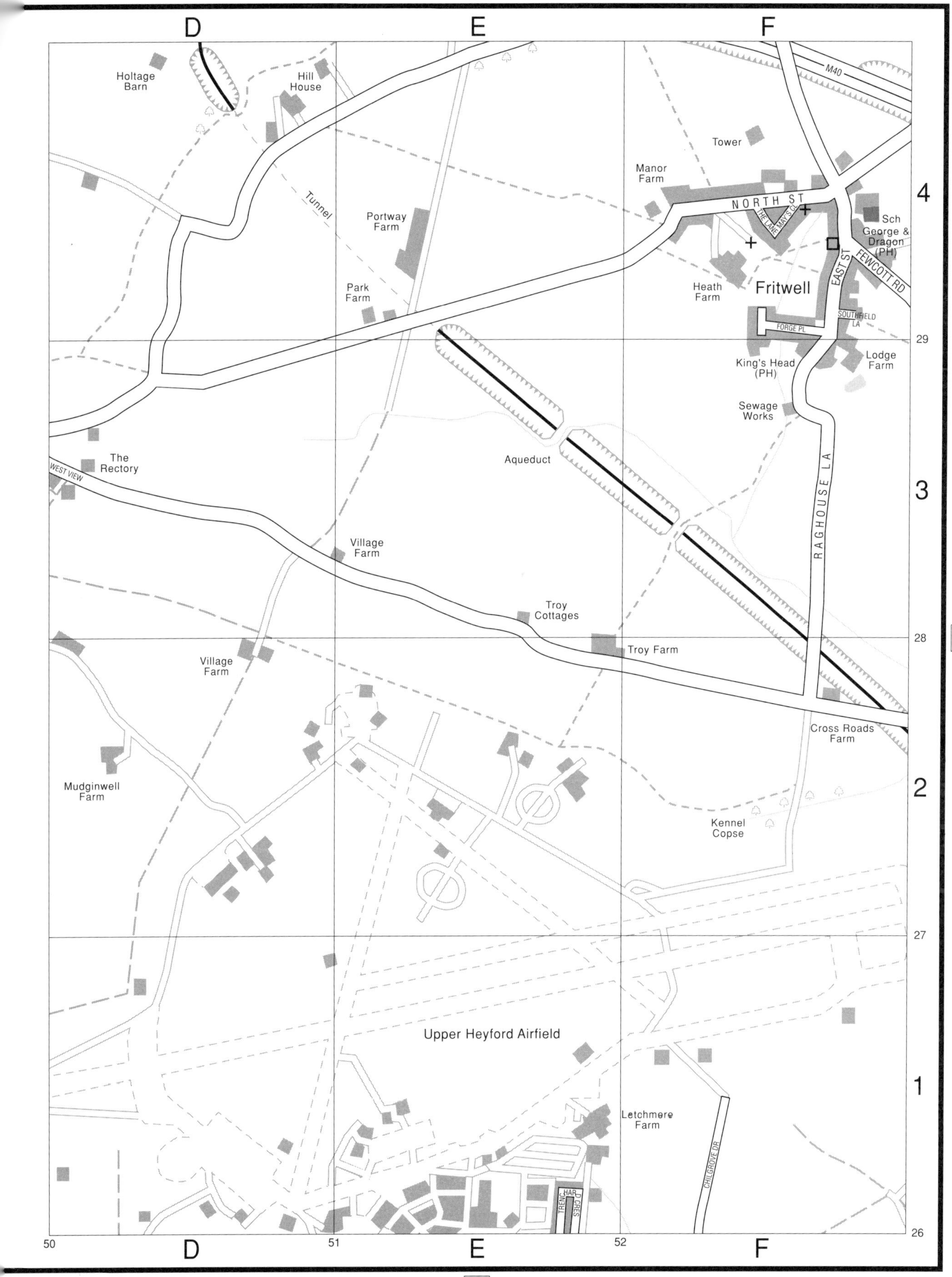
D
E
F
Holtage Barn
Hill House
Tunnel
Portway Farm
Park Farm
M40
Tower
Manor Farm
NORTH ST
THE LANE
MAY'S CL
Sch
George & Dragon (PH)
FEWCOTT RD
EAST ST
Heath Farm
Fritwell
SOUTHFIELD LA
FORGE PL
King's Head (PH)
Lodge Farm
Sewage Works
4
29
3
The Rectory
WEST VIEW
Aqueduct
RAGHOUSE LA
Village Farm
Troy Cottages
Troy Farm
28
Village Farm
Cross Roads Farm
Mudginwell Farm
2
Kennel Copse
27
Upper Heyford Airfield
1
Letchmere Farm
CHILGROVE DR
TRENCHARD CRES
26
50
51
52

50

63

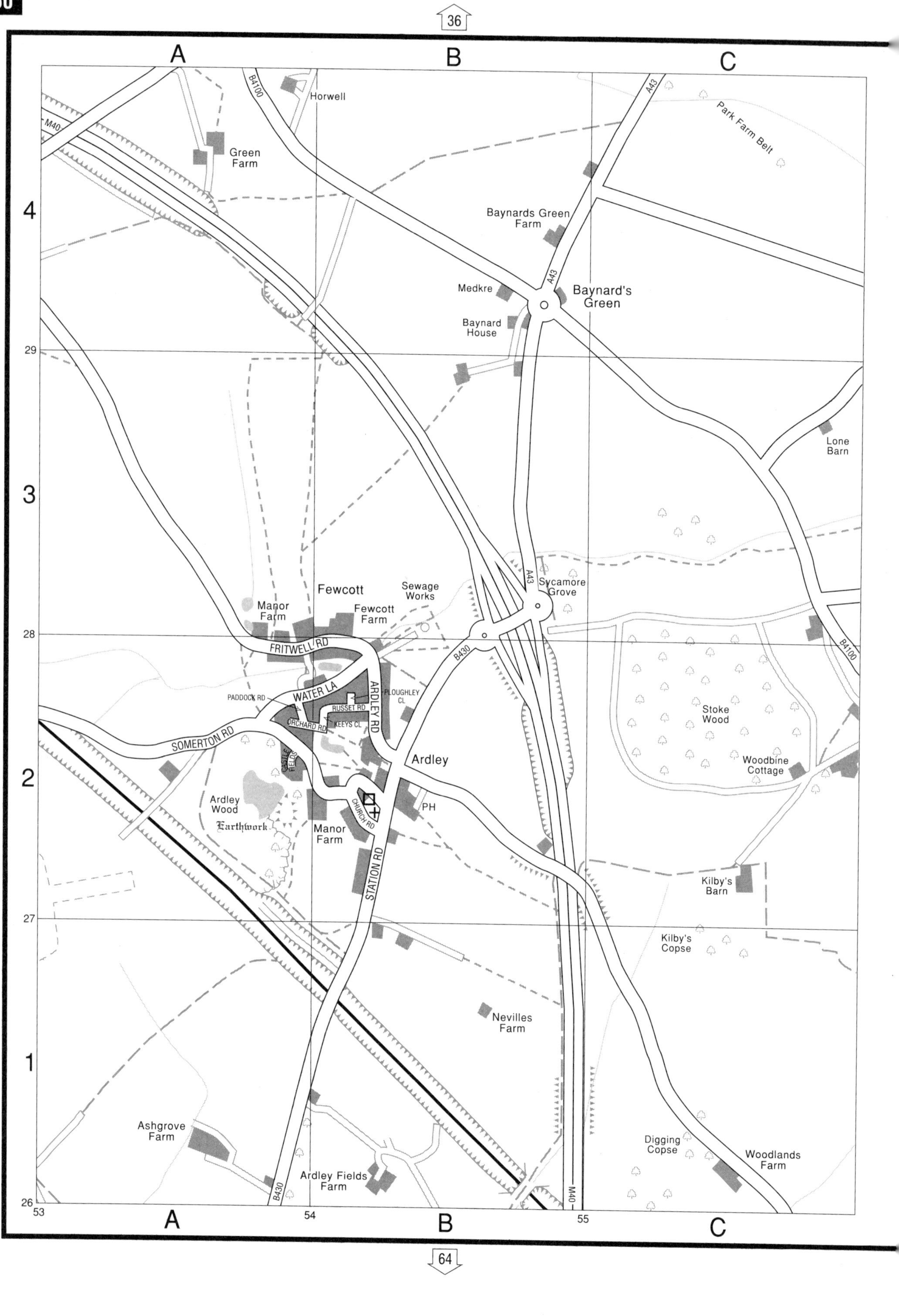
36
A
B
C
4
3
2
1
29
28
27
26
53
54
55
49
64
M40
B4100
Horwell
Green Farm
A43
Park Farm Belt
Baynards Green Farm
Medkre
Baynard's Green
Baynard House
Lone Barn
Fewcott
Manor Farm
Fewcott Farm
Sewage Works
Sycamore Grove
FRITWELL RD
B430
WATER LA
PADDOCK RD
RUSSET RD
PLOUGHLEY CL
ORCHARD RD
KEEYS CL
ARDLEY RD
SOMERTON RD
CASTLE FIELDS
Ardley
Stoke Wood
Woodbine Cottage
Ardley Wood
Earthwork
Manor Farm
CHURCH RD
PH
STATION RD
Kilby's Barn
Kilby's Copse
Nevilles Farm
Ashgrove Farm
Ardley Fields Farm
Digging Copse
Woodlands Farm

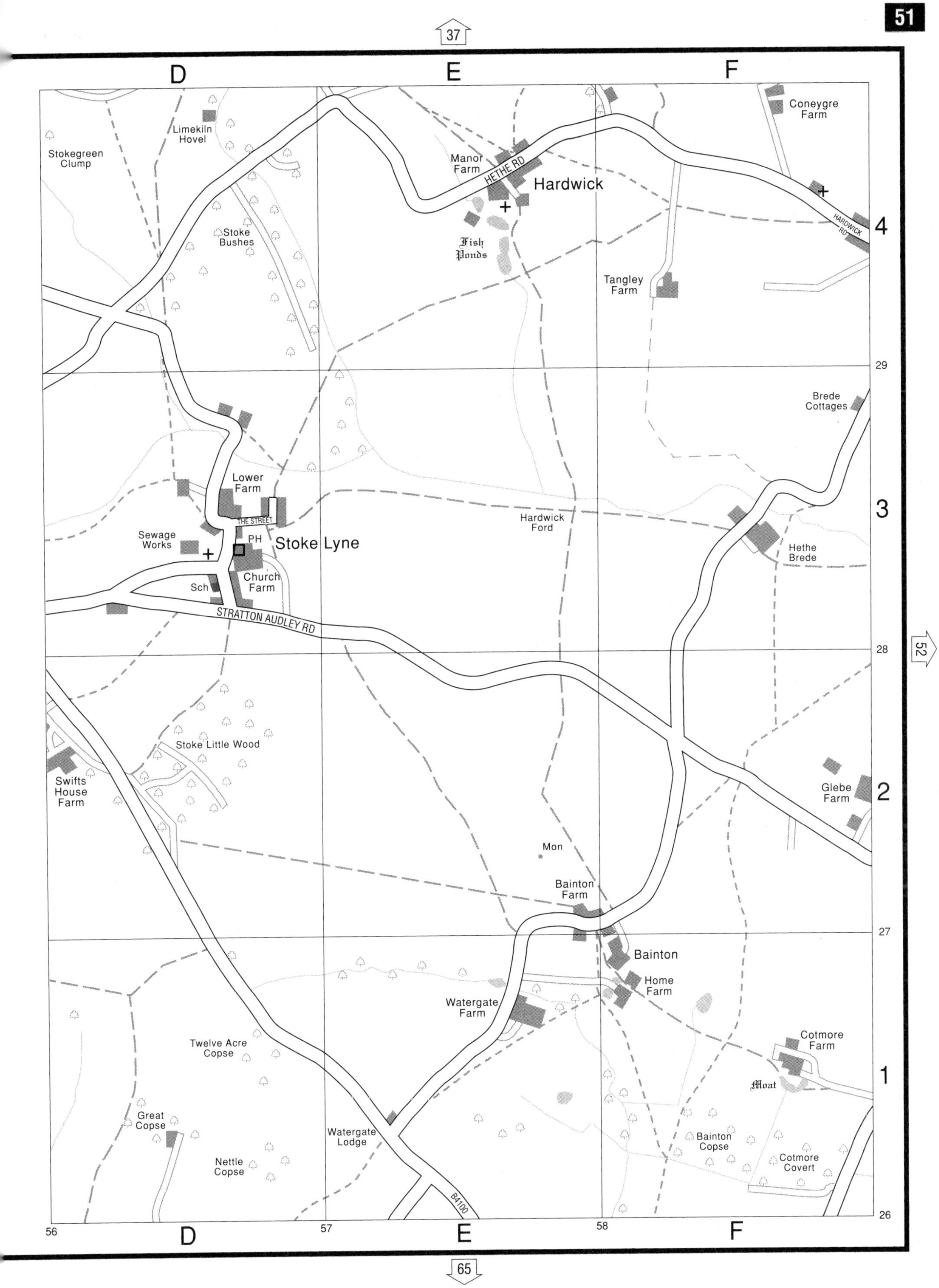
37
D
E
F
Coneygre Farm
Limekiln Hovel
Stokegreen Clump
Manor Farm
HETHE RD
Hardwick
HARDWICK RD
4
Stoke Bushes
Fish Ponds
Tangley Farm
29
Brede Cottages
Lower Farm
THE STREET
3
Hardwick Ford
Sewage Works
PH
Stoke Lyne
Hethe Brede
Sch
Church Farm
STRATTON AUDLEY RD
28
52
Stoke Little Wood
Swifts House Farm
Glebe Farm
2
Mon
Bainton Farm
27
Bainton
Home Farm
Watergate Farm
Cotmore Farm
Twelve Acre Copse
Moat
1
Great Copse
Watergate Lodge
Bainton Copse
Nettle Copse
Cotmore Covert
B4100
26
56
D
57
E
58
F
65

38

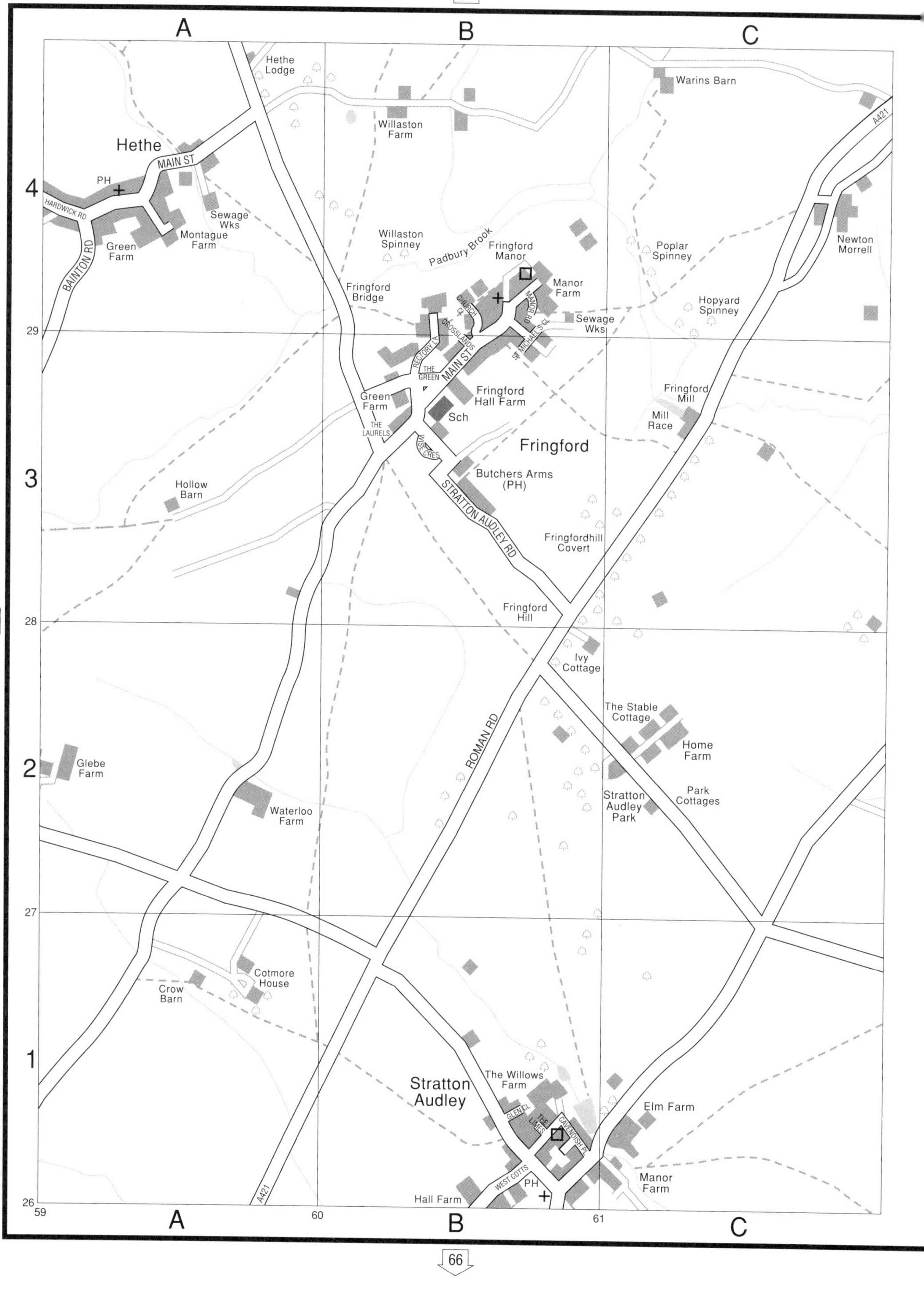
A
B
C
4
3
2
1
29
28
27
26
59
60
61
Hethe Lodge
Willaston Farm
Warins Barn
Hethe
MAIN ST
PH
HARDWICK RD
BAINTON RD
Green Farm
Sewage Wks
Montague Farm
Willaston Spinney
Padbury Brook
Fringford Manor
Manor Farm
Poplar Spinney
Newton Morrell
A421
Fringford Bridge
CHURCH CL
MANOR RD
Sewage Wks
Hopyard Spinney
CROSSLANDS
RECTORY LA
ST MICHAEL'S CL
THE GREEN
MAIN ST
Fringford Hall Farm
Fringford Mill
Green Farm
Sch
Mill Race
THE LAURELS
WISE CRES
Fringford
Butchers Arms (PH)
Hollow Barn
STRATTON AUDLEY RD
Fringfordhill Covert
Fringford Hill
Ivy Cottage
The Stable Cottage
Home Farm
ROMAN RD
Glebe Farm
Stratton Audley Park
Park Cottages
Waterloo Farm
Cotmore House
Crow Barn
The Willows Farm
Stratton Audley
GLEN CL
THE LIMES
CAVENDISH PL
Elm Farm
WEST COTTS
PH
Manor Farm
Hall Farm
A421

51

66

39

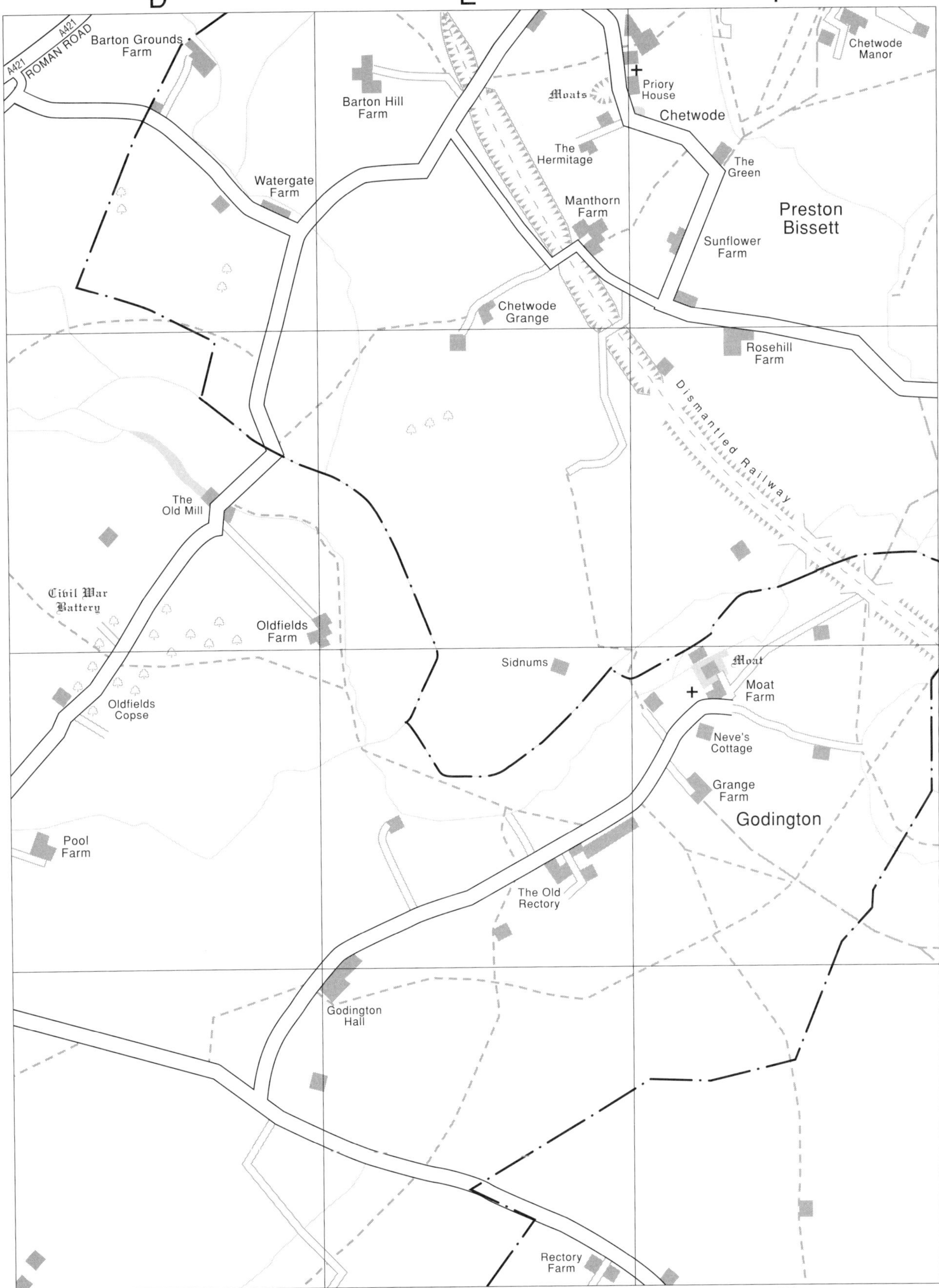

not continued, see key diagram

67

40

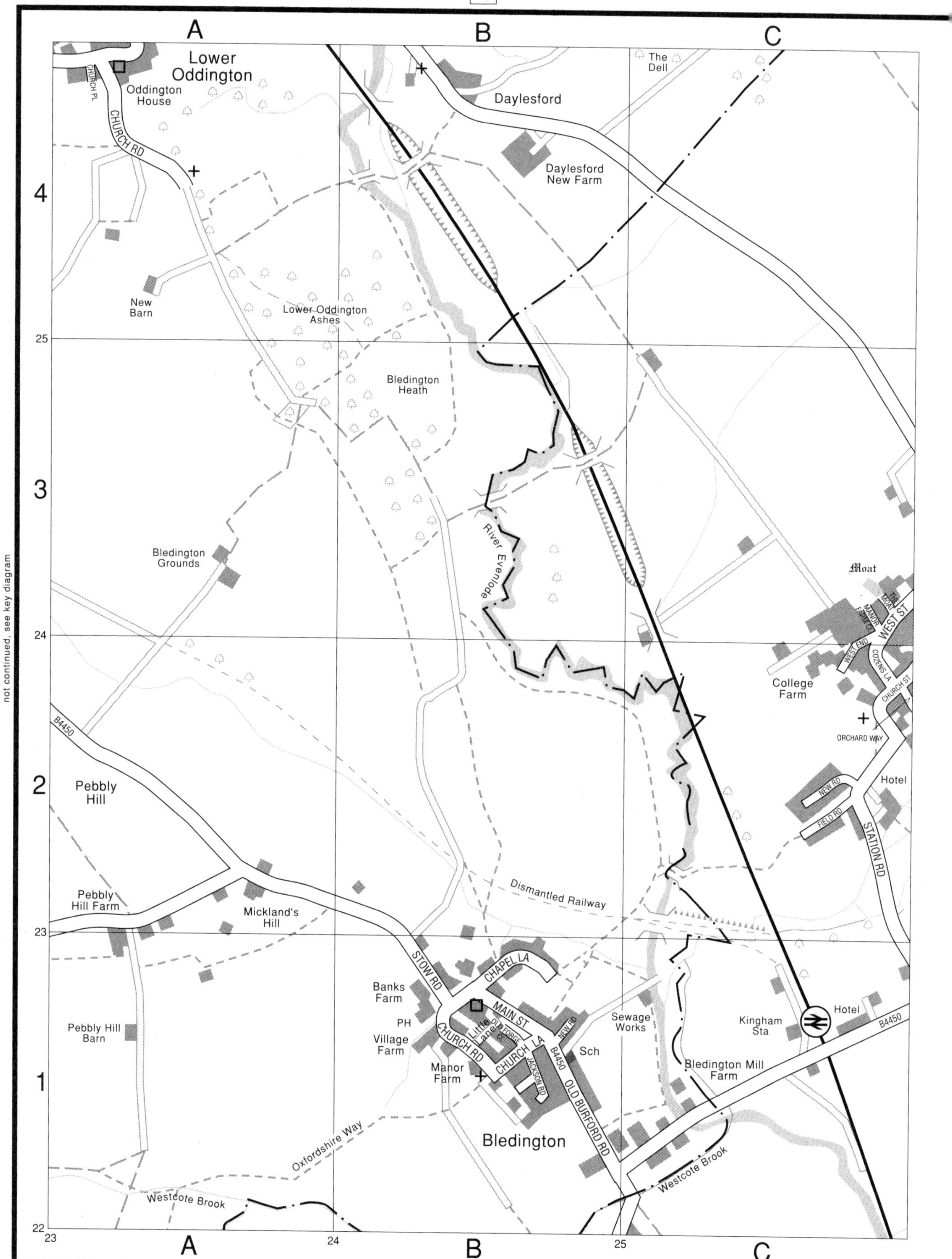
Lower Oddington
Oddington House
CHURCH PL
CHURCH RD
Daylesford
The Dell
Daylesford New Farm
New Barn
Lower Oddington Ashes
Bledington Heath
Bledington Grounds
River Evenlode
Moat
THE MOAT
MANOR FARM CT
WEST ST
WEST END
COZENS LA
CHURCH ST
College Farm
ORCHARD WAY
NEW RD
FIELD RD
STATION RD
Hotel
B4450
Pebbly Hill
Pebbly Hill Farm
Mickland's Hill
Dismantled Railway
STOW RD
CHAPEL LA
MAIN ST
Banks Farm
PH
Village Farm
Little Lane
OLD FORGE CT
CHURCH RD
CHURCH LA
JACKSON RD
NEW RD
B4450
OLD BURFORD RD
Sch
Sewage Works
Kingham Sta
Hotel
B4450
Bledington Mill Farm
Manor Farm
Pebbly Hill Barn
Bledington
Oxfordshire Way
Westcote Brook
Westcote Brook
A
B
C
1
2
3
4
22
23
24
25
not continued, see key diagram

69

41

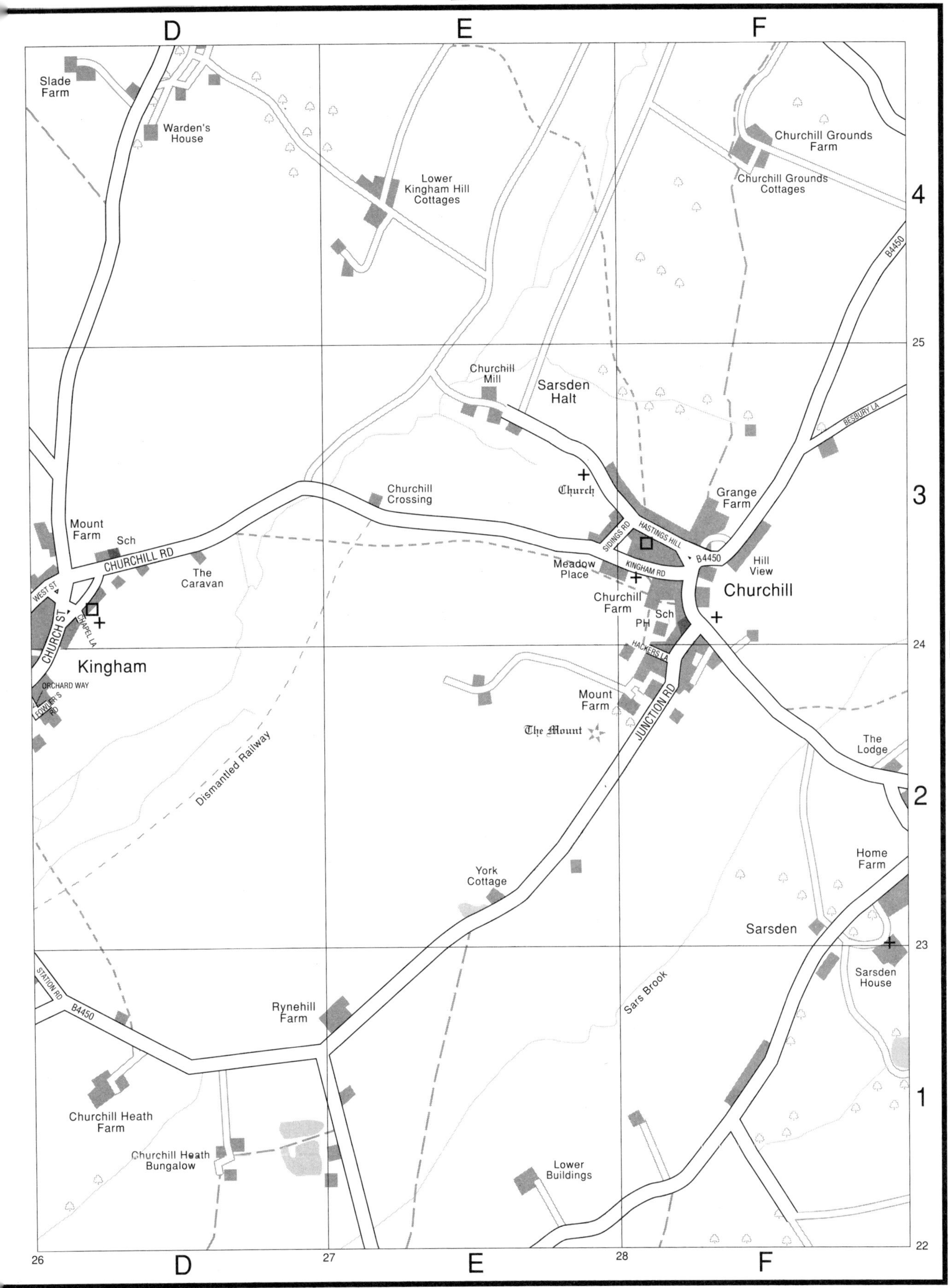
D
E
F
Slade Farm
Warden's House
Lower Kingham Hill Cottages
Churchill Grounds Farm
Churchill Grounds Cottages
4
B4450
25
Churchill Mill
Sarsden Halt
BESBURY LA
Church
3
Churchill Crossing
Grange Farm
Mount Farm
Sch
CHURCHILL RD
The Caravan
SIDINGS RD
HASTINGS HILL
B4450
Hill View
Meadow Place
KINGHAM RD
Churchill
Churchill Farm
Sch
PH
WEST ST
CHURCH ST
CHAPEL LA
Kingham
24
HACKERS LA
ORCHARD WAY
FOWLER'S RD
Mount Farm
JUNCTION RD
The Mount
The Lodge
Dismantled Railway
2
Home Farm
York Cottage
Sarsden
23
Sarsden House
STATION RD
B4450
Sars Brook
Rynehill Farm
1
Churchill Heath Farm
Churchill Heath Bungalow
Lower Buildings
22
26
27
28
D
E
F

56

70

42

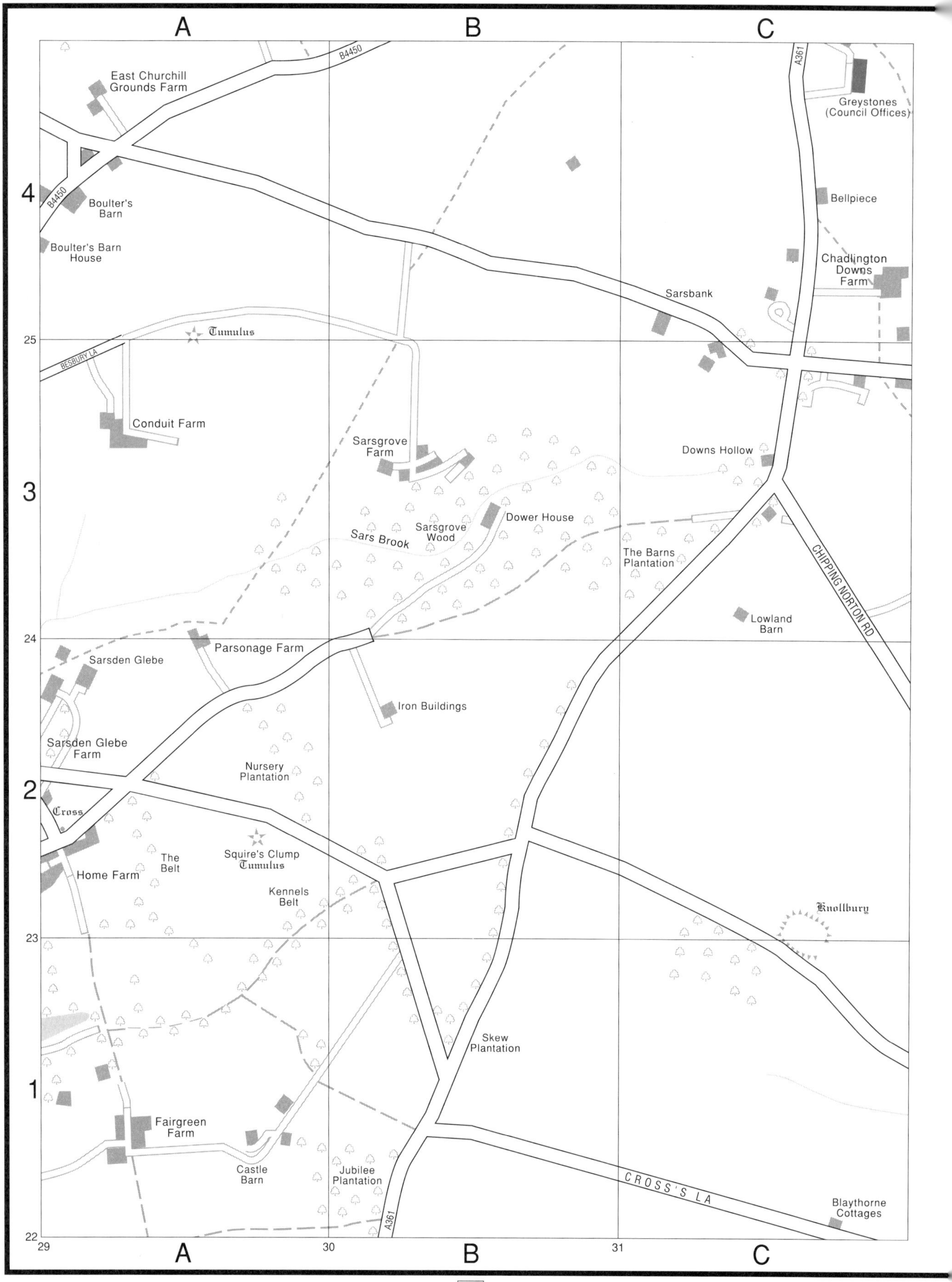
A
B
C
East Churchill Grounds Farm
B4450
Greystones (Council Offices)
A361
Boulter's Barn
Boulter's Barn House
Bellpiece
Chadlington Downs Farm
Sarsbank
Tumulus
BESBURY LA
Conduit Farm
Sarsgrove Farm
Downs Hollow
Dower House
Sarsgrove Wood
Sars Brook
The Barns Plantation
CHIPPING NORTON RD
Lowland Barn
Parsonage Farm
Sarsden Glebe
Iron Buildings
Sarsden Glebe Farm
Nursery Plantation
Cross
Squire's Clump Tumulus
The Belt
Home Farm
Kennels Belt
Knollbury
Skew Plantation
Fairgreen Farm
Castle Barn
Jubilee Plantation
CROSS'S LA
Blaythorne Cottages
4
25
3
24
2
23
1
22
29
30
31

55

71

43

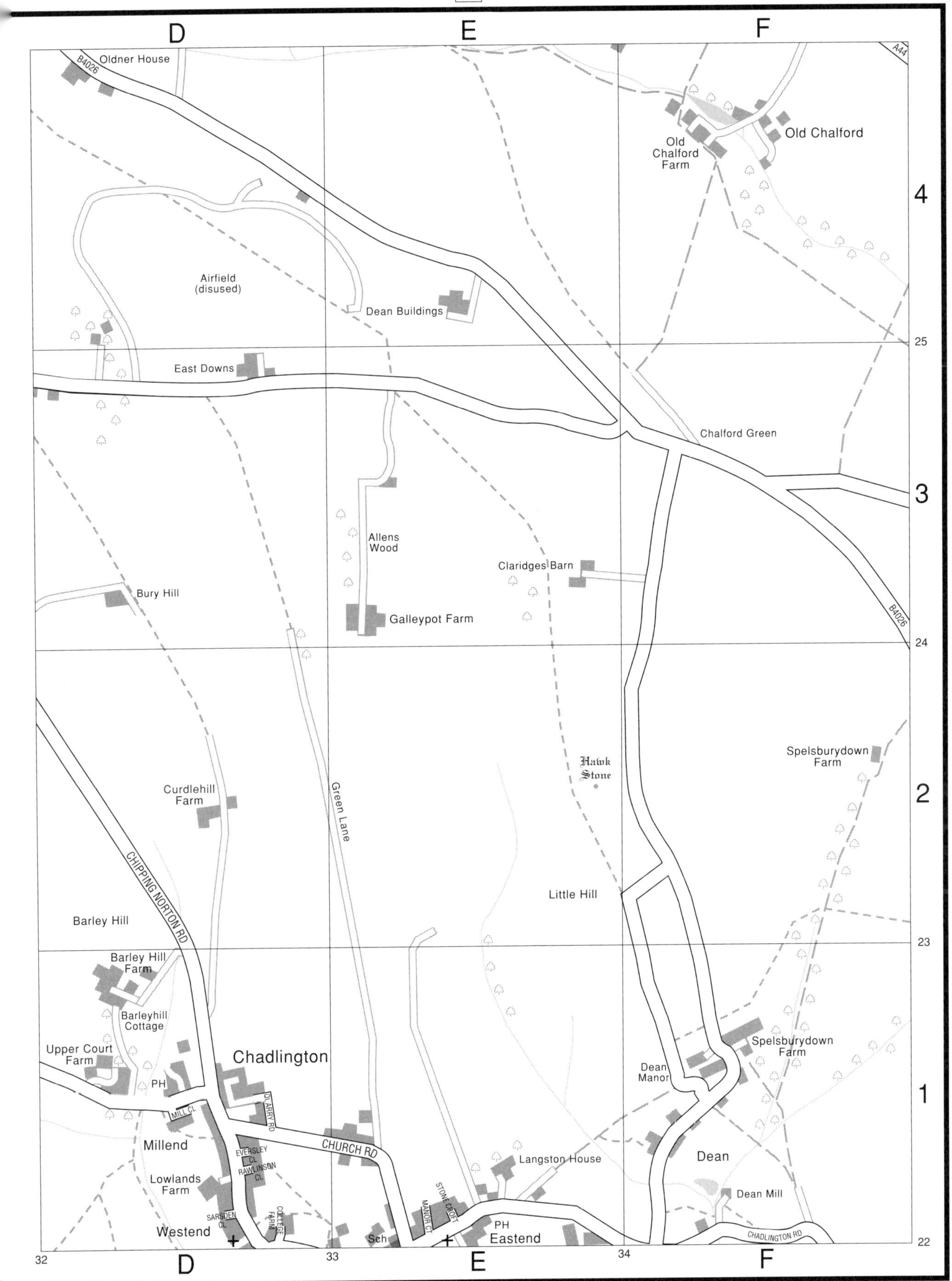

D
E
F
B4026
Oldner House
A44
Old Chalford
Old Chalford Farm
4
Airfield (disused)
Dean Buildings
25
East Downs
Chalford Green
3
Allens Wood
Claridges Barn
Bury Hill
Galleypot Farm
B4026
24
Spelsburydown Farm
Hawk Stone
2
Curdlehill Farm
Green Lane
CHIPPING NORTON RD
Little Hill
Barley Hill
23
Barley Hill Farm
Barleyhill Cottage
Upper Court Farm
Chadlington
Spelsburydown Farm
Dean Manor
PH
1
MILL CL
QUARRY RD
Millend
CHURCH RD
EVERSLEY CL
RAWLINSON CL
Langston House
Dean
Lowlands Farm
STONE CROFT
MANOR CT
Dean Mill
SARSDEN CL
COLLEGE FARM
PH
Westend
Sch
Eastend
CHADLINGTON RD
22
32
33
34
D
E
F

58

72

44

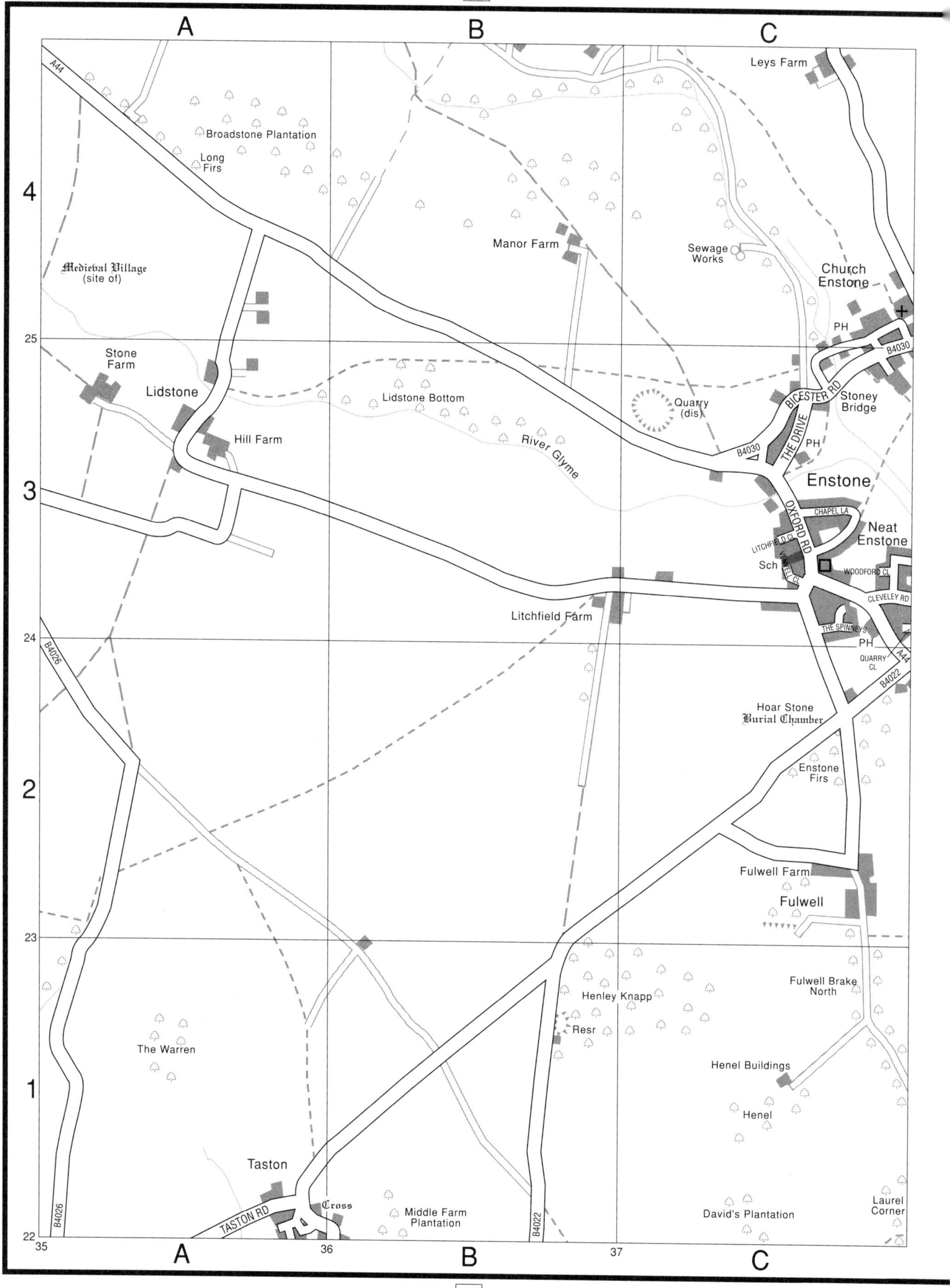
A
B
C
4
3
2
1
25
24
23
22
35
36
37
A44
Broadstone Plantation
Long Firs
Medieval Village (site of)
Manor Farm
Sewage Works
Leys Farm
Church Enstone
PH
B4030
Stone Farm
Lidstone
Hill Farm
Lidstone Bottom
River Glyme
Quarry (dis)
BICESTER RD
THE DRIVE
Stoney Bridge
PH
Enstone
OXFORD RD
CHAPEL LA
LITCHFIELD CL
Neat Enstone
Sch
WOODFORD CL
CLEVELEY RD
Litchfield Farm
THE SPINNEYS
PH
QUARRY CL
A44
B4022
B4026
Hoar Stone Burial Chamber
Enstone Firs
Fulwell Farm
Fulwell
Henley Knapp
Fulwell Brake North
Resr
The Warren
Henel Buildings
Henel
Taston
Cross
TASTON RD
Middle Farm Plantation
B4026
B4022
David's Plantation
Laurel Corner

57

73

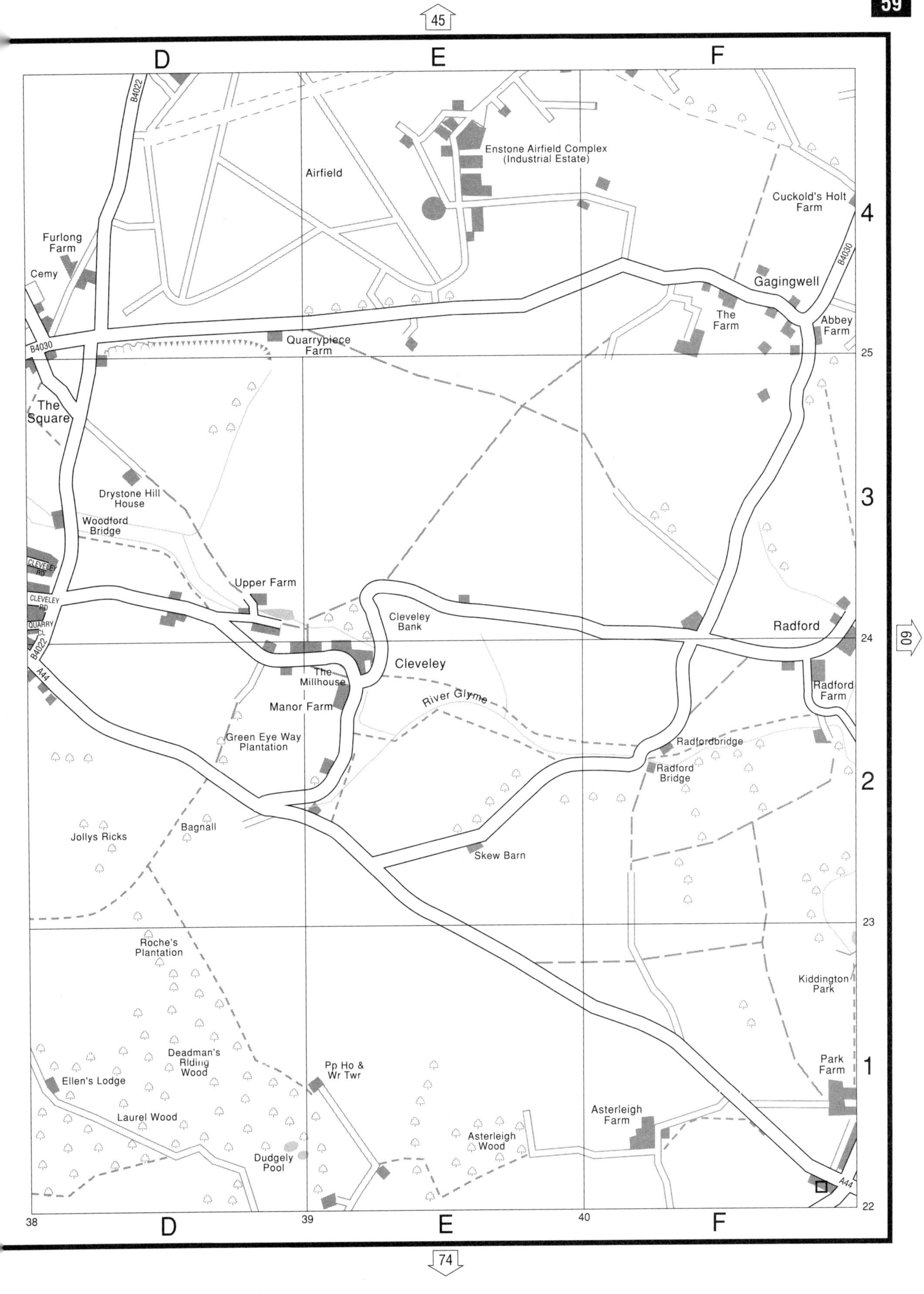
45
D
E
F
Enstone Airfield Complex
(Industrial Estate)
Airfield
Cuckold's Holt
Farm
4
Furlong
Farm
Cemy
B4022
B4030
Gagingwell
The
Farm
Abbey
Farm
Quarrypiece
Farm
25
The
Square
Drystone Hill
House
3
Woodford
Bridge
CLEVELEY
RD
Upper Farm
Radford
Cleveley
Bank
QUARRY
CL
24
60
Cleveley
The
Millhouse
A44
Manor Farm
River Glyme
Radford
Farm
Green Eye Way
Plantation
Radfordbridge
Radford
Bridge
2
Jollys Ricks
Bagnall
Skew Barn
23
Roche's
Plantation
Kiddington
Park
Deadman's
Riding
Wood
Pp Ho &
Wr Twr
Park
Farm
1
Ellen's Lodge
Laurel Wood
Asterleigh
Farm
Asterleigh
Wood
Dudgely
Pool
22
38
39
40
74

46

59

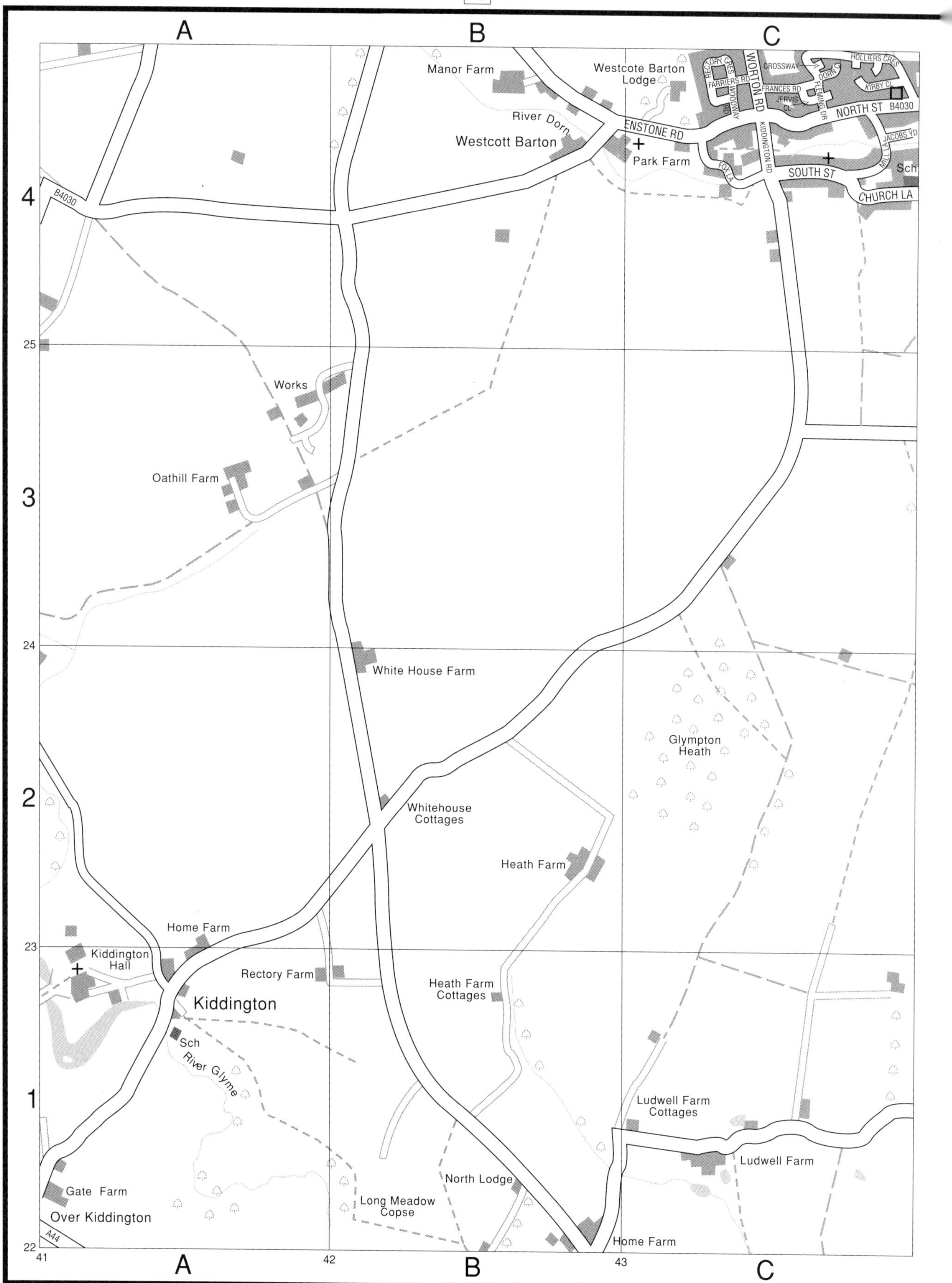
A
B
C
Manor Farm
Westcote Barton Lodge
River Dorn
Westcott Barton
RECTORY CRES
FARRIERS RD
WOODWAY RD
WORTON RD
CROSSWAY
FRANCES RD
JERVIS CL
DORN CL
FLEMING DR
HOLLIERS CRES
KIRBY CL
NORTH ST
B4030
ENSTONE RD
KIDDINGTON RD
Park Farm
FOX LA
SOUTH ST
MILL LA
JACOBS YD
Sch
CHURCH LA
4
B4030
25
Works
Oathill Farm
3
24
White House Farm
Glympton Heath
2
Whitehouse Cottages
Heath Farm
Home Farm
23
Kiddington Hall
Rectory Farm
Heath Farm Cottages
Kiddington
Sch
River Glyme
1
Ludwell Farm Cottages
Ludwell Farm
North Lodge
Gate Farm
Long Meadow Copse
Over Kiddington
A44
Home Farm
22
41
42
43
A
B
C

75

47

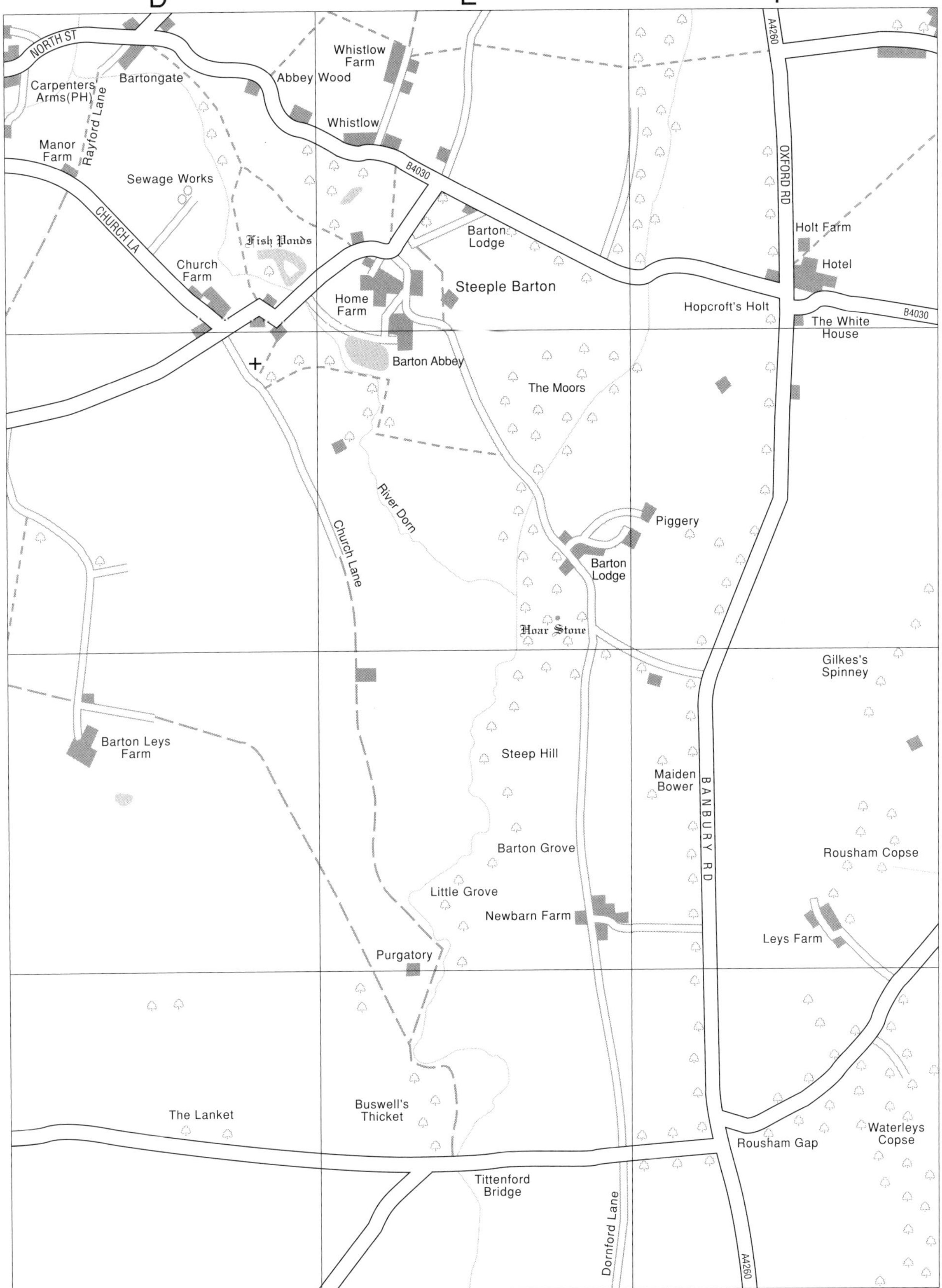
D
E
F
NORTH ST
Carpenters Arms(PH)
Bartongate
Rayford Lane
Manor Farm
Sewage Works
CHURCH LA
Church Farm
Fish Ponds
Abbey Wood
Whistlow Farm
Whistlow
B4030
Barton Lodge
Steeple Barton
Home Farm
Barton Abbey
The Moors
A4260
OXFORD RD
Holt Farm
Hotel
Hopcroft's Holt
The White House
B4030
River Dorn
Church Lane
Piggery
Barton Lodge
Hoar Stone
Gilkes's Spinney
Barton Leys Farm
Steep Hill
Maiden Bower
BANBURY RD
Barton Grove
Rousham Copse
Little Grove
Newbarn Farm
Leys Farm
Purgatory
The Lanket
Buswell's Thicket
Rousham Gap
Waterleys Copse
Tittenford Bridge
Dornford Lane
A4260
4
3
2
1
25
24
23
22
44
45
46
D
E
F

62

76

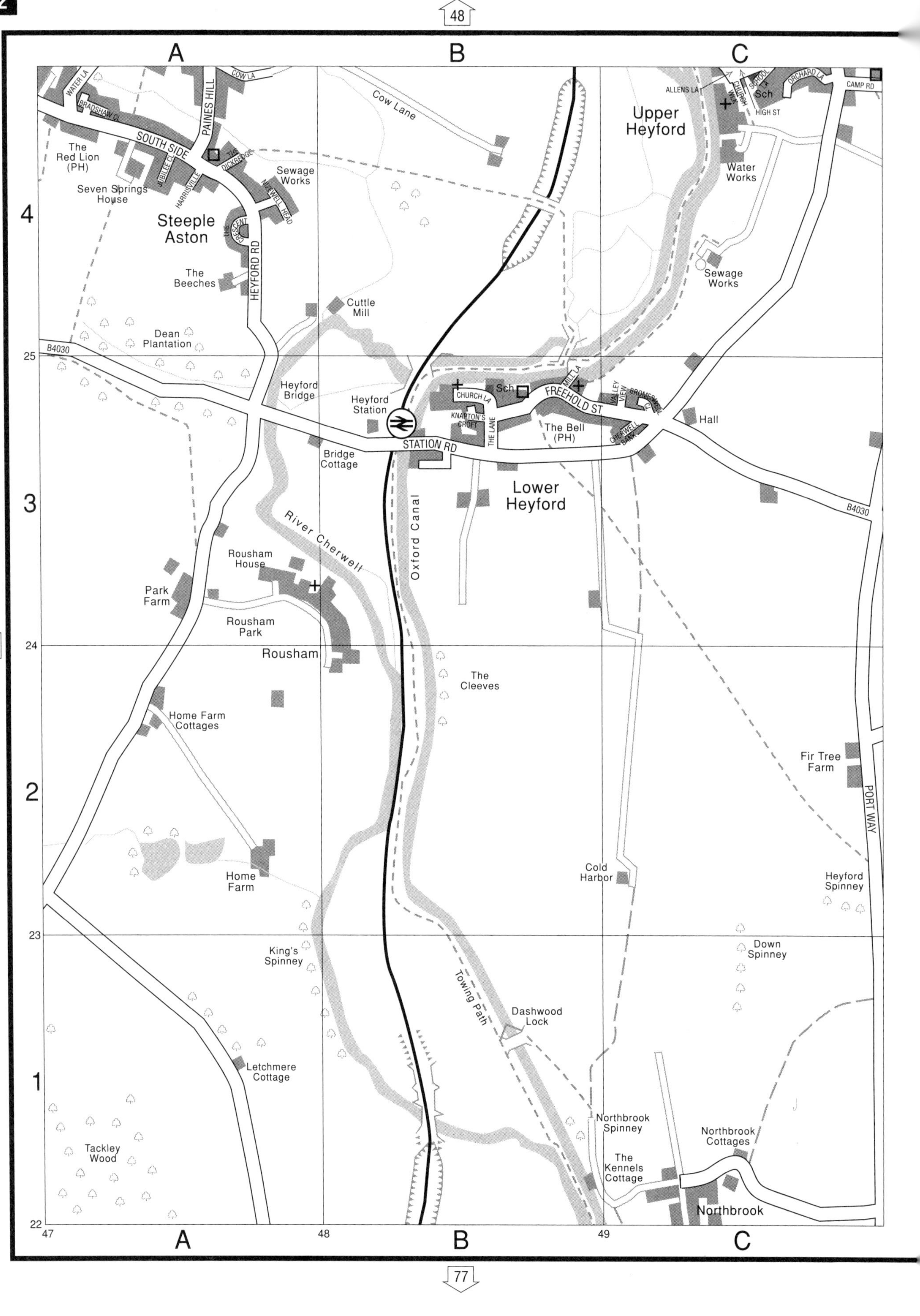
48
A
B
C
Upper
Heyford
Steeple
Aston
The
Red Lion
(PH)
Seven Springs
House
Sewage
Works
Water
Works
Cow Lane
SOUTH SIDE
PAINES HILL
HEYFORD RD
The
Beeches
Cuttle
Mill
Dean
Plantation
B4030
Heyford
Bridge
Heyford
Station
STATION RD
Bridge
Cottage
Lower
Heyford
FREEHOLD ST
The Bell
(PH)
Hall
Sch
River Cherwell
Oxford Canal
Rousham
House
Park
Farm
Rousham
Park
Rousham
The
Cleeves
Home Farm
Cottages
Fir Tree
Farm
PORT WAY
Home
Farm
Cold
Harbor
Heyford
Spinney
King's
Spinney
Down
Spinney
Towing Path
Dashwood
Lock
Letchmere
Cottage
Northbrook
Spinney
Northbrook
Cottages
The
Kennels
Cottage
Tackley
Wood
Northbrook
47
48
49
22
23
24
25
1
2
3
4
61
77

49

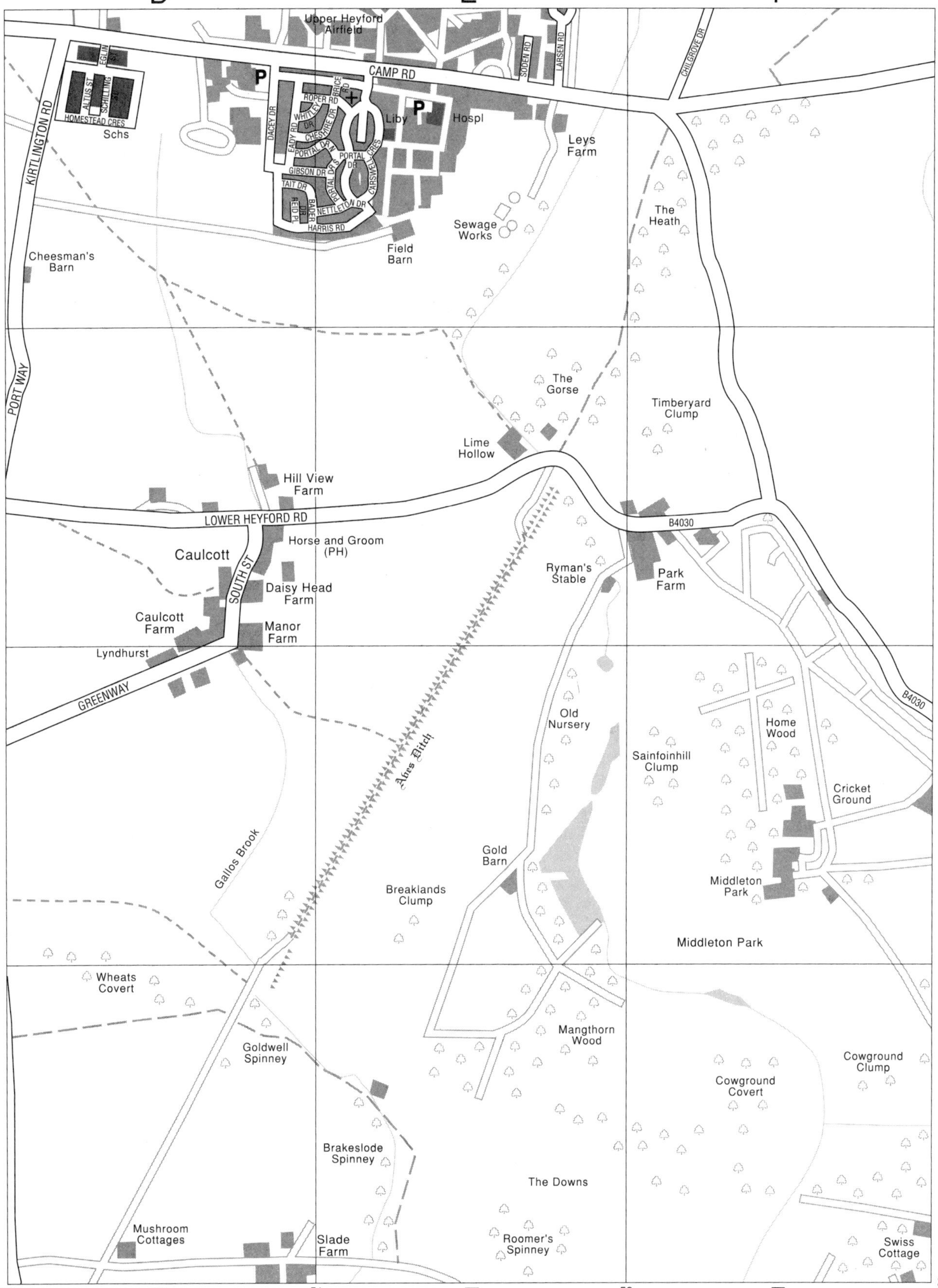

D
E
F
Upper Heyford Airfield
CAMP RD
KIRTLINGTON RD
EGLIN ST
ALTUS ST
SCHILLING ST
HOMESTEAD CRES
Schs
P
DACEY DR
ROPER RD
BRICE RD
WHITLEY DR
CHESHIRE DR
EADY RD
PORTAL DR N
PORTAL DR
GIBSON DR
TAIT DR
REID PL
BADER DR
NETTLETON DR
HARRIS RD
CARSWELL CRES
Liby
Hospl
SODEN RD
LARSEN RD
CHILGROVE DR
Leys Farm
Sewage Works
Field Barn
The Heath
Cheesman's Barn
4
25
PORT WAY
The Gorse
Timberyard Clump
Lime Hollow
Hill View Farm
3
LOWER HEYFORD RD
B4030
Caulcott
Horse and Groom (PH)
SOUTH ST
Daisy Head Farm
Ryman's Stable
Park Farm
Caulcott Farm
Manor Farm
Lyndhurst
24
GREENWAY
B4030
Old Nursery
Home Wood
Sainfoinhill Clump
Aves Ditch
Cricket Ground
2
Gallos Brook
Gold Barn
Middleton Park
Breaklands Clump
Middleton Park
23
Wheats Covert
Mangthorn Wood
Goldwell Spinney
Cowground Clump
Cowground Covert
1
Brakeslode Spinney
The Downs
Mushroom Cottages
Slade Farm
Roomer's Spinney
Swiss Cottage
22
50
51
52

64

78

50

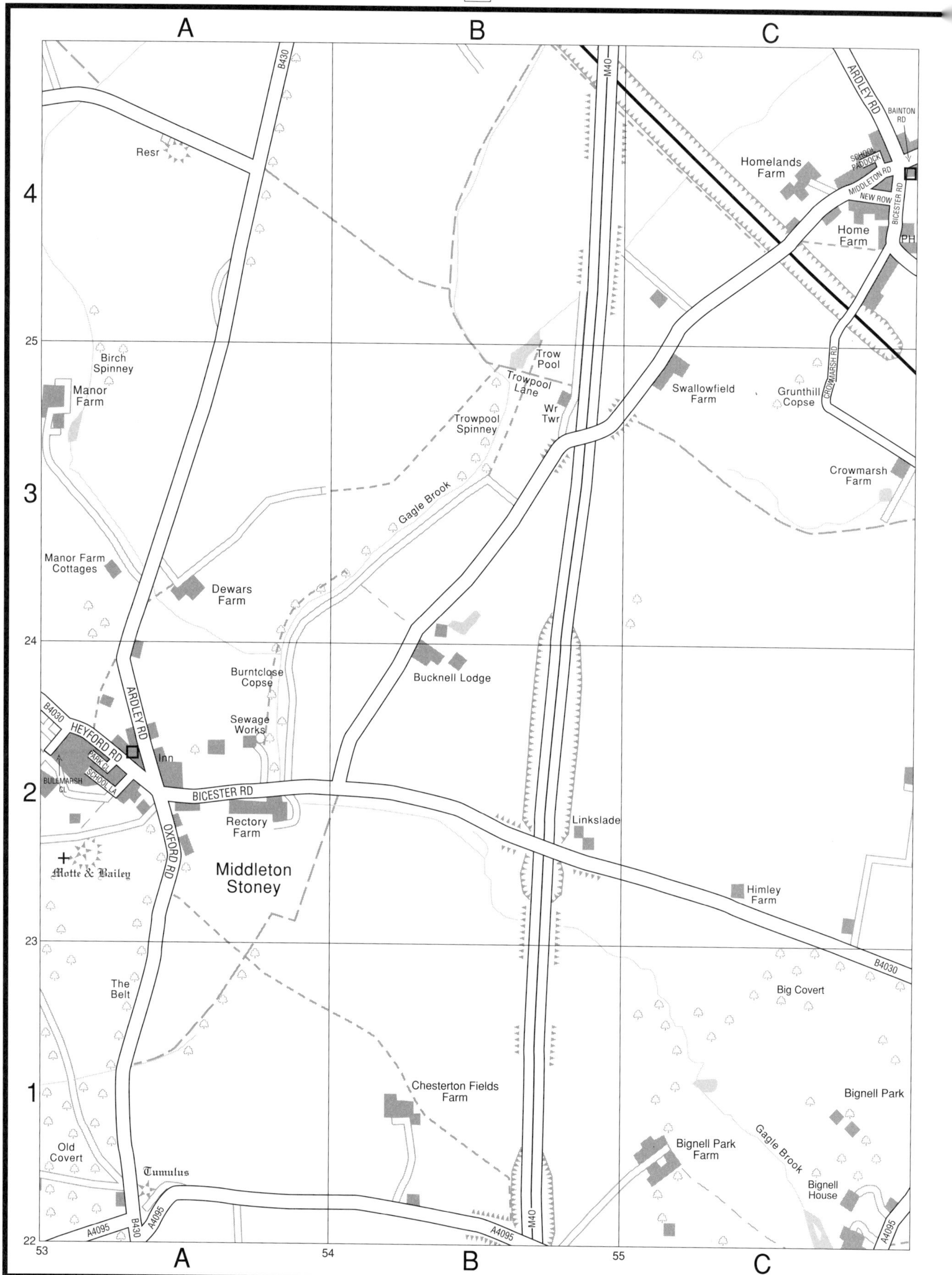
A
B
C
4
3
2
1
25
24
23
22
53
54
55
B430
M40
ARDLEY RD
BAINTON RD
SCHOOL PADDOCK
MIDDLETON RD
NEW ROW
BICESTER RD
Homelands Farm
Home Farm
PH
Resr
Birch Spinney
Manor Farm
Trow Pool
Trowpool Lane
Wr Twr
Trowpool Spinney
Swallowfield Farm
Grunthill Copse
CROWMARSH RD
Crowmarsh Farm
Gagle Brook
Manor Farm Cottages
Dewars Farm
Bucknell Lodge
Burntclose Copse
Sewage Works
B4030
HEYFORD RD
ARDLEY RD
PARK CL
SCHOOL LA
BULLMARSH CL
Inn
BICESTER RD
Rectory Farm
OXFORD RD
Linkslade
Motte & Bailey
Middleton Stoney
Himley Farm
B4030
Big Covert
The Belt
Chesterton Fields Farm
Bignell Park
Bignell Park Farm
Gagle Brook
Bignell House
Old Covert
Tumulus
A4095
B430
A4095
A4095
M40
A4095
A
B
C

63

79

51

D
E
F
Manor Farm
BAINTON RD
Lower Farm
Bucknell Manor Farm
Manor House
Bucknell
B4100
Lodge
Caversfield House
Caversfield
Home Farm
BICESTER RD
SPRINGFIELD RD
FAIRHAVEN RD
ELDERFIELD RD
OLD SCHOOL CL
WILSON WAY
THOMPSON DR
BAKER CL
CASTLE CL
DAVIS GDNS
PAYNES END
SHEEN CL
MANZEL RD
CUCKOO CL
BLENCOWE CL
BARNFIELD CL
SKIMMINGDISH LA
Bricknells Farm
Hawkwell Farm
4
25
3
Oxford Lodge
A421
1 WALNUT CL
2 SOUTHWOLD
3 SPINDLESIDE
4 LARCH CL
5 CHESTNUT END
South Farm
Aldershot Farm
Lord's Farm
24
Slade Farm
COLERIDGE CL 1
COWPER CL 2
GOLDSMITH CL 3
KEATS CL 4
KINGSLEY RD 5
WORDSWORTH CL 6
WALPOLE CL 7
Gowell Farm
BICESTER
LIME CRES
SYCAMORE GDNS
WILLOW DR
WINDMILL AVE
HAZEL DR
OAK CL
FAIR CL
SOMERVILLE DR
ST PETER'S CR
ST HUGH'S CL
CHURCHILL RD
Sch
Himley Farm
FLEMING CL
BROWNING DR
WESLEY CL
BUNYAN RD
KIPLING CL
BUCHAN RD
BROOK RD
SWIFT CL
STEVENSON CL
RAYMOND RD
MAUD CL
MARGARET CL
KITCHENER CL
JANE CL
EWART CL
BARRY AVE
BUCKNELL RD
Woodfield
BANBURY RD
TAYLOR CL
BRASHFIELD RD
BLAKE RD
ROMAN ROAD
BUCKINGHAM RD
BUCKINGHAM CRES
STABLE RD
2
DERWENT RD
DRYDEN AVE
TWEED CRES
TAMAR CRES
TRENT CRES
DOVE GREEN
SEVERN CL
WYE CL
BECKDALE CL
THAMES AVE
GREENWOOD DR
WINSLOW CRES
SHAKESPEARE DR
BYRON WAY
SHELLEY CL
MILTON CL
BURNS CL
SPENSER CL
MACAULAY CL
SCOTT CL
ORCHARD WAY
LONGFELLOW CL
THE OVAL
GRAHAM RD
ALMOND RD
ROWAN RD
THE APPROACH
MARKET END WAY
WEST ST
THE CRESCENT
HUDSON ST
EAST ST
1 MACKENZIE CL
2 MASEFIELD CL
Highfield
DICKENS CL
MEREDITH CL
STONEBURGE CRES
CEDAR CL
MAGDALEN CL
BALLIOL RD
BASSETT AVE
WADHAM CL
TRINITY CL
PEMBROKE WAY
RUSKIN WALK
ORIEL WAY
KEBLE RD
NUFFIELD CL
MERTON WLK
HERTFORD CL
MURDOCK RD
Bicester North Station
Ind Est
23
BLENHEIM DR
ROOKERY WAY
REDMOOR CT
BROMWELL CL
HUXLEY CL
OSBORNE CL
DUMAS CL
SHAW CL
HEMINGWAY DR
AUSTEN WLK
LAWRENCE WAY
MELVILLE CL
DANES RD
LANGFORD GDNS
LEACH RD
WINDLE GDNS
ASHBY RD
Schs
CROCKWELL CL
NEW ST
ROMAN WAY
FIELD ST
NORTH ST
ST JOHN'S ST
CHICHESTER CL
CAMPBELL CL
DRAYMANS CROFT
BROWNING RD
MAPLE RD
WITHINGTON RD
LINDEN RD
MOOR POND CL
LONGFIELDS
Sch
BECKDALE CL
WELLAND CROFT
BLYTHE PL
AVON CRES
BOWMONT SQ
WAVENEY CL
MEDINA GDNS
ISIS AVE
WANSBECK DR
HAMBLESIDE
EDEN WAY
SHANNON RD
WEAR RD
B4030
A4095
Bignell Belt
Coll
ST EDITH'S WAY
ALDBOURNE CL
WINTERBOURNE CL
Ct
F Sta
WESLEY LA
HUNT CL
MANORSFIELD RD
SHEEP ST
BURE PL
CROWN WLK
BARDWELL TERR
Cattle Market
VICTORIA RD
FALLOWFIELDS
GREEN CL
LAUNTON RD
1
BUCKNELL RD
TUBB CL
KENNEDY RD
ST EDBURG'S CL
ASHDENE RD
ALDERBATE RD
ST MARY'S CL
VILLIERS RD
KINGSCLERE RD
CHALVEY RD
WINDRUSH CL
EVENLODE CL
CHERWELL CL
FOX LA
KING'S AVE
COLNE CL
BOURNE CL
KENNET CL
BAY RD
FINCHE CL
QUEENS AVE
THE QUADRANGLE
KING'S END
COKER CL
PIGGY LA
CEMETERY RD
CHURCH ST
CAUSEWAY
MARKET SQ
HANOVER GDNS
MIDDLETON STONEY RD
CHALVEY CL
KING'S END
Sch
Hospl
King's End
A421
OXFORD RD
Cemy
CHURCH LA
Liby
PRIORY RD
PRIORY LA
CHAPEL ST
LONDON RD
B4100
WESTHOLM CT
Garth Park
Bicester Crossing
ALCHESTER TERR
MCKAY TRADING EST
STATION APPR
OLD PLACE YD
PRIORY CT
Whitelands Farm
22
56
57
58

66

80

52

65

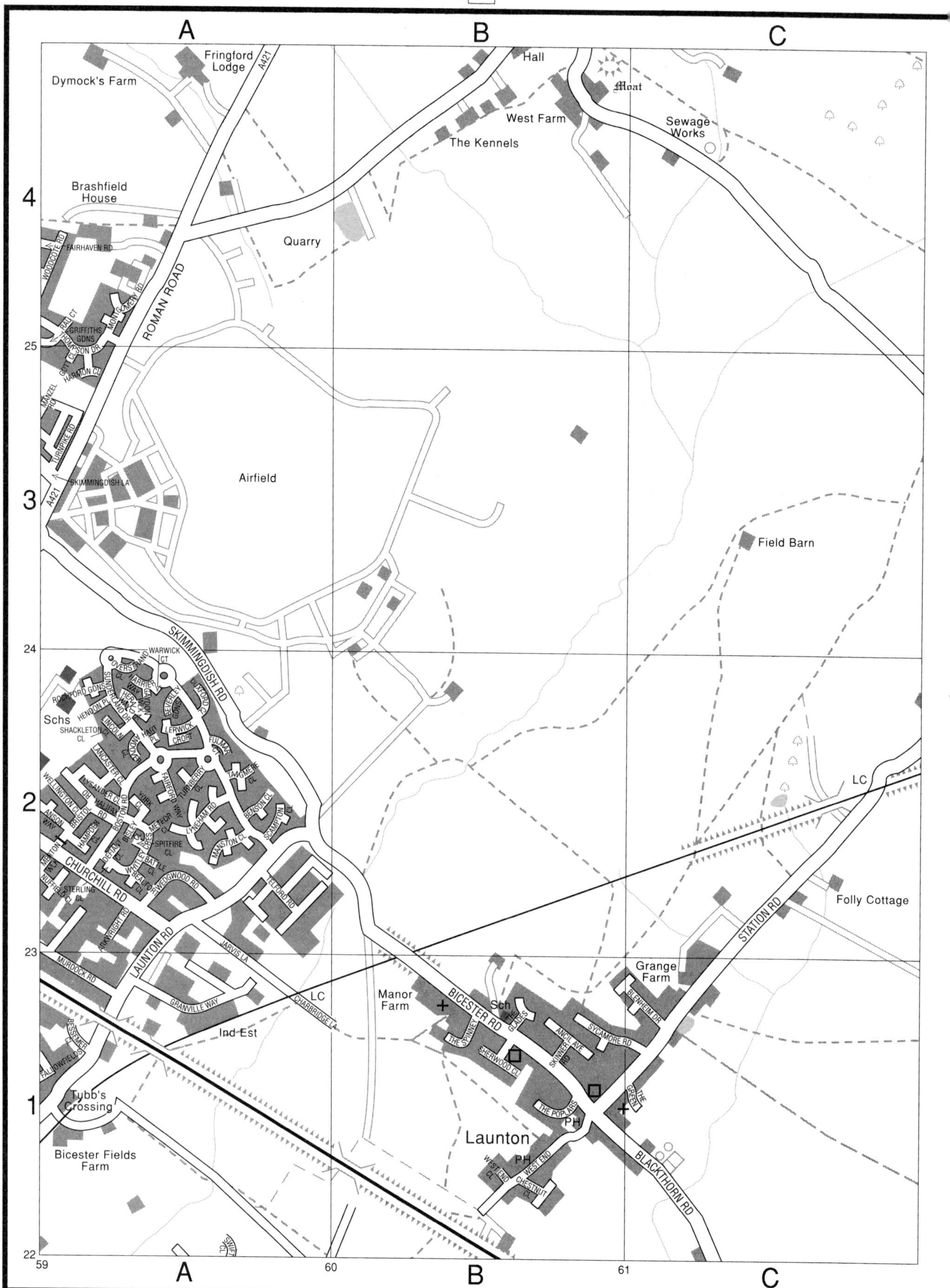
A
B
C
4
3
2
1
25
24
23
22
59
60
61
Fringford Lodge
A421
Hall
Dymock's Farm
Moat
West Farm
Sewage Works
The Kennels
Brashfield House
Quarry
FAIRHAVEN RD
WOODCOTE RD
MONTGOMERY RD
ROMAN ROAD
RAU CT
GRIFFITHS GDNS
THOMPSON DR
GOTT CL
HARMON CL
MANZEL RD
TURNPIKE RD
SKIMMINGDISH LA
Airfield
Field Barn
SKIMMINGDISH RD
WARWICK CT
ROCKFORD GDNS
HENDON PL
Schs
SHACKLETON CL
LINCOLN
LERWICK CROFT
FULMAR CT
LANCASTER CL
LYSANDER CL
WELLINGTON CL
ANSON WAY
BRISTOL RD
HAMPDEN CL
HALIFAX
BOSTON RD
YORK CL
FAIRFORD WAY
LYNEHAM RD
TURNBERRY CL
TANGMERE CL
BENSON CL
SCAMPTON CL
MANSTON CL
SPITFIRE CL
METEOR
BATTLE CL
BEAUFORT
WEDGWOOD RD
CHURCHILL RD
NUFFIELD CL
STERLING CL
ARKWRIGHT RD
MURDOCK RD
LAUNTON RD
JARVIS LA
TELFORD RD
GRANVILLE WAY
LC
CHARBRIDGE LA
Ind Est
BESSEMER CL
FALLOWFIELDS
Tubb's Crossing
Bicester Fields Farm
Manor Farm
BICESTER RD
Sch
THE GLADES
THE SPINNEY
SHERWOOD CL
SKINNER RD
ANCIL AVE
SYCAMORE RD
BLENHEIM DR
Grange Farm
STATION RD
Folly Cottage
THE POPLARS
PH
THE GREEN
Launton
WEST END
WEST END CL
CHESTNUT CL
BLACKTHORN RD

81

53

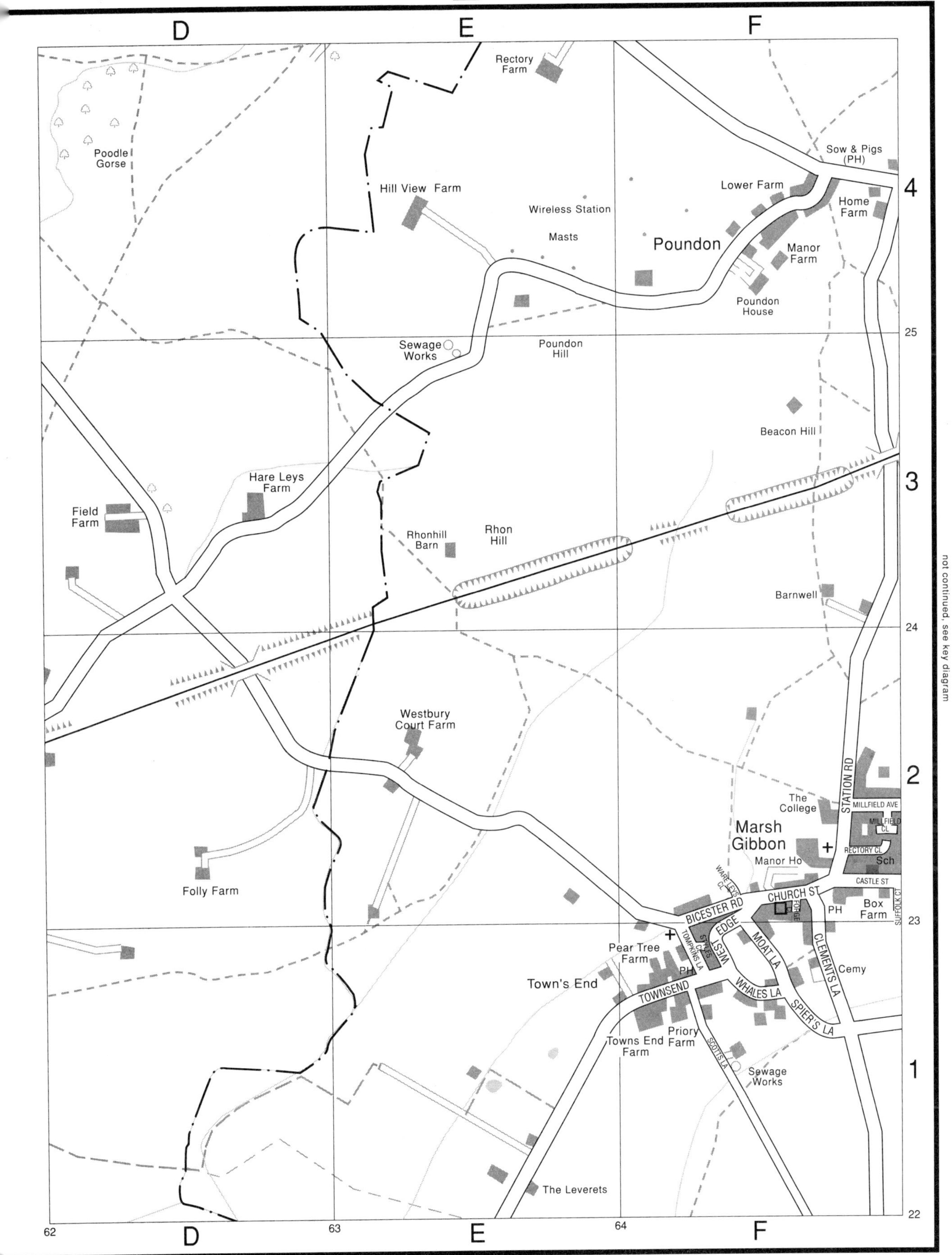
D
E
F
Rectory Farm
Poodle Gorse
Hill View Farm
Wireless Station
Masts
Sow & Pigs (PH)
Lower Farm
Home Farm
Poundon
Manor Farm
Poundon House
4
25
Sewage Works
Poundon Hill
Beacon Hill
3
Hare Leys Farm
Field Farm
Rhonhill Barn
Rhon Hill
Barnwell
24
Westbury Court Farm
2
The College
STATION RD
MILLFIELD AVE
MILLFIELD CL
Marsh Gibbon
RECTORY CL
Manor Ho
Sch
CASTLE ST
WARLEYS CL
CHURCH ST
BICESTER RD
FORGE
PH
Box Farm
SUFFOLK CT
23
Folly Farm
Pear Tree Farm
STYLES CL
TOMPKINS LA
WEST EDGE
MOAT LA
CLEMENTS LA
Cemy
PH
Town's End
TOWNSEND
WHALES LA
SPIER'S LA
Towns End Farm
Priory Farm
SCOTTS LA
Sewage Works
1
The Leverets
22
62
63
64
not continued, see key diagram

82

not continued, see key diagram

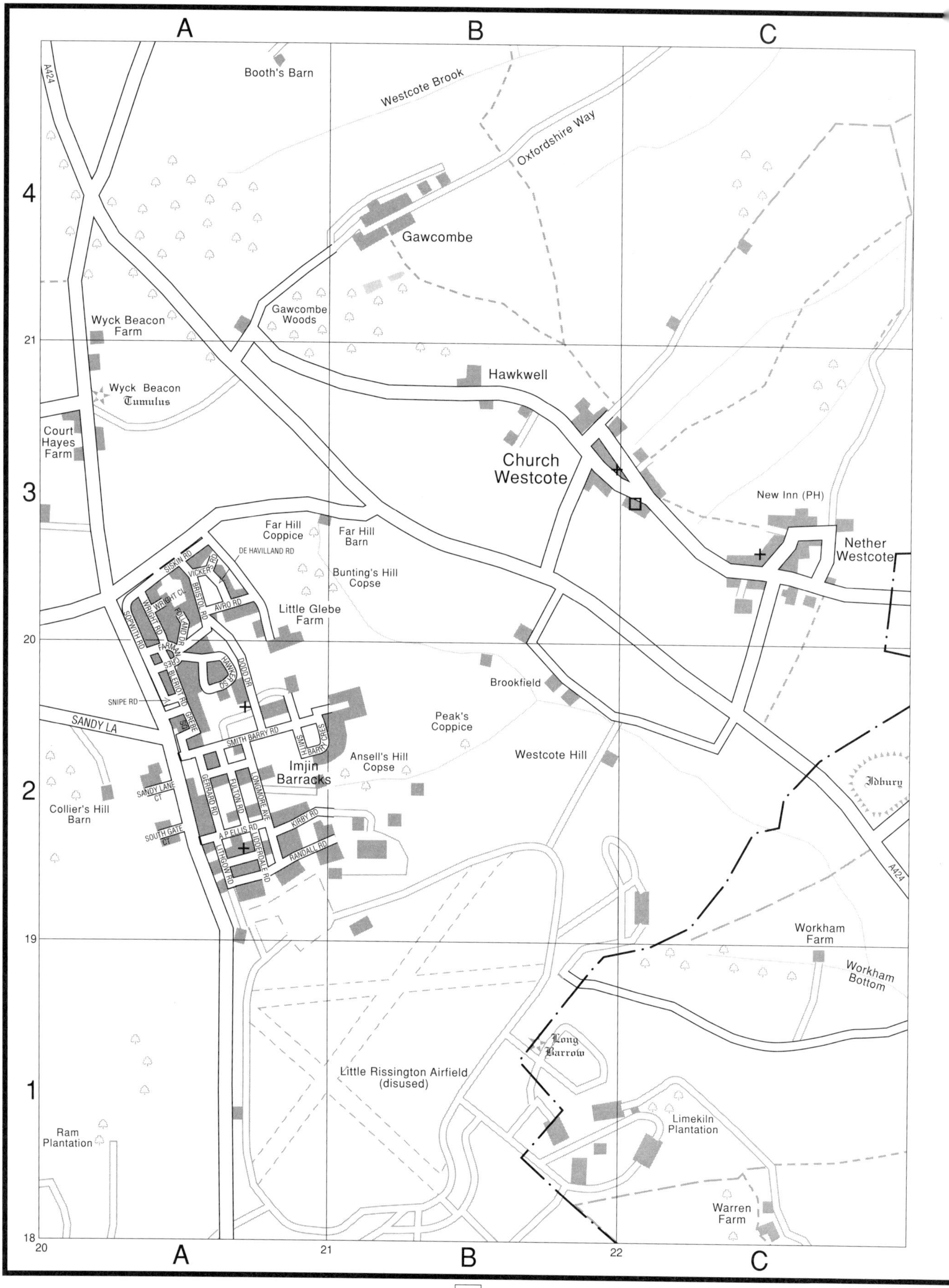

not continued, see key diagram

54

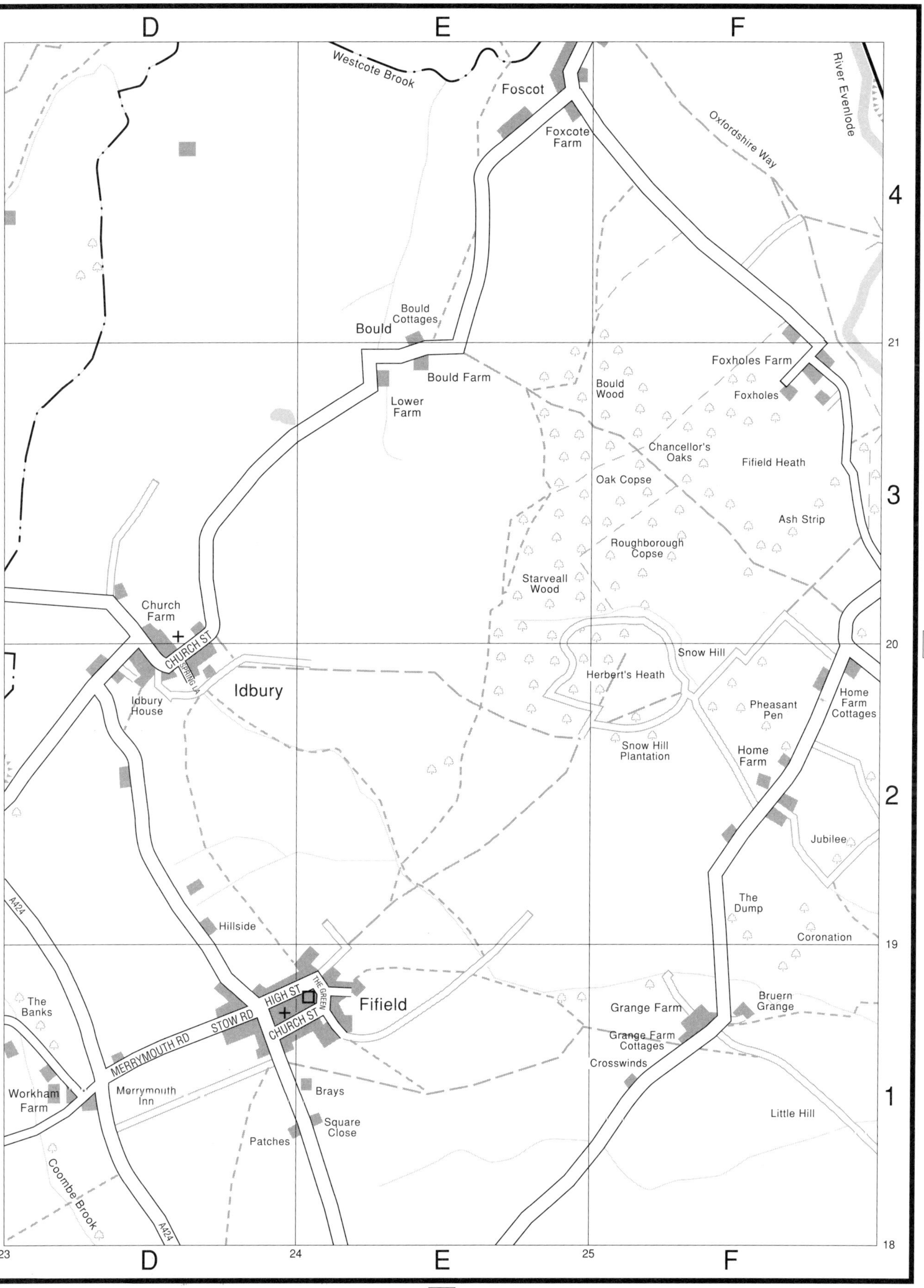
D
E
F
Westcote Brook
Foscot
Foxcote Farm
River Evenlode
Oxfordshire Way
4
Bould Cottages
Bould
21
Foxholes Farm
Bould Farm
Lower Farm
Bould Wood
Foxholes
Chancellor's Oaks
Fifield Heath
Oak Copse
3
Ash Strip
Roughborough Copse
Starveall Wood
Church Farm
CHURCH ST
20
Snow Hill
SPRING LA
Idbury
Herbert's Heath
Home Farm Cottages
Idbury House
Pheasant Pen
Snow Hill Plantation
Home Farm
2
Jubilee
A424
The Dump
Hillside
Coronation
19
The Banks
HIGH ST
THE GREEN
Fifield
Grange Farm
Bruern Grange
STOW RD
CHURCH ST
MERRYMOUTH RD
Grange Farm Cottages
Crosswinds
Workham Farm
Merrymouth Inn
Brays
1
Little Hill
Square Close
Patches
Coombe Brook
A424
18
23
24
25
D
E
F

70

84

55

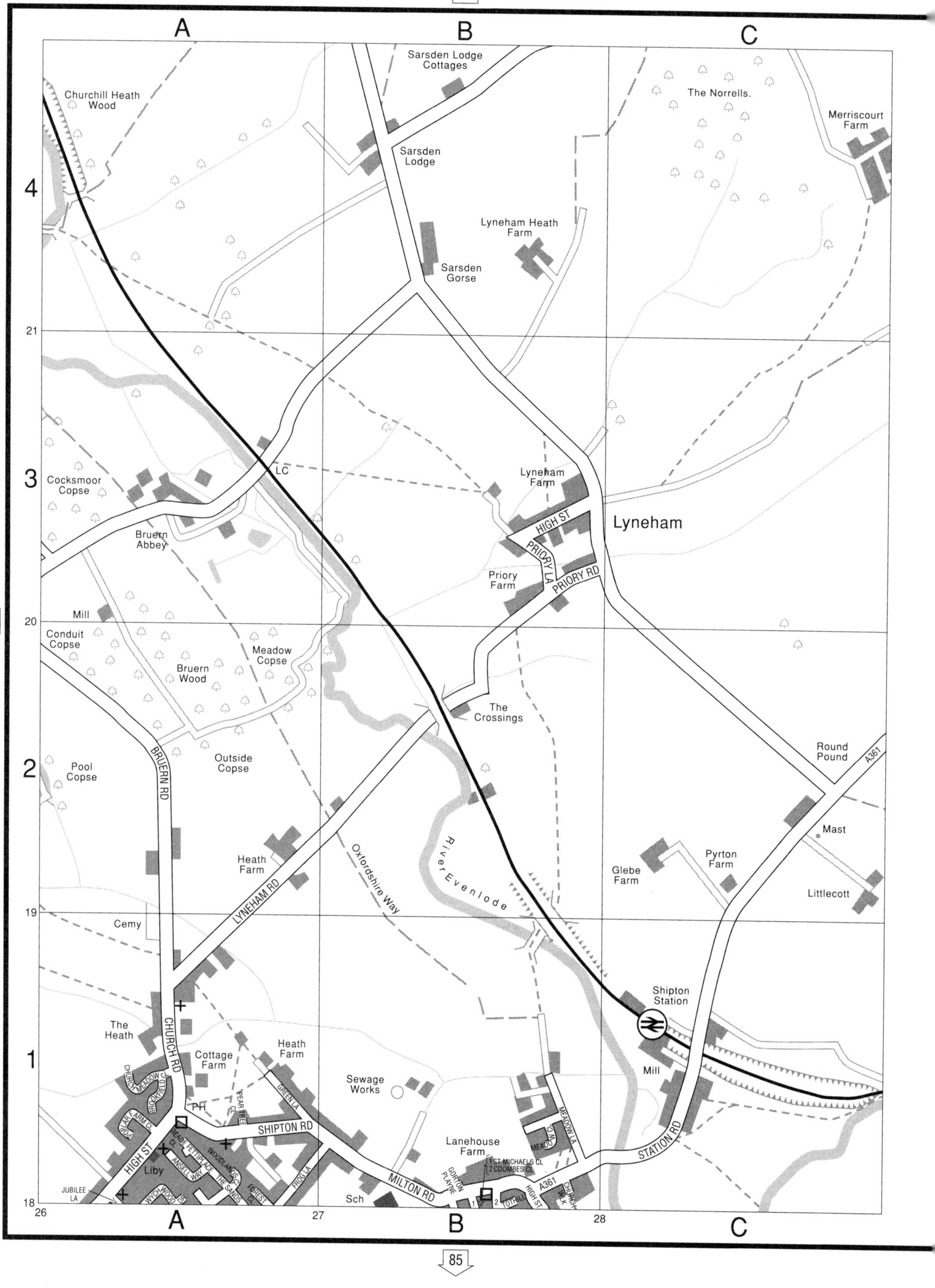
A
B
C
1
2
3
4
26
27
28
18
19
20
21
Churchill Heath Wood
Sarsden Lodge Cottages
The Norrells.
Merriscourt Farm
Sarsden Lodge
Lyneham Heath Farm
Sarsden Gorse
LC
Cocksmoor Copse
Lyneham Farm
HIGH ST
Lyneham
PRIORY LA
PRIORY RD
Bruern Abbey
Priory Farm
Mill
Conduit Copse
Meadow Copse
Bruern Wood
The Crossings
Outside Copse
Pool Copse
BRUERN RD
Round Pound
A361
Mast
Heath Farm
Oxfordshire Way
River Evenlode
Pyrton Farm
Glebe Farm
Littlecott
LYNEHAM RD
Cemy
Shipton Station
The Heath
CHURCH RD
Cottage Farm
Heath Farm
Mill
Sewage Works
PH
SHIPTON RD
PEAR TREE CL
GREEN LA
MEADOW LA
STATION RD
Lanehouse Farm
1 ST MICHAELS CL
2 COOMBES CL
HIGH ST
Liby
JUBILEE LA
WOODLANDS CL
ANSELL WAY
THE SANDS
FROG LA
Sch
MILTON RD
GORTON PLAYNE
TOTHILL
A361
CHURCH WALK
CHURCH MEADOW
BROOKFIELD CL
POPLAR FARM CL

69

85

56

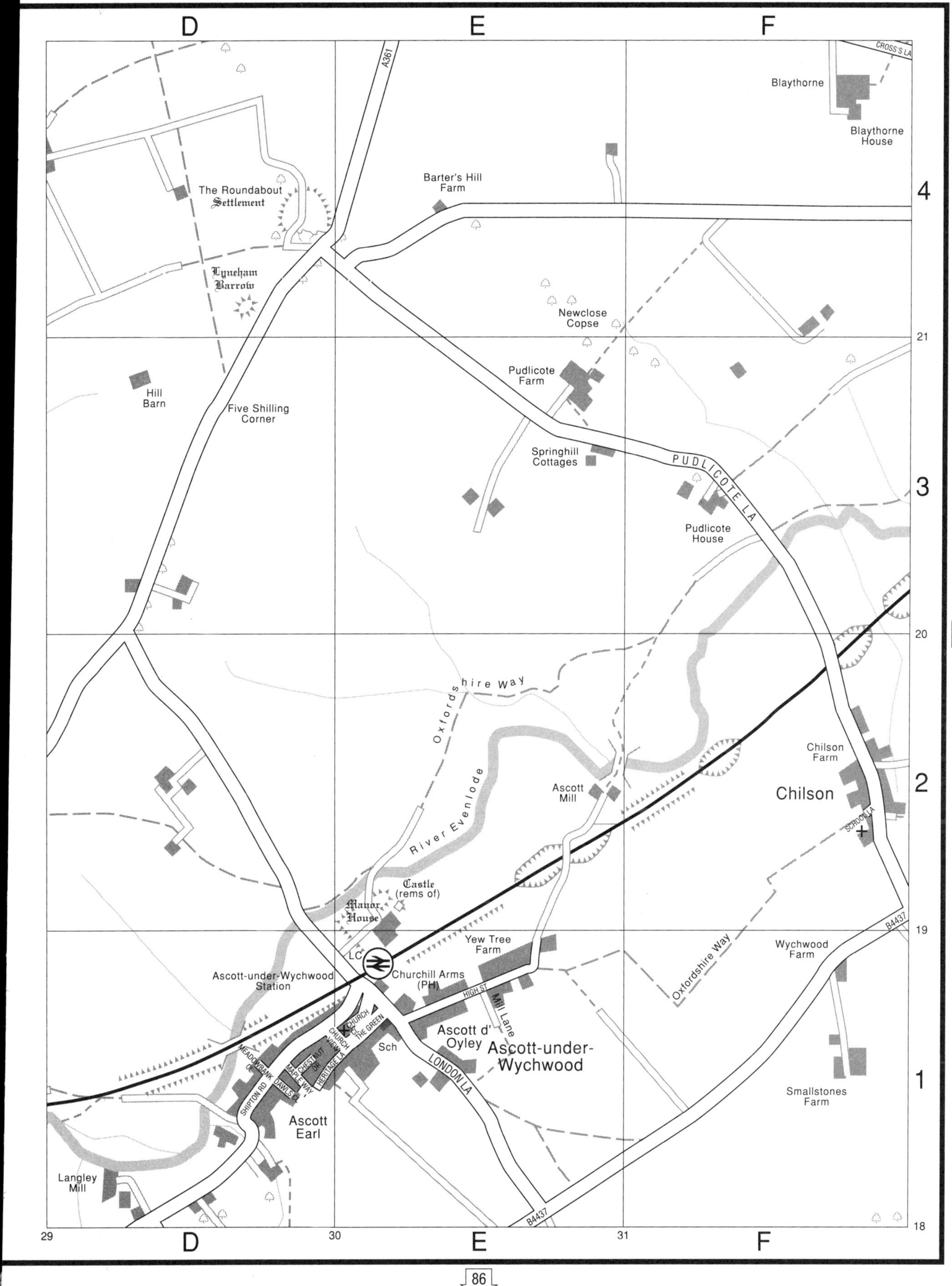
D
E
F
A361
CROSS'S LA
Blaythorne
Blaythorne House
Barter's Hill Farm
The Roundabout Settlement
Lyneham Barrow
Newclose Copse
Pudlicote Farm
Hill Barn
Five Shilling Corner
Springhill Cottages
PUDLICOTE LA
Pudlicote House
Oxfordshire Way
River Evenlode
Ascott Mill
Chilson Farm
Chilson
SCHOOL LA
Castle (rems of)
Manor House
Yew Tree Farm
LC
Churchill Arms (PH)
Ascott-under-Wychwood Station
HIGH ST
Mill Lane
Oxfordshire Way
Wychwood Farm
B4437
CHURCH
THE GREEN
Sch
Ascott d' Oyley
Ascott-under-Wychwood
MEADOWBANK CL
SHIPTON RD
DAWLS CL
MAPLE WAY
CHESTNUT DR
CHURCH VIEW
HERITAGE LA
LONDON LA
Ascott Earl
Langley Mill
Smallstones Farm
B4437
4
3
2
1
21
20
19
18
29
30
31
D
E
F

72

86

57

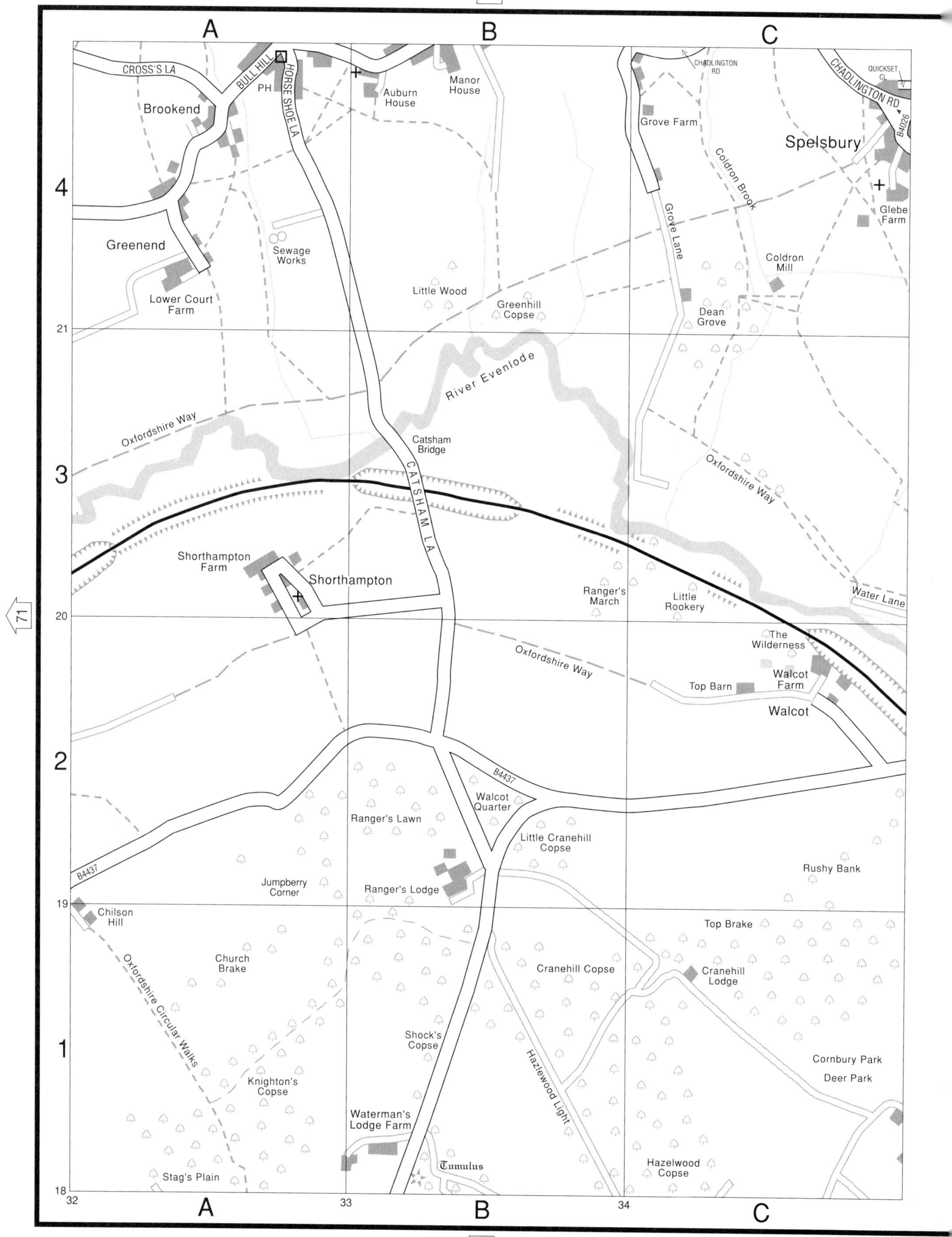
A
B
C
4
3
2
1
21
20
19
18
32
33
34
CROSS'S LA
BULL HILL
HORSE SHOE LA
PH
Brookend
Auburn House
Manor House
CHADLINGTON RD
QUICKSET CL
CHADLINGTON RD
B4026
Grove Farm
Spelsbury
Coldron Brook
Glebe Farm
Greenend
Sewage Works
Grove Lane
Coldron Mill
Lower Court Farm
Little Wood
Greenhill Copse
Dean Grove
River Evenlode
Oxfordshire Way
Catsham Bridge
CATSHAM LA
Oxfordshire Way
Shorthampton Farm
Shorthampton
Ranger's March
Little Rookery
Water Lane
The Wilderness
Oxfordshire Way
Walcot Farm
Top Barn
Walcot
B4437
Walcot Quarter
Ranger's Lawn
Little Cranehill Copse
Rushy Bank
B4437
Jumpberry Corner
Ranger's Lodge
Chilson Hill
Top Brake
Church Brake
Cranehill Copse
Cranehill Lodge
Oxfordshire Circular Walks
Shock's Copse
Hazlewood Light
Cornbury Park
Deer Park
Knighton's Copse
Waterman's Lodge Farm
Tumulus
Hazelwood Copse
Stag's Plain
71

87

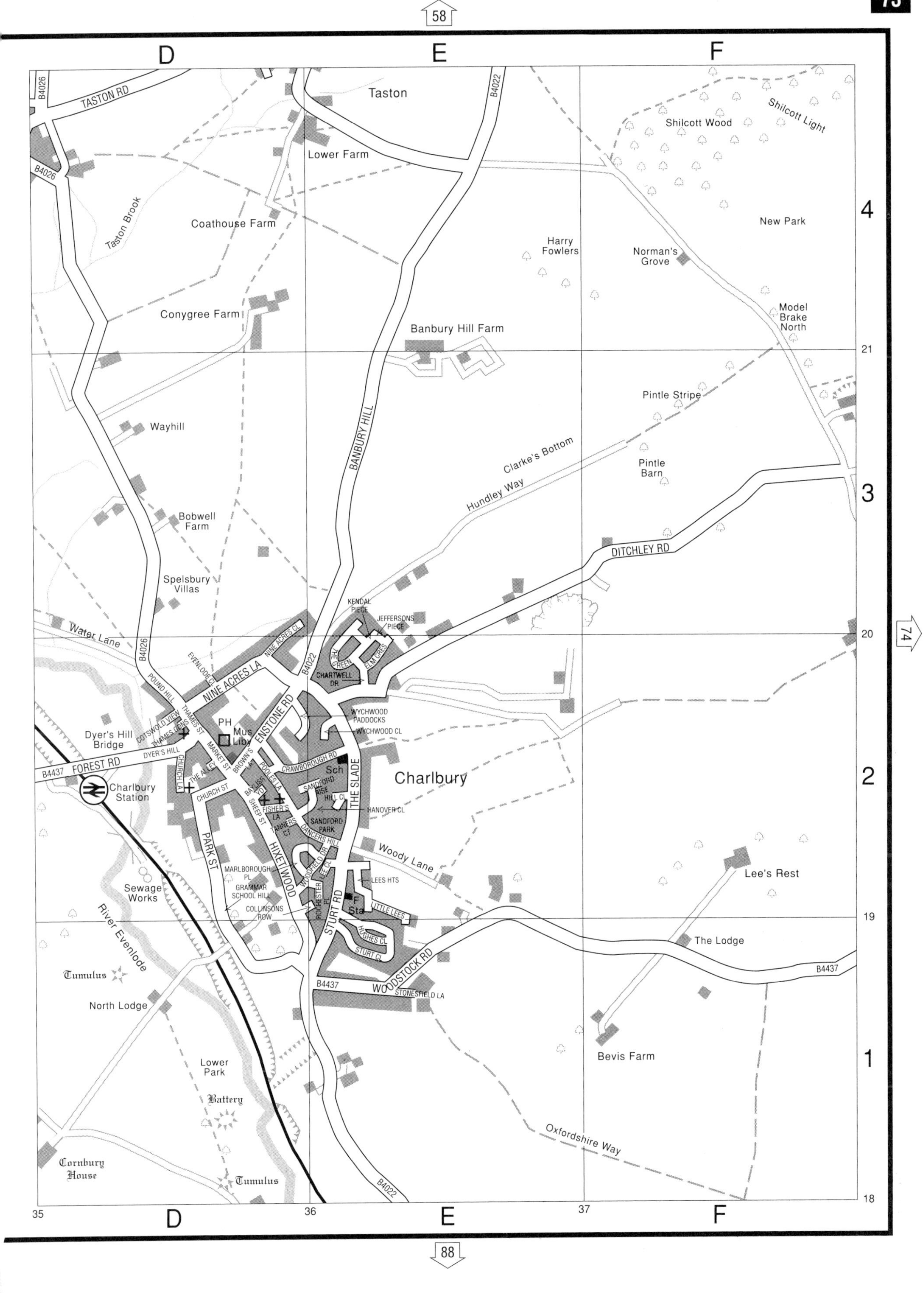
58
D
E
F
Taston
TASTON RD
B4026
B4022
Lower Farm
Shilcott Wood
Shilcott Light
Taston Brook
Coathouse Farm
New Park
Harry Fowlers
Norman's Grove
Conygree Farm
Banbury Hill Farm
Model Brake North
Pintle Stripe
Wayhill
Clarke's Bottom
Hundley Way
Pintle Barn
BANBURY HILL
Bobwell Farm
DITCHLEY RD
Spelsbury Villas
KENDAL PIECE
JEFFERSONS PIECE
Water Lane
THE GREEN
ELM CRES
CHARTWELL DR
NINE ACRES LA
NINE ACRES CL
EVENLODE CL
POUND HILL
WYCHWOOD PADDOCKS
WYCHWOOD CL
ENSTONE RD
COTSWOLD VIEW
THAMES GDNS
THAMES ST
PH
Mus
Liby
Dyer's Hill Bridge
DYER'S HILL
CHURCH LA
MARKET ST
BROWN'S LA
CRAWBOROUGH RD
Sch
Charlbury
B4437
FOREST RD
Charlbury Station
THE ALLEY
CHURCH ST
POOLES LA
SANDFORD RISE
HILL CL
THE SLADE
BAYLISS YD
FISHER'S LA
HANOVER CL
SHEEP ST
TANNERS CT
SANDFORD PARK
DANCERS HILL
PARK ST
HIXET WOOD
Woody Lane
Sewage Works
MARLBOROUGH PL
WOODFIELD DR
LEES CL
LEES HTS
Lee's Rest
GRAMMAR SCHOOL HILL
COLLINSONS ROW
ROCHESTER PL
STURT RD
F Sta
LITTLE LEES
River Evenlode
HUGHES CL
STURT CL
The Lodge
Tumulus
WOODSTOCK RD
STONESFIELD LA
North Lodge
Bevis Farm
Lower Park
Battery
Oxfordshire Way
Cornbury House
Tumulus
35
36
37
21
20
19
18
4
3
2
1
74
88

59

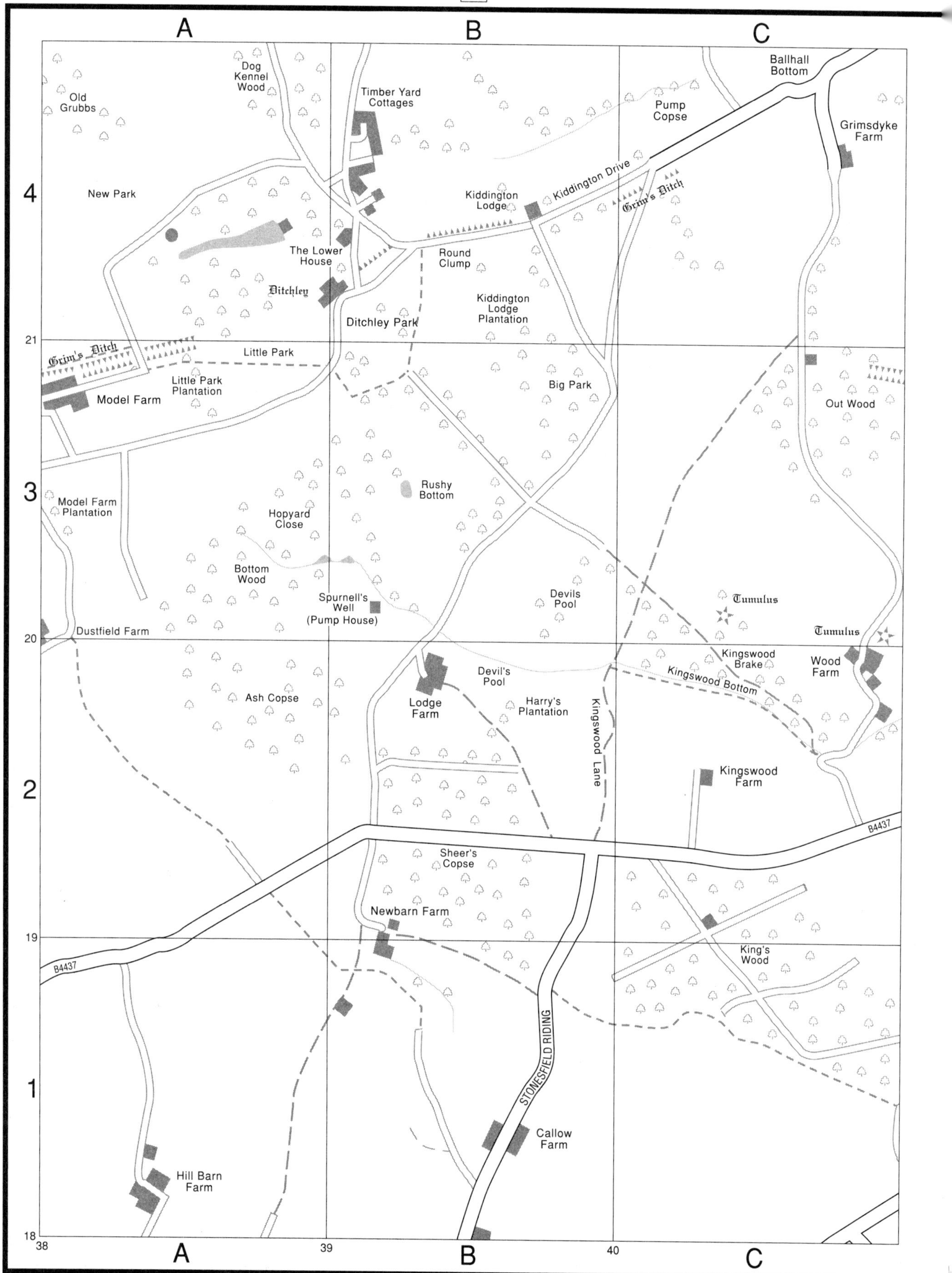

A
B
C
4
3
2
1
21
20
19
18
38
39
40
Old Grubbs
Dog Kennel Wood
Timber Yard Cottages
Ballhall Bottom
Pump Copse
Grimsdyke Farm
New Park
Kiddington Drive
Kiddington Lodge
Grim's Ditch
The Lower House
Round Clump
Ditchley
Kiddington Lodge Plantation
Ditchley Park
Little Park
Big Park
Little Park Plantation
Model Farm
Out Wood
Rushy Bottom
Model Farm Plantation
Hopyard Close
Bottom Wood
Devils Pool
Tumulus
Spurnell's Well (Pump House)
Tumulus
Dustfield Farm
Kingswood Brake
Wood Farm
Kingswood Bottom
Devil's Pool
Ash Copse
Lodge Farm
Harry's Plantation
Kingswood Lane
Kingswood Farm
B4437
Sheer's Copse
Newbarn Farm
King's Wood
B4437
STONESFIELD RIDING
Callow Farm
Hill Barn Farm

73

89

60

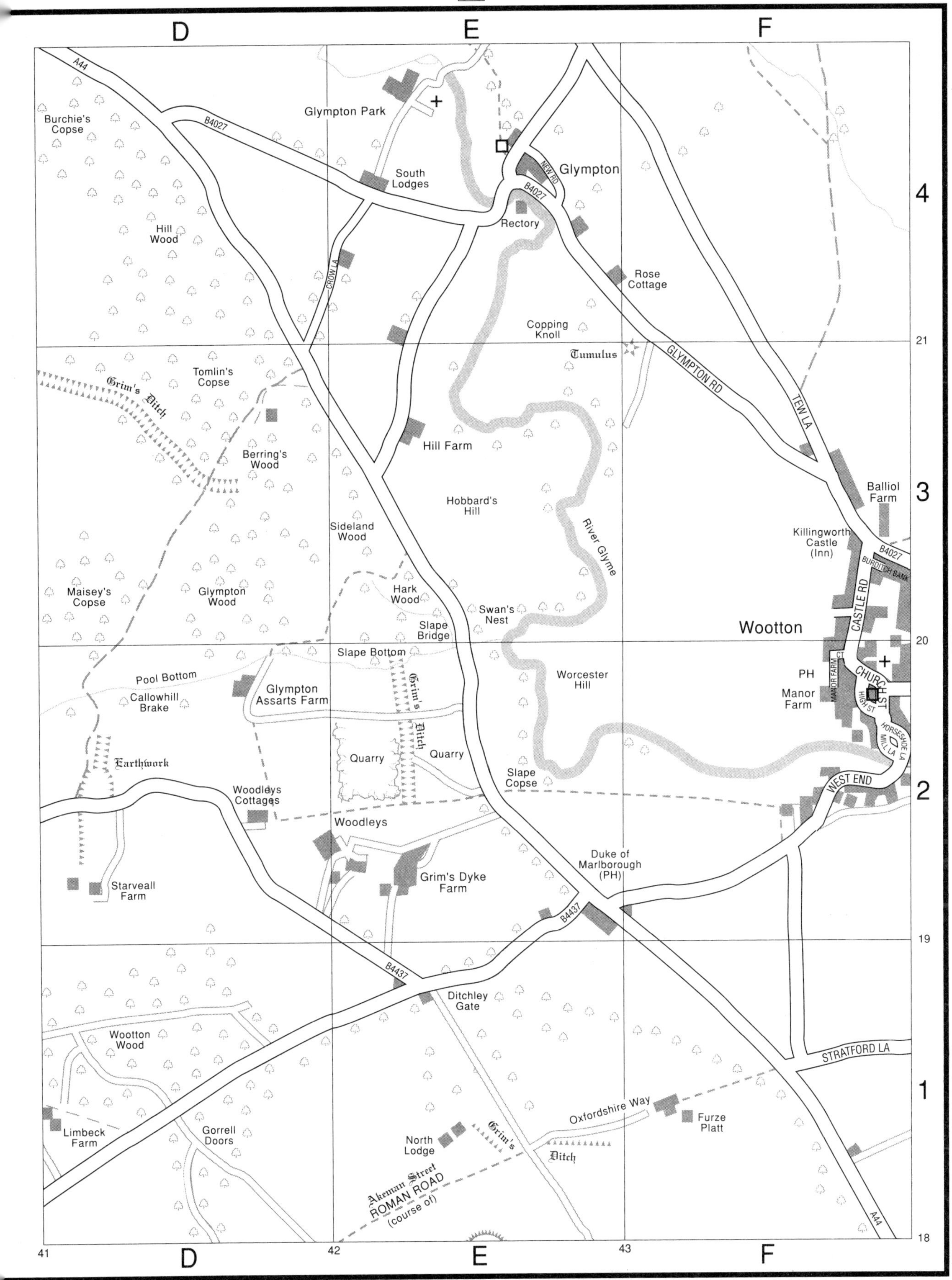
D
E
F
A44
B4027
Burchie's Copse
Glympton Park
South Lodges
Glympton
NEW RD
Rectory
Hill Wood
CROW LA
Rose Cottage
Copping Knoll
Tumulus
GLYMPTON RD
TEW LA
Tomlin's Copse
Grim's Ditch
Berring's Wood
Hill Farm
Hobbard's Hill
Balliol Farm
Sideland Wood
River Glyme
Killingworth Castle (Inn)
BURDITCH BANK
Maisey's Copse
Glympton Wood
Hark Wood
Swan's Nest
Slape Bridge
CASTLE RD
Wootton
Slape Bottom
Pool Bottom
Callowhill Brake
Glympton Assarts Farm
Worcester Hill
PH
Manor Farm
MANOR FARM CT
CHURCH ST
HIGH ST
HORSESHOE LA
MILL LA
Quarry
Earthwork
Slape Copse
WEST END
Woodleys Cottages
Woodleys
Starveall Farm
Grim's Dyke Farm
Duke of Marlborough (PH)
B4437
Ditchley Gate
Wootton Wood
STRATFORD LA
Oxfordshire Way
Furze Platt
Limbeck Farm
Gorrell Doors
North Lodge
Akeman Street
ROMAN ROAD (course of)
4
3
2
1
21
20
19
18
41
42
43

76

90

61

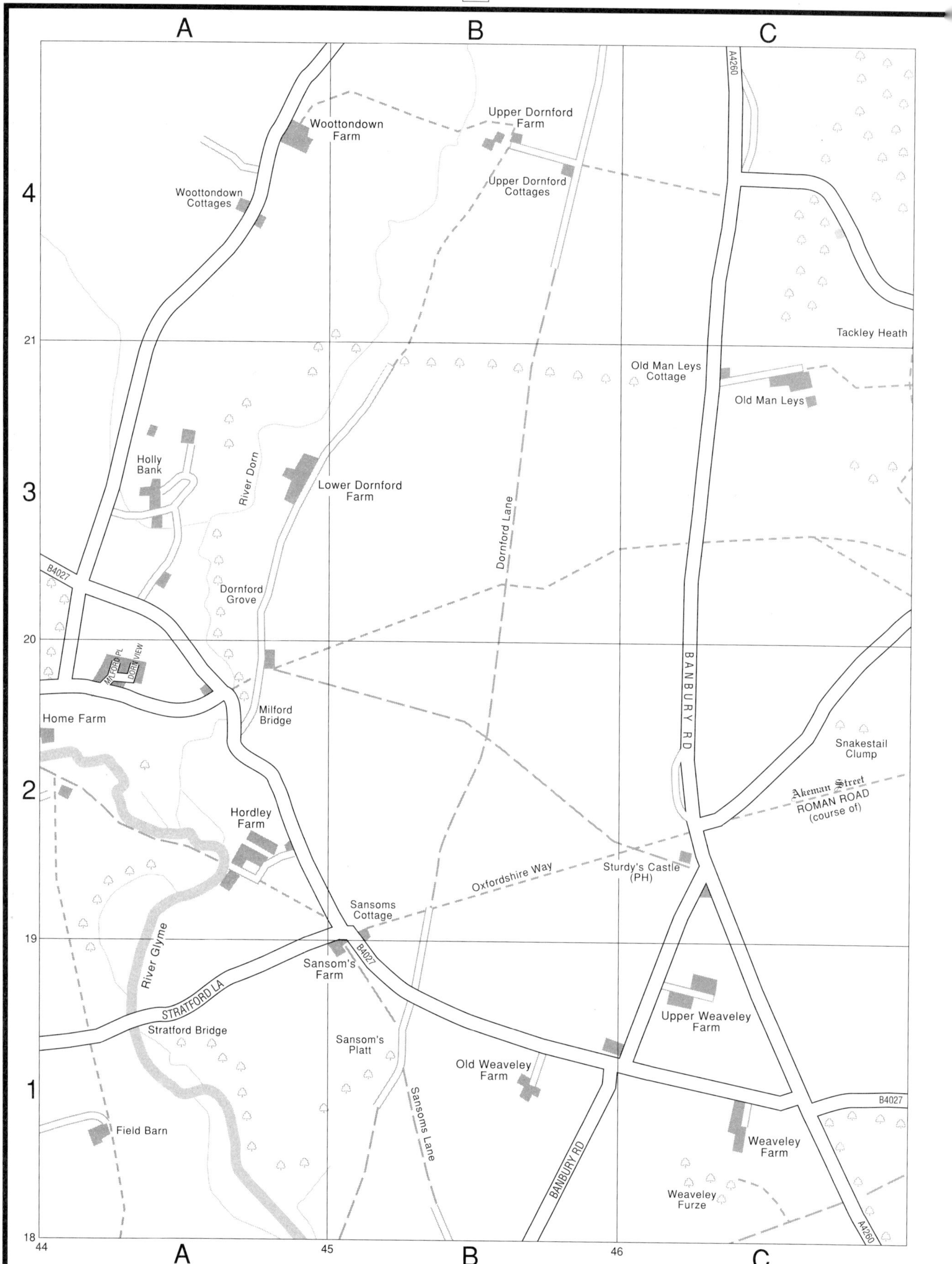
A
B
C
4
3
2
1
21
20
19
18
44
45
46
Woottondown Farm
Upper Dornford Farm
Woottondown Cottages
Upper Dornford Cottages
A4260
Tackley Heath
Old Man Leys Cottage
Old Man Leys
Holly Bank
River Dorn
Lower Dornford Farm
Dornford Lane
B4027
Dornford Grove
MILFORD PL
DORN VIEW
Home Farm
Milford Bridge
BANBURY RD
Snakestail Clump
Akeman Street
ROMAN ROAD (course of)
Hordley Farm
Oxfordshire Way
Sturdy's Castle (PH)
Sansoms Cottage
River Glyme
Sansom's Farm
STRATFORD LA
Upper Weaveley Farm
Stratford Bridge
Sansom's Platt
Old Weaveley Farm
B4027
Sansoms Lane
Field Barn
BANBURY RD
Weaveley Farm
Weaveley Furze
A4260

75

91

62

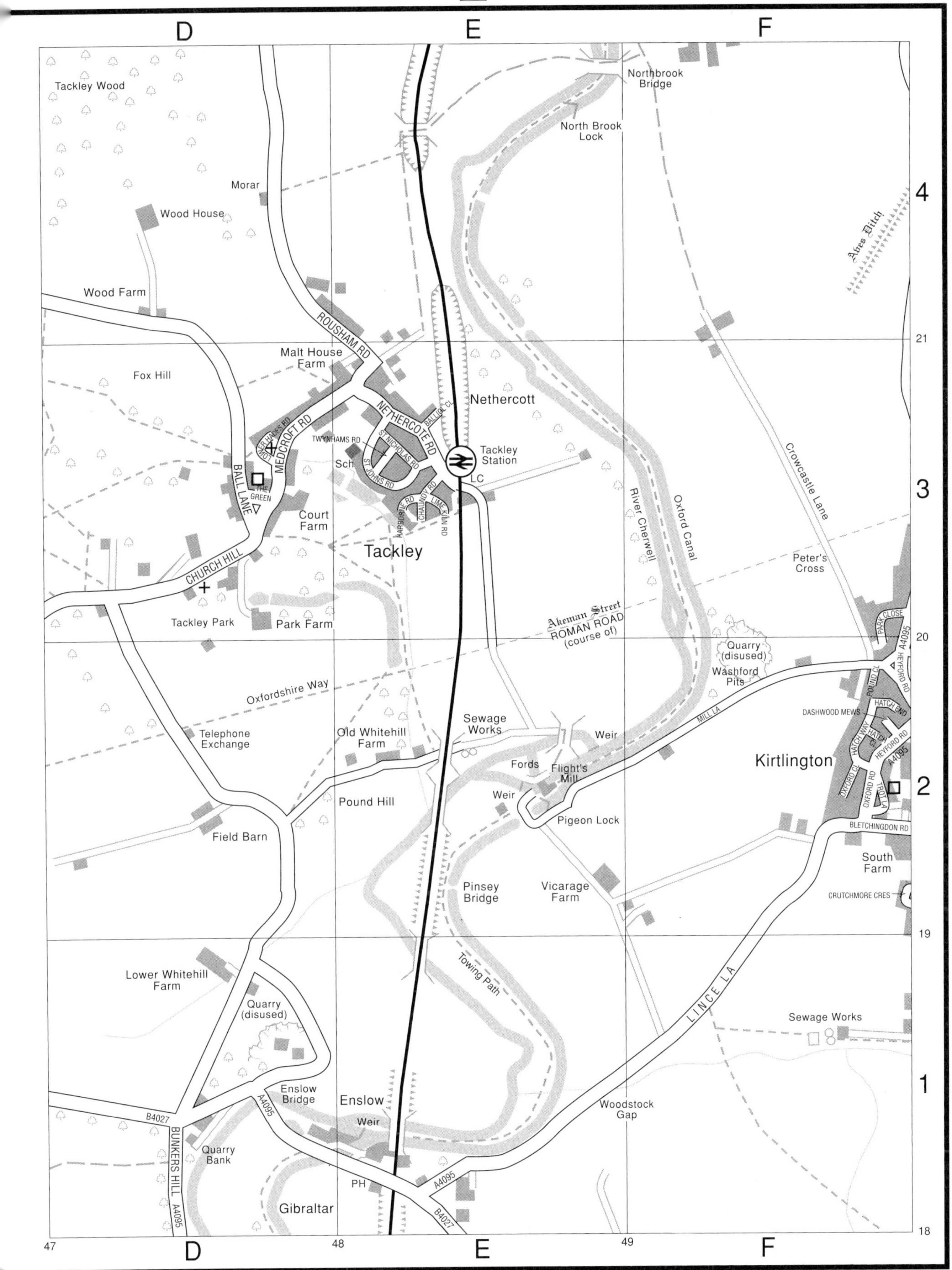
D
E
F
Tackley Wood
Northbrook Bridge
North Brook Lock
Morar
Wood House
4
Ashes Ditch
Wood Farm
ROUSHAM RD
21
Malt House Farm
Fox Hill
Nethercott
NETHERCOTE RD
BALLIOL CL
MEDCROFT RD
TWYNHAMS RD
ST NICHOLAS RD
Tackley Station
Sch
ST JOHNS RD
LC
BALL LANE
THE GREEN
Crowcastle Lane
3
River Cherwell
Oxford Canal
Court Farm
HARBORNE RD
CHAUNDY RD
LIME KILN RD
Tackley
CHURCH HILL
Peter's Cross
Akeman Street
ROMAN ROAD (course of)
Tackley Park
Park Farm
PARK CLOSE
A4095
20
Quarry (disused)
Washford Pits
POUND CL
HEYFORD RD
Oxfordshire Way
MILL LA
HATCH END
DASHWOOD MEWS
Sewage Works
Weir
Telephone Exchange
Old Whitehill Farm
HATCH WAY
HATCH CL
HEYFORD RD
Kirtlington
Fords
Flight's Mill
OXFORD CL
OXFORD RD
TROY LA
A4095
2
Pound Hill
Weir
Pigeon Lock
BLETCHINGDON RD
Field Barn
South Farm
Pinsey Bridge
Vicarage Farm
CRUTCHMORE CRES
19
Towing Path
Lower Whitehill Farm
LINCE LA
Quarry (disused)
Sewage Works
1
Enslow Bridge
Enslow
Woodstock Gap
B4027
A4095
Weir
BUNKERS HILL
Quarry Bank
PH
A4095
Gibraltar
B4027
A4095
18
47
48
49
D
E
F

78

92

63

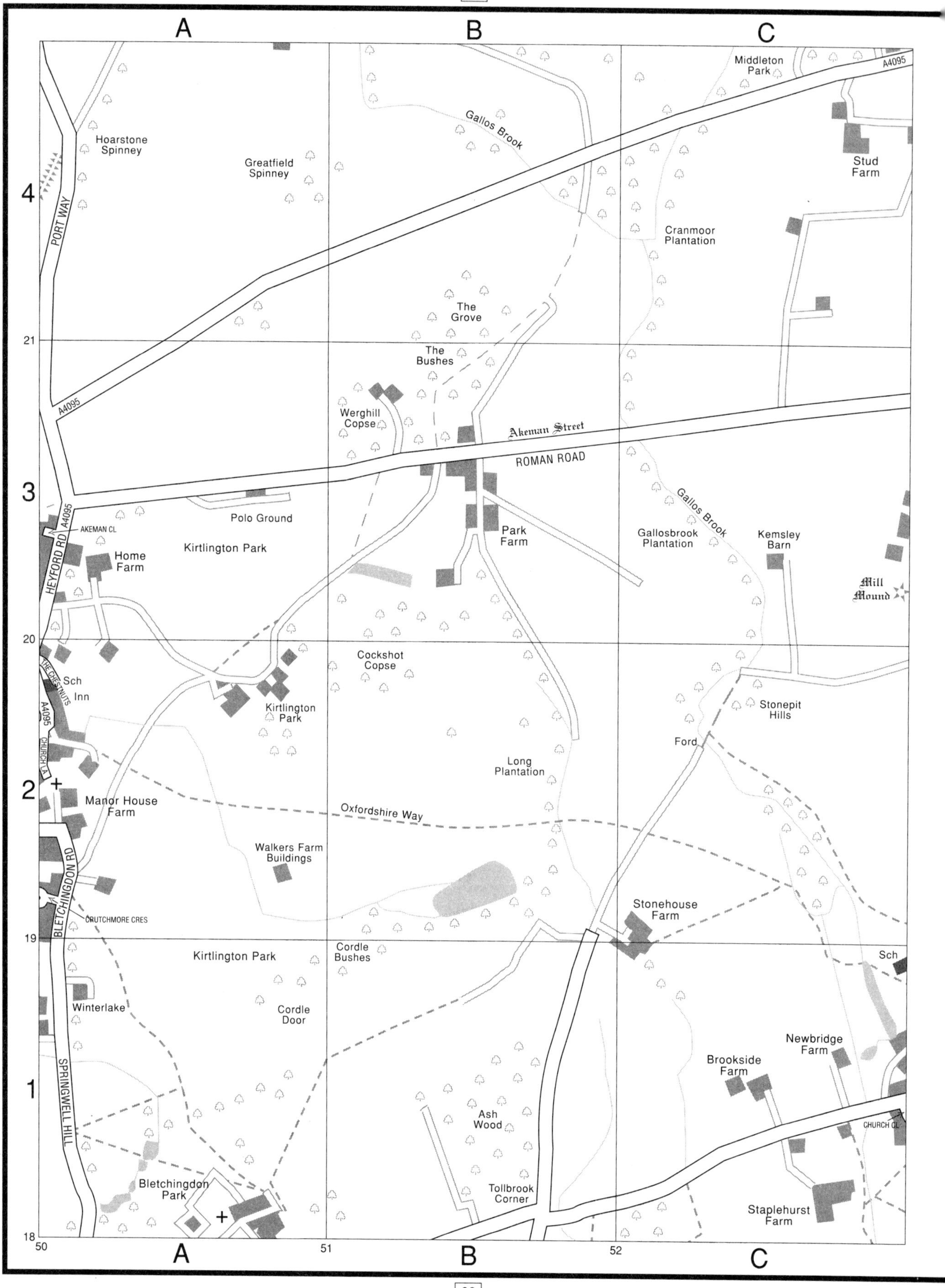
A
B
C
4
3
2
1
21
20
19
18
50
51
52
Hoarstone Spinney
PORT WAY
Greatfield Spinney
Gallos Brook
Middleton Park
A4095
Stud Farm
Cranmoor Plantation
The Grove
The Bushes
Werghill Copse
Akeman Street
ROMAN ROAD
A4095
Polo Ground
Kirtlington Park
Home Farm
AKEMAN CL
HEYFORD RD
A4095
Park Farm
Gallos Brook
Gallosbrook Plantation
Kemsley Barn
Mill Mound
Cockshot Copse
Kirtlington Park
Sch
Inn
THE CHESTNUTS
A4095
CHURCH LA
Stonepit Hills
Ford
Long Plantation
Manor House Farm
Oxfordshire Way
Walkers Farm Buildings
BLETCHINGDON RD
CRUTCHMORE CRES
Stonehouse Farm
Kirtlington Park
Cordle Bushes
Sch
Winterlake
Cordle Door
SPRINGWELL HILL
Newbridge Farm
Brookside Farm
Ash Wood
CHURCH CL
Bletchingdon Park
Tollbrook Corner
Staplehurst Farm

77

93

64

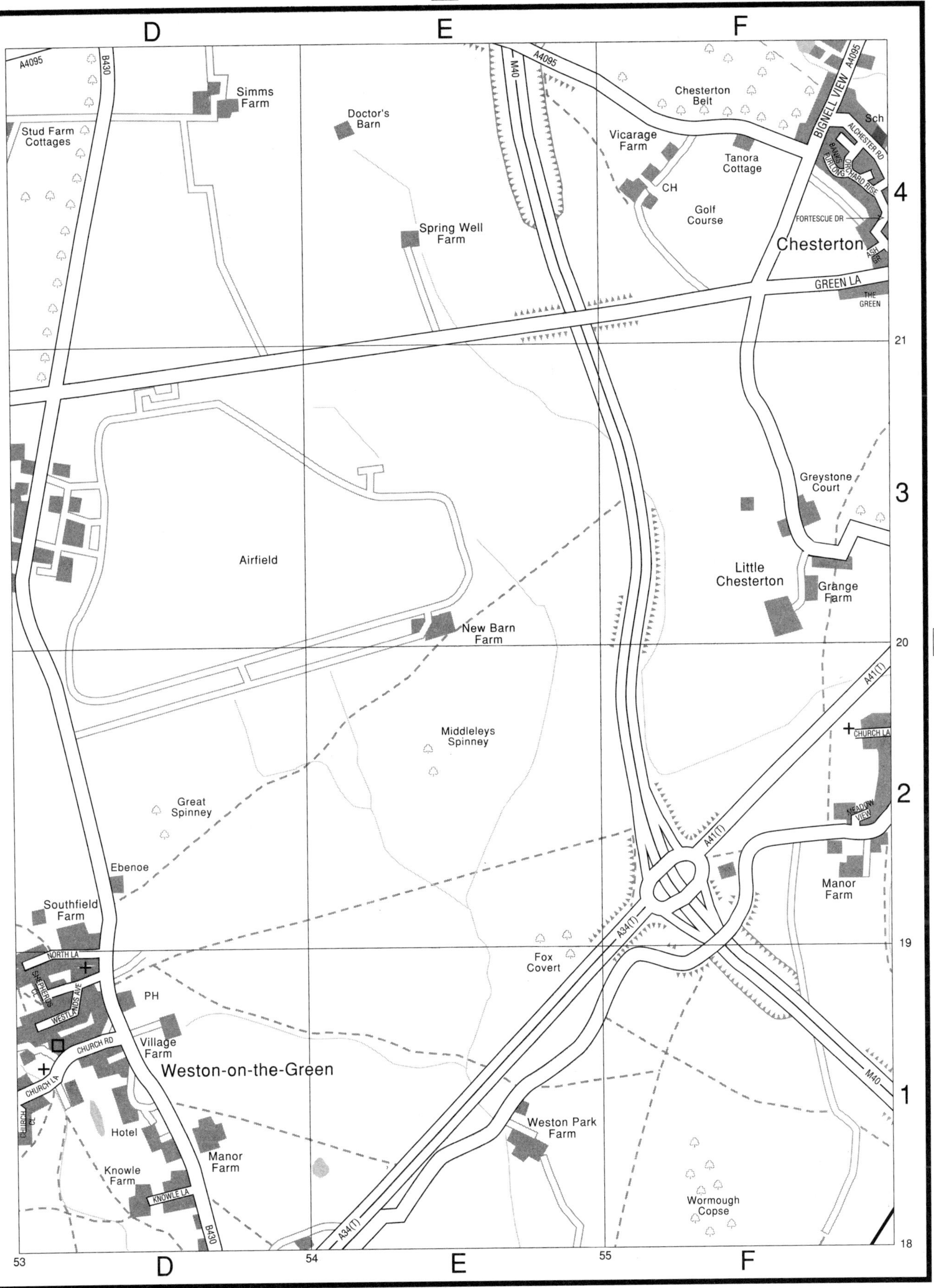
D
E
F
A4095
B430
Simms Farm
Stud Farm Cottages
Doctor's Barn
M40
Chesterton Belt
BIGNELL VIEW
Sch
ALCHESTER RD
Vicarage Farm
Tanora Cottage
BANKS FURLONG
ORCHARD RISE
CH
Golf Course
4
FORTESCUE DR
Spring Well Farm
Chesterton
ASH GR
GREEN LA
THE GREEN
21
Greystone Court
3
Airfield
Little Chesterton
Grange Farm
New Barn Farm
20
A41(T)
Middleleys Spinney
CHURCH LA
Great Spinney
2
MEADOW VIEW
Ebenoe
Manor Farm
Southfield Farm
A34(T)
Fox Covert
19
NORTH LA
SHEPHERDS CL
WESTLANDS AVE
PH
Village Farm
CHURCH RD
Weston-on-the-Green
CHURCH LA
CHURCH CL
M40
1
Weston Park Farm
Hotel
Knowle Farm
Manor Farm
KNOWLE LA
Wormough Copse
B430
18
53
54
55
D
E
F

80

94

65

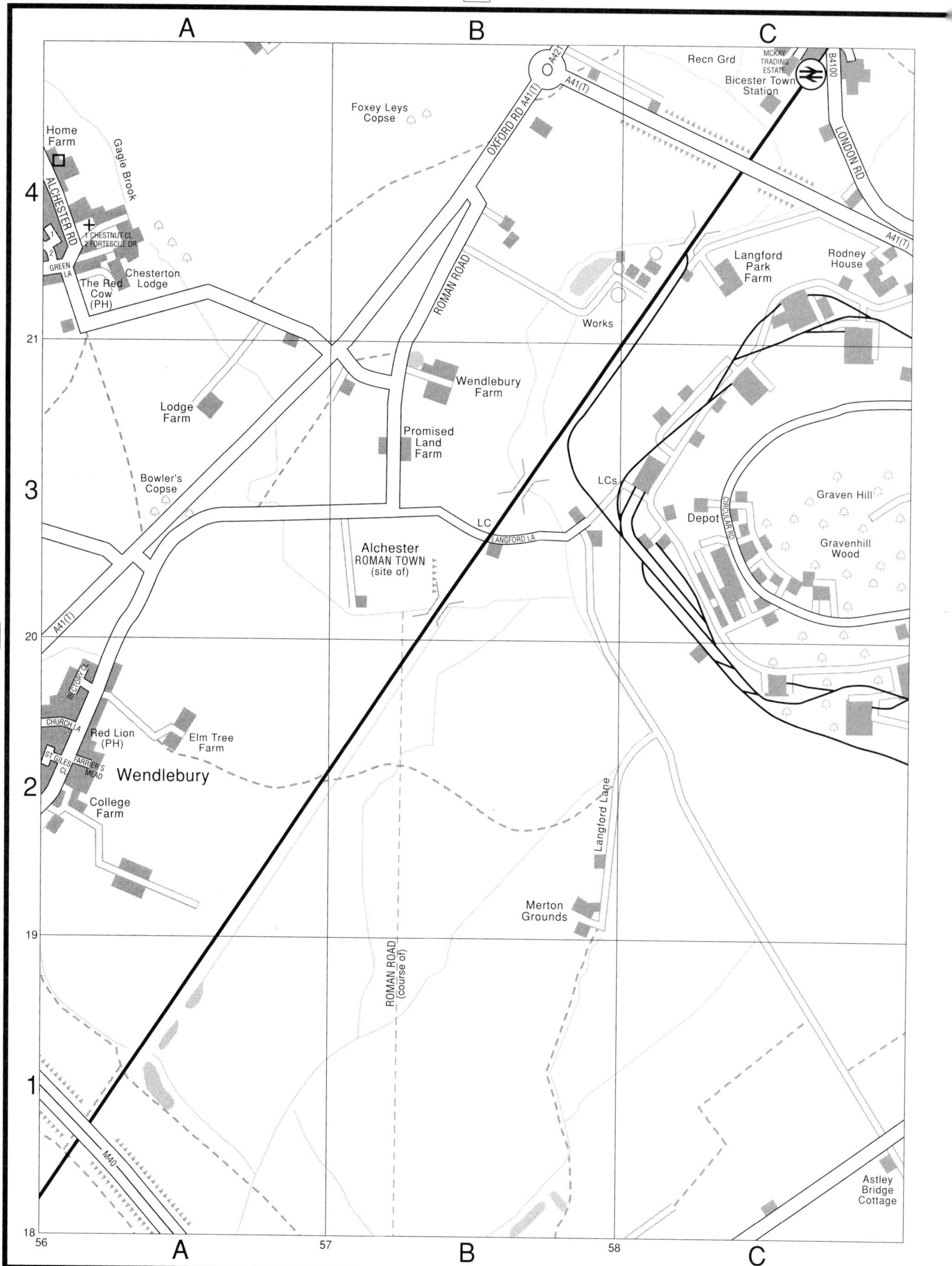
A
B
C
Recn Grd
MCKAY TRADING ESTATE
Bicester Town Station
B4100
A421
A41(T)
OXFORD RD A41(T)
Foxey Leys Copse
Home Farm
Gagle Brook
LONDON RD
4
ALCHESTER RD
1 CHESTNUT CL
2 FORTESCUE DR
GREEN LA
Chesterton Lodge
The Red Cow (PH)
ROMAN ROAD
Langford Park Farm
Rodney House
Works
21
Wendlebury Farm
Lodge Farm
Promised Land Farm
3
Bowler's Copse
LCs
LC
Graven Hill
Depot
CIRCULAR RD
LANGFORD LA
Gravenhill Wood
Alchester
ROMAN TOWN
(site of)
A41(T)
20
RECTORY CL
CHURCH LA
Red Lion (PH)
Elm Tree Farm
ST GILES CL
FARRIER'S MEAD
Wendlebury
2
College Farm
Langford Lane
Merton Grounds
19
ROMAN ROAD (course of)
1
M40
Astley Bridge Cottage
18
56
57
58
A
B
C

79

95

66

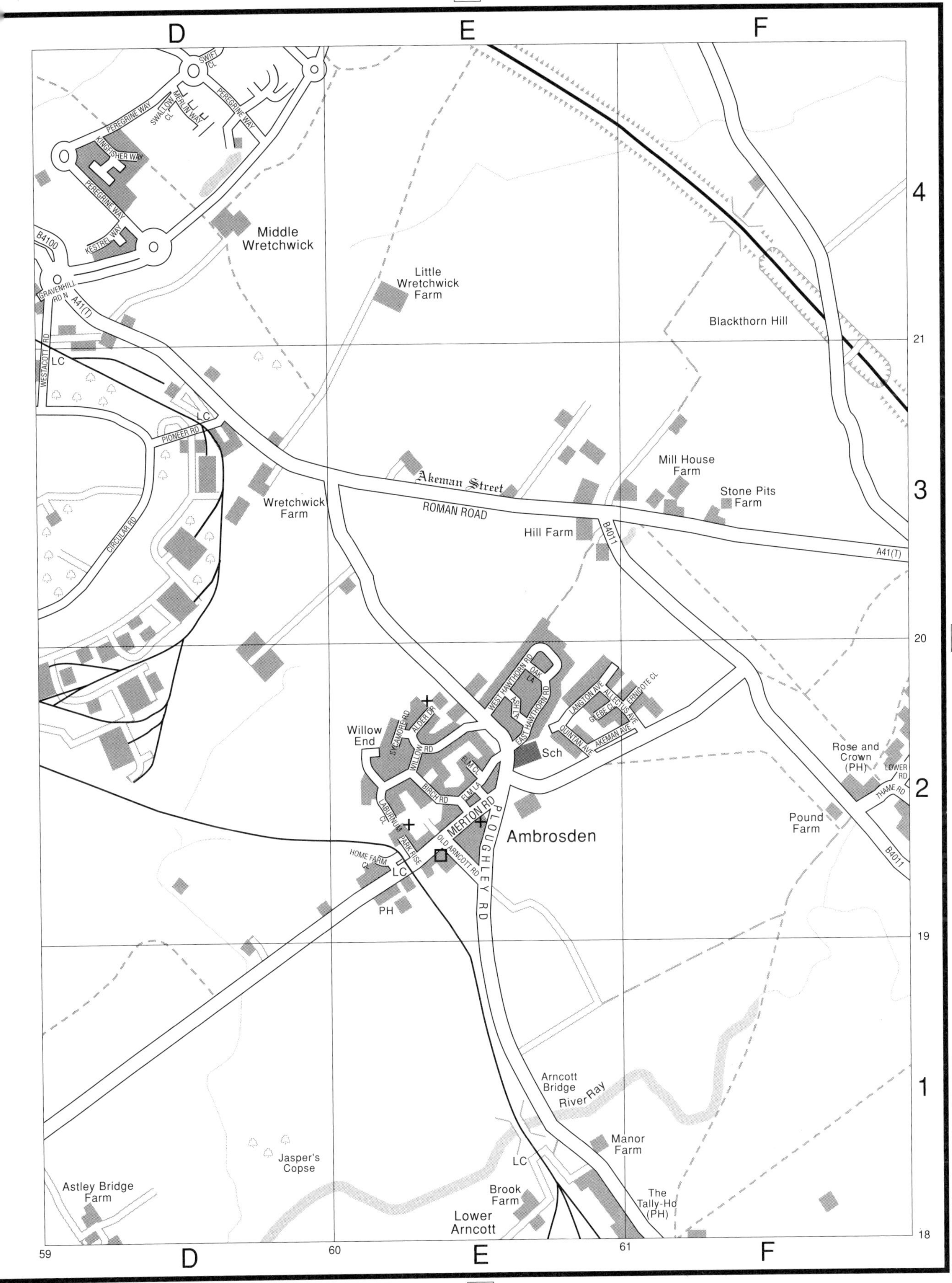
D
E
F
4
3
2
1
21
20
19
18
59
60
61
PEREGRINE WAY
SWIFT CL
SWALLOW CL
MERLIN WAY
KINGFISHER WAY
KESTREL WAY
B4100
GRAVENHILL RD N
A41(T)
Middle Wretchwick
Little Wretchwick Farm
Blackthorn Hill
WESTACOTT RD
LC
PIONEER RD
CIRCULAR RD
Akeman Street
ROMAN ROAD
Wretchwick Farm
Mill House Farm
Stone Pits Farm
Hill Farm
B4011
WEST HAWTHORN RD
OAK LA
ASH LA
EAST HAWTHORN RD
LANGTON AVE
ALLECTUS AVE
ERNICOTE CL
GLEBE CT
QUINTAN AVE
AKEMAN AVE
Sch
Willow End
SYCAMORE RD
ALDER DR
WILLOW RD
ELM CL
BIRCH RD
ELM LA
LABURNUM CL
MERTON RD
PARK RISE
OLD ARNCOTT RD
HOME FARM CL
PLOUGHLEY RD
Ambrosden
PH
Rose and Crown (PH)
LOWER RD
THAME RD
Pound Farm
Arncott Bridge
River Ray
Manor Farm
Jasper's Copse
Astley Bridge Farm
Brook Farm
Lower Arncott
The Tally-Ho (PH)

82

96

67

81

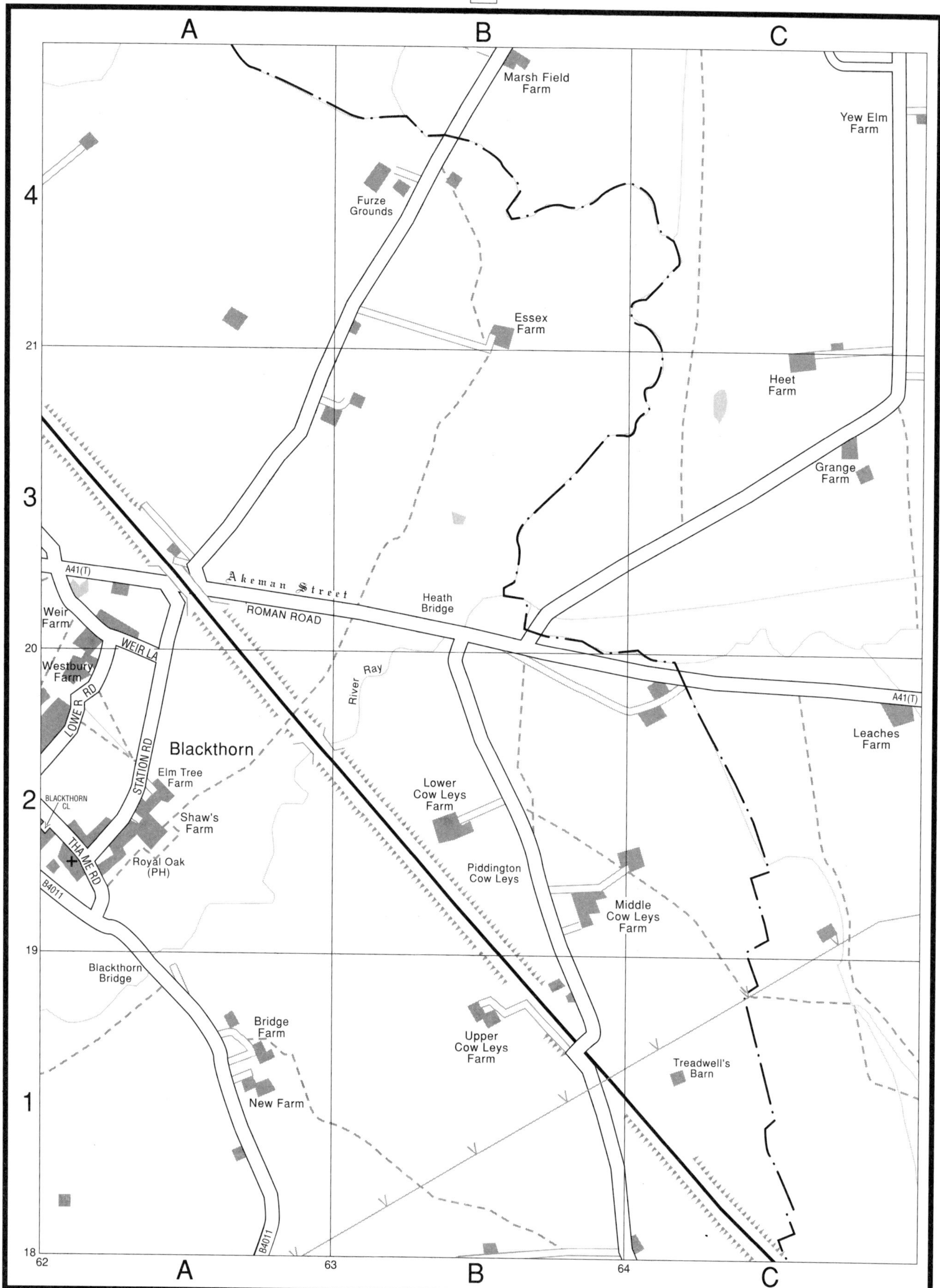

not continued, see key diagram

97

68

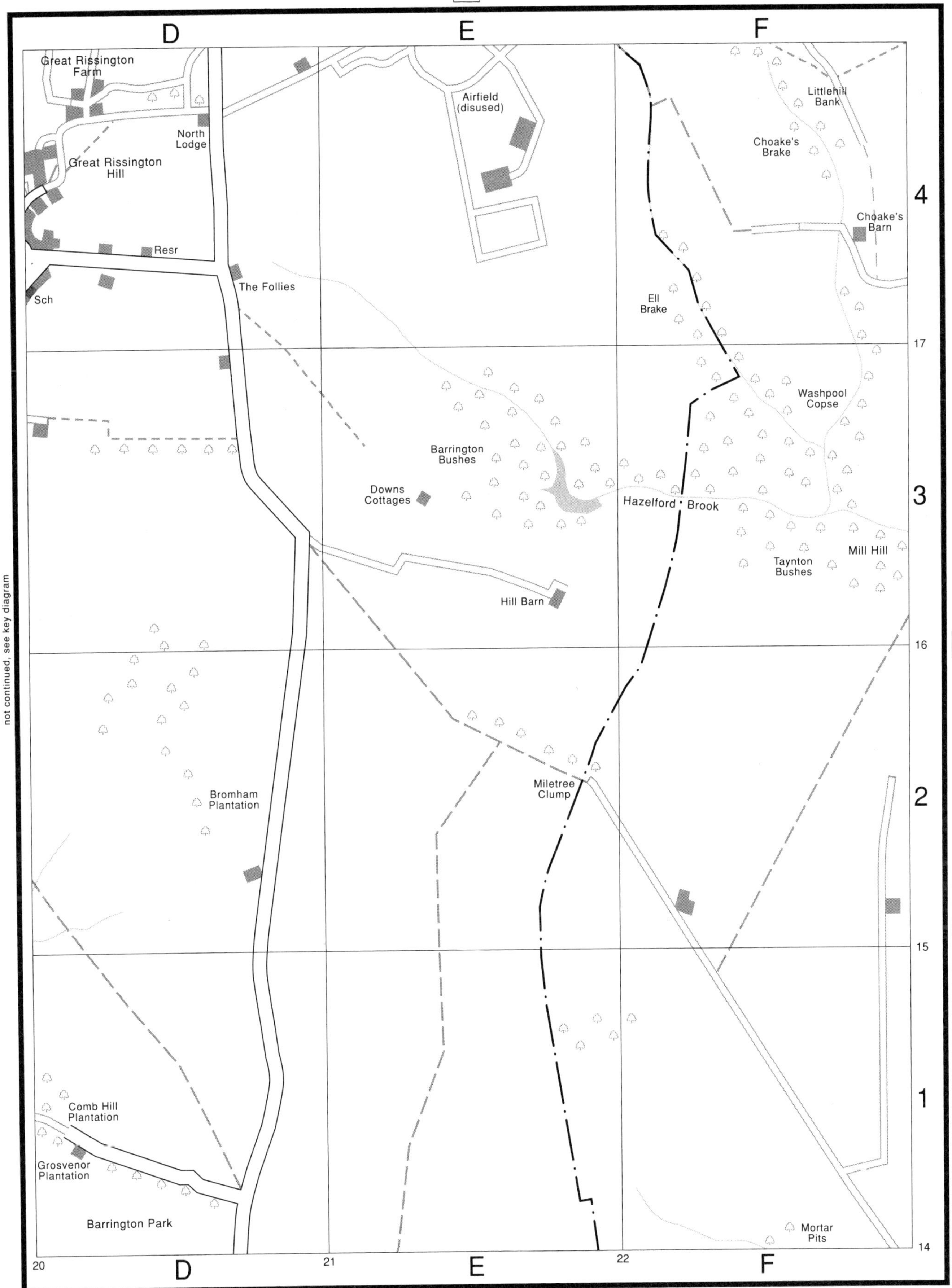

84

not continued, see key diagram

99

69

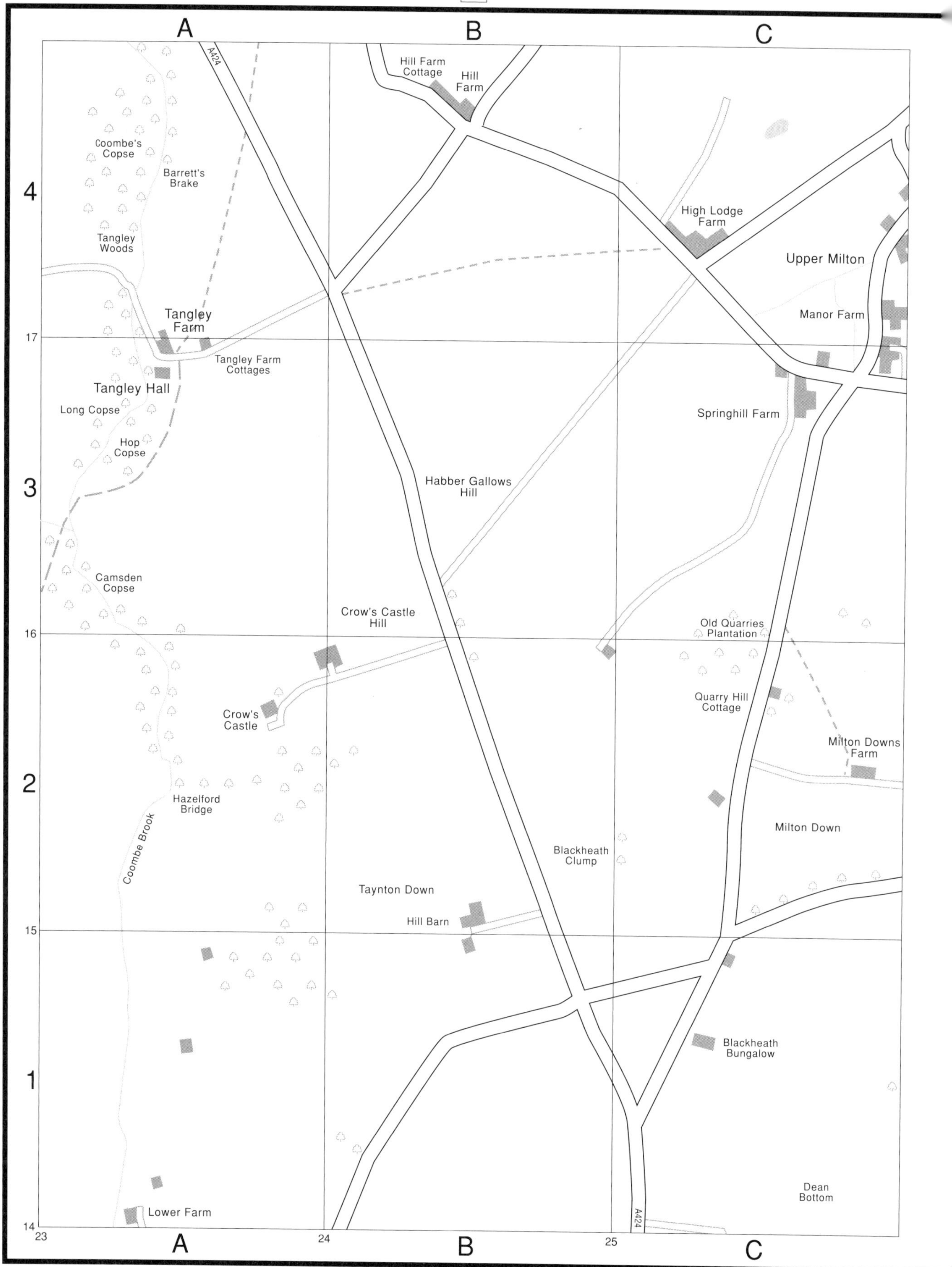
A
B
C
A424
Hill Farm Cottage
Hill Farm
Coombe's Copse
Barrett's Brake
4
High Lodge Farm
Tangley Woods
Upper Milton
Tangley Farm
Manor Farm
17
Tangley Farm Cottages
Tangley Hall
Long Copse
Springhill Farm
Hop Copse
3
Habber Gallows Hill
Camsden Copse
Crow's Castle Hill
Old Quarries Plantation
16
Quarry Hill Cottage
Crow's Castle
Milton Downs Farm
2
Hazelford Bridge
Coombe Brook
Milton Down
Blackheath Clump
Taynton Down
Hill Barn
15
Blackheath Bungalow
1
Dean Bottom
Lower Farm
A424
14
23
24
25
A
B
C

83

100

70

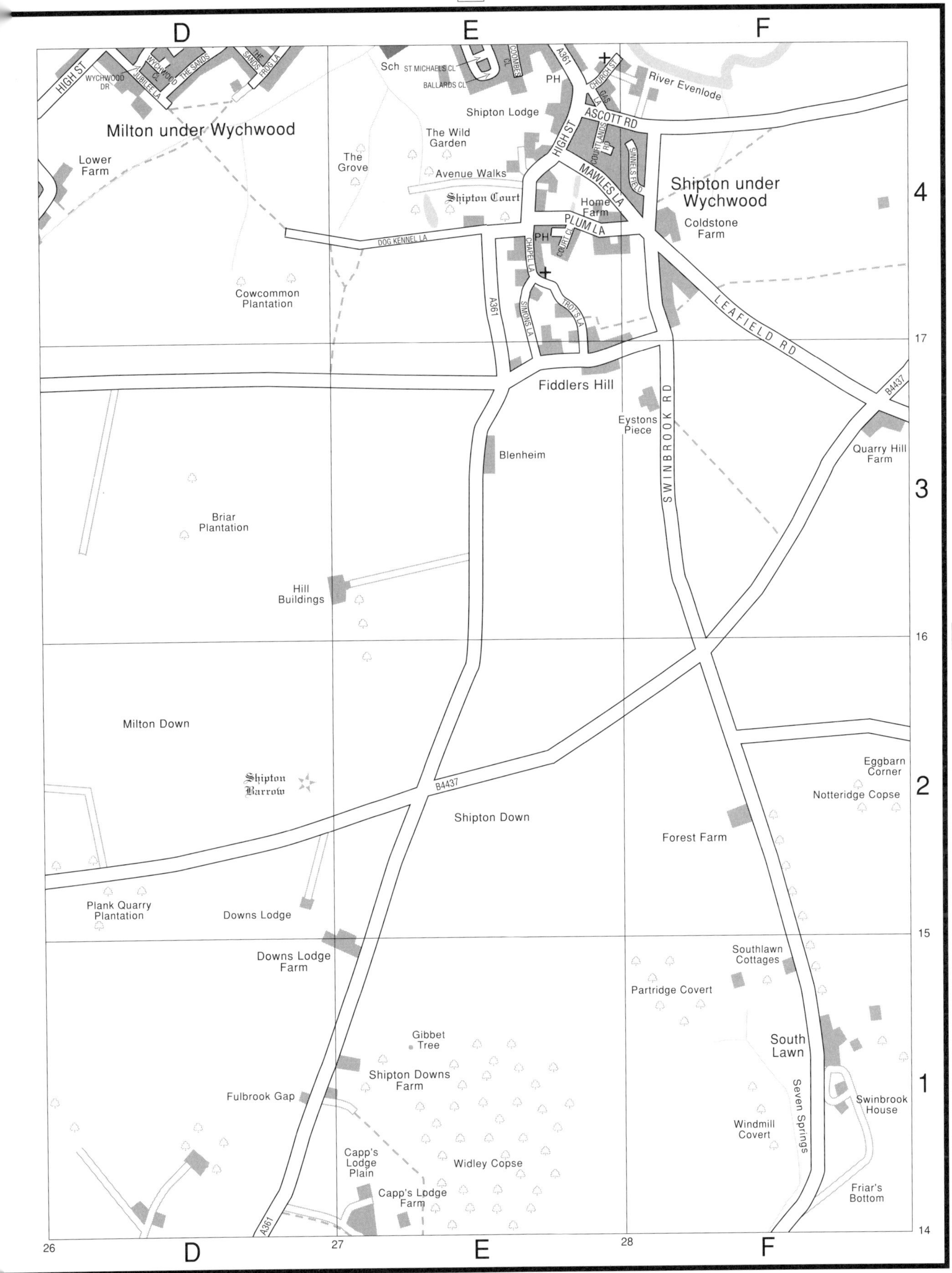

D
E
F
HIGH ST
WYCHWOOD DR
WYCHWOOD CL
JUBILEE LA
THE SANDS
FROG LA
Sch
ST MICHAELS CL
BALLARDS CL
COOMBES CL
A361
PH
CHURCH ST
GAS LA
River Evenlode
ASCOTT RD
Shipton Lodge
Milton under Wychwood
The Wild Garden
HIGH ST
COURTLANDS RD
SINNELS FIELD
Lower Farm
The Grove
Avenue Walks
MAWLES LA
Shipton under Wychwood
Shipton Court
Home Farm
Coldstone Farm
PLUM LA
PH
COURT CL
DOG KENNEL LA
CHAPEL LA
Cowcommon Plantation
A361
SIMONS LA
TROT'S LA
LEAFIELD RD
Fiddlers Hill
B4437
SWINBROOK RD
Eystons Piece
Blenheim
Quarry Hill Farm
Briar Plantation
Hill Buildings
Milton Down
Eggbarn Corner
Shipton Barrow
B4437
Notteridge Copse
Shipton Down
Forest Farm
Plank Quarry Plantation
Downs Lodge
Downs Lodge Farm
Southlawn Cottages
Partridge Covert
Gibbet Tree
South Lawn
Shipton Downs Farm
Fulbrook Gap
Seven Springs
Swinbrook House
Windmill Covert
Capp's Lodge Plain
Widley Copse
Capp's Lodge Farm
Friar's Bottom
A361
4
3
2
1
17
16
15
14
26
27
28
D
E
F

86

101

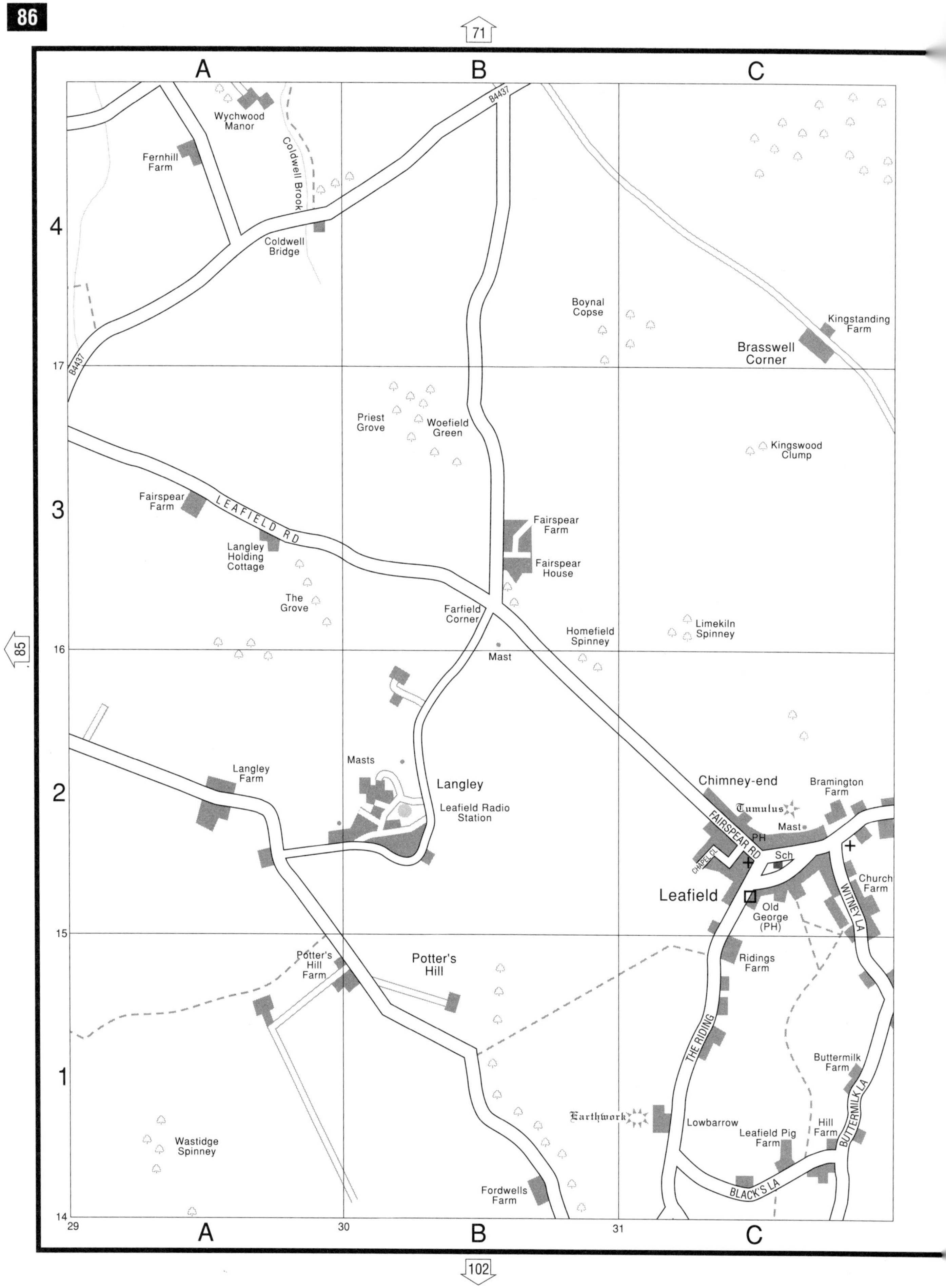
71
A
B
C
4
3
2
1
17
16
15
14
29
30
31
85
102
B4437
Wychwood Manor
Fernhill Farm
Coldwell Brook
Coldwell Bridge
Boynal Copse
Kingstanding Farm
Brasswell Corner
Priest Grove
Woefield Green
Kingswood Clump
Fairspear Farm
LEAFIELD RD
Langley Holding Cottage
Fairspear Farm
Fairspear House
The Grove
Farfield Corner
Homefield Spinney
Limekiln Spinney
Mast
Masts
Langley
Langley Farm
Leafield Radio Station
Chimney-end
Bramington Farm
Tumulus
Mast
FAIRSPEAR RD
PH
Sch
CHAPEL CL
Church Farm
WITNEY LA
Leafield
Old George (PH)
Potter's Hill Farm
Potter's Hill
Ridings Farm
THE RIDING
Buttermilk Farm
BUTTERMILK LA
Earthwork
Lowbarrow
Leafield Pig Farm
Hill Farm
BLACK'S LA
Wastidge Spinney
Fordwells Farm

72

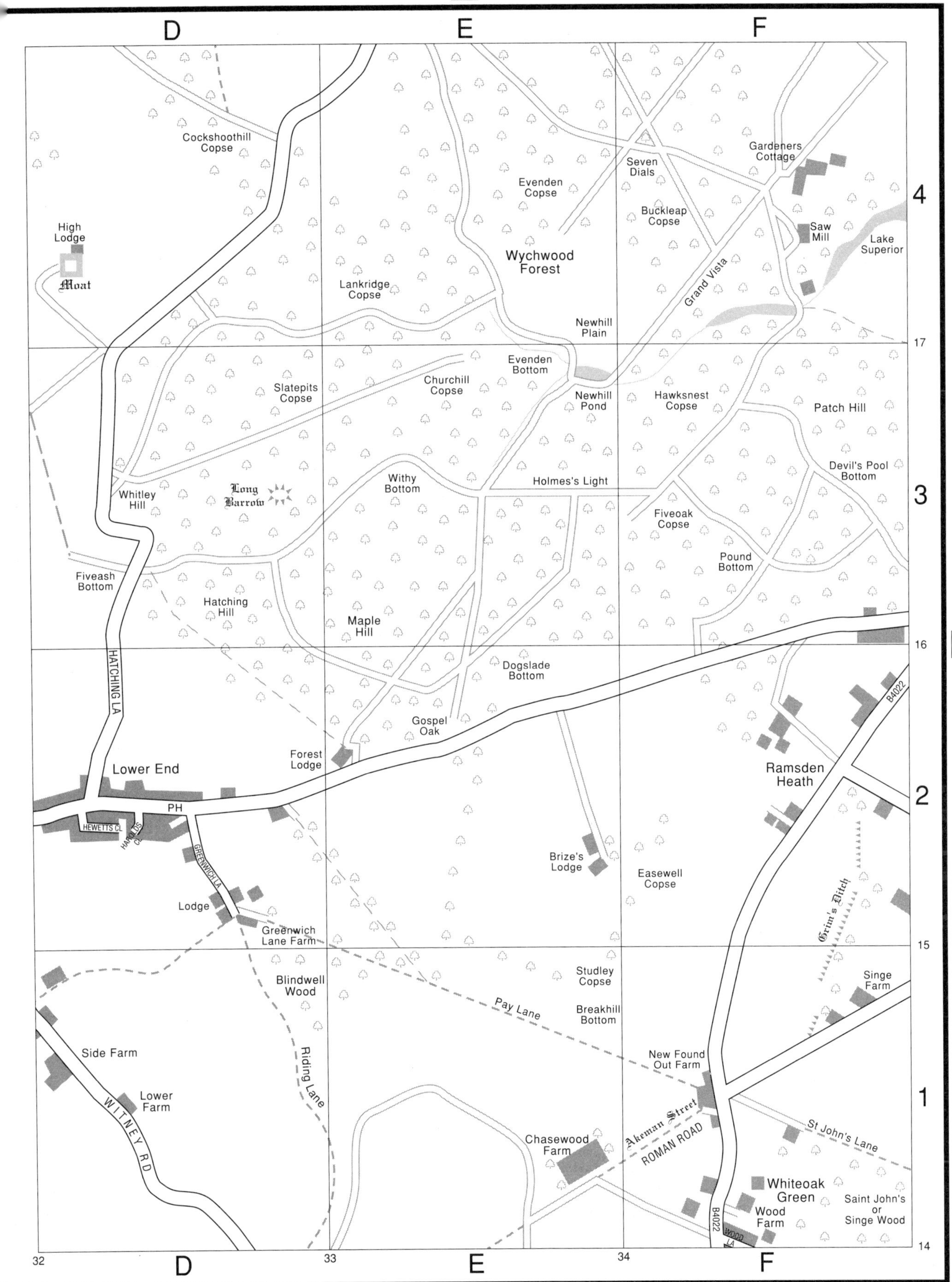
D
E
F
4
3
2
1
17
16
15
14
32
33
34
Cockshoothill Copse
High Lodge
Moat
Seven Dials
Gardeners Cottage
Evenden Copse
Buckleap Copse
Saw Mill
Lake Superior
Wychwood Forest
Grand Vista
Lankridge Copse
Newhill Plain
Evenden Bottom
Slatepits Copse
Churchill Copse
Newhill Pond
Hawksnest Copse
Patch Hill
Devil's Pool Bottom
Withy Bottom
Holmes's Light
Whitley Hill
Long Barrow
Fiveoak Copse
Pound Bottom
Fiveash Bottom
Hatching Hill
Maple Hill
Dogslade Bottom
HATCHING LA
Gospel Oak
Forest Lodge
Lower End
PH
HEWETTS CL
HAROLDS CL
GREENWICH LA
Ramsden Heath
B4022
Brize's Lodge
Easewell Copse
Lodge
Greenwich Lane Farm
Grim's Ditch
Blindwell Wood
Studley Copse
Singe Farm
Pay Lane
Breakhill Bottom
Side Farm
New Found Out Farm
Riding Lane
Lower Farm
Akeman Street
ROMAN ROAD
St John's Lane
WITNEY RD
Chasewood Farm
Whiteoak Green
Wood Farm
Saint John's or Singe Wood
WOOD LA

88
103

73

87

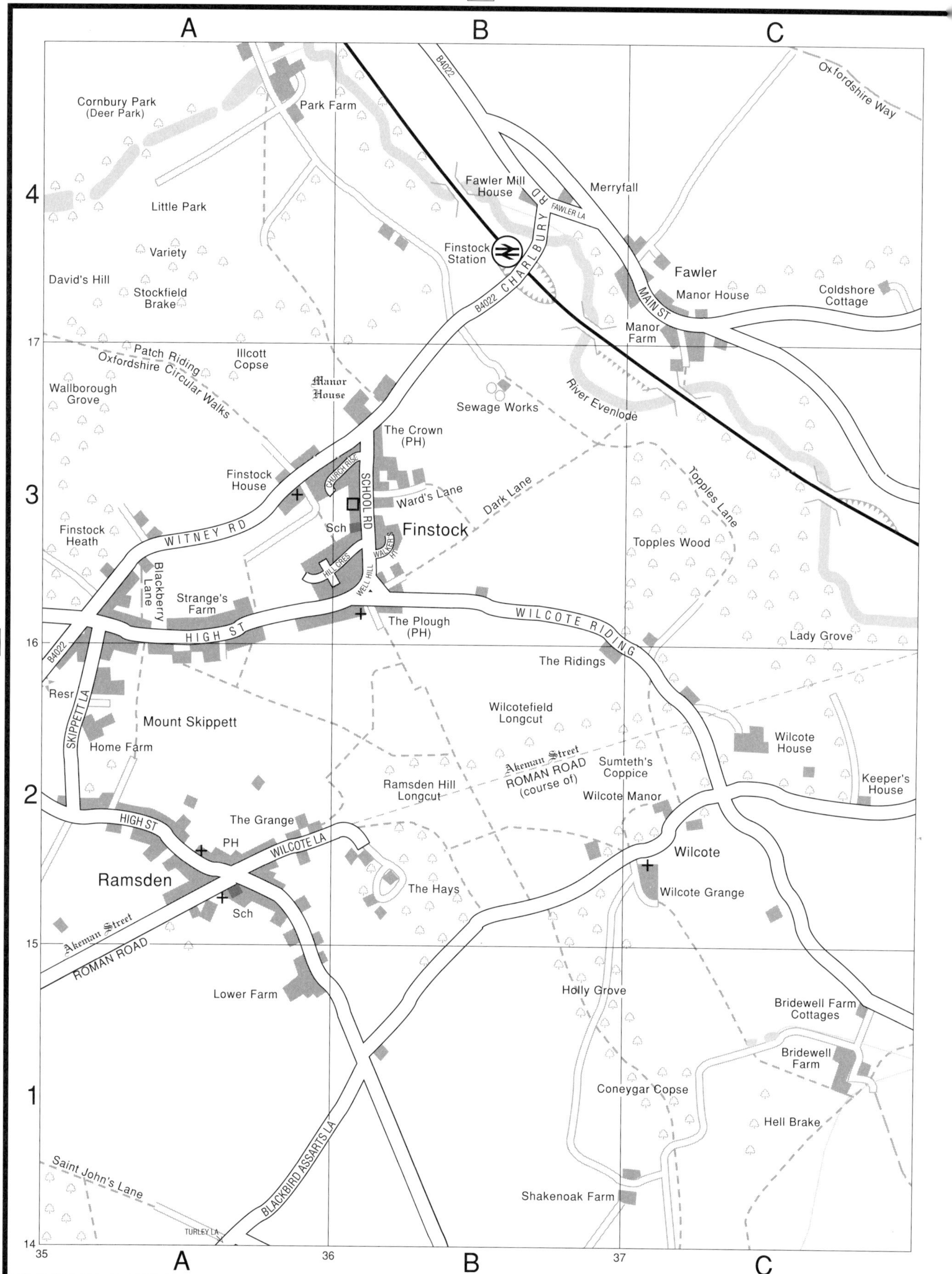
A
B
C
4
3
2
1
17
16
15
14
35
36
37
Cornbury Park
(Deer Park)
Park Farm
B4022
Oxfordshire Way
Little Park
Fawler Mill
House
Merryfall
FAWLER LA
Variety
Finstock
Station
CHARLBURY RD
Fawler
David's Hill
Stockfield
Brake
Manor House
Coldshore
Cottage
MAIN ST
Manor
Farm
Patch Riding
Oxfordshire Circular Walks
Illcott
Copse
Wallborough
Grove
Manor
House
Sewage Works
River Evenlode
The Crown
(PH)
Finstock
House
CHURCH RISE
SCHOOL RD
Ward's Lane
Dark Lane
Topples Lane
Finstock
Heath
WITNEY RD
Sch
Finstock
WALKERS HT
Topples Wood
HILL CRES
Blackberry
Lane
Strange's
Farm
WELL HILL
HIGH ST
The Plough
(PH)
WILCOTE RIDING
Lady Grove
The Ridings
Resr
Mount Skippett
Wilcotefield
Longcut
Wilcote
House
SKIPPETT LA
Home Farm
Akeman Street
ROMAN ROAD
(course of)
Sumteth's
Coppice
Keeper's
House
Ramsden Hill
Longcut
Wilcote Manor
The Grange
HIGH ST
PH
WILCOTE LA
Wilcote
Ramsden
The Hays
Wilcote Grange
Sch
Akeman Street
ROMAN ROAD
Lower Farm
Holly Grove
Bridewell Farm
Cottages
Bridewell
Farm
Coneygar Copse
Hell Brake
Saint John's Lane
BLACKBIRD ASSARTS LA
Shakenoak Farm
TURLEY LA

104

74

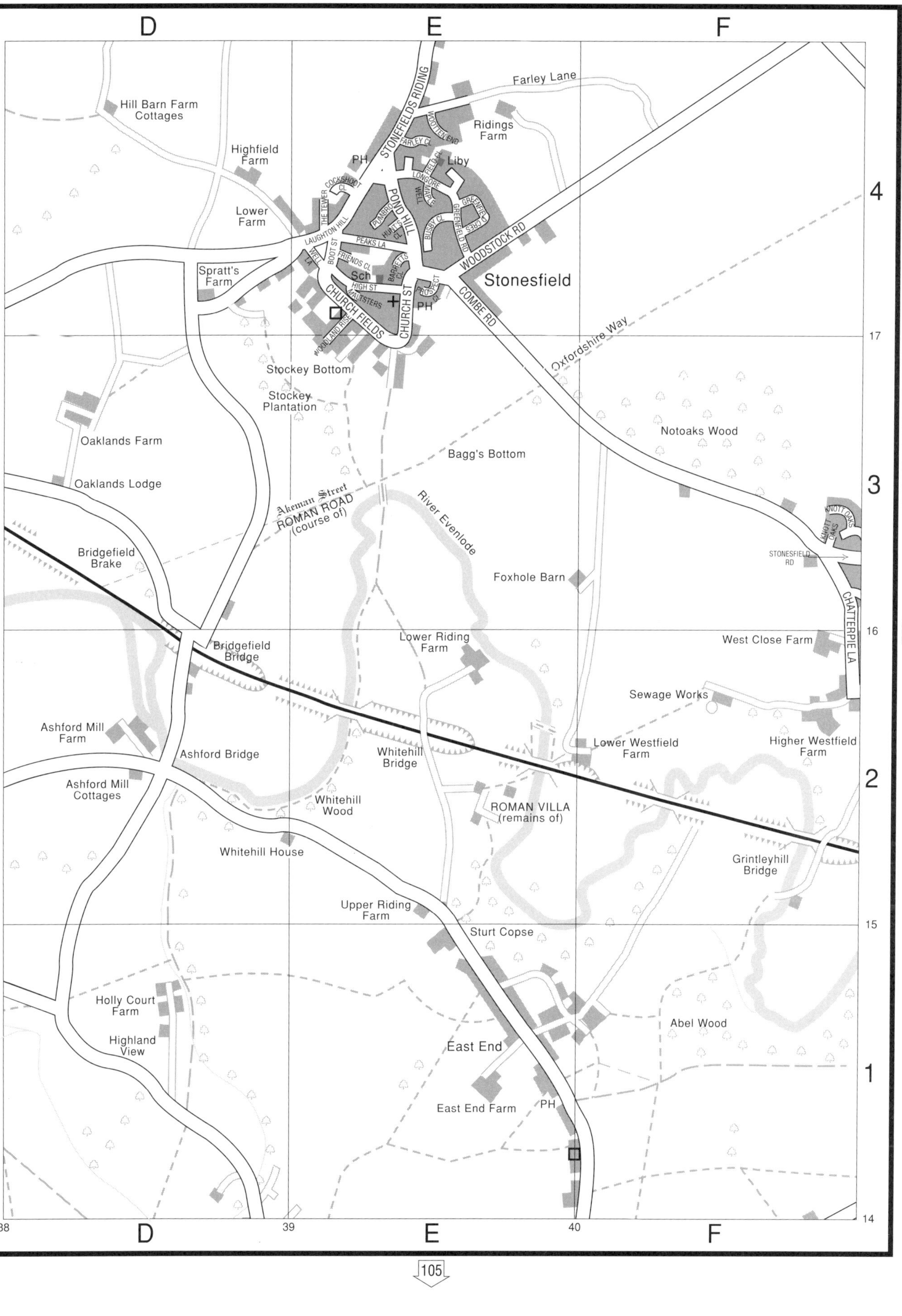
D
E
F
Hill Barn Farm Cottages
Highfield Farm
Lower Farm
Spratt's Farm
Farley Lane
Ridings Farm
Liby
PH
Sch
Stonesfield
STONESFIELDS RIDING
POND HILL
CHURCH ST
CHURCH FIELDS
WOODSTOCK RD
COMBE RD
Oxfordshire Way
Stockey Bottom
Stockey Plantation
Oaklands Farm
Oaklands Lodge
Notoaks Wood
Bagg's Bottom
Akeman Street
ROMAN ROAD (course of)
River Evenlode
Bridgefield Brake
Foxhole Barn
STONESFIELD RD
CHATTERPIE LA
Bridgefield Bridge
Lower Riding Farm
West Close Farm
Sewage Works
Ashford Mill Farm
Ashford Bridge
Whitehill Bridge
Lower Westfield Farm
Higher Westfield Farm
Ashford Mill Cottages
Whitehill Wood
ROMAN VILLA (remains of)
Whitehill House
Grintleyhill Bridge
Upper Riding Farm
Sturt Copse
Holly Court Farm
Highland View
East End
Abel Wood
East End Farm
4
3
2
1
17
16
15
14
38
39
40

90

105

75

89

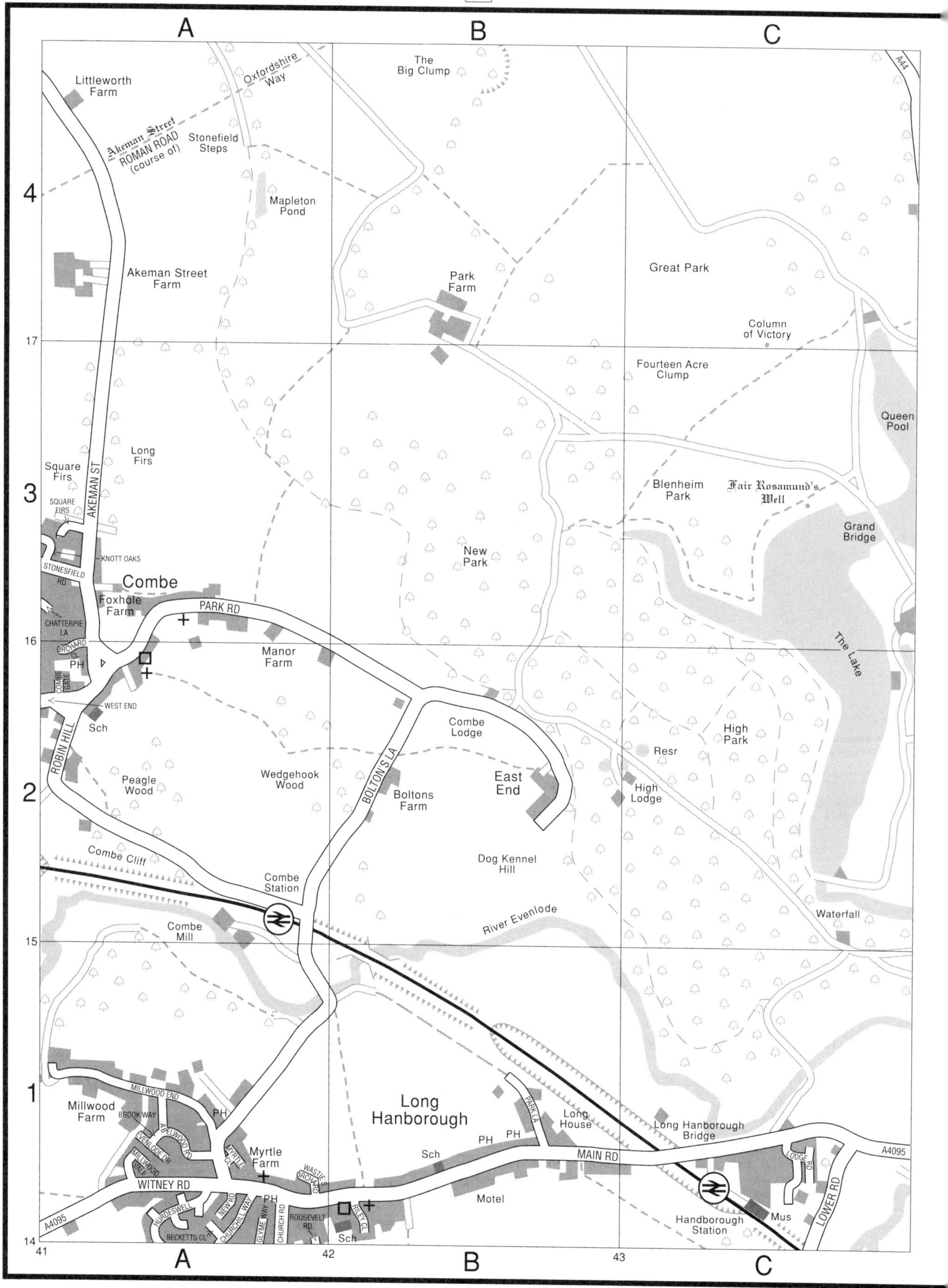
A
B
C
4
3
2
1
17
16
15
14
41
42
43
Littleworth Farm
Oxfordshire Way
Akeman Street
ROMAN ROAD (course of)
Stonefield Steps
The Big Clump
A44
Mapleton Pond
Akeman Street Farm
Park Farm
Great Park
Column of Victory
Fourteen Acre Clump
Queen Pool
Long Firs
Square Firs
AKEMAN ST
SQUARE FIRS
Blenheim Park
Fair Rosamund's Well
Grand Bridge
New Park
KNOTT OAKS
STONESFIELD RD
Combe
Foxhole Farm
PARK RD
CHATTERPIE LA
ORCHARD CL
PH
COMBE GATE
Manor Farm
The Lake
WEST END
Sch
ROBIN HILL
Combe Lodge
High Park
Resr
Peagle Wood
Wedgehook Wood
BOLTON'S LA
Boltons Farm
East End
High Lodge
Combe Cliff
Dog Kennel Hill
Combe Station
River Evenlode
Waterfall
Combe Mill
Millwood Farm
MILLWOOD END
BROOK WAY
ABELWOOD RD
EVENLODE DR
MILLWOOD VALE
PH
MYRTLE CL
Myrtle Farm
Long Hanborough
PARK LA
Long House
Long Hanborough Bridge
PH
PH
Sch
MAIN RD
A4095
WASTIE'S ORCHARD
LODGE RD
WITNEY RD
HURDESWELL
NEW RD
CHURCHILL WAY
GLYME WAY
CHURCH RD
ROOSEVELT RD
RILEY CL
PH
Motel
Handborough Station
Mus
LOWER RD
A4095
BECKETTS CL
Sch

106

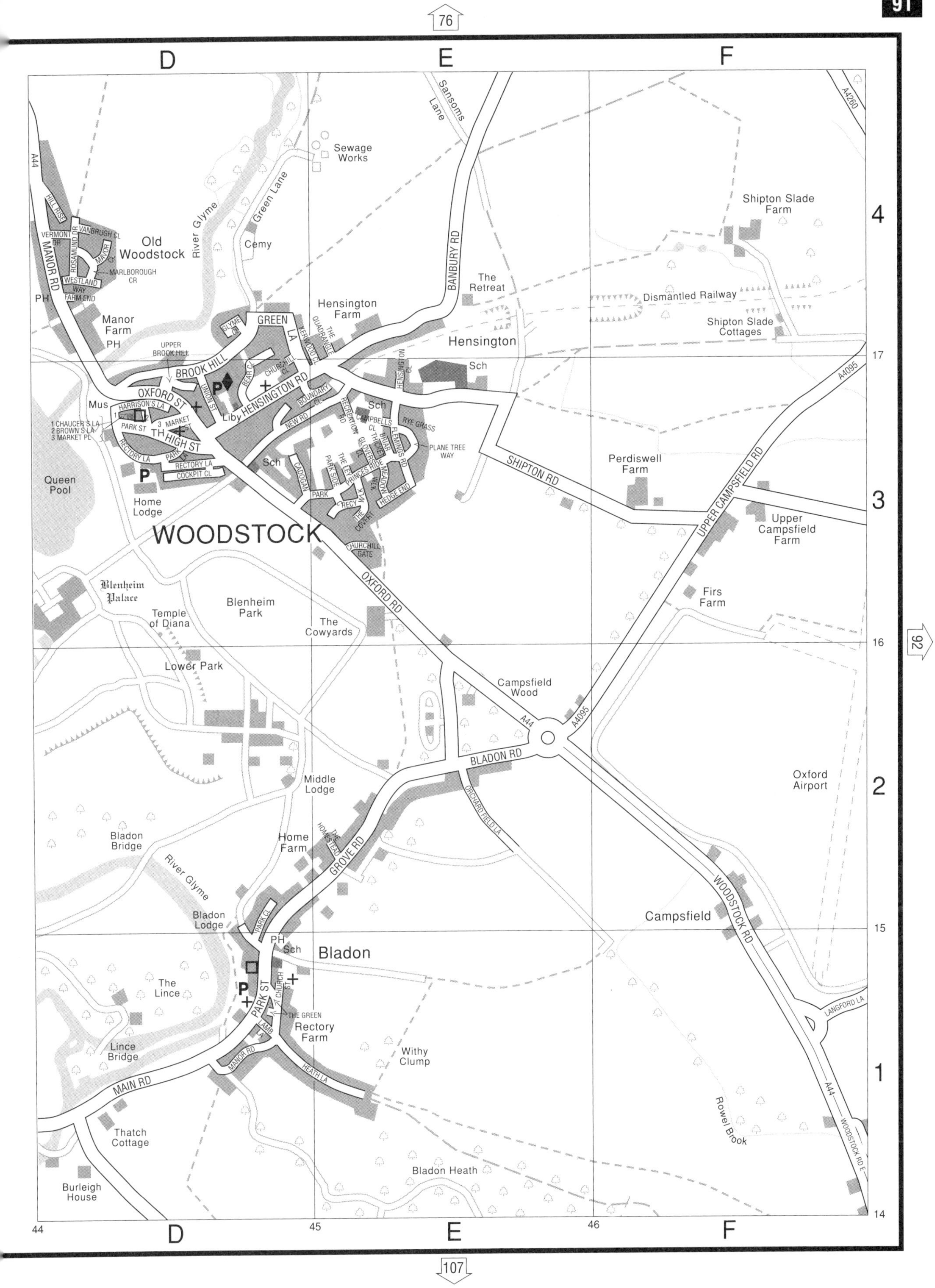
76
D
E
F
Sansoms Lane
A4260
Sewage Works
Green Lane
Shipton Slade Farm
4
A44
HILL RISE
VERMON DR
VANBRUGH CL
ROSAMUND DR
MAVOR
MARLBOROUGH CR
WESTLAND WAY
FARM END
MANOR RD
Old Woodstock
River Glyme
Cemy
BANBURY RD
The Retreat
Dismantled Railway
PH
Manor Farm
PH
Hensington Farm
Shipton Slade Cottages
GLYME CL
GREEN LA
KERWOOD CL
THE QUADRANGLE
Hensington
UPPER BROOK HILL
BROOK HILL
17
HENSINGTON CL
Sch
A4095
UNION ST
BEAR CL
CHURCHILL CL
HENSINGTON RD
Mus
OXFORD ST
HARRISON'S LA
BOUNDARY CL
RECREATION RD
Sch
CAMPBELLS CL
RYE GRASS
1 CHAUCER'S LA
2 BROWN'S LA
3 MARKET PL
PARK ST
3 MARKET ST
TH
HIGH ST
Liby
NEW RD
GLOVERS CL
THE THICKET
BRIARS
FLEMINGS RD
PLANE TREE WAY
RECTORY LA
PARK LA
Sch
MEADOW WALK
PRINCES RIDE
THE LEY
PARK SIDE
CADOGAN PARK
RECTORY LA
COCKPIT CL
SHIPTON RD
Perdiswell Farm
UPPER CAMPSFIELD RD
Queen Pool
P
HEDGE END
RECY
THE COVERT
3
Home Lodge
WOODSTOCK
Upper Campsfield Farm
CHURCHILL GATE
Blenheim Palace
Blenheim Park
OXFORD RD
Firs Farm
Temple of Diana
The Cowyards
92
16
Lower Park
Campsfield Wood
A44
A4095
BLADON RD
Middle Lodge
Oxford Airport
2
ORCHARD FIELD LA
Bladon Bridge
Home Farm
THE HOMESTEAD
GROVE RD
River Glyme
WOODSTOCK RD
Bladon Lodge
PARK CL
Campsfield
15
PH
Sch
Bladon
The Lince
P
PARK ST
CHURCH ST
THE GREEN
LANGFORD LA
Rectory Farm
LAMB LA
MANOR RD
Lince Bridge
Withy Clump
1
HEATH LA
MAIN RD
A44
Rowel Brook
WOODSTOCK RD E
Thatch Cottage
Bladon Heath
Burleigh House
14
44
D
45
E
46
F
107

77

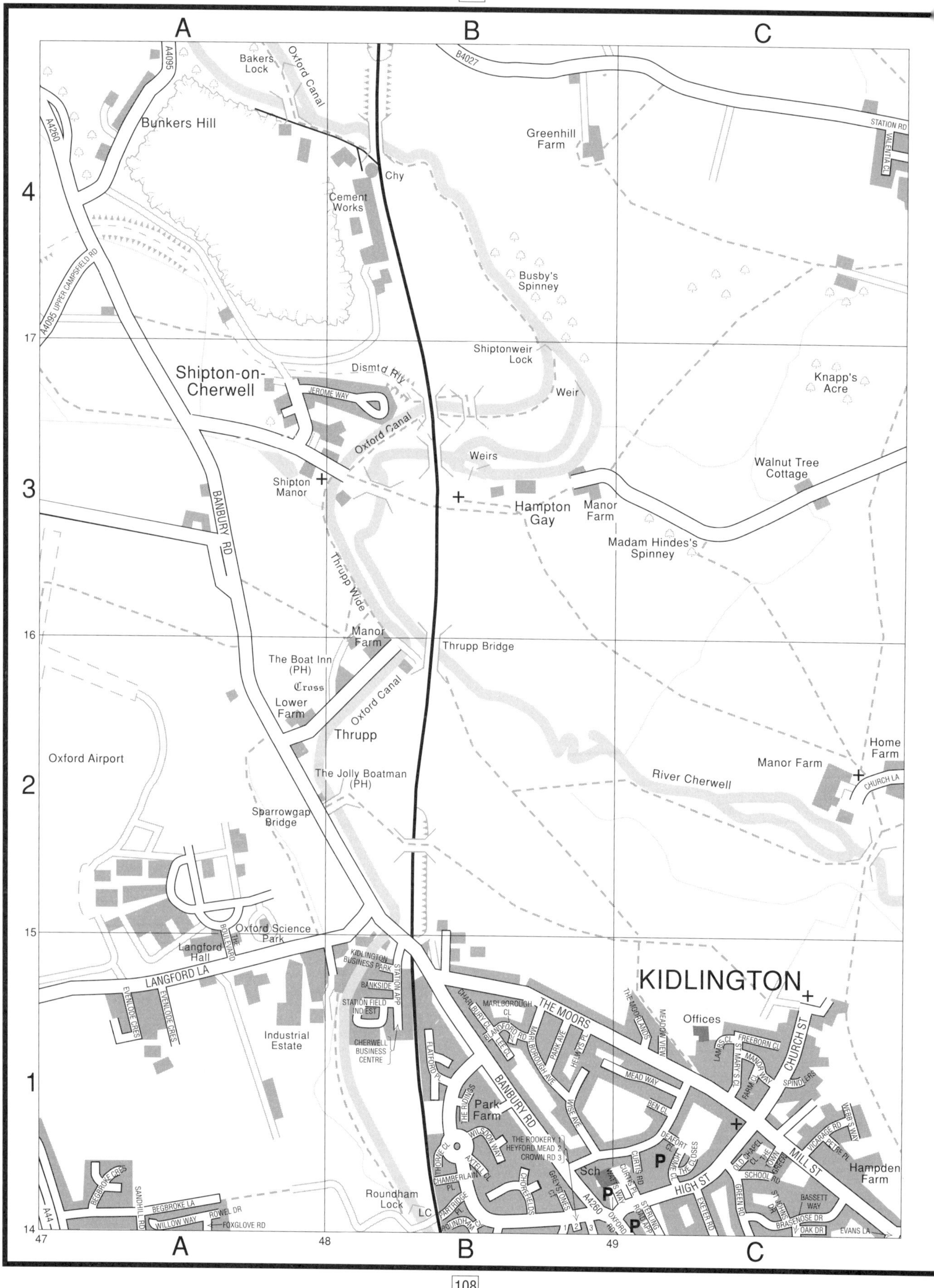

A
B
C
Bakers Lock
Oxford Canal
B4027
A4095
A4260
Bunkers Hill
Greenhill Farm
STATION RD
VALENTIA CL
Chy
Cement Works
4
Busby's Spinney
A4095 UPPER CAMPSFIELD RD
17
Shiptonweir Lock
Shipton-on-Cherwell
Dismtd Rly
JEROME WAY
Weir
Knapp's Acre
Oxford Canal
Weirs
Walnut Tree Cottage
Shipton Manor
3
Hampton Gay
Manor Farm
BANBURY RD
Madam Hindes's Spinney
Thrupp Wide
16
Manor Farm
Thrupp Bridge
The Boat Inn (PH)
Cross
Lower Farm
Oxford Canal
Thrupp
Home Farm
Oxford Airport
Manor Farm
CHURCH LA
River Cherwell
2
The Jolly Boatman (PH)
Sparrowgap Bridge
Oxford Science Park
15
Langford Hall
THE BOULEVARD
KIDLINGTON BUSINESS PARK
STATION APP
LANGFORD LA
BANKSIDE
KIDLINGTON
STATION FIELD IND EST
THE MOORS
MARLBOROUGH CL
CHARLBURY CL
BLANDFORD RD
EVENLODE CRES
Offices
Industrial Estate
CHERWELL BUSINESS CENTRE
THE MOORLANDS
MEADOW VIEW
LAMBS CL
FREEBORN CL
ST MARY'S CL
MANOR WAY
CHURCH ST
FLATFORD PL
LEE CL
MARLBOROUGH AVE
PARK AVE
HEWITTS PL
MEAD WAY
FARM CL
SPINDLERS
1
BANBURY RD
THE RIDINGS
Park Farm
WISE AVE
BEN CL
WILSON WAY
THE ROOKERY 1
HEYFORD MEAD 2
CROWN RD 3
DEAFORT CL
THE CLOSES
OLD CHAPEL CL
THE TOWN GREEN
VICARAGE RD
PETRE PL
WEBBS WAY
MILL ST
THORNE CL
AXTELL CL
Sch
CURTIS RD
P
HOLME CL
Hampden Farm
BEGBROKE CRES
CHAMBERLAIN PL
CHOREFIELDS
GREYSTONES CT
WATTS WAY
CURTIS PL
HIGH ST
SCHOOL RD
Roundham Lock
SANDHILL RD
BEGBROKE LA
PARTRIDGE PL
A4260
STERLING RD APP
EXETER RD
GREEN RD
ST JOHNS DR
BASSETT WAY
BRASENOSE DR
ROWEL DR
WILLOW WAY
FOXGLOVE RD
LC
ROUNDHAM CL
OXFORD RD
OAK DR
EVANS LA
A44
14
47
48
49

91

108

78

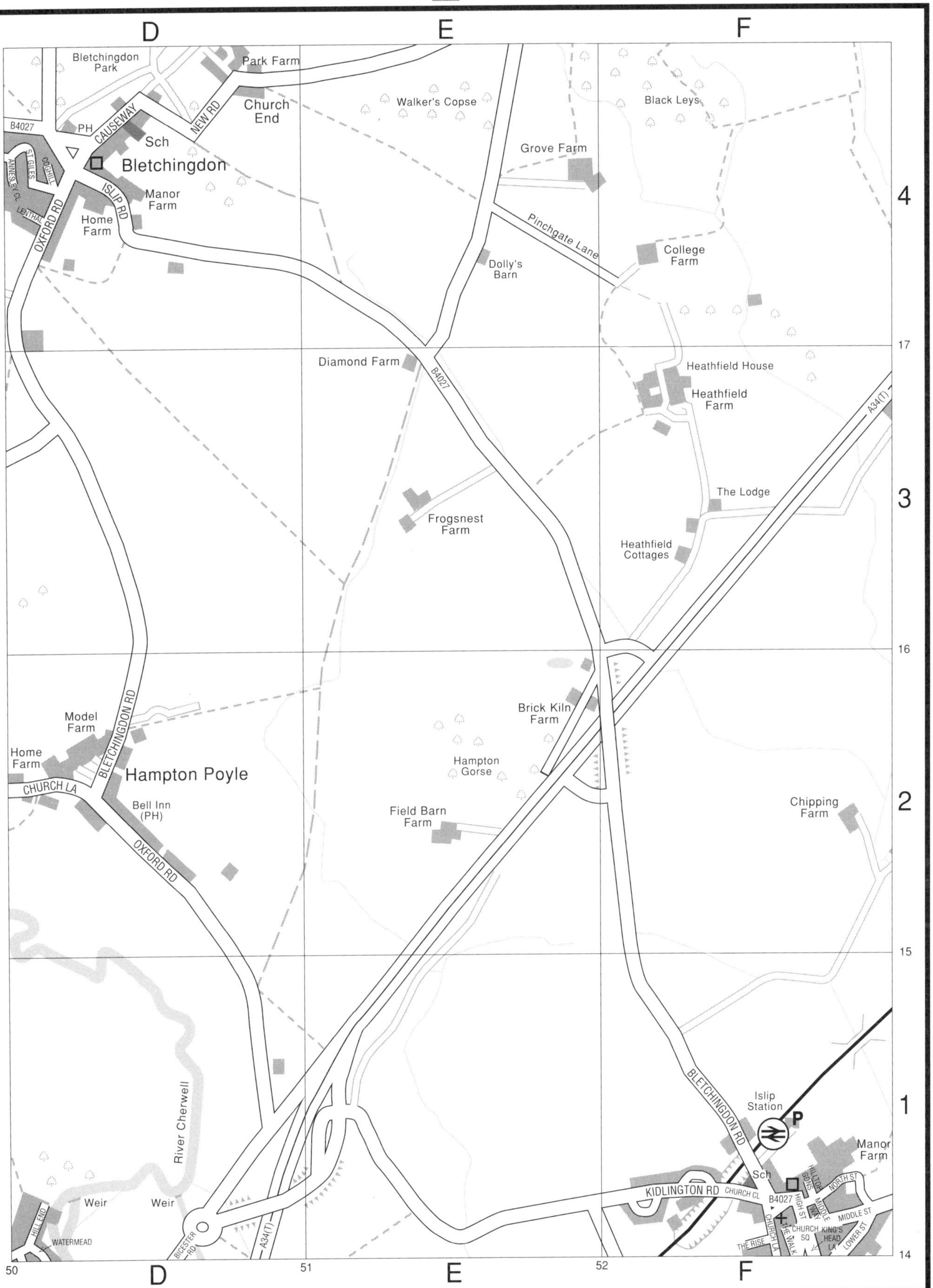
D
E
F
Bletchingdon Park
Park Farm
Walker's Copse
Black Leys
Church End
NEW RD
CAUSEWAY
B4027
PH
Sch
Bletchingdon
ST GILES
COGHILL
ANNESLEY CL
LENTHAL
OXFORD RD
ISLIP RD
Manor Farm
Home Farm
Grove Farm
Pinchgate Lane
Dolly's Barn
College Farm
Diamond Farm
B4027
Heathfield House
Heathfield Farm
A34(T)
The Lodge
Frogsnest Farm
Heathfield Cottages
Brick Kiln Farm
Hampton Gorse
Model Farm
Home Farm
BLETCHINGDON RD
Hampton Poyle
CHURCH LA
Bell Inn (PH)
Field Barn Farm
Chipping Farm
OXFORD RD
River Cherwell
BLETCHINGDON RD
Islip Station
P
Manor Farm
Sch
KIDLINGTON RD
CHURCH CL
B4027
HILLTOP GDNS
HIGH ST
MIDDLE WAY
NORTH ST
MIDDLE ST
CHURCH LA
THE WALK
CHURCH SQ
KING'S HEAD LA
LOWER ST
THE RISE
Weir
Weir
HILL END
WATERMEAD
BICESTER RD
A34(T)
4
17
3
16
2
15
1
14
50
51
52
D
E
F

94

109

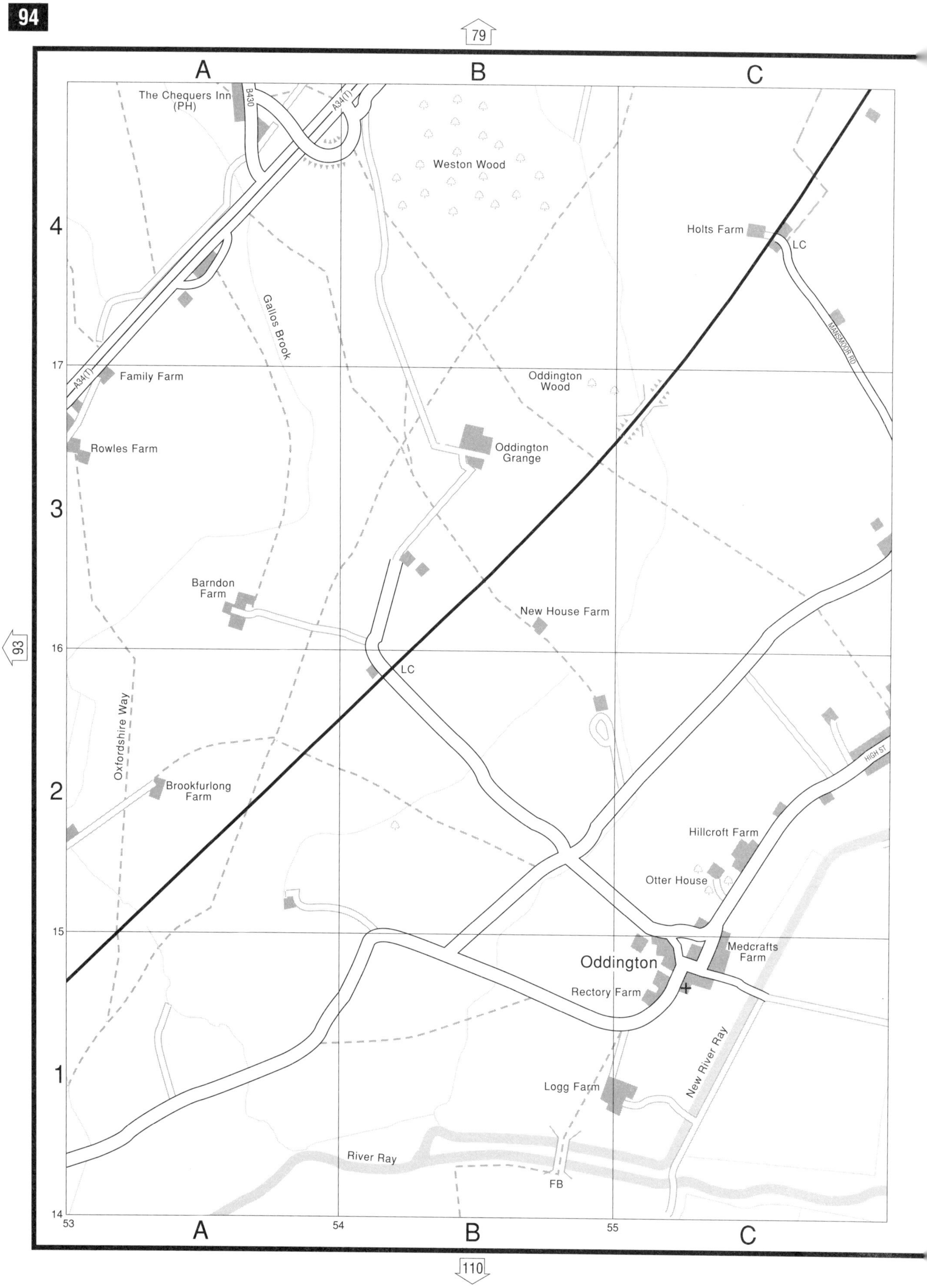
79
A
B
C
The Chequers Inn (PH)
B430
A34(T)
Weston Wood
4
Holts Farm
LC
Gallos Brook
MANSMOOR RD
17
A34(T)
Family Farm
Oddington Wood
Rowles Farm
Oddington Grange
3
Barndon Farm
New House Farm
93
16
LC
Oxfordshire Way
HIGH ST
2
Brookfurlong Farm
Hillcroft Farm
Otter House
15
Medcrafts Farm
Oddington
Rectory Farm
New River Ray
1
Logg Farm
River Ray
FB
14
53
54
55
A
B
C
110

80

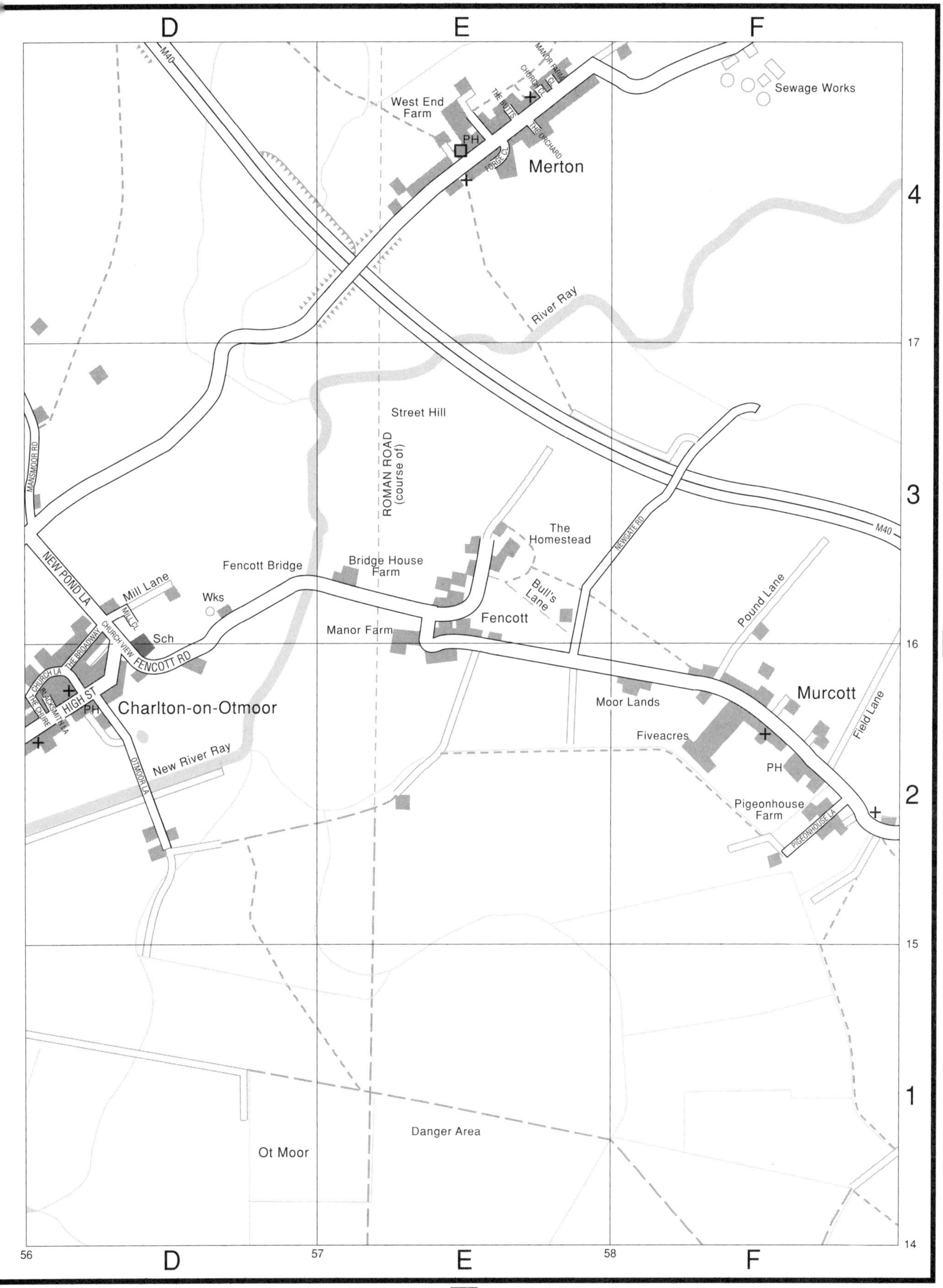
D
E
F
D
E
F
4
3
2
1
17
16
15
14
56
57
58
M40
Manor Farm
Church Cl
The Butts
West End
Farm
PH
The Orchard
Forge Cl
Merton
Sewage Works
River Ray
Street Hill
ROMAN ROAD
(course of)
Mansmoor Rd
New Pond La
The Homestead
Newgate Rd
M40
Fencott Bridge
Bridge House
Farm
Bull's
Lane
Mill Lane
Wks
Mill Cl
Sch
Fencott
Manor Farm
Pound Lane
Church View
Fencott Rd
The Broadway
Church La
High St
Blacksmith La
The Chure
PH
Charlton-on-Otmoor
Moor Lands
Murcott
Field Lane
Fiveacres
PH
New River Ray
Otmoor La
Pigeonhouse
Farm
Pigeonhouse La
Danger Area
Ot Moor

96

111

81

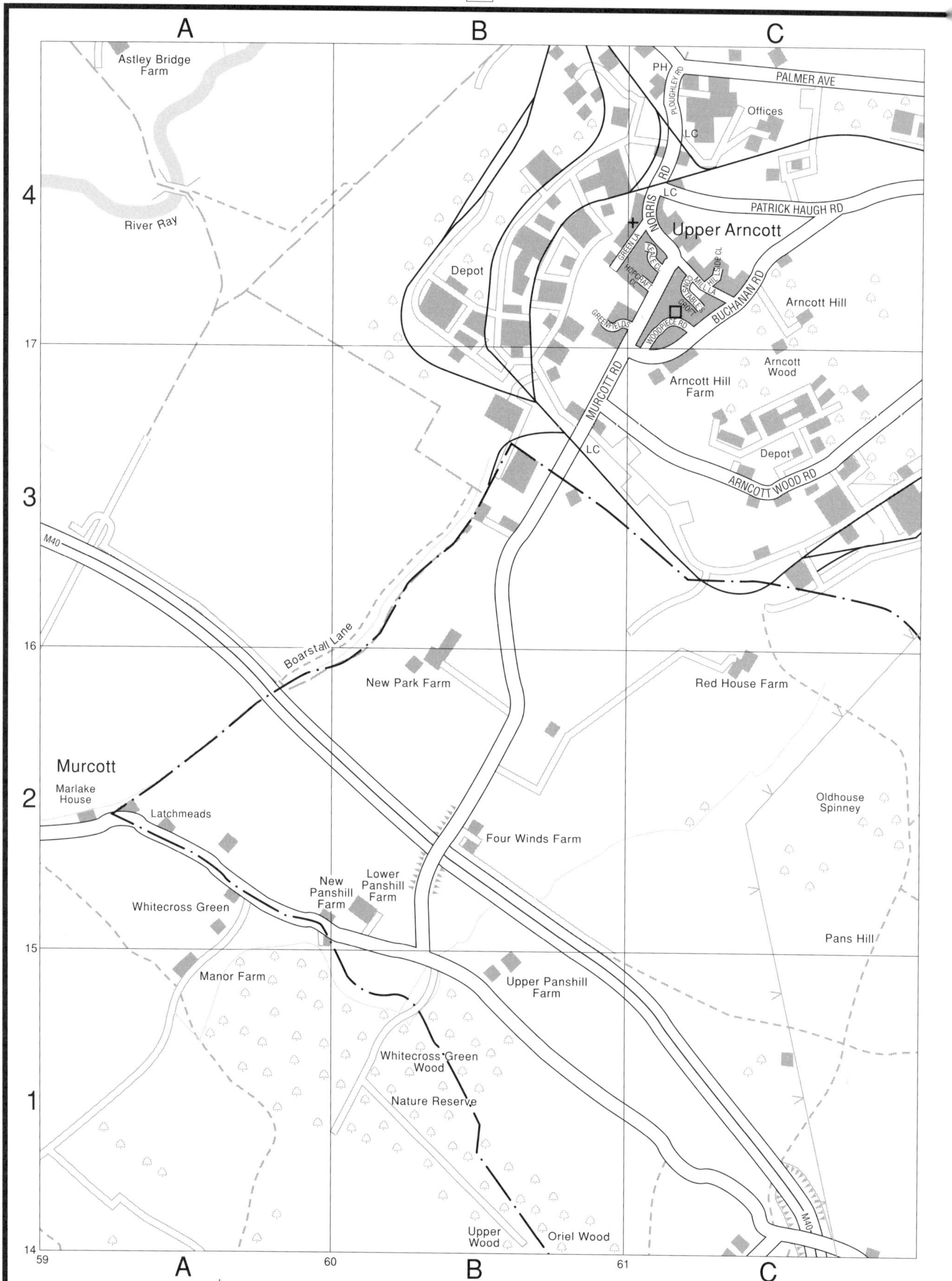
A
B
C
4
3
2
1
17
16
15
14
59
60
61
Astley Bridge Farm
River Ray
Depot
PH
PLOUGHLEY RD
PALMER AVE
Offices
LC
NORRIS RD
PATRICK HAUGH RD
Upper Arncott
GREEN LA
TEALE CL
HOPCRAFT CL
MILL LA
HILLSIDE CL
CONSTABLE'S CROFT
BUCHANAN RD
GREENFIELDS
WOODPIECE RD
Arncott Hill
Arncott Wood
Arncott Hill Farm
MURCOTT RD
Depot
ARNCOTT WOOD RD
M40
Boarstall Lane
New Park Farm
Red House Farm
Murcott
Marlake House
Latchmeads
Four Winds Farm
Oldhouse Spinney
New Panshill Farm
Lower Panshill Farm
Whitecross Green
Pans Hill
Manor Farm
Upper Panshill Farm
Whitecross Green Wood
Nature Reserve
Upper Wood
Oriel Wood

95

112

82

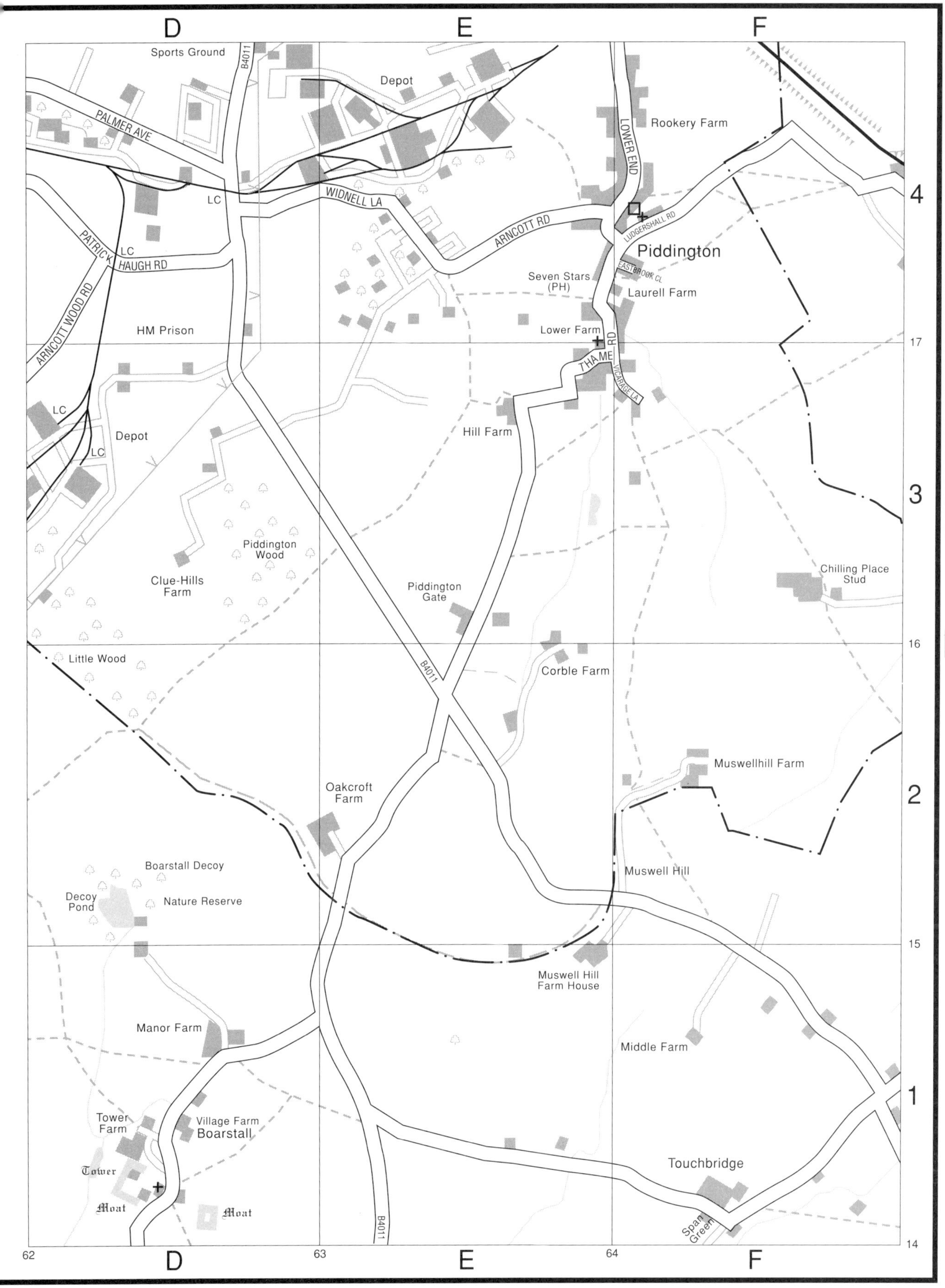

98

not continued, see key diagram

not continued, see key diagram

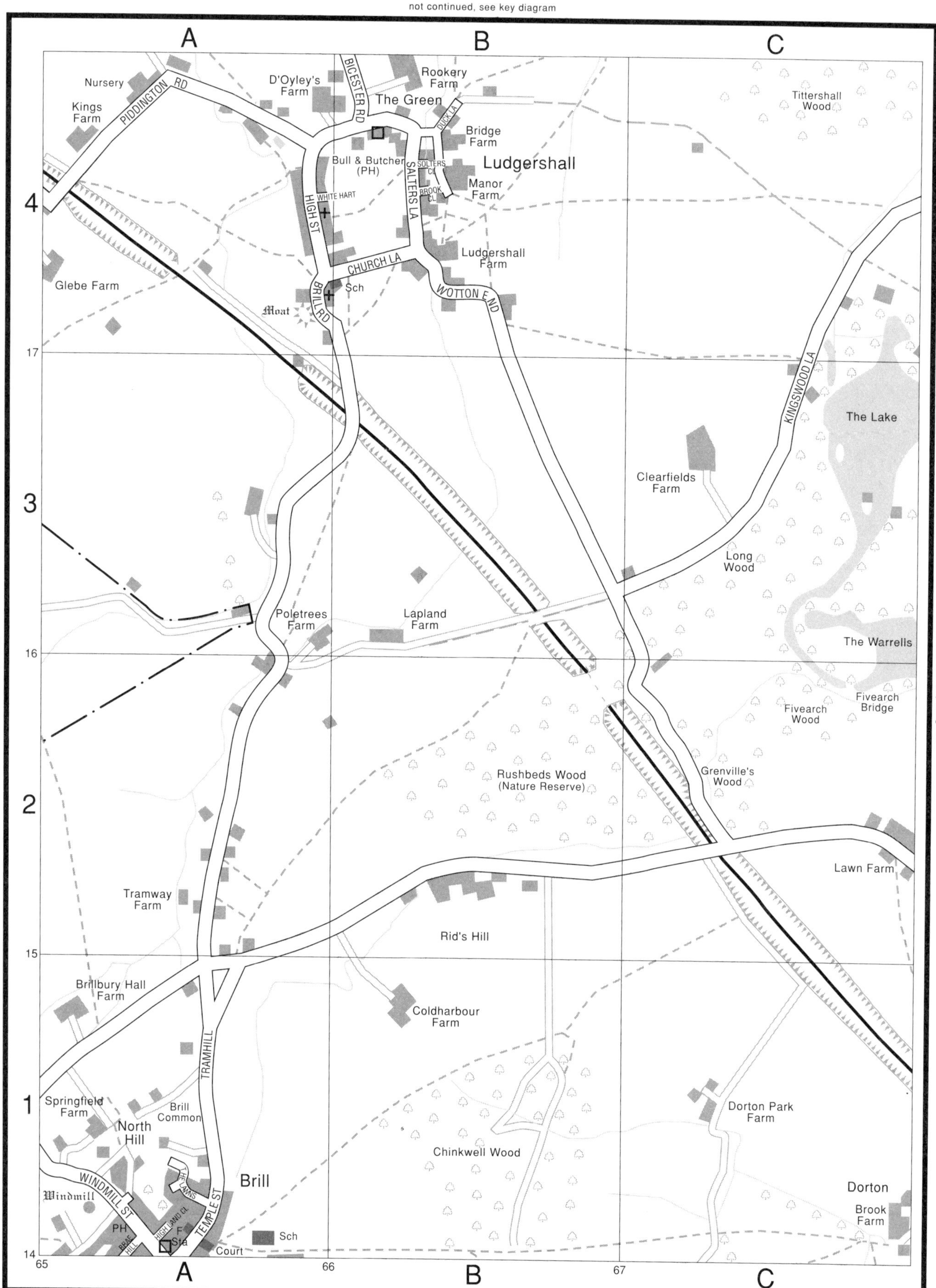

not continued, see key diagram

not continued, see key diagram

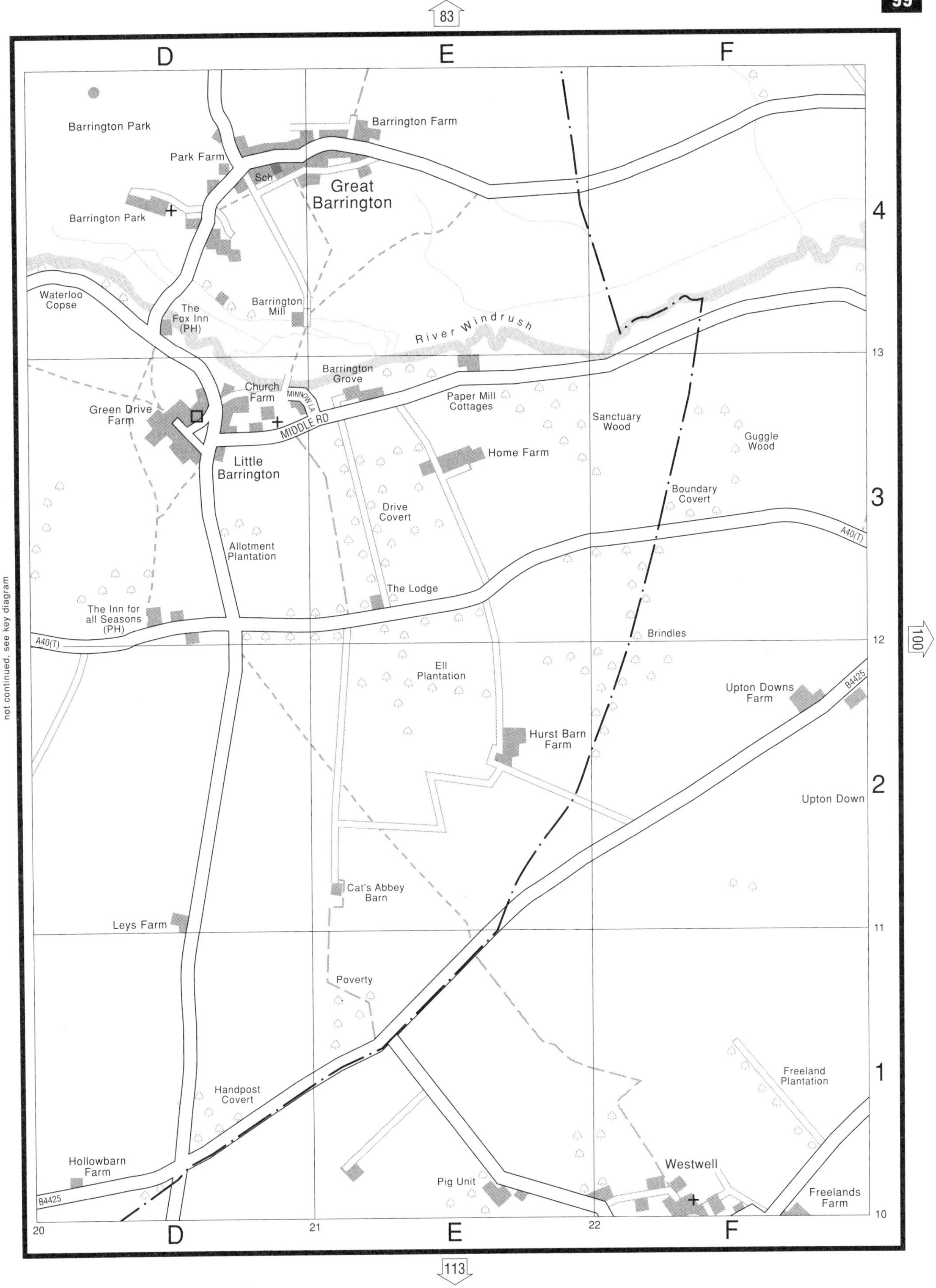
83
D
E
F
Barrington Park
Barrington Farm
Park Farm
Sch
Great Barrington
Barrington Park
Waterloo Copse
The Fox Inn (PH)
Barrington Mill
River Windrush
Barrington Grove
Church Farm
MINNOW LA
Green Drive Farm
Paper Mill Cottages
MIDDLE RD
Sanctuary Wood
Guggle Wood
Little Barrington
Home Farm
Boundary Covert
Drive Covert
Allotment Plantation
A40(T)
The Lodge
The Inn for all Seasons (PH)
Brindles
Ell Plantation
Upton Downs Farm
B4425
Hurst Barn Farm
Upton Down
Cat's Abbey Barn
Leys Farm
Poverty
Handpost Covert
Freeland Plantation
Hollowbarn Farm
Westwell
Pig Unit
Freelands Farm
4
13
3
12
2
11
1
10
20
21
22
100
113
not continued, see key diagram

84

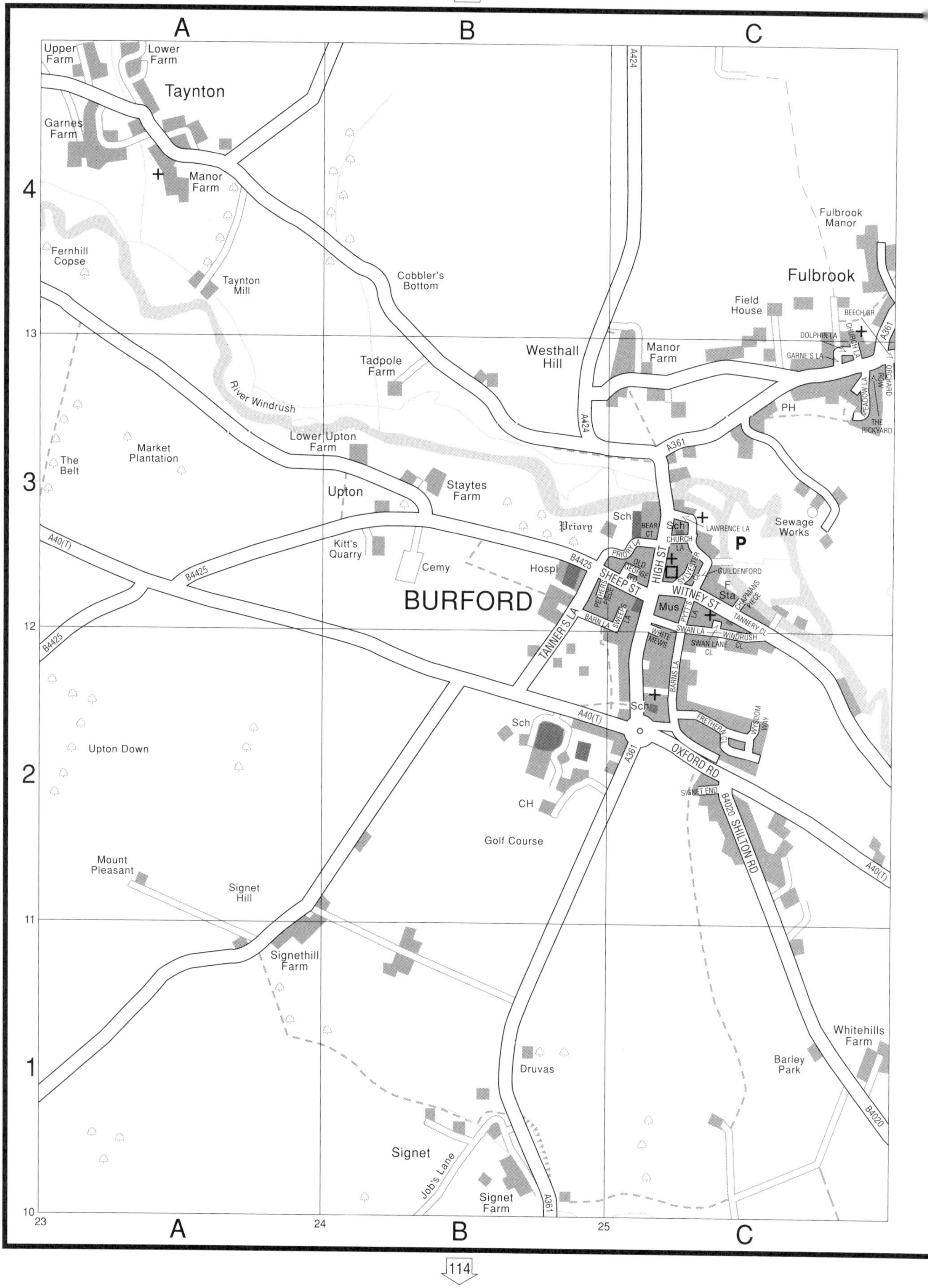

A
B
C
Upper Farm
Lower Farm
Taynton
Garnes Farm
Manor Farm
4
Fernhill Copse
Taynton Mill
Cobbler's Bottom
A424
Fulbrook Manor
Fulbrook
Field House
BEECH GR
DOLPHIN LA
CHURCH LA
GARNE'S LA
A361
Westhall Hill
Manor Farm
MEADOW LA
ORCHARD ROW
Tadpole Farm
13
River Windrush
PH
THE RICKYARD
A424
A361
Lower Upton Farm
Market Plantation
The Belt
3
Upton
Staytes Farm
Sch
Priory
Sch
LAWRENCE LA
Sewage Works
BEAR CT
CHURCH LA
P
A40(T)
Kitt's Quarry
Cemy
PRIORY LA
B4425
OLD GEORGE YD
HIGH ST
SYLVESTER CL
GUILDENFORD
B4425
Hospl
SHEEP ST
WITNEY ST
F Sta
CHAPMANS PIECE
BURFORD
PETHERS PIECE
SWEEPS LA
Mus
PYTTS LA
TANNERY CL
BARN LA
SWAN LA
WINDRUSH CL
12
B4425
TANNER'S LA
WHITE MEWS
SWAN LANE CL
BARNS LA
Sch
A40(T)
Sch
FRETHERNE CL
WYSDOM WAY
Upton Down
A361
OXFORD RD
2
SIGNET END
B4020 SHILTON RD
CH
Golf Course
A40(T)
Mount Pleasant
Signet Hill
11
Signethill Farm
Whitehills Farm
Barley Park
1
Druvas
B4020
Signet
Job's Lane
Signet Farm
A361
10
23
A
24
B
25
C

99

114

85

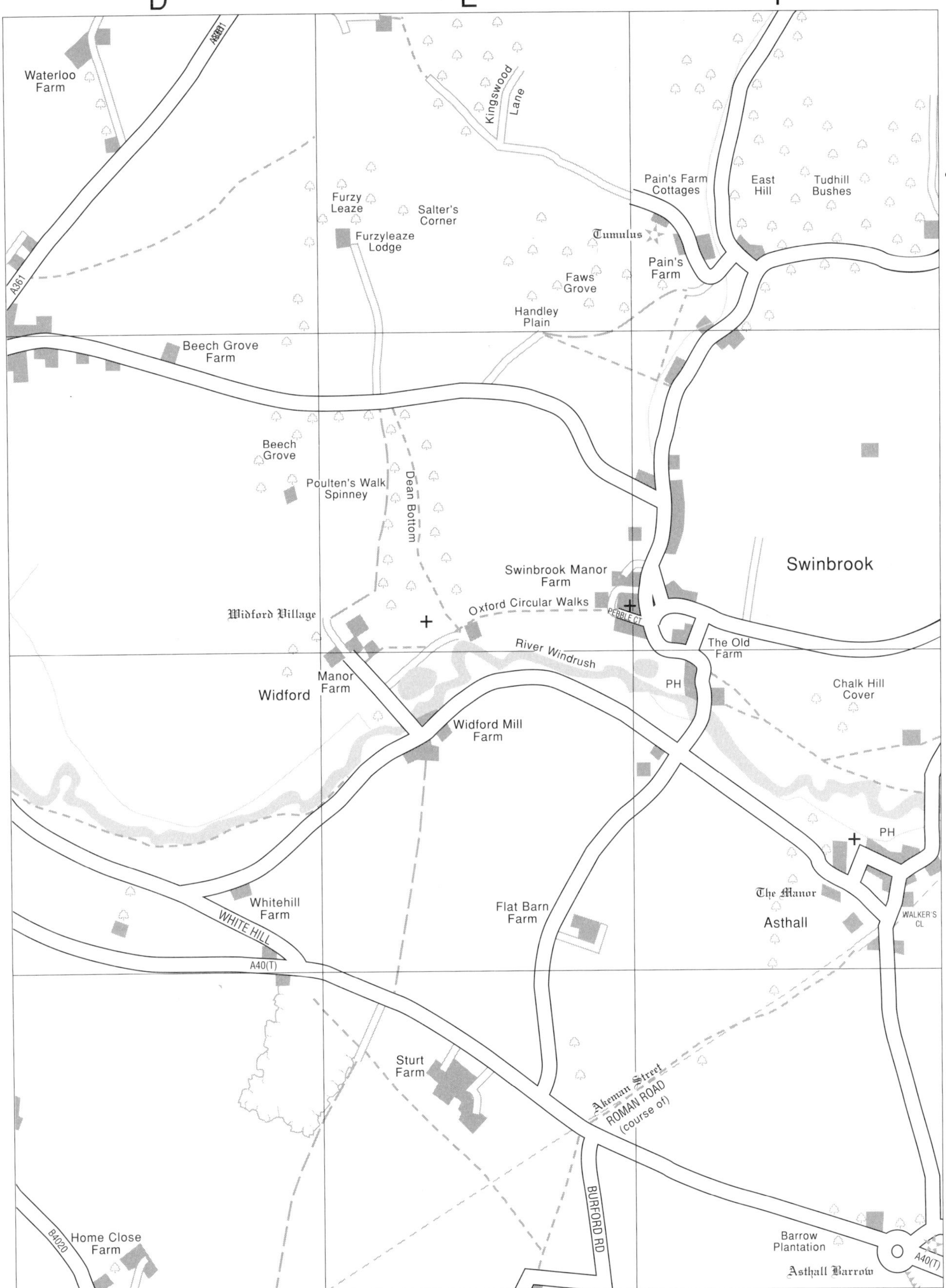
D
E
F
Waterloo Farm
A361
Kingswood Lane
Furzy Leaze
Salter's Corner
Furzyleaze Lodge
Pain's Farm Cottages
East Hill
Tudhill Bushes
Tumulus
Pain's Farm
Faws Grove
Handley Plain
Beech Grove Farm
Beech Grove
Poulten's Walk Spinney
Dean Bottom
Swinbrook
Swinbrook Manor Farm
Widford Village
Oxford Circular Walks
PEBBLE CT
The Old Farm
River Windrush
Manor Farm
Widford
PH
Chalk Hill Cover
Widford Mill Farm
PH
Whitehill Farm
White Hill
Flat Barn Farm
The Manor
Asthall
WALKER'S CL
A40(T)
Sturt Farm
Akeman Street
ROMAN ROAD (course of)
BURFORD RD
B4020
Home Close Farm
Barrow Plantation
A40(T)
Asthall Barrow
4
13
3
12
2
11
1
10
26
27
28

102

115

86

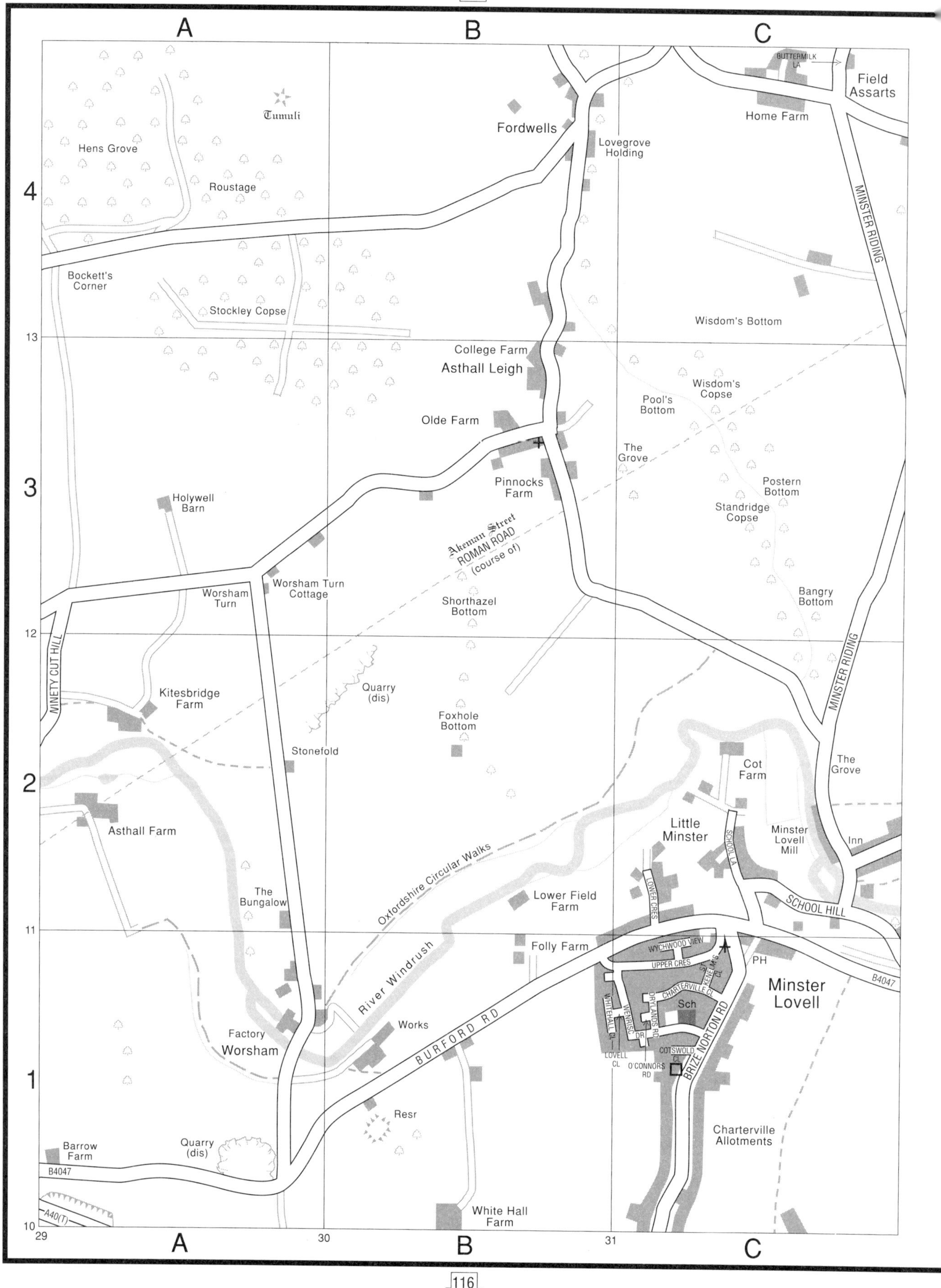
A
B
C
Tumuli
Hens Grove
Roustage
Fordwells
Lovegrove Holding
BUTTERMILK LA
Field Assarts
Home Farm
MINSTER RIDING
Bockett's Corner
Stockley Copse
Wisdom's Bottom
College Farm
Asthall Leigh
Wisdom's Copse
Pool's Bottom
Olde Farm
The Grove
Pinnocks Farm
Postern Bottom
Standridge Copse
Holywell Barn
Akeman Street
ROMAN ROAD
(course of)
Worsham Turn Cottage
Worsham Turn
Shorthazel Bottom
Bangry Bottom
MINETY CUT HILL
Kitesbridge Farm
Quarry (dis)
Foxhole Bottom
Stonefold
Cot Farm
The Grove
Asthall Farm
Little Minster
SCHOOL LA
Minster Lovell Mill
Inn
Oxfordshire Circular Walks
LOWER CRES
SCHOOL HILL
The Bungalow
Lower Field Farm
Folly Farm
WYCHWOOD VIEW
UPPER CRES
ST KENELMS CL
CHARTERVILLE CL
PH
B4047
River Windrush
WHITEHALL CL
WENRISC DR
DRYLANDS RD
Sch
Minster Lovell
Factory
Worsham
Works
BURFORD RD
LOVELL CL
O'CONNORS RD
COTSWOLD CL
BRIZE NORTON RD
Resr
Charterville Allotments
Barrow Farm
Quarry (dis)
B4047
A40(T)
White Hall Farm
4
3
2
1
13
12
11
10
29
30
31

101

116

87

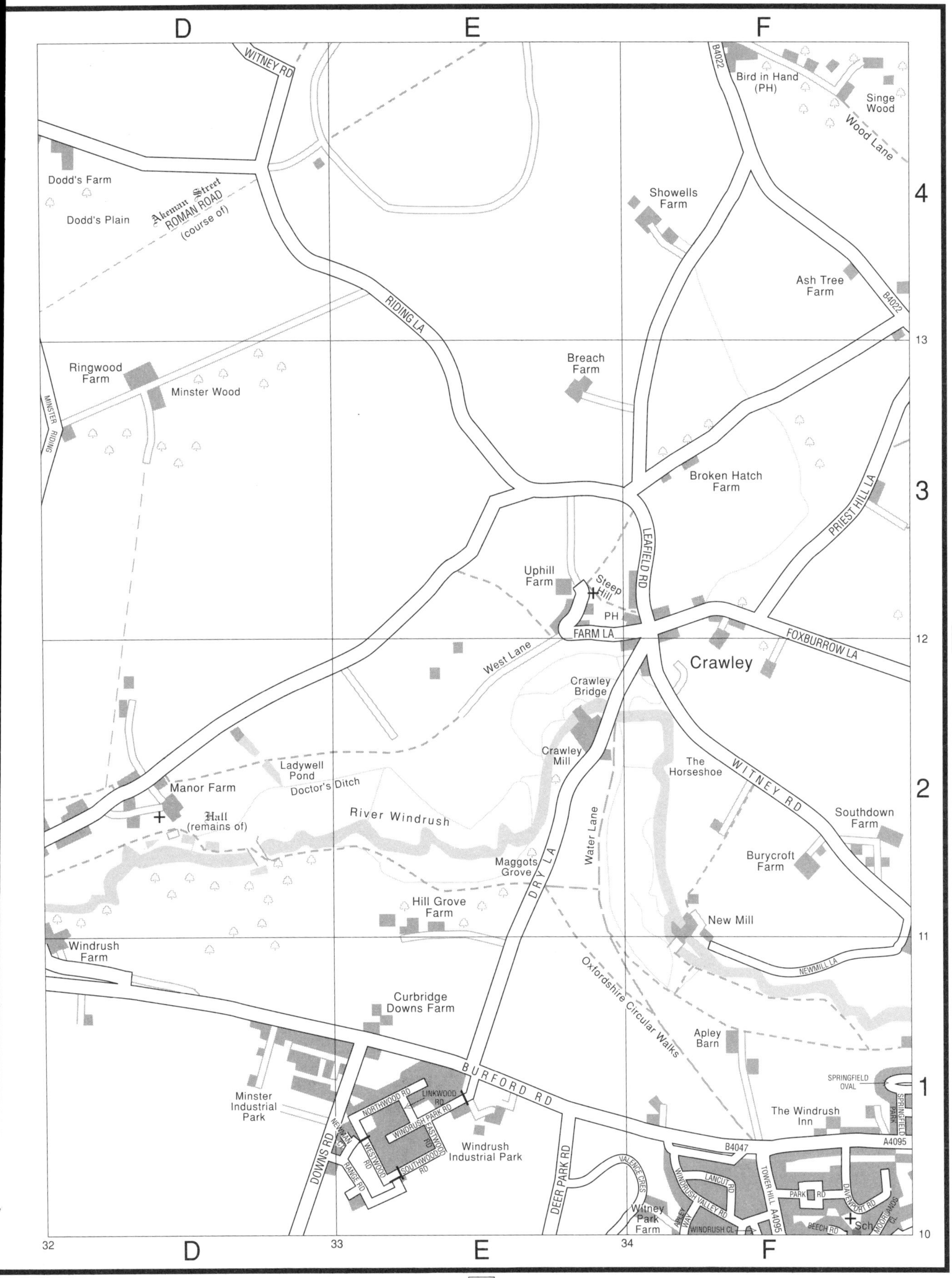
D
E
F
4
3
2
1
13
12
11
10
32
33
34
WITNEY RD
B4022
Bird in Hand
(PH)
Singe
Wood
Wood Lane
Dodd's Farm
Dodd's Plain
Akeman Street
ROMAN ROAD
(course of)
Showells
Farm
Ash Tree
Farm
B4022
RIDING LA
Ringwood
Farm
Minster Wood
MINSTER RIDING
Breach
Farm
Broken Hatch
Farm
PRIEST HILL LA
LEAFIELD RD
Uphill
Farm
Steep
Hill
PH
FARM LA
FOXBURROW LA
West Lane
Crawley
Crawley
Bridge
Crawley
Mill
The
Horseshoe
WITNEY RD
Southdown
Farm
Ladywell
Pond
Doctor's Ditch
Manor Farm
Hall
(remains of)
River Windrush
Water Lane
DRY LA
Maggots
Grove
Burycroft
Farm
Hill Grove
Farm
New Mill
Windrush
Farm
NEWMILL LA
Oxfordshire Circular Walks
Curbridge
Downs Farm
Apley
Barn
BURFORD RD
SPRINGFIELD
OVAL
SPRINGFIELD PARK
Minster
Industrial
Park
NORTHWOOD RD
LINKWOOD
RD
WINDRUSH PARK RD
EASTWOOD RD
WESTWOOD RD
SOUTHWOOD RD
RANGE RD
DOWNS RD
Windrush
Industrial Park
The Windrush
Inn
B4047
A4095
DEER PARK RD
VALENCE CRES
LANCUT RD
TOWER HILL
WINDRUSH VALLEY RD
A4095
PARK RD
DAVENPORT RD
MOORLANDS CL
Witney
Park
Farm
WINDRUSH CL
BEECH RD
Sch

104

117

88

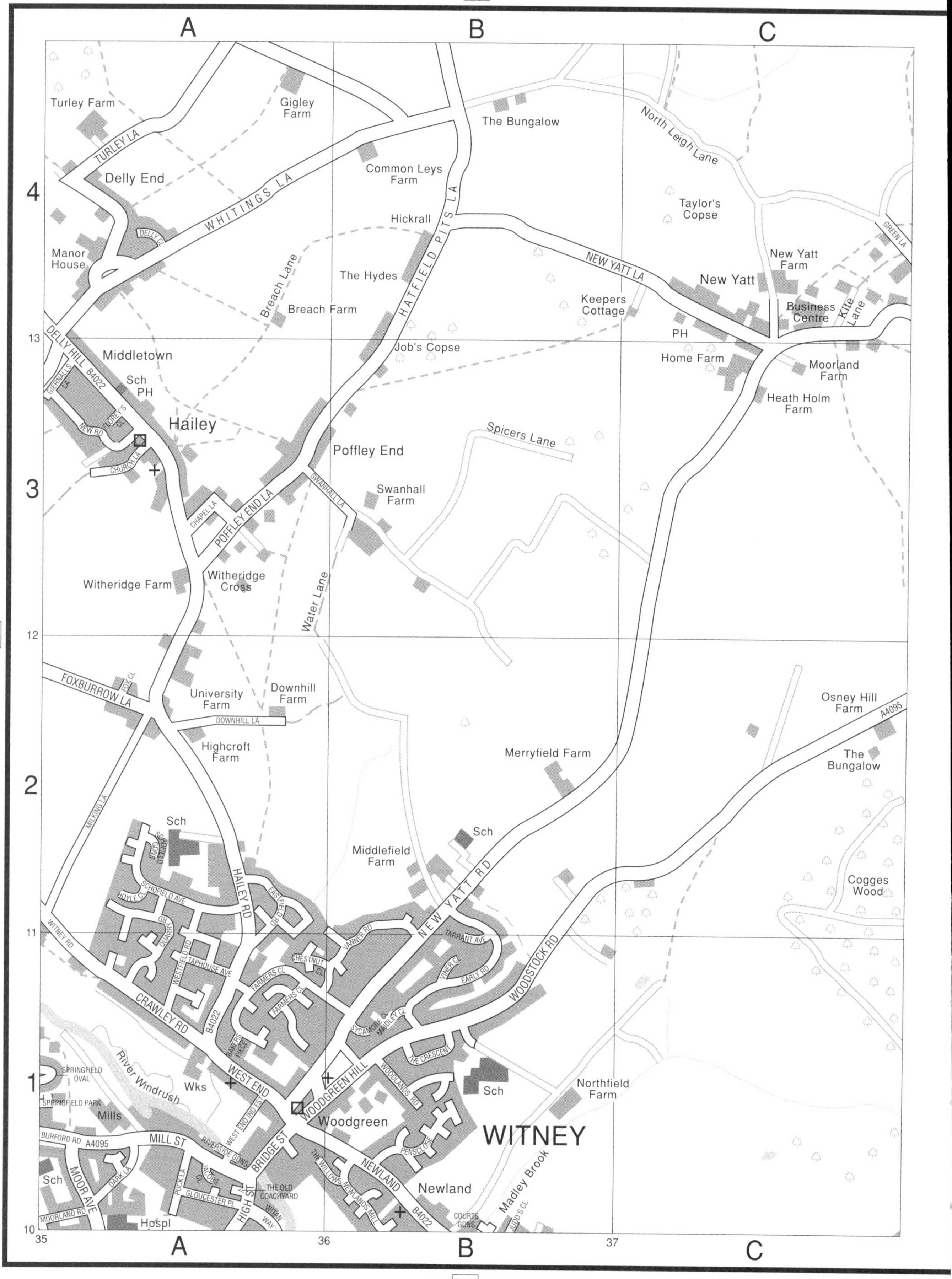
A
B
C
4
3
2
1
13
12
11
10
35
36
37
Turley Farm
Gigley Farm
TURLEY LA
Delly End
WHITINGS LA
DELLY CL
Manor House
The Bungalow
Common Leys Farm
Hickrall
North Leigh Lane
Taylor's Copse
GREEN LA
New Yatt Farm
New Yatt
NEW YATT LA
Keepers Cottage
Business Centre
Kite Lane
The Hydes
Breach Lane
Breach Farm
HATFIELD PITS LA
DELLY HILL B4022
Middletown
GIERNALLS LA
FLOREYS CL
NEW RD
Sch
PH
Hailey
CHURCH LA
Job's Copse
PH
Home Farm
Moorland Farm
Heath Holm Farm
Spicers Lane
Poffley End
SWANHALL LA
Swanhall Farm
CHAPEL LA
POFFLEY END LA
Witheridge Farm
Witheridge Cross
Water Lane
FOXBURROW LA
FOX CL
University Farm
Downhill Farm
DOWNHILL LA
Highcroft Farm
Osney Hill Farm
A4095
The Bungalow
Merryfield Farm
MILKING LA
Sch
SCHOFIELD GDNS
Sch
Middlefield Farm
HOYLE CL
SCHOFIELD AVE
HAILEY RD
EASTFIELD RD
NEW YATT RD
Cogges Wood
WITNEY RD
QUARRY RD
WESTFIELD RD
TAPHOUSE AVE
CHESTNUT CL
VANNER RD
TARRANT AVE
FARMERS CL
VINER CL
EARLY RD
WOODSTOCK RD
CRAWLEY RD
B4022
BAKERS PIECE
SYCAMORE CL
MADLEY CL
SPRINGFIELD OVAL
River Windrush
Wks
WEST END
WOODGREEN HILL
WOODLANDS RD
THE CRESCENT
Sch
Northfield Farm
SPRINGFIELD PARK
Mills
WEST END IND EST
Woodgreen
WITNEY
BURFORD RD
A4095
MILL ST
RIVERSIDE GDNS
BRIDGE ST
THE WILLOWS
NEWLAND
PENSCLOSE
Sch
MOOR AVE
DARK LA
PUCK LA
JACOBS CL
GLOUCESTER PL
HIGH ST
THE OLD COACHYARD
WITAN WAY
NEWLANDS MILL
Newland
Madley Brook
B4022
COURTS GDNS
JUDD'S CL
MOORLAND RD
Hospl

103

118

89

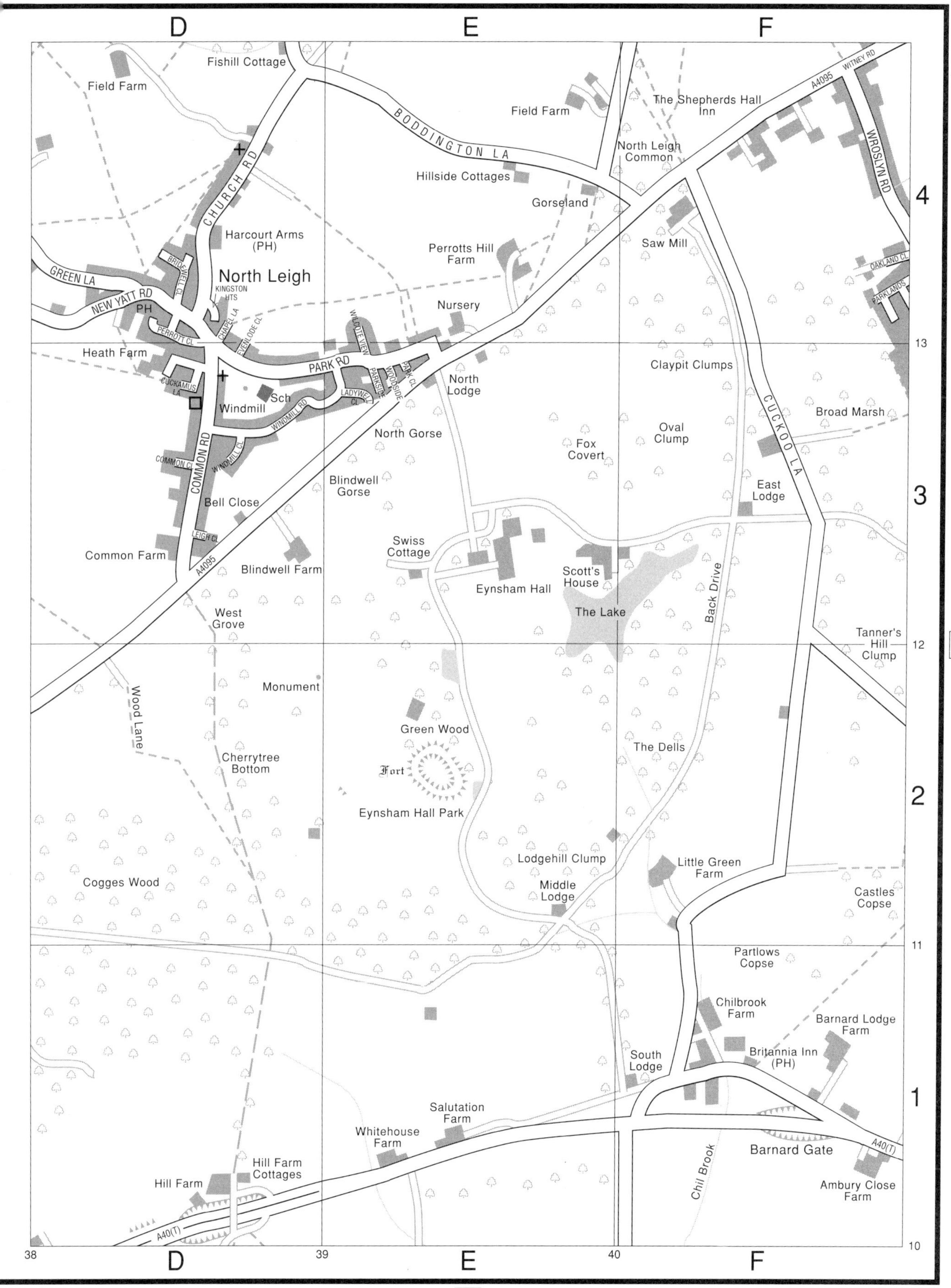
D
E
F
Field Farm
Fishill Cottage
BODDINGTON LA
Field Farm
The Shepherds Hall Inn
A4095
WITNEY RD
WROSLYN RD
North Leigh Common
Hillside Cottages
Gorseland
CHURCH RD
Harcourt Arms (PH)
Perrotts Hill Farm
Saw Mill
GREEN LA
BRIDEWELL CL
North Leigh
KINGSTON HTS
NEW YATT RD
PH
CHAPEL LA
EVENLODE CL
PERROTT CL
Nursery
WILCOTE VIEW
OAKLAND CL
PARKLANDS
Heath Farm
CUCKAMUS LA
PARK RD
PARKSIDE
WOODSIDE
PARK CL
Sch
Windmill
WINDMILL RD
LADYWELL CL
North Lodge
Claypit Clumps
CUCKOO LA
Broad Marsh
North Gorse
Fox Covert
Oval Clump
COMMON CL
COMMON RD
WINDMILL CL
Blindwell Gorse
East Lodge
Bell Close
LEIGH CL
Swiss Cottage
Common Farm
A4095
Blindwell Farm
Eynsham Hall
Scott's House
Back Drive
The Lake
West Grove
Tanner's Hill Clump
Monument
Wood Lane
Green Wood
The Dells
Cherrytree Bottom
Fort
Eynsham Hall Park
Lodgehill Clump
Little Green Farm
Coggés Wood
Middle Lodge
Castles Copse
Partlows Copse
Chilbrook Farm
Barnard Lodge Farm
South Lodge
Britannia Inn (PH)
Salutation Farm
Whitehouse Farm
A40(T)
Barnard Gate
Chil Brook
Hill Farm Cottages
Hill Farm
Ambury Close Farm
A40(T)
4
13
3
12
2
11
1
10
38
39
40

106

119

90

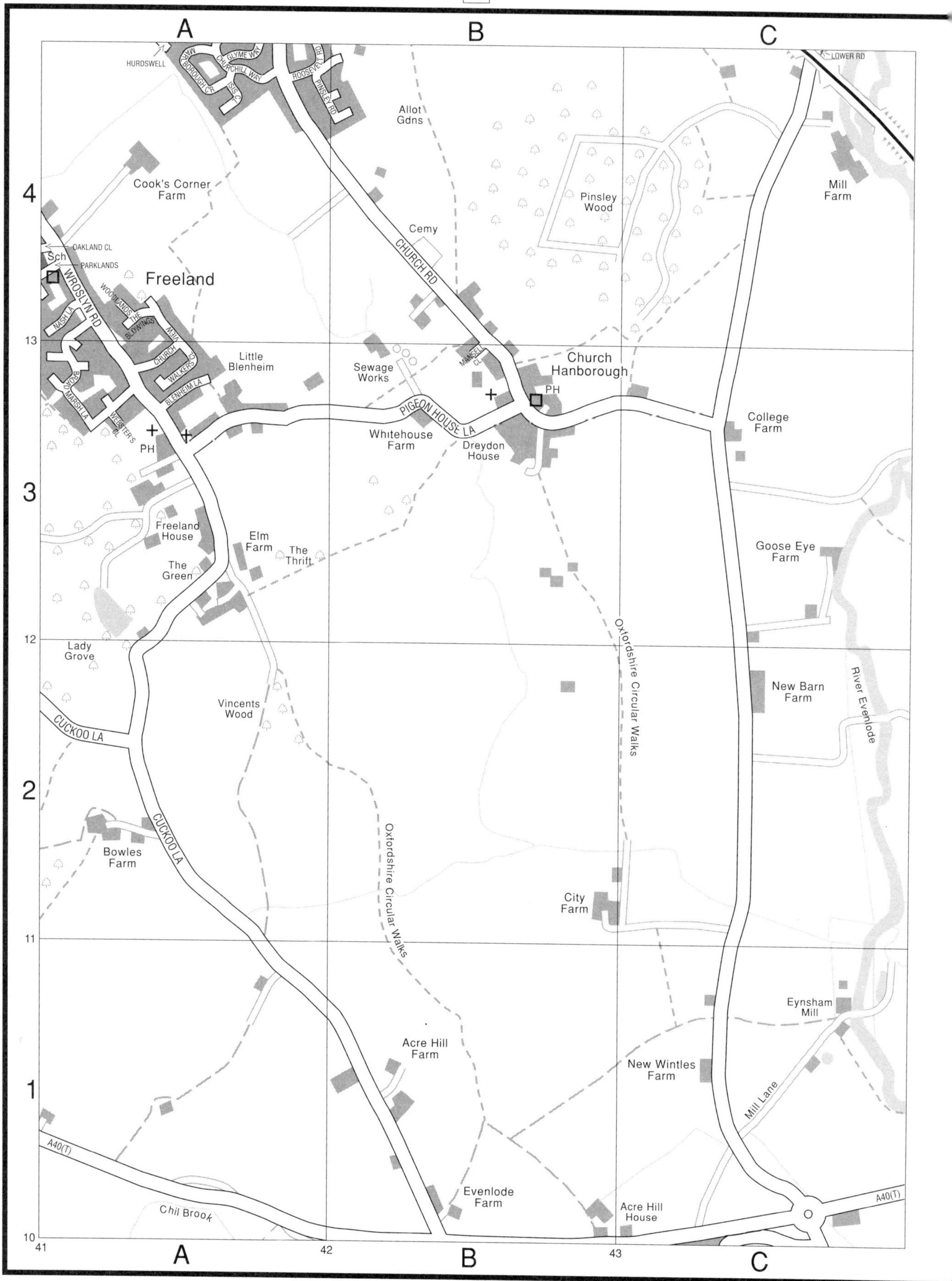

A
B
C
HURDSWELL
MARLBOROUGH CR
GLYME WAY
CHURCHILL WAY
ISIS CL
ROOSEVELT RD
PINSLEY RD
LOWER RD
Allot Gdns
Cook's Corner Farm
Mill Farm
Pinsley Wood
4
Cemy
CHURCH RD
OAKLAND CL
PARKLANDS
Sch
Freeland
WROSLYN RD
WOODLANDS
THE BLOWINGS
WIHA
NASH LA
13
CHURCH
WALKERS CL
MANSELL CL
Little Blenheim
Sewage Works
Church Hanborough
PH
BLENHEIM LA
MARSH LA
WEBSTER'S CL
PIGEON HOUSE LA
College Farm
PH
Whitehouse Farm
Dreydon House
3
Freeland House
Elm Farm
The Thrift
Goose Eye Farm
The Green
Oxfordshire Circular Walks
12
Lady Grove
River Evenlode
New Barn Farm
Vincents Wood
CUCKOO LA
2
CUCKOO LA
Oxfordshire Circular Walks
Bowles Farm
City Farm
11
Eynsham Mill
Acre Hill Farm
New Wintles Farm
1
Mill Lane
A40(T)
A40(T)
Evenlode Farm
Chil Brook
Acre Hill House
10
41
A
42
B
43
C

105

120

91

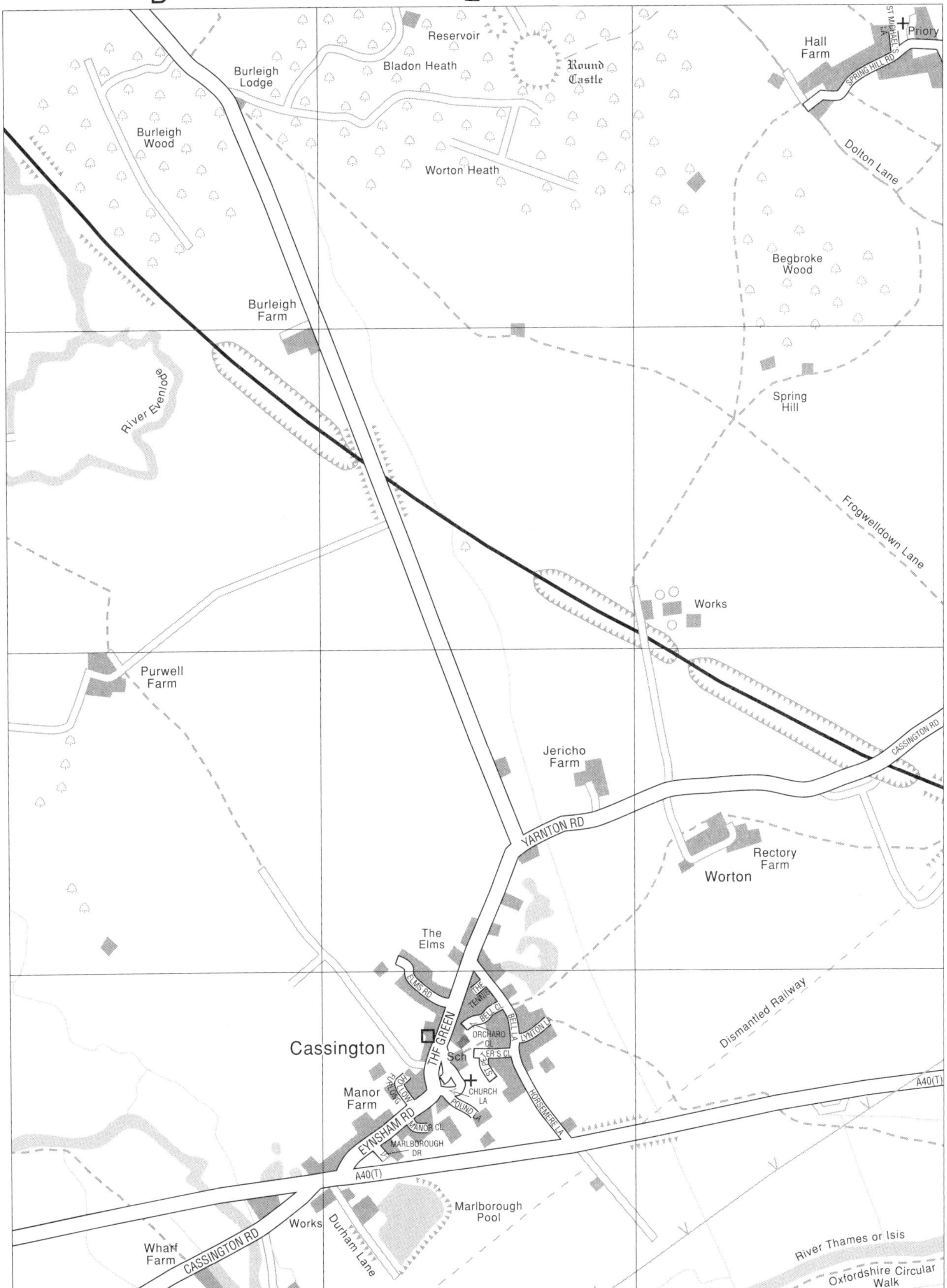
D
E
F
Reservoir
Bladon Heath
Round Castle
Burleigh Lodge
Hall Farm
Priory
ST MICHAEL'S LA
SPRING HILL RD
Burleigh Wood
Worton Heath
Dolton Lane
4
Begbroke Wood
Burleigh Farm
13
Spring Hill
River Evenlode
3
Frogwelldown Lane
Works
12
Purwell Farm
CASSINGTON RD
Jericho Farm
2
YARNTON RD
Rectory Farm
Worton
The Elms
11
ELMS RD
THE TENTINS
BELL CL
BELL LA
ORCHARD CL
LYNTON LA
Dismantled Railway
Cassington
THE GREEN
Sch
ST PETER'S CL
FURLONG
HOLLOW
CHURCH LA
Manor Farm
POUND LA
HORSEMERE LA
A40(T)
1
EYNSHAM RD
MANOR CL
MARLBOROUGH DR
A40(T)
Marlborough Pool
Works
Durham Lane
Wharf Farm
CASSINGTON RD
River Thames or Isis
Oxfordshire Circular Walk
44
45
46
D
E
F

108

121

92

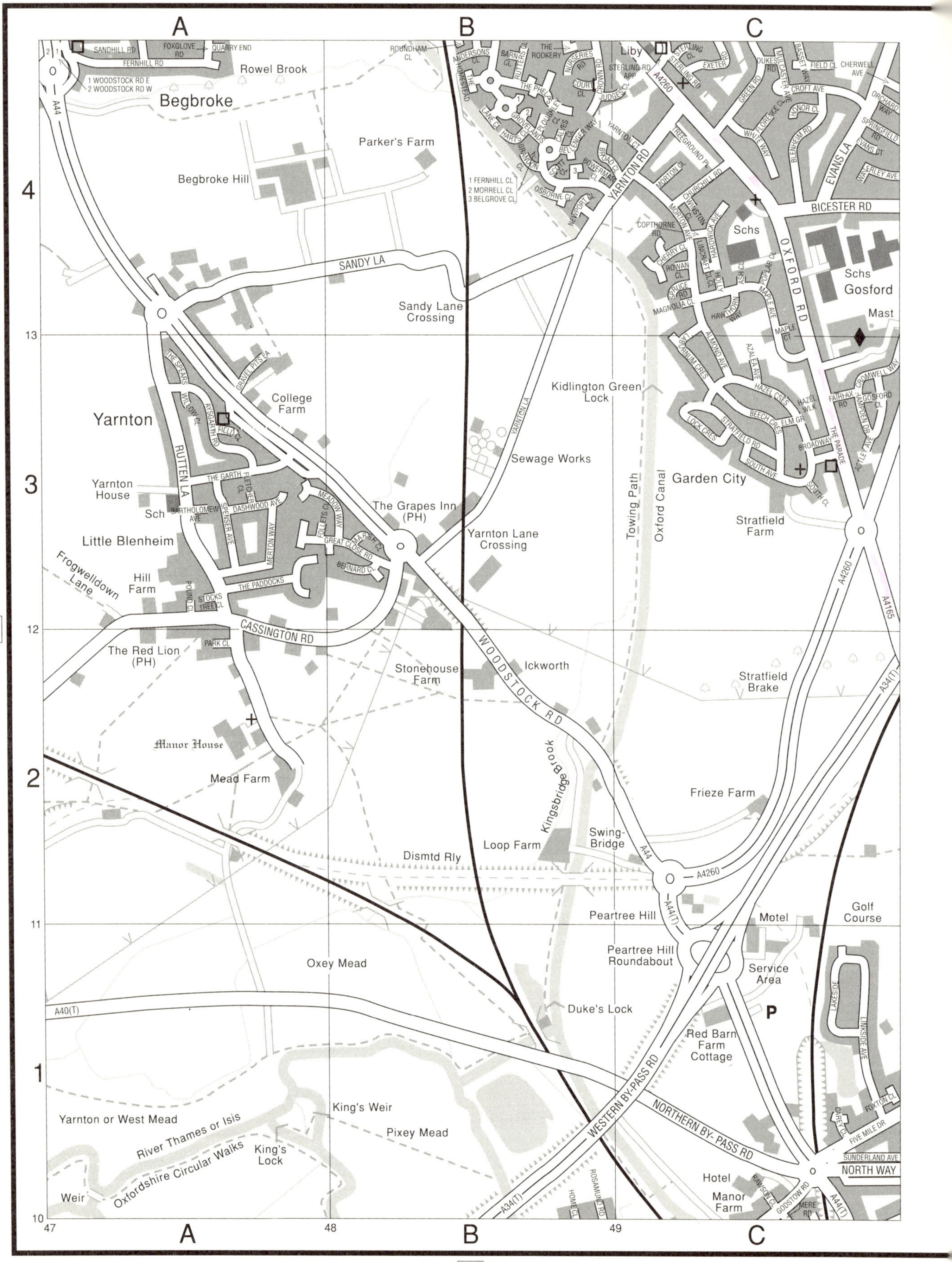

A
B
C
Begbroke
Rowel Brook
Parker's Farm
Begbroke Hill
SANDHILL RD
FOXGLOVE RD
QUARRY END
FERNHILL RD
1 WOODSTOCK RD E
2 WOODSTOCK RD W
A44
ROUNDHAM CL
THE ROOKERY
Liby
STERLING RD APP
YARNTON RD
YARNTON CT
1 FERNHILL CL
2 MORRELL CL
3 BELGROVE CL
OSBORNE CL
NEWPORT CL
A4260
EXETER RD
GREEN RD
WHITE WAY
CROFT AVE
FIELD CL
CHERWELL AVE
ORCHARD WAY
SPRINGFIELD RD
EVANS CT
EVANS LA
BLENHEIM RD
MORTON CL
CHURCHILL RD
TREEGROUND PL
BICESTER RD
COPTHORNE RD
MORTON AVE
CHERRY CL
ROWAN CL
SPRUCE RD
MAGNOLIA CL
HAWTHORN WAY
ASH CL
POPLAR CL
MAPLE AVE
MAPLE CT
Schs
OXFORD RD
Schs
Gosford
Mast
SANDY LA
Sandy Lane Crossing
4
13
College Farm
Yarnton
Kidlington Green Lock
YARNTON LA
Sewage Works
GRAVEL PITS LA
THE SPEARS
WILLOW CL
AYSGARTH RD
RUTTEN LA
THE GARTH
FLETCHER CL
DASHWOOD AVE
MEADOW WAY
FOLLETS CL
GREAT CLOSE RD
MARSH CL
BERNARD CL
MERTON WAY
SPENSER AVE
BARTHOLOMEW AVE
THE PADDOCKS
POUND CL
STOCKS TREE CL
Yarnton House
Sch
Little Blenheim
Hill Farm
Frogwelldown Lane
The Grapes Inn (PH)
Yarnton Lane Crossing
Towing Path
Oxford Canal
Garden City
Stratfield Farm
AZALEA AVE
ALMOND AVE
LABURNUM CRES
HAZEL CRES
BEECH CRES
ELM GR
HAZEL WLK
LOCK CRES
STRATFIELD RD
SOUTH AVE
BROADWAY
THE PARADE
SOUTH CL
FAIRHAX RD
CROMWELL WAY
GOSFORD CL
ASTLEY AVE
3
12
CASSINGTON RD
PARK CL
The Red Lion (PH)
Stonehouse Farm
WOODSTOCK RD
Ickworth
Stratfield Brake
A4260
A4165
A34(T)
Manor House
Mead Farm
Kingsbridge Brook
Frieze Farm
2
Swing-Bridge
Loop Farm
Dismtd Rly
A44
A4260
A44(T)
Peartree Hill
Motel
Golf Course
11
Oxey Mead
Peartree Hill Roundabout
Service Area
P
LAKESIDE
LINKSIDE AVE
A40(T)
Duke's Lock
Red Barn Farm Cottage
1
WESTERN BY-PASS RD
NORTHERN BY- PASS RD
King's Weir
Yarnton or West Mead
River Thames or Isis
Pixey Mead
Oxfordshire Circular Walks
King's Lock
Weir
A34(T)
HOME CL
ROSAMUND RD
Hotel
Manor Farm
RAWSON CL
GODSTOW RD
MERE RD
A44(T)
CAREY CL
FOXTON CL
FIVE MILE DR
SUNDERLAND AVE
NORTH WAY
10
47
48
49
A
B
C

107

122

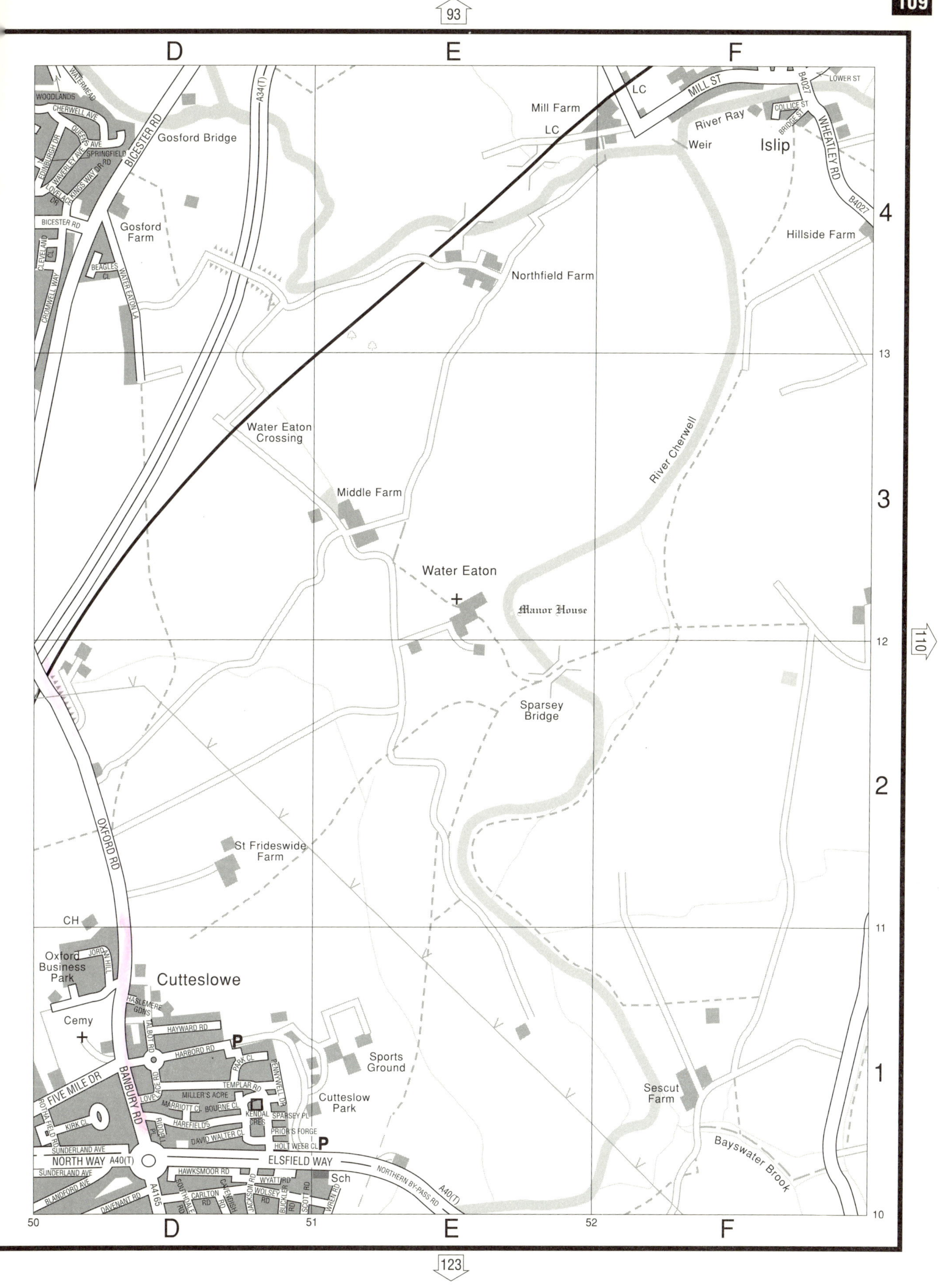
93
D
E
F
4
3
2
1
13
12
11
10
50
51
52
110
123
Mill Farm
LC
MILL ST
River Ray
Weir
Islip
COLLICE ST
BRIDGE ST
WHEATLEY RD
B4027
LOWER ST
Hillside Farm
Gosford Bridge
Gosford Farm
BICESTER RD
WATER EATON LA
A34(T)
WOODLANDS
CHERWELL AVE
WATERMEAD
QUEEN'S AVE
SPRINGFIELD RD
EDINBURGH DR
WAVERLEY AVE
KINGS WAY DR
LOVELACE DR
CLEVELAND
CROMWELL WAY
BEAGLES CL
Northfield Farm
Water Eaton Crossing
Middle Farm
Water Eaton
Manor House
River Cherwell
Sparsey Bridge
OXFORD RD
St Frideswide Farm
CH
Oxford Business Park
JORDAN HILL
Cutteslowe
Cemy
HASLEMERE GDNS
HAYWARD RD
HARBORD RD
TALBOT RD
PARK CL
PENNYWELL DR
TEMPLAR RD
MILLER'S ACRE
MARRIOTT CL
BOURNE CL
KENDAL CRES
SPARSEY PL
PRIOR'S FORGE
HOLT WEEB CL
HAREFIELDS
DAVID WALTER CL
RIDDELL PL
LOVELACE RD
BANBURY RD
FIVE MILE DR
ROTHAFIELD RD
KIRK CL
SUNDERLAND AVE
NORTH WAY
A40(T)
ELSFIELD WAY
NORTHERN BY-PASS RD
HAWKSMOOR RD
WYATT RD
CARLTON RD
CAVENDISH RD
JACKSON RD
WOLSEY RD
BUCKLER RD
SCOTT RD
WREN RD
SOUTHDALE RD
DAVENANT RD
BLANDFORD AVE
A4165
Sch
P
Sports Ground
Cutteslow Park
Sescut Farm
Bayswater Brook

94

109

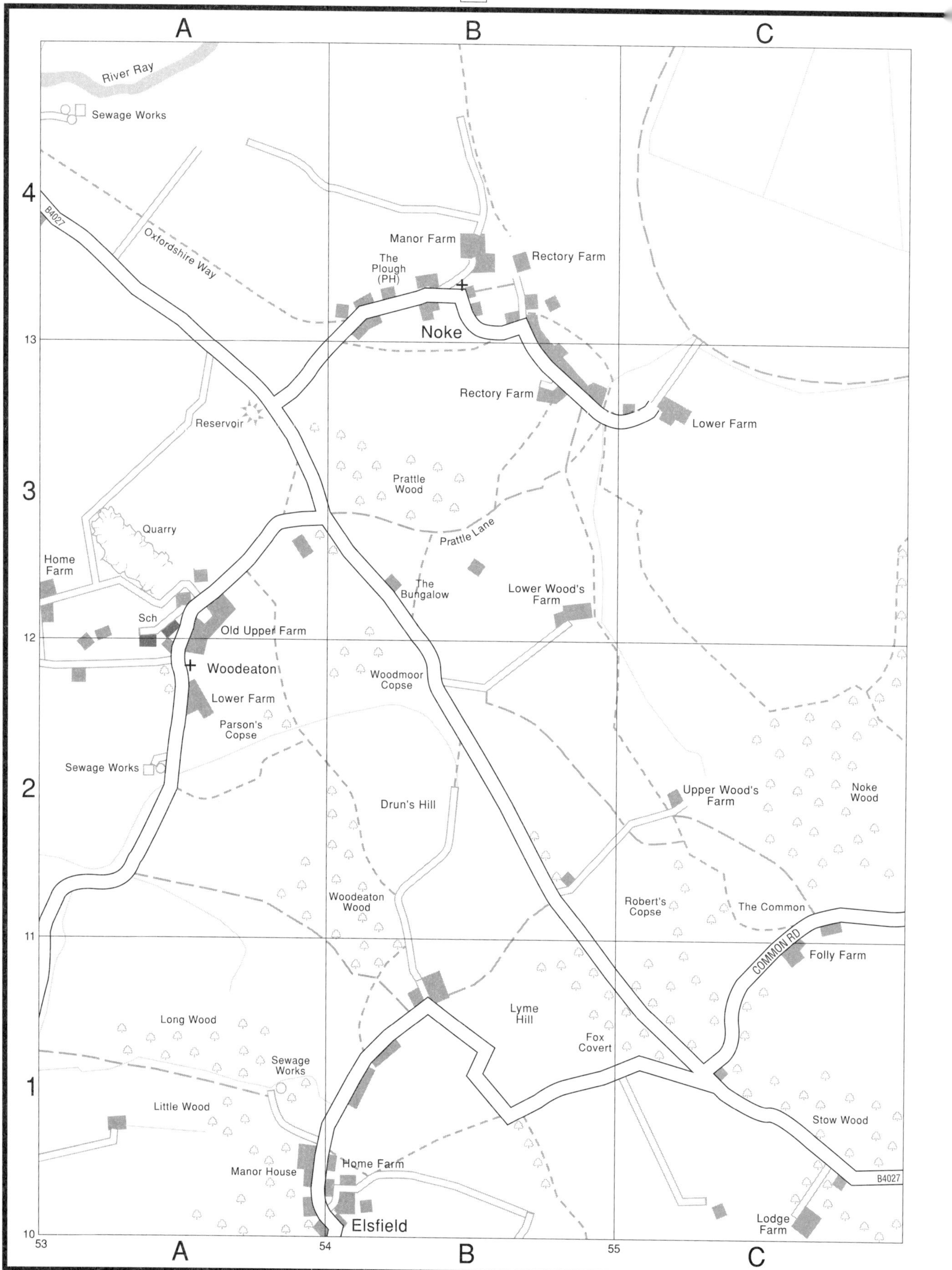

A
B
C
River Ray
Sewage Works
4
B4027
Oxfordshire Way
Manor Farm
Rectory Farm
The Plough (PH)
Noke
13
Rectory Farm
Lower Farm
Reservoir
Prattle Wood
3
Quarry
Prattle Lane
Home Farm
The Bungalow
Lower Wood's Farm
Sch
Old Upper Farm
12
Woodeaton
Woodmoor Copse
Lower Farm
Parson's Copse
Sewage Works
2
Drun's Hill
Upper Wood's Farm
Noke Wood
Woodeaton Wood
Robert's Copse
The Common
11
COMMON RD
Folly Farm
Long Wood
Lyme Hill
Fox Covert
Sewage Works
1
Little Wood
Stow Wood
Manor House
Home Farm
B4027
Elsfield
Lodge Farm
10
53
54
55
A
B
C

124

95

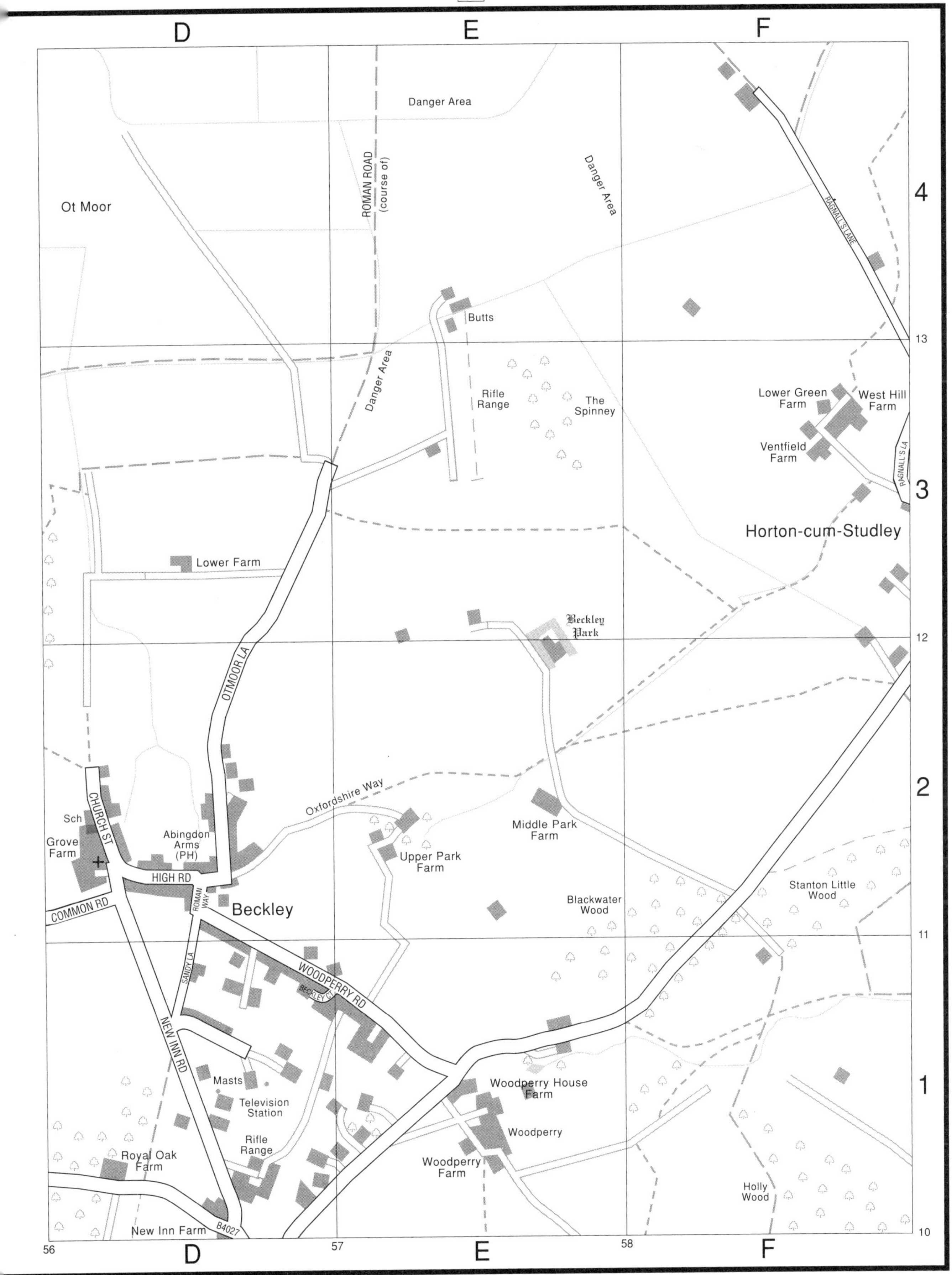

D
E
F
Danger Area
ROMAN ROAD (course of)
Danger Area
Ot Moor
RAGNALL'S LANE
4
13
Butts
Danger Area
Rifle Range
The Spinney
Lower Green Farm
West Hill Farm
Ventfield Farm
RAGNALL'S LA
3
Horton-cum-Studley
Lower Farm
Beckley Park
12
OTMOOR LA
2
Oxfordshire Way
Sch
CHURCH ST
Grove Farm
Abingdon Arms (PH)
HIGH RD
Upper Park Farm
Middle Park Farm
Blackwater Wood
Stanton Little Wood
COMMON RD
ROMAN WAY
Beckley
11
SANDY LA
WOODPERRY RD
BECKLEY CT
NEW INN RD
Masts
Television Station
Woodperry House Farm
1
Woodperry
Rifle Range
Royal Oak Farm
Woodperry Farm
Holly Wood
New Inn Farm
B4027
10
56
57
58
D
E
F

112

125

96

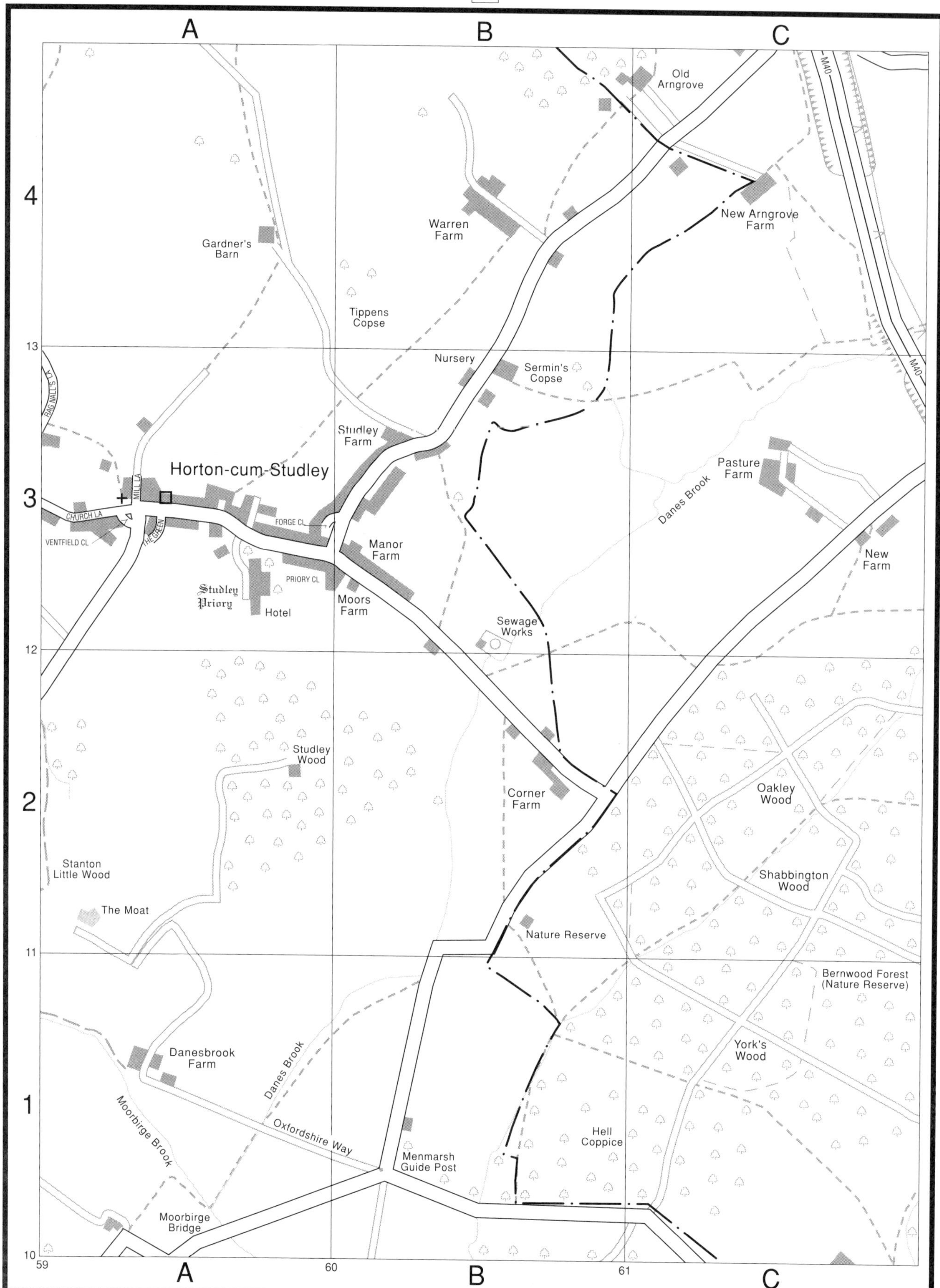

111

not continued, see key diagram

126

99

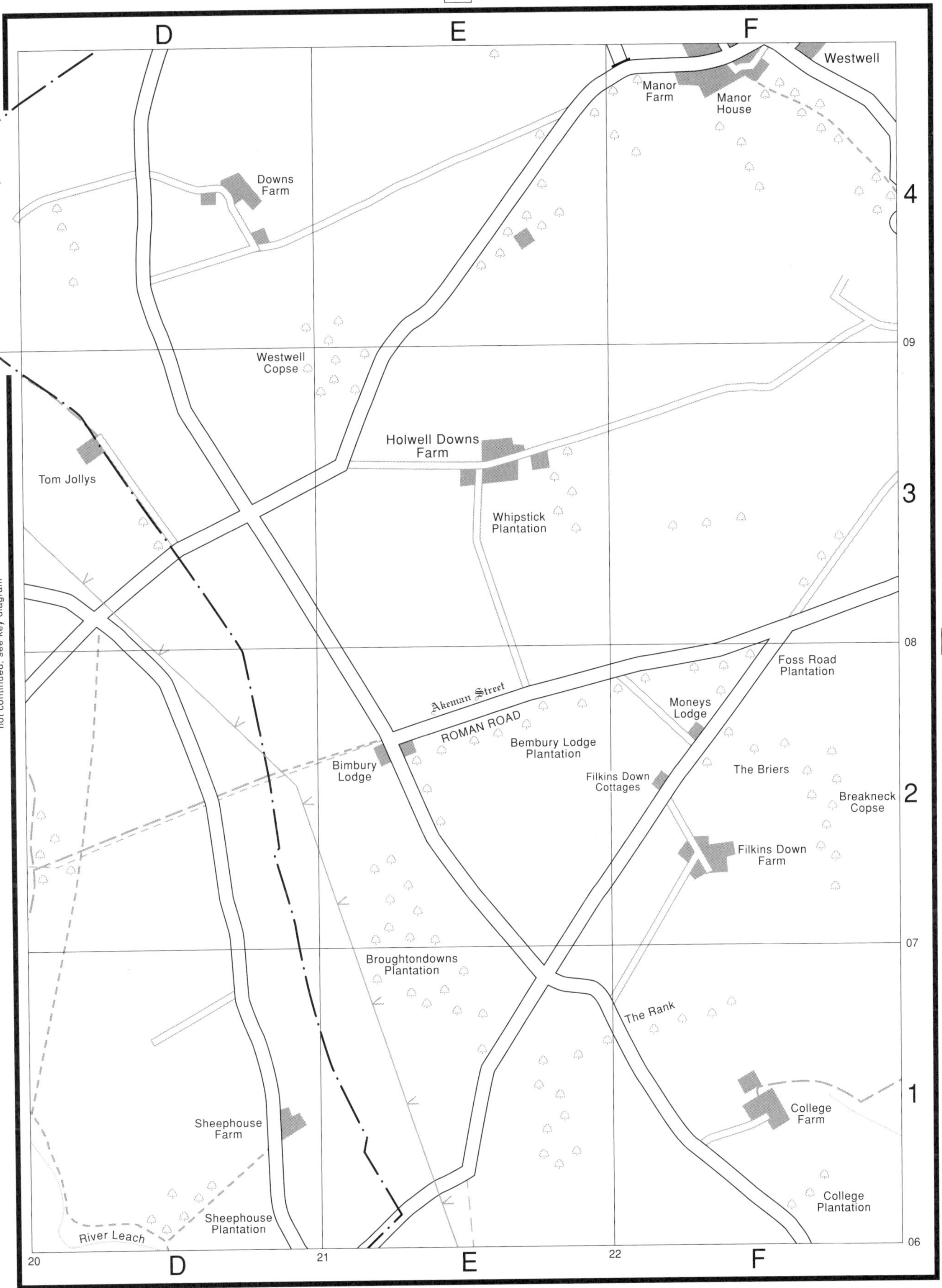
D
E
F
Westwell
Manor Farm
Manor House
Downs Farm
4
09
Westwell Copse
Holwell Downs Farm
Tom Jollys
Whipstick Plantation
3
not continued, see key diagram
08
Akeman Street
ROMAN ROAD
Foss Road Plantation
Moneys Lodge
Bembury Lodge Plantation
Bimbury Lodge
Filkins Down Cottages
The Briers
Breakneck Copse
2
Filkins Down Farm
07
Broughtondowns Plantation
The Rank
1
College Farm
Sheephouse Farm
College Plantation
Sheephouse Plantation
River Leach
06
20
D
21
E
22
F

114

131

100

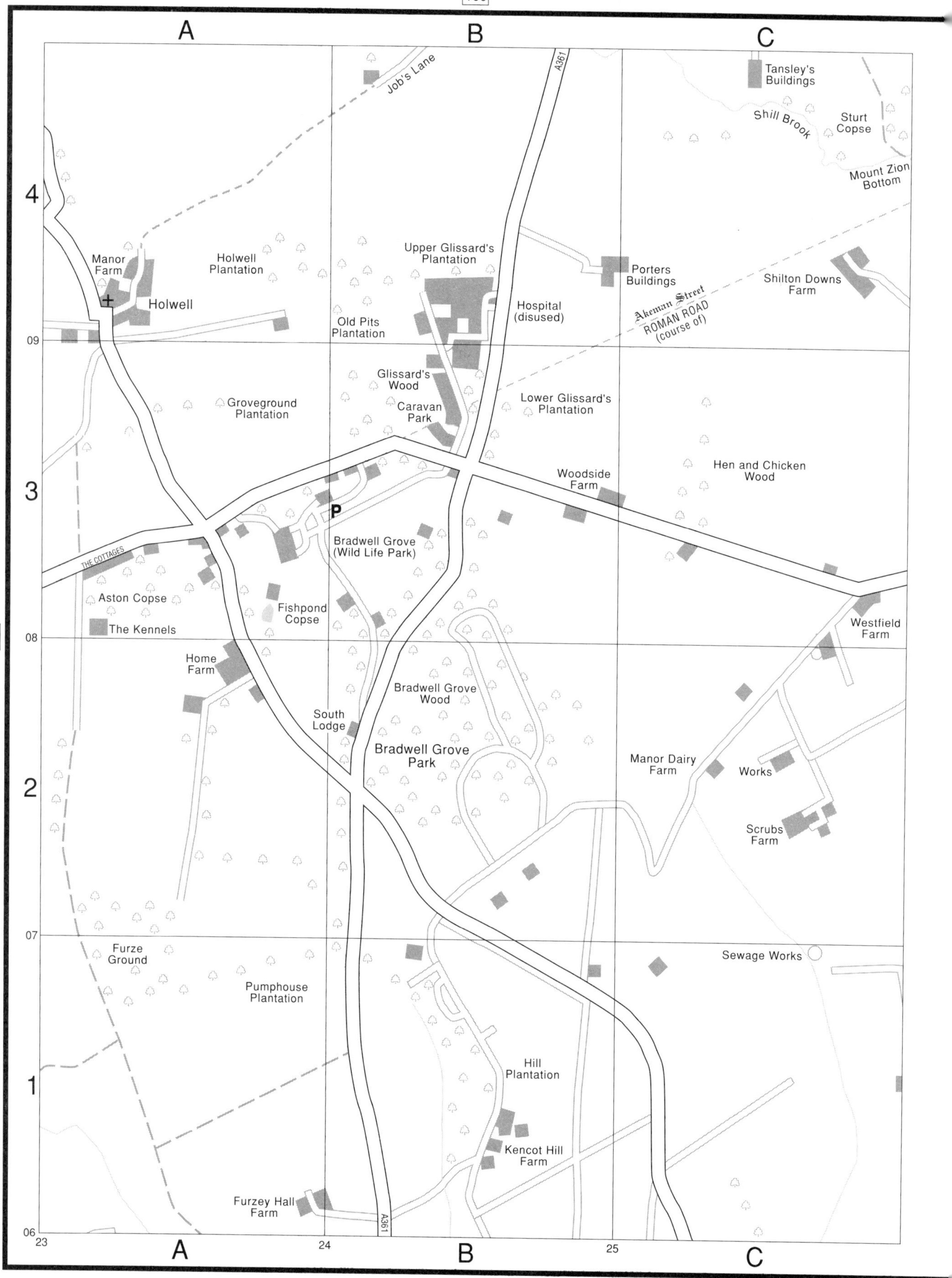
A
B
C
Tansley's Buildings
Job's Lane
A361
Shill Brook
Sturt Copse
Mount Zion Bottom
4
Manor Farm
Holwell Plantation
Upper Glissard's Plantation
Porters Buildings
Shilton Downs Farm
Holwell
Old Pits Plantation
Hospital (disused)
Akeman Street
ROMAN ROAD (course of)
09
Glissard's Wood
Groveground Plantation
Caravan Park
Lower Glissard's Plantation
Hen and Chicken Wood
Woodside Farm
3
P
Bradwell Grove (Wild Life Park)
THE COTTAGES
Aston Copse
Fishpond Copse
The Kennels
Westfield Farm
08
Home Farm
Bradwell Grove Wood
South Lodge
Bradwell Grove Park
Manor Dairy Farm
Works
2
Scrubs Farm
07
Furze Ground
Sewage Works
Pumphouse Plantation
1
Hill Plantation
Kencot Hill Farm
Furzey Hall Farm
A361
06
23
24
25
A
B
C

113

132

101

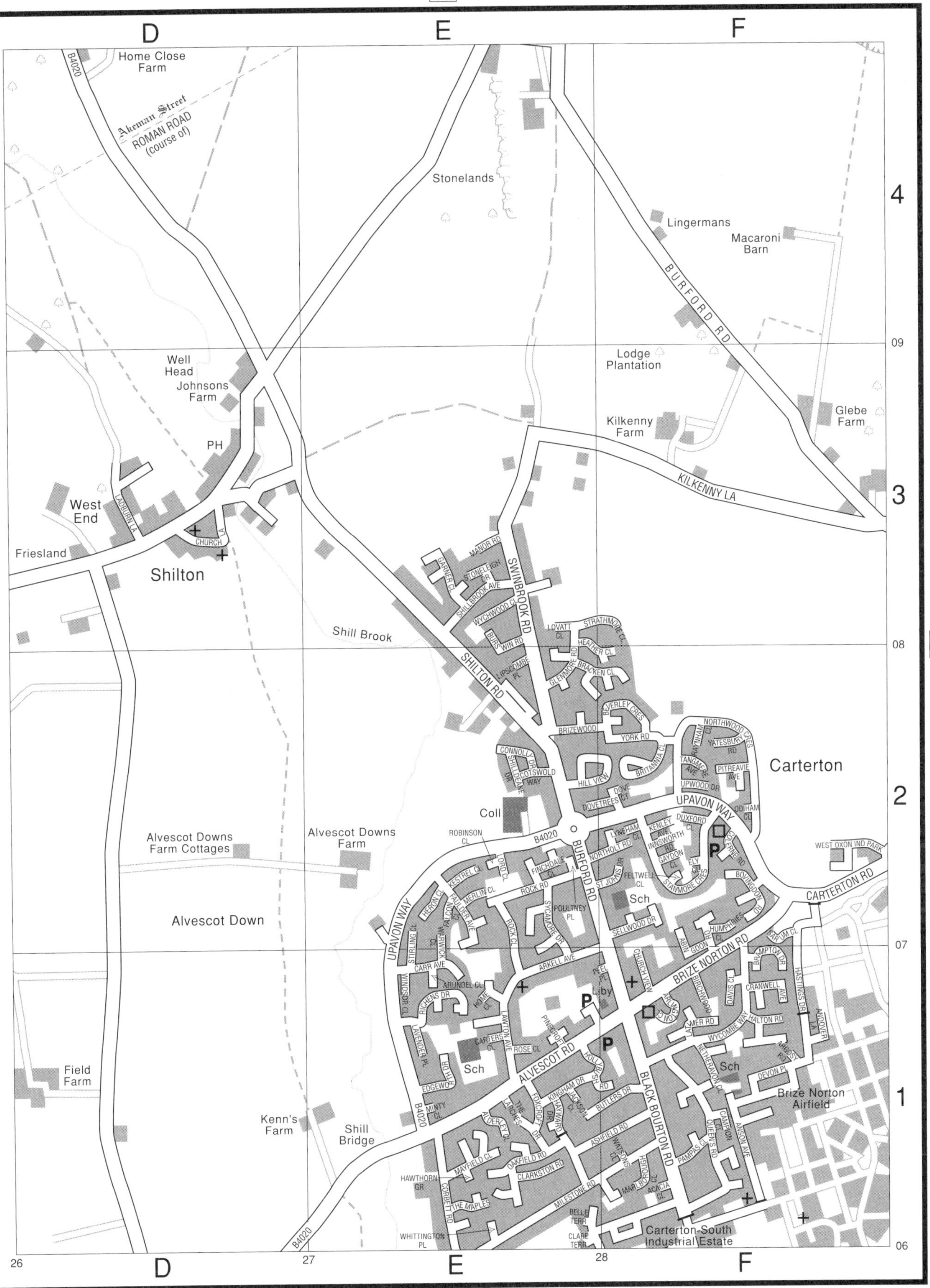

D
E
F
4
3
2
1
09
08
07
06
26
27
28
Home Close Farm
B4020
Akeman Street
ROMAN ROAD (course of)
Stonelands
Lingermans
Macaroni Barn
BURFORD RD
Lodge Plantation
Glebe Farm
Kilkenny Farm
KILKENNY LA
Well Head
Johnsons Farm
PH
West End
LADBURN LA
CHURCH LA
Friesland
Shilton
Shill Brook
SHILTON RD
SWINBROOK RD
MANOR RD
GARNER CL
STONELEIGH DR
SHILBROOK AVE
WYCHWOOD CL
BURSWIN RD
LIPSCOMBE PL
LOVATT CL
STRATHMORE CL
HEATHER CL
GLENMORE RD
BRACKEN CL
BEVERLEY CRES
BRIZEWOOD
YORK RD
BRITANNIA CL
HILL VIEW
DOVE CT
DOVETREES
CONNOLLY DR
SHILLBROOK AVE
COTSWOLD WAY
Coll
Carterton
NORTHWOOD CRES
YATESBURY RD
BRAYNHAM CL
TANGMERE AVE
PITREAVIE AVE
UPWOOD DR
UPAVON WAY
ODIHAM CL
WEST OXON IND PARK
CARTERTON RD
Alvescot Downs Farm Cottages
Alvescot Downs Farm
Alvescot Down
ROBINSON CL
B4020
BURFORD RD
LYNEHAM CL
KENLEY AVE
DUXFORD CL
INNSWORTH RD
GAYDON CL
ELY CL
COLERNE RD
NORTHOLT RD
FELTWELL CL
STANMORE CRES
BOULDGON RD
ST JOHNS DR
Sch
FINCHDALE CL
LORD CL
KESTREL CL
MERLIN CL
ROCK RD
HERON CL
FALCON CL
FAULDER AVE
WARWICK
POULTNEY PL
SYCAMORE DR
ROCK CL
SELLWOOD DR
ABINGDON
HUMPHRIES CL
SARUM CL
BRAMPTON DR
UPAVON WAY
STIRLING CL
CARR AVE
ARUNDEL CL
ARKELL AVE
PEEL PL
Liby
CHURCH VIEW
BRIZE NORTON RD
BIRCHWOOD
DAVIS CL
CRANWELL AVE
HASTINGS DR
ANDOVER LA
WINDSOR CL
RICHENS DR
HOME CL
LAWTON AVE
PINECROFT
ARLINGTON
LARMER RD
WYCOMBE WAY
HALTON RD
ARGOSY RD
LAVENDER PL
CARTERS CL
ROSE CL
ALVESCOT RD
HOLLYBUSH RD
NETHERAVON CL
DEVON PL
Sch
EDGEWO
MINTY CL
B4020
Field Farm
Kenn's Farm
Shill Bridge
ALDERLEY CL
THE LARCHES
FOXCROFT DR
KINGHAM DR
HAYWARD DR
JACKSON CL
BUTLERS DR
BLACK BOURTON RD
ASHFIELD RD
WATSONS CL
PAMPAS CL
QUEENS RD
CAMPION
ANSON AVE
Brize Norton Airfield
MAYFIELD CL
OAKFIELD RD
CLARKSTON RD
HAWTHORN GR
CORBETT RD
THE MAPLES
MILESTONE RD
MARLBOROUGH CL
ACACIA CL
BELLE TERR
CLARE TERR
WHITTINGTON PL
Carterton South Industrial Estate
B4020

116

133

102

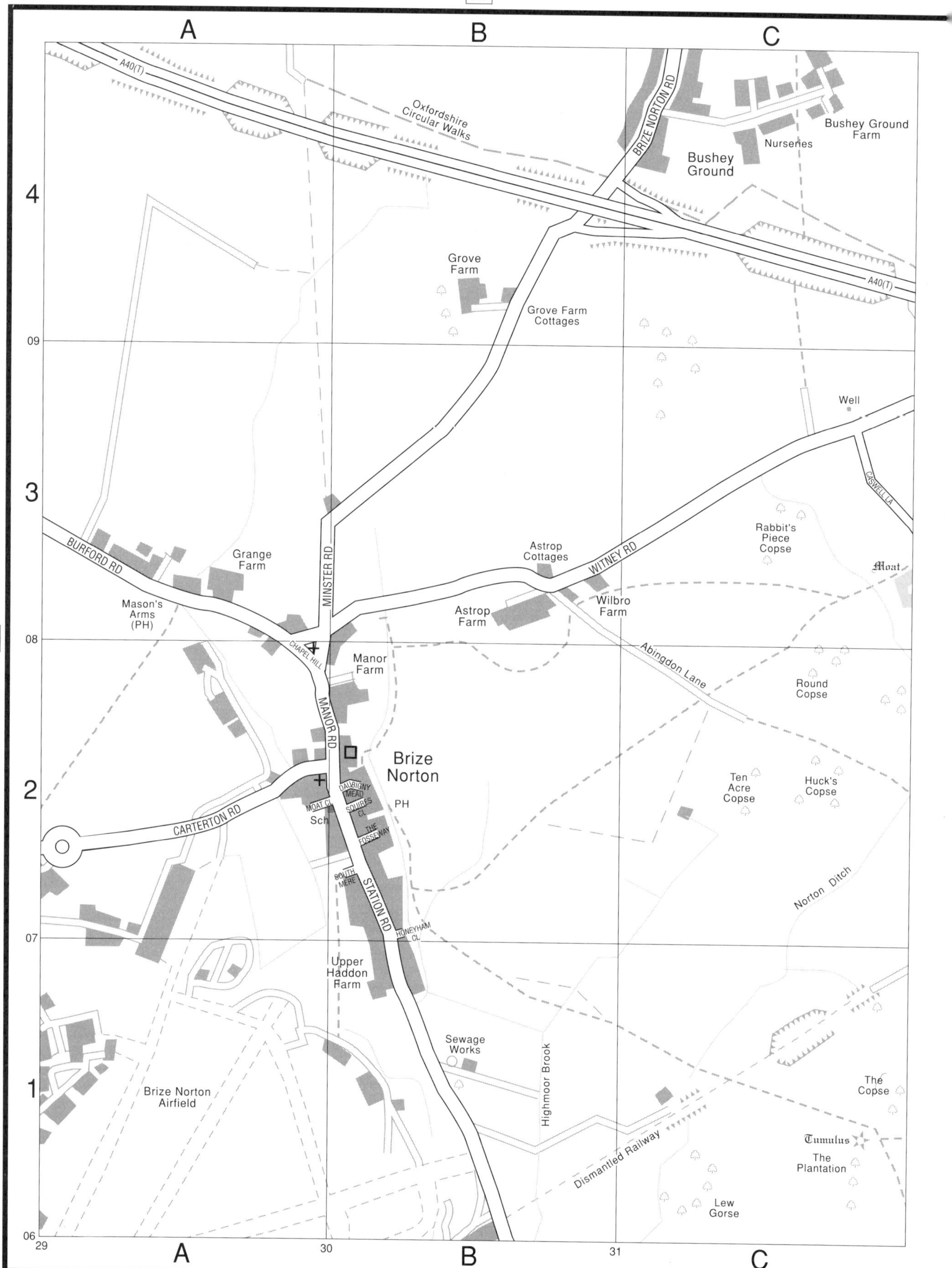
A
B
C
4
3
2
1
09
08
07
06
29
30
31
A40(T)
Oxfordshire Circular Walks
BRIZE NORTON RD
Bushey Ground
Nurseries
Bushey Ground Farm
Grove Farm
Grove Farm Cottages
Well
CASWELL LA
Rabbit's Piece Copse
Moat
BURFORD RD
Grange Farm
MINSTER RD
Astrop Cottages
WITNEY RD
Mason's Arms (PH)
Astrop Farm
Wilbro Farm
CHAPEL HILL
Manor Farm
Abingdon Lane
Round Copse
MANOR RD
Brize Norton
DAUBIGNY MEAD
SQUIRES CL
MOAT CL
Sch
PH
THE FOSSEWAY
CARTERTON RD
Ten Acre Copse
Huck's Copse
SOUTH MERE
STATION RD
HONEYHAM CL
Norton Ditch
Upper Haddon Farm
Sewage Works
Highmoor Brook
Brize Norton Airfield
The Copse
Tumulus
Dismantled Railway
The Plantation
Lew Gorse
A
B
C

115

134

103

D
E
F
Sewage Works
Sch
VALENCE CRES
EDINGTON RD
WYCHWOOD CL
APLEY WAY
WENHAM RD
FETTIPLACE RD
WINDRUSH CL
A4095
TOWER HILL
UNION WAY
BEECH RD
RISE
MOORLAND RD
Cemy
CORN ST
SHERBOURNE RD
RISSINGTON DR
VALE RD
MIRFIELD RD
FIELDMERE CL
A415
DEER PARK RD
RAGLEGH CRES
WESTCOTE CL
IDBURY CL
DONNINGTON CL
ALDSWORTH CT
BOURTON CL
BARRINGTON CL
COTSWOLD MEADOW
CURBRIDGE RD
FAIRFIELD DR
FRENCH CL
CHURCH VIEW RD
SOUTHLAWN
DUCKLINGTON LA
ELM CL
CORNFIELD
BURWELL CL
THORNEY LEYS
ABBEY RD
ELM DR
MOUNTFIELD RD
HOLFORD RD
BURWELL DR
WILSON AVE
COLWELL DR
MEADOW
Oxfordshire Circular Walks
Peashell Farm
Colwell Brook
4
09
PH
Charity Farm
Manor Farm
Ind Est
A40(T)
WELL LA
Curbridge
A4095
3
CASWELL LA
Caswell Farm
Sewage Works
Black Moat
Duttons Farm
08
Dismantled Railway
BAMPTON RD
Glebe Farm
Coursehill Farm
2
Abingdon Lane
Davis's Copse
Moulden's Wood
07
Barleypark Farm
Hill View
1
Lew
Morgans Farm
Lew House
Lower Farm
Manor Farm
Elm Bank Ditch
Barleypark Wood
A4095
06
32
33
34

118

135

104

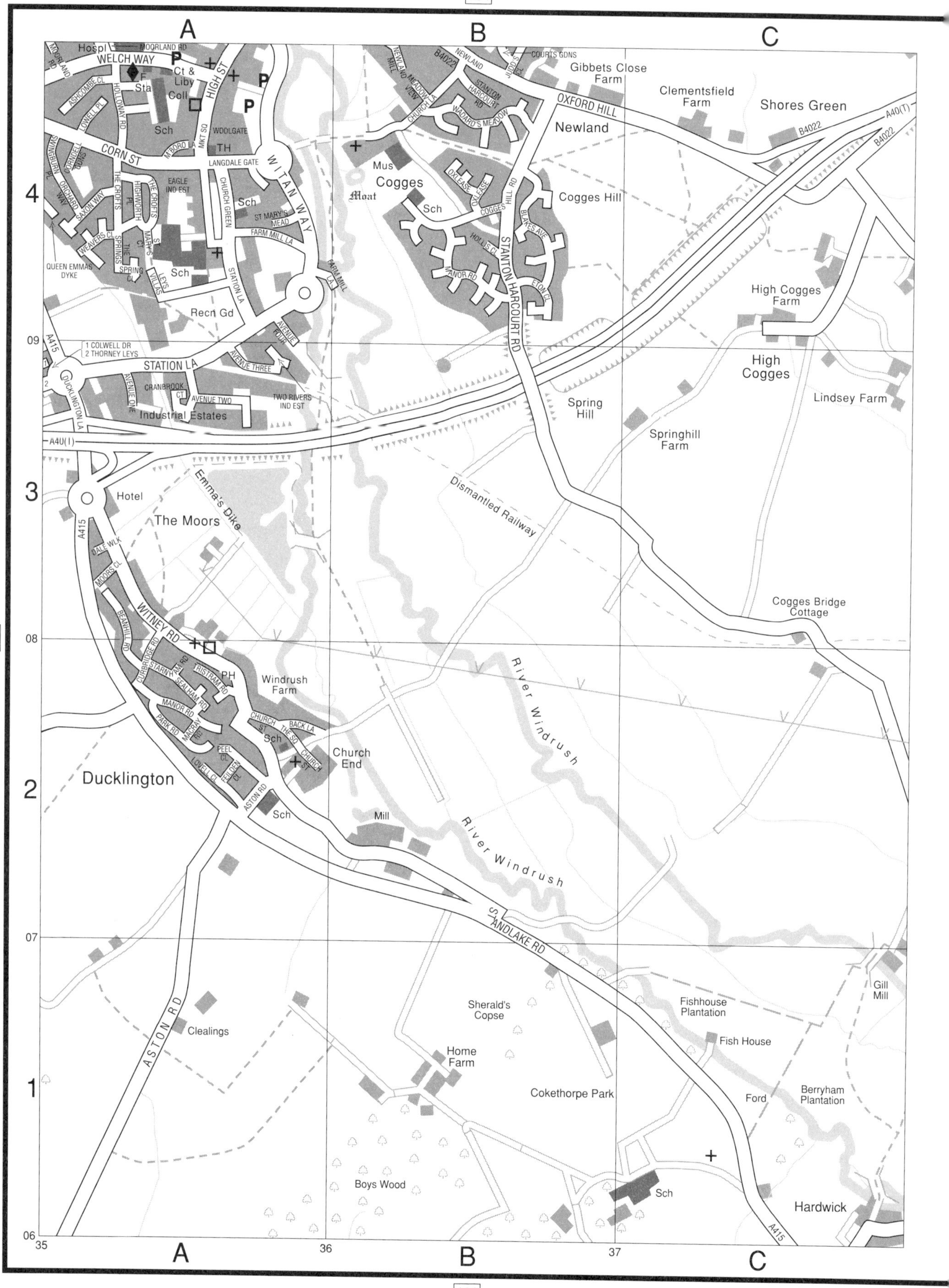
A
B
C
Hospl
MOORLAND RD
WELCH WAY
P
Ct & Liby
Sta
Coll
HIGH ST
P
P
Sch
WOOLGATE
TH
MKT SQ
M'BORO LA
CORN ST
LANGDALE GATE
WITAN WAY
ASHCOMBE CL
LOWELL PL
HOLLOWAY RD
SWINGBURN PL
CORNDELL GDNS
ORCHARD WAY
SAXON WAY
THE CROFTS
HIGHWORTH PL
EAGLE IND EST
CHURCH GREEN
Sch
ST MARY'S MEAD
FARM MILL LA
WEAVERS CL
SPRINGS
THE SPRING CL
LEYS VILLAS
Sch
STATION LA
QUEEN EMMAS DYKE
Recn Gd
AVENUE FOUR
FARM MILL LA
A415
1 COLWELL DR
2 THORNEY LEYS
STATION LA
AVENUE THREE
CRANBROOK CT
AVENUE ONE
AVENUE TWO
Industrial Estates
TWO RIVERS IND EST
DUCKLINGTON LA
A40(T)
Hotel
The Moors
Emma's Dike
A415
DALE WLK
MOORS CL
WITNEY RD
BEANHILL RD
CURBRIDGE RD
STARNHAM RD
TRISTRAM RD
SEALHAM RD
PH
Windrush Farm
MANOR RD
PARK RD
MACRAY RD
CHURCH ST
BACK LA
THE SQ
Sch
CHURCH ST
PEEL CL
LOWELL CL
FEILDEN CL
Church End
Ducklington
ASTON RD
Sch
Mill
NEWLAND
NEWLAND MILL
MEADOW VIEW
B4022
JUDD'S CL
COURTS GDNS
Gibbets Close Farm
CHURCH LA
STANTON HARCOURT RD
WADARD'S MEADOW
OXFORD HILL
Newland
Mus
Cogges
Moat
Sch
OXLEASE
COGGES HILL RD
Cogges Hill
BLAKES AVE
HOLLIS CL
MANOR RD
STANTON HARCOURT RD
ETON CL
Clementsfield Farm
Shores Green
A40(T)
B4022
B4022
High Cogges Farm
High Cogges
Lindsey Farm
Spring Hill
Springhill Farm
Dismantled Railway
Cogges Bridge Cottage
River Windrush
River Windrush
STANDLAKE RD
Gill Mill
Sherald's Copse
Fishhouse Plantation
Fish House
ASTON RD
Clealings
Home Farm
Cokethorpe Park
Ford
Berryham Plantation
Boys Wood
Sch
Hardwick
A415
4
09
3
08
2
07
1
06
35
36
37

117

136

105

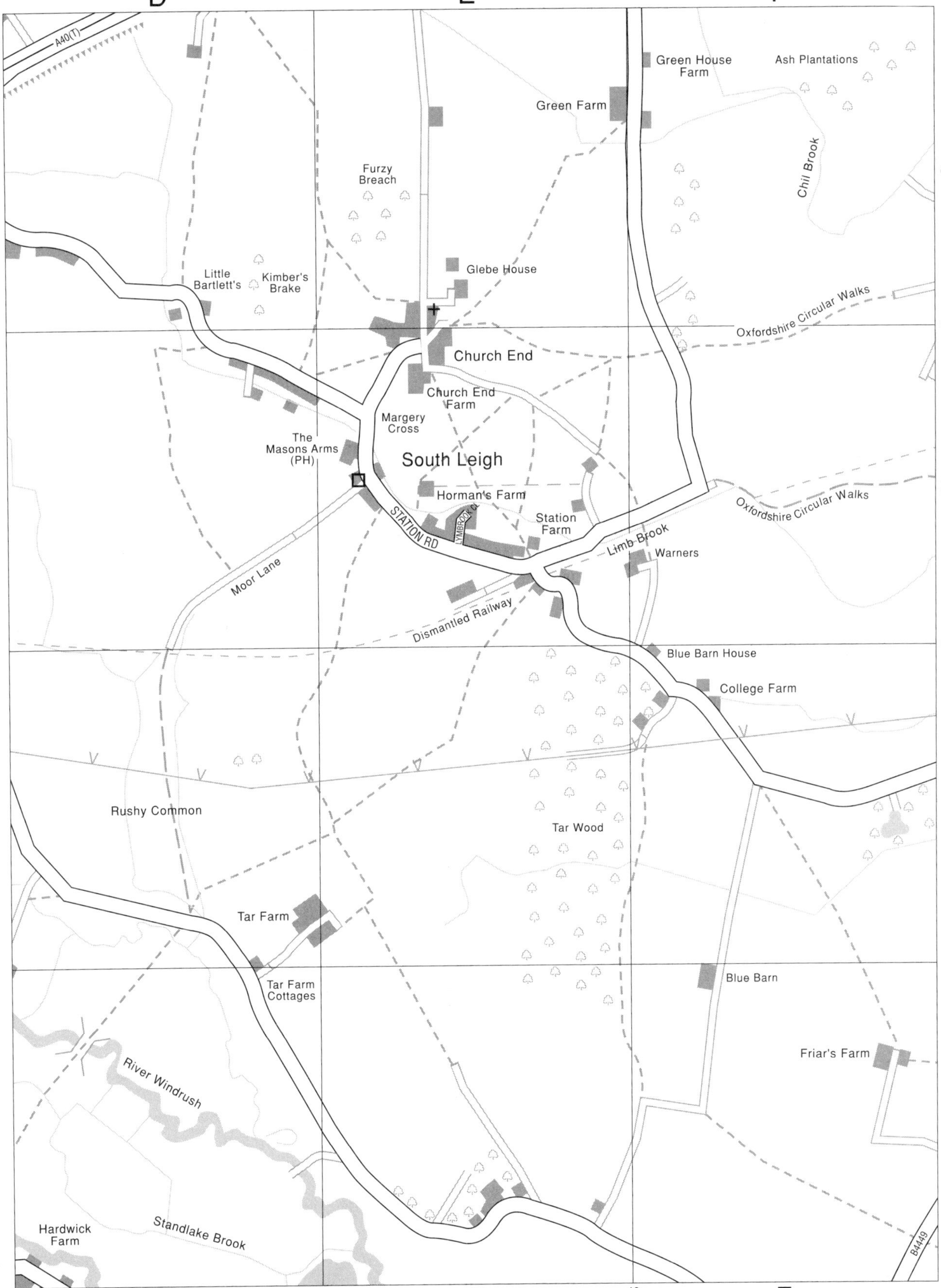

D
E
F
A40(T)
Green House Farm
Ash Plantations
Green Farm
Chil Brook
4
Furzy Breach
Glebe House
Little Bartlett's
Kimber's Brake
Oxfordshire Circular Walks
09
Church End
Church End Farm
Margery Cross
The Masons Arms (PH)
South Leigh
3
Horman's Farm
STATION RD
LYMBROOK CL
Station Farm
Limb Brook
Oxfordshire Circular Walks
Warners
Moor Lane
Dismantled Railway
08
Blue Barn House
College Farm
2
Rushy Common
Tar Wood
Tar Farm
07
Tar Farm Cottages
Blue Barn
Friar's Farm
River Windrush
1
Hardwick Farm
Standlake Brook
B4449
06
38
39
40
D
E
F

120

137

106

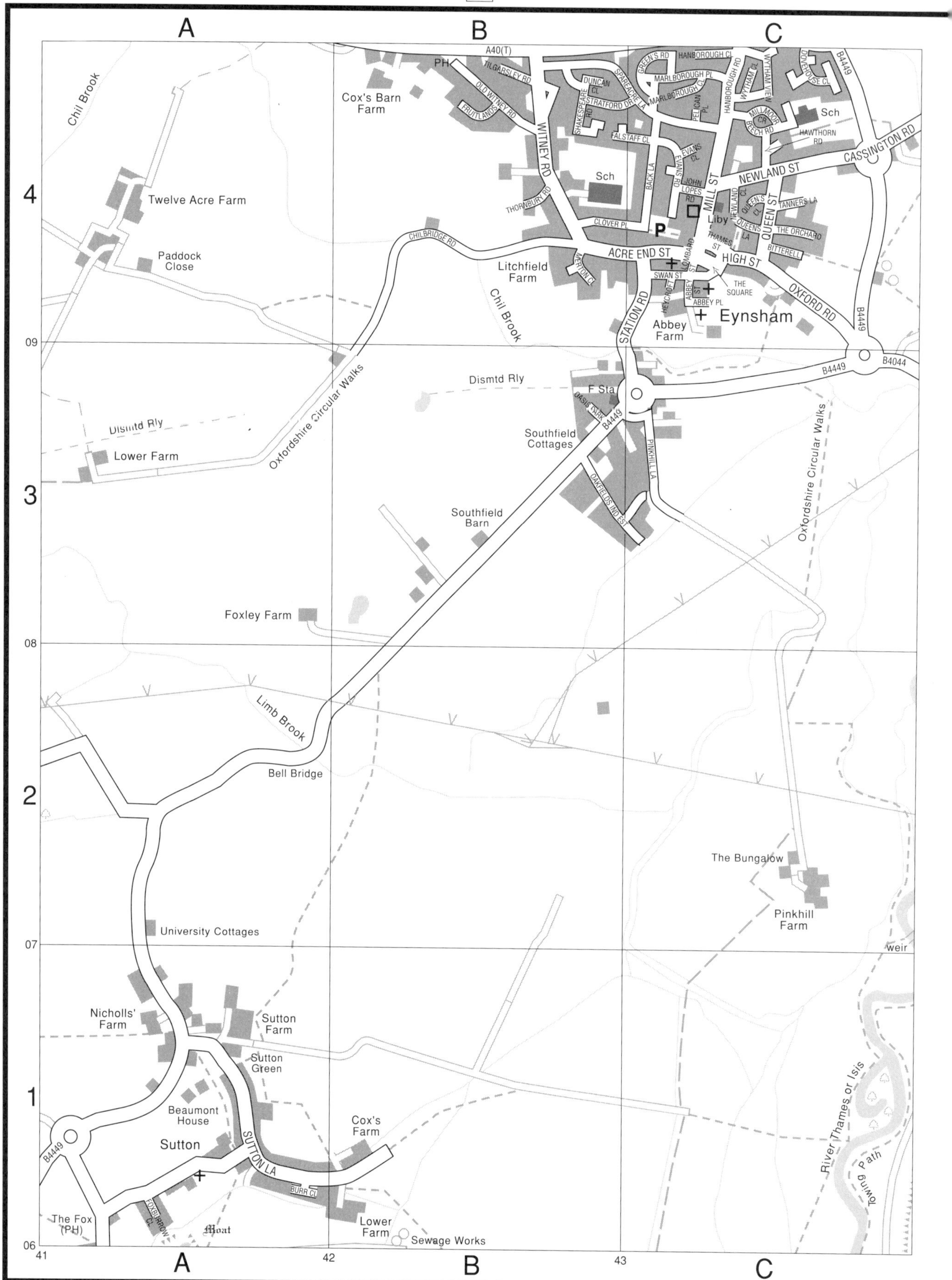
A
B
C
A40(T)
PH
TILGARSLEY RD
OLD WITNEY RD
FRUITLANDS
Cox's Barn Farm
WITNEY RD
GREEN'S RD
HANBOROUGH CL
DUNCAN CL
SPAREACRE LA
MARLBOROUGH PL
MARLBOROUGH CL
SHAKESPEARE RD
STRATFORD DR
PELICAN PL
HANBOROUGH RD
WYTHAM CL
WYTHAM VIEW
DOVEHOUSE CL
B4449
Sch
MILLMOOR CR
BEECH RD
HAWTHORN RD
CASSINGTON RD
FALSTAFF CL
EVANS CL
EVANS RD
JOHN LOPES RD
BACK LA
MILL ST
NEWLAND ST
NEWLAND
QUEEN'S CL
QUEEN ST
TANNERS LA
QUEENS LA
THE ORCHARD
Chil Brook
Twelve Acre Farm
THORNBURY RD
CLOVER PL
Liby
P
THAMES ST
CHILBRIDGE RD
Paddock Close
Litchfield Farm
MERTON CL
ACRE END ST
LOMBARD ST
HIGH ST
BITTERELL
SWAN ST
ABBEY ST
THE SQUARE
OXFORD RD
HEYCROFT
ABBEY PL
STATION RD
Abbey Farm
Eynsham
09
B4044
Dismtd Rly
F Sta
OASIS PARK
B4449
Oxfordshire Circular Walks
Dismtd Rly
Southfield Cottages
PINKHILL LA
Lower Farm
OAKFIELDS IND EST
3
Southfield Barn
Foxley Farm
08
Limb Brook
Bell Bridge
2
The Bungalow
Pinkhill Farm
University Cottages
07
weir
Nicholls' Farm
Sutton Farm
Sutton Green
1
River Thames or Isis
Beaumont House
Cox's Farm
Sutton
SUTTON LA
Towing Path
B4449
BURR CL
The Fox (PH)
FOXBURROW CL
Moat
Lower Farm
Sewage Works
06
41
42
43
4

119

138

107

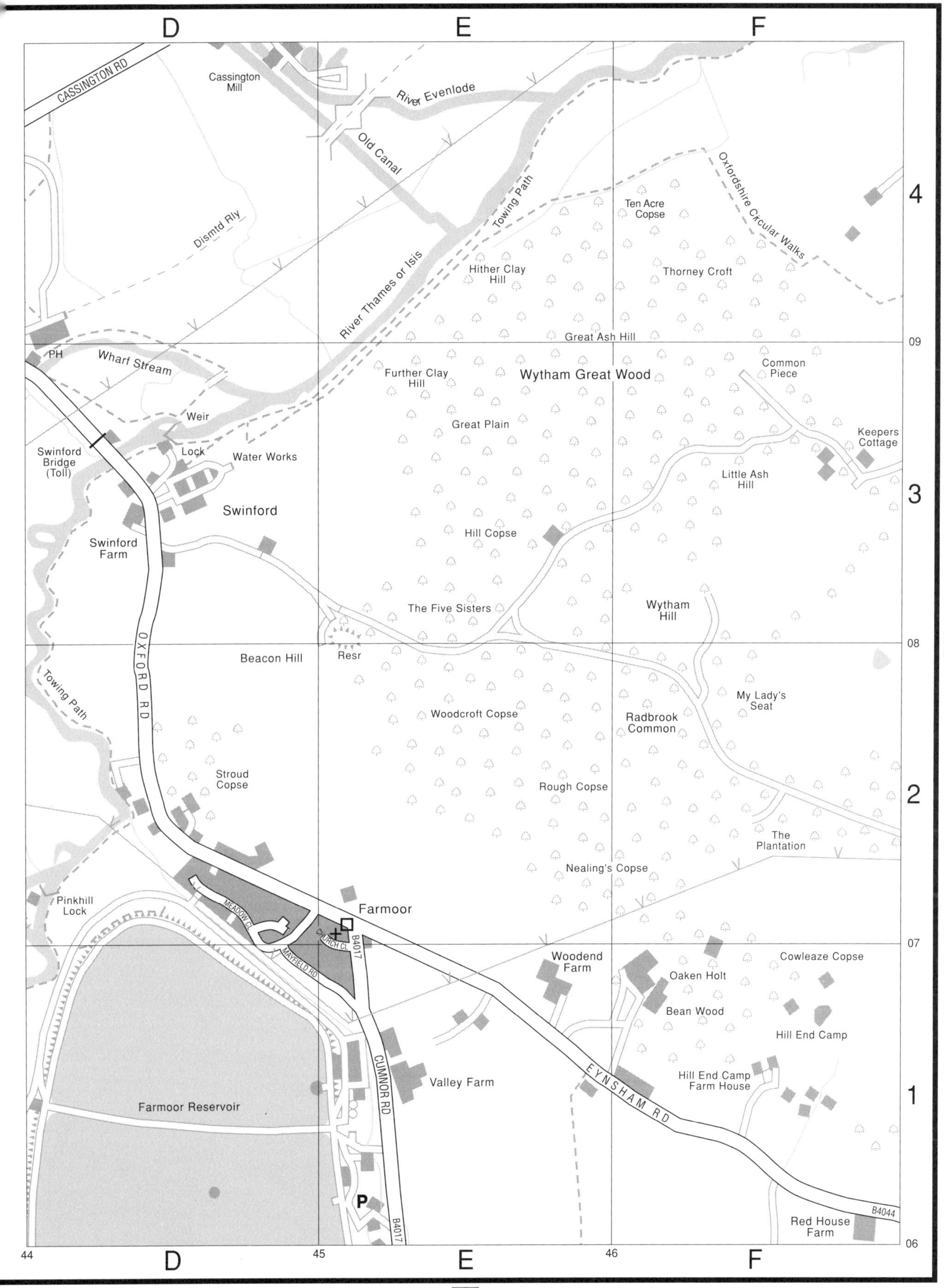
D
E
F
CASSINGTON RD
Cassington Mill
River Evenlode
Old Canal
Oxfordshire Circular Walks
Towing Path
Dismtd Rly
River Thames or Isis
Ten Acre Copse
Hither Clay Hill
Thorney Croft
Great Ash Hill
4
09
PH
Wharf Stream
Further Clay Hill
Wytham Great Wood
Common Piece
Weir
Great Plain
Keepers Cottage
Swinford Bridge (Toll)
Lock
Water Works
Little Ash Hill
3
Swinford
Swinford Farm
Hill Copse
The Five Sisters
Wytham Hill
OXFORD RD
08
Beacon Hill
Resr
Towing Path
My Lady's Seat
Woodcroft Copse
Radbrook Common
Stroud Copse
Rough Copse
2
The Plantation
Nealing's Copse
Pinkhill Lock
MEADOW CL
Farmoor
CHURCH CL
B4017
MAYFIELD RD
07
Woodend Farm
Cowleaze Copse
Oaken Holt
Bean Wood
Hill End Camp
CUMMOR RD
Valley Farm
EYNSHAM RD
Hill End Camp Farm House
1
Farmoor Reservoir
P
B4017
B4044
Red House Farm
06
44
45
46
D
E
F

122

139

108

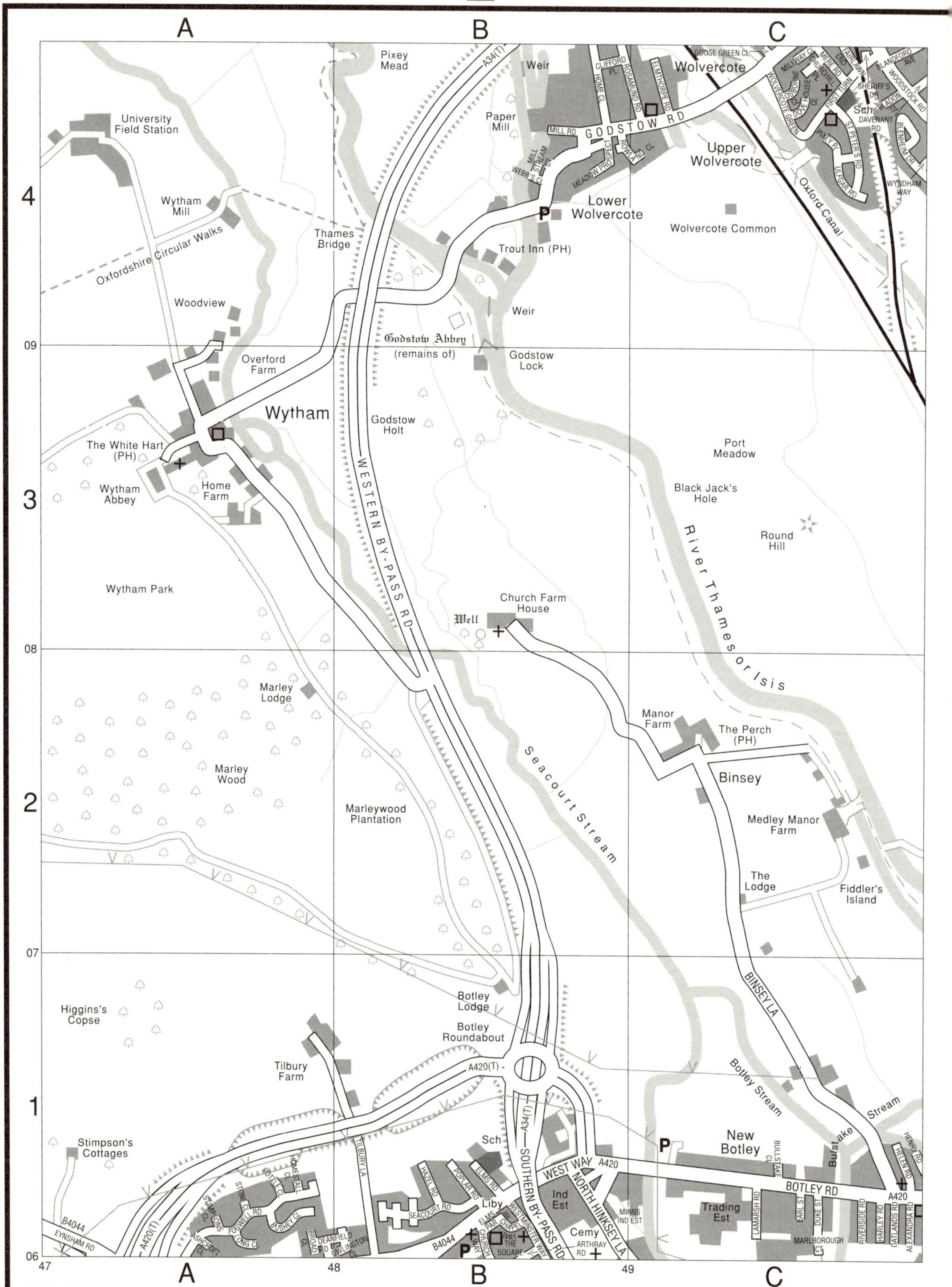
A
B
C
1
2
3
4
06
07
08
09
47
48
49
Pixey Mead
Weir
Wolvercote
University Field Station
Paper Mill
GODSTOW RD
MILL RD
Upper Wolvercote
Oxford Canal
Wytham Mill
Lower Wolvercote
Wolvercote Common
Thames Bridge
Trout Inn (PH)
Oxfordshire Circular Walks
Woodview
Weir
Godstow Abbey
(remains of)
Godstow Lock
Overford Farm
Wytham
Godstow Holt
The White Hart (PH)
Wytham Abbey
Home Farm
WESTERN BY-PASS RD
Port Meadow
Black Jack's Hole
Round Hill
River Thames or Isis
Wytham Park
Church Farm House
Well
Marley Lodge
Manor Farm
The Perch (PH)
Binsey
Marley Wood
Seacourt Stream
Marleywood Plantation
Medley Manor Farm
The Lodge
Fiddler's Island
Higgins's Copse
Botley Lodge
Botley Roundabout
BINSEY LA
Tilbury Farm
A420(T)
Botley Stream
Bulstake Stream
Stimpson's Cottages
Sch
New Botley
A34(T)
SOUTHERN BY-PASS RD
WEST WAY
A420
NORTH HINKSEY LA
BOTLEY RD
Ind Est
Trading Est
Liby
Cemy
SEACOURT RD
B4044
EYNSHAM RD
A420(T)
TILBURY LA
ARTHRAY RD
MINNS IND EST
MARLBOROUGH CT
LAMARSH RD
EARL ST
DUKE ST
RIVERSIDE RD
HARLEY RD
OATLANDS RD
ALEXANDRA RD
HELEN RD
HENRY RD
BULSTAKE CL
Sch

121

140

109

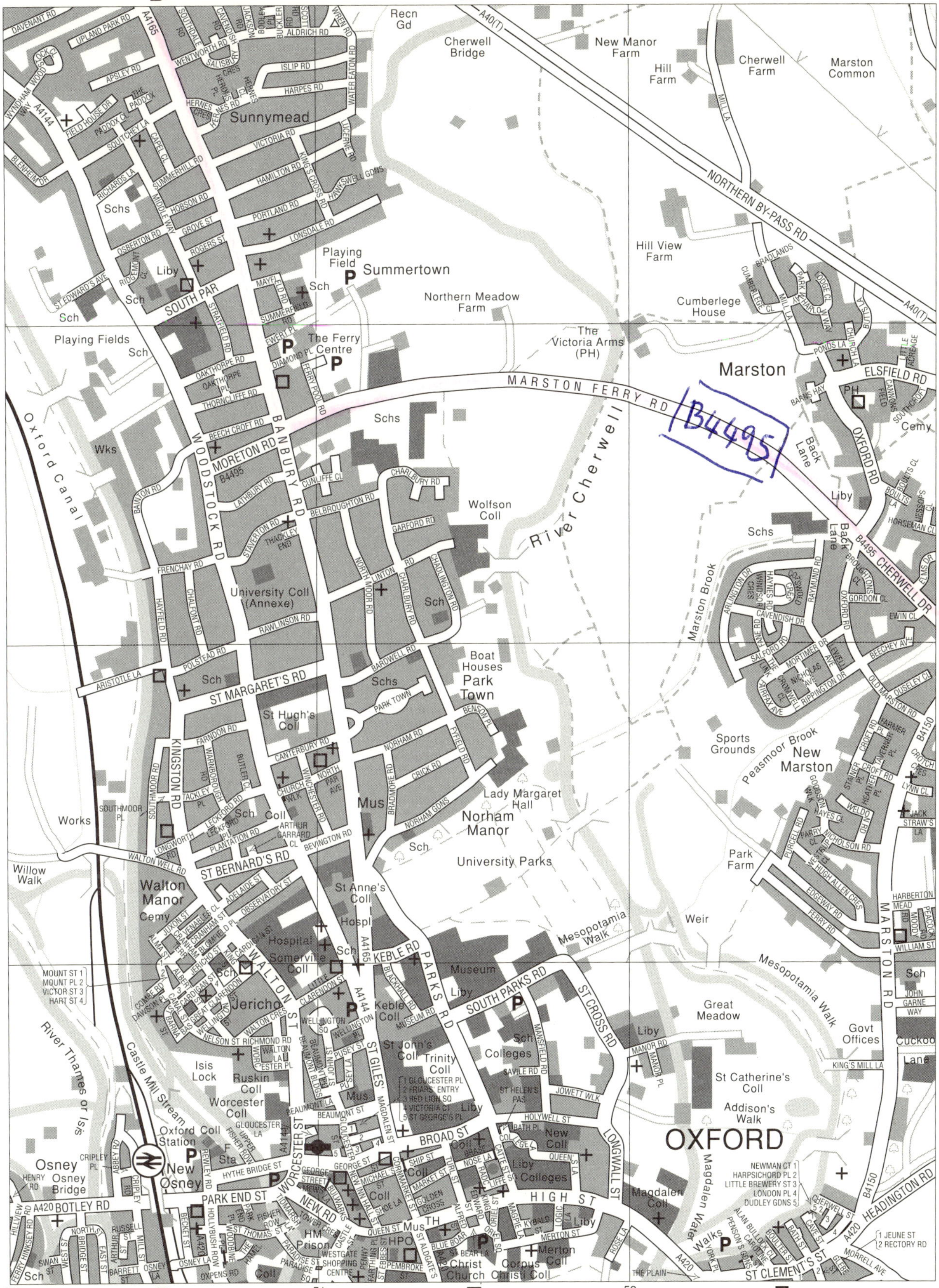
D
E
F
4
3
2
1
09
08
07
06
50
51
52
Recn Gd
Cherwell Bridge
New Manor Farm
Hill Farm
Cherwell Farm
Marston Common
Sunnymead
Schs
Liby
Sch
Playing Field
Summertown
Northern Meadow Farm
Hill View Farm
Cumberlege House
NORTHERN BY-PASS RD
A40(T)
Playing Fields
The Ferry Centre
The Victoria Arms (PH)
Marston
ELSFIELD RD
MARSTON FERRY RD
B4495
Oxford Canal
Wks
Wolfson Coll
River Cherwell
Cemy
Back Lane
OXFORD RD
CHERWELL DR
University Coll (Annexe)
Marston Brook
Boat Houses
Park Town
St Hugh's Coll
Sports Grounds
Peasmoor Brook
New Marston
Works
Mus
Lady Margaret Hall
Norham Manor
University Parks
Park Farm
Willow Walk
Walton Manor
Cemy
St Anne's Coll
Hospl
Hospital
Somerville Coll
Mesopotamia Walk
Weir
Museum
Great Meadow
Govt Offices
Cuckoo Lane
Jericho
Keble Coll
Liby
Colleges
St Catherine's Coll
Addison's Walk
River Thames or Isis
Castle Mill Stream
Isis Lock
Ruskin Coll
Worcester Coll
St John's Coll
Trinity Coll
Oxford Coll
Station
New Osney
Osney
Osney Bridge
BROAD ST
New Coll
OXFORD
Magdalen Water Walks
Magdalen Coll
HIGH ST
HM Prison
HPO
Christ Church
Corpus Christi Coll
Merton Coll
ST CLEMENT'S ST
BOTLEY RD
PARK END ST
BANBURY RD
WOODSTOCK RD
ST MARGARET'S RD
ST BERNARD'S RD
KEBLE RD
PARKS RD
SOUTH PARKS RD
ST CROSS RD
LONGWALL ST
WALTON ST
ST GILES'
MARSTON RD
HEADINGTON RD
D
E
F

124

141

110

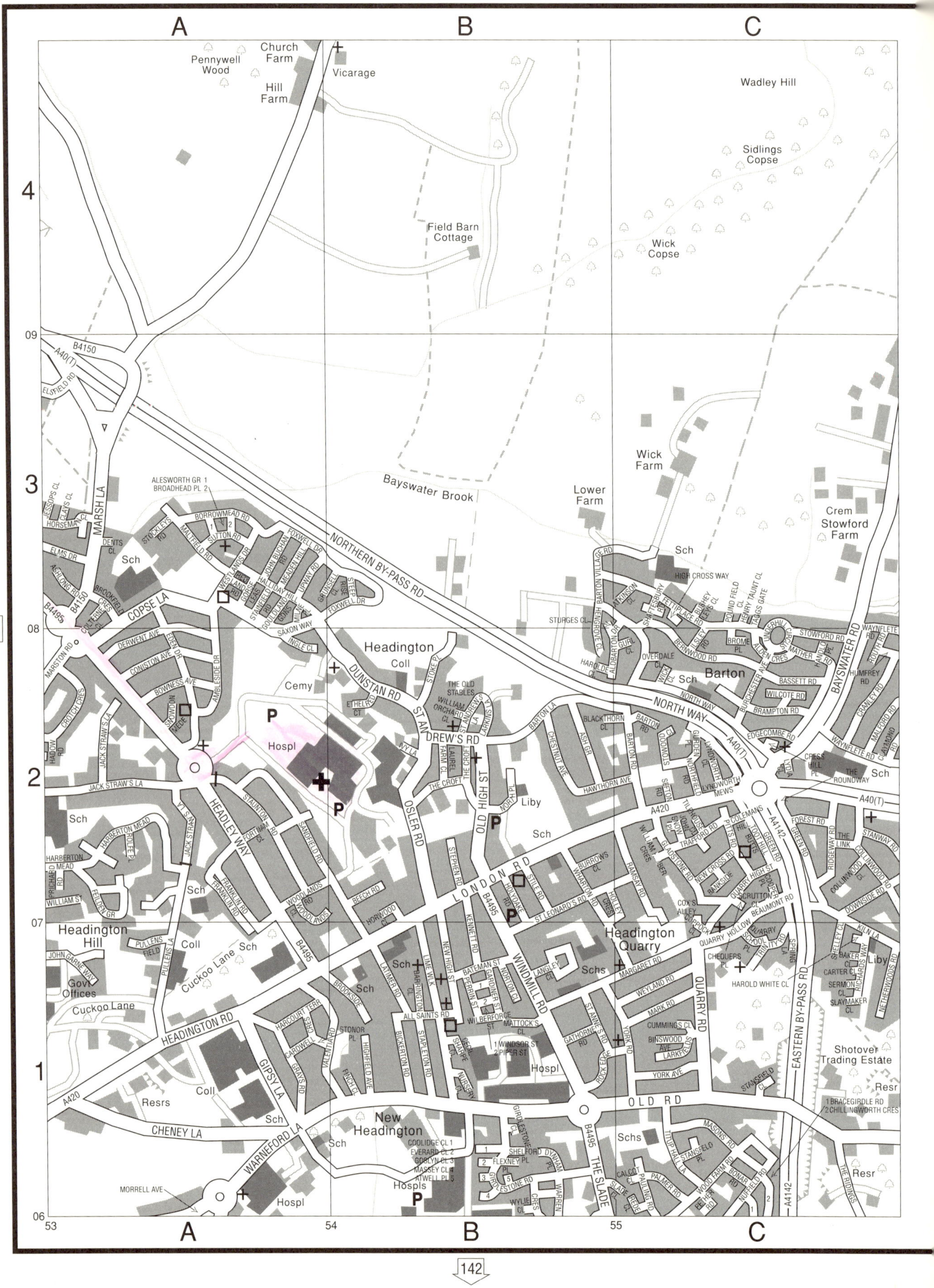

A
B
C
Pennywell Wood
Church Farm
Hill Farm
Vicarage
Wadley Hill
Sidlings Copse
Field Barn Cottage
Wick Copse
Wick Farm
Lower Farm
Crem
Stowford Farm
Bayswater Brook
NORTHERN BY-PASS RD
B4150
A40(T)
MARSH LA
COPSE LA
Headington
Coll
Cemy
Hospl
DUNSTAN RD
ST ANDREW'S RD
OSLER RD
OLD HIGH ST
Liby
Sch
Barton
NORTH WAY
BAYSWATER RD
BARTON VILLAGE RD
HIGH CROSS WAY
A4142
A420
JACK STRAW'S LA
HEADLEY WAY
LONDON RD
B4495
WINDMILL RD
Headington Quarry
QUARRY RD
EASTERN BY-PASS RD
Headington Hill
Govt Offices
Cuckoo Lane
HEADINGTON RD
GIPSY LA
CHENEY LA
Resrs
OLD RD
THE SLADE
New Headington
Hospls
Schs
WARNEFORD LA
Shotover Trading Estate
Resr
MORRELL AVE
09
08
07
06
53
54
55
4
3
2
1

123

142

111

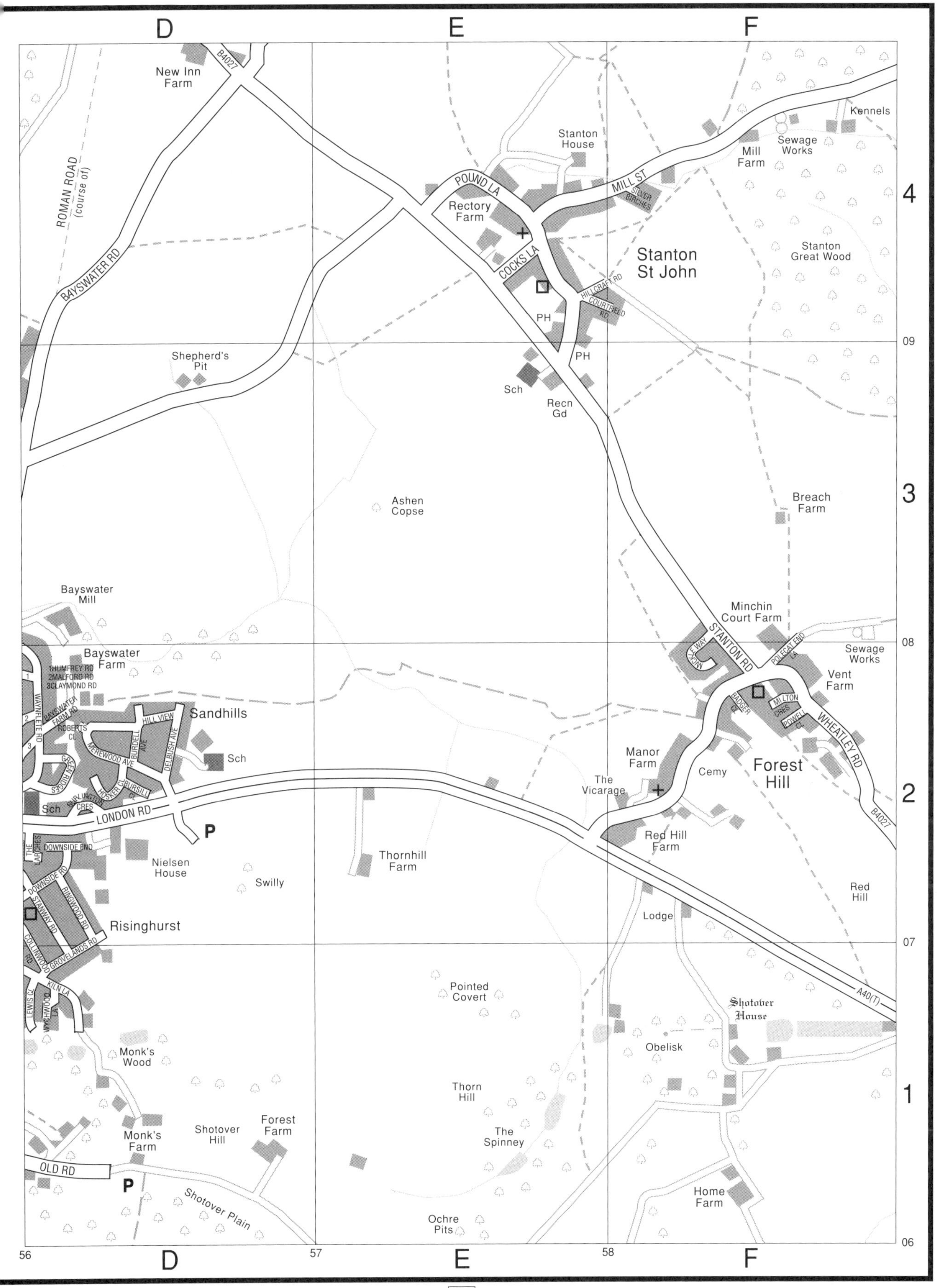
D
E
F
New Inn Farm
B4027
ROMAN ROAD (course of)
BAYSWATER RD
Stanton House
Kennels
Mill Farm
Sewage Works
POUND LA
Rectory Farm
MILL ST
SILVER BIRCHES
Stanton St John
Stanton Great Wood
COCKS LA
HILLCRAFT RD
COURTFIELD RD
PH
Shepherd's Pit
Sch
Recn Gd
Ashen Copse
Breach Farm
Bayswater Mill
Minchin Court Farm
STANTON RD
POLECAT END LA
Sewage Works
Bayswater Farm
1HUMFREY RD
2MALFORD RD
3CLAYMOND RD
NICKLE WAY
Vent Farm
BADGER CL
MILTON CRES
POWELL CL
WHEATLEY RD
WAYNFLETE RD
BAYSWATER FARM RD
ROBERTS CL
Sandhills
HILL VIEW
DELBUSH AVE
BURDELL AVE
MEREWOOD AVE
Sch
Manor Farm
Cemy
Forest Hill
The Vicarage
HOWE CL
BURSILL CL
BURLINGTON CRES
LONDON RD
Sch
P
Red Hill Farm
THE LARCHES
DOWNSIDE END
Nielsen House
Thornhill Farm
DOWNSIDE RD
STANWAY RD
RINGWOOD RD
Swilly
Red Hill
Lodge
Risinghurst
COLLINWOOD RD
GROVELANDS RD
Pointed Covert
A40(T)
Shotover House
KILN LA
LEWIS CL
WYCHWOOD LA
Monk's Wood
Obelisk
Thorn Hill
Monk's Farm
Shotover Hill
Forest Farm
The Spinney
OLD RD
P
Shotover Plain
Home Farm
Ochre Pits
4
3
2
1
09
08
07
06
56
57
58
D
E
F

126

143

112

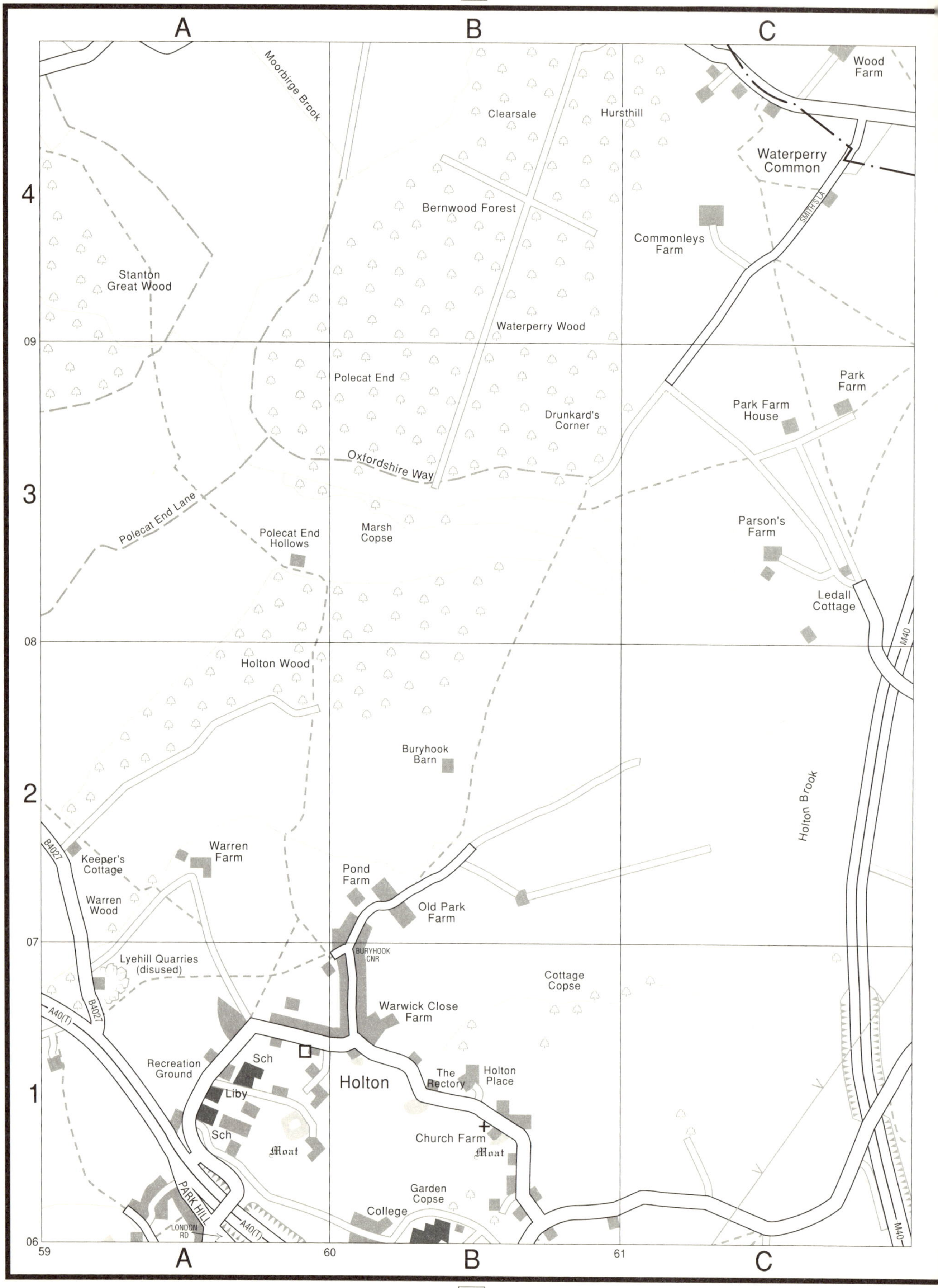
A
B
C
4
3
2
1
09
08
07
06
59
60
61
Moorbirge Brook
Wood Farm
Clearsale
Hursthill
Waterperry Common
Smiths La
Bernwood Forest
Commonleys Farm
Stanton Great Wood
Waterperry Wood
Polecat End
Park Farm
Park Farm House
Drunkard's Corner
Oxfordshire Way
Polecat End Lane
Polecat End Hollows
Marsh Copse
Parson's Farm
Ledall Cottage
M40
Holton Wood
Buryhook Barn
Holton Brook
Warren Farm
Keeper's Cottage
B4027
Pond Farm
Old Park Farm
Warren Wood
Lyehill Quarries (disused)
Buryhook Cnr
Cottage Copse
Warwick Close Farm
A40(T)
Recreation Ground
Sch
Holton
Liby
The Rectory
Holton Place
Church Farm
Moat
Garden Copse
College
Park Hill
London Rd

125

144

not continued, see key diagram

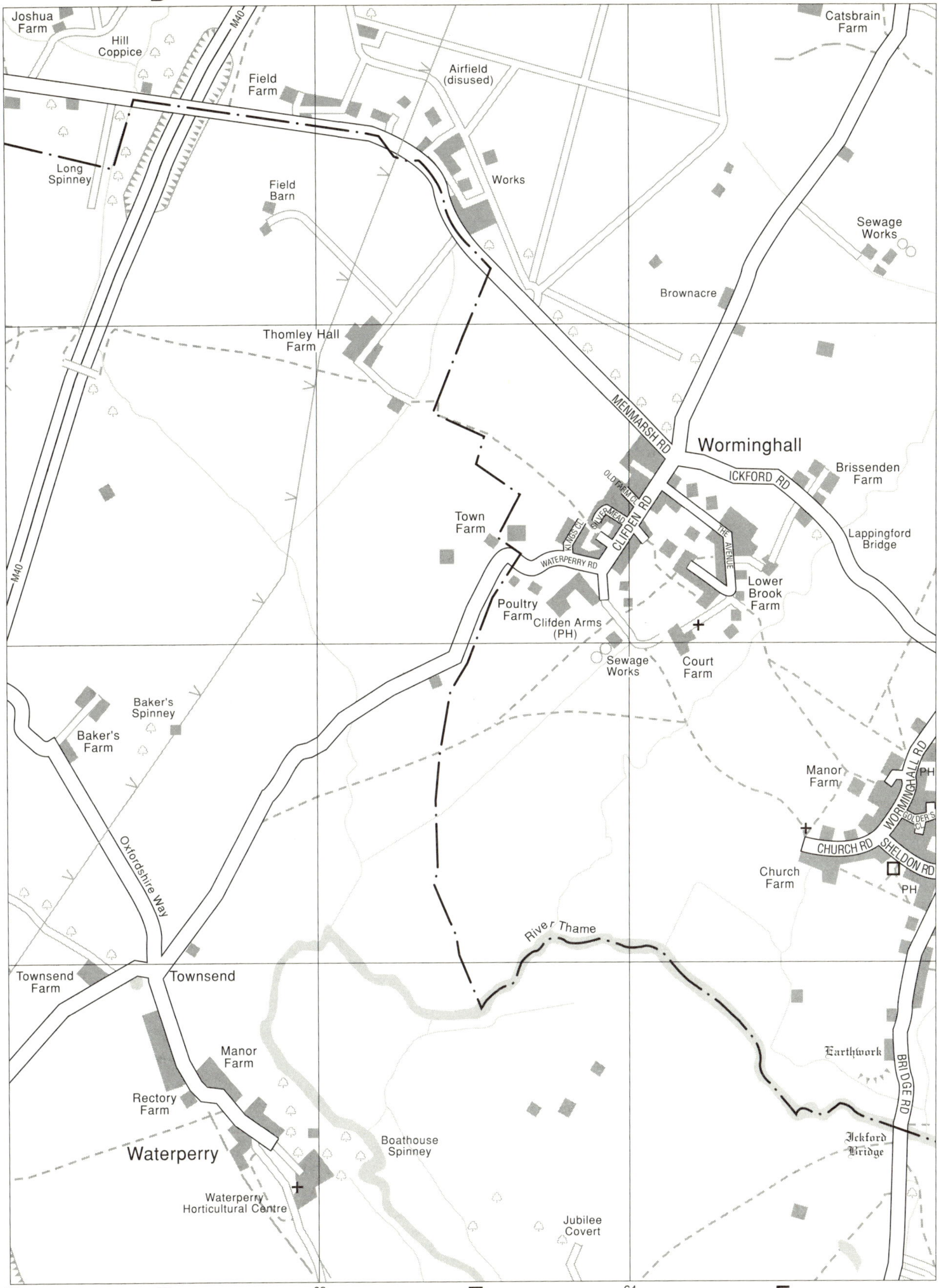

128

145

not continued, see key diagram

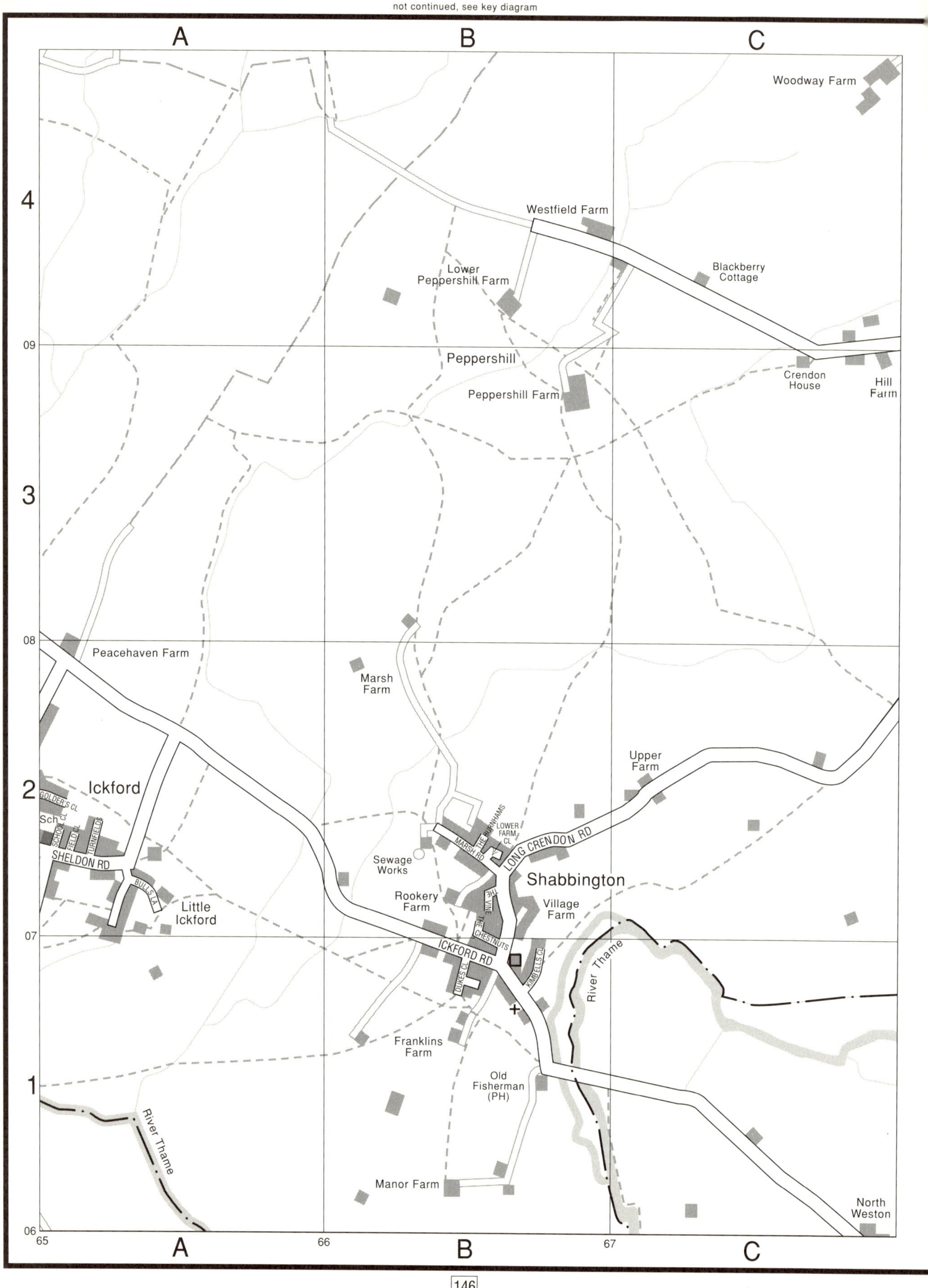

127

146

not continued, see key diagram

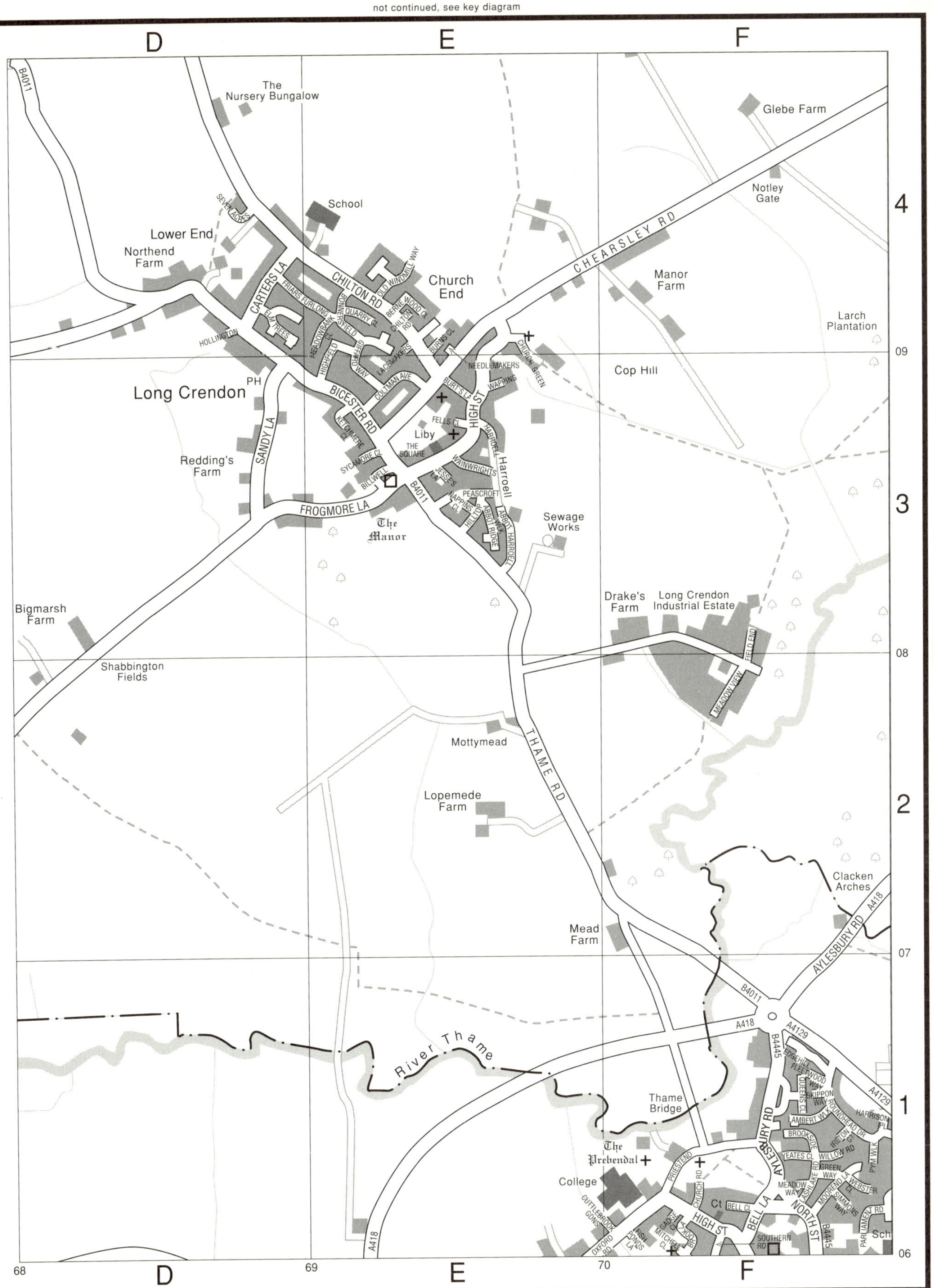

not continued, see key diagram

129

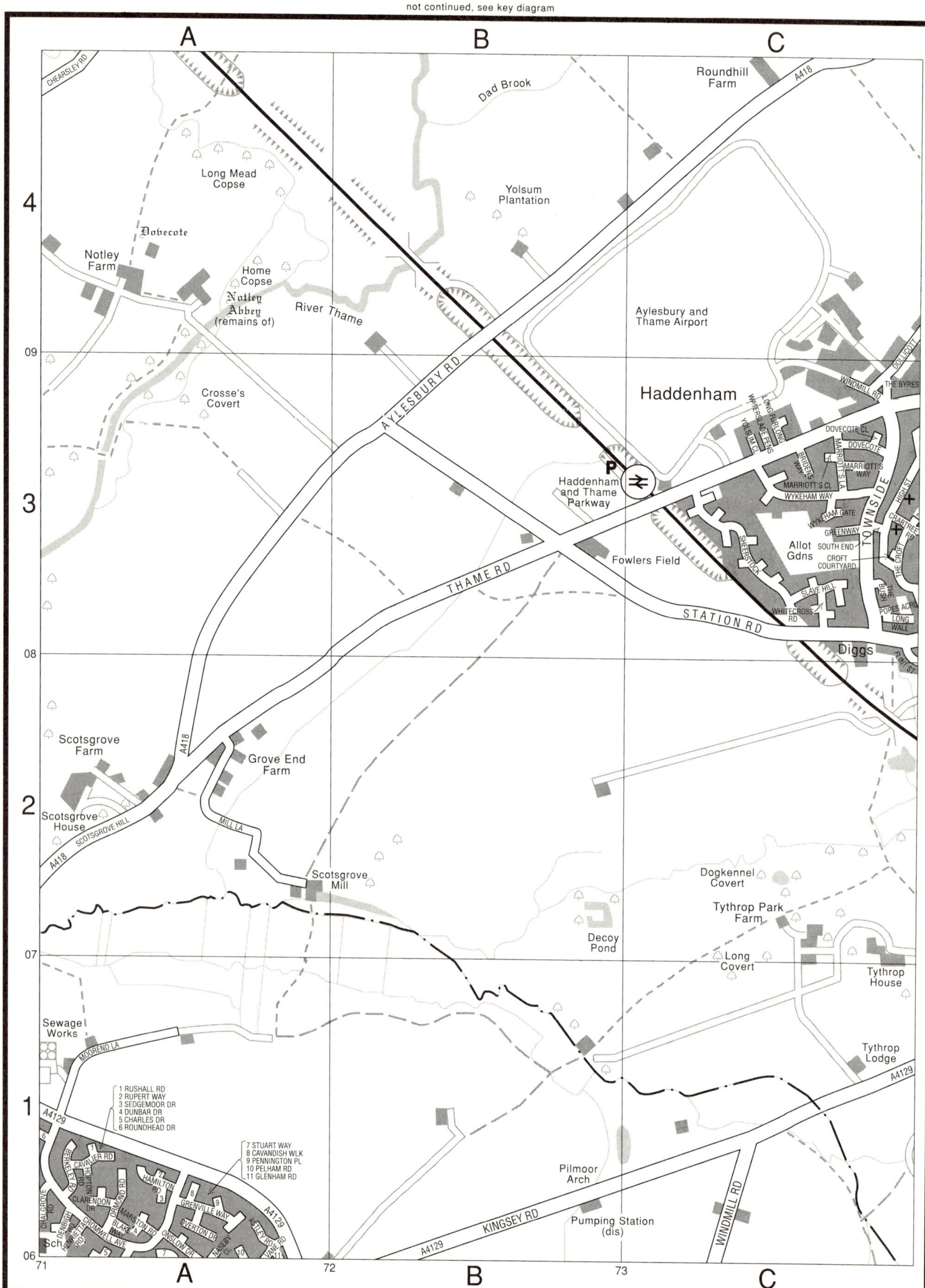

not continued, see key diagram

113

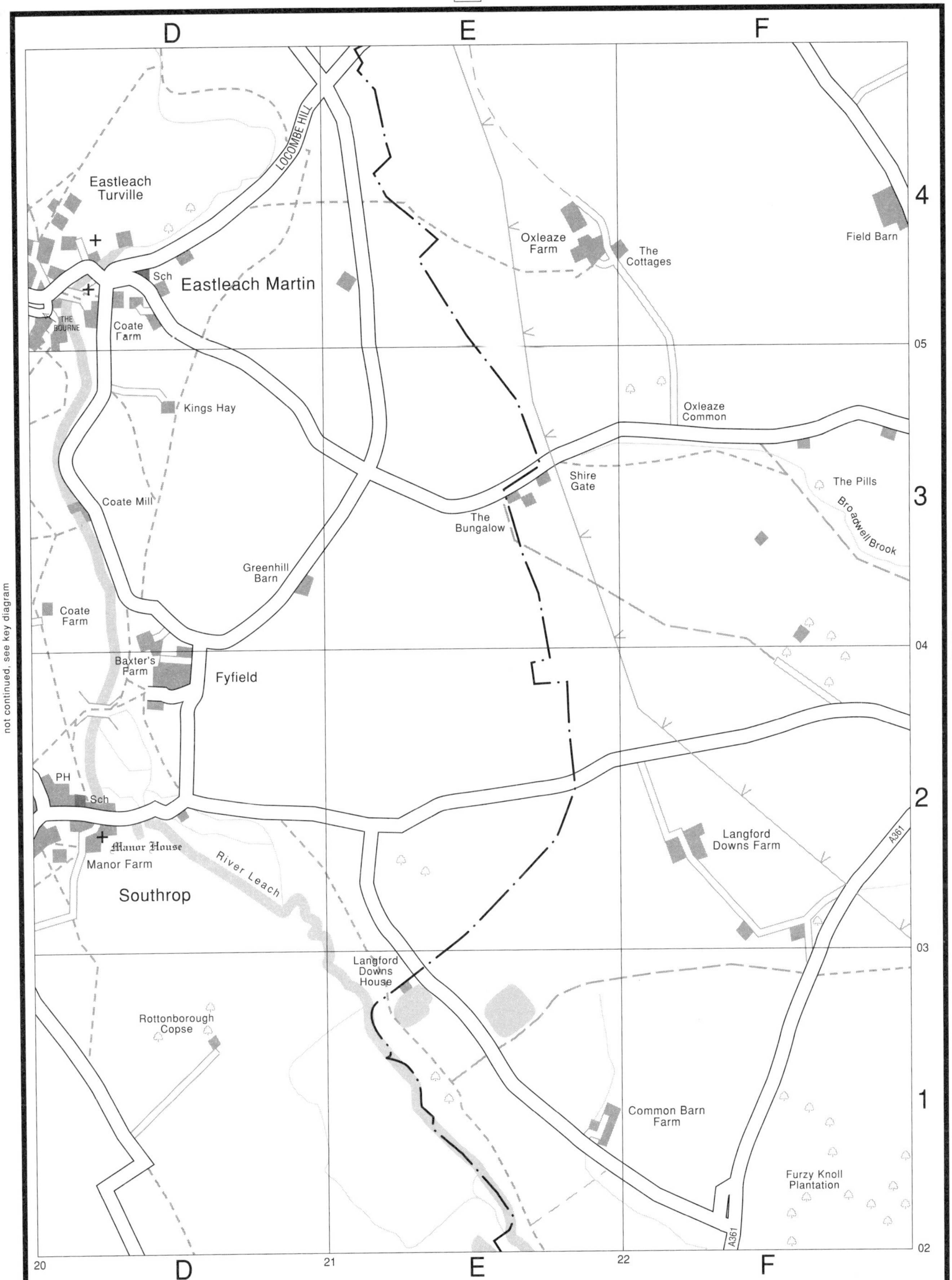

not continued, see key diagram

132

150

114

131

A
B
C
4
3
2
1
05
04
03
02
23
24
25
A361
Hillview Farm
Peartree Farm
Filkins
Home Farm
Asthall Farm
Kencot
Filkins Farm
CROSS TREE LA
Filkins Hall
Manor Farm
BULL CL
ROUSES LA
HAZELLS LA
Mus
Factory
PH
Sch
KINGS LA
Manor Farm
Broughton Poggs
Broughton Hall
Broadwell
Lower Farm
Filkins Mill
Broadshire Bridge
Broadwell Brook
Holly Cottage
CALCROFT LA
FILKINS RD
BROADWELL RD
Langford
Ansells Farm
LECHLADE RD
THE ELMS
CHURCH LA
Broadwell Mill
Rectory Farm
Lower Farm
Leys View
Little Faringdon Wood
Hulse Grounds Farm

151

115

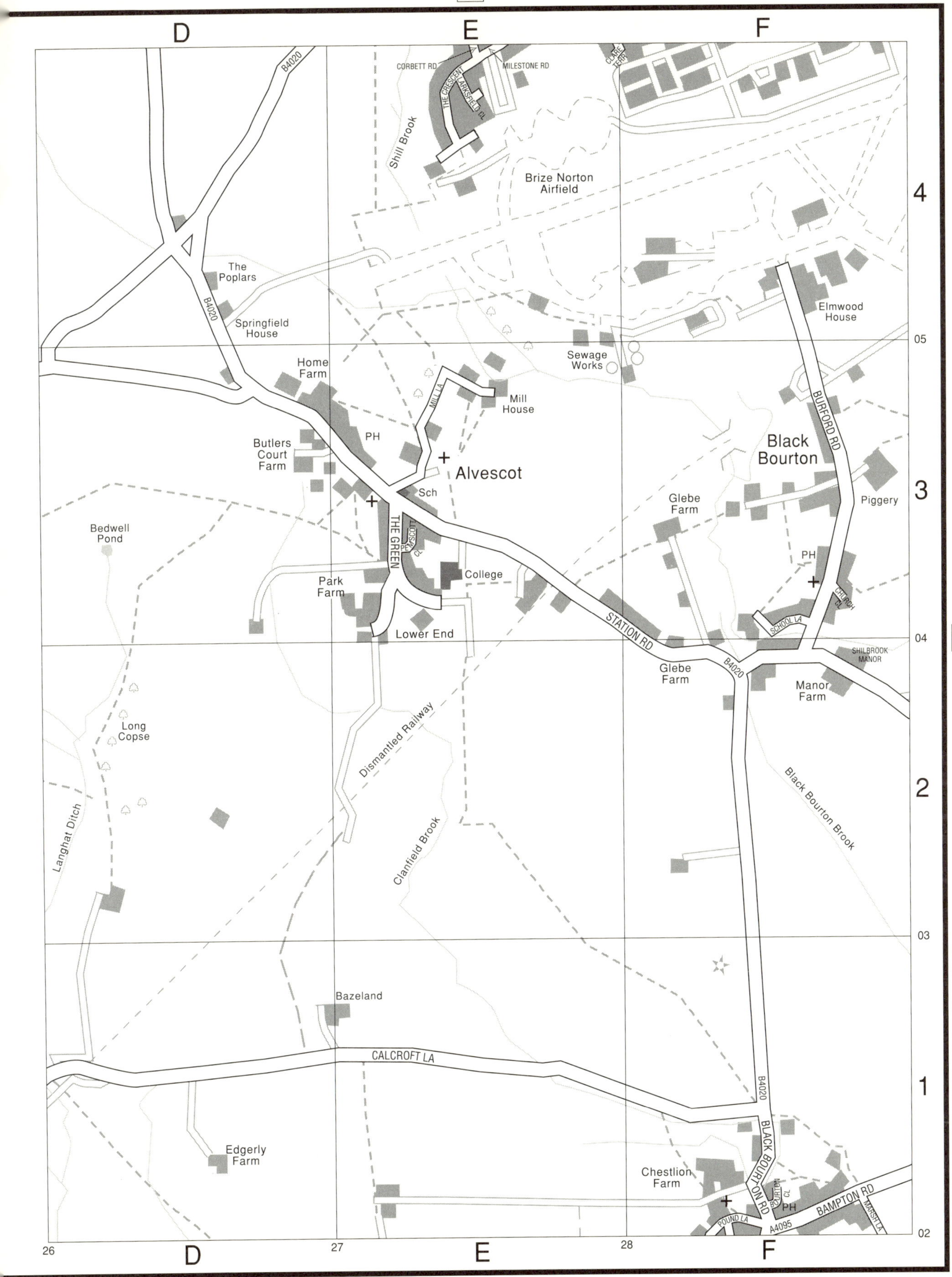
D
E
F
CORBETT RD
THE CRESCENT
LARKSFIELD CL
MILESTONE RD
CLARE TERR
B4020
Shill Brook
Brize Norton
Airfield
4
The
Poplars
Springfield
House
Elmwood
House
05
Sewage
Works
Home
Farm
MILL LA
Mill
House
PH
Butlers
Court
Farm
Alvescot
Black
Bourton
BURFORD RD
Sch
3
Piggery
Glebe
Farm
Bedwell
Pond
THE GREEN
PEYSCOTT CL
College
PH
CHURCH CL
Park
Farm
STATION RD
SCHOOL LA
Lower End
04
SHILBROOK
MANOR
Glebe
Farm
B4020
Manor
Farm
Long
Copse
Dismantled Railway
2
Black Bourton Brook
Langhat Ditch
Clanfield Brook
03
Bazeland
CALCROFT LA
1
B4020
BLACK BOURTON RD
Edgerly
Farm
Chestlion
Farm
BOURTON CL
PH
BAMPTON RD
MARSH LA
POUND LA
A4095
02
26
27
28
D
E
F

134

152

116

133

A
B
C
4
3
2
1
05
04
03
02
29
30
31
Ven Bridge
Lower Haddon Farm
Piggery
A4095
Dismantled Railway
Lew Heath House
Wind Pump
STATION RD
Deanery Farm
Hobbs Buildings
Garson's Copse
Mill Farm
The Plantation
Highmoor Brook
Field Cottage
The Windmill
Bampton
Sch
Cemy
F Sta
Shill Brook
NEW RD
BUSHY ROW
BROAD ST
CHURCH VIEW
Liby
HIGH ST
ASTON RD
B4449
BUCKLAND RD
Ham Court
PH
BRIDGE ST
The Grange
Shill Brook
Cowleaze Corner
Weald Manor
Weald Manor Farm
WEALD ST
Blackhouse Farm
Weald Farm
Weald
Glebe Farm
Black Bourton Brook

153

117

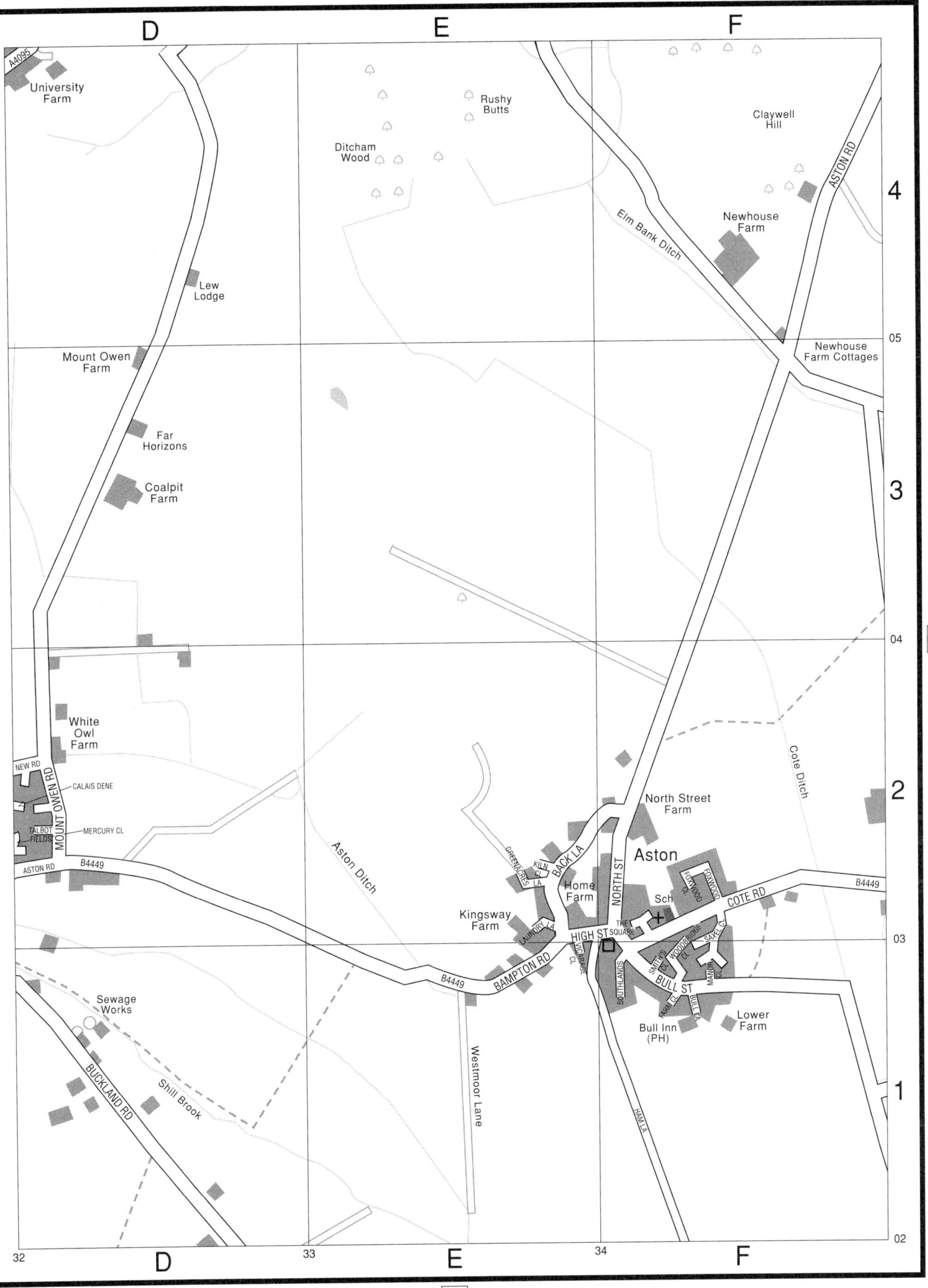
D
E
F
A4095
University Farm
Rushy Butts
Ditcham Wood
Claywell Hill
ASTON RD
4
Elm Bank Ditch
Newhouse Farm
Lew Lodge
05
Newhouse Farm Cottages
Mount Owen Farm
Far Horizons
Coalpit Farm
3
04
White Owl Farm
Cote Ditch
NEW RD
MOUNT OWEN RD
CALAIS DENE
TALBOT FIELDS
MERCURY CL
2
North Street Farm
Aston
ASTON RD
B4449
Aston Ditch
GREENACRES
KILN CL
LA
BACK LA
NORTH ST
Home Farm
FOXWOOD CL
FOXWOOD
Sch
COTE RD
B4449
Kingsway Farm
LAUNDRY LA
HIGH ST
THE SQUARE
WOODBRIDGE CL
SAXEL CL
SMITH'S CL
03
VICARAGE CL
BAMPTON RD
B4449
SOUTHLANDS
MANOR CL
BULL ST
FARM CL
BULL LA
Sewage Works
Lower Farm
Bull Inn (PH)
Westmoor Lane
1
BUCKLAND RD
Shill Brook
HAM LA
02
32
33
34

136

154

118

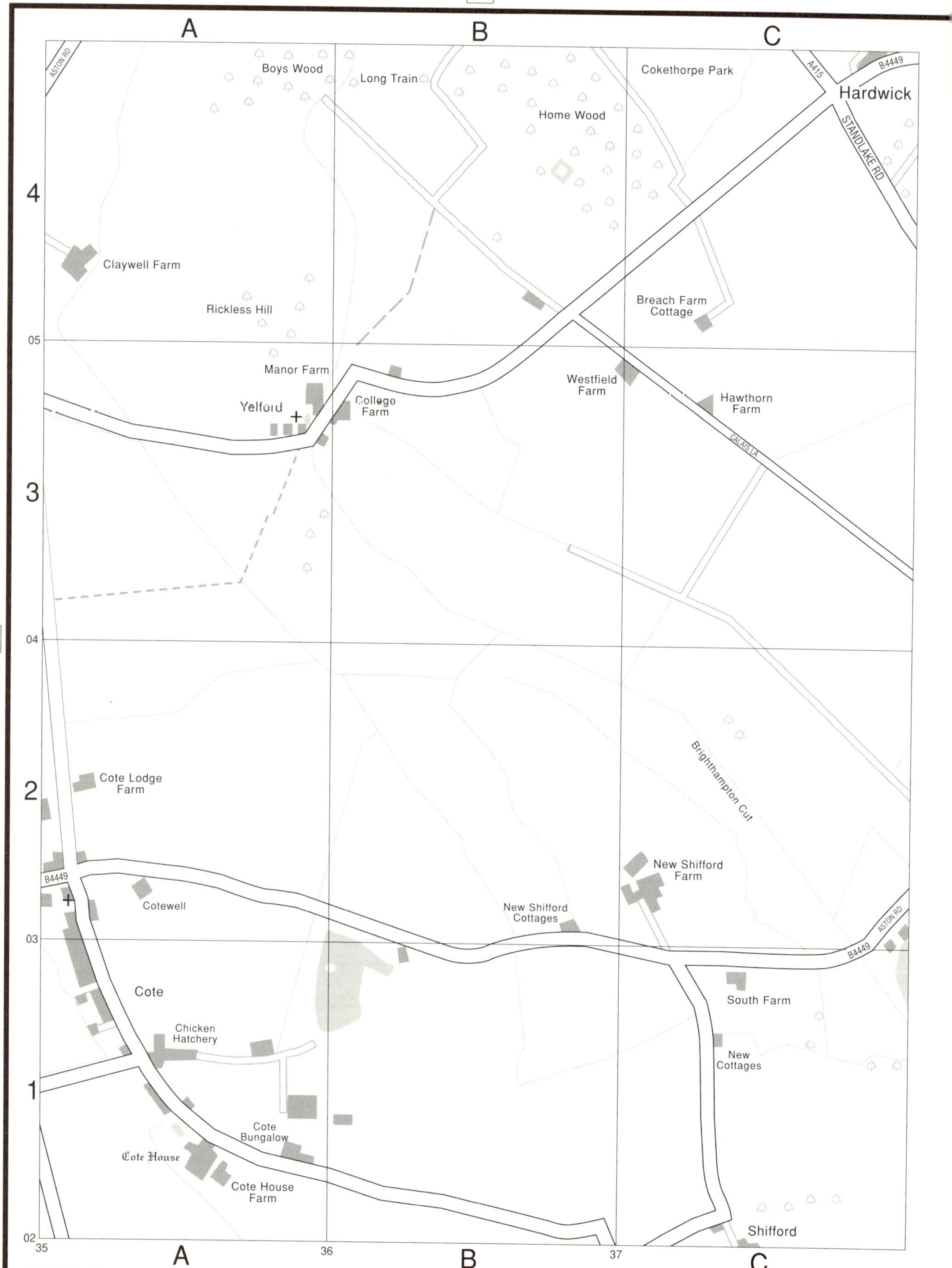
A
B
C
ASTON RD
Boys Wood
Long Train
Cokethorpe Park
A415
B4449
Hardwick
Home Wood
STANDLAKE RD
4
Claywell Farm
Rickless Hill
Breach Farm
Cottage
05
Manor Farm
Westfield
Farm
Yelford
College
Farm
Hawthorn
Farm
CALAIS LA
3
04
Brighthampton Cut
2
Cote Lodge
Farm
B4449
New Shifford
Farm
Cotewell
New Shifford
Cottages
ASTON RD
03
B4449
Cote
South Farm
Chicken
Hatchery
New
Cottages
1
Cote
Bungalow
Cote House
Cote House
Farm
Shifford
02
35
36
37
A
B
C

135

155

119

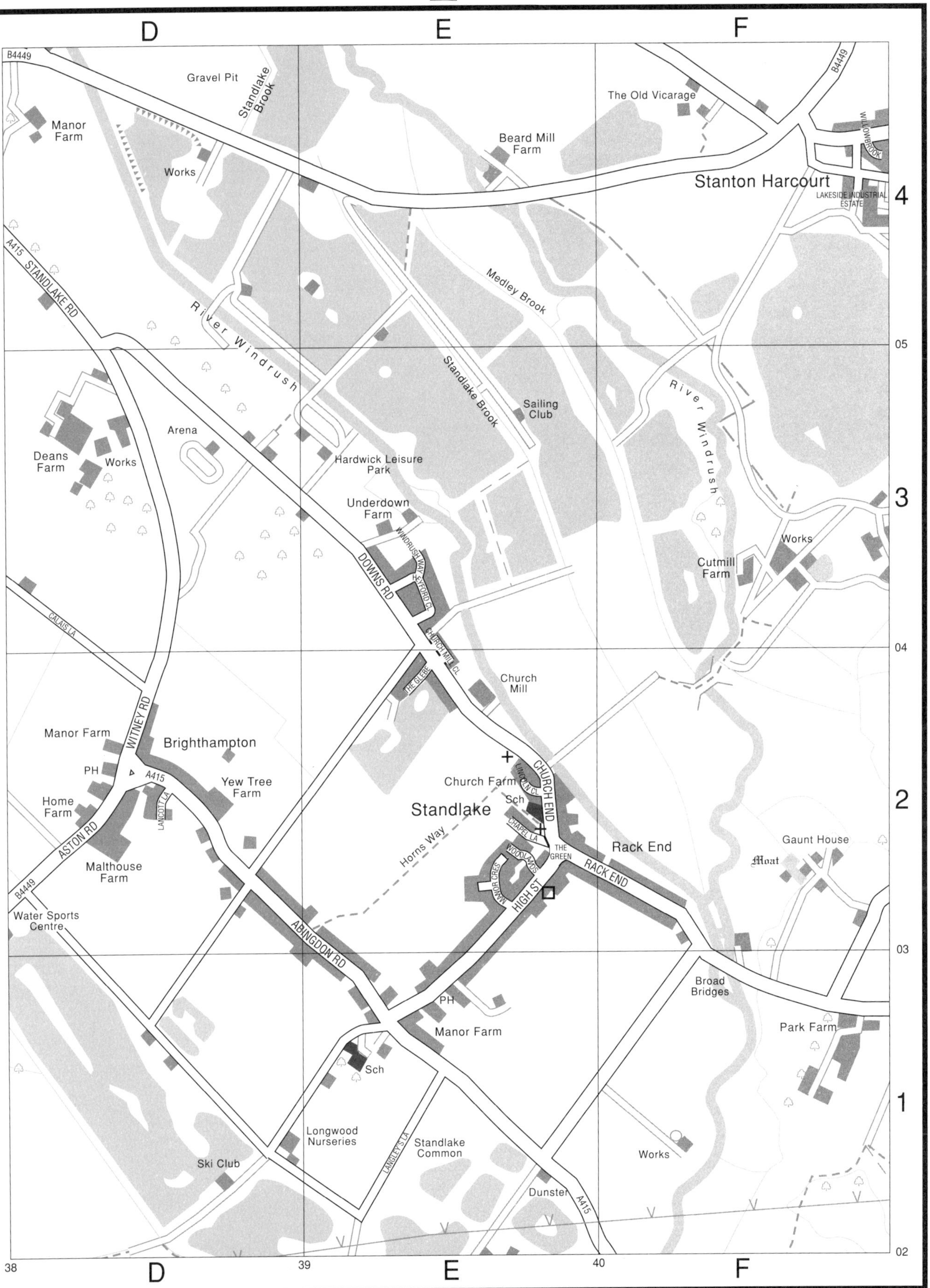
D
E
F
B4449
Gravel Pit
Standlake Brook
Manor Farm
Works
The Old Vicarage
Beard Mill Farm
Stanton Harcourt
WILLOWBROOK
LAKESIDE INDUSTRIAL ESTATE
4
A415 STANDLAKE RD
River Windrush
Medley Brook
05
Standlake Brook
Sailing Club
Arena
Deans Farm
Works
Hardwick Leisure Park
River Windrush
3
Underdown Farm
WINDRUSH WAY
HALEYFORD CL
DOWNS RD
Works
Cutmill Farm
CALAIS LA
CHURCH MILL CL
04
THE GLEBE
Church Mill
WITNEY RD
Manor Farm
Brighthampton
PH
A415
Yew Tree Farm
Home Farm
LANCOTT LA
ASTON RD
Malthouse Farm
Church Farm
LINCOLN CL
CHURCH END
Sch
Standlake
CHAPEL LA
2
Horns Way
WOODLANDS
THE GREEN
Rack End
RACK END
Gaunt House
Moat
MANOR CRES
HIGH ST
B4449
Water Sports Centre
ABINGDON RD
03
Broad Bridges
PH
Manor Farm
Park Farm
Sch
1
Longwood Nurseries
Standlake Common
LANGLEY'S LA
Works
Ski Club
Dunstey
A415
38
39
40
02
D
E
F

138

156

120

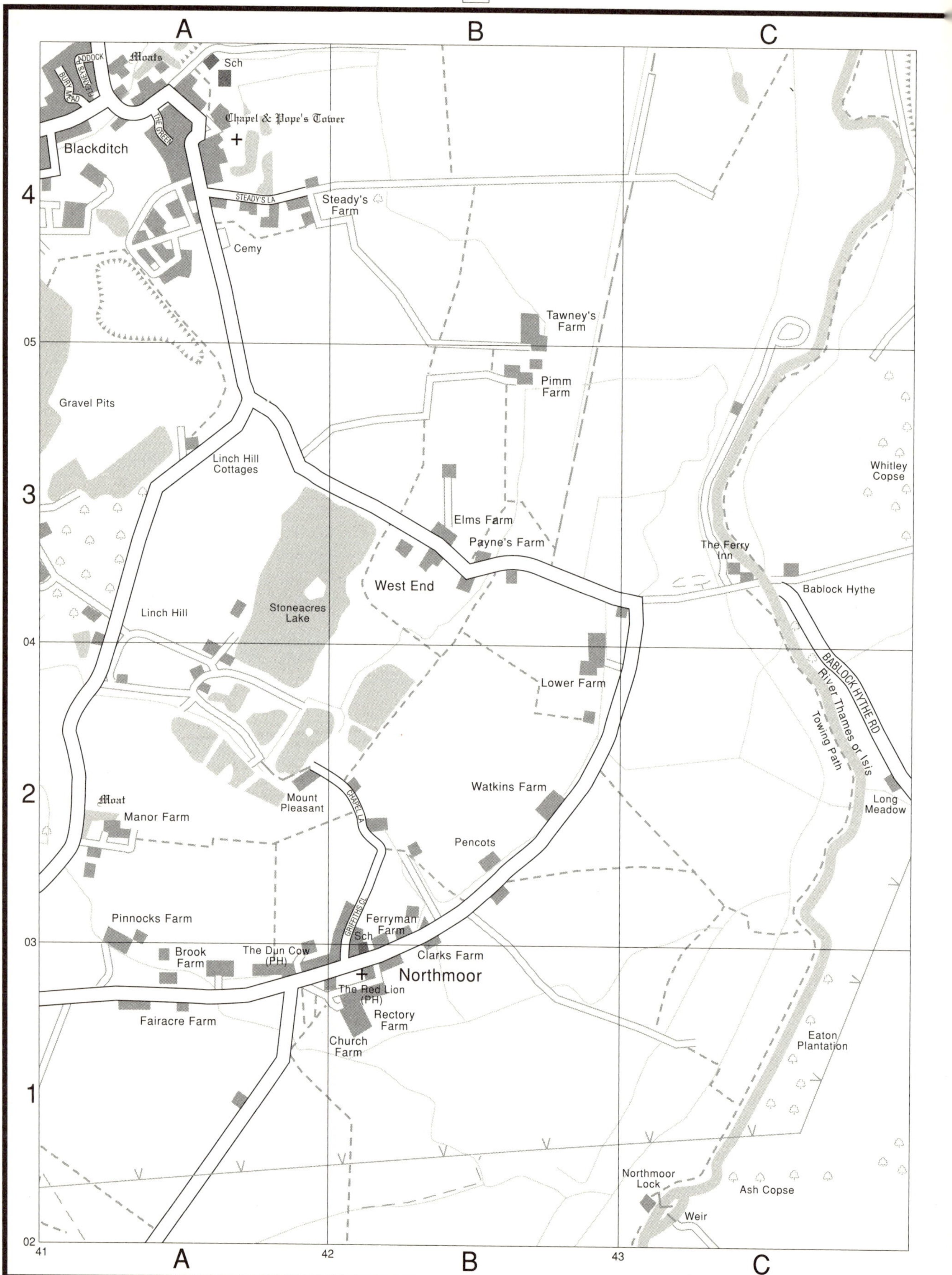

A
B
C
Moats
Sch
Chapel & Pope's Tower
BURY MEAD
THE GREEN
Blackditch
4
STEADY'S LA
Steady's Farm
Cemy
Tawney's Farm
05
Pimm Farm
Gravel Pits
Linch Hill Cottages
Whitley Copse
3
Elms Farm
Payne's Farm
The Ferry Inn
West End
Bablock Hythe
Stoneacres Lake
Linch Hill
04
Lower Farm
BABLOCK HYTHE RD
River Thames or Isis
Towing Path
Watkins Farm
2
Moat
Mount Pleasant
CHAPEL LA
Long Meadow
Manor Farm
Pencots
Pinnocks Farm
GRIFFITHS CL
Ferryman Farm
Sch
03
Brook Farm
The Dun Cow (PH)
Clarks Farm
Northmoor
The Red Lion (PH)
Rectory Farm
Fairacre Farm
Eaton Plantation
Church Farm
1
Northmoor Lock
Ash Copse
Weir
02
41
42
43

137

157

121

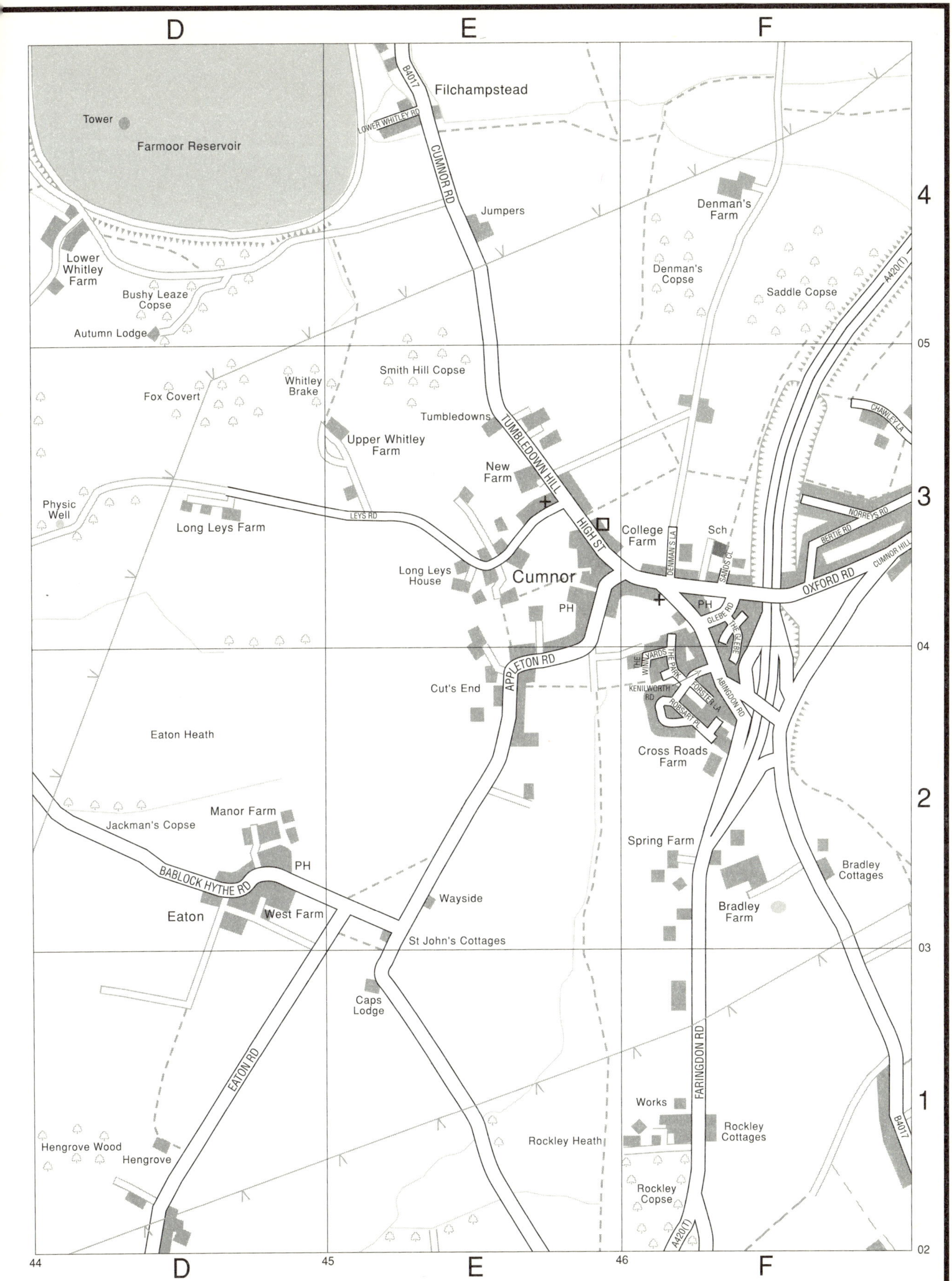

D
E
F
4
3
2
1
05
04
03
02
44
45
46
Filchampstead
B4017
LOWER WHITLEY RD
CUMNOR RD
Tower
Farmoor Reservoir
Jumpers
Denman's Farm
Lower Whitley Farm
Bushy Leaze Copse
Autumn Lodge
Denman's Copse
Saddle Copse
A420(T)
Smith Hill Copse
Whitley Brake
Fox Covert
Tumbledowns
TUMBLEDOWN HILL
CHAWLEY LA
Upper Whitley Farm
New Farm
Physic Well
Long Leys Farm
LEYS RD
HIGH ST
College Farm
Sch
NORREYS RD
BERTIE RD
DENMAN'S LA
SANDS CL
Long Leys House
Cumnor
OXFORD RD
CUMNOR HILL
PH
GLEBE RD
THE GLEBE
APPLETON RD
THE WINNYARDS
THE PARK
KENILWORTH RD
FORSTER LA
ROBSART PL
ABINGDON RD
Cut's End
Eaton Heath
Cross Roads Farm
Manor Farm
Jackman's Copse
Spring Farm
BABLOCK HYTHE RD
Bradley Cottages
Wayside
Bradley Farm
Eaton
West Farm
St John's Cottages
Caps Lodge
FARINGDON RD
EATON RD
Works
Rockley Cottages
Hengrove Wood
Hengrove
Rockley Heath
Rockley Copse
B4017
A420(T)

140

158

122

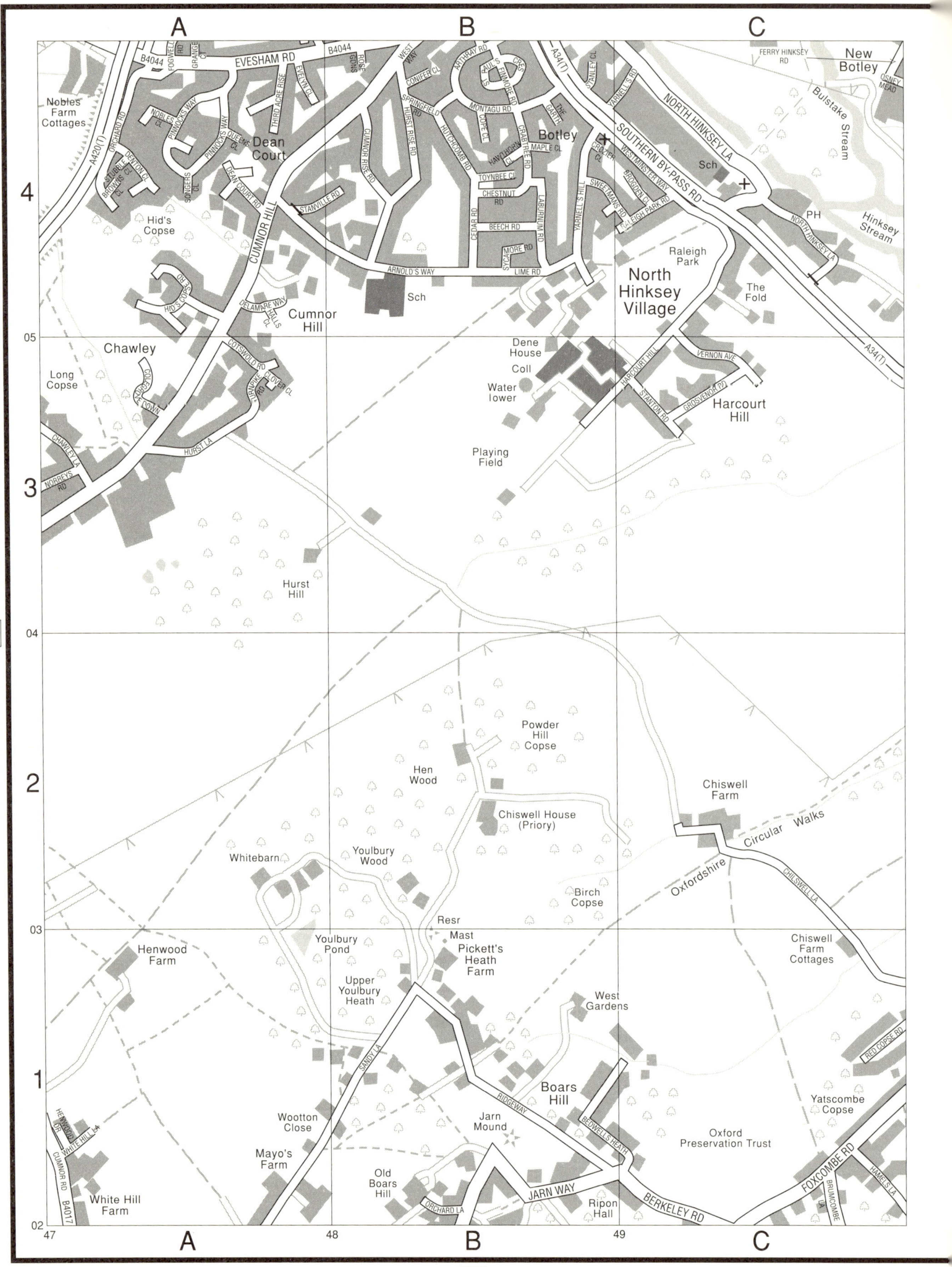
A
B
C
New Botley
Nobles Farm Cottages
Dean Court
Botley
Sch
PH
Bulstake Stream
Hinksey Stream
Hid's Copse
Raleigh Park
North Hinksey Village
The Fold
Cumnor Hill
Chawley
Long Copse
Dene House
Coll
Water Tower
Harcourt Hill
Playing Field
Hurst Hill
Powder Hill Copse
Hen Wood
Chiswell Farm
Chiswell House (Priory)
Oxfordshire Circular Walks
Whitebarn
Youlbury Wood
Birch Copse
Resr
Mast
Henwood Farm
Youlbury Pond
Pickett's Heath Farm
Chiswell Farm Cottages
Upper Youlbury Heath
West Gardens
Boars Hill
Yatscombe Copse
Wootton Close
Jarn Mound
Oxford Preservation Trust
Mayo's Farm
Old Boars Hill
Ripon Hall
White Hill Farm
EVESHAM RD
B4044
A420(T)
A34(T)
SOUTHERN BY-PASS RD
NORTH HINKSEY LA
FERRY HINKSEY RD
CUMNOR HILL
ARNOLD'S WAY
LIME RD
HURST LA
CHAWLEY LA
NORREYS RD
COTSWOLD RD
HARCOURT HILL
VERNON AVE
GROSVENOR RD
STANTON RD
CHILSWELL LA
SANDY LA
RIDGEWAY
BEDWELLS HEATH
JARN WAY
BERKELEY RD
FOXCOMBE RD
BRUMCOMBE LA
HAMELS LA
RED COPSE RD
ORCHARD LA
WHITE HILL LA
HENWOOD DR
CUMNOR RD
B4017
05
04
03
02
47
48
49
4
3
2
1

139

159

123

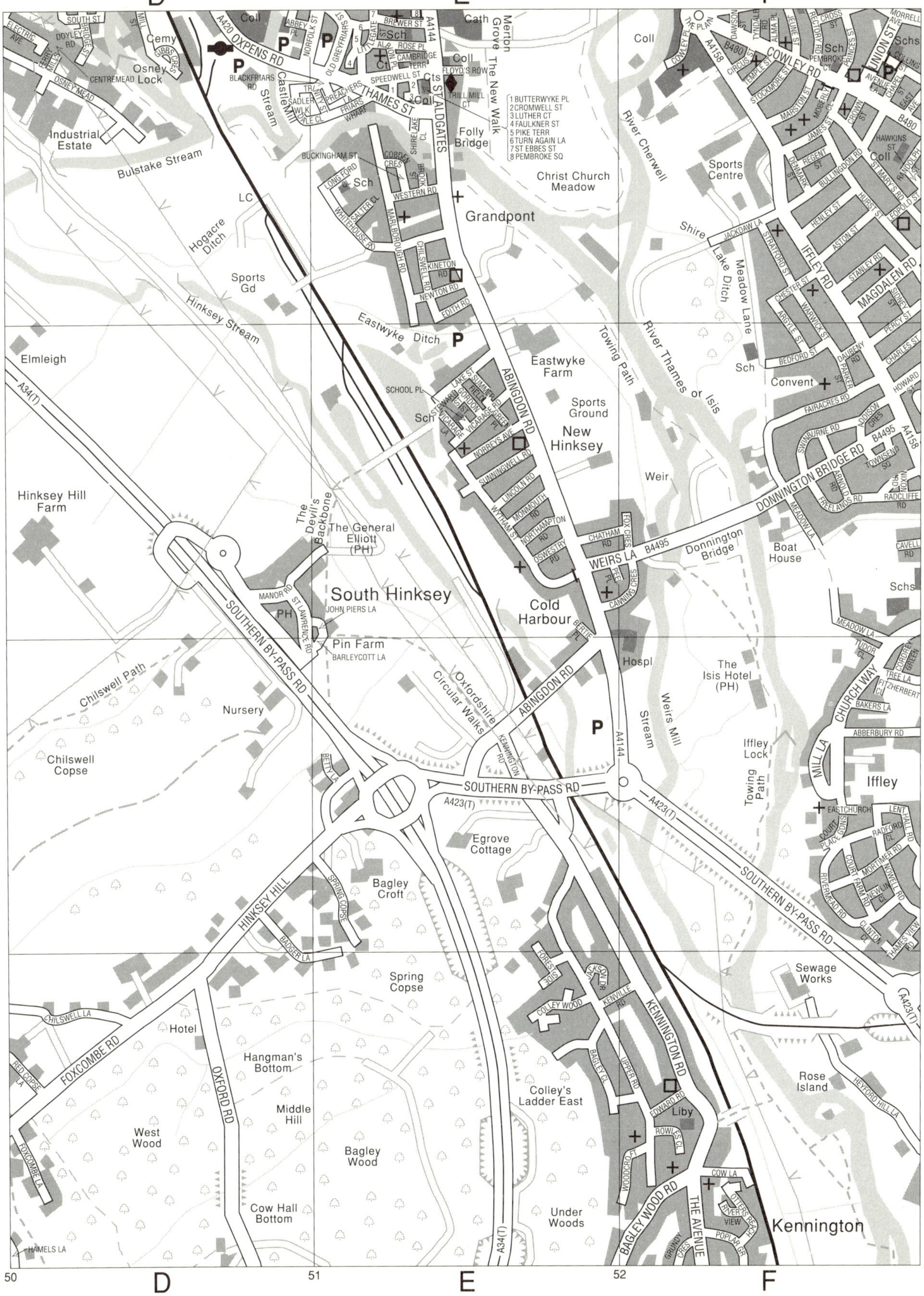
D
E
F
Coll
Cath
Merton Grove
The New Walk
Cemy
Osney Lock
Osney Mead
Industrial Estate
Centremead
Electric Ave
South St
Doyley Rd
Bridge St
Mill St
Gibbs Cres
A420 Oxpens Rd
Blackfriars Rd
Castle Mill Stream
Abbey Pl
Norfolk St
Old Greyfriars St
Littlegate St
Brewer St
Sch
Rose Pl
Cambridge Terr
Speedwell St
Thames St
Preachers La
Friars Wharf
Trinity St
Sadler Wlk
Floyd's Row
Trill Mill Ct
St Aldgates
A4144
Cts
Ct
1 Butterwyke Pl
2 Cromwell St
3 Luther Ct
4 Faulkner St
5 Pike Terr
6 Turn Again La
7 St Ebbes St
8 Pembroke Sq
Folly Bridge
Christ Church Meadow
River Cherwell
Bulstake Stream
Buckingham St
Long Ford Cl
Cobden Cres
Shirelake Cl
Brook St
Western Rd
Salter Cl
Whitehouse Rd
Marlborough Rd
Chilswell Rd
Kineton Rd
Newton Rd
Edith Rd
Grandpont
LC
Hogacre Ditch
Sports Gd
Hinksey Stream
Eastwyke Ditch
Elmleigh
A34(T)
School Pl
Lake St
Summerfield
Gordon St
Vicarage Rd
Vicarage La
Green Pl
Norreys Ave
Sunningwell Rd
Lincoln Rd
Monmouth Rd
Northampton Rd
Oswestry Rd
Wytham St
Abingdon Rd
Eastwyke Farm
Sports Ground
New Hinksey
Towing Path
River Thames or Isis
Weir
Sports Centre
Shire Lake Ditch
Meadow Lane
Jackdaw La
Sch
Convent
Cowley Pl
The Plain
A4158
B480
Circus St
Temple St
Cowley Rd
Stockmore St
Marston St
Moberly Cl
James St
Denmark St
Regent St
Bullingdon Rd
Henley St
Hurst St
Aston St
Stratford St
Iffley Rd
Chester St
Warwick St
Argyle St
Bedford St
Daubeny Rd
Parker St
Magdalen Rd
Stanley Rd
Sidney St
Percy St
Charles St
Howard St
Fairacres Rd
Swinburne Rd
Addison Cres
B4495
Townsend Sq
Donnington Bridge Rd
Arnold Rd
Freelands Rd
Radcliffe Rd
Meadow La
Union St
Pembroke St
Princes St
Cross St
Morrell Ave
Schs
Collins St
Chapel St
East Ave
Hawkins St
Randolph St
St Mary's Rd
Leopold St
Crown St
Avenue La
Hinksey Hill Farm
The Devil's Backbone
The General Elliott (PH)
South Hinksey
Manor Rd
St Lawrence Rd
John Piers La
PH
Pin Farm
Barleycott La
Chatham Rd
Fox Cres
Weirs La
B4495
Donnington Bridge
Peel Pl
Canning Cres
Cold Harbour
Bertie Pl
Boat House
Cavell Rd
Schs
Meadow La
Tudor Cl
Cordrey Green
Tree La
Fitzherbert Cl
Bakers La
Church Way
Abberbury Rd
Chilswell Path
Nursery
Oxfordshire Circular Walks
Hospl
The Isis Hotel (PH)
Weirs Mill Stream
Chilswell Copse
Betty La
Kennington Rd
Southern By-Pass Rd
A423(T)
Iffley Lock
Towing Path
Mill La
Iffley
Eastchurch
Court Place Gdns
Lenthall Rd
Radford Cl
Mortimer Rd
Court Farm Rd
Newlin Cl
Nowell Rd
Rivermead Rd
Clinton Cl
Thames View Rd
Egrove Cottage
Bagley Croft
Spring Copse
Hinksey Hill
Badger La
Spring Copse
Sewage Works
Forest Side
Jackson Dr
Colley Wood
Kenville Rd
Chilswell La
Hotel
Foxcombe Rd
Red Copse La
Oxford Rd
Hangman's Bottom
Middle Hill
Bagley Cl
Upper Rd
Colley's Ladder East
Liby
Edward Rd
Rowles Cl
Rose Island
Heyford Hill La
West Wood
Foxcombe La
Bagley Wood
Woodcroft
Cow Hall Bottom
Under Woods
Bagley Wood Rd
The Avenue
Cow La
Otters Reach
Riverview
Poplar Gr
Grundy Cres
Kennington
Hamels La
Hospl
A34(T)
4
3
2
1
05
04
03
02
50
51
52

142

160

124

141

A
B
C
4
3
2
1
05
04
03
02
53
54
55
MORRELL AVE
Hospital
DIVINITY RD
CH
Boundary Brook
Golf Course
Hospital
WARREN CRES
THE SLADE
Open Magdalen
1 BRACEGIRDLE RD
1 ABBOTS WOOD (W)
2 ABBOTS WOOD (E)
Brasenose Wood
Sports Gd
Conv
MAGDALEN RD
COWLEY RD
Sch
HOWARD ST
Barracks La
Cowley Marsh
F Sta
Hospital
HORSPATH DRIFTWAY
Brasenose Farm
Industrial Estate
Allot Gdns
MARSH RD
CRESCENT RD
HOLLOW WAY
HORSPATH RD
OXFORD RD
Schs
Temple Cowley
Liby
Florence Park
IFFLEY RD
RYMERS LA
1 RADCLIFFE RD
Works
EASTERN BY-PASS RD
John Allen Centre
BETWEEN TOWNS RD
CHURCH COWLEY RD
Cowley
TURN
Cemy
GARSINGTON RD
ROSE HILL
1 SHEEPWAY CT
2 WEST VIEW
Rose Hill
Stadium
WATLINGTON RD
COUNTY TRADING EST
1 PRUNUS CL
2 PINE CL
Recn Gd
SANDY LA W
BLACKBIRD LEYS RD
CUDDESDON WAY
Park
Blackbird Leys
Ind Est
Playing Field
Littlemore
SANDFORD RD
Hospital
Littlemore Brook
Minchery Farm
Northfield Brook
Blackbird Leys Farm
Sewage Works
1 STRAWBERRY PATH
2 BUTTERWORTH PL
1 JASMINE CL
2 TIMOTHY WAY
3 REST HARROW
4 STARWORT PATH
5 PERIWINKLE PL
A4142
A4158
A423(T)
B480
B4495

161

125

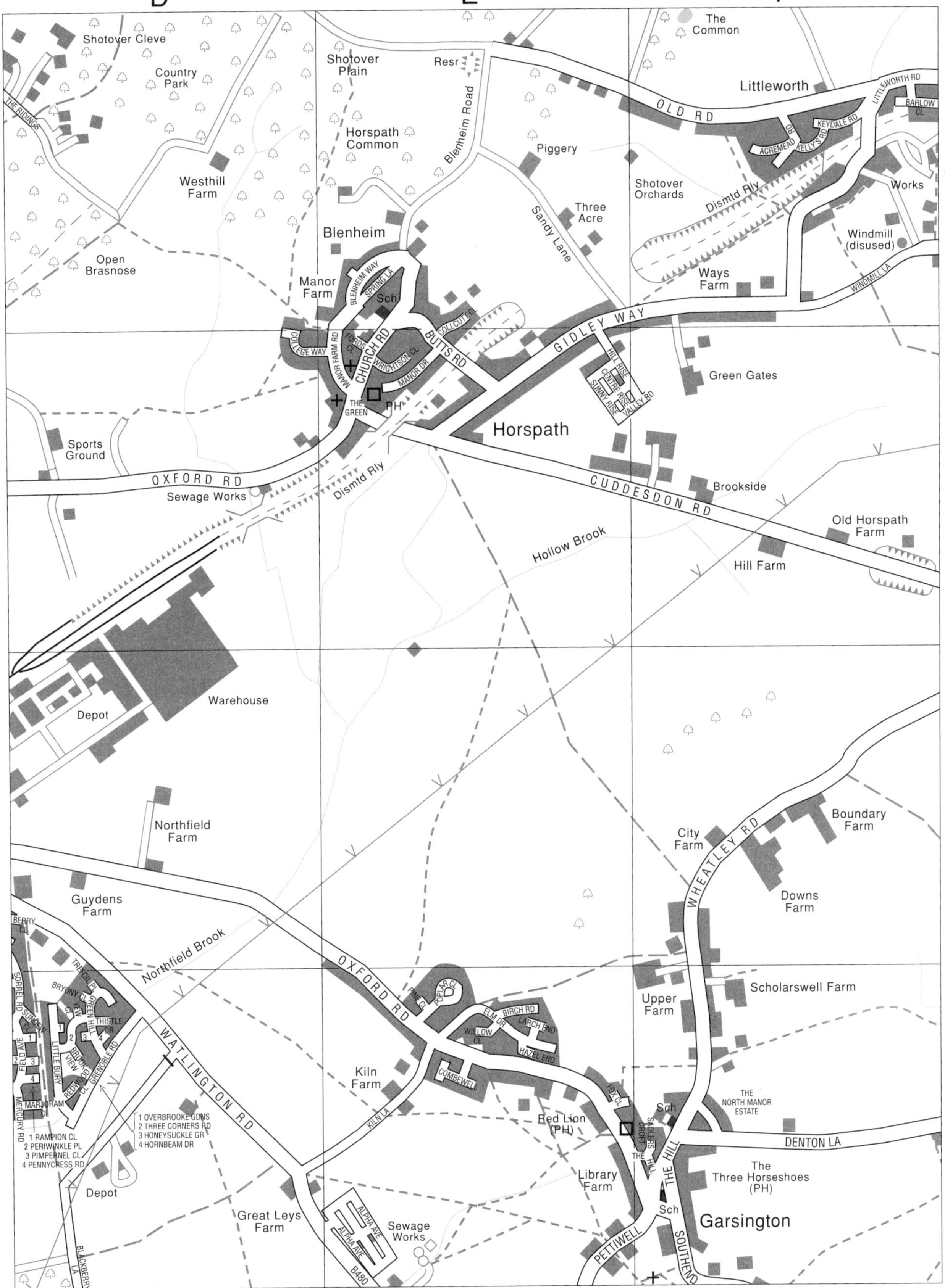
D
E
F
Shotover Cleve
Country Park
Shotover Plain
Resr
Blenheim Road
Horspath Common
The Common
Littleworth
OLD RD
LITTLEWORTH RD
BARLOW CL
KEYDALE RD
ACREMEAD RD
KELLY'S RD
THE RIDINGS
Westhill Farm
Piggery
Shotover Orchards
Dismtd Rly
Works
Three Acre
Sandy Lane
Windmill (disused)
Blenheim
Open Brasnose
Manor Farm
BLENHEIM WAY
SPRING LA
Sch
Ways Farm
WINDMILL LA
COLLCUTT CL
GIDLEY WAY
COLLEGE WAY
MANOR FARM RD
FORDS CL
CHURCH RD
BUTTS RD
WRIGHTSON CL
MANOR DR
HILL RISE
CENTRE RISE
SUNNY RISE
VALLEY RD
Green Gates
THE GREEN
PH
Horspath
Sports Ground
OXFORD RD
Sewage Works
Dismtd Rly
CUDDESDON RD
Brookside
Old Horspath Farm
Hollow Brook
Hill Farm
Warehouse
Depot
Northfield Farm
Boundary Farm
City Farm
WHEATLEY RD
Downs Farm
Guydens Farm
BERRY CL
Northfield Brook
OXFORD RD
TREVOR PL
SORREL RD
SUNNY RISE
BRYONY CL
GREEN HILL
THISTLE DR
FIELD AVE
LITTLE BURY
BROOK VIEW
REDWOOD CL
GRENOBLE RD
MARJORAM CL
MERCURY RD
1 RAMPION CL
2 PERIWINKLE PL
3 PIMPERNEL CL
4 PENNYCRESS RD
1 OVERBROOKE GDNS
2 THREE CORNERS RD
3 HONEYSUCKLE GR
4 HORNBEAM DR
WATLINGTON RD
Depot
BLACKBERRY LA
Upper Farm
Scholarswell Farm
PINE CL
POPLAR CL
ELM DR
BIRCH RD
LARCH END
WILLOW CL
HAZEL END
Kiln Farm
COMBEWELL
KILN LA
FOX CL
Red Lion (PH)
Sch
THE CROFT
SOLLERS HILL
THE HILL
THE NORTH MANOR ESTATE
DENTON LA
The Three Horseshoes (PH)
Library Farm
Great Leys Farm
ALPHA AVE
Sewage Works
B480
PETTIWELL
Sch
SOUTHEND
Garsington
05
04
03
02
4
3
2
1
56
57
58

144

162

126

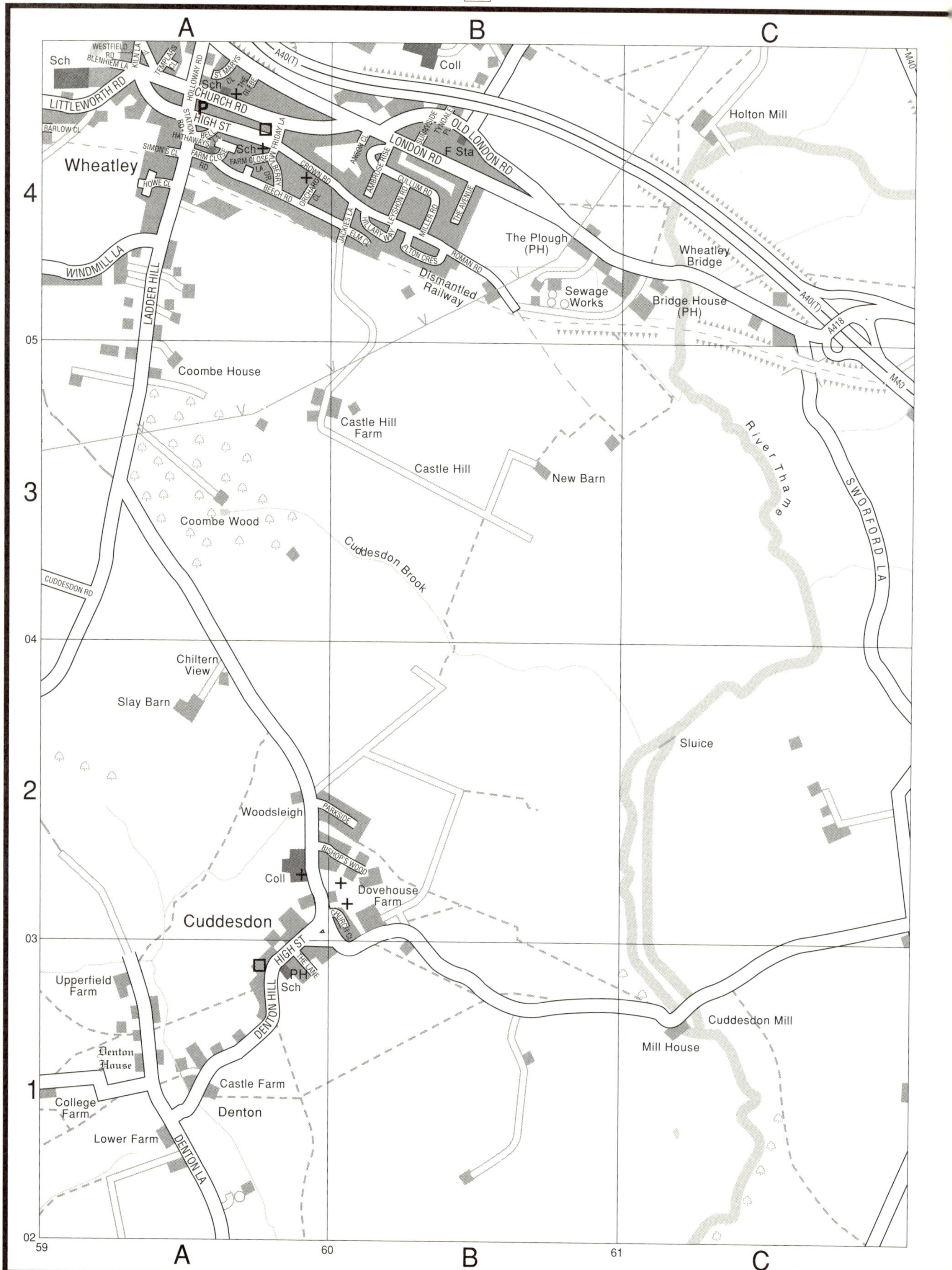
A
B
C
A
B
C
4
3
2
1
05
04
03
02
59
60
61
Sch
WESTFIELD RD
BLENHEIM LA
KILN LA
TEMPLARS CL
HOLLOWAY RD
ST MARY'S CL
THE GLEBE
LITTLEWORTH RD
CHURCH RD
BARLOW CL
HIGH ST
STATION RD
BELL LA
HATHAWAYS
FRIDAY LA
SIMON'S CL
FARM CLOSE RD
FARM CLOSE LA
MULBERRY DR
CROWN RD
ORCHARD CL
BEECH RD
Wheatley
HOWE CL
A40(T)
Coll
SUNNYSIDE
TYNDALE PL
OLD LONDON RD
LONDON RD
F Sta
ANSON CL
AMBROSE RISE
CULLUM RD
LEYSHON RD
MILLER RD
THE AVENUE
JACKIES LA
HILLARY WAY
ELM CL
ELTON CRES
ROMAN RD
Dismantled Railway
WINDMILL LA
LADDER HILL
The Plough (PH)
Sewage Works
Holton Mill
Wheatley Bridge
Bridge House (PH)
A418
M40
Coombe House
Castle Hill Farm
Castle Hill
New Barn
Coombe Wood
Cuddesdon Brook
River Thame
SWORFORD LA
CUDDESDON RD
Chiltern View
Slay Barn
Sluice
Woodsleigh
PARKSIDE
BISHOP'S WOOD
Coll
Dovehouse Farm
CHURCH CL
Cuddesdon
HIGH ST
THE LANE
PH
Sch
Upperfield Farm
DENTON HILL
Cuddesdon Mill
Mill House
Denton House
Castle Farm
College Farm
Denton
Lower Farm
DENTON LA

143

163

127

D
E
F
M40
Waterstock House
Stockwell Lane
Waterstock
Manor Farm
Draycot
Albury Farm
Bow Bridge
River Thame
Waterstock Mill
Home Farm
Oxfordshire Way
ICKFORD RD
NORTH CL
BROOKSIDE CL
The Fox (PH)
Tiddington
A418
Hyde Spinney
ALBURY VIEW
A418
OXFORD RD
Lower Farm
05
Walter's Farm
Chilworth House
Dismantled Railway
4
Holloway Farm
3
M40
Sandylane Farm
Lower Chilworth Farm
SANDY LA
LONDON RD
04
Chilworth Farm
Camp Corner
Branscrouch
Trindalls Farm
OLD LONDON RD
SWORFORD LA
CHILWORTH RD
2
M40
Sewage Works
Heath Farm
Tripps Farm
Orpwoods Farm
LOWER END
A329
POTTS CL
Sch
Kings Head (PH)
03
PEGSWELL LA
HIGH ST
GREEN HITCHINGS
FULLERS FIELD
Mount Pleasant Farm
Sch
THAME RD
Green Ways
Great Milton
CHURCH RD
Mill House
1
The Views
THE FORTIES
LYCH GATE LA
Windmill (disused)
Milton Common
Romeyns Court
Manor Farm
Haseley Estate
Glebe Farm
A329
02
62
63
64
D
E
F

146

164

128

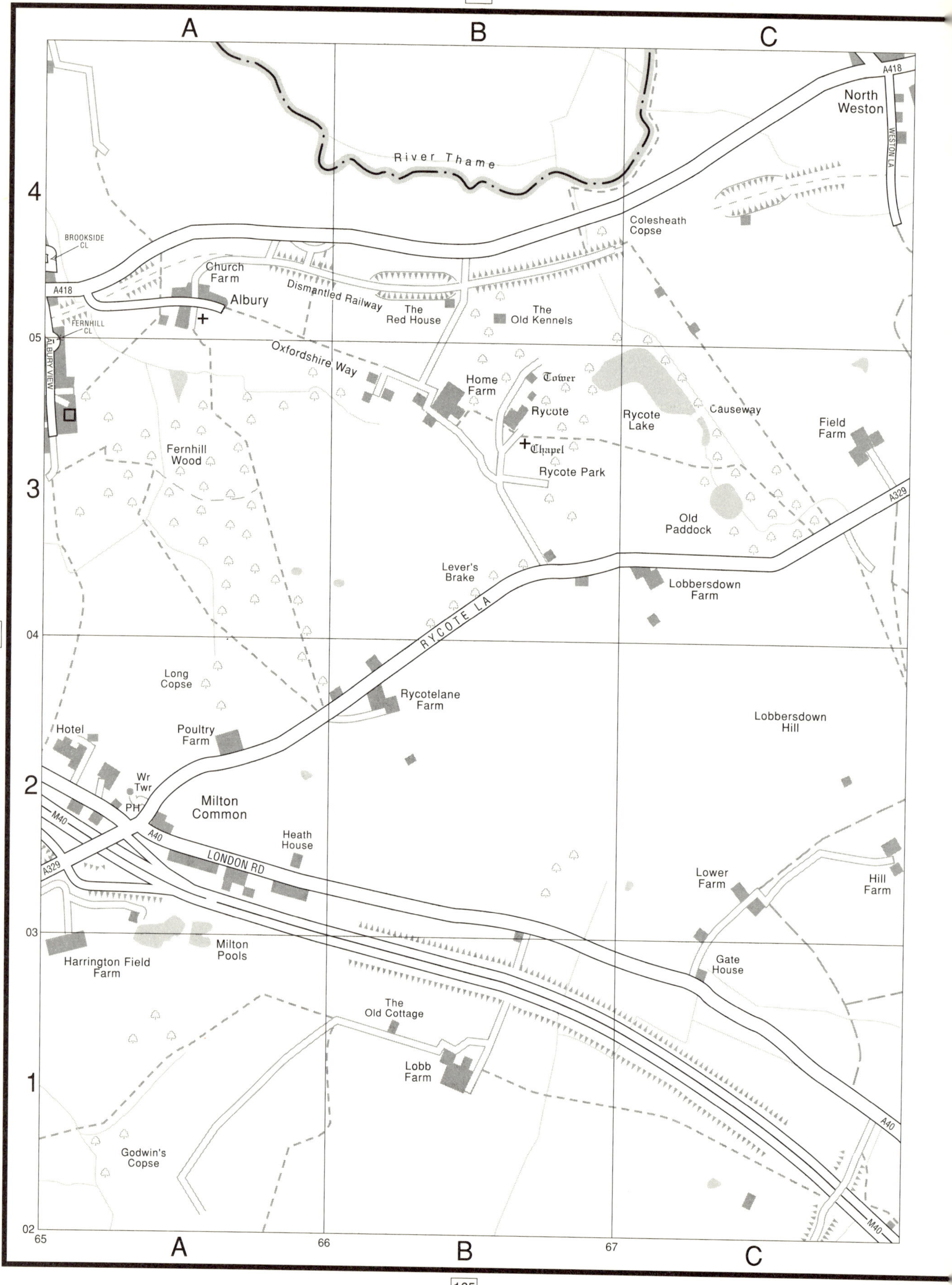
A
B
C
River Thame
A418
North Weston
WESTON LA
4
BROOKSIDE CL
Colesheath Copse
Church Farm
A418
Albury
Dismantled Railway
The Red House
The Old Kennels
FERNHILL CL
05
ALBURY VIEW
Oxfordshire Way
Home Farm
Tower
Rycote
Rycote Lake
Causeway
Field Farm
Chapel
Fernhill Wood
Rycote Park
3
A329
Old Paddock
Lever's Brake
Lobbersdown Farm
RYCOTE LA
04
Long Copse
Rycotelane Farm
Lobbersdown Hill
Hotel
Poultry Farm
2
Wr Twr
PH
Milton Common
M40
A40
Heath House
A329
LONDON RD
Lower Farm
Hill Farm
03
Milton Pools
Harrington Field Farm
Gate House
The Old Cottage
1
Lobb Farm
A40
Godwin's Copse
M40
02
65
66
67
A
B
C

145

165

129

D
E
F
A418
A329
OXFORD RD
RYCOTE LA
B4012
B4445
Sch
Abbey Farm
Manor Farm
Dismantled Railway
Works
Depot
BROOK LA
MITCHELL CL
SPRING PATH
BEECH RD
CHESTNUT AVE
HAZEL AVE
SYCAMORE DR
CEDAR CRES
HAWTHORN AVE
Recn Gd
SHARMAN BEER CT
THAME
WELLINGTON ST
UPPER HIGH ST
NORTH ST
BUTTER MARKET
CORN MARKET
HIGH ST
HAZELTON CL
LINCOLN PL
DORCHESTER PL
SOUTHERN RD
ROOKS LA
NELSON ST
SWAN WK
PLAYHOUSE CT
ST ANDREW CT
KING'S
EAST ST
PARK ST
BELMONT MEWS
GOODSONS IND MEWS
F Sta
Liby
HOLLIERS CL
MORETON LA
ARNOLD WAY
PEARCE CT
COOMBE HILL CRES
CONDUIT HILL RISE
WINDMILL RD
ELMS RD
BROOK WATERS
HAMPDEN AVE
VAN DIEMAN'S RD
Recn Gd
Depot
Batesleys Farm
Moreton Farm
THE FURLONGS
Leys Farm
Elmtree Farm
Chestnut Farm
PH
Moreton
Meadowbrook Farm
Cuttle Brook
Greys Mead
Lobbersdown-hill Farm
Parkgrange Farm
Thame Park
Moreton Gap
Oxfordshire Way
Moretonfield Farm
Moretongap Wood
Lodges
Musgrave's Covert
Osierbed Wood
Horsenden Hill
Judd's Lane
Spencer's Farm
Tetsworth Common
Sewage Works
Fox Covert
Upper Atlington Wood
HIGH ST
A40
MARSH END
05
04
03
02
4
3
2
1
68
69
70

148

166

130

147

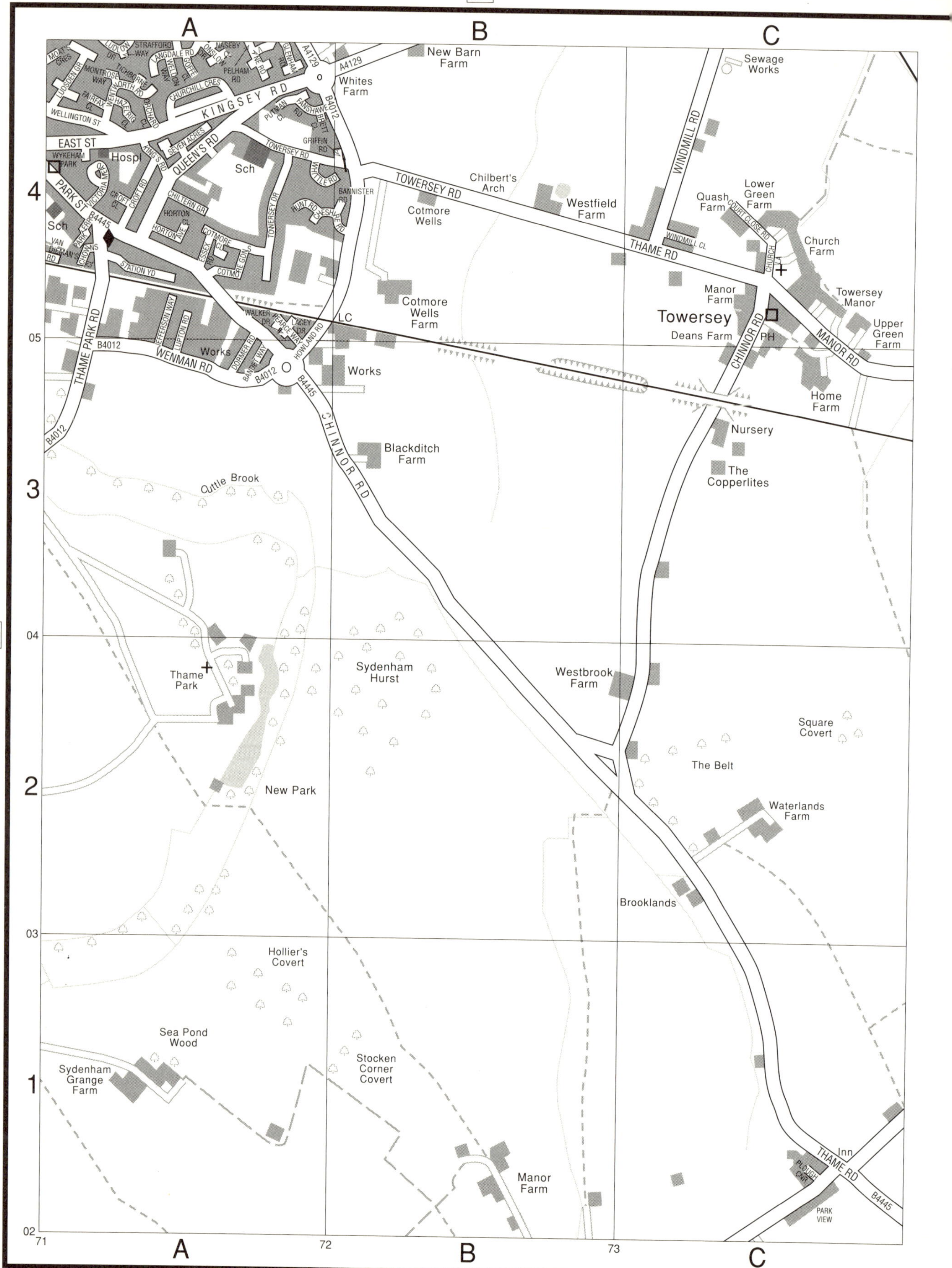
A
B
C
4
3
2
1
05
04
03
02
71
72
73
New Barn Farm
Whites Farm
Sewage Works
A4129
B4012
KINGSEY RD
EAST ST
WELLINGTON ST
WYKEHAM PARK
Hospl
Sch
QUEEN'S RD
SEVEN ACRES
TOWERSEY RD
PARK ST
VICTORIA MEAD
CHILTERN GR
HORTON CL
COTMORE CL
ESSEX RD
TOWERSEY DR
STATION YD
VAN DIEMAN'S RD
B4445
THAME PARK RD
WENMAN RD
JEFFERSON WAY
LUPTON RD
Works
DORMER RD
BANDET WAY
HOWLAND RD
WALKER DR
PEARCE WAY
LACEY DR
LC
BANNISTER RD
GRIFFIN RD
WHITTLE RD
HUNT RD
CHESHIRE RD
FANSHAWE RD
PUTMAN CL
BRETT CL
STRAFFORD WAY
NASEBY CL
LUDLOW DR
MOATS CRES
LUDSDEN GR
MONTROSE WAY
FAIRFAX CL
CHURCHILL CRES
PELHAM RD
LANGDALE RD
TICHBORNE
WENTWORTH RD
HAZEL RD
ORCHARD CL
Chilbert's Arch
Cotmore Wells
Westfield Farm
Cotmore Wells Farm
WINDMILL RD
WINDMILL CL
THAME RD
Quash Farm
Lower Green Farm
COURT CLOSE RD
Church Farm
CHURCH LA
Manor Farm
Towersey Manor
Towersey
Deans Farm
PH
Upper Green Farm
MANOR RD
CHINNOR RD
Home Farm
Nursery
The Copperlites
Blackditch Farm
CHINNOR RD
Cuttle Brook
Thame Park
Sydenham Hurst
Westbrook Farm
Square Covert
The Belt
New Park
Waterlands Farm
Brooklands
Hollier's Covert
Sea Pond Wood
Sydenham Grange Farm
Stocken Corner Covert
Manor Farm
Inn
THAME RD
PLOUGH CNR
PARK VIEW
B4445

167

not continued, see key diagram

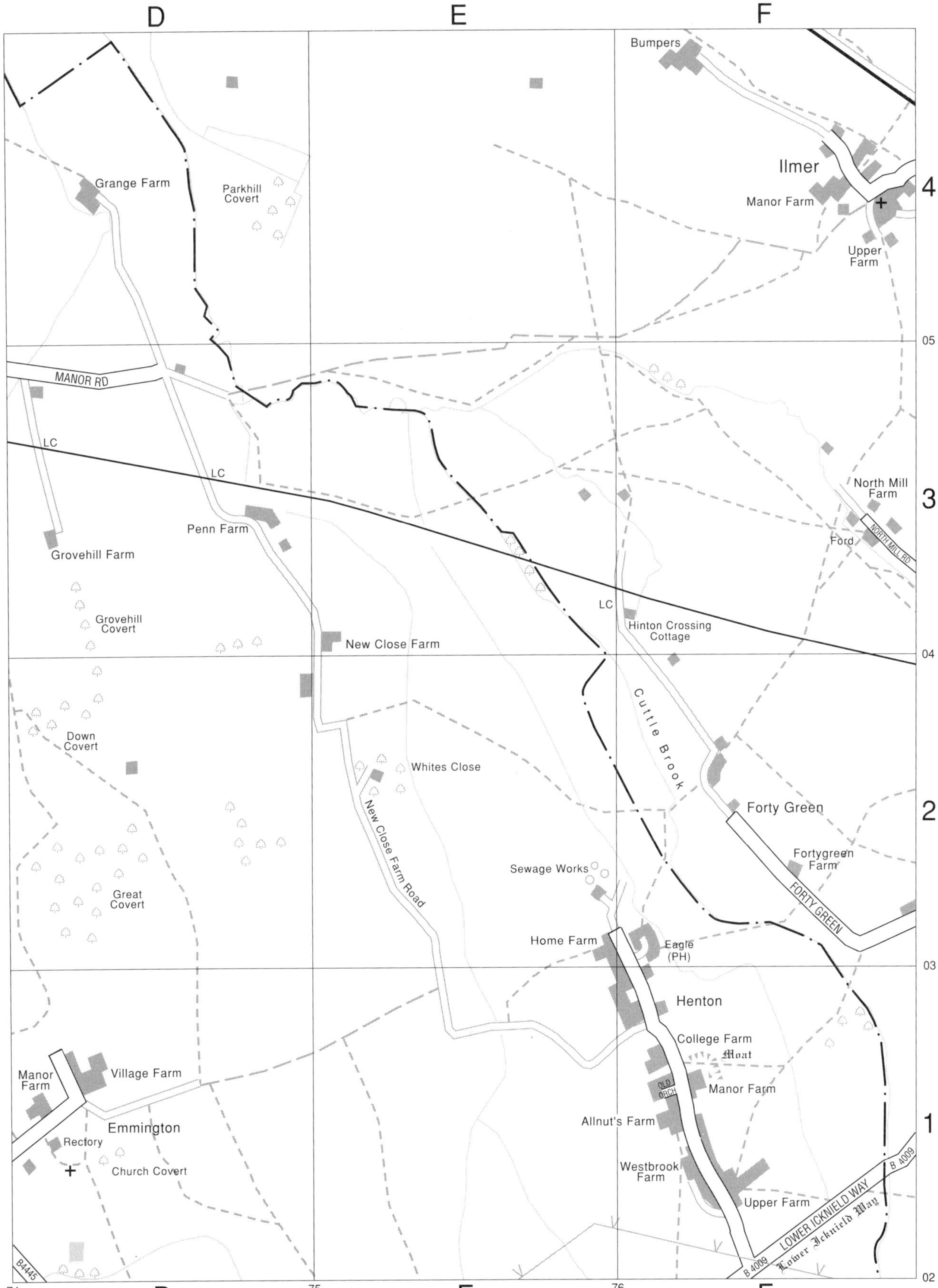

not continued, see key diagram

168

131

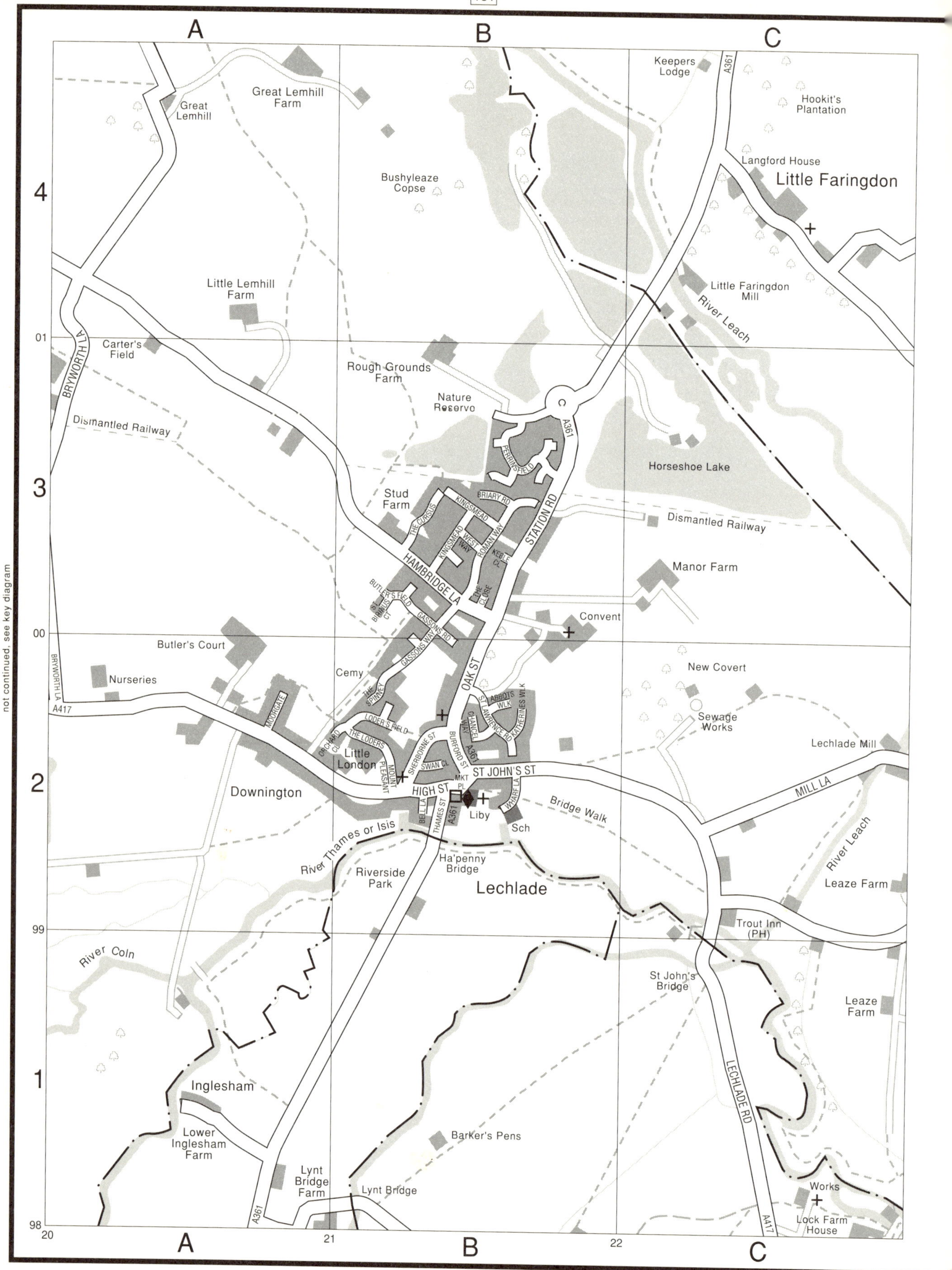
A
B
C
4
3
2
1
01
00
99
98
20
21
22
Great Lemhill
Great Lemhill Farm
Bushyleaze Copse
Keepers Lodge
Hookit's Plantation
Langford House
Little Faringdon
Little Faringdon Mill
River Leach
Little Lemhill Farm
Carter's Field
BRYWORTH LA
Rough Grounds Farm
Nature Reserve
Dismantled Railway
Horseshoe Lake
Stud Farm
PERRINSFIELD
BRIARY RD
KINGSMEAD
THE CURSUS
WEST WAY
ROMAN WAY
KEBLE CL
STATION RD
A361
HAMBRIDGE LA
THE CLOSE
Manor Farm
BUTLER'S FIELD
GASSONS RD
GASSONS WAY
Convent
Butler's Court
Nurseries
Cemy
OAK ST
New Covert
A417
MOORGATE
THE SPINNEY
LODER'S FIELD
THE LODERS
ORCHARD CL
ABBOTS WLK
ST LAWRENCE RD
KATHERINES WLK
CHANCEL WAY
BURFORD ST
SHERBORNE ST
SWAN CL
Sewage Works
Lechlade Mill
Little London
MOUNT PLEASANT
MKT PL
ST JOHN'S ST
MILL LA
Downington
HIGH ST
BELL LA
THAMES ST
Liby
WHARF LA
Sch
Bridge Walk
River Thames or Isis
Ha'penny Bridge
Riverside Park
Lechlade
Leaze Farm
Trout Inn (PH)
River Coln
St John's Bridge
Leaze Farm
Inglesham
LECHLADE RD
Lower Inglesham Farm
Barker's Pens
Lynt Bridge Farm
Lynt Bridge
Works
Lock Farm House
not continued, see key diagram

170

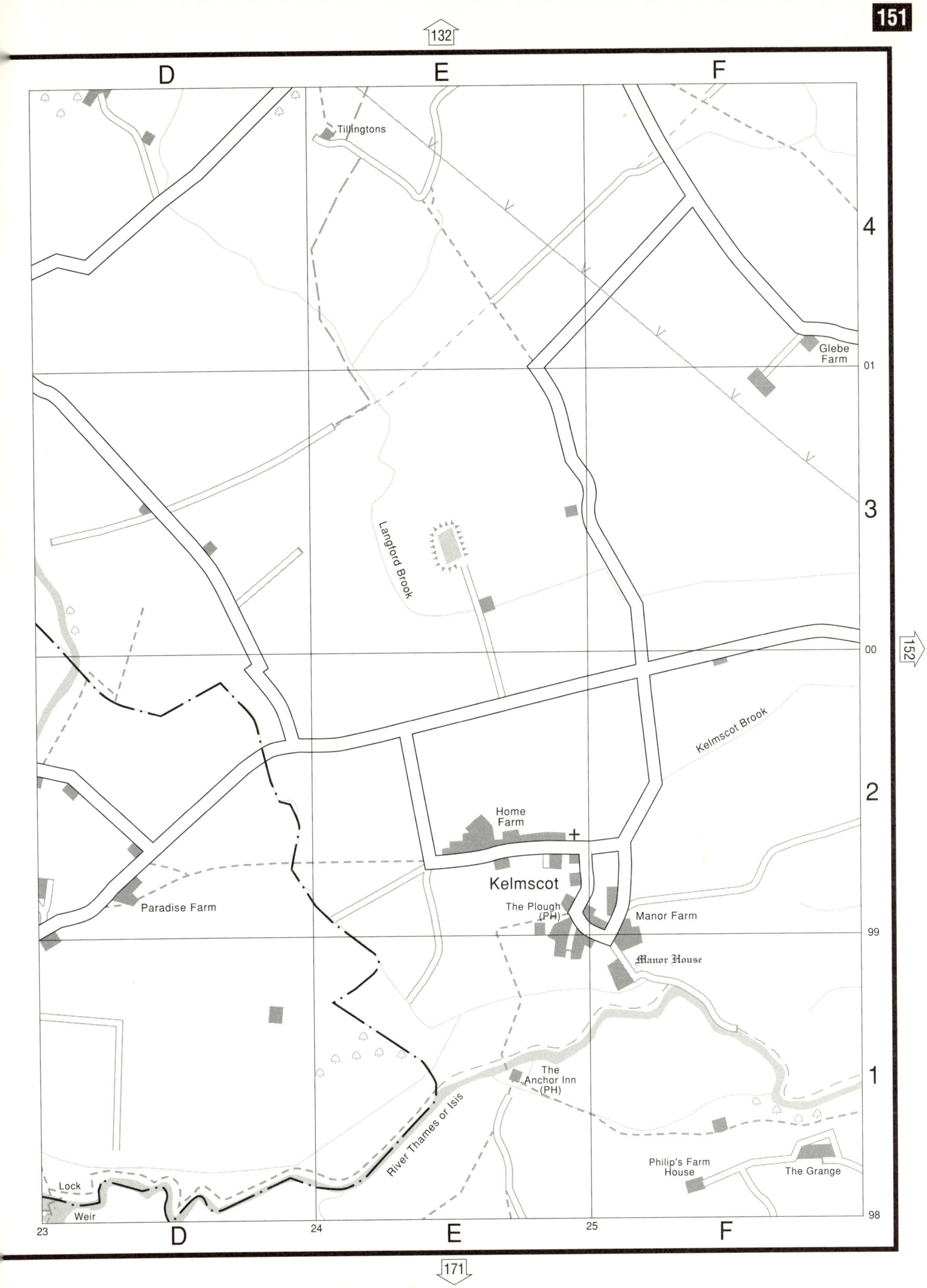
132
D
E
F
Tillingtons
4
Glebe Farm
01
3
Langford Brook
00
152
Kelmscot Brook
2
Home Farm
Kelmscot
The Plough (PH)
Manor Farm
Paradise Farm
99
Manor House
1
The Anchor Inn (PH)
River Thames or Isis
Philip's Farm House
The Grange
Lock
Weir
98
23
24
25
D
E
F
171

133

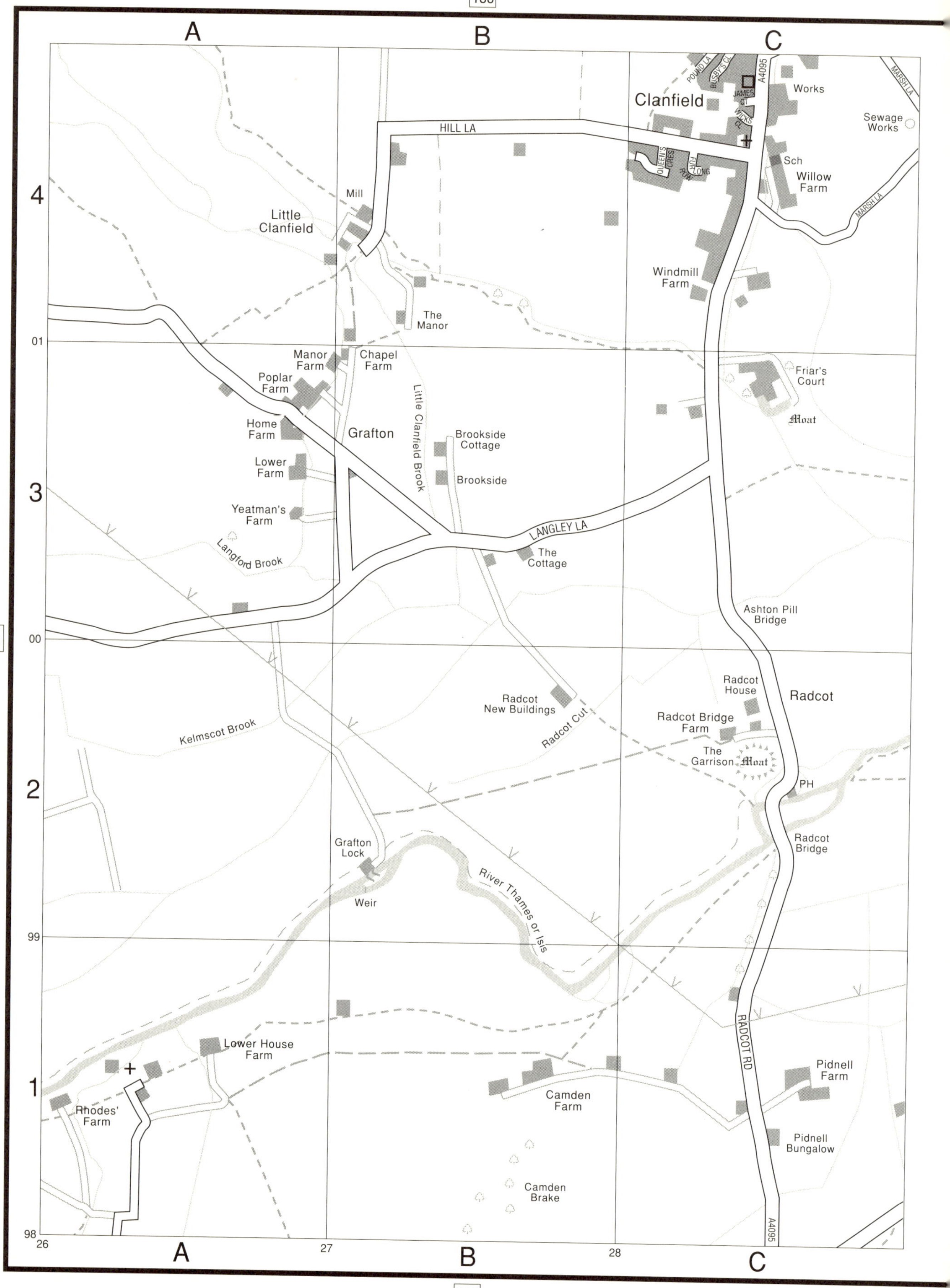
A
B
C
Clanfield
POUND LA
BUSBY'S CL
JAMES CT
WICKS CL
A4095
Works
MARSH LA
Sewage Works
HILL LA
QUEEN'S CRES
FURLONG ROW
Sch
Willow Farm
Mill
Little Clanfield
Windmill Farm
The Manor
Friar's Court
Moat
Manor Farm
Chapel Farm
Poplar Farm
Home Farm
Grafton
Little Clanfield Brook
Brookside Cottage
Lower Farm
Brookside
Yeatman's Farm
LANGLEY LA
The Cottage
Langford Brook
Ashton Pill Bridge
Radcot House
Radcot
Radcot New Buildings
Radcot Bridge Farm
Kelmscot Brook
Radcot Cut
The Garrison
Moat
PH
Radcot Bridge
Grafton Lock
Weir
River Thames or Isis
RADCOT RD
Lower House Farm
Pidnell Farm
Camden Farm
Rhodes' Farm
Pidnell Bungalow
Camden Brake
A4095
4
3
2
1
01
00
99
98
26
27
28

151

172

134

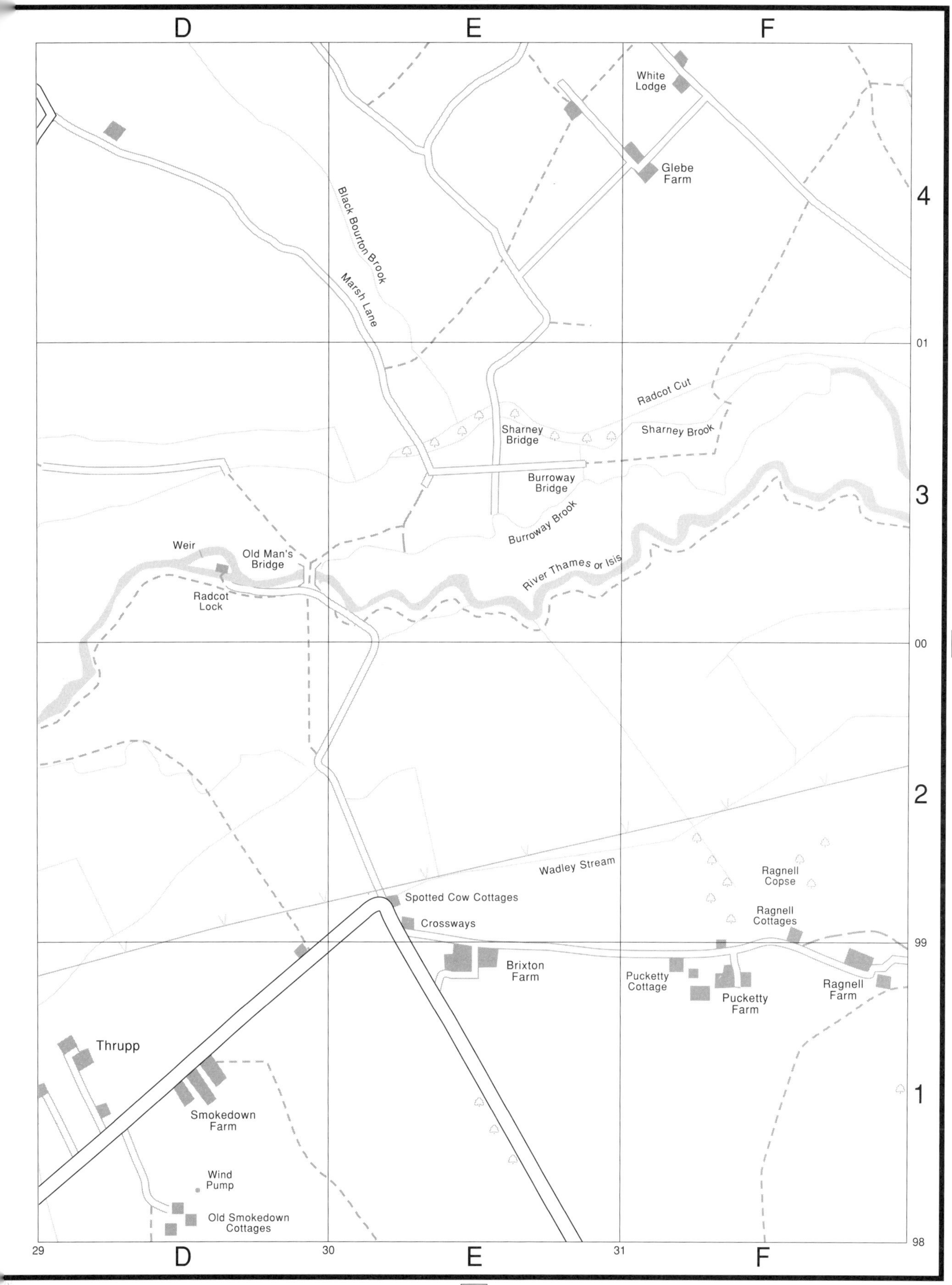
D
E
F
White Lodge
Glebe Farm
4
Black Bourton Brook
Marsh Lane
01
Radcot Cut
Sharney Bridge
Sharney Brook
Burroway Bridge
3
Burroway Brook
Weir
Old Man's Bridge
Radcot Lock
River Thames or Isis
00
2
Wadley Stream
Ragnell Copse
Spotted Cow Cottages
Crossways
Ragnell Cottages
99
Brixton Farm
Pucketty Cottage
Pucketty Farm
Ragnell Farm
Thrupp
1
Smokedown Farm
Wind Pump
Old Smokedown Cottages
29
30
31
98
D
E
F

154

173

135

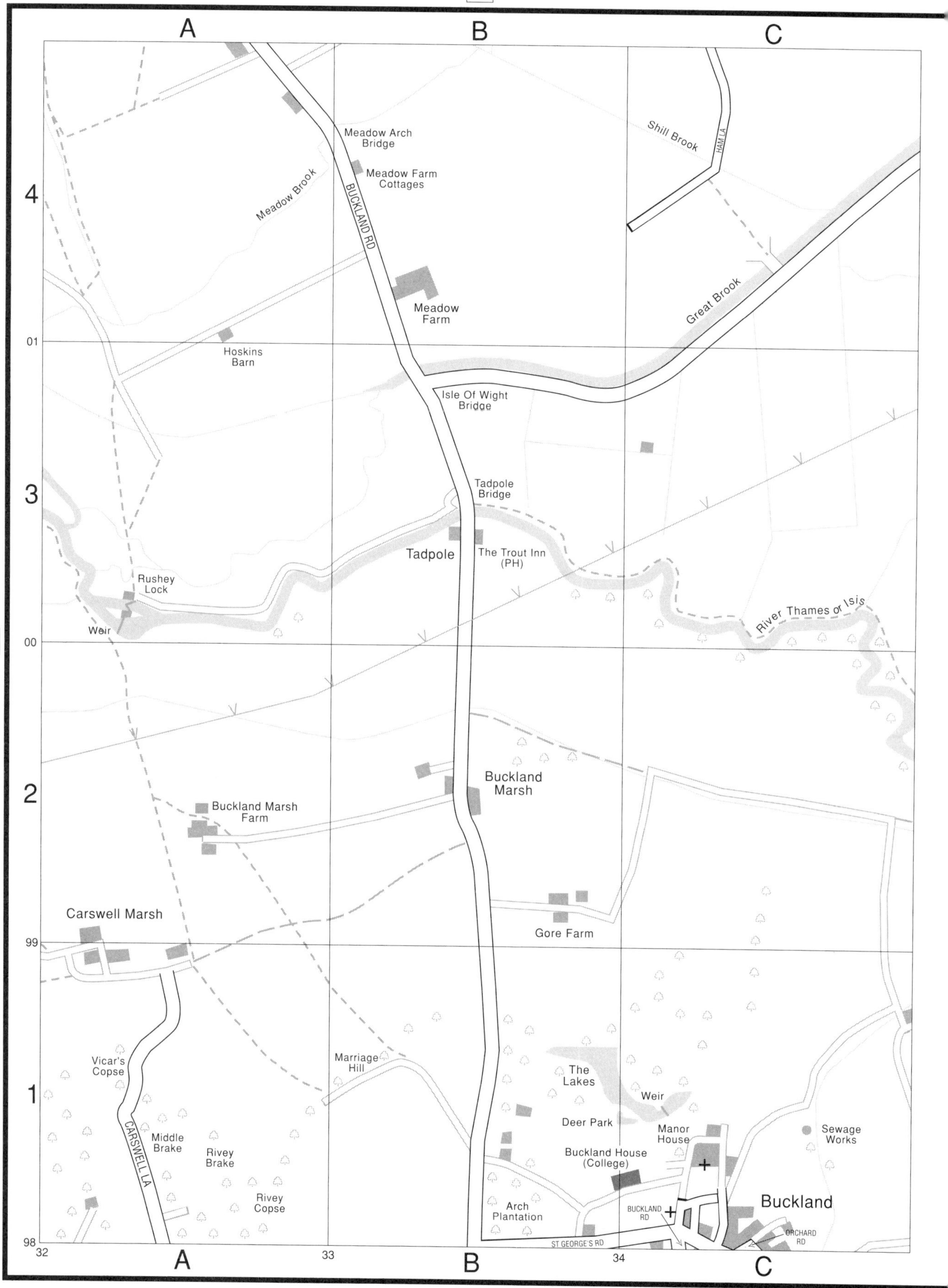
A
B
C
4
3
2
1
01
00
99
98
32
33
34
Meadow Arch Bridge
Meadow Farm Cottages
Meadow Brook
BUCKLAND RD
Shill Brook
HAM LA
Great Brook
Meadow Farm
Hoskins Barn
Isle Of Wight Bridge
Tadpole Bridge
Tadpole
The Trout Inn (PH)
Rushey Lock
Weir
River Thames or Isis
Buckland Marsh
Buckland Marsh Farm
Carswell Marsh
Gore Farm
Vicar's Copse
Marriage Hill
The Lakes
Weir
Deer Park
Manor House
Sewage Works
CARSWELL LA
Middle Brake
Rivey Brake
Rivey Copse
Buckland House (College)
Arch Plantation
Buckland
BUCKLAND RD
ORCHARD RD
ST GEORGE'S RD

153

174

136

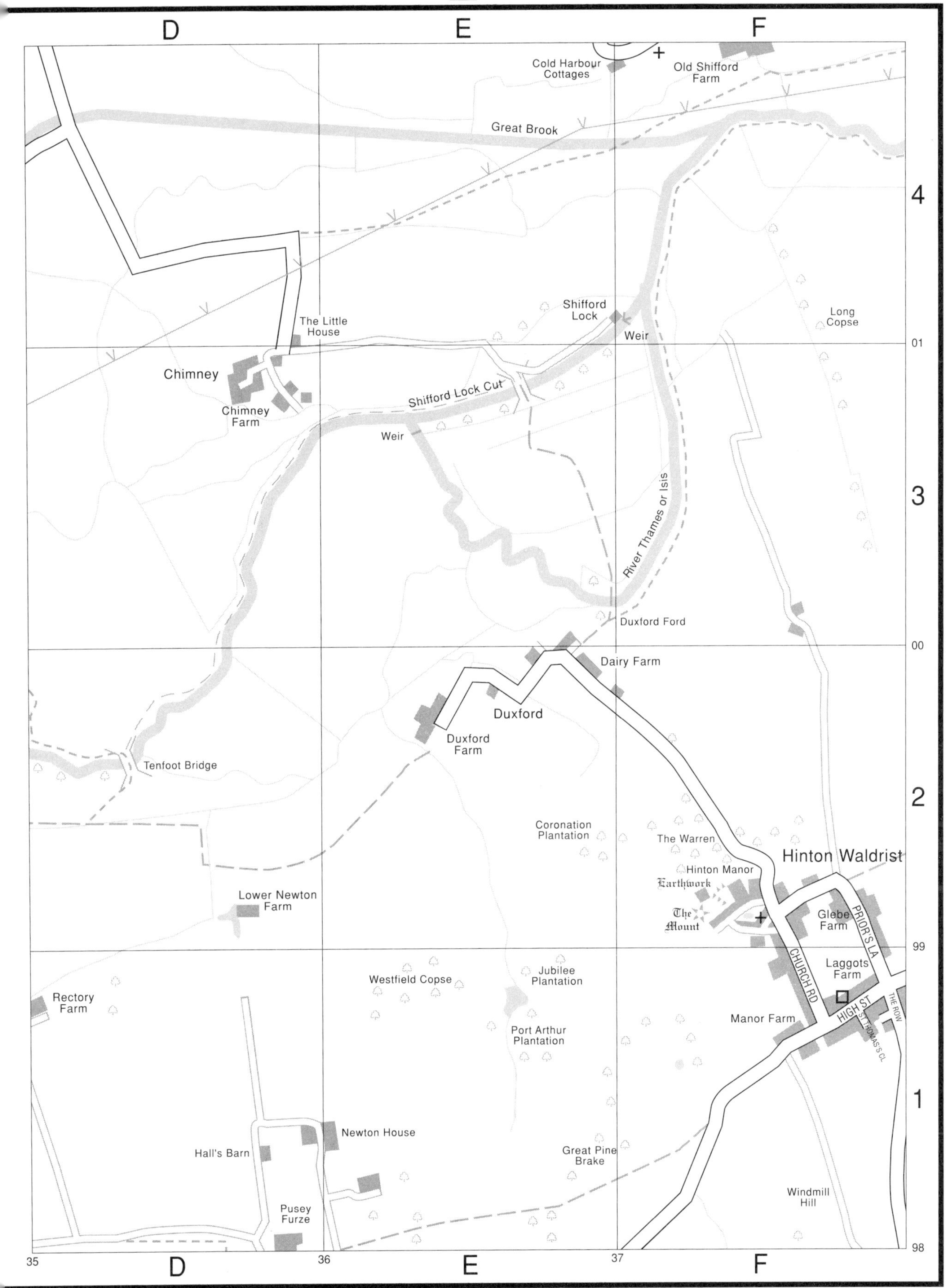
D
E
F
Cold Harbour Cottages
Old Shifford Farm
Great Brook
4
Shifford Lock
Long Copse
The Little House
Weir
01
Chimney
Chimney Farm
Shifford Lock Cut
Weir
3
River Thames or Isis
Duxford Ford
00
Dairy Farm
Duxford
Duxford Farm
Tenfoot Bridge
2
Coronation Plantation
The Warren
Hinton Waldrist
Hinton Manor
Earthwork
The Mount
Lower Newton Farm
Glebe Farm
PRIOR'S LA
CHURCH RD
99
Laggots Farm
Westfield Copse
Jubilee Plantation
Rectory Farm
HIGH ST
THE ROW
ST THOMAS'S CL
Manor Farm
Port Arthur Plantation
1
Newton House
Hall's Barn
Great Pine Brake
Windmill Hill
Pusey Furze
98
35
36
37
D
E
F

156

175

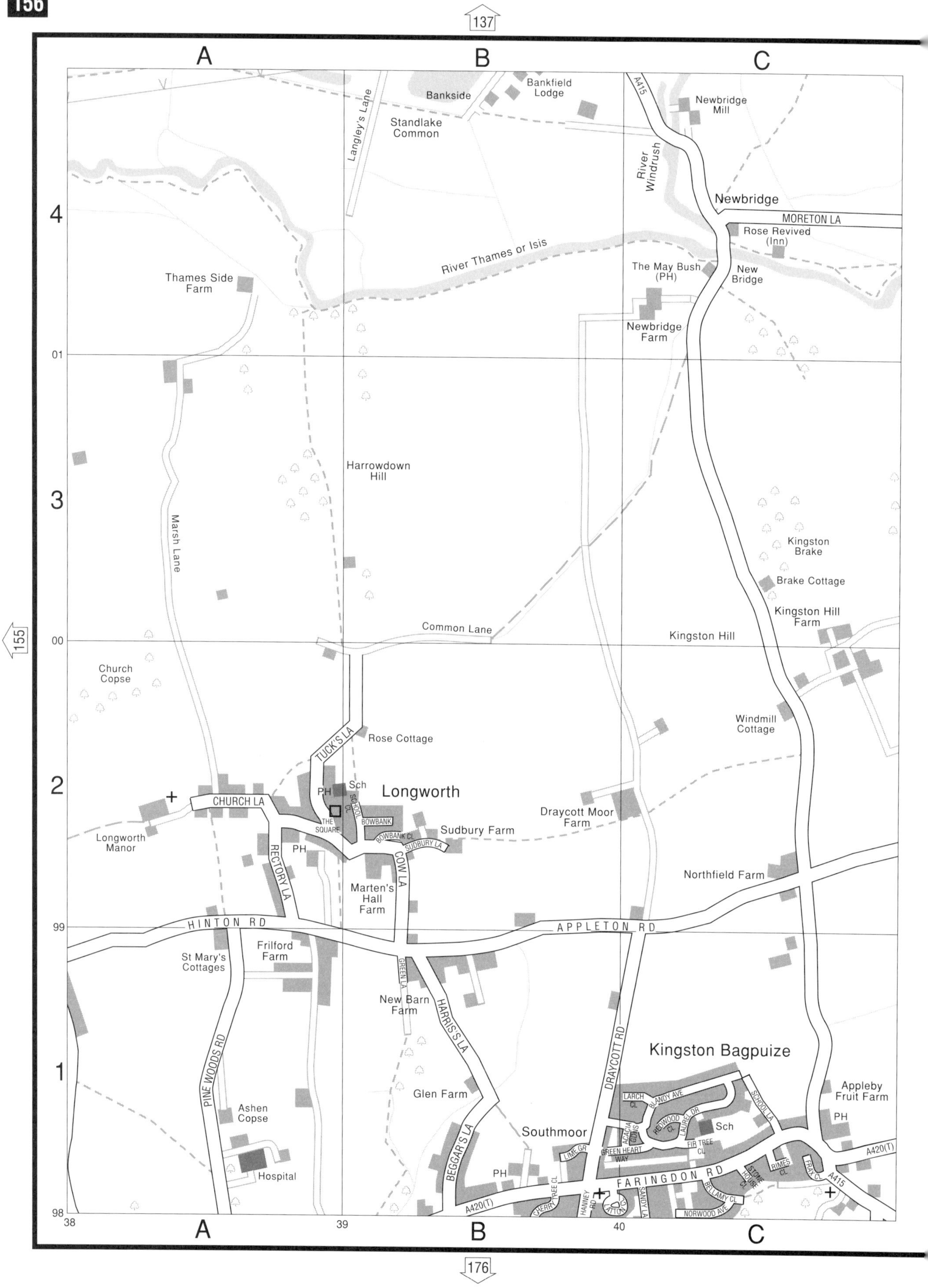
137
155
176
A
B
C
4
3
2
1
01
00
99
98
38
39
40
Bankside
Bankfield Lodge
Newbridge Mill
Standlake Common
Langley's Lane
River Windrush
A415
Newbridge
MORETON LA
Rose Revived (Inn)
River Thames or Isis
The May Bush (PH)
New Bridge
Thames Side Farm
Newbridge Farm
Harrowdown Hill
Marsh Lane
Kingston Brake
Brake Cottage
Kingston Hill Farm
Common Lane
Kingston Hill
Church Copse
Windmill Cottage
TUCK'S LA
Rose Cottage
Longworth
PH
Sch
CHURCH LA
THE SQUARE
SCHOOL CL
BOWBANK
BOWBANK CL
SUDBURY LA
Sudbury Farm
Draycott Moor Farm
Longworth Manor
RECTORY LA
PH
COW LA
Marten's Hall Farm
Northfield Farm
HINTON RD
APPLETON RD
St Mary's Cottages
Frilford Farm
GREEN LA
New Barn Farm
HARRIS'S LA
Kingston Bagpuize
DRAYCOTT RD
PINE WOODS RD
Glen Farm
Appleby Fruit Farm
Ashen Copse
LARCH CL
BLANDY AVE
SCHOOL LA
REDWOOD CL
LAUREL DR
Sch
PH
Southmoor
BEGGAR'S LA
ACACIA GDNS
LIME GR
GREEN HEART WAY
FIR TREE CL
RIMES CL
FRAX CL
A420(T)
A415
Hospital
PH
CHERRY TREE CL
FARINGDON RD
STONE HOUSE CL
BELLAMY CL
A420(T)
HANNEY RD
LATTON CL
SANDY LA
NORWOOD AVE

138

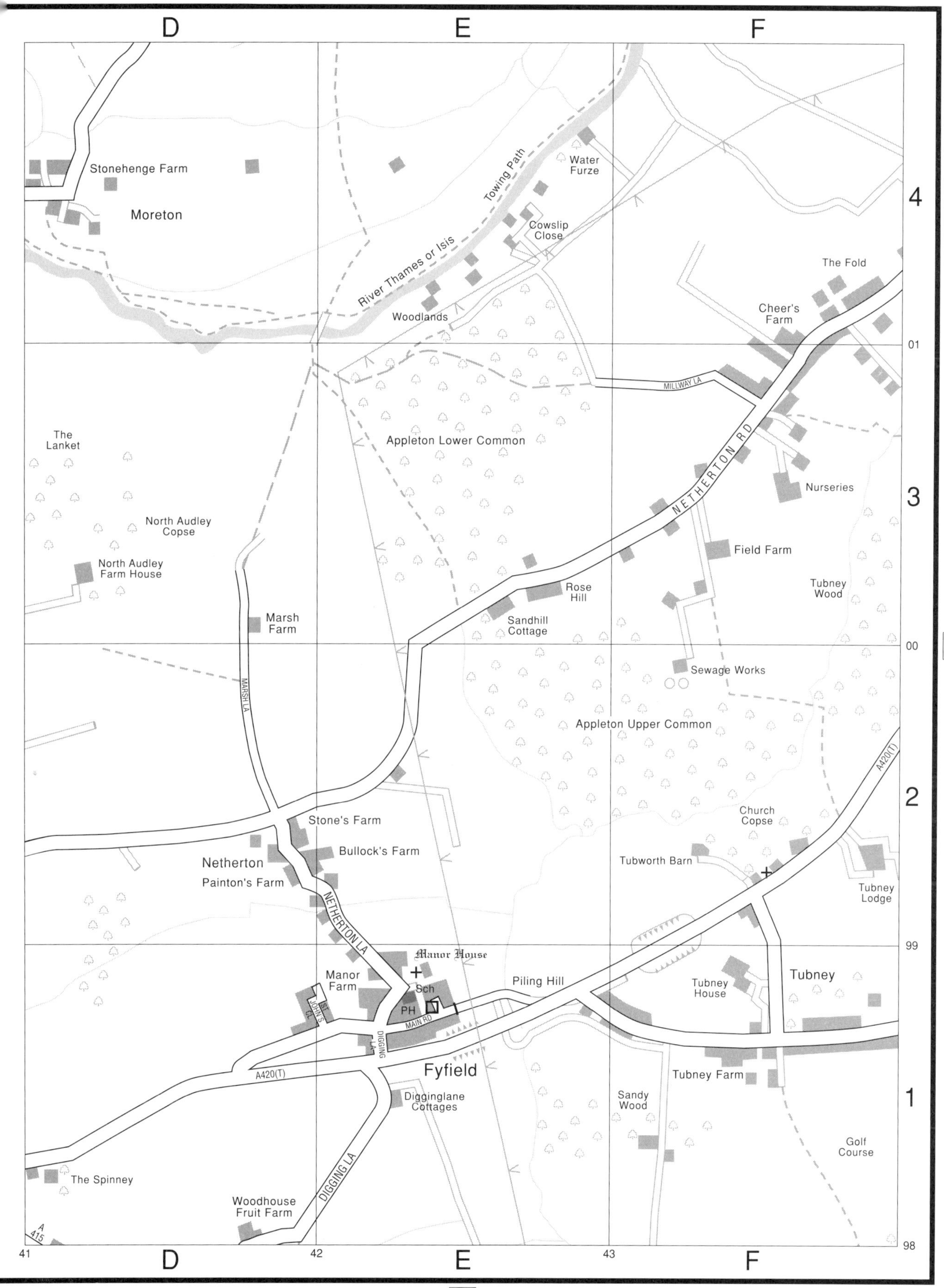

D
E
F
Stonehenge Farm
Moreton
Towing Path
River Thames or Isis
Water
Furze
Cowslip
Close
Woodlands
The Fold
Cheer's
Farm
MILLWAY LA
The
Lanket
Appleton Lower Common
NETHERTON RD
Nurseries
North Audley
Copse
North Audley
Farm House
Field Farm
Rose
Hill
Tubney
Wood
Marsh
Farm
Sandhill
Cottage
Sewage Works
MARSH LA
Appleton Upper Common
A420(T)
Stone's Farm
Church
Copse
Bullock's Farm
Netherton
Tubworth Barn
Painton's Farm
Tubney
Lodge
NETHERTON LA
Manor House
Manor
Farm
Sch
PH
ST JOHN'S CL
MAIN RD
Piling Hill
Tubney
Tubney
House
DIGGING LA
A420(T)
Fyfield
Tubney Farm
Digginglane
Cottages
Sandy
Wood
The Spinney
Golf
Course
Woodhouse
Fruit Farm
DIGGING LA
A 415
4
01
3
00
2
99
1
98
41
42
43

158

177

139

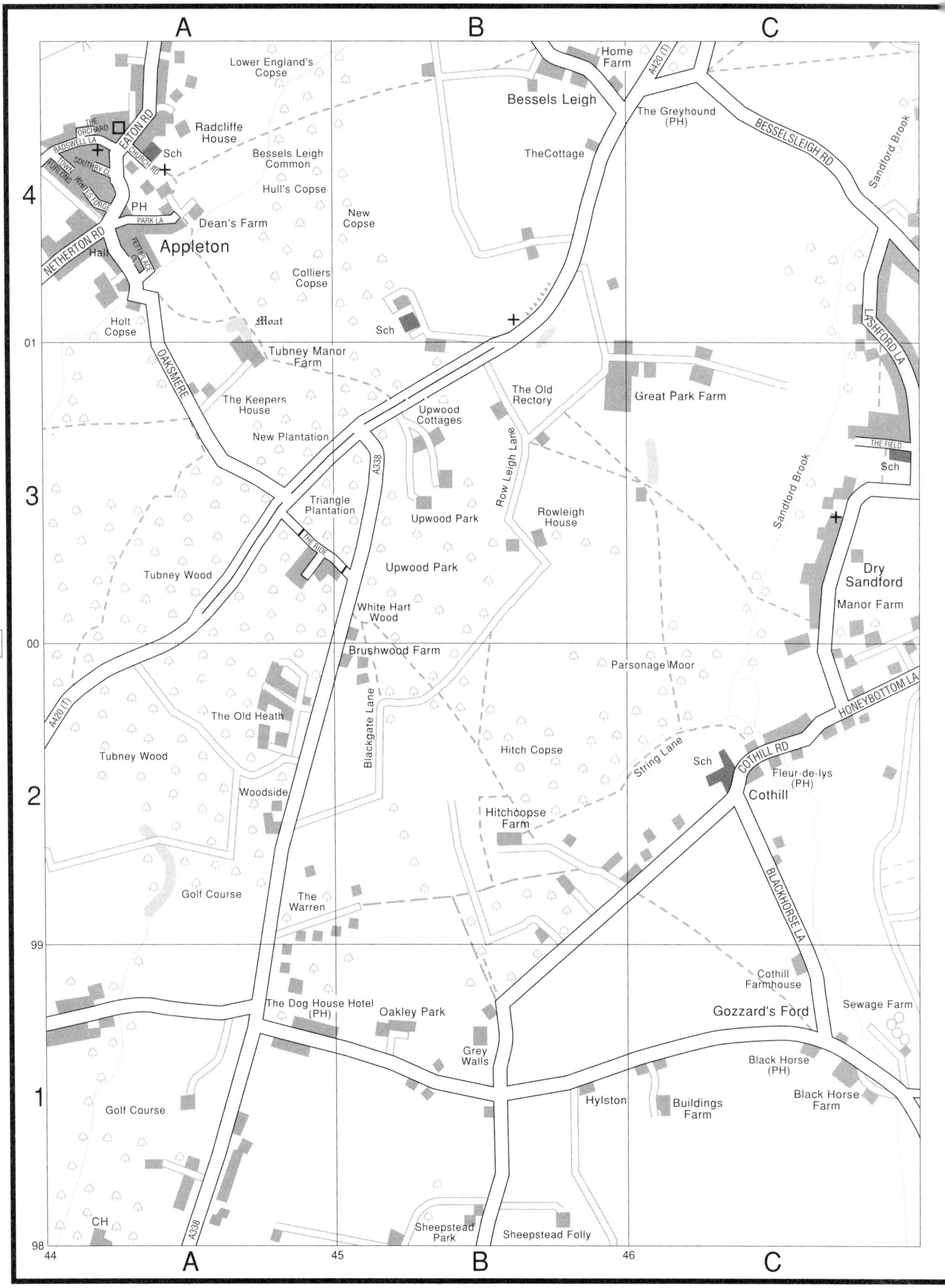
A
B
C
Home Farm
A420 (T)
Lower England's Copse
Bessels Leigh
The Greyhound (PH)
THE ORCHARD
EATON RD
Radcliffe House
BESSELSLEIGH RD
Sandford Brook
BADSWELL LA
Sch
CHURCH RD
Bessels Leigh Common
TheCottage
TOWN FURLONG
SOUTHBY CL
WHITES FORGE
Hull's Copse
4
PH
PARK LA
New Copse
Dean's Farm
NETHERTON RD
Hall
FETTIPLACE CL
Appleton
Colliers Copse
LASHFORD LA
Holt Copse
Moat
Sch
01
Tubney Manor Farm
OAKSMERE
The Old Rectory
Great Park Farm
The Keepers House
Upwood Cottages
New Plantation
A338
THE FIELD
Sch
Row Leigh Lane
Sandford Brook
3
Triangle Plantation
Upwood Park
Rowleigh House
THE RIDE
Tubney Wood
Upwood Park
Dry Sandford
Manor Farm
White Hart Wood
00
Brushwood Farm
Parsonage Moor
HONEYBOTTOM LA
A420 (T)
The Old Heath
Blackgate Lane
Hitch Copse
Tubney Wood
String Lane
Sch
COTHILL RD
Fleur-de-lys (PH)
2
Woodside
Cothill
Hitchcopse Farm
BLACKHORSE LA
Golf Course
The Warren
99
Cothill Farmhouse
The Dog House Hotel (PH)
Oakley Park
Gozzard's Ford
Sewage Farm
Grey Walls
Black Horse (PH)
1
Black Horse Farm
Hylston
Buildings Farm
Golf Course
CH
A338
Sheepstead Park
Sheepstead Folly
98
44
45
46
A
B
C

157

178

140

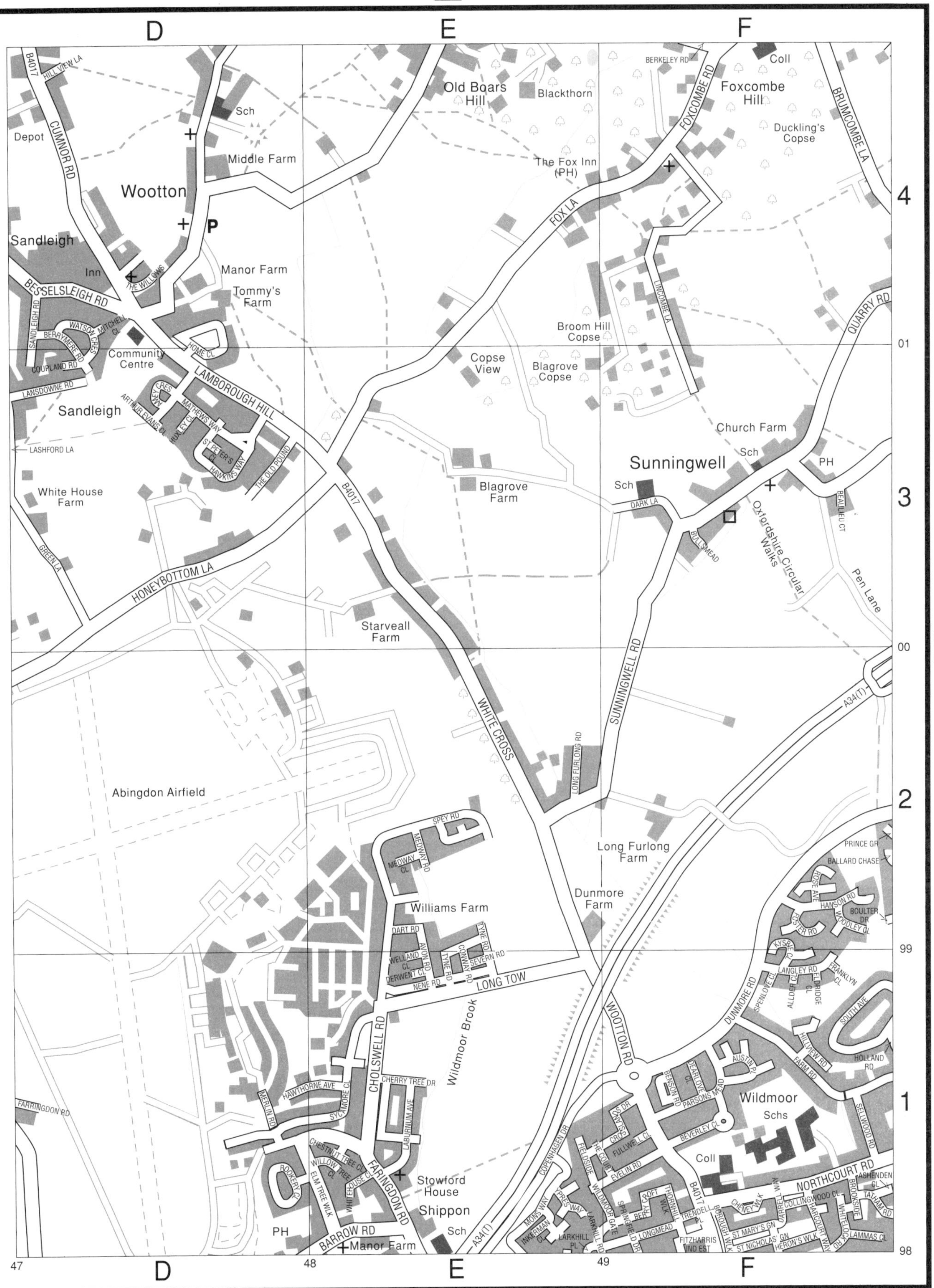
D
E
F
Wootton
Sandleigh
Old Boars Hill
Blackthorn
Foxcombe Hill
Coll
Sch
Depot
Middle Farm
Duckling's Copse
The Fox Inn (PH)
Manor Farm
Tommy's Farm
Inn
Community Centre
Broom Hill Copse
Copse View
Blagrove Copse
Church Farm
Sunningwell
PH
White House Farm
Blagrove Farm
Oxfordshire Circular Walks
Pen Lane
Starveall Farm
Abingdon Airfield
Long Furlong Farm
Dunmore Farm
Williams Farm
Wildmoor Brook
Wildmoor
Schs
Stowford House
Shippon
Manor Farm
CUMNOR RD
B4017
HILL VIEW LA
BESSELSLEIGH RD
LAMBOROUGH HILL
HONEYBOTTOM LA
FOX LA
FOXCOMBE RD
BERKELEY RD
BRUMCOMBE LA
LINCOMBE LA
QUARRY RD
DARK LA
BULLSMEAD
BEAULIEU CT
SUNNINGWELL RD
WHITE CROSS
LONG FURLONG RD
A34(T)
LASHFORD LA
GREEN LA
LANSDOWNE RD
COUPLAND RD
SANDLEIGH RD
BERRYMERE RD
WATSON CRES
MITCHELL CL
THE WILLOWS
HOME CL
MATHEWS WAY
HUXLEY CL
ST PETER'S CL
HAWKINS WAY
THE OLD POUND
ARTHUR EVANS CL
SPEY RD
MEDWAY RD
MEDWAY CL
DART RD
AVON RD
WELLAND CL
DERWENT CL
TYNE RD
CONWAY RD
SEVERN RD
NENE RD
LONG TOW
CHOLSWELL RD
CHERRY TREE DR
LABURNUM AVE
HAWTHORNE AVE
SYCAMORE CL
MERLIN RD
FARRINGDON RD
CHESTNUT TREE CL
WILLOW TREE CL
ELM TREE WLK
WHITEHOUSE CL
ROOKERY CL
FARINGDON RD
BARROW RD
WOOTTON RD
DUNMORE RD
PRINCE GR
BALLARD CHASE
ROSE AVE
HANSON RD
BOULTER DR
WOODLEY CL
KYSBIE CL
LANGLEY RD
FRANKLYN CL
SPENLOVE CL
ALLDER CL
ELDRIDGE CL
SOUTH AVE
HILLVIEW RD
FARM RD
HOLLAND RD
SELWOOD RD
AUSTIN PL
TEARLOVE CL
BENSON RD
PARSONS MEAD
BEVERLEY CL
FULLWELL CL
EVELIN RD
COPENHAGEN DR
FIELDSIDE
THE CROFT
WILDMOOR GATE
SPRINGFIELD DR
LONGMEAD
THORNHILL WLK
TRENDELL PL
FITZHARRIS IND EST
BOROUGH WLK
CHIEVELEY WLK
ST MARY'S GN
ST NICHOLAS' GN
HERON'S WLK
CARRELL WAY
COLLINGWOOD CL
HARCOURT WAY
BROOKSIDE
WHITELOCK RD
LAMMAS CL
NORTHCOURT RD
ASHENDEN CL
TATHAM RD
MONS WAY
INKERMAN CL
LARKHILL PL
LARKHILL RD
ARMY WAY
4
3
2
1
01
00
99
98
47
48
49

160

179

141

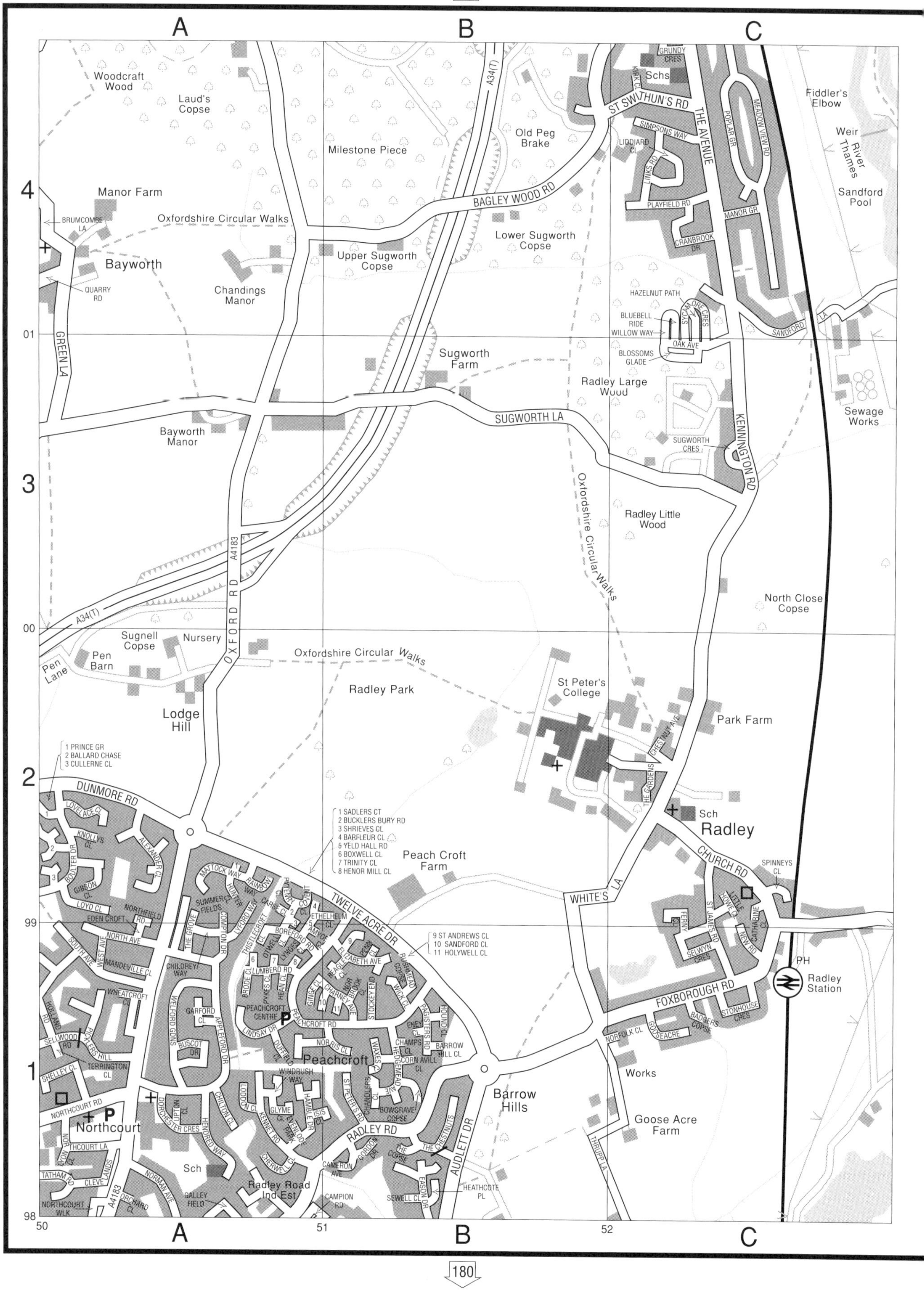

A
B
C
4
3
2
1
01
00
99
98
50
51
52
Woodcraft Wood
Laud's Copse
Milestone Piece
Old Peg Brake
Schs
GRUNDY CRES
KIRK CL
ST SWITHUN'S RD
SIMPSONS WAY
LIDDIARD CL
LINKS RD
THE AVENUE
POPLAR GR
MEADOW VIEW RD
Fiddler's Elbow
Weir
River Thames
Sandford Pool
Manor Farm
BRUMCOMBE LA
Oxfordshire Circular Walks
BAGLEY WOOD RD
A34(T)
PLAYFIELD RD
MANOR GR
CRANBROOK DR
Lower Sugworth Copse
Bayworth
Upper Sugworth Copse
QUARRY RD
Chandings Manor
HAZELNUT PATH
BLUEBELL RIDE
WILLOW WAY
SYCAMORE CRES
OAK AVE
BLOSSOMS GLADE
SANDFORD LA
GREEN LA
Sugworth Farm
Radley Large Wood
Sewage Works
Bayworth Manor
SUGWORTH LA
SUGWORTH CRES
KENNINGTON RD
Oxfordshire Circular Walks
Radley Little Wood
A4183
OXFORD RD
North Close Copse
Sugnell Copse
Nursery
Pen Barn
Pen Lane
Oxfordshire Circular Walks
Radley Park
St Peter's College
Park Farm
CHESTNUT AVE
THE GARDENS
Lodge Hill
1 PRINCE GR
2 BALLARD CHASE
3 CULLERNE CL
DUNMORE RD
LOVELACE CL
KNOLLYS CL
ALEXANDER CL
BOULTER DR
GIBSON CL
LOYD CL
NORTHFIELD RD
EDEN CROFT
NORTH AVE
SOUTH AVE
WEST AVE
MANDEVILLE CL
WHEATCROFT CL
HOLLAND RD
SELLWOOD RD
PICKERS HILL
TERRINGTON CL
SHELLEY CL
NORTHCOURT RD
Northcourt
NORTHCOURT LA
TATHAM RD
CLEVE
NORTHCOURT WLK
ORCHARD CL
A4183
Sch
Sch
Radley
1 SADLERS CT
2 BUCKLERS BURY RD
3 SHRIEVES CL
4 BARFLEUR CL
5 YELD HALL RD
6 BOXWELL CL
7 TRINITY CL
8 HENOR MILL CL
Peach Croft Farm
MATTOCK WAY
RAINBOW WAY
HUNTER CL
SUMMER FIELDS
COMPTON DR
THE GROVE
CHILDREY WAY
WELFORD GDNS
GARFORD CL
APPLEFORD DR
BUSCOT DR
DORCHESTER CRES
HENDRED WAY
CHILTON CL
GALLEY FIELD
NORMAN AVE
LYFORD WAY
THISTLECROFT CL
OTWELL CL
LUMBERD RD
BRODE CL
PYKES CL
HEATH CL
PEACHCROFT CENTRE
PEACHCROFT RD
LINDSAY DR
DUFFIELD CL
NORRIS CL
Peachcroft
WINDRUSH WAY
LODDON CL
GLYME CL
KENNET RD
CHERWELL CL
ISIS CL
HAMBLE DR
EVENLODE PARK
Radley Road Ind Est
CAMERON AVE
CAMPION RD
TWELVE ACRE DR
ETHELHELM CL
AMYCE
BOREFORD RD
ELIZABETH AVE
CHARNEY AVE
NOR BROOK CL
STOCKEY END
BUSHMEAD COPSE
WICK CL
9 ST ANDREWS CL
10 SANDFORD CL
11 HOLYWELL CL
PAGISTERS RD
HOUND CL
ENEY CL
CHAMPS CL
BARROW HILL CL
CORN AVILL CL
HEDGEMEAD AVE
WAXES CL
ST PETERS RD
CHANDLERS CL
BOWGRAVE COPSE
RADLEY RD
GORDON DR
THE COPSE
THE CHESTNUTS
EASON DR
SEWELL CL
AUDLETT DR
HEATHCOTE PL
Barrow Hills
WHITE'S LA
CHURCH RD
SPINNEYS CL
LITTLE HOWE CL
FERNY CL
ST JAMES RD
SELWYN CRES
NEW RD
CATHARINE CL
PH
Radley Station
FOXBOROUGH RD
STONHOUSE CRES
BADGERS COPSE
GOOSEACRE
NORFOLK CL
Works
Goose Acre Farm
THRUPP LA

159

180

142

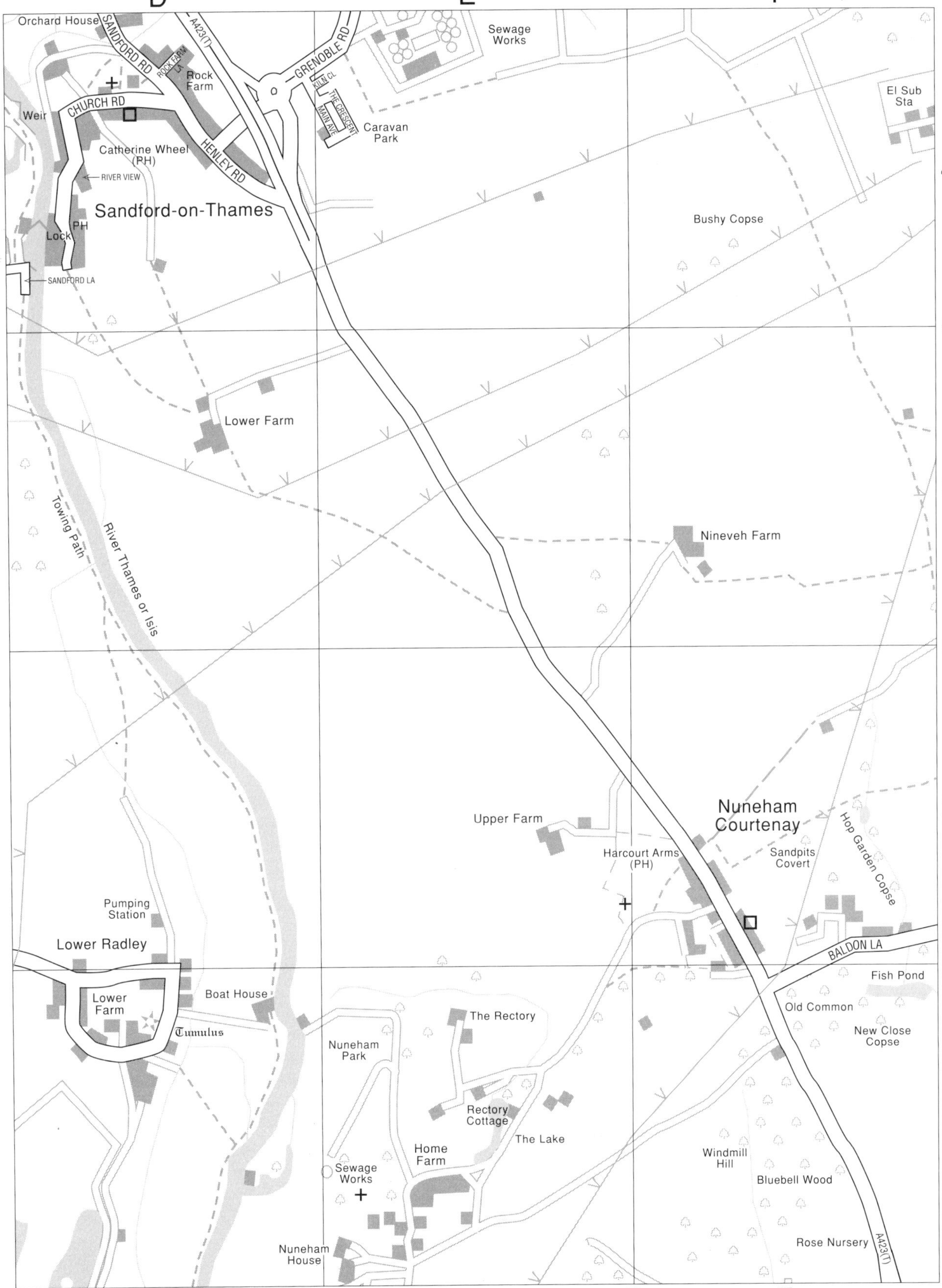
D
E
F
Orchard House
SANDFORD RD
ROCK FARM LA
Rock Farm
A423(T)
GRENOBLE RD
KILN CL
THE CRESCENT
MAIN AVE
Sewage Works
Caravan Park
El Sub Sta
Weir
CHURCH RD
Catherine Wheel (PH)
HENLEY RD
RIVER VIEW
Sandford-on-Thames
PH
Lock
SANDFORD LA
Bushy Copse
4
01
Lower Farm
3
Towing Path
River Thames or Isis
Nineveh Farm
00
2
Nuneham Courtenay
Upper Farm
Harcourt Arms (PH)
Sandpits Covert
Hop Garden Copse
Pumping Station
Lower Radley
BALDON LA
99
Fish Pond
Lower Farm
Boat House
Tumulus
The Rectory
Old Common
New Close Copse
Nuneham Park
Rectory Cottage
1
The Lake
Home Farm
Windmill Hill
Sewage Works
Bluebell Wood
Nuneham House
Rose Nursery
A423(T)
98
53
54
55
D
E
F

162

181

143

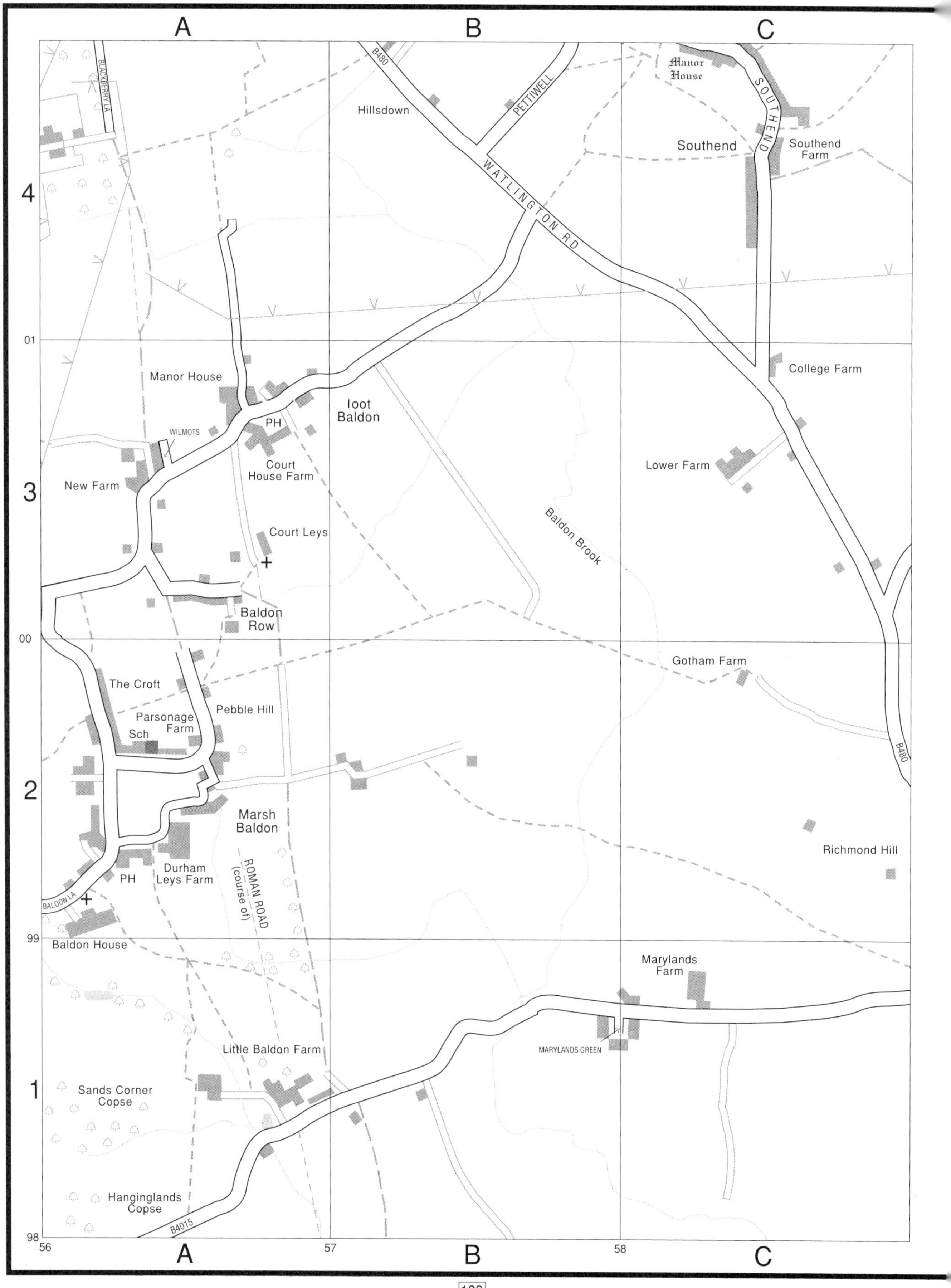

A
B
C
4
3
2
1
01
00
99
98
56
57
58
BLACKBERRY LA
B480
PETTIWELL
Manor House
SOUTHEND
Hillsdown
Southend
Southend Farm
WATLINGTON RD
Manor House
WILMOTS
PH
Ioot Baldon
College Farm
New Farm
Court House Farm
Lower Farm
Court Leys
Baldon Brook
Baldon Row
Gotham Farm
The Croft
Pebble Hill
Parsonage Farm
Sch
B480
Marsh Baldon
Richmond Hill
PH
Durham Leys Farm
ROMAN ROAD (course of)
BALDON LA
Baldon House
Marylands Farm
MARYLANDS GREEN
Little Baldon Farm
Sands Corner Copse
Hanginglands Copse
B4015

161

182

144

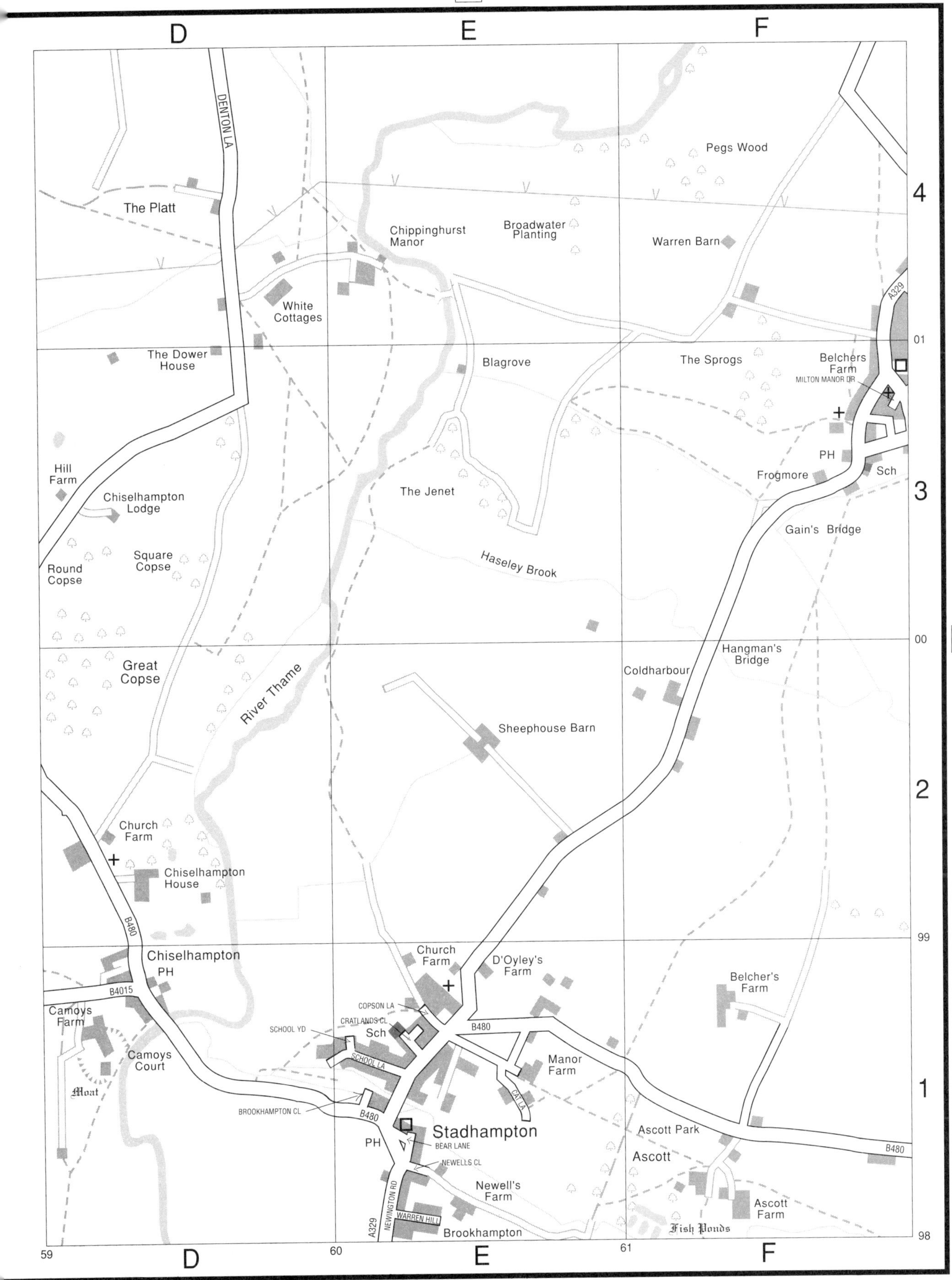
D
E
F
DENTON LA
The Platt
Chippinghurst Manor
Broadwater Planting
Pegs Wood
Warren Barn
White Cottages
A329
The Dower House
Blagrove
The Sprogs
Belchers Farm
MILTON MANOR DR
Hill Farm
Chiselhampton Lodge
The Jenet
PH
Frogmore
Sch
Gain's Bridge
Square Copse
Round Copse
Haseley Brook
Great Copse
River Thame
Coldharbour
Hangman's Bridge
Sheephouse Barn
Church Farm
Chiselhampton House
B480
Chiselhampton
PH
Church Farm
D'Oyley's Farm
Belcher's Farm
B4015
Camoys Farm
COPSON LA
CRATLANDS CL
SCHOOL YD
Sch
B480
SCHOOL LA
Camoys Court
Manor Farm
Moat
CAT LA
BROOKHAMPTON CL
B480
Stadhampton
PH
BEAR LANE
Ascott Park
Ascott
B480
NEWELLS CL
Newell's Farm
NEWINGTON RD
WARREN HILL
A329
Ascott Farm
Fish Ponds
Brookhampton
4
01
3
00
2
99
1
98
59
60
61
D
E
F

164

183

145

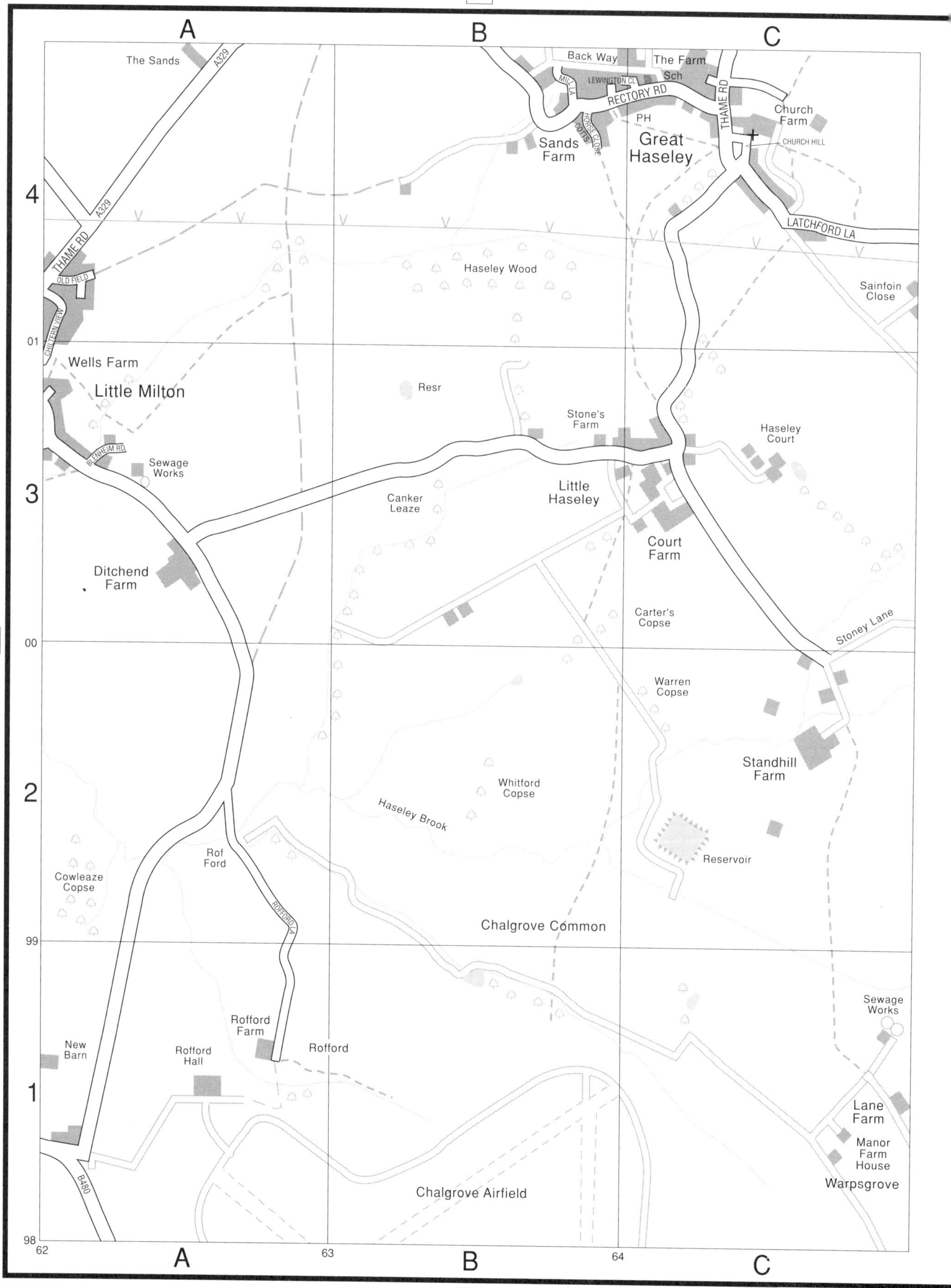
A
B
C
The Sands
A329
Back Way
The Farm
Sch
MILL LA
LEWINGTON CL
RECTORY RD
THAME RD
Church Farm
PH
HORSE CLOSE
COTTS
Sands Farm
Great Haseley
CHURCH HILL
4
THAME RD
LATCHFORD LA
OLD FIELD
Haseley Wood
Sainfoin Close
CHILTERN VIEW
01
Wells Farm
Little Milton
Resr
Stone's Farm
Haseley Court
BLENHEIM RD
Sewage Works
3
Canker Leaze
Little Haseley
Court Farm
Ditchend Farm
Carter's Copse
Stoney Lane
00
Warren Copse
Standhill Farm
2
Whitford Copse
Haseley Brook
Rof Ford
Reservoir
Cowleaze Copse
ROFFORD LA
Chalgrove Common
99
Sewage Works
Rofford Farm
New Barn
Rofford Hall
Rofford
1
Lane Farm
Manor Farm House
B480
Warpsgrove
Chalgrove Airfield
98
62
63
64

163

184

146

D
E
F
M40
Manor Farm
Goldpits Farm
Jointer's Farm
Latchford House
4
Oxhouse Farm
LATCHFORD LA
Latchford Farm
Latchford
Latchford Copse
Haseley Brook
01
Sheepbridge Copse
Peggs Farm
3
Cornwell Copse
Stoke Grange
The Island
00
Poppets Hill
Oxfordshire Way
2
Poppets Hill Farm
Stoke Talmage
Manor Farm
Stoney Lane
99
North Farm
Clare
1
Clare Copse
South Farm
98
65
66
67
D
E
F

166

185

147

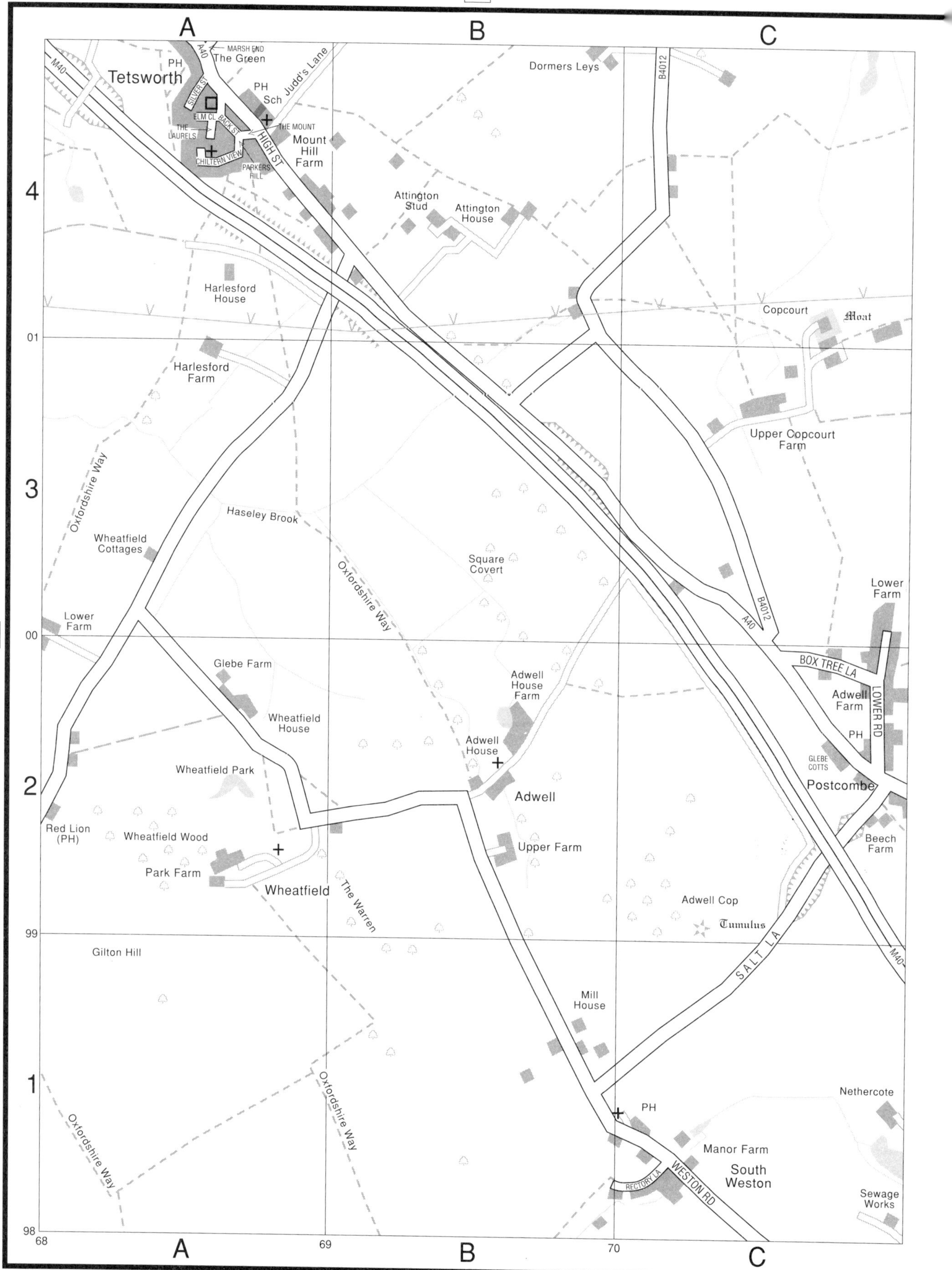
A
B
C
Tetsworth
PH
M40
A40
MARSH END
The Green
Judd's Lane
SILVER ST
ELM CL
BACK ST
THE LAURELS
CHILTERN VIEW
PH
Sch
THE MOUNT
HIGH ST
PARKERS HILL
Mount Hill Farm
Dormers Leys
B4012
Attington Stud
Attington House
4
Harlesford House
Copcourt
Moat
01
Harlesford Farm
Upper Copcourt Farm
Oxfordshire Way
3
Haseley Brook
Wheatfield Cottages
Square Covert
Oxfordshire Way
Lower Farm
Lower Farm
B4012
A40
00
BOX TREE LA
Glebe Farm
Adwell House Farm
Adwell Farm
LOWER RD
Wheatfield House
PH
Adwell House
GLEBE COTTS
Wheatfield Park
Postcombe
2
Adwell
Red Lion (PH)
Wheatfield Wood
Upper Farm
Beech Farm
Park Farm
Wheatfield
The Warren
Adwell Cop
Tumulus
99
M40
Gilton Hill
SALT LA
Mill House
1
Oxfordshire Way
Nethercote
Oxfordshire Way
PH
Manor Farm
South Weston
RECTORY LA
WESTON RD
Sewage Works
98
68
69
70
A
B
C

165

186

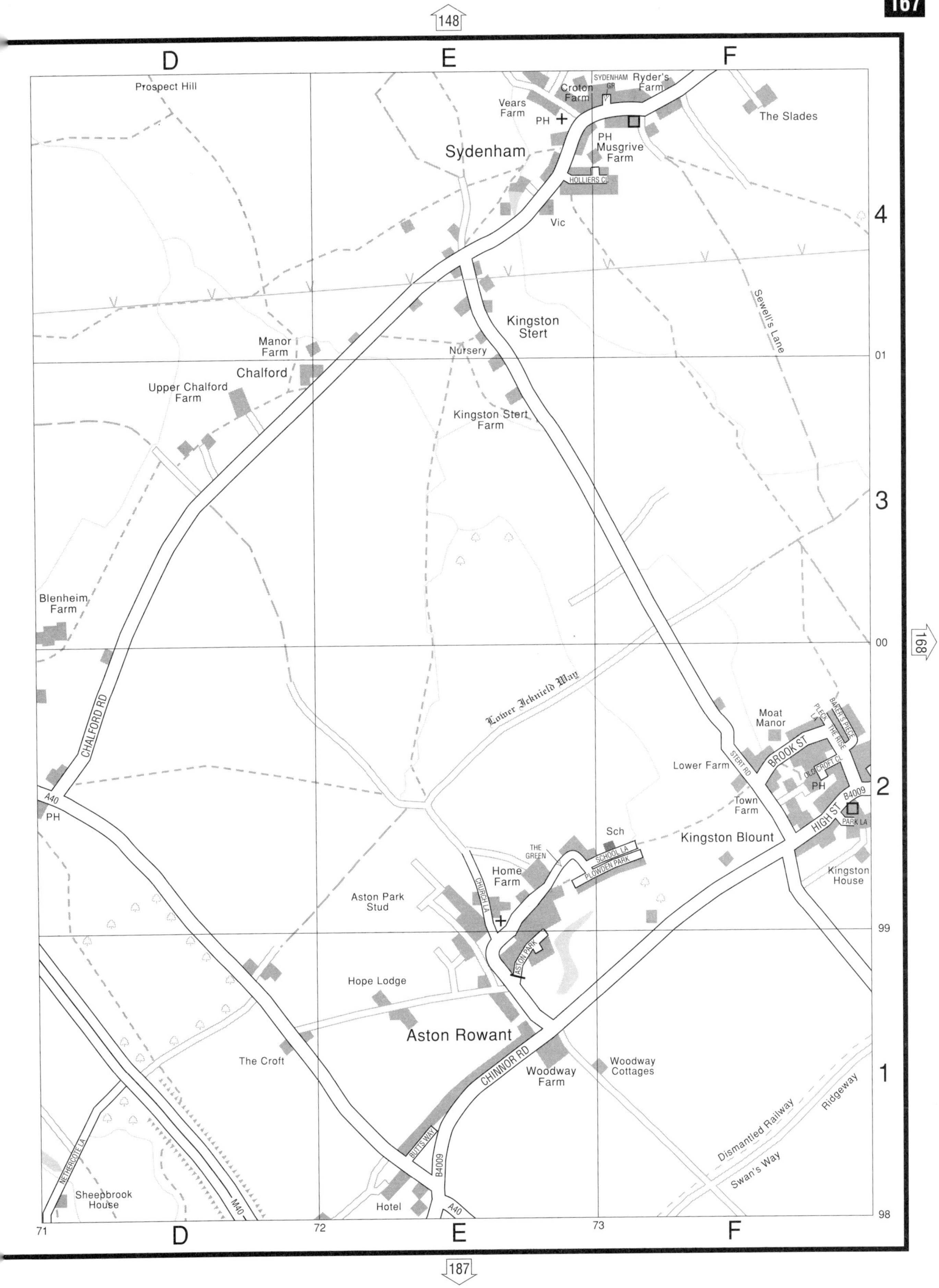
148
D
E
F
Prospect Hill
Vears Farm
Croton Farm
SYDENHAM GR
Ryder's Farm
The Slades
PH
Sydenham
PH Musgrive Farm
HOLLIERS CL
Vic
Sewell's Lane
Kingston Stert
Manor Farm
Nursery
Chalford
Upper Chalford Farm
Kingston Stert Farm
Blenheim Farm
Lower Icknield Way
CHALFORD RD
A40
PH
Moat Manor
PLECK LA
BAKER'S PIECE
THE RISE
BROOK ST
STERT RD
Lower Farm
OLD CROFT CL
PH
B4009
Town Farm
HIGH ST
PARK LA
Sch
THE GREEN
SCHOOL LA
PLOWDEN PARK
Kingston Blount
Home Farm
CHURCH LA
Aston Park Stud
Kingston House
ASTON PARK
Hope Lodge
Aston Rowant
The Croft
CHINNOR RD
Woodway Farm
Woodway Cottages
Dismantled Railway
Ridgeway
Swan's Way
NETHERCOTE LA
Sheepbrook House
M40
BUTTS WAY
B4009
Hotel
A40
4
3
2
1
01
00
99
98
71
72
73
168
187

149

167

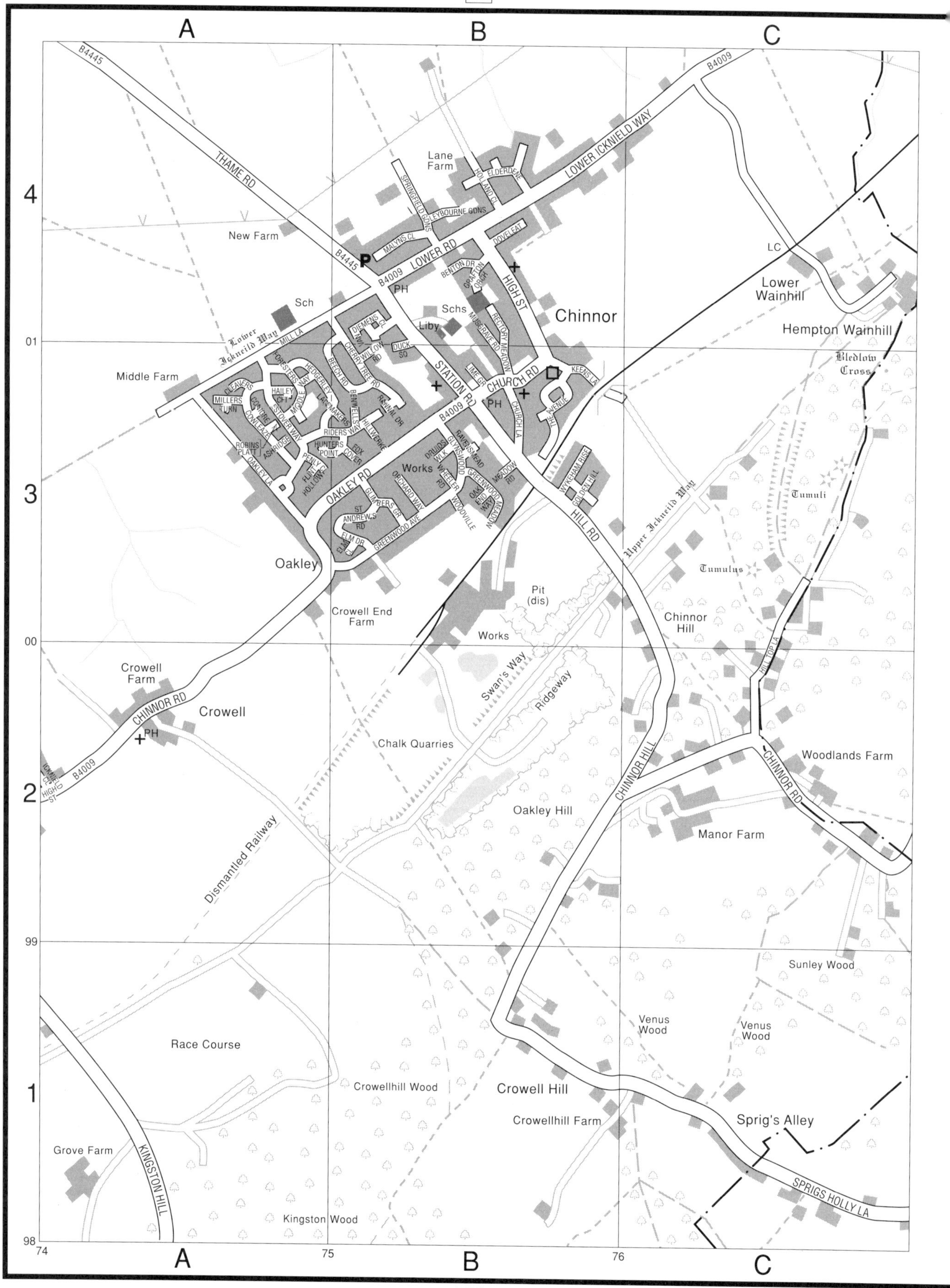
A
B
C
4
3
2
1
01
00
99
98
74
75
76
B4445
THAME RD
B4009
LOWER ICKNIELD WAY
Lane Farm
New Farm
HOLLAND CL
ELDERDENE
SPRINGFIELD GDNS
EYBOURNE GDNS
MALYNS CL
LOWER RD
DOVELEAT
BENTON DR
GRAFTON ORCH
HIGH ST
PH
Sch
Schs
Chinnor
Liby
MUSGRAVE RD
RECTORY MEADOW
Lower Icknield Way
MILL LA
DIEMENS CL
DUCK SQ
CHERRY TREE RD
WILLOW RD
STATION RD
CHURCH RD
KEENS LA
LIME GR
Middle Farm
CLEAVERS
MILLERS TURN
HAILEY CFT
FORSTERS WAY
HEDGERLEY
BEECH RD
BENWELLS
RENDAL DR
CHURCH LA
THE AVENUE
CONLEAZE
ASHRIDGE
ROBINS PLATT
RIDERS WAY
HUNTERS POINT
FOX COVER
HILLWERKE
OAKLEY LA
HOLLOWAY
Works
OAKLEY RD
DRUIDS WLK
WHEELER RD
RAVENSMEAD
ORCHARD WAY
GREENWOOD MEADOW
MEADOW RD
WYKEHAM RISE
GOLDEN HILL
HILL RD
ST ANDREWS RD
GREENWOOD AVE
WOODVILLE
ELM DR
Oakley
Crowell End Farm
Pit (dis)
Works
Upper Icknield Way
Chinnor Hill
HILL TOP LA
Lower Wainhill
LC
Hempton Wainhill
Bledlow Cross
Tumuli
Tumulus
Crowell Farm
Crowell
CHINNOR RD
PH
HIGH ST
Swan's Way
Ridgeway
Chalk Quarries
Oakley Hill
CHINNOR HILL
Woodlands Farm
CHINNOR RD
Manor Farm
Dismantled Railway
Sunley Wood
Race Course
Venus Wood
Venus Wood
Crowellhill Wood
Crowell Hill
Crowellhill Farm
Sprig's Alley
Grove Farm
KINGSTON HILL
SPRIGS HOLLY LA
Kingston Wood

188

not continued, see key diagram

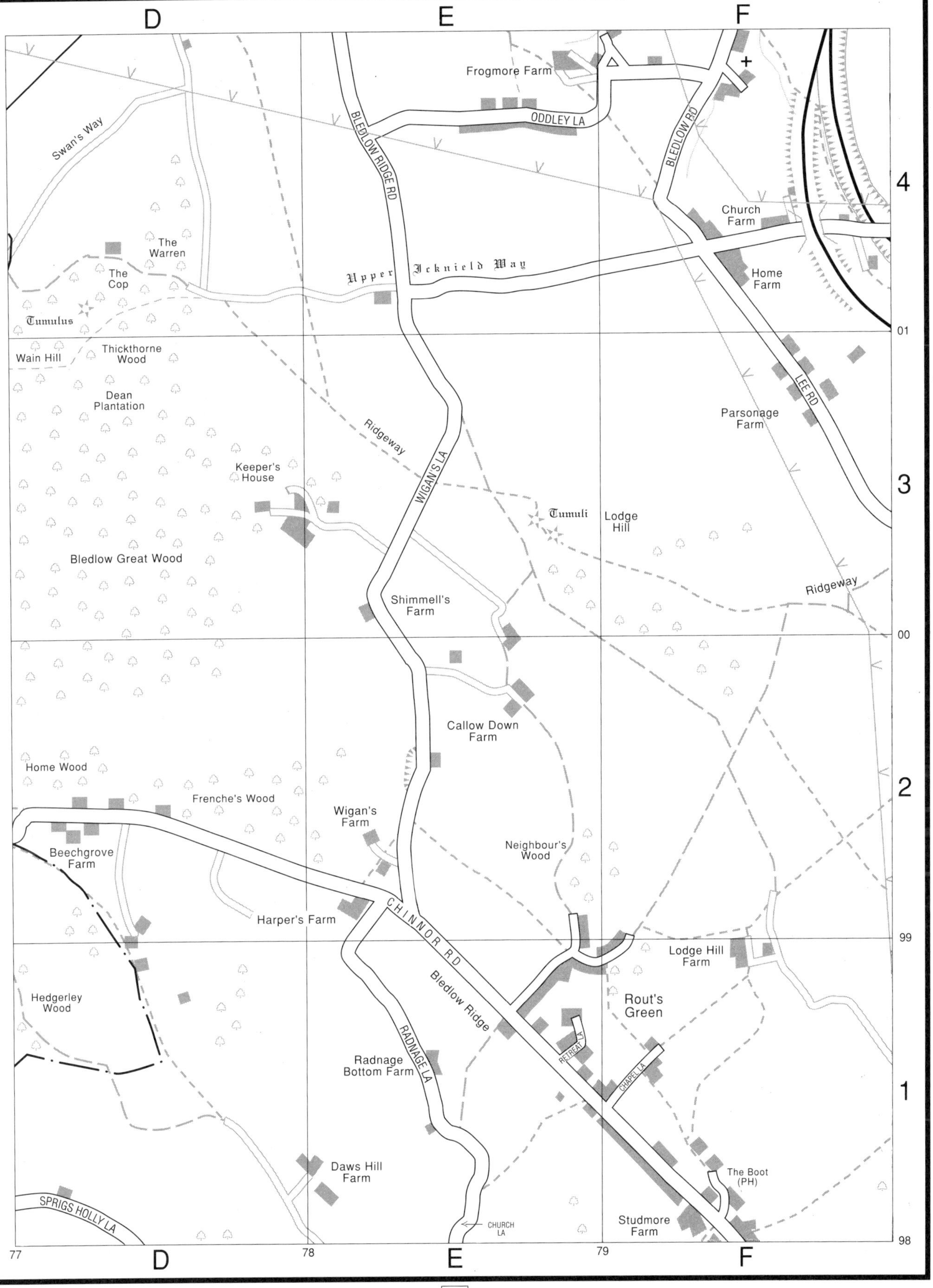

not continued, see key diagram

150

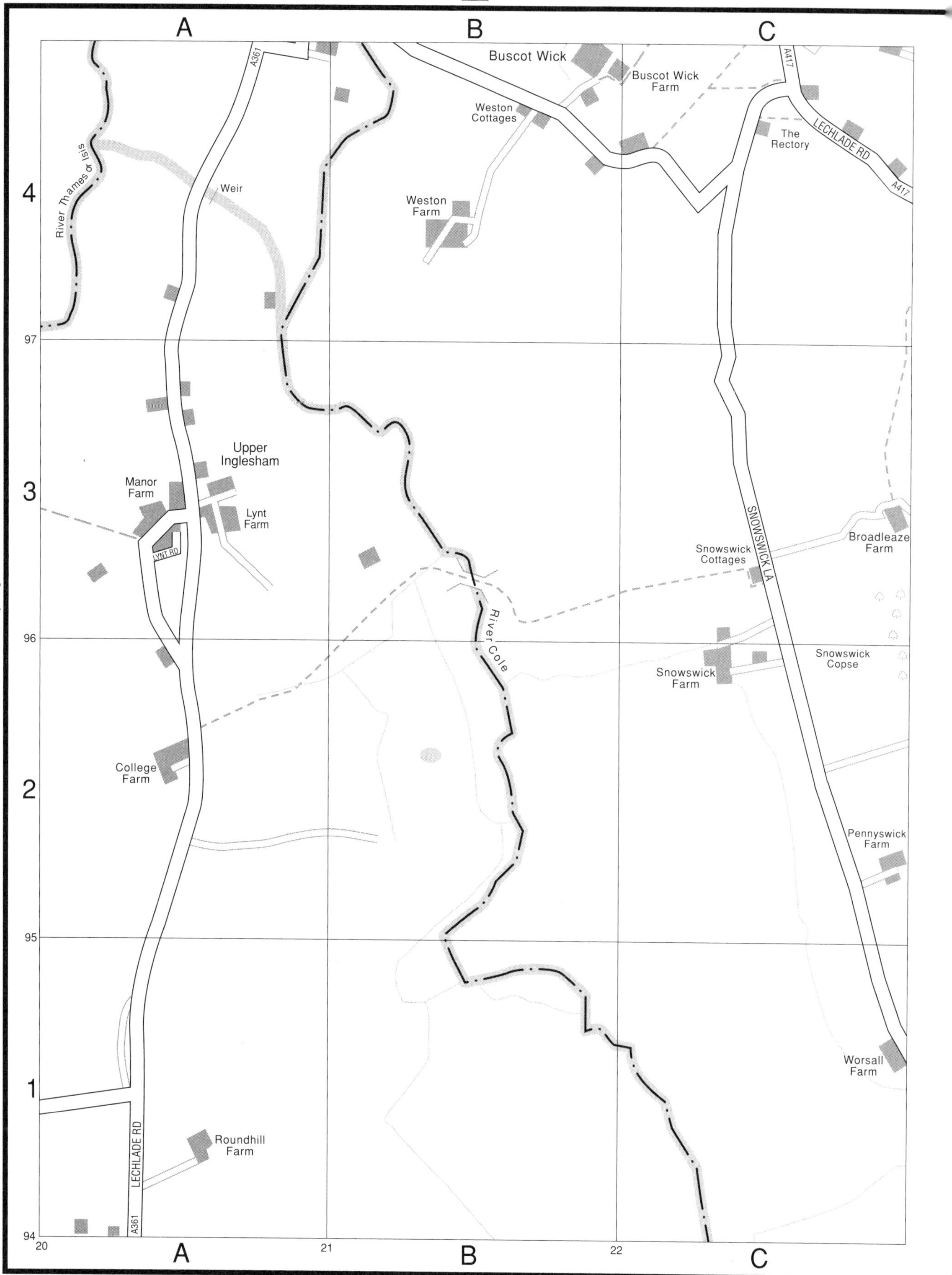

not continued, see key diagram

190

151

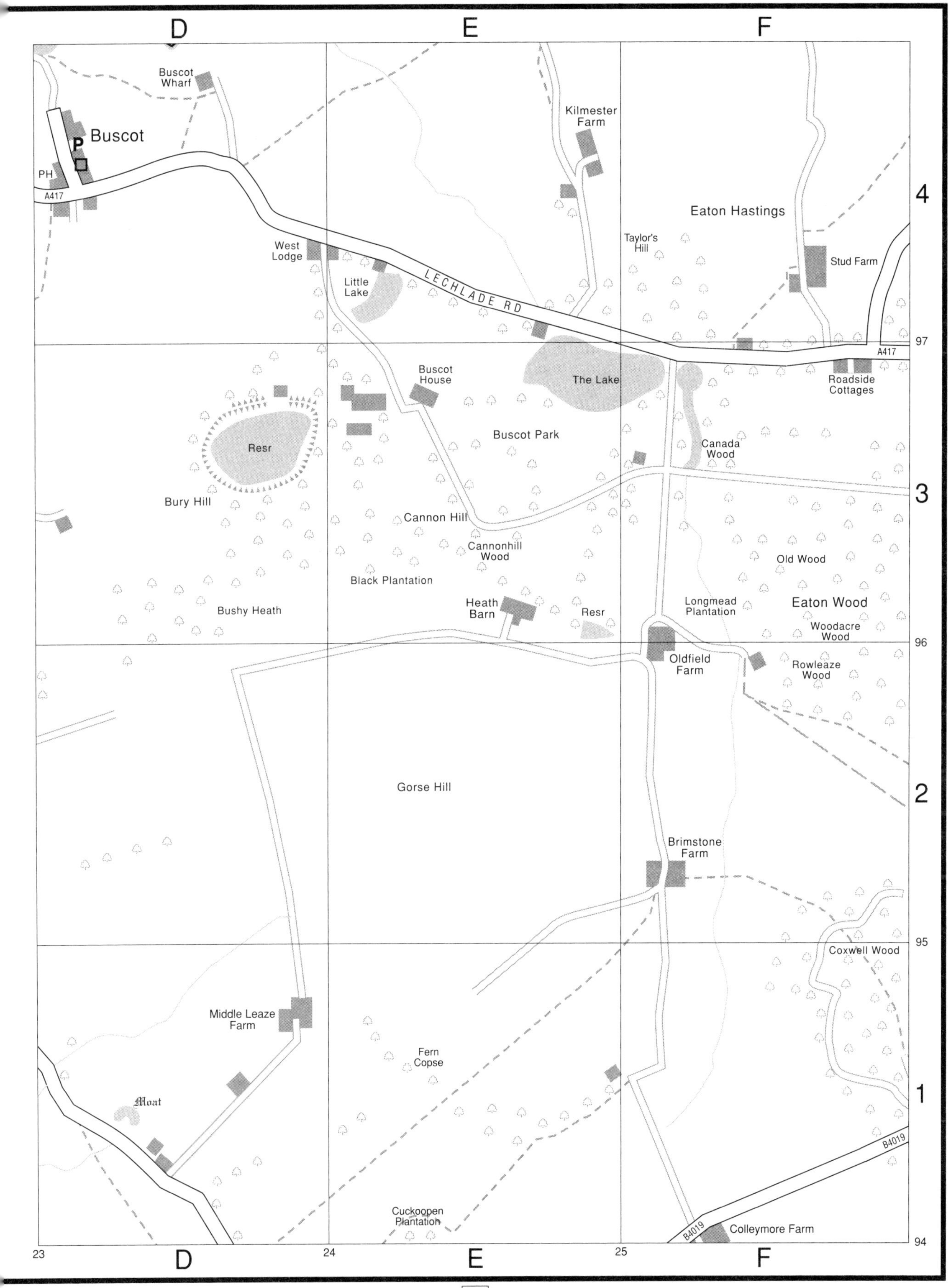

D
E
F
Buscot Wharf
Buscot
P
PH
A417
Kilmester Farm
Eaton Hastings
4
West Lodge
Taylor's Hill
Stud Farm
Little Lake
LECHLADE RD
97
A417
Buscot House
The Lake
Roadside Cottages
Resr
Buscot Park
Canada Wood
Bury Hill
3
Cannon Hill
Cannonhill Wood
Old Wood
Black Plantation
Heath Barn
Resr
Longmead Plantation
Eaton Wood
Bushy Heath
Woodacre Wood
96
Oldfield Farm
Rowleaze Wood
Gorse Hill
2
Brimstone Farm
95
Coxwell Wood
Middle Leaze Farm
Fern Copse
1
Moat
B4019
Cuckoopen Plantation
B4019
Colleymore Farm
94
23
24
25
D
E
F

172

191

152

171

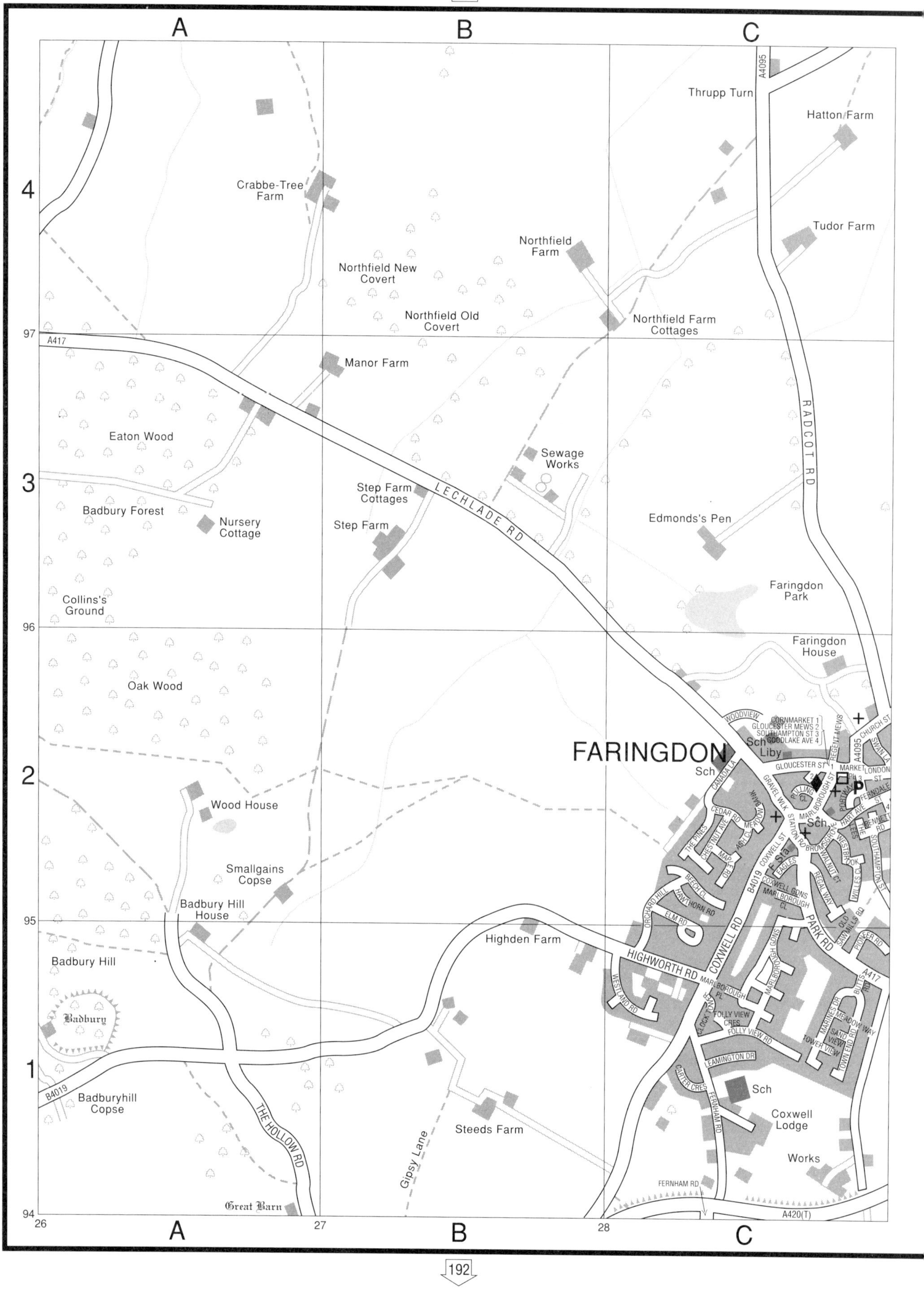
A
B
C
4
3
2
1
97
96
95
94
26
27
28
Thrupp Turn
A4095
Hatton Farm
Crabbe-Tree Farm
Tudor Farm
Northfield Farm
Northfield New Covert
Northfield Old Covert
Northfield Farm Cottages
A417
Manor Farm
RADCOT RD
Eaton Wood
Sewage Works
Step Farm Cottages
LECHLADE RD
Badbury Forest
Nursery Cottage
Step Farm
Edmonds's Pen
Faringdon Park
Collins's Ground
Faringdon House
Oak Wood
WOODVIEW
CORNMARKET 1
GLOUCESTER MEWS 2
SOUTHAMPTON ST 3
GOODLAKE AVE 4
REGENT MEWS
CHURCH ST
FARINGDON
Sch
Liby
GLOUCESTER ST
MARKET
LONDON ST
Wood House
CANADA LA
GRAVEL WLK
CEDAR RD
MEADOW BANK
STATION RD
THE PINES
CHESTNUT AVE
COXWELL ST
Sta
PARK RD
Smallgains Copse
B4019
BEECH CL
HAWTHORN RD
ORCHARD HILL
ELM RD
Badbury Hill House
Highden Farm
HIGHWORTH RD
COXWELL RD
MARLBOROUGH GDNS
Badbury Hill
WESTLAND RD
FOLLY VIEW CRES
FOLLY VIEW RD
TOWER VIEW
TOWN END RD
MEADOW WAY
Badbury
LEAMINGTON DR
B4019
Badburyhill Copse
CARTER CRES
FERNHAM RD
Sch
Coxwell Lodge
THE HOLLOW RD
Steeds Farm
Gipsy Lane
Works
FERNHAM RD
Great Barn
A420(T)

192

153
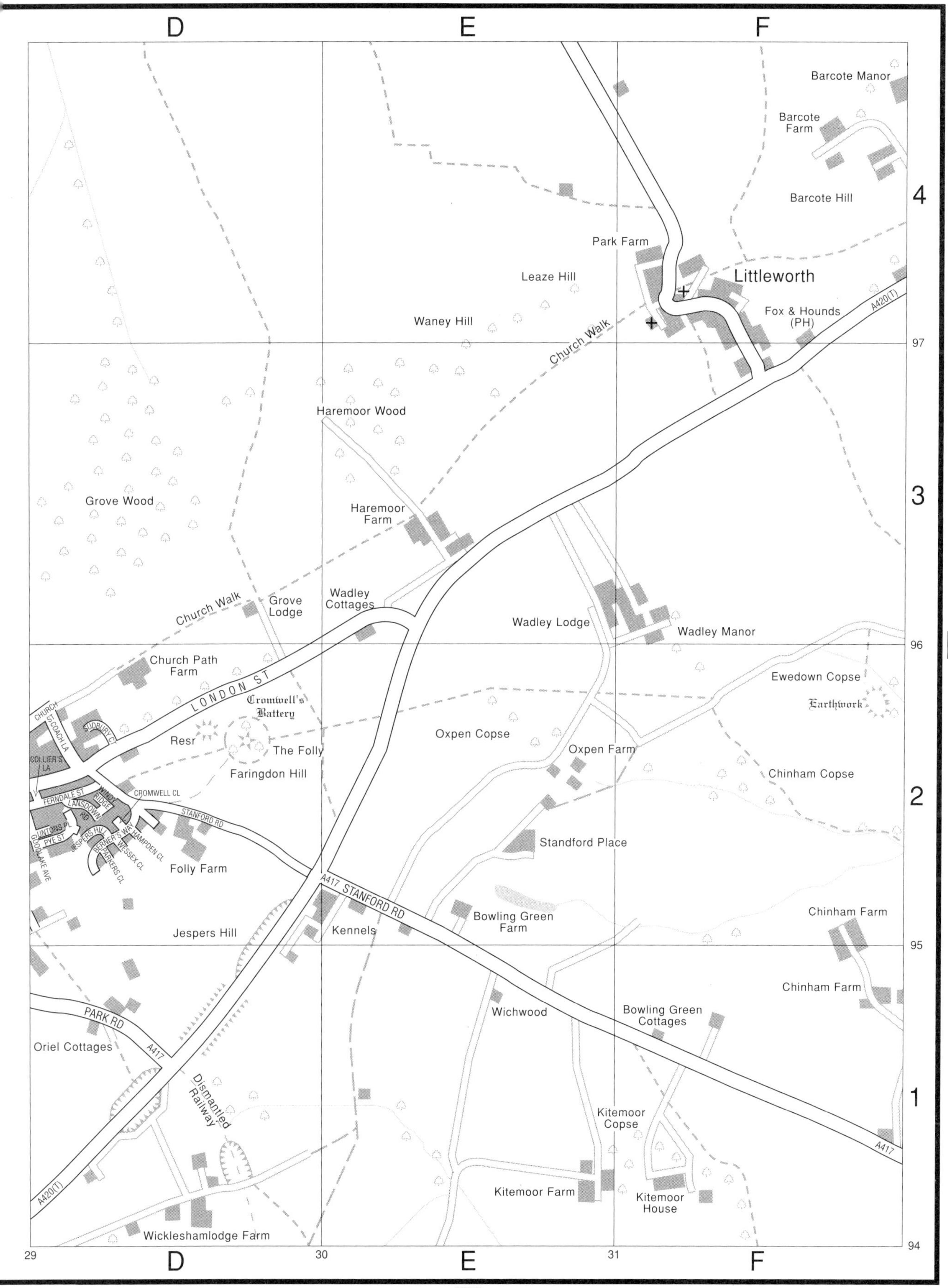
D
E
F
Barcote Manor
Barcote Farm
Barcote Hill
4
Park Farm
Leaze Hill
Littleworth
Fox & Hounds (PH)
A420(T)
Waney Hill
Church Walk
97
Haremoor Wood
3
Grove Wood
Haremoor Farm
Church Walk
Grove Lodge
Wadley Cottages
Wadley Lodge
Wadley Manor
96
Church Path Farm
LONDON ST
Cromwell's Battery
Ewedown Copse
Earthwork
CHURCH ST
COACH LA
SUDBURY CT
Resr
The Folly
Oxpen Copse
Oxpen Farm
COLLIER'S LA
Faringdon Hill
Chinham Copse
CROMWELL CL
2
FERNDALE ST
WINDRIDGE
LANSDOWN RD
STANFORD RD
GUNTONS PL
PYE ST
JESPERS HILL
BERNER'S WAY
WESSEX CL
HAMPDEN CL
PARKERS CL
GOODLAKE AVE
Standford Place
Folly Farm
A417 STANFORD RD
Bowling Green Farm
Kennels
Chinham Farm
Jespers Hill
95
Chinham Farm
PARK RD
Wichwood
Bowling Green Cottages
A417
Oriel Cottages
Dismantled Railway
1
Kitemoor Copse
A417
A420(T)
Kitemoor Farm
Kitemoor House
Wickleshamlodge Farm
94
29
30
31
D
E
F
174
193

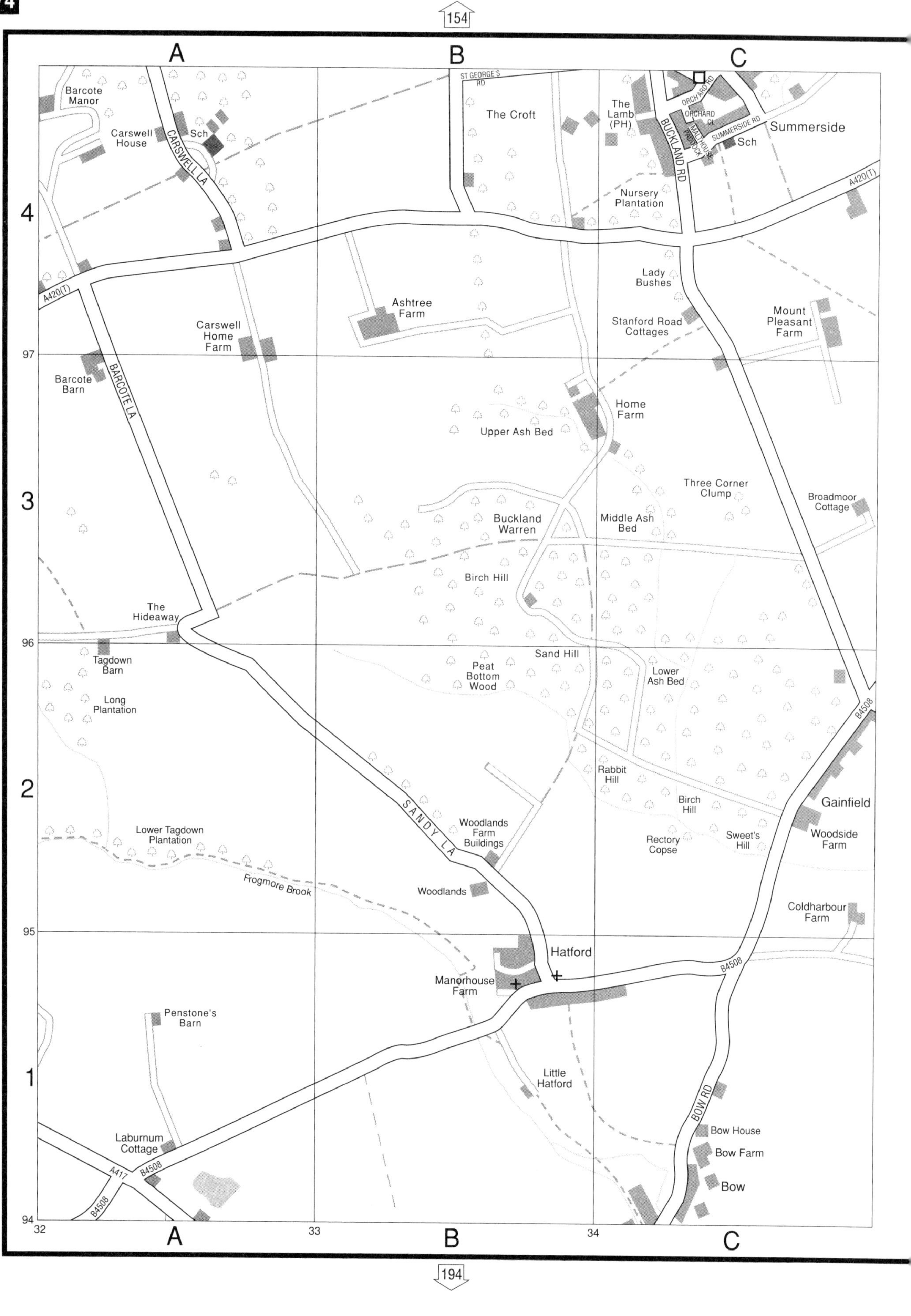
154
A
B
C
Barcote Manor
Carswell House
Sch
CARSWELL LA
ST GEORGE'S RD
The Croft
The Lamb (PH)
BUCKLAND RD
ORCHARD RD
ORCHARD CL
MALTHOUSE PADDOCK
SUMMERSIDE RD
Summerside
Sch
Nursery Plantation
A420(T)
4
Lady Bushes
A420(T)
Ashtree Farm
Stanford Road Cottages
Mount Pleasant Farm
Carswell Home Farm
97
Barcote Barn
BARCOTE LA
Home Farm
Upper Ash Bed
3
Three Corner Clump
Broadmoor Cottage
Buckland Warren
Middle Ash Bed
Birch Hill
The Hideaway
173
96
Tagdown Barn
Sand Hill
Peat Bottom Wood
Lower Ash Bed
Long Plantation
B4508
2
Rabbit Hill
SANDY LA
Birch Hill
Gainfield
Woodlands Farm Buildings
Lower Tagdown Plantation
Rectory Copse
Sweet's Hill
Woodside Farm
Frogmore Brook
Woodlands
Coldharbour Farm
95
Hatford
B4508
Manorhouse Farm
Penstone's Barn
1
Little Hatford
BOW RD
Bow House
Laburnum Cottage
Bow Farm
A417
B4508
Bow
B4508
94
32
33
34
A
B
C
194

155

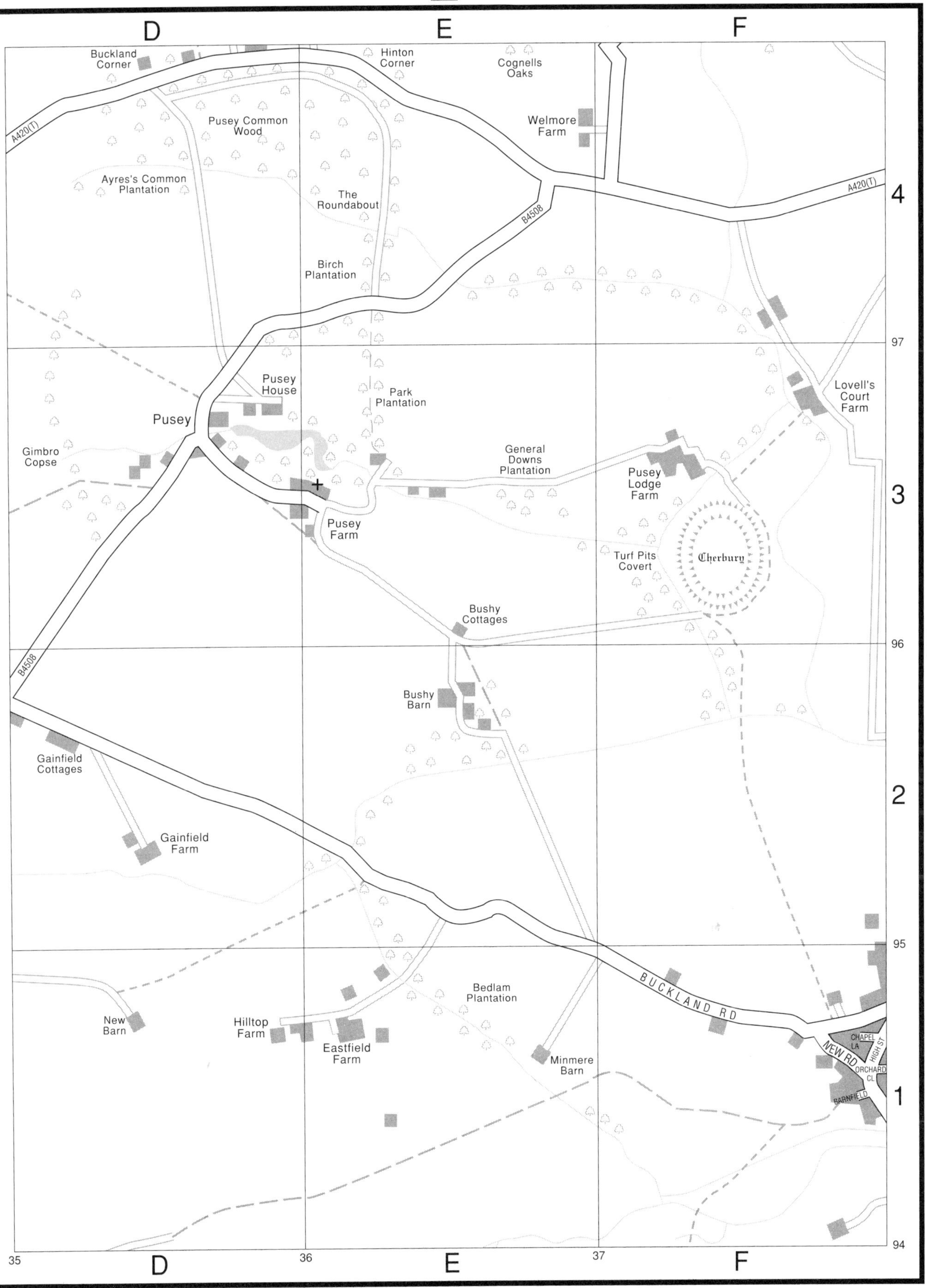
D
E
F
Buckland Corner
Hinton Corner
Cognells Oaks
A420(T)
Pusey Common Wood
Welmore Farm
Ayres's Common Plantation
The Roundabout
A420(T)
4
B4508
Birch Plantation
97
Pusey House
Park Plantation
Lovell's Court Farm
Pusey
Gimbro Copse
General Downs Plantation
Pusey Lodge Farm
3
Pusey Farm
Cherbury
Turf Pits Covert
Bushy Cottages
96
B4508
Bushy Barn
Gainfield Cottages
2
Gainfield Farm
95
BUCKLAND RD
Bedlam Plantation
New Barn
Hilltop Farm
Eastfield Farm
Minmere Barn
CHAPEL LA
HIGH ST
NEW RD
ORCHARD CL
BARNFIELD
1
94
35
D
36
E
37
F

176

195

156

175

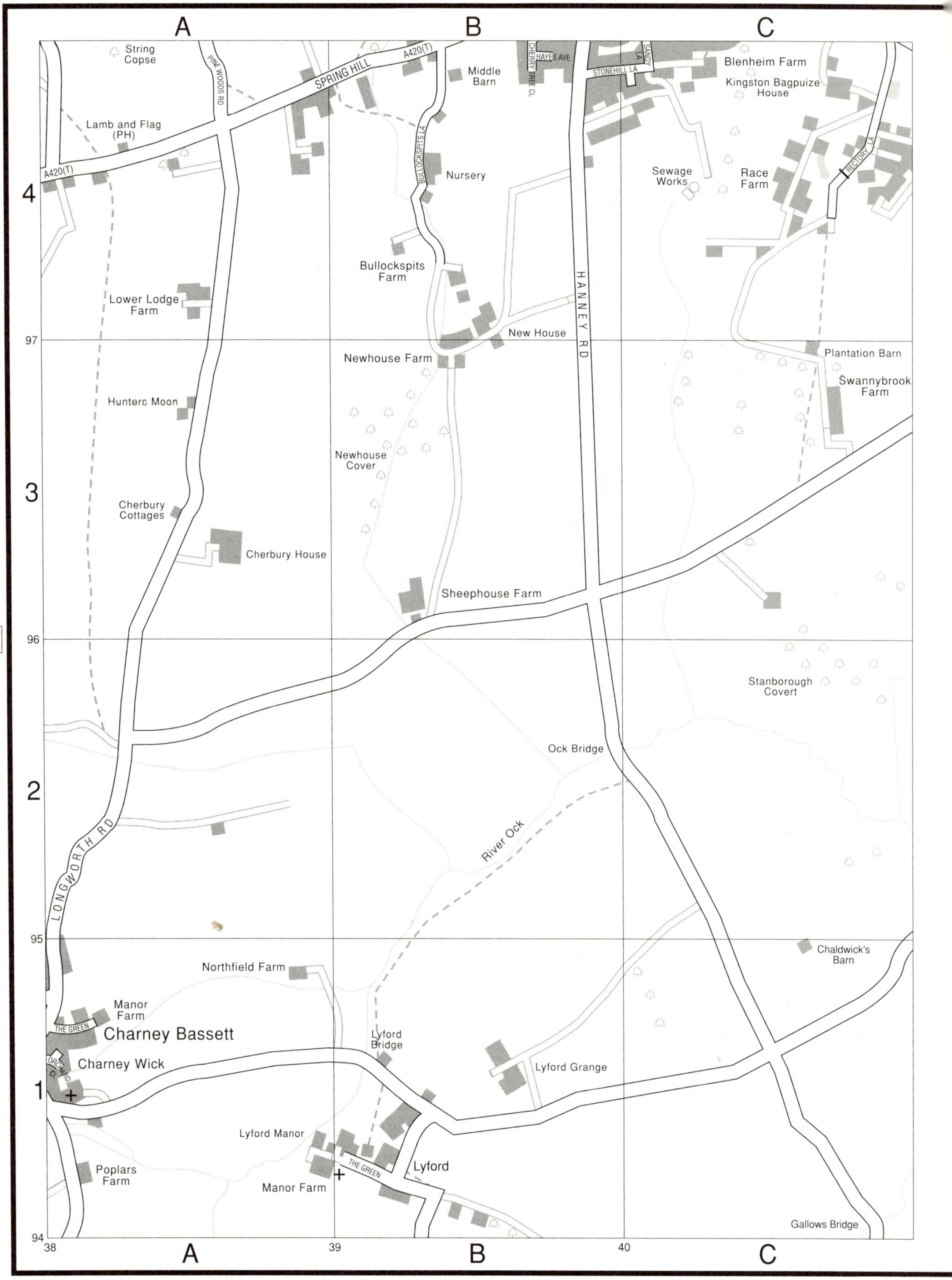

A
B
C
String Copse
PINE WOODS RD
SPRING HILL
A420(T)
Middle Barn
CHERRY TREE CL
HAYES AVE
STONEHILL LA
SANDY LA
Blenheim Farm
Kingston Bagpuize House
Lamb and Flag (PH)
A420(T)
BULLOCKSPITS LA
Nursery
Sewage Works
Race Farm
RECTORY LA
4
Bullockspits Farm
Lower Lodge Farm
HANNEY RD
New House
97
Newhouse Farm
Plantation Barn
Swannybrook Farm
Hunters Moon
Newhouse Cover
3
Cherbury Cottages
Cherbury House
Sheephouse Farm
96
Stanborough Covert
Ock Bridge
2
River Ock
LONGWORTH RD
95
Chaldwick's Barn
Northfield Farm
Manor Farm
THE GREEN
Charney Bassett
Lyford Bridge
ORCHARD CL
Charney Wick
Lyford Grange
1
Lyford Manor
Poplars Farm
THE GREEN
Lyford
Manor Farm
Gallows Bridge
94
38
39
40
A
B
C

196

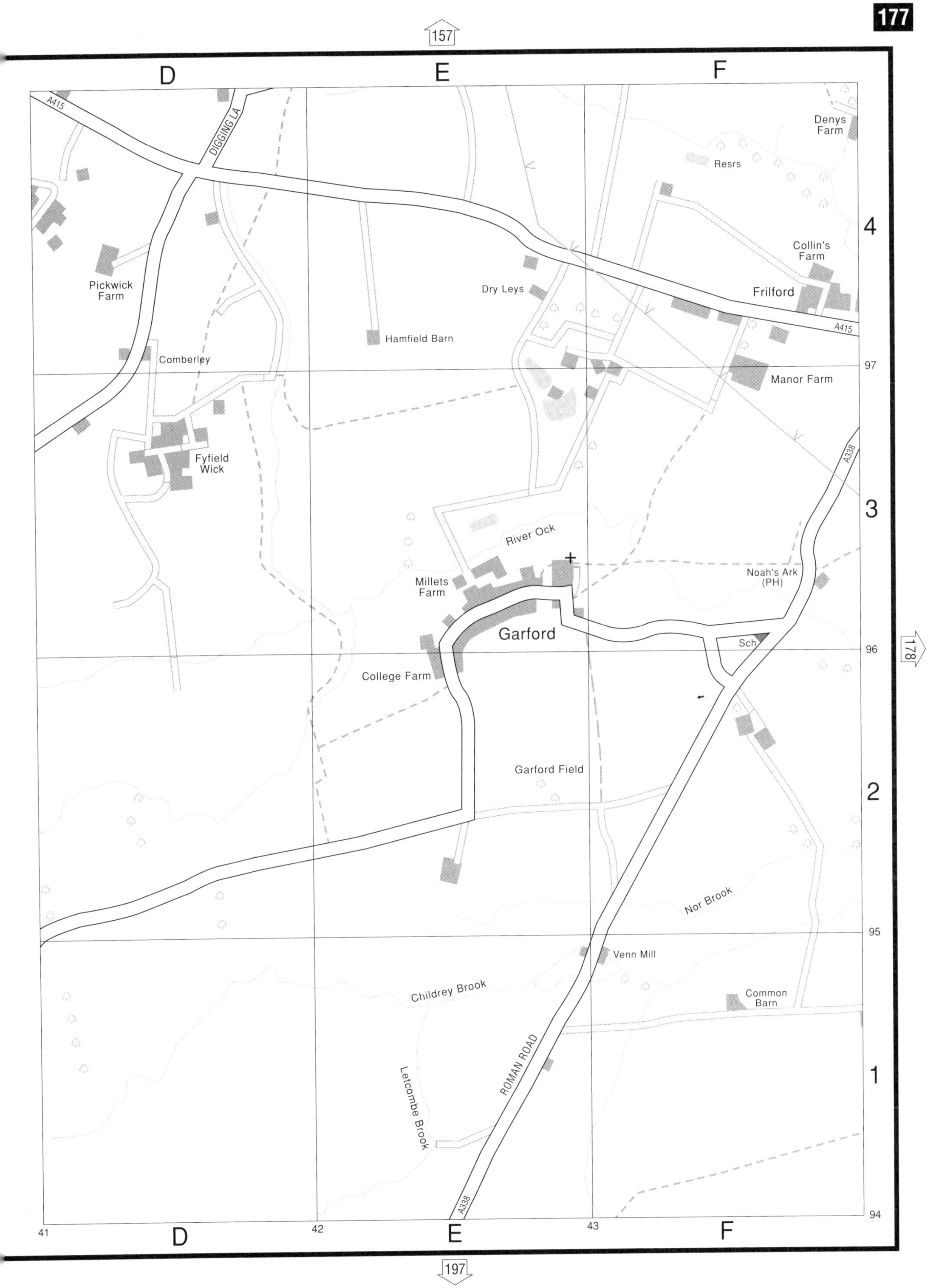
157
D
E
F
A415
DIGGING LA
Denys Farm
Resrs
4
Collin's Farm
Pickwick Farm
Dry Leys
Frilford
A415
Hamfield Barn
Comberley
97
Manor Farm
Fyfield Wick
A338
3
River Ock
Noah's Ark (PH)
Millets Farm
Garford
Sch
96
178
College Farm
Garford Field
2
Nor Brook
95
Venn Mill
Childrey Brook
Common Barn
ROMAN ROAD
1
Letcombe Brook
A338
94
41
D
42
E
43
F
197

158

177

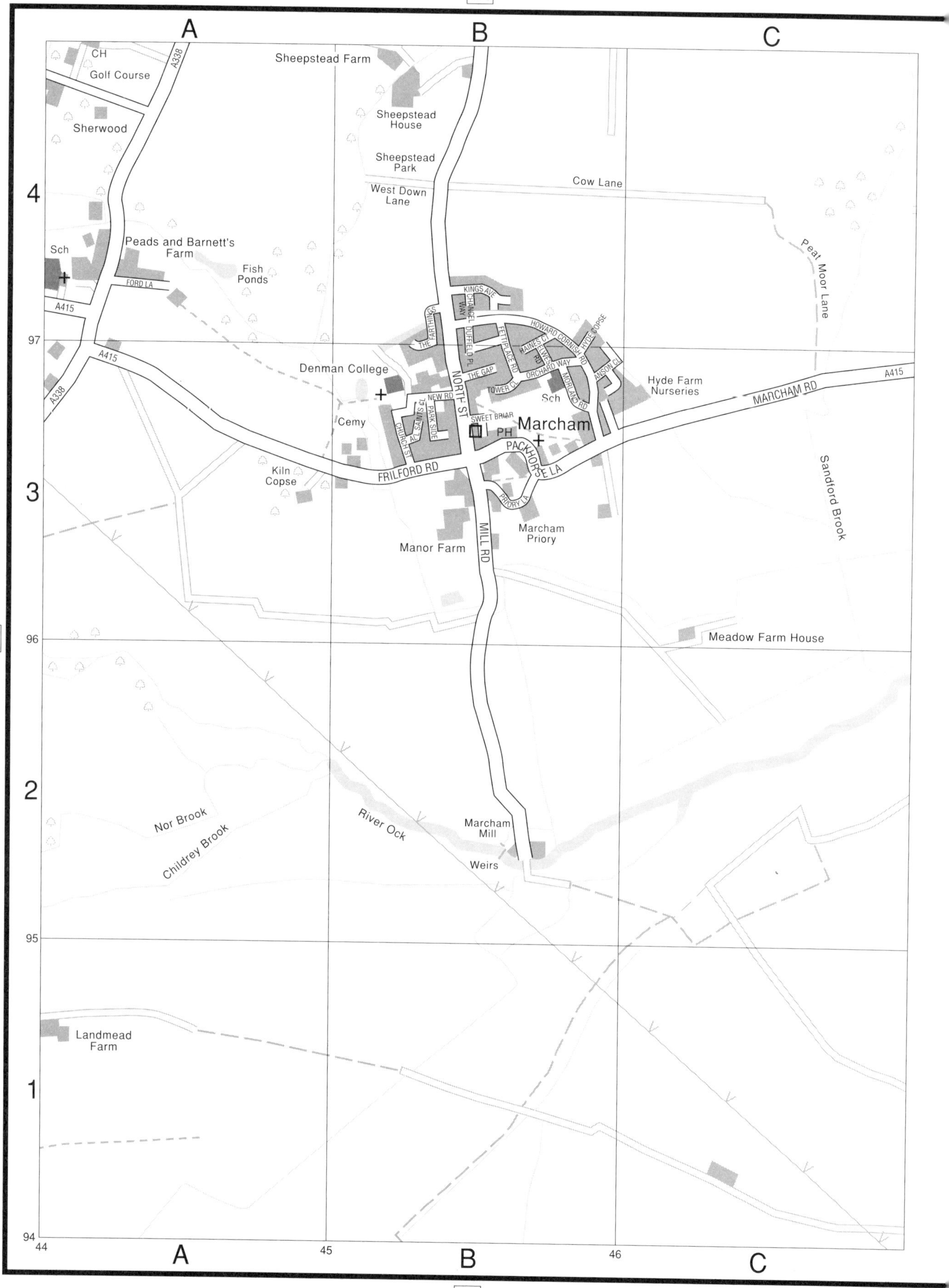
A
B
C
4
3
2
1
97
96
95
94
44
45
46
CH
Golf Course
A338
Sheepstead Farm
Sheepstead House
Sherwood
Sheepstead Park
West Down Lane
Cow Lane
Sch
Peads and Barnett's Farm
Fish Ponds
FORD LA
A415
Peat Moor Lane
KINGS AVE
CHANCEL WAY
THE FARTHINGS
DUFFIELD PL
FETTIPLACE RD
HAINES CT
HOWARD CORNISH RD
HYDE COPSE
ORCHARD WAY
MORLAND RD
ANSON CL
THE GAP
TOWER CL
Denman College
NEW RD
NORTH ST
Sch
Hyde Farm Nurseries
MARCHAM RD
Cemy
CHURCH ST
ALL SAINTS
PARK SIDE
SWEET BRIAR
PH
Marcham
PACKHORSE LA
Kiln Copse
FRILFORD RD
PRIORY LA
Sandford Brook
Marcham Priory
Manor Farm
MILL RD
Meadow Farm House
Nor Brook
Childrey Brook
River Ock
Marcham Mill
Weirs
Landmead Farm

198

159

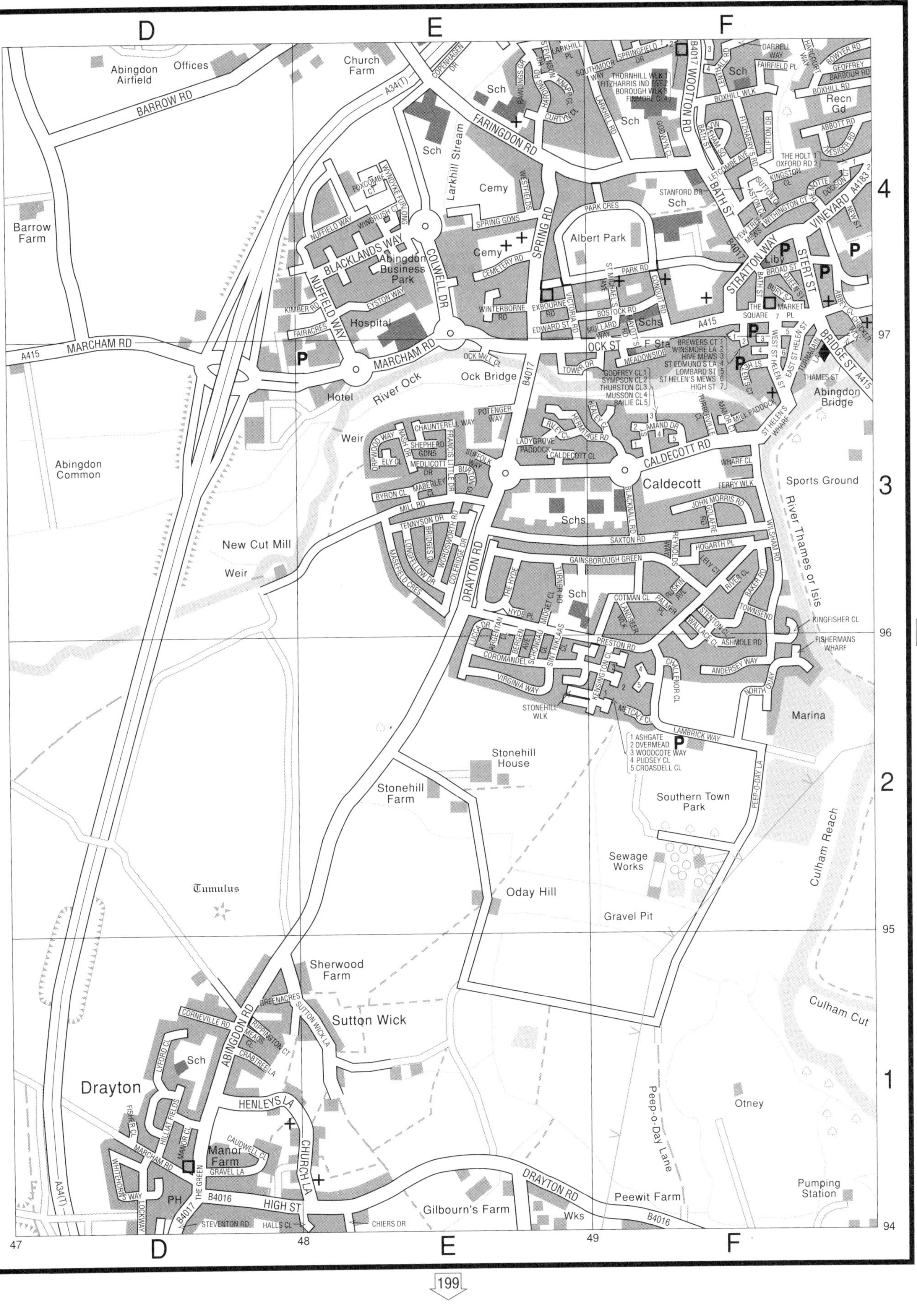
D
E
F
Abingdon Airfield
Offices
Church Farm
BARROW RD
Barrow Farm
A34(T)
Sch
FARINGDON RD
Larkhill Stream
Cemy
SPRING RD
Albert Park
Sch
B4017 WOOTTON RD
BATH ST
STRATTON WAY
VINEYARD
STERT ST
Recn Gd
Liby
BLACKLANDS WAY
Abingdon Business Park
COLWELL DR
NUFFIELD WAY
Hospital
A415
MARCHAM RD
OCK ST
F Sta
Schs
THE SQUARE
MARKET PL
BRIDGE ST
Abingdon Bridge
THAMES ST
Hotel
River Ock
Ock Bridge
B4017
Weir
Abingdon Common
CALDECOTT RD
Caldecott
Sports Ground
River Thames or Isis
Schs
New Cut Mill
Weir
DRAYTON RD
SAXTON RD
GAINSBOROUGH GREEN
Sch
PRESTON RD
KINGFISHER CL
FISHERMANS WHARF
Marina
LAMBRICK WAY
1 ASHGATE
2 OVERMEAD
3 WOODCOTE WAY
4 PUDSEY CL
5 CROASDELL CL
Stonehill House
Stonehill Farm
Southern Town Park
PEEP-O-DAY LA
Culham Reach
Sewage Works
Oday Hill
Tumulus
Gravel Pit
Sherwood Farm
Culham Cut
Sutton Wick
ABINGDON RD
SUTTON WICK LA
Sch
Drayton
HENLEYS LA
Otney
Peep-o-Day Lane
Manor Farm
CHURCH LA
DRAYTON RD
Pumping Station
PH
B4016
HIGH ST
Gilbourn's Farm
Peewit Farm
Wks
B4016
STEVENTON RD
HALLS CL
CHIERS DR
1
2
3
4
47
48
49
94
95
96
97

180

199

160

179

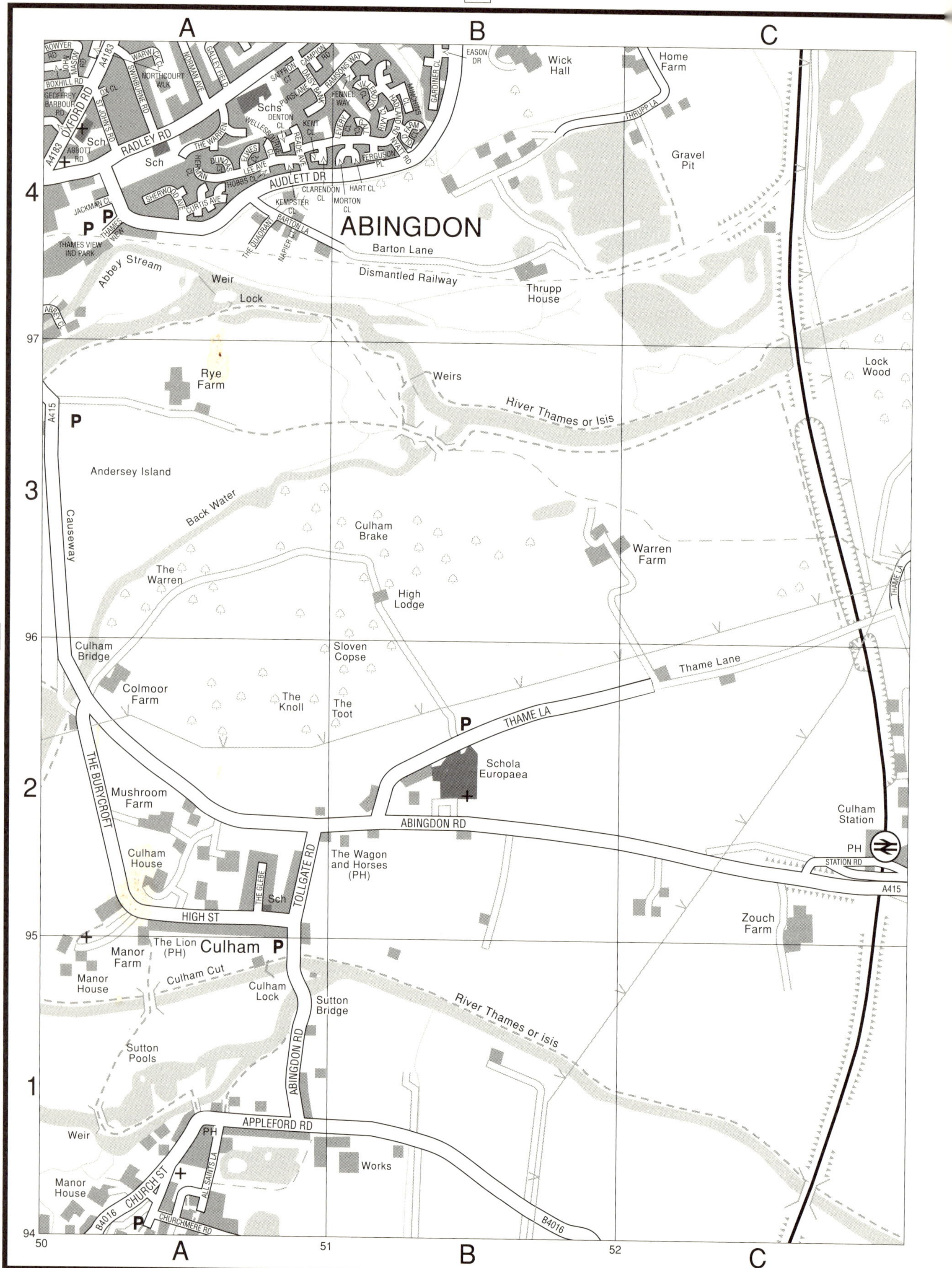
A
B
C
ABINGDON
BOWYER RD
JOHN MASON RD
BOXHILL RD
GEOFFREY BARBOUR RD
OXFORD RD
A4183
ST JOHNS RD
SWINBURNE RD
WARWICK CL
NORTHCOURT WLK
NORMAN AVE
GALLEY FIELD
RADLEY RD
Sch
Schs
SAFFRON CT
CAMPION RD
DAISY BANK
PURSLANE
DENTON CL
WELLESBOURNE CL
KENT CL
RAMSONS WAY
FENNEL WAY
LEVERY CL
HADLAND RD
GARDINER CL
MINCHINS CL
NYATT RD
FERGUSON PL
THE WARREN
HERMAN CL
DUNLAS CL
FAWES CL
LEE AVE
HOBBS CL
READE AVE
AUDLETT DR
CLARENDON CL
HART CL
MORTON CL
KEMPSTER CL
BARTON LA
SHERWOOD AVE
CURTIS AVE
JACKMAN CL
ABBOTT RD
THAMES VIEW
THAMES VIEW IND PARK
THE QUADRANT
NAPIER CT
EASON DR
Wick Hall
Home Farm
THRUPP LA
Gravel Pit
Barton Lane
Dismantled Railway
Thrupp House
Abbey Stream
Weir
Lock
ABBEY CL
97
Rye Farm
Weirs
River Thames or Isis
Lock Wood
A415
Andersey Island
Back Water
Causeway
Culham Brake
Warren Farm
The Warren
High Lodge
96
Culham Bridge
Sloven Copse
Thame Lane
Colmoor Farm
The Knoll
The Toot
THAME LA
THE BURYCROFT
Schola Europaea
Mushroom Farm
ABINGDON RD
Culham Station
PH
STATION RD
Culham House
TOLLGATE RD
THE GLEBE
The Wagon and Horses (PH)
HIGH ST
Zouch Farm
95
The Lion (PH)
Culham
Manor Farm
Manor House
Culham Cut
Culham Lock
Sutton Bridge
Sutton Pools
1
2
3
4
Weir
APPLEFORD RD
Works
CHURCH ST
ALL SAINTS LA
B4016
CHURCHMERE RD
94
50
51
52

200

161

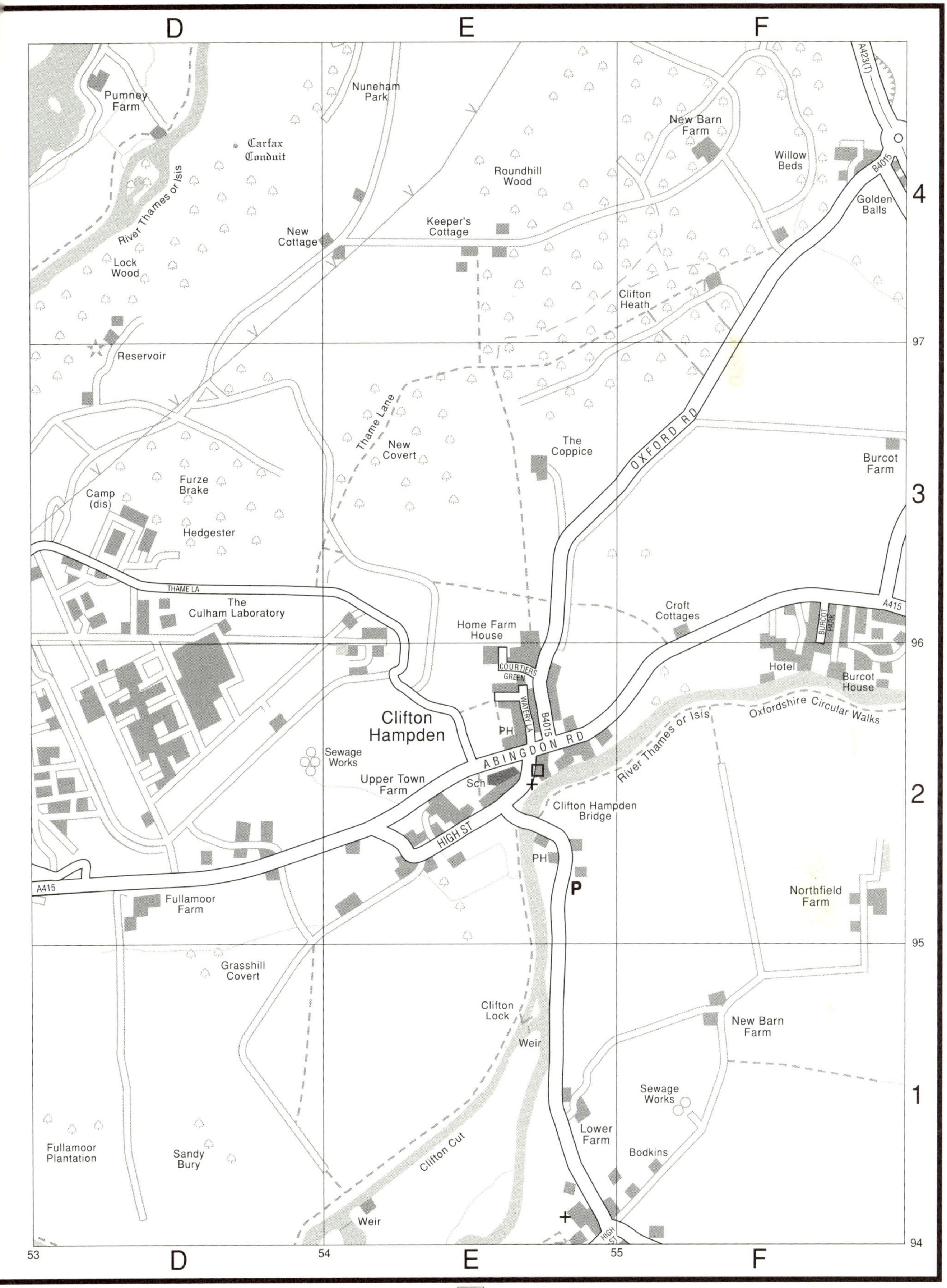
D
E
F
Pumney Farm
Carfax Conduit
River Thames or Isis
Lock Wood
Nuneham Park
Roundhill Wood
New Barn Farm
Willow Beds
A423(T)
B4015
Golden Balls
New Cottage
Keeper's Cottage
Clifton Heath
Reservoir
Thame Lane
New Covert
The Coppice
OXFORD RD
Burcot Farm
Camp (dis)
Furze Brake
Hedgester
THAME LA
The Culham Laboratory
Croft Cottages
A415
BURCOT PARK
Home Farm House
COURTIERS GREEN
WATERY LA
B4015
Hotel
Burcot House
Clifton Hampden
Oxfordshire Circular Walks
River Thames or Isis
PH
ABINGDON RD
Sewage Works
Upper Town Farm
Sch
Clifton Hampden Bridge
HIGH ST
PH
P
A415
Fullamoor Farm
Northfield Farm
Grasshill Covert
Clifton Lock
New Barn Farm
Weir
Sewage Works
Lower Farm
Bodkins
Fullamoor Plantation
Sandy Bury
Clifton Cut
Weir
HIGH ST
4
97
3
96
2
95
1
94
53
54
55
D
E
F

182

201

162

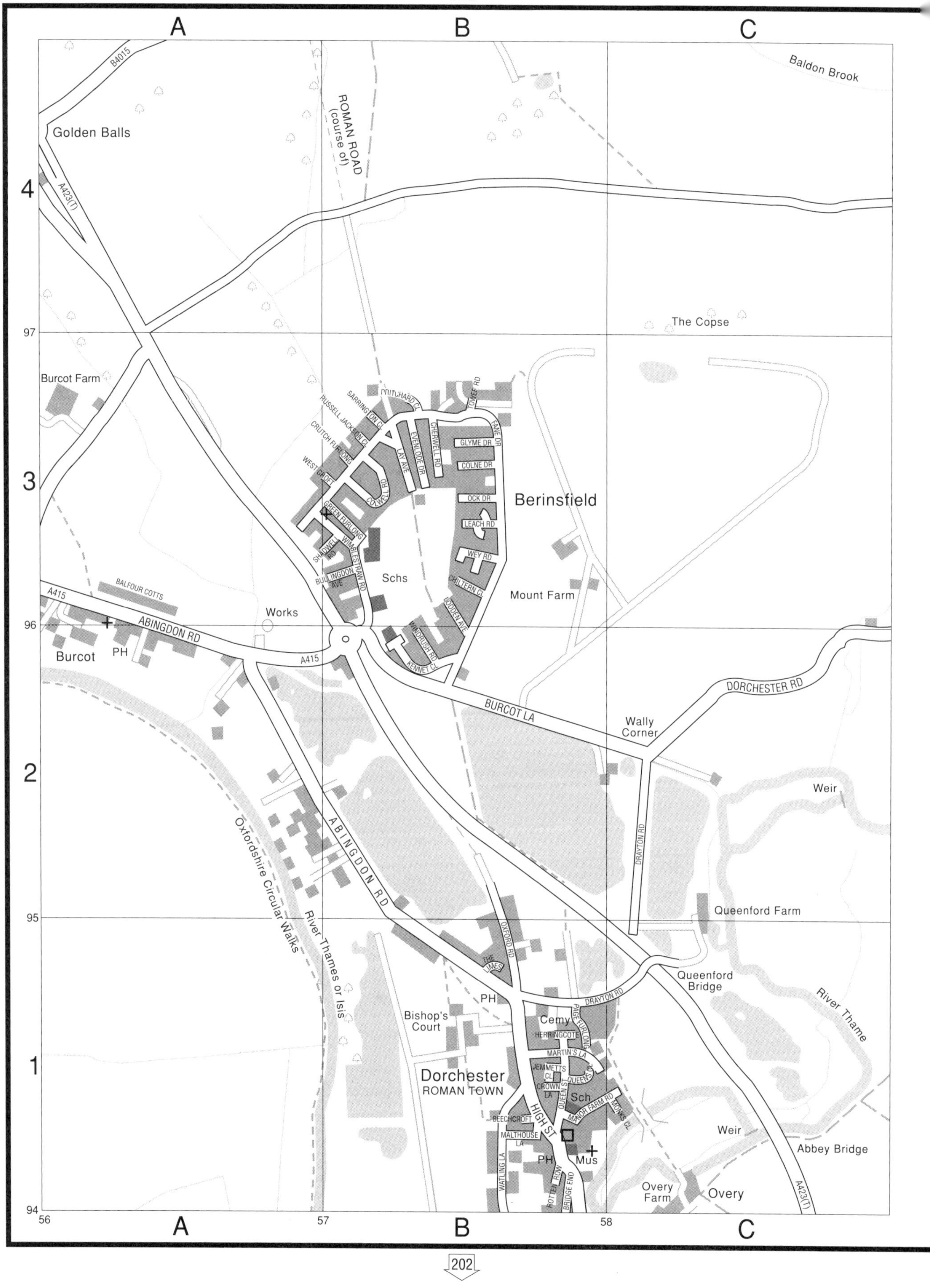
A
B
C
4
3
2
1
97
96
95
94
56
57
58
Baldon Brook
B4015
Golden Balls
ROMAN ROAD (course of)
A423(T)
The Copse
Burcot Farm
PRITCHARD CL
SARRINGTON CL
RUSSELL JACKSON CL
CRUTCH FURLONG
WEST CROFT
GREEN FURLONG
SHADWELL RD
WIMBLESTRAW RD
BULLINGDON AVE
COLWELL RD
LAY AVE
EVENLODE DR
CHERWELL RD
GLYME DR
COLNE DR
OCK DR
LEACH RD
WEY RD
CHILTERN CL
LODDEN AVE
WINDRUSH RD
KENNET CL
FANE DR
TOWEF RD
Berinsfield
Schs
Mount Farm
BALFOUR COTTS
A415
ABINGDON RD
Works
Burcot
PH
BURCOT LA
DORCHESTER RD
Wally Corner
Weir
DRAYTON RD
Oxfordshire Circular Walks
River Thames or Isis
ABINGDON RD
OXFORD RD
THE LIMES
Queenford Farm
Queenford Bridge
River Thame
DRAYTON RD
PH
Bishop's Court
Cemy
PAGE FURLONG
HERRINGCOTE
MARTIN'S LA
JEMMETTS CL
QUEEN ST
QUEENS CL
CROWN LA
Sch
MANOR FARM RD
MONKS CL
Dorchester
ROMAN TOWN
BEECHCROFT
HIGH ST
MALTHOUSE LA
WATLING LA
ROTTEN ROW
BRIDGE END
PH
Mus
Weir
Abbey Bridge
Overy Farm
Overy

181

202

163

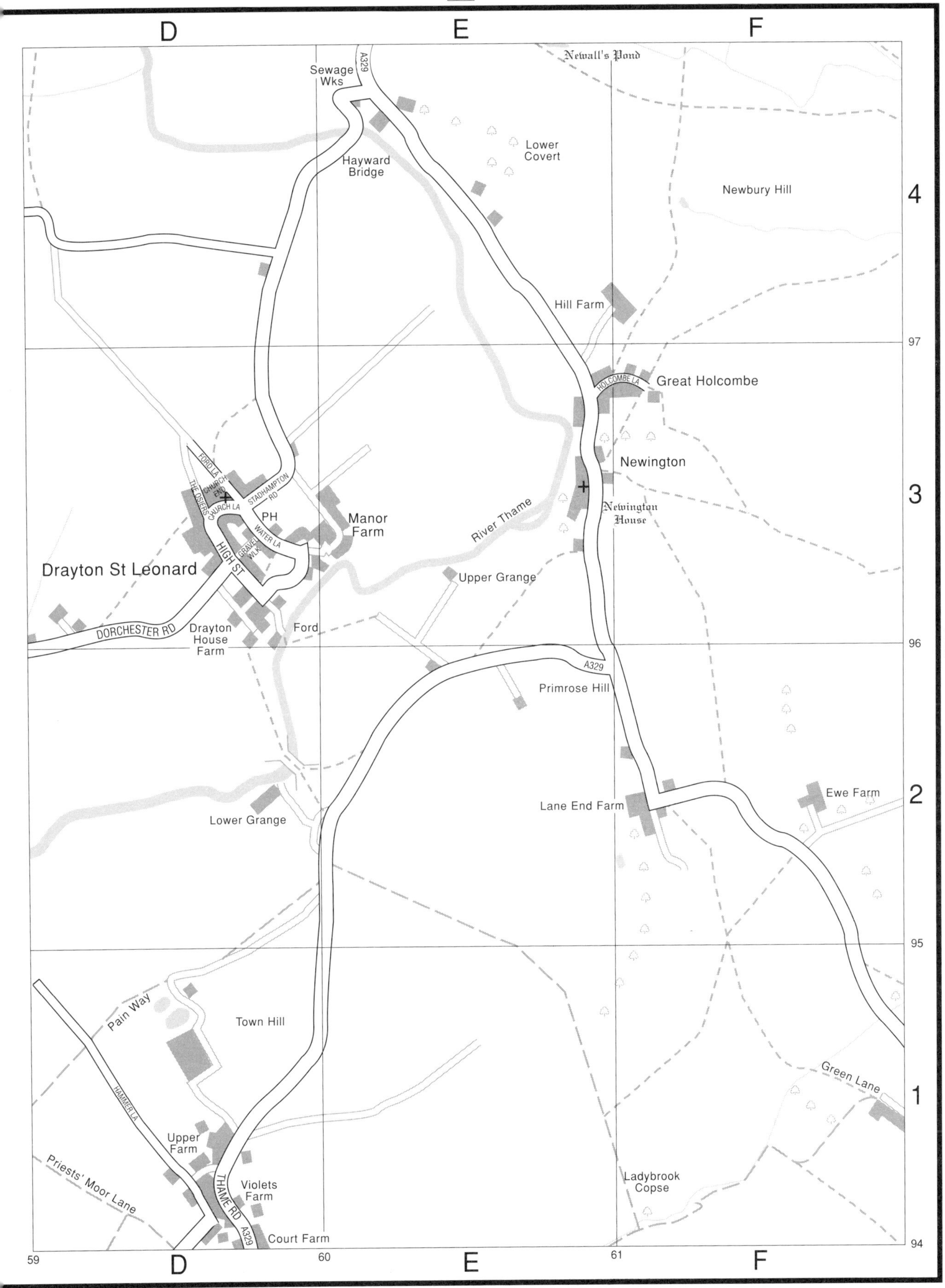
D
E
F
Newall's Pond
Sewage Wks
A329
Lower Covert
Hayward Bridge
Newbury Hill
4
Hill Farm
97
HOLCOMBE LA
Great Holcombe
Newington
FORD LA
CHURCH END
STADHAMPTON RD
THE OSIERS
CHURCH LA
PH
Manor Farm
3
Newington House
River Thame
WATER LA
GRAVEL WLK
HIGH ST
Drayton St Leonard
Upper Grange
DORCHESTER RD
Drayton House Farm
Ford
96
A329
Primrose Hill
Ewe Farm
2
Lane End Farm
Lower Grange
95
Pain Way
Town Hill
Green Lane
1
HAMMER LA
Upper Farm
Priests' Moor Lane
THAME RD
Violets Farm
A329
Court Farm
Ladybrook Copse
94
59
60
61
D
E
F

184

203

164

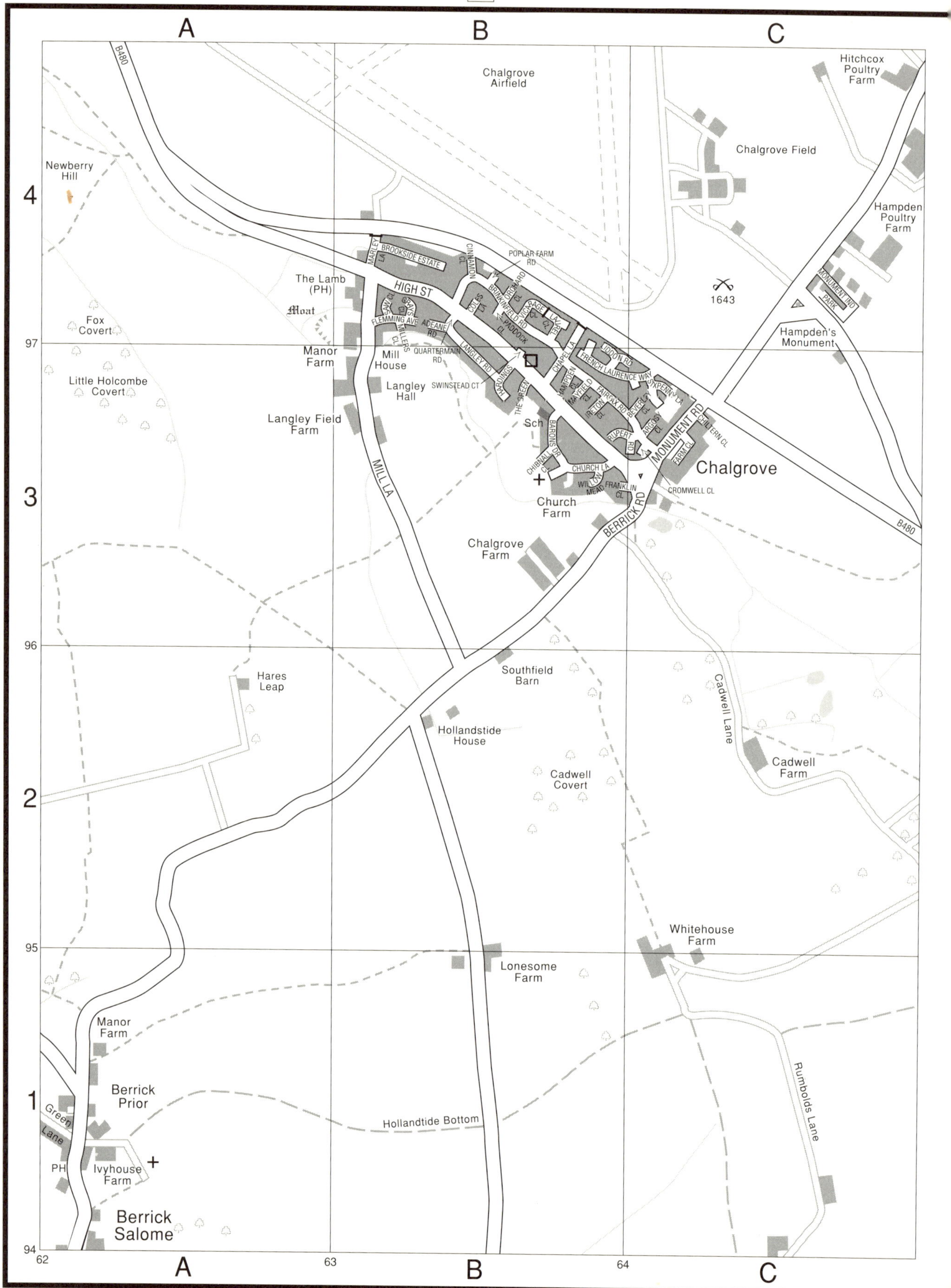
A
B
C
Chalgrove Airfield
Hitchcox Poultry Farm
Chalgrove Field
Newberry Hill
Hampden Poultry Farm
B480
MARLEY LA
BROOKSIDE ESTATE
CINNAMON CL
POPLAR FARM RD
The Lamb (PH)
HIGH ST
1643
Moat
Fox Covert
FLEMMING AVE
ADEANE RD
Hampden's Monument
MONUMENT IND PARK
Manor Farm
Mill House
QUARTERMAIN RD
LANGLEY RD
CHAPEL LA
FRENCH LAURENCE WAY
Little Holcombe Covert
Langley Hall
SWINSTEAD CT
HARDINGS
THE GREEN
Langley Field Farm
Sch
BARONS DR
RUPERT RD
MONUMENT RD
CHILTERN CL
FARM CL
Chalgrove
CHIBNALL CL
CHURCH LA
WILLOW MEAD
FRANKLIN CL
CROMWELL CL
MILL LA
Church Farm
BERRICK RD
Chalgrove Farm
Southfield Barn
Hares Leap
Cadwell Lane
Hollandstide House
Cadwell Farm
Cadwell Covert
Whitehouse Farm
Lonesome Farm
Manor Farm
Rumbolds Lane
Berrick Prior
Green Lane
Hollandtide Bottom
PH
Ivyhouse Farm
Berrick Salome
4
97
3
96
2
95
1
94
62
63
64

183

204

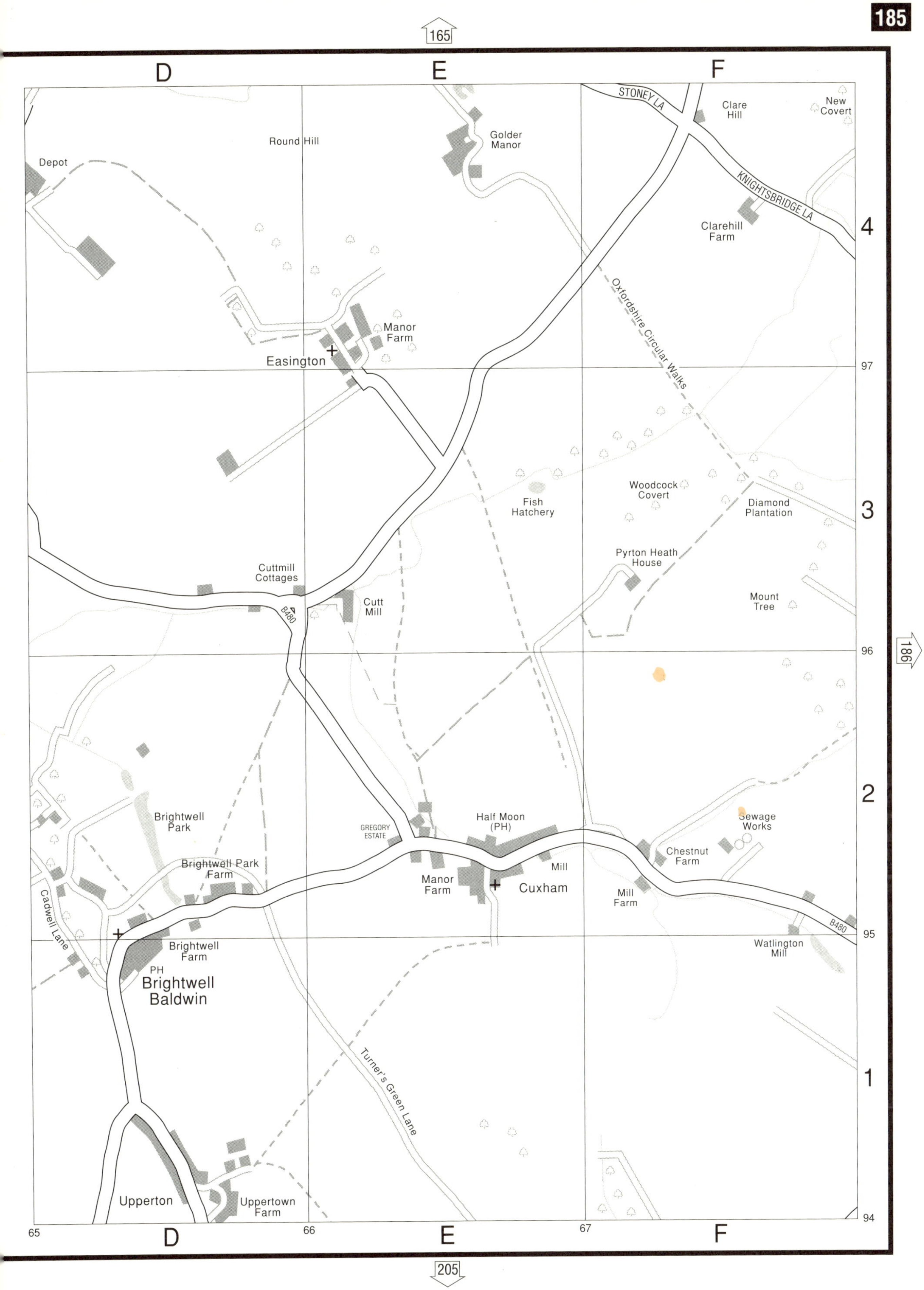
165
D
E
F
STONEY LA
Clare Hill
New Covert
Golder Manor
Round Hill
Depot
KNIGHTSBRIDGE LA
Clarehill Farm
4
Oxfordshire Circular Walks
Manor Farm
Easington
97
Woodcock Covert
Fish Hatchery
Diamond Plantation
3
Pyrton Heath House
Cuttmill Cottages
Mount Tree
Cutt Mill
B480
96
186
2
Brightwell Park
Half Moon (PH)
GREGORY ESTATE
Sewage Works
Brightwell Park Farm
Chestnut Farm
Mill
Manor Farm
Cuxham
Mill Farm
Cadwell Lane
B480
95
Brightwell Farm
Watlington Mill
PH
Brightwell Baldwin
1
Turner's Green Lane
Upperton
Uppertown Farm
94
65
66
67
D
E
F
205

166

185

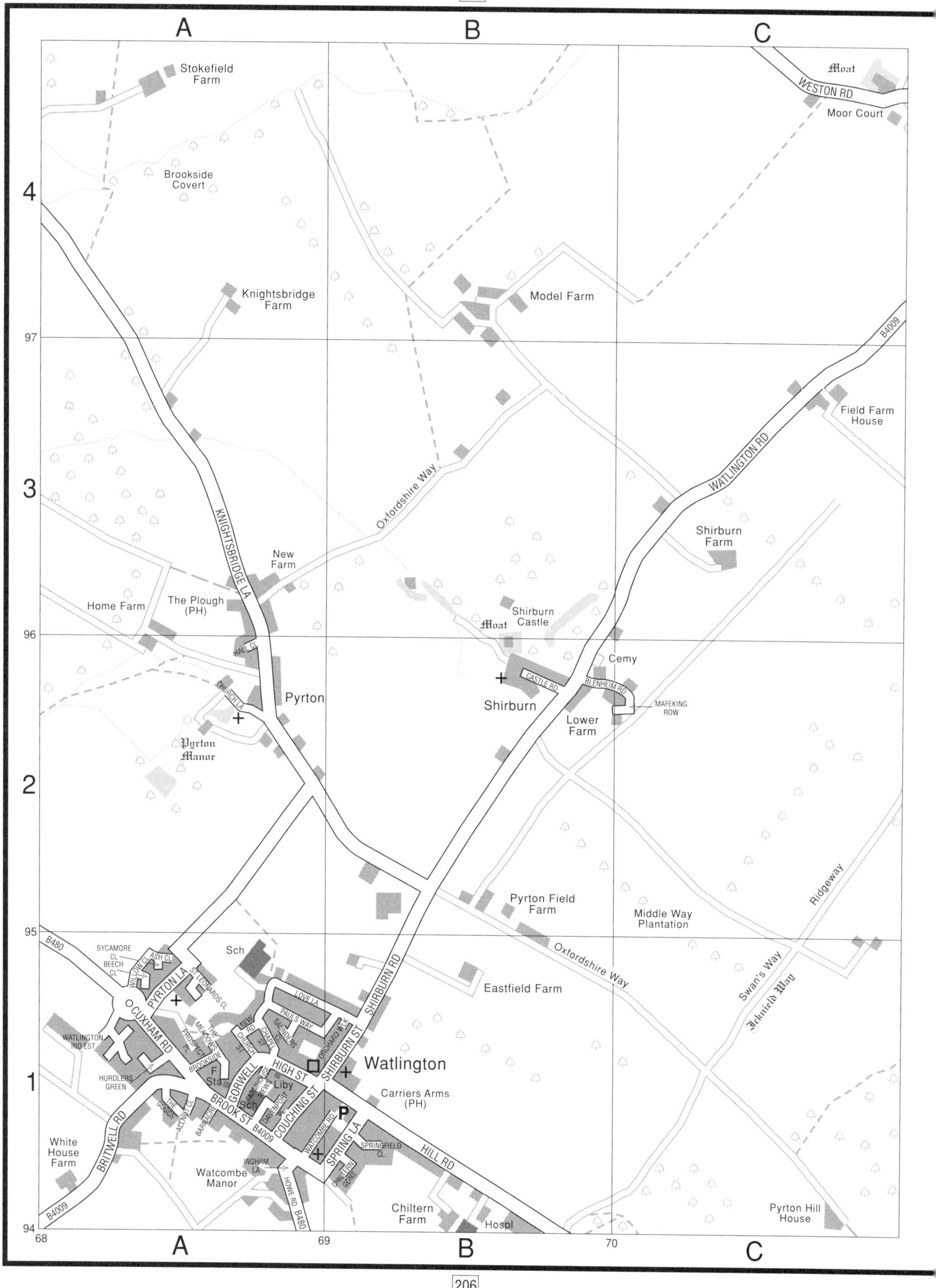
A
B
C
4
3
2
1
97
96
95
94
68
69
70
Stokefield Farm
Moat
WESTON RD
Moor Court
Brookside Covert
Knightsbridge Farm
Model Farm
B4009
Field Farm House
WATLINGTON RD
Oxfordshire Way
KNIGHTSBRIDGE LA
New Farm
Shirburn Farm
Home Farm
The Plough (PH)
Shirburn Castle
Moat
HAL CL
Cemy
CASTLE RD
BLENHEIM RD
MAFEKING ROW
CHURCH LA
Pyrton
Shirburn
Lower Farm
Pyrton Manor
Pyrton Field Farm
Middle Way Plantation
Ridgeway
B480
SYCAMORE CL
BEECH CL
WILLOW CL
ASH CL
PYRTON LA
ST LEONARDS CL
Sch
LOVE LA
PAULS WAY
SAUNDERS
ORCHARD WLK
SHIRBURN RD
Eastfield Farm
Oxfordshire Way
Swan's Way
Icknield Way
CUXHAM RD
WATLINGTON IND EST
PROSPECT PL
THE MEADOWS
BROOKSIDE
NEW RD
CHURCH ST
CHAPEL ST
HIGH ST
SHIRBURN ST
Watlington
F
Sta
GORWELL
Liby
Sch
HURDLERS GREEN
COUCHING ST
DAVENPORT PL
P
Carriers Arms (PH)
BRITWELL RD
THE GOGGS
ALLNUT CL
BARNACRE
BROOK ST
B4009
WATCOMBE RD
SPRING LA
SPRINGFIELD CL
HILL RD
White House Farm
INGHAM LA
Watcombe Manor
HOWE RD B480
CHILTERN GDNS
Chiltern Farm
Hospl
Pyrton Hill House
B4009

206

167

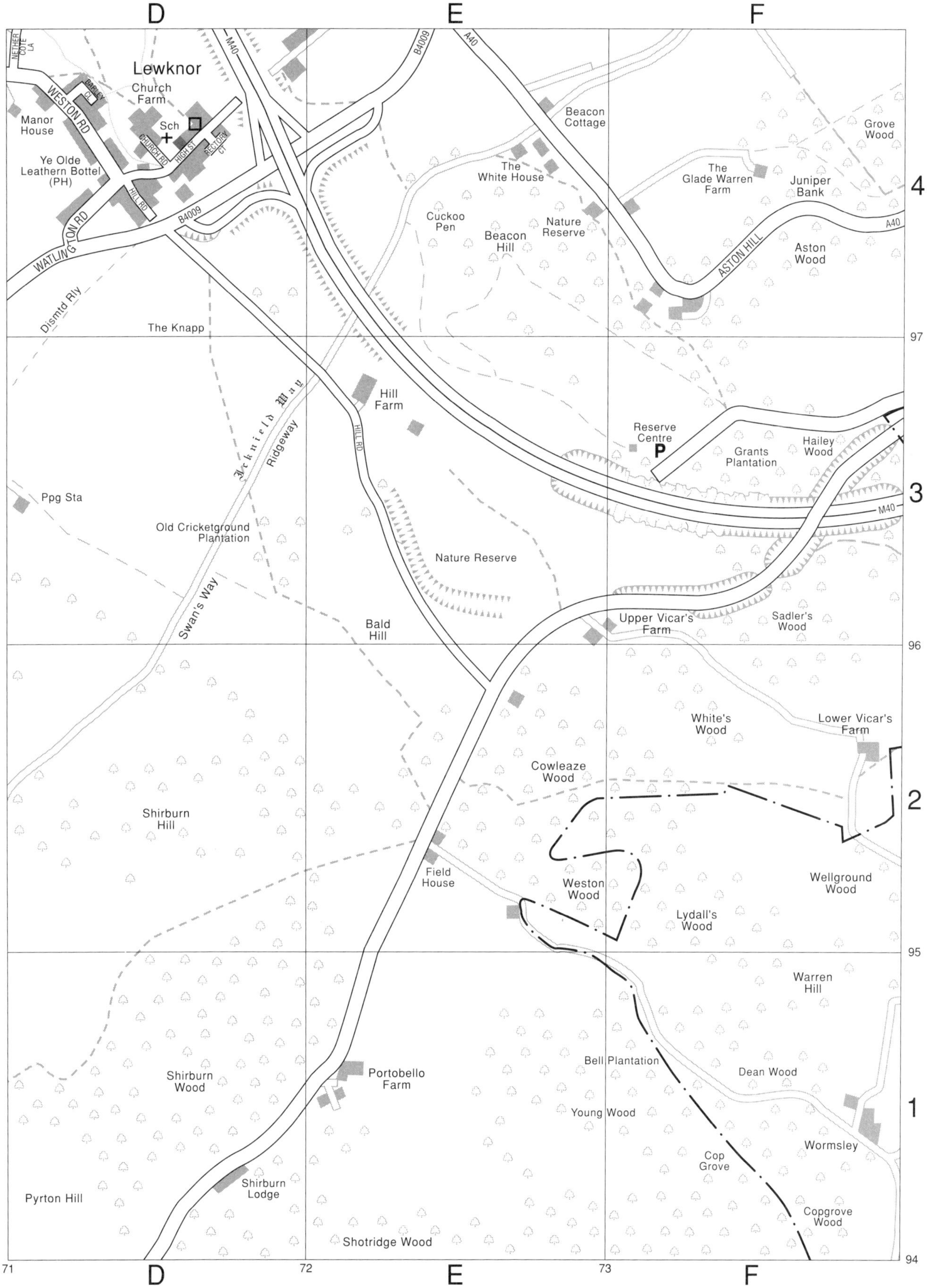
D
E
F
NETHER COTE LA
Lewknor
Church Farm
BARLEY CL
WESTON RD
Manor House
Sch
CHURCH RD
HIGH ST
RECTORY CT
Ye Olde Leathern Bottel (PH)
HILL RD
WATLINGTON RD
B4009
M40
A40
Beacon Cottage
The White House
Cuckoo Pen
Beacon Hill
Nature Reserve
The Glade Warren Farm
Grove Wood
Juniper Bank
ASTON HILL
Aston Wood
Dismtd Rly
The Knapp
Hill Farm
Icknield Way
Ridgeway
Reserve Centre
P
Grants Plantation
Hailey Wood
Ppg Sta
Old Cricketground Plantation
Nature Reserve
Swan's Way
Bald Hill
Upper Vicar's Farm
Sadler's Wood
White's Wood
Lower Vicar's Farm
Cowleaze Wood
Shirburn Hill
Field House
Weston Wood
Lydall's Wood
Wellground Wood
Warren Hill
Bell Plantation
Dean Wood
Shirburn Wood
Portobello Farm
Young Wood
Wormsley
Cop Grove
Copgrove Wood
Shirburn Lodge
Pyrton Hill
Shotridge Wood
4
3
2
1
97
96
95
94
71
72
73

188

207

168

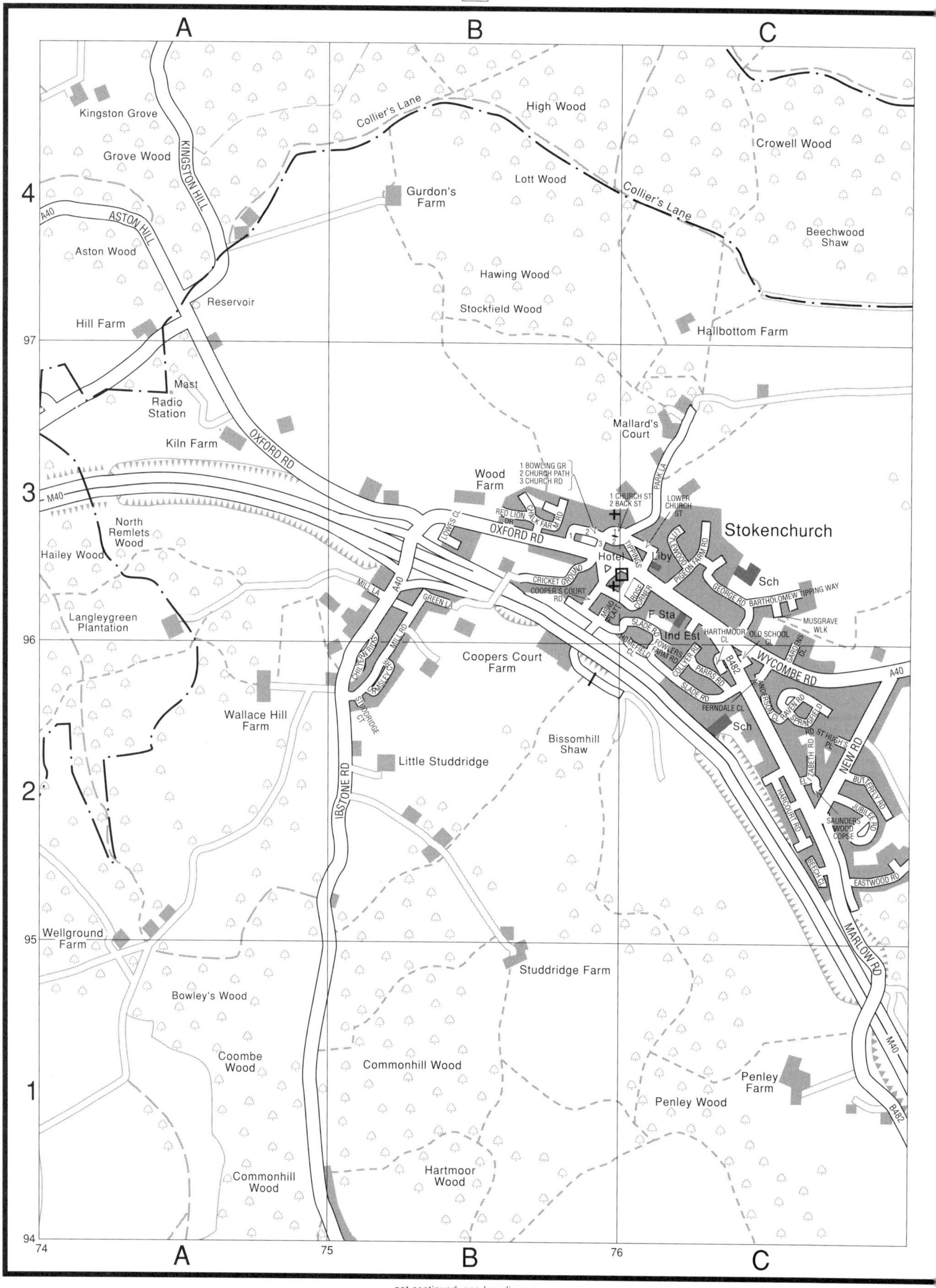

187

not continued, see key diagram

169

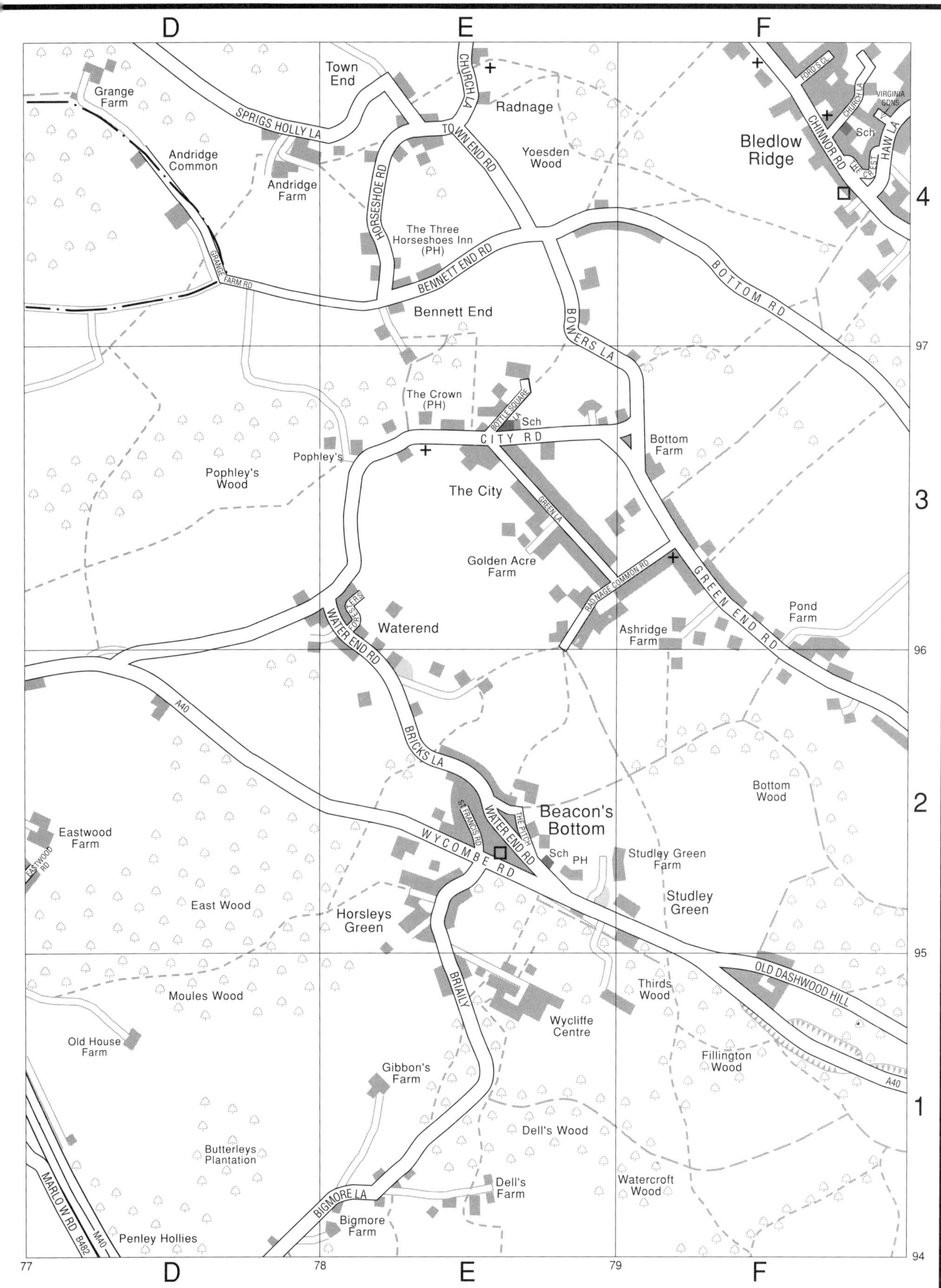

not continued, see key diagram

not continued, see key diagram

170

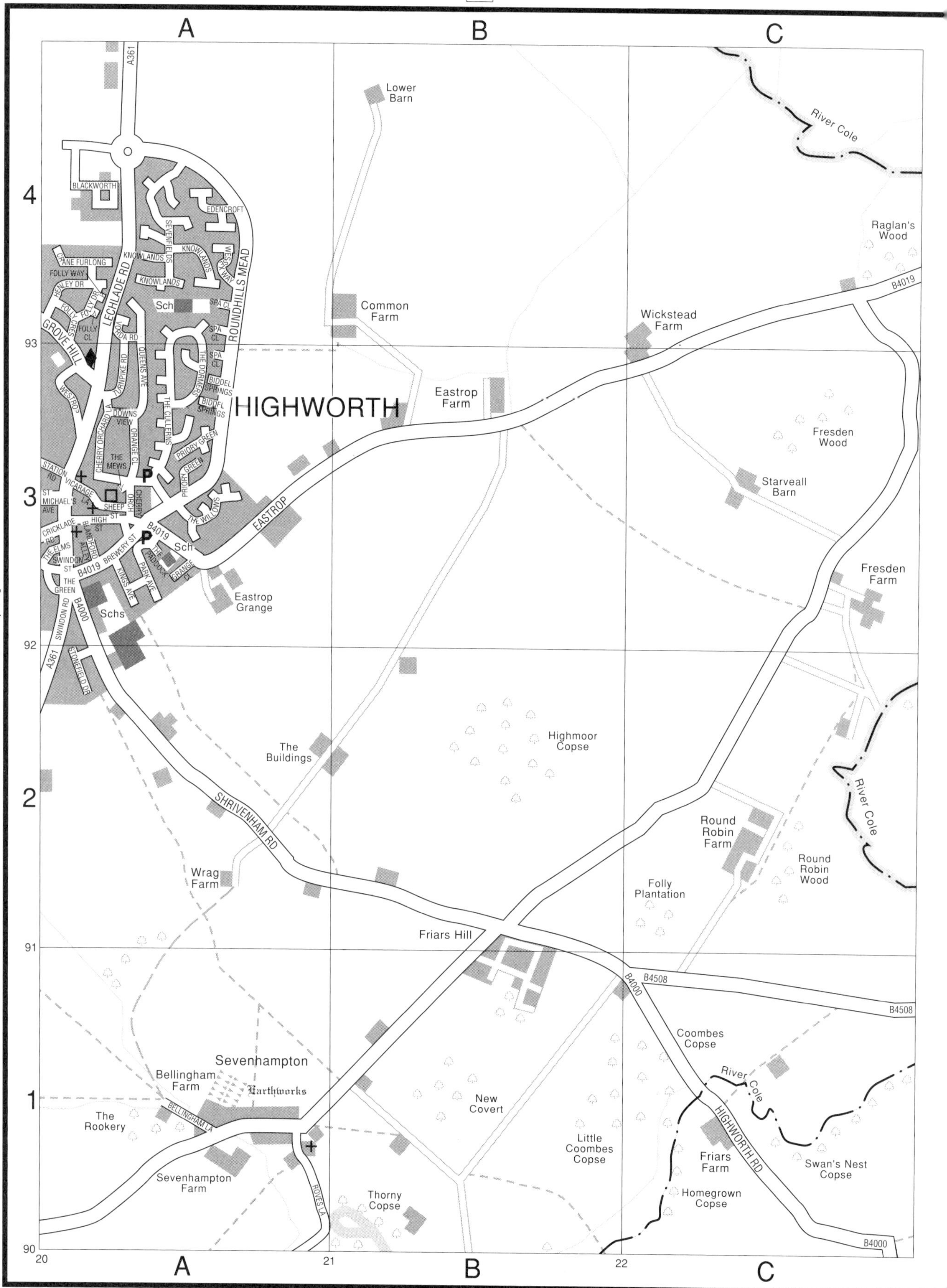

208

not continued, see key diagram

171

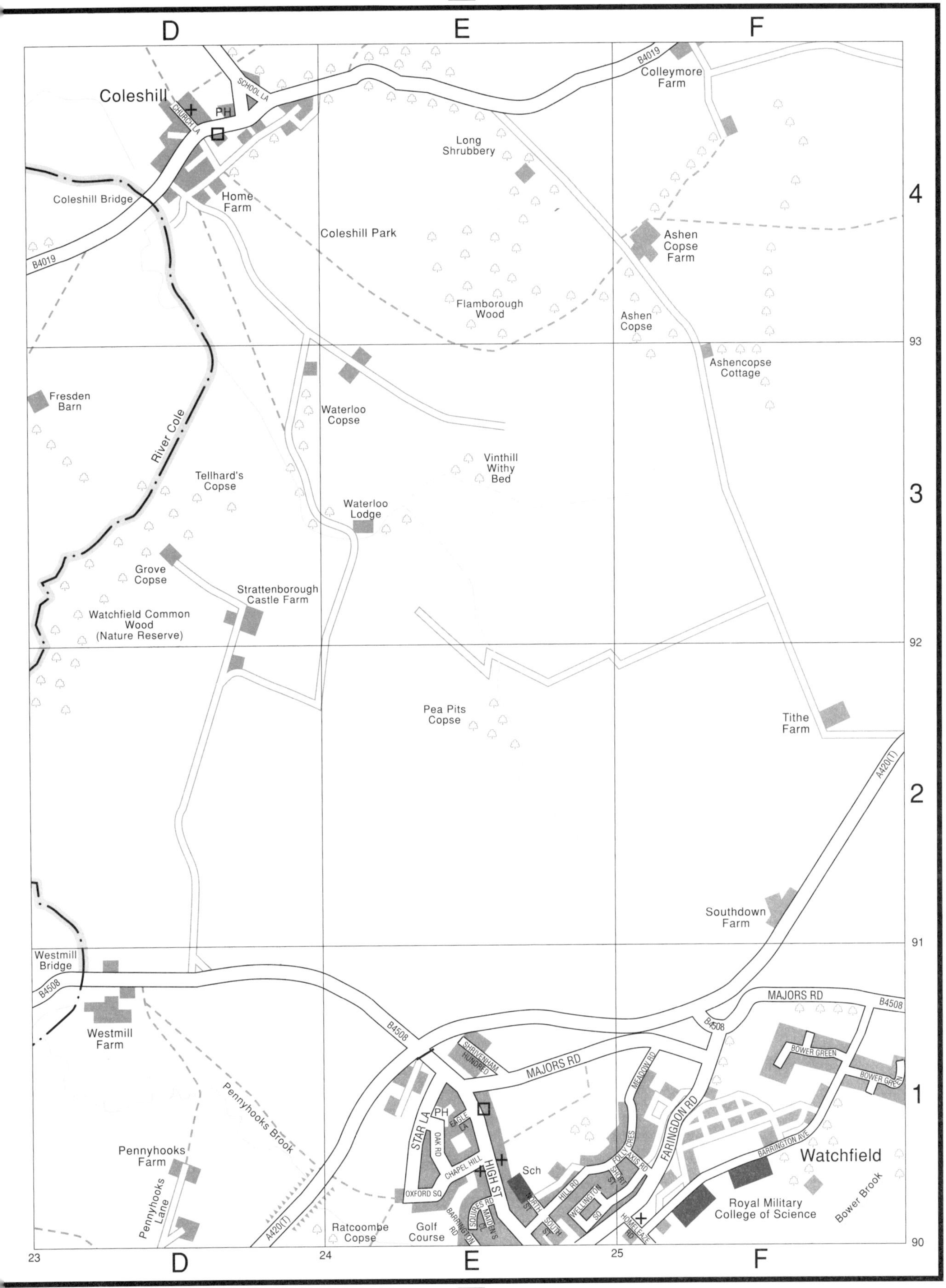
D
E
F
Coleshill
PH
CHURCH LA
SCHOOL LA
B4019
Colleymore
Farm
Long
Shrubbery
Coleshill Bridge
Home
Farm
Coleshill Park
Ashen
Copse
Farm
Flamborough
Wood
Ashen
Copse
4
93
Ashencopse
Cottage
Fresden
Barn
Waterloo
Copse
River Cole
Vinthill
Withy
Bed
Tellhard's
Copse
3
Waterloo
Lodge
Grove
Copse
Strattenborough
Castle Farm
Watchfield Common
Wood
(Nature Reserve)
92
Pea Pits
Copse
Tithe
Farm
A420(T)
2
Southdown
Farm
91
Westmill
Bridge
B4508
MAJORS RD
Westmill
Farm
SHRIVENHAM
HUNDRED
MAJORS RD
MEADOW RD
BOWER GREEN
BOWER GREEN
1
Pennyhooks Brook
STAR LA
PH
EAGLE LA
OAK RD
FOLLY CRES
AXIS RD
FARINGDON RD
BARRINGTON AVE
Watchfield
Pennyhooks
Farm
CHAPEL HILL
HIGH ST
Sch
HILL RD
WELLINGTON SQ
SHORT ST
OXFORD SQ
NORTH ST
SOUTH ST
SQUIRES RD
MAIDEN'S CL
BARRINGTON RD
HOMELEAZE RD
Royal Military
College of Science
Bower Brook
Pennyhooks
Lane
A420(T)
Ratcoombe
Copse
Golf
Course
90
23
24
25

192

209

172

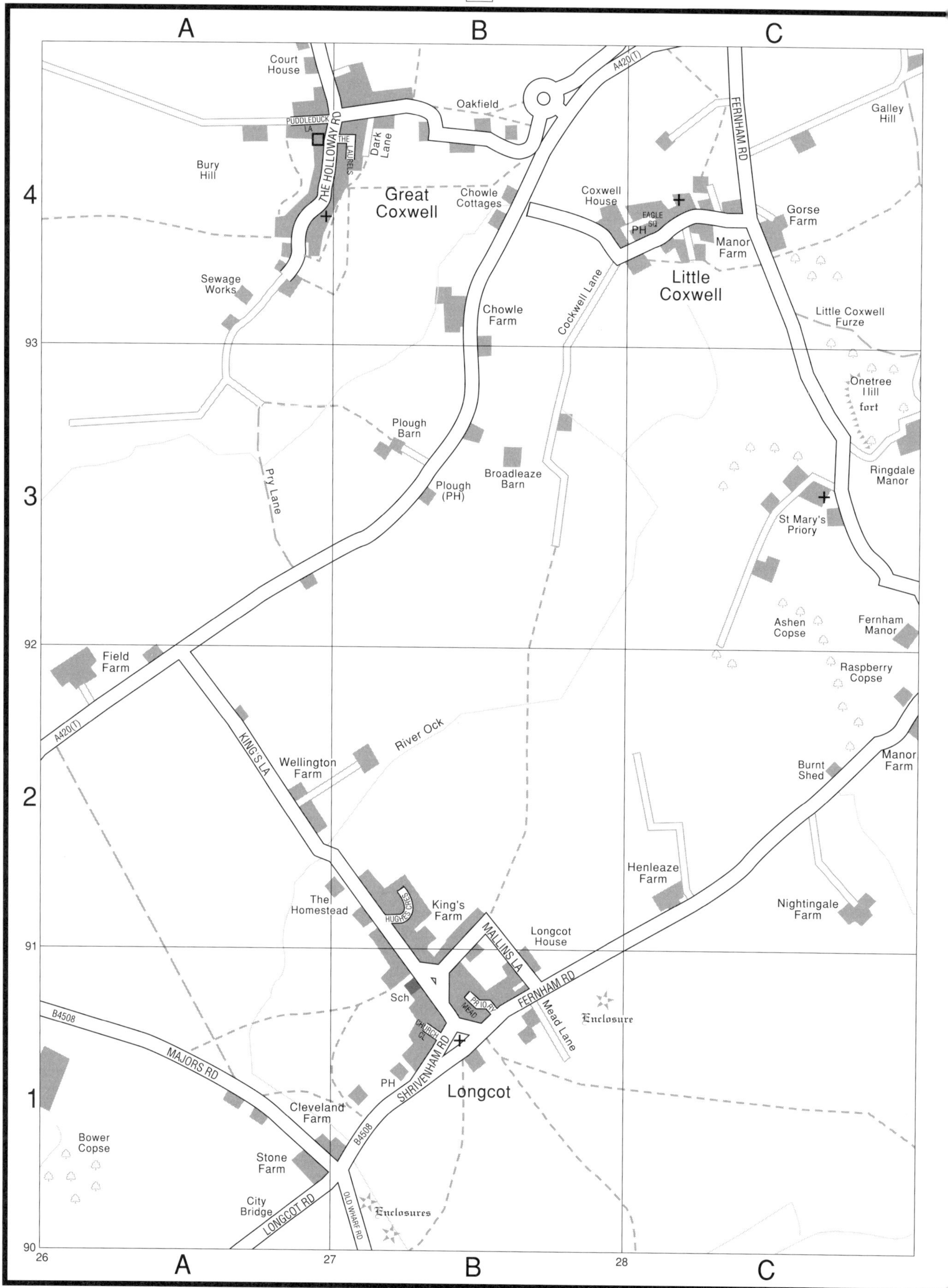
A
B
C
4
3
2
1
93
92
91
90
26
27
28
Court House
Puddleduck La
The Holloway Rd
The Laurels
Dark Lane
Oakfield
A420(T)
Fernham Rd
Galley Hill
Bury Hill
Great Coxwell
Chowle Cottages
Coxwell House
Eagle Sq
PH
Gorse Farm
Manor Farm
Little Coxwell
Sewage Works
Chowle Farm
Cockwell Lane
Little Coxwell Furze
Onetree Hill
fort
Plough Barn
Broadleaze Barn
Plough (PH)
Pry Lane
Ringdale Manor
St Mary's Priory
Ashen Copse
Fernham Manor
Field Farm
Raspberry Copse
River Ock
King's La
Wellington Farm
Burnt Shed
Manor Farm
Henleaze Farm
Nightingale Farm
The Homestead
Hughes Cres
King's Farm
Mallins La
Longcot House
Sch
Priory Mead
Fernham Rd
Mead Lane
Enclosure
B4508
Majors Rd
Church Cl
Shrivenham Rd
PH
Longcot
Cleveland Farm
Bower Copse
Stone Farm
B4508
City Bridge
Longcot Rd
Old Wharf Rd
Enclosures
A
B
C

191

210

173

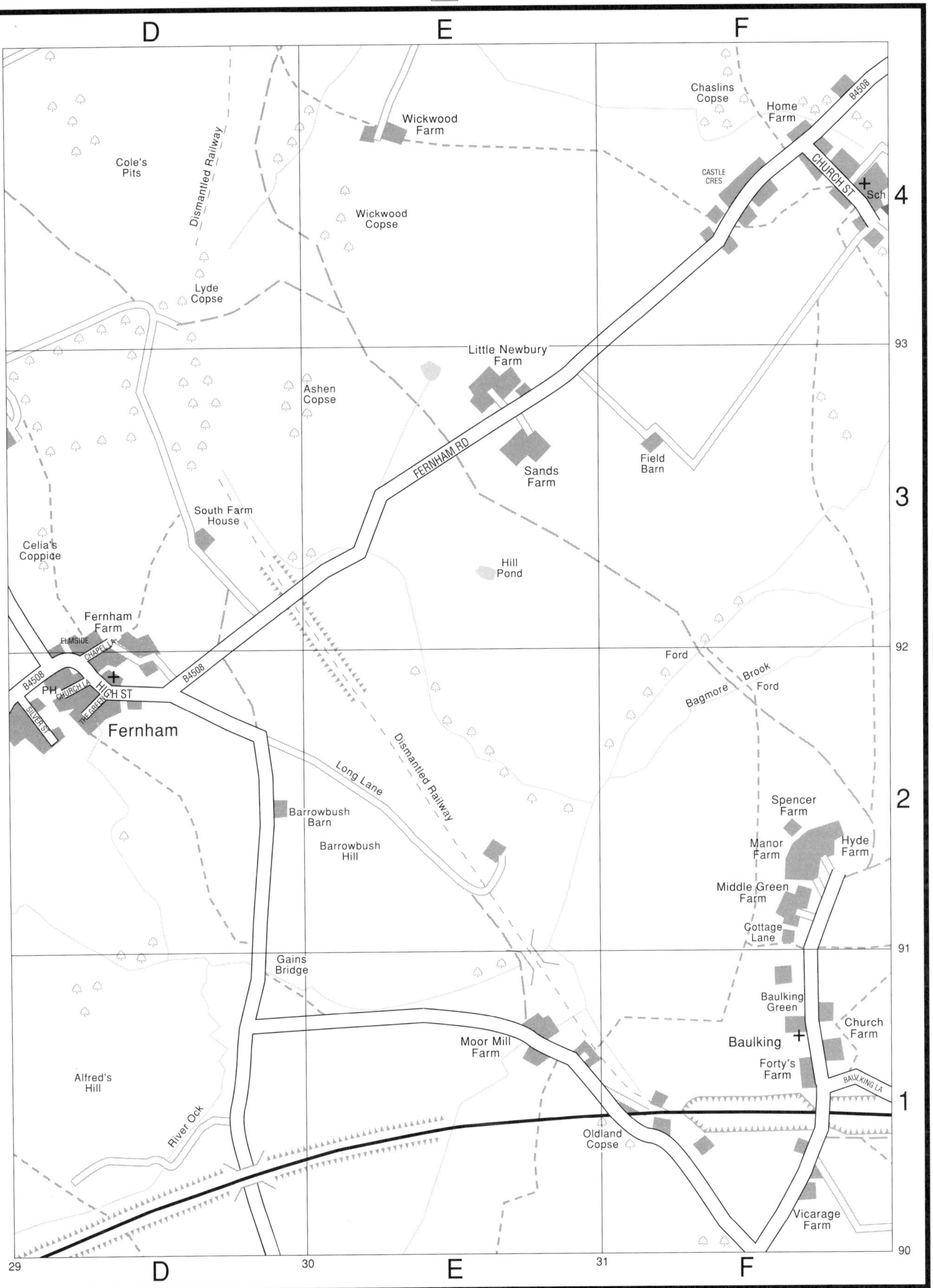

D
E
F
Chaslins Copse
Home Farm
B4508
Wickwood Farm
Cole's Pits
Dismantled Railway
CASTLE CRES
CHURCH ST
Sch
4
Wickwood Copse
Lyde Copse
93
Little Newbury Farm
Ashen Copse
FERNHAM RD
Sands Farm
Field Barn
3
South Farm House
Celia's Coppice
Hill Pond
Fernham Farm
ELMSIDE
CHAPEL LA
92
Ford
B4508
PH
CHURCH LA
HIGH ST
Bagmore Brook
Ford
SILVER ST
THE GREEN
Fernham
Long Lane
Dismantled Railway
Spencer Farm
2
Barrowbush Barn
Barrowbush Hill
Manor Farm
Hyde Farm
Middle Green Farm
Cottage Lane
91
Gains Bridge
Baulking Green
Church Farm
Moor Mill Farm
Baulking
Alfred's Hill
Forty's Farm
BAULKING LA
1
River Ock
Oldland Copse
Vicarage Farm
90
29
30
31
D
E
F

194

211

174

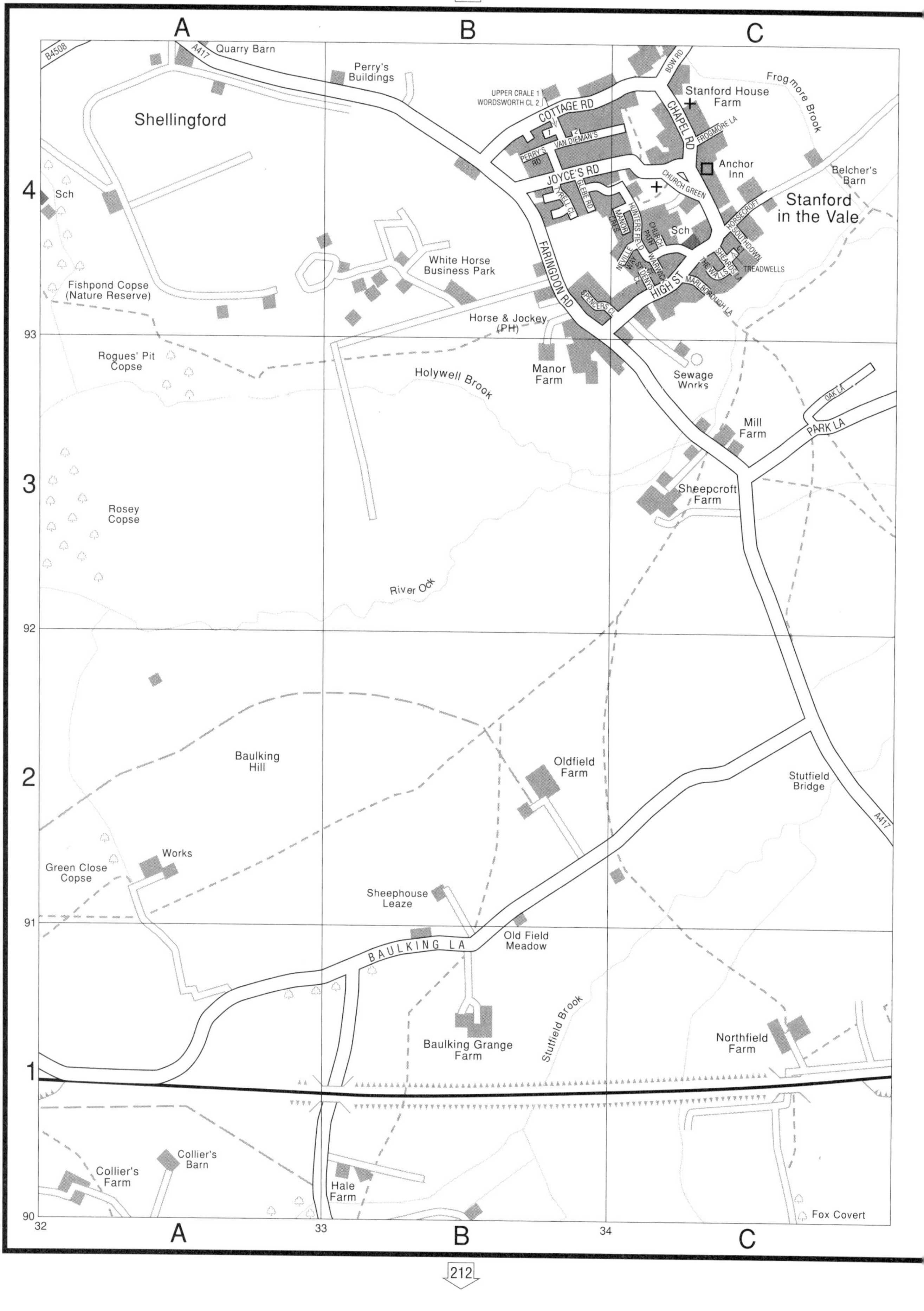

A
B
C
B4508
A417
Quarry Barn
Perry's Buildings
UPPER CRALE 1
WORDSWORTH CL 2
COTTAGE RD
BOW RD
CHAPEL RD
Stanford House Farm
Frogmore Brook
FROGMORE LA
VAN DIEMAN'S
PERRY'S RD
Shellingford
JOYCE'S RD
CHURCH GREEN
Anchor Inn
Belcher's Barn
Stanford in the Vale
4
Sch
TYRELL CL
GLEBE RD
MANOR CRES
HUNTERS FIELD
CHURCH PATH
WARWICK
NEVILLE WAY
ST DENYS
HORSECROFT
SOUTHDOWN
SHEARDS
THE WALLS
TREADWELLS
HIGH ST
MARLBOROUGH LA
SPENCERS CL
FARINGDON RD
Fishpond Copse (Nature Reserve)
White Horse Business Park
Horse & Jockey (PH)
93
Rogues' Pit Copse
Manor Farm
Sewage Works
Holywell Brook
OAK LA
PARK LA
Mill Farm
3
Sheepcroft Farm
Rosey Copse
River Ock
92
Baulking Hill
Oldfield Farm
2
Stutfield Bridge
Works
Green Close Copse
Sheephouse Leaze
91
BAULKING LA
Old Field Meadow
Baulking Grange Farm
Stutfield Brook
Northfield Farm
1
Collier's Barn
Collier's Farm
Hale Farm
Fox Covert
90
32
33
34

193

212

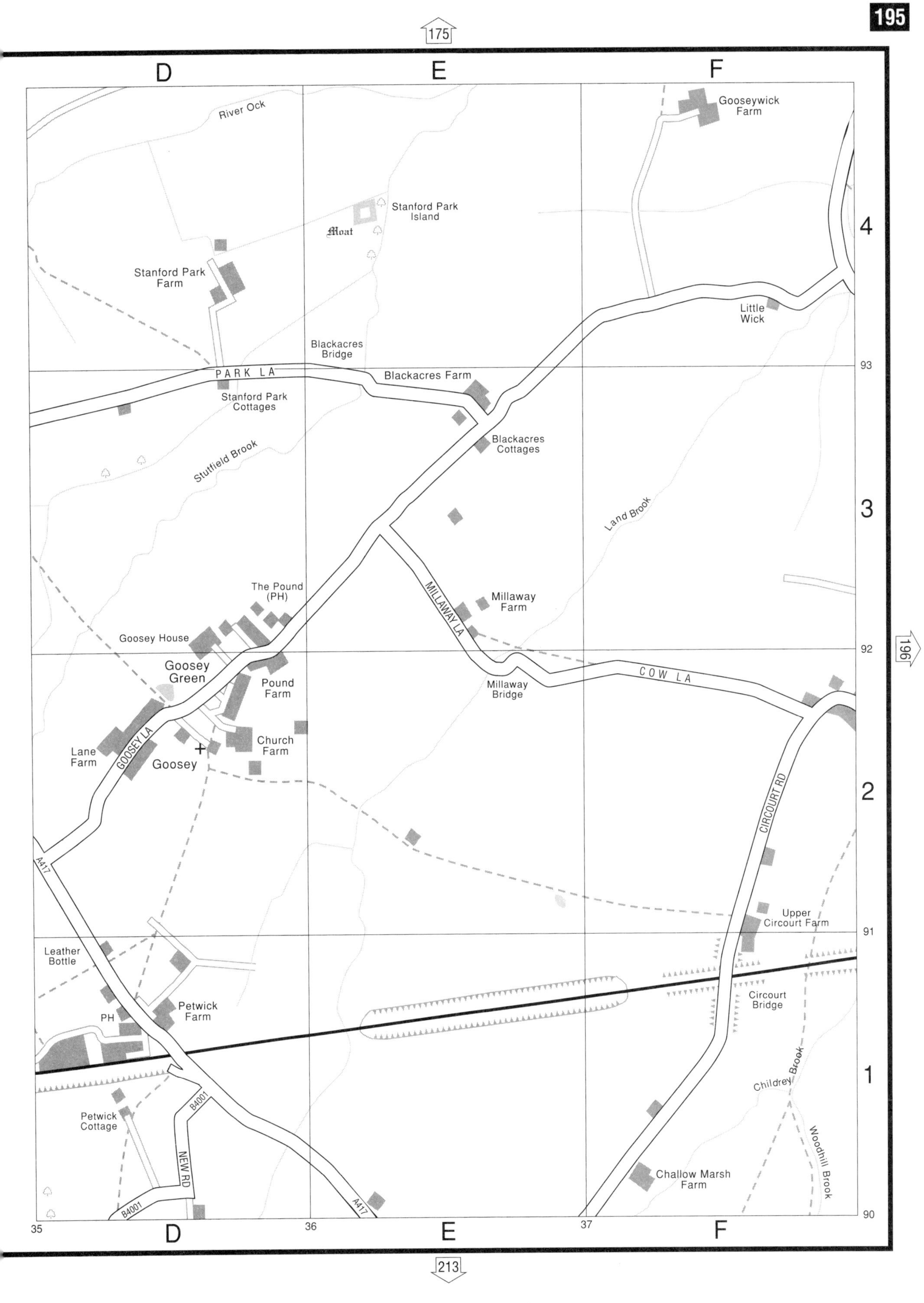
175
D
E
F
River Ock
Gooseywick Farm
Stanford Park Island
Moat
4
Stanford Park Farm
Little Wick
Blackacres Bridge
PARK LA
Blackacres Farm
93
Stanford Park Cottages
Blackacres Cottages
Stutfield Brook
Land Brook
3
The Pound (PH)
Millaway Farm
MILLAWAY LA
Goosey House
92
196
Goosey Green
Pound Farm
Millaway Bridge
COW LA
Lane Farm
GOOSEY LA
Church Farm
Goosey
CIRCOURT RD
2
A417
Upper Circourt Farm
91
Leather Bottle
Circourt Bridge
PH
Petwick Farm
Childrey Brook
1
B4001
Petwick Cottage
NEW RD
Woodhill Brook
Challow Marsh Farm
B4001
A417
90
35
36
37
213

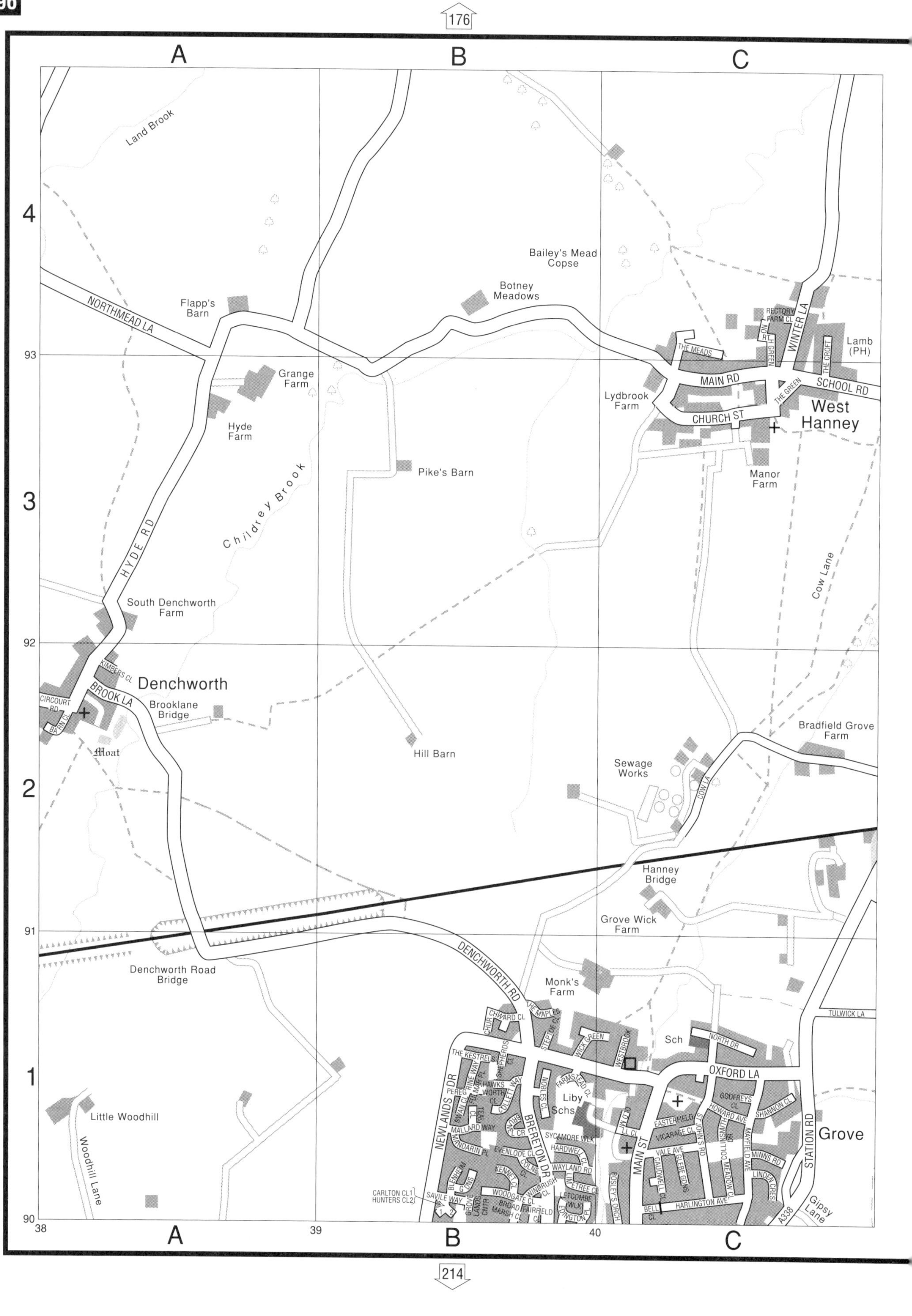
176
195
214
A
B
C
4
3
2
1
93
92
91
90
38
39
40
Land Brook
Northmead La
Flapp's Barn
Botney Meadows
Bailey's Mead Copse
Grange Farm
Hyde Farm
Pike's Barn
Childrey Brook
Hyde Rd
South Denchworth Farm
Denchworth
Kimbers Cl
Brook La
Circourt Rd
Barn Cl
Brooklane Bridge
Moat
Hill Barn
Denchworth Road Bridge
Denchworth Rd
Little Woodhill
Woodhill Lane
The Meads
Rectory Farm Cl
North Green
Winter La
Lamb (PH)
The Croft
Main Rd
School Rd
The Green
Lydbrook Farm
Church St
West Hanney
Manor Farm
Cow Lane
Bradfield Grove Farm
Sewage Works
Cow La
Hanney Bridge
Grove Wick Farm
Monk's Farm
Tulwick La
The Maples
Churchward Cl
Steptoe Cl
Wick Green
Westbrook
Sch
North Dr
Oxford La
The Kestrels
Shepherds Cl
Newlands Dr
Hawksworth Cl
Collett Way
Nobles Cl
Farmstead Cl
Liby
Schs
Godfreys Cl
Howard Ave
Shannon Cl
Station Rd
Grove
Easterfield
Vicarage Cl
St John's Rd
Mallard Way
Mandarin Pl
Brereton Dr
Sycamore Wlk
Hardwell Cl
Evenlode Cl
Colne Cl
Kennet Cl
Wayland Rd
Main St
Vale Ave
Glebe Gdns
Meadow Cl
Mayfield Ave
Minns Rd
Linden Cres
Blenheim Gdns
Windrush Cl
Limetree Cl
Letcombe Wlk
Carlton Cl 1
Hunters Cl 2
Savile Way
Grove
Woodgate Cl
Fairfield Cl
Broad Marsh Cl
Edington Pl
Bosley's Orch
Bell Cl
Harlington Ave
A338
Gipsy Lane

177

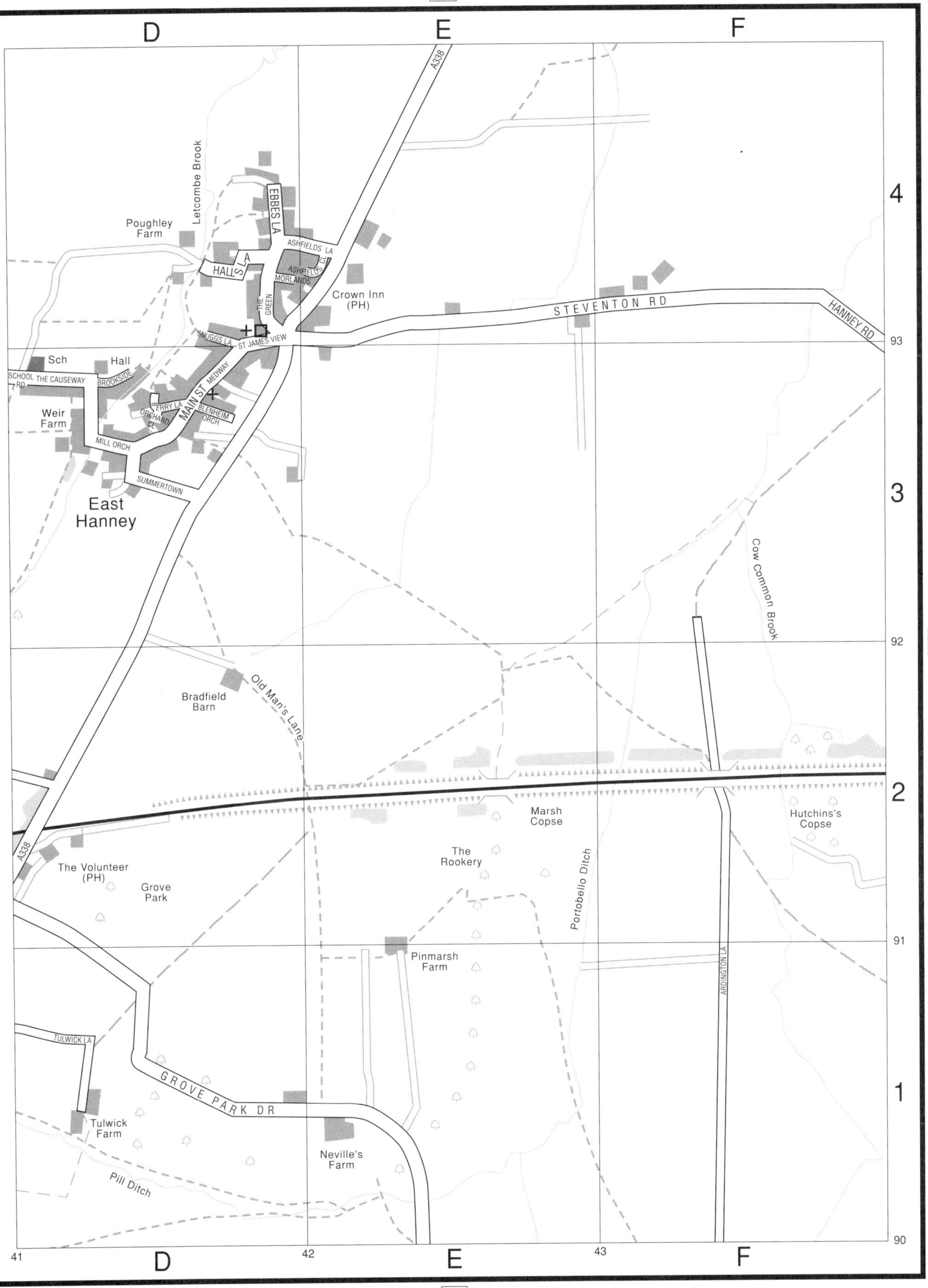
D
E
F
A338
Letcombe Brook
EBBES LA
Poughley
Farm
ASHFIELDS LA
ASHFIELDS CL
HALLS LA
MORLANDS
THE GREEN
Crown Inn
(PH)
STEVENTON RD
HANNEY RD
SNUGGS LA
ST JAMES VIEW
Sch
Hall
SCHOOL RD
THE CAUSEWAY
BROOKSIDE
MEDWAY
MAIN ST
BERRY LA
ORCHARD CL
BLENHEIM ORCH
Weir
Farm
MILL ORCH
SUMMERTOWN
East
Hanney
Cow Common Brook
Bradfield
Barn
Old Man's Lane
Marsh
Copse
Hutchins's
Copse
The Volunteer
(PH)
Grove
Park
The
Rookery
Portobello Ditch
Pinmarsh
Farm
ARDINGTON LA
TULWICK LA
GROVE PARK DR
Tulwick
Farm
Neville's
Farm
Pill Ditch
4
3
2
1
93
92
91
90
41
42
43

198

215

178

197

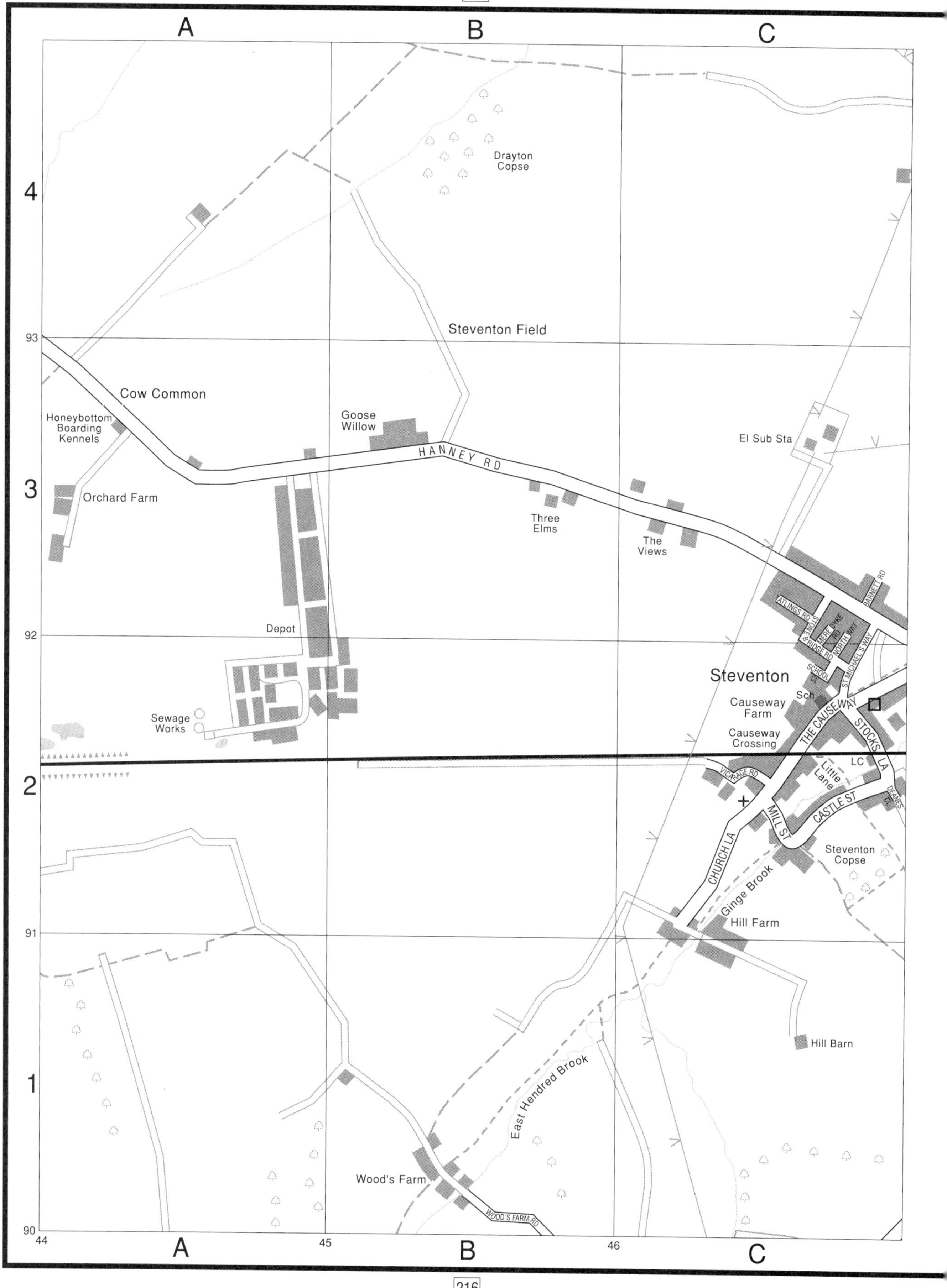
A
B
C
4
3
2
1
93
92
91
90
44
45
46
Drayton
Copse
Steventon Field
Cow Common
Honeybottom
Boarding
Kennels
Goose
Willow
HANNEY RD
El Sub Sta
Orchard Farm
Three
Elms
The
Views
Depot
Sewage
Works
ATLINGS RD
STONE BRIDGE RD
MERE DYKE RD
NORTH WAY
BARNETT RD
ST MICHAEL'S WAY
SCHOOL CL
Steventon
Sch
Causeway
Farm
Causeway
Crossing
THE CAUSEWAY
STOCKS LA
LC
VICARAGE RD
Little
Lane
CASTLE ST
DEANES CL
MILL ST
CHURCH LA
Steventon
Copse
Ginge Brook
Hill Farm
Hill Barn
East Hendred Brook
Wood's Farm
WOOD'S FARM RD
A
B
C

216

179

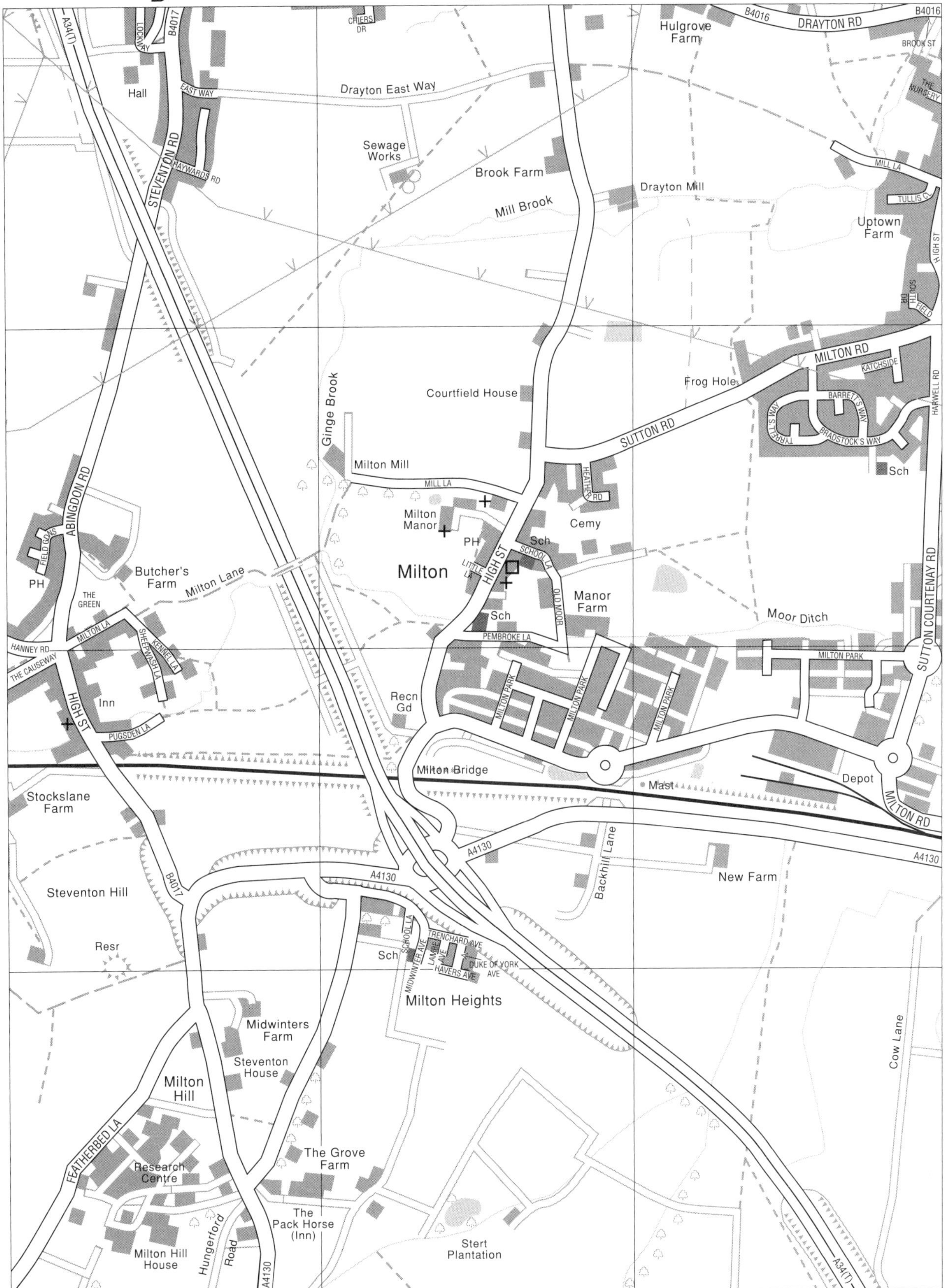
D
E
F
Hulgrove Farm
B4016 DRAYTON RD
BROOK ST
THE NURSERY
Hall
EAST WAY
Drayton East Way
STEVENTON RD
HAYWARDS RD
Sewage Works
Brook Farm
Mill Brook
Drayton Mill
MILL LA
TULLIS CL
Uptown Farm
HIGH ST
SOUTH FIELD DR
4
93
MILTON RD
KATCHSIDE
Frog Hole
Courtfield House
Ginge Brook
SUTTON RD
BARRETT'S WAY
TYRRELL'S WAY
BRADSTOCK'S WAY
HARWELL RD
Sch
3
Milton Mill
MILL LA
HEATHER RD
ABINGDON RD
FIELD GDNS
Milton Manor
Cemy
PH
Sch
SCHOOL LA
Butcher's Farm
Milton Lane
Milton
LITTLE LA
HIGH ST
OLD MOOR
Manor Farm
PH
THE GREEN
Sch
Moor Ditch
SUTTON COURTENAY RD
MILTON LA
SHEPHERDS LA
KENNEL LA
PEMBROKE LA
HANNEY RD
THE CAUSEWAY
MILTON PARK
92
HIGH ST
Inn
Recn Gd
PUGSDEN LA
Milton Bridge
Mast
Depot
Stockslane Farm
2
MILTON RD
A4130
A4130
Steventon Hill
B4017
A4130
New Farm
Backhill Lane
Resr
Sch
SCHOOL LA
TRENCHARD AVE
LAMBE AVE
DUKE OF YORK AVE
HAVERS AVE
MIDWINTER AVE
91
Milton Heights
Midwinters Farm
Cow Lane
Steventon House
Milton Hill
1
FEATHERBED LA
The Grove Farm
Research Centre
The Pack Horse (Inn)
Stert Plantation
Milton Hill House
Hungerford Road
A4130
A34(T)
90
47
48
49
D
E
F

200
217

180

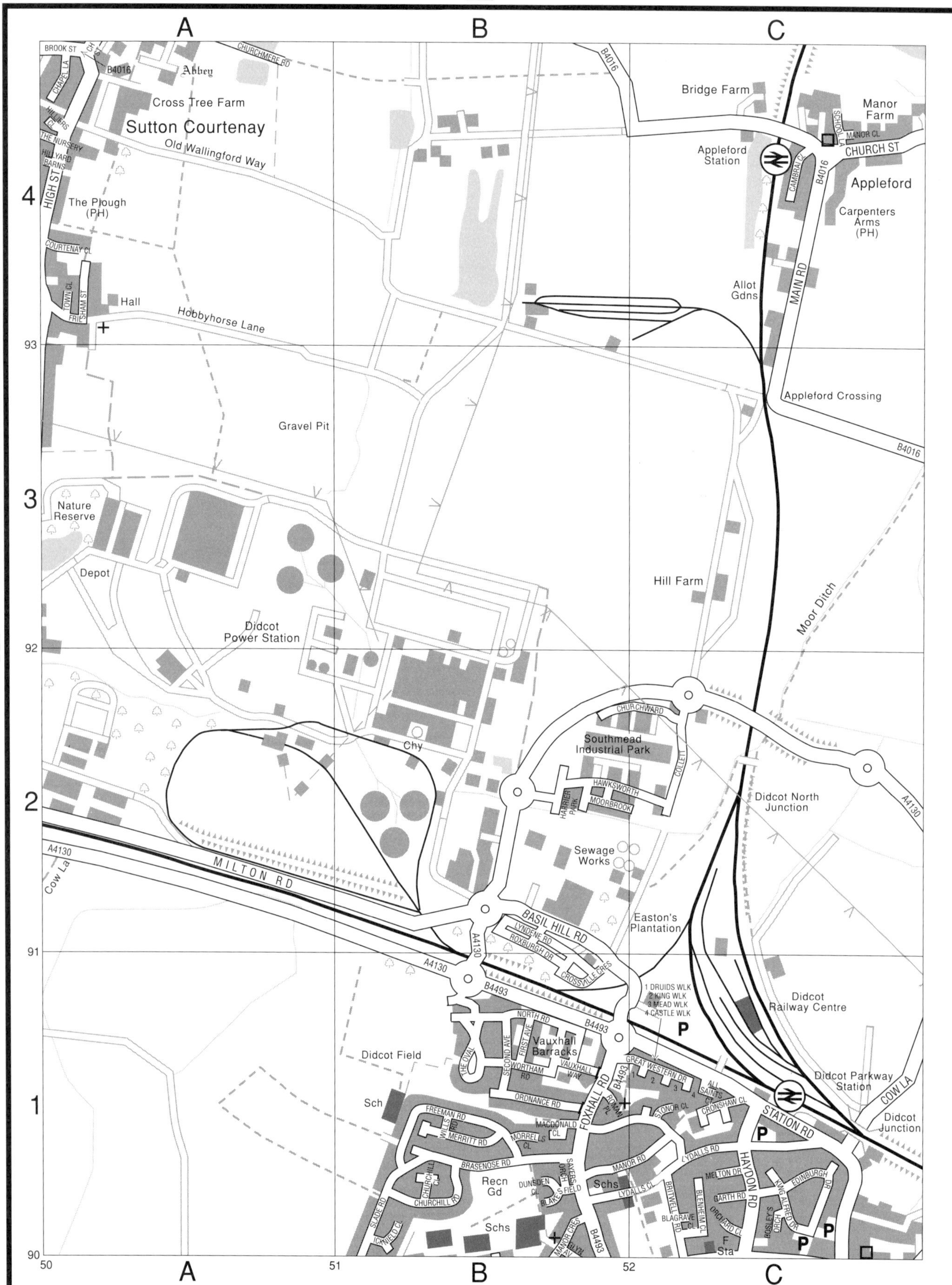
A
B
C
Sutton Courtenay
Cross Tree Farm
Abbey
Old Wallingford Way
The Plough (PH)
Hall
Hobbyhorse Lane
Gravel Pit
Nature Reserve
Depot
Didcot Power Station
Chy
Bridge Farm
Appleford Station
Manor Farm
Appleford
Carpenters Arms (PH)
Allot Gdns
Appleford Crossing
Hill Farm
Moor Ditch
Southmead Industrial Park
Didcot North Junction
Sewage Works
Easton's Plantation
Didcot Railway Centre
Didcot Parkway Station
Didcot Junction
Vauxhall Barracks
Didcot Field
Sch
Recn Gd
Schs
F Sta
MILTON RD
BASIL HILL RD
STATION RD
HAYDON RD
FOXHALL RD
MAIN RD
CHURCH ST
COW LA
Cow La
A4130
B4016
B4493
1 DRUIDS WLK
2 KING WLK
3 MEAD WLK
4 CASTLE WLK
4
3
2
1
93
92
91
90
50
51
52

199

218

181

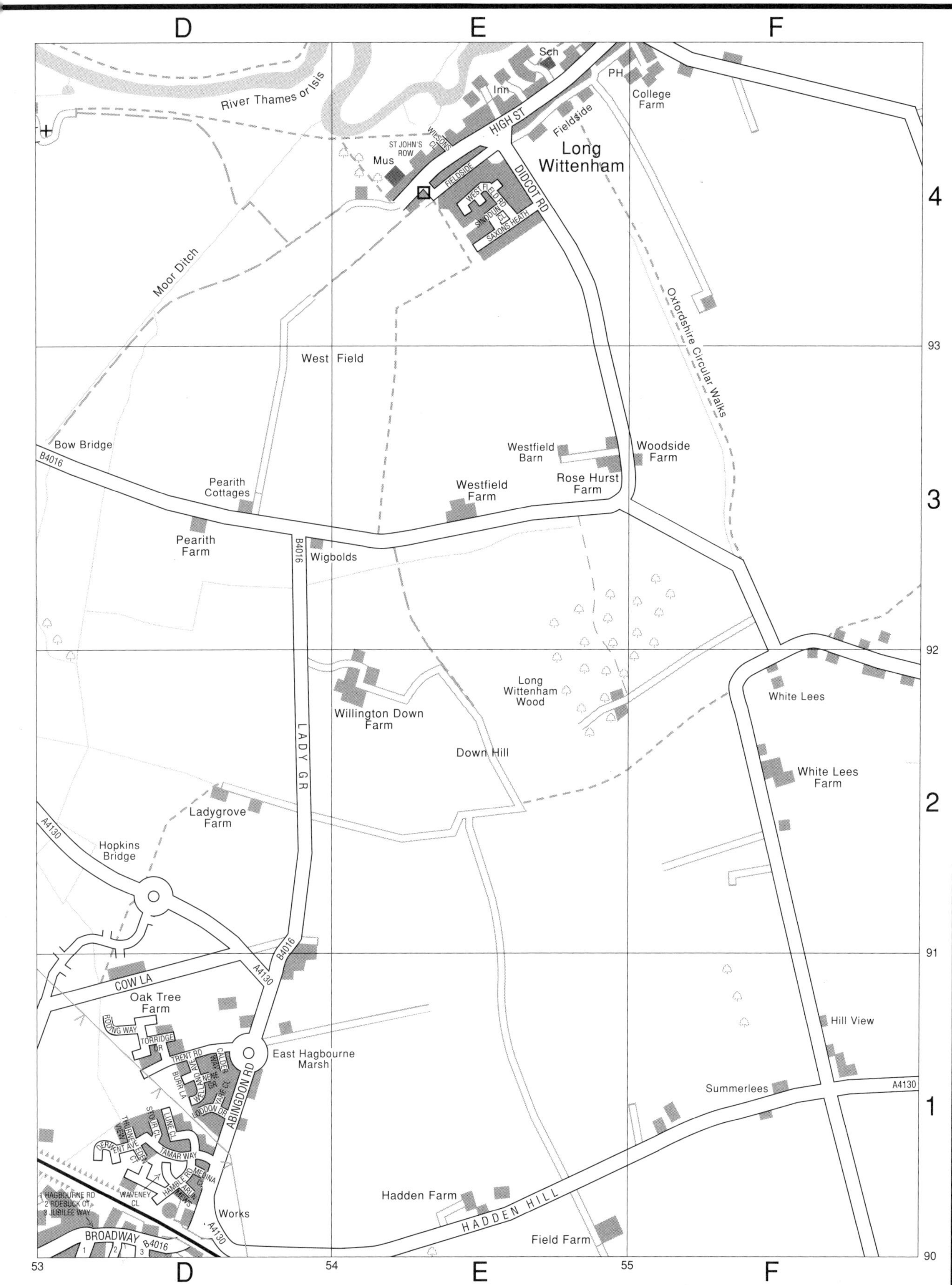

D
E
F
River Thames or Isis
Sch
Inn
PH
College Farm
HIGH ST
WILSONS CL
ST JOHN'S ROW
Mus
Fieldside
FIELDSIDE
Long Wittenham
DIDCOT RD
WEST FIELD RD
SINODUN CL
SAXONS HEATH
Moor Ditch
Oxfordshire Circular Walks
West Field
93
4
Bow Bridge
B4016
Westfield Barn
Woodside Farm
Pearith Cottages
Westfield Farm
Rose Hurst Farm
3
Pearith Farm
Wigbolds
92
Long Wittenham Wood
White Lees
Willington Down Farm
LADY GR
Down Hill
White Lees Farm
2
Ladygrove Farm
A4130
Hopkins Bridge
91
COW LA
Oak Tree Farm
RODING WAY
TORRIDGE DR
TRENT RD
CALDER WAY
BURR LA
WELLAND AVE
NENE GR
YARE CL
LODDON DR
ABINGDON RD
East Hagbourne Marsh
Hill View
Summerlees
A4130
1
STOUR CL
LUNE CL
DERWENT AVE
EDEN CL
TAMAR WAY
MEDINA CL
HAMBLE RD
ARUN MEWS
WAVENEY CL
1 HAGBOURNE RD
2 ROEBUCK CT
3 JUBILEE WAY
Hadden Farm
HADDEN HILL
Works
Field Farm
BROADWAY
B4016
90
53
54
55

202

219

182

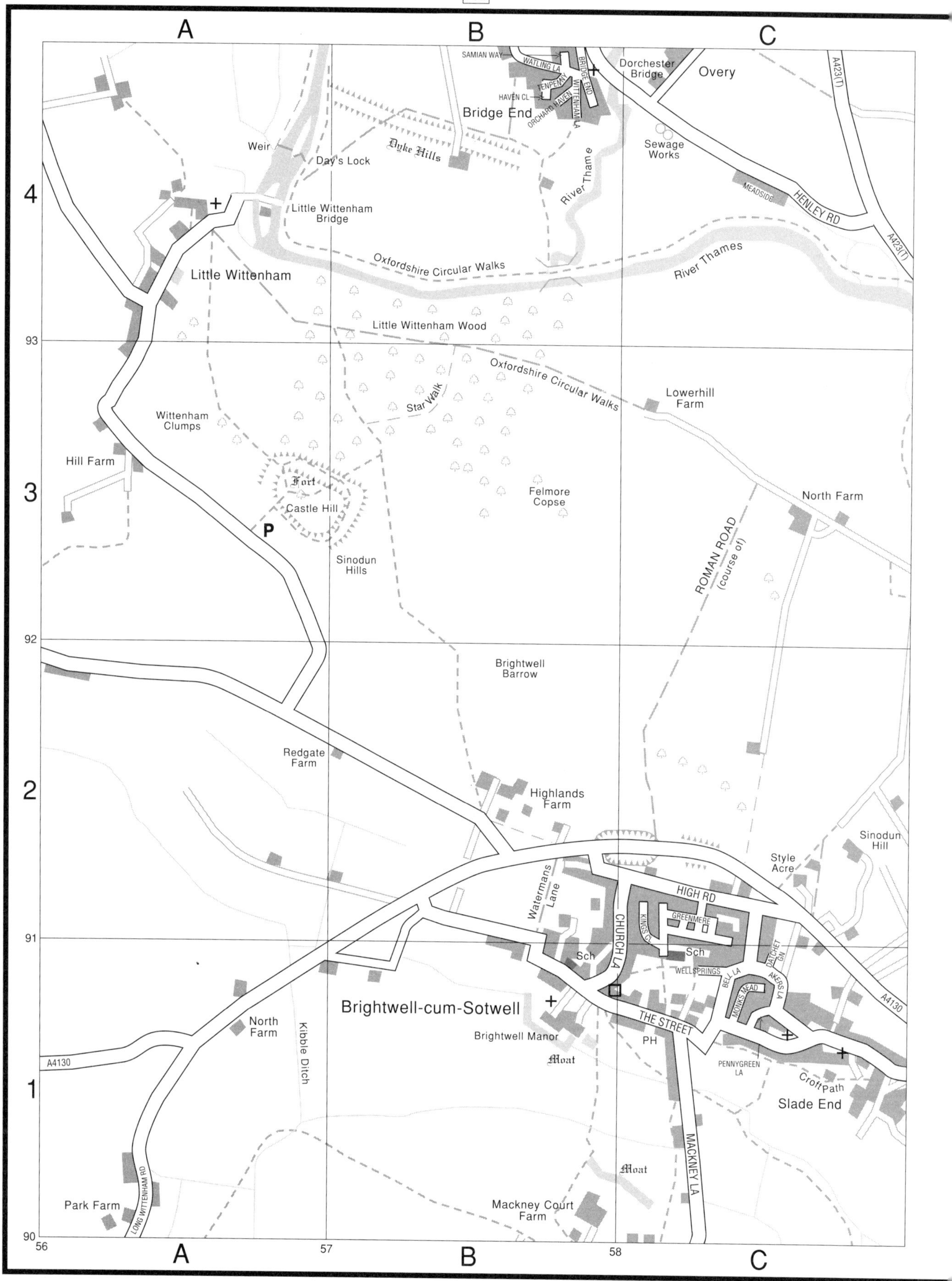

A
B
C
4
3
2
1
93
92
91
90
56
57
58
SAMIAN WAY
WATLING LA
BRIDGE END
TENPENNY
HAVEN CL
ORCHARD HAVEN
WITTENHAM LA
Bridge End
Dorchester Bridge
Overy
A423(T)
Weir
Day's Lock
Dyke Hills
Sewage Works
River Thame
MEADSIDE
HENLEY RD
Little Wittenham Bridge
Little Wittenham
Oxfordshire Circular Walks
River Thames
Little Wittenham Wood
Star Walk
Lowerhill Farm
Wittenham Clumps
Hill Farm
Fort
Castle Hill
P
Sinodun Hills
Felmore Copse
North Farm
ROMAN ROAD (course of)
Brightwell Barrow
Redgate Farm
Highlands Farm
Sinodun Hill
Style Acre
Watermans Lane
HIGH RD
CHURCH LA
Sch
WELLSPRINGS
BELL LA
DATCHET GN
AKERS LA
MONKS MEAD
A4130
Brightwell-cum-Sotwell
THE STREET
PH
Brightwell Manor
Moat
North Farm
Kibble Ditch
PENNYGREEN LA
Croft Path
Slade End
MACKNEY LA
Moat
Mackney Court Farm
Park Farm
LONG WITTENHAM RD

201

220

183

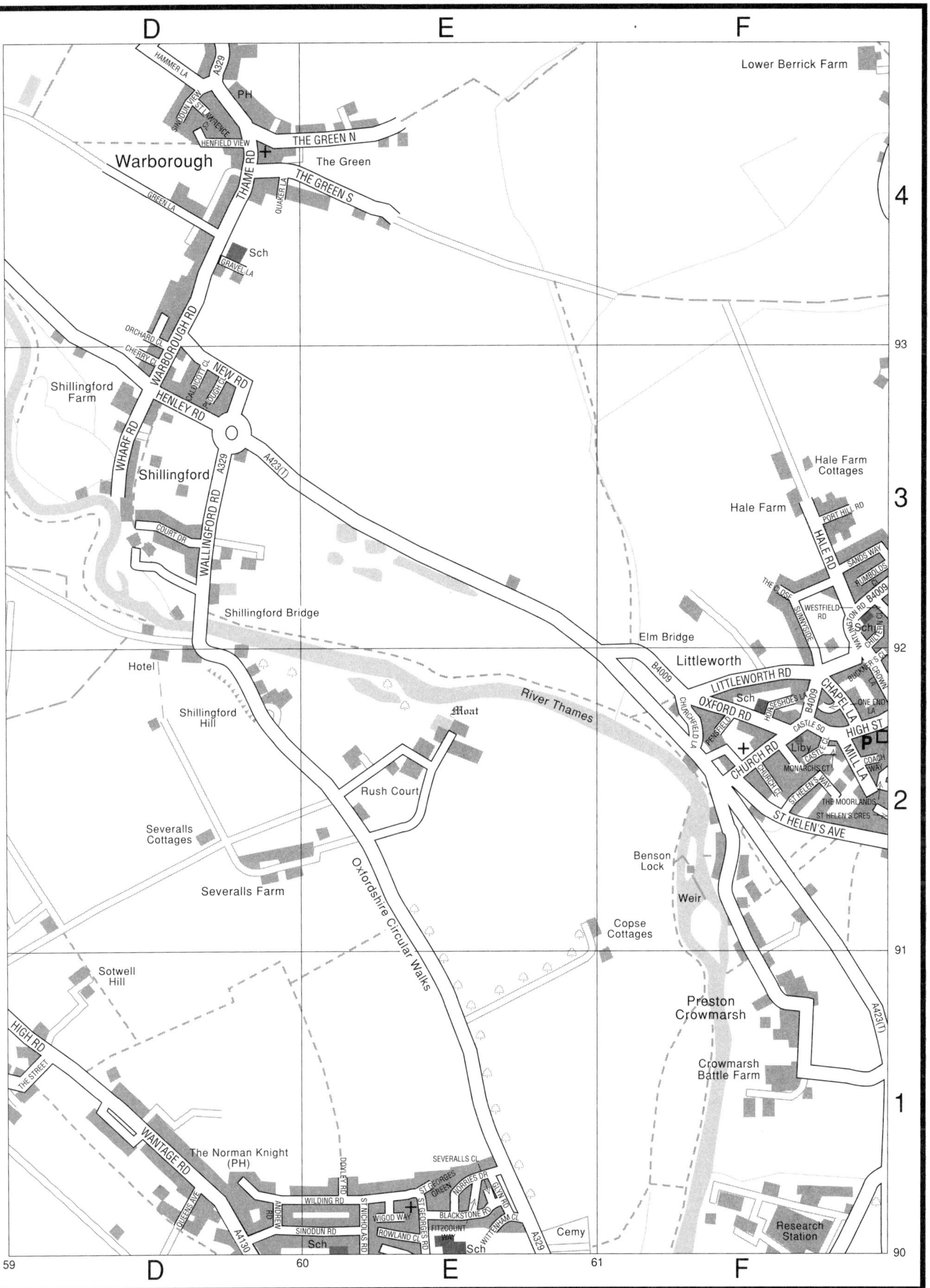

D
E
F
Lower Berrick Farm
HAMMER LA
A329
PH
SINODUN VIEW
ST LAWRENCE CL
HENFIELD VIEW
THE GREEN N
The Green
Warborough
THAME RD
THE GREEN S
QUAKER LA
GREEN LA
Sch
GRAVEL LA
4
ORCHARD CL
CHERRY CL
WARBOROUGH RD
CALDICOTT CL
PLOUGH CL
NEW RD
HENLEY RD
93
Shillingford Farm
WHARF RD
A329
A423(T)
Shillingford
WALLINGFORD RD
COURT DR
Hale Farm Cottages
Hale Farm
3
PORT HILL RD
HALE RD
SANDS WAY
RUMBOLDS CL
THE CLOSE
SUNNYSIDE
WESTFIELD RD
B4009
Sch
Shillingford Bridge
Elm Bridge
92
Hotel
Littleworth
B4009
LITTLEWORTH RD
Sch
OXFORD RD
HORSESHOES LA
CHAPEL LA
ONE END LA
CROWN LA
River Thames
Moat
Shillingford Hill
CHURCHFIELD LA
PENSFIELD
CASTLE SQ
HIGH ST
P
CHURCH RD
Liby
CASTLE CL
MONARCHS CT
MILL LA
COACH WAY
CHURCH CL
ST HELEN'S WAY
THE MOORLANDS
ST HELEN'S CRES
ST HELEN'S AVE
Rush Court
2
Severalls Cottages
Benson Lock
Oxfordshire Circular Walks
Severalls Farm
Weir
Copse Cottages
91
Sotwell Hill
Preston Crowmarsh
A423(T)
HIGH RD
THE STREET
Crowmarsh Battle Farm
1
WANTAGE RD
The Norman Knight (PH)
DOYLEY RD
SEVERALLS CL
ST GEORGES GREEN
NORRIES DR
GLYN RD
QUEENS AVE
ANDREW RD
WILDING RD
ST NICHOLAS RD
WIGOD WAY
ST GEORGES RD
BLACKSTONE RD
WITTENHAM CL
A4130
SINODUN RD
ROWLAND CL
FITZCOUNT WAY
A329
Cemy
Sch
Sch
Research Station
90
59
60
61

204

221

184

203

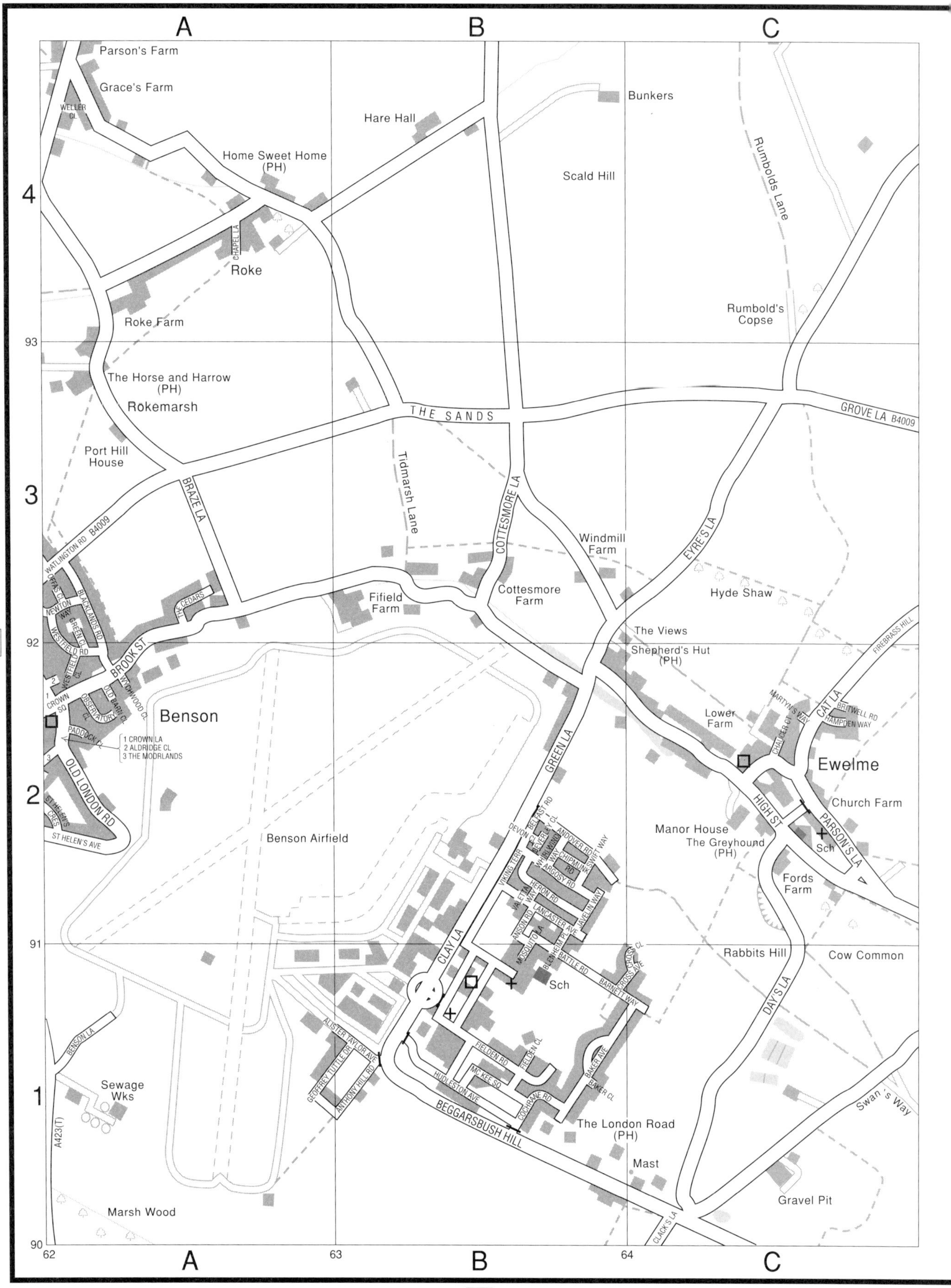
A
B
C
4
3
2
1
93
92
91
90
62
63
64
Parson's Farm
Grace's Farm
WELLER CL
Hare Hall
Bunkers
Home Sweet Home (PH)
Scald Hill
Rumbolds Lane
CHAPEL LA
Roke
Roke Farm
Rumbold's Copse
The Horse and Harrow (PH)
Rokemarsh
THE SANDS
GROVE LA B4009
Port Hill House
Tidmarsh Lane
BRAZE LA
COTTESMORE LA
EYRE'S LA
WATLINGTON RD B4009
Windmill Farm
THE CEDARS
Fifield Farm
Cottesmore Farm
Hyde Shaw
The Views
Shepherd's Hut (PH)
FIREBRASS HILL
BROOK ST
Benson
Lower Farm
MARTYN'S WAY
CAT LA
BRITWELL RD
HAMPDEN WAY
CHAUCER CT
Ewelme
1 CROWN LA
2 ALDRIDGE CL
3 THE MOORLANDS
GREEN LA
OLD LONDON RD
ST HELEN'S AVE
Church Farm
HIGH ST
PARSON'S LA
Manor House
The Greyhound (PH)
Benson Airfield
Sch
Fords Farm
CLAY LA
Rabbits Hill
Cow Common
Sch
DAY'S LA
BENSON LA
ALISTER TAYLOR AVE
GEOFFREY TUTTLE DR
ANTHONY HILL RD
FIELDEN RD
FIELDEN CL
MC KEE SQ
HUDLESTON AVE
COCHRANE RD
BAKER AVE
BAKER CR
BEGGARSBUSH HILL
Sewage Wks
The London Road (PH)
Swan's Way
A423(T)
Mast
Marsh Wood
CLACK'S LA
Gravel Pit

222

185

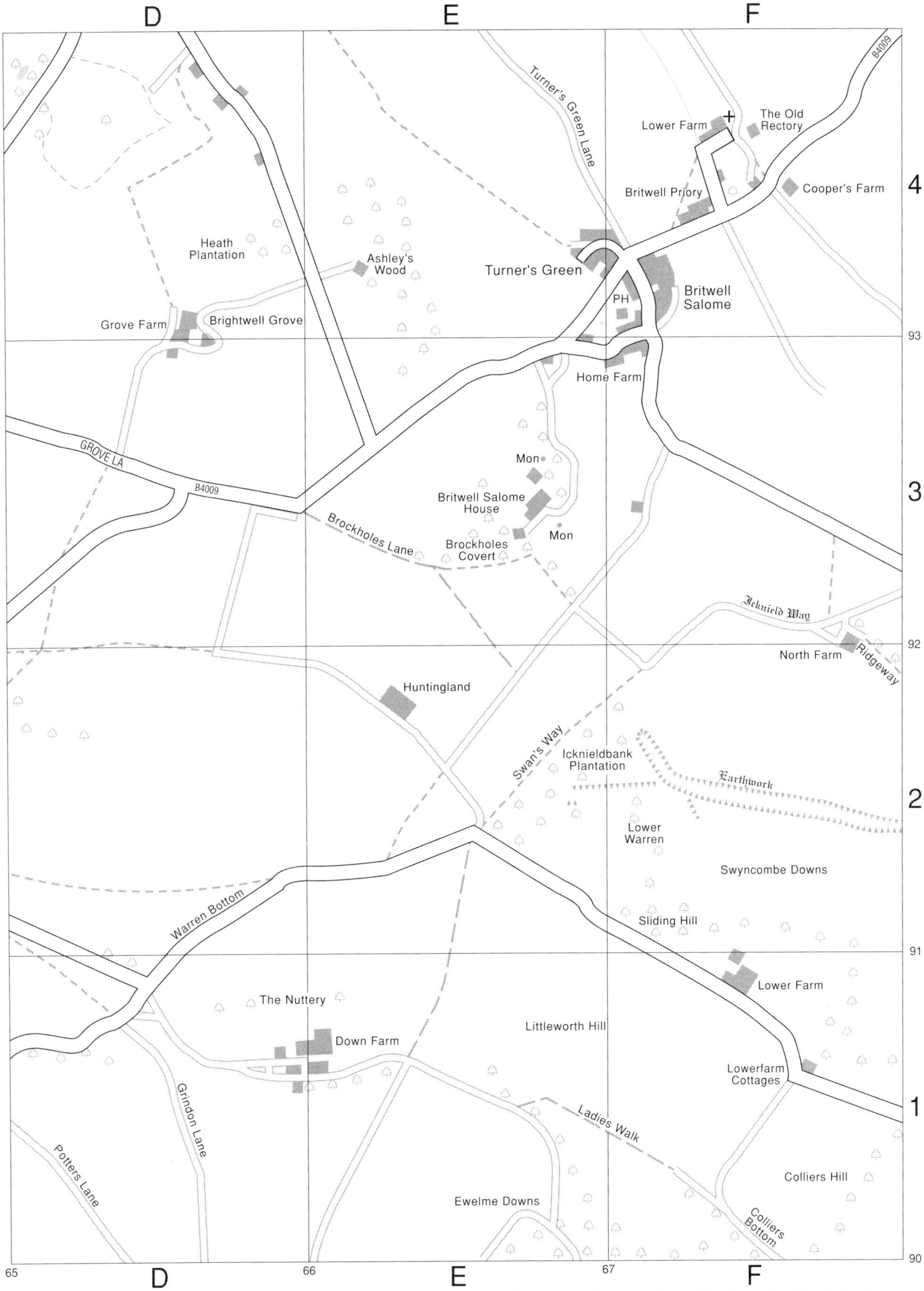
D
E
F
Turner's Green Lane
B4009
Lower Farm
The Old Rectory
Britwell Priory
Cooper's Farm
Heath Plantation
Ashley's Wood
Turner's Green
Britwell Salome
PH
Grove Farm
Brightwell Grove
Home Farm
GROVE LA
B4009
Mon
Britwell Salome House
Mon
Brockholes Lane
Brockholes Covert
Icknield Way
North Farm
Ridgeway
Huntingland
Swan's Way
Icknieldbank Plantation
Earthwork
Lower Warren
Swyncombe Downs
Warren Bottom
Sliding Hill
Lower Farm
The Nuttery
Down Farm
Littleworth Hill
Lowerfarm Cottages
Grindon Lane
Ladies Walk
Potters Lane
Colliers Hill
Ewelme Downs
Colliers Bottom
4
3
2
1
93
92
91
90
65
66
67
D
E
F

206

223

186

205

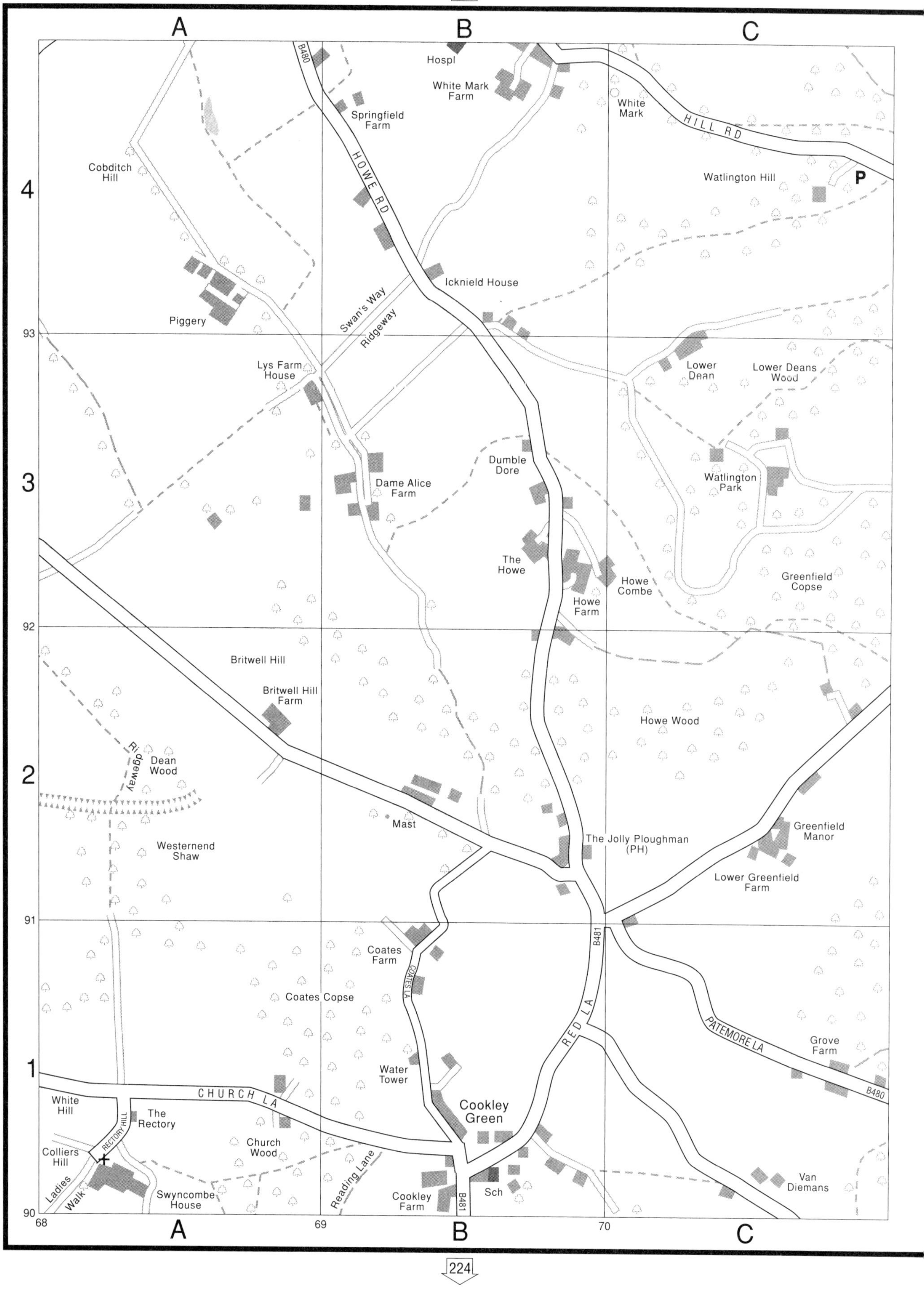
A
B
C
4
3
2
1
93
92
91
90
68
69
70
Hospl
White Mark Farm
Springfield Farm
White Mark
HILL RD
Watlington Hill
P
Cobditch Hill
HOWE RD
B480
Icknield House
Piggery
Swan's Way
Ridgeway
Lys Farm House
Lower Dean
Lower Deans Wood
Dumble Dore
Dame Alice Farm
Watlington Park
The Howe
Howe Combe
Howe Farm
Greenfield Copse
Britwell Hill
Britwell Hill Farm
Howe Wood
Ridgeway
Dean Wood
Mast
Westernend Shaw
The Jolly Ploughman (PH)
Greenfield Manor
Lower Greenfield Farm
Coates Farm
COATES LA
B481
Coates Copse
RED LA
PATEMORE LA
Grove Farm
B480
Water Tower
CHURCH LA
White Hill
The Rectory
RECTORY HILL
Cookley Green
Colliers Hill
Church Wood
Ladies Walk
Swyncombe House
Reading Lane
Cookley Farm
B481
Sch
Van Diemans

224

187

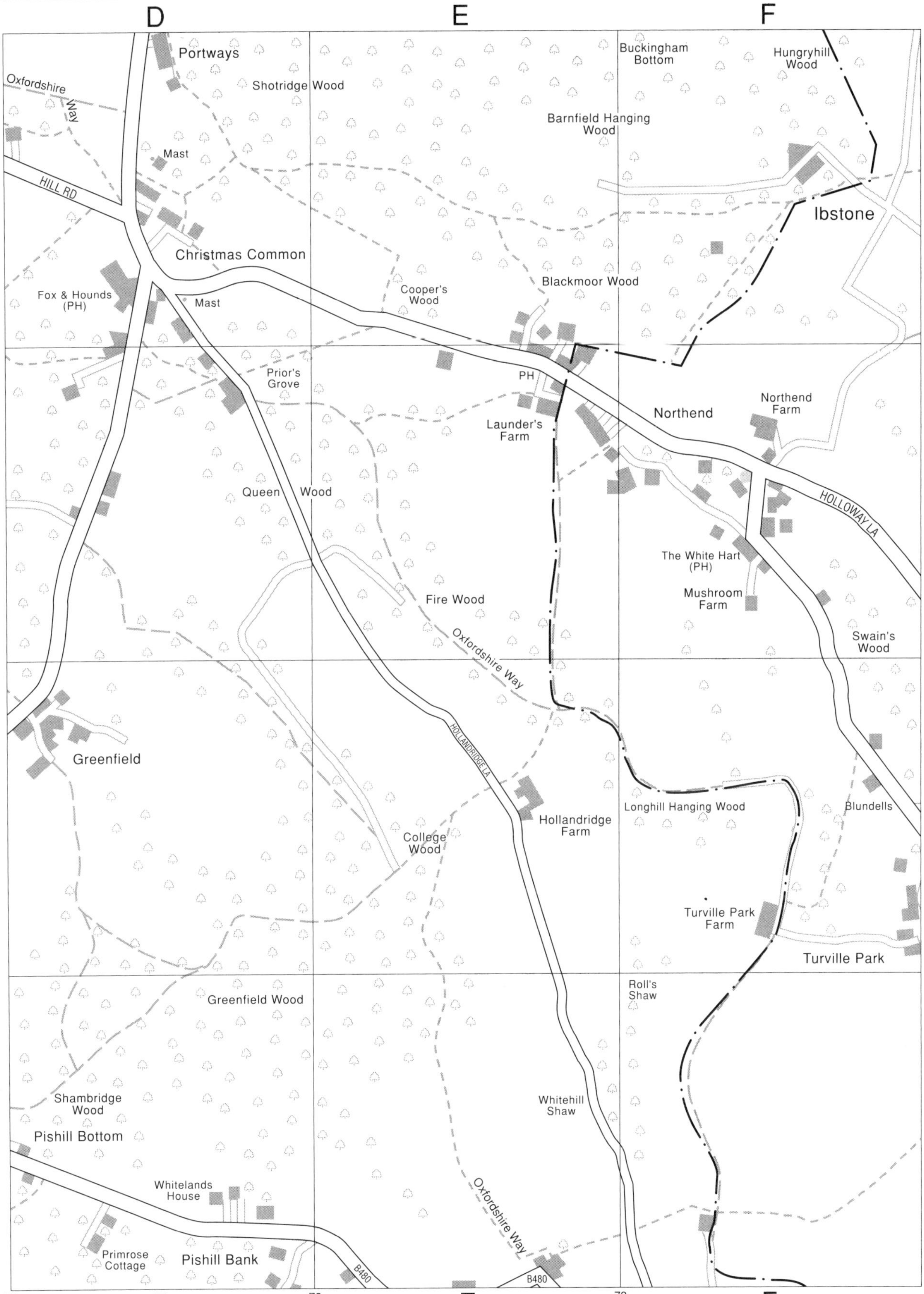

not continued, see key diagram

225

190

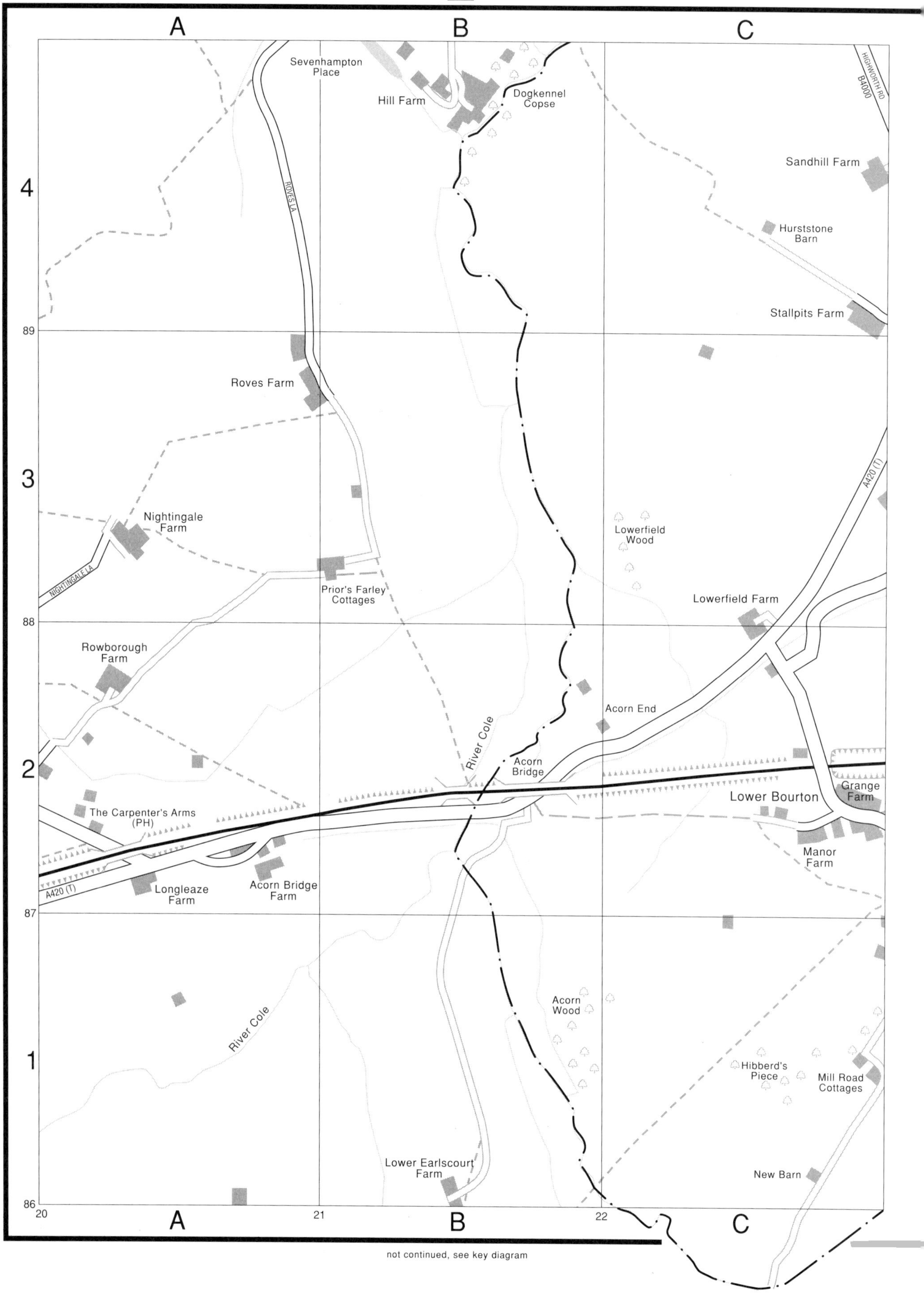

not continued, see key diagram

not continued, see key diagram

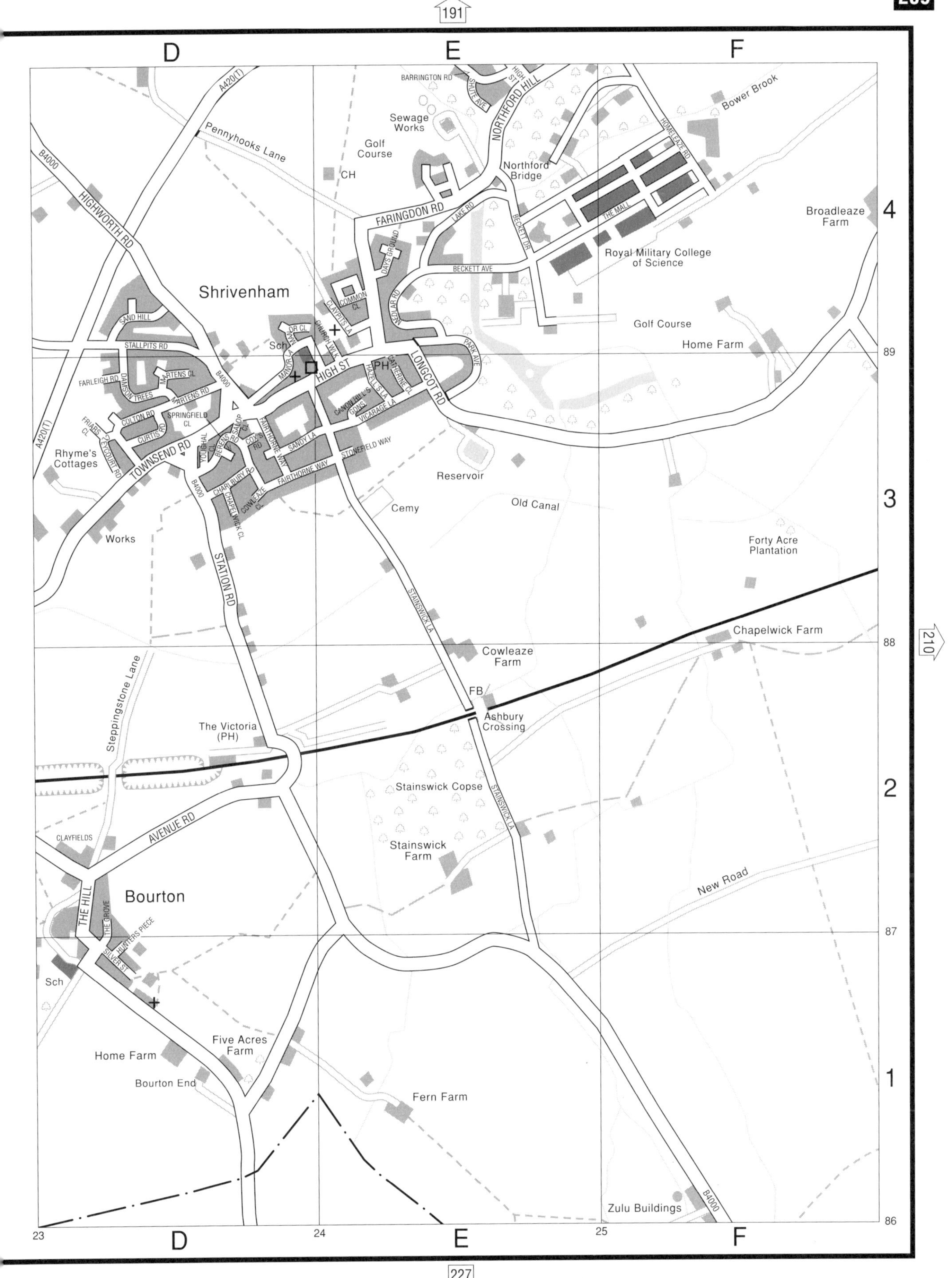
191
D
E
F
Shrivenham
Bourton
Pennyhooks Lane
Golf Course
Sewage Works
CH
Northford Bridge
Bower Brook
Broadleaze Farm
Royal Military College of Science
Golf Course
Home Farm
FARINGDON RD
NORTHFORD HILL
HIGHWORTH RD
HIGH ST
LONGCOT RD
TOWNSEND RD
STATION RD
Rhyme's Cottages
Works
Reservoir
Cemy
Old Canal
Forty Acre Plantation
Chapelwick Farm
Cowleaze Farm
FB
Ashbury Crossing
The Victoria (PH)
Steppingstone Lane
Stainswick Copse
Stainswick Farm
AVENUE RD
New Road
THE HILL
Sch
Home Farm
Five Acres Farm
Bourton End
Fern Farm
Zulu Buildings
B4000
A420(T)
4
3
2
1
89
88
87
86
23
24
25
210
227

192

209

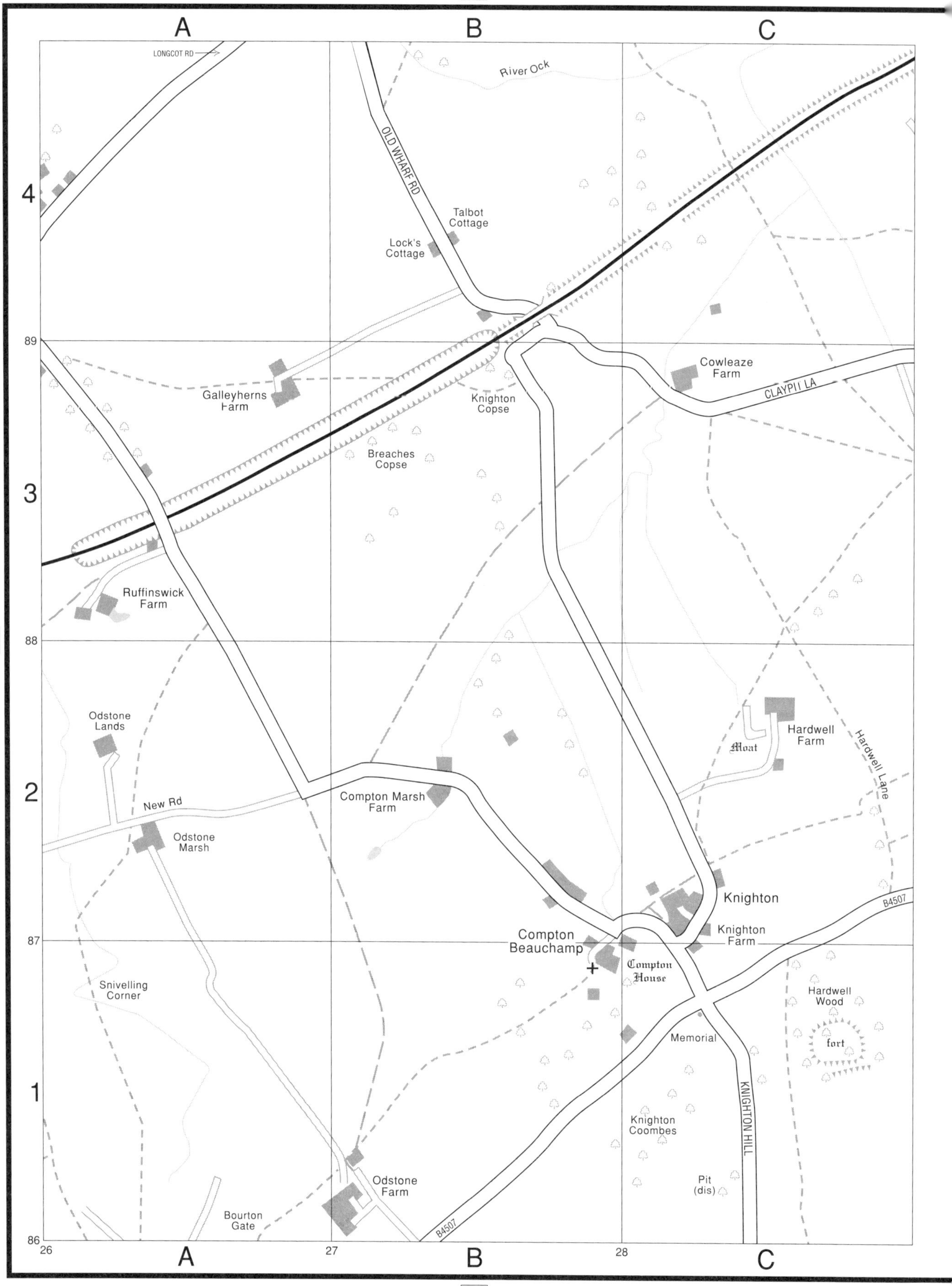
A
B
C
4
3
2
1
89
88
87
86
26
27
28
LONGCOT RD
River Ock
OLD WHARF RD
Talbot Cottage
Lock's Cottage
Galleyherns Farm
Knighton Copse
Cowleaze Farm
CLAYPIT LA
Breaches Copse
Ruffinswick Farm
Odstone Lands
Hardwell Farm
Moat
Hardwell Lane
New Rd
Compton Marsh Farm
Odstone Marsh
Knighton
Compton Beauchamp
Knighton Farm
B4507
Compton House
Snivelling Corner
Hardwell Wood
fort
Memorial
KNIGHTON HILL
Knighton Coombes
Pit (dis)
Odstone Farm
Bourton Gate

228

193

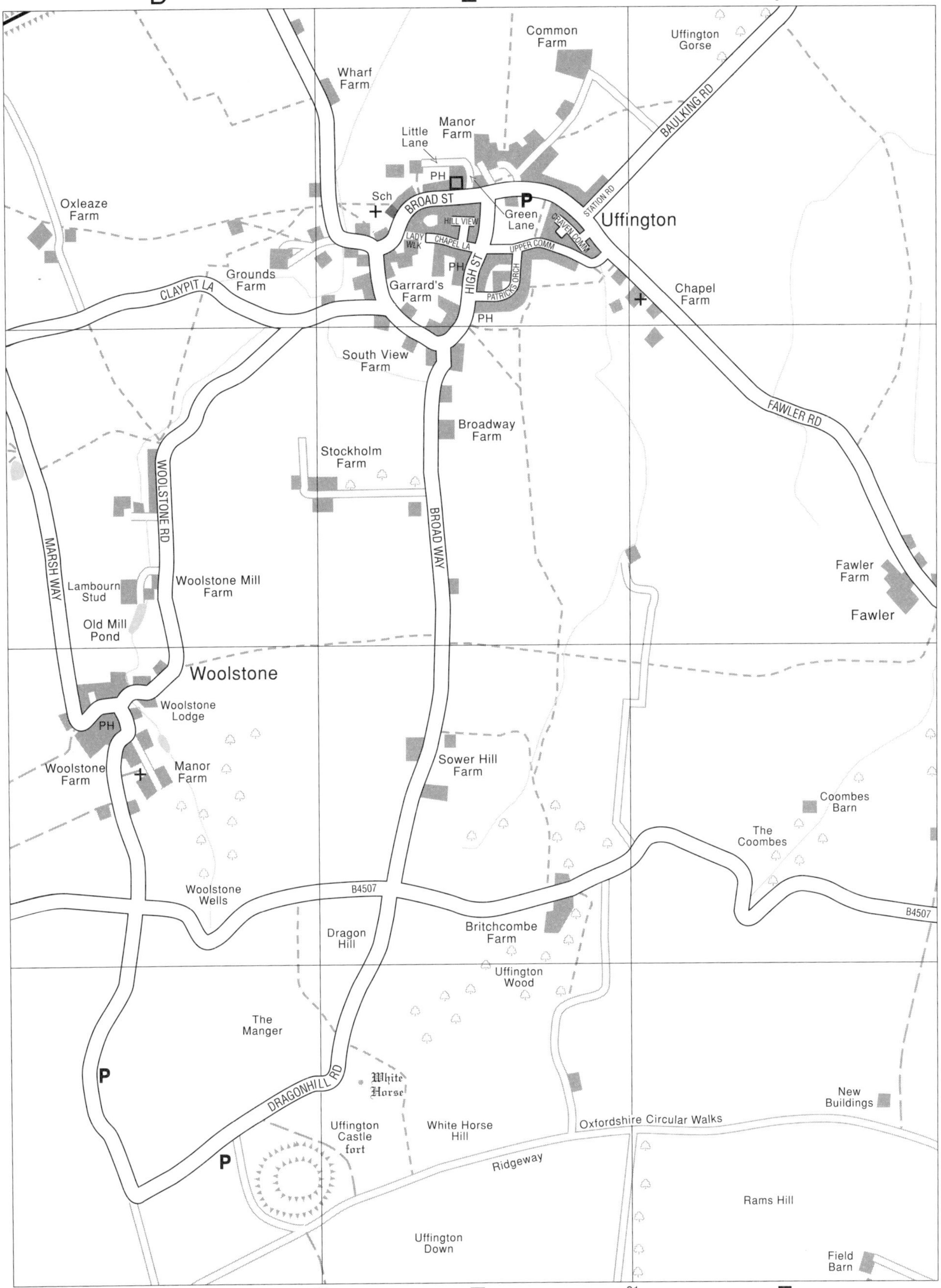
D
E
F
Common Farm
Uffington Gorse
Wharf Farm
Manor Farm
Little Lane
PH
Sch
BROAD ST
BAULKING RD
STATION RD
Uffington
Green Lane
CRAVEN COMM
HILL VIEW
LADY WLK
CHAPEL LA
UPPER COMM
HIGH ST
PATRICKS ORCH
Oxleaze Farm
Grounds Farm
CLAYPIT LA
Garrard's Farm
Chapel Farm
South View Farm
FAWLER RD
Broadway Farm
Stockholm Farm
WOOLSTONE RD
BROAD WAY
MARSH WAY
Lambourn Stud
Woolstone Mill Farm
Fawler Farm
Fawler
Old Mill Pond
Woolstone
Woolstone Lodge
Woolstone Farm
Manor Farm
Sower Hill Farm
Coombes Barn
The Coombes
Woolstone Wells
B4507
Dragon Hill
Britchcombe Farm
Uffington Wood
The Manger
DRAGONHILL RD
White Horse
New Buildings
Uffington Castle fort
White Horse Hill
Oxfordshire Circular Walks
Ridgeway
Rams Hill
Uffington Down
Field Barn
4
3
2
1
89
88
87
86
29
30
31
P

212

229

194

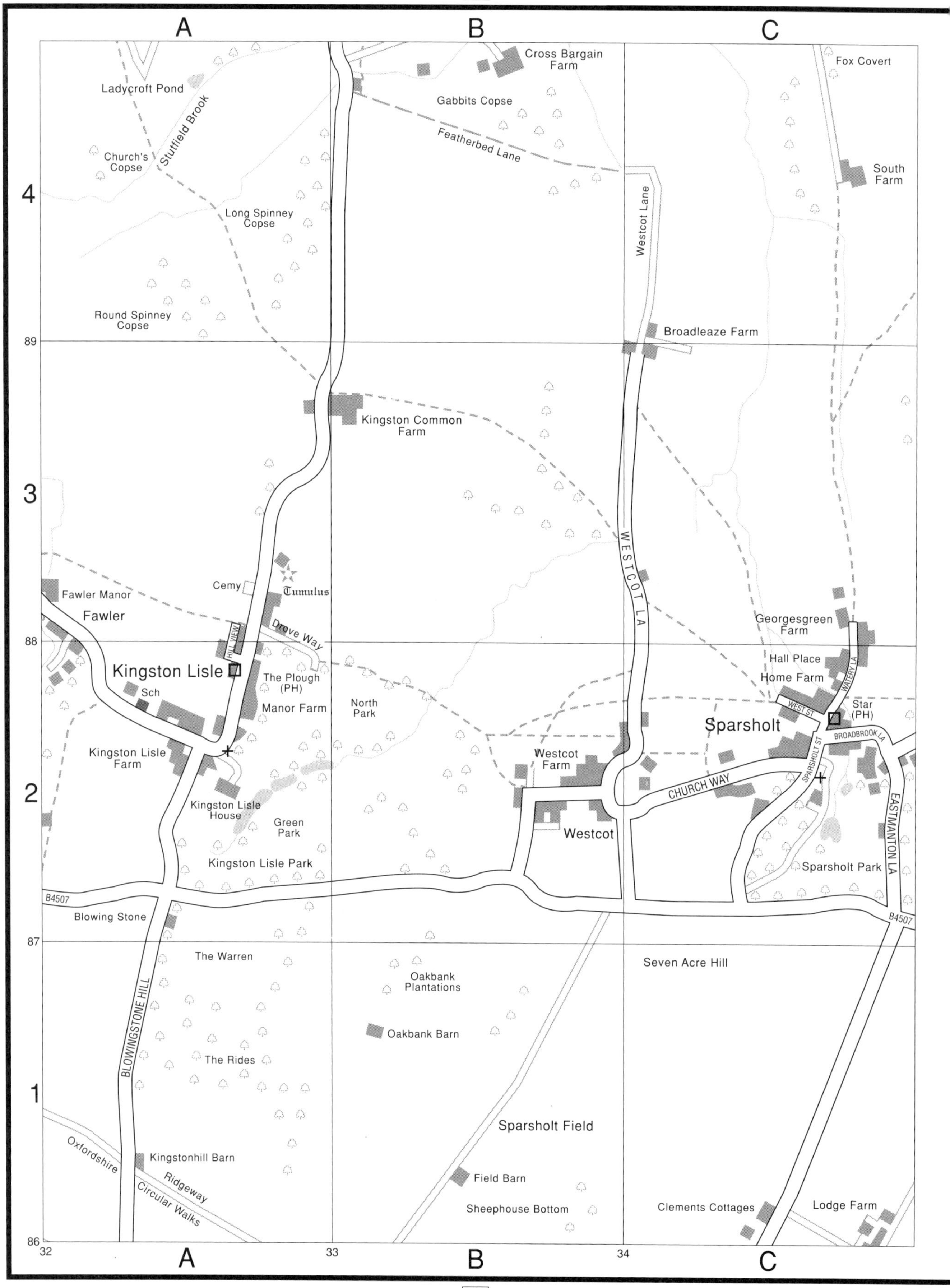

A
B
C
4
3
2
1
89
88
87
86
32
33
34
Ladycroft Pond
Stutfield Brook
Church's Copse
Long Spinney Copse
Round Spinney Copse
Cross Bargain Farm
Gabbits Copse
Featherbed Lane
Westcot Lane
Fox Covert
South Farm
Broadleaze Farm
Kingston Common Farm
Cemy
Tumulus
Fawler Manor
Fawler
Drove Way
HILL VIEW
Kingston Lisle
The Plough (PH)
Sch
Manor Farm
North Park
Kingston Lisle Farm
Kingston Lisle House
Green Park
Kingston Lisle Park
WESTCOT LA
Georgesgreen Farm
Hall Place
Home Farm
WATERY LA
WEST ST
Star (PH)
Sparsholt
BROADBROOK LA
SPARSHOLT ST
Westcot Farm
CHURCH WAY
Westcot
EASTMANTON LA
Sparsholt Park
B4507
Blowing Stone
The Warren
Oakbank Plantations
Seven Acre Hill
Oakbank Barn
BLOWINGSTONE HILL
The Rides
Sparsholt Field
Kingstonhill Barn
Oxfordshire Ridgeway Circular Walks
Field Barn
Sheephouse Bottom
Clements Cottages
Lodge Farm

211

230

195

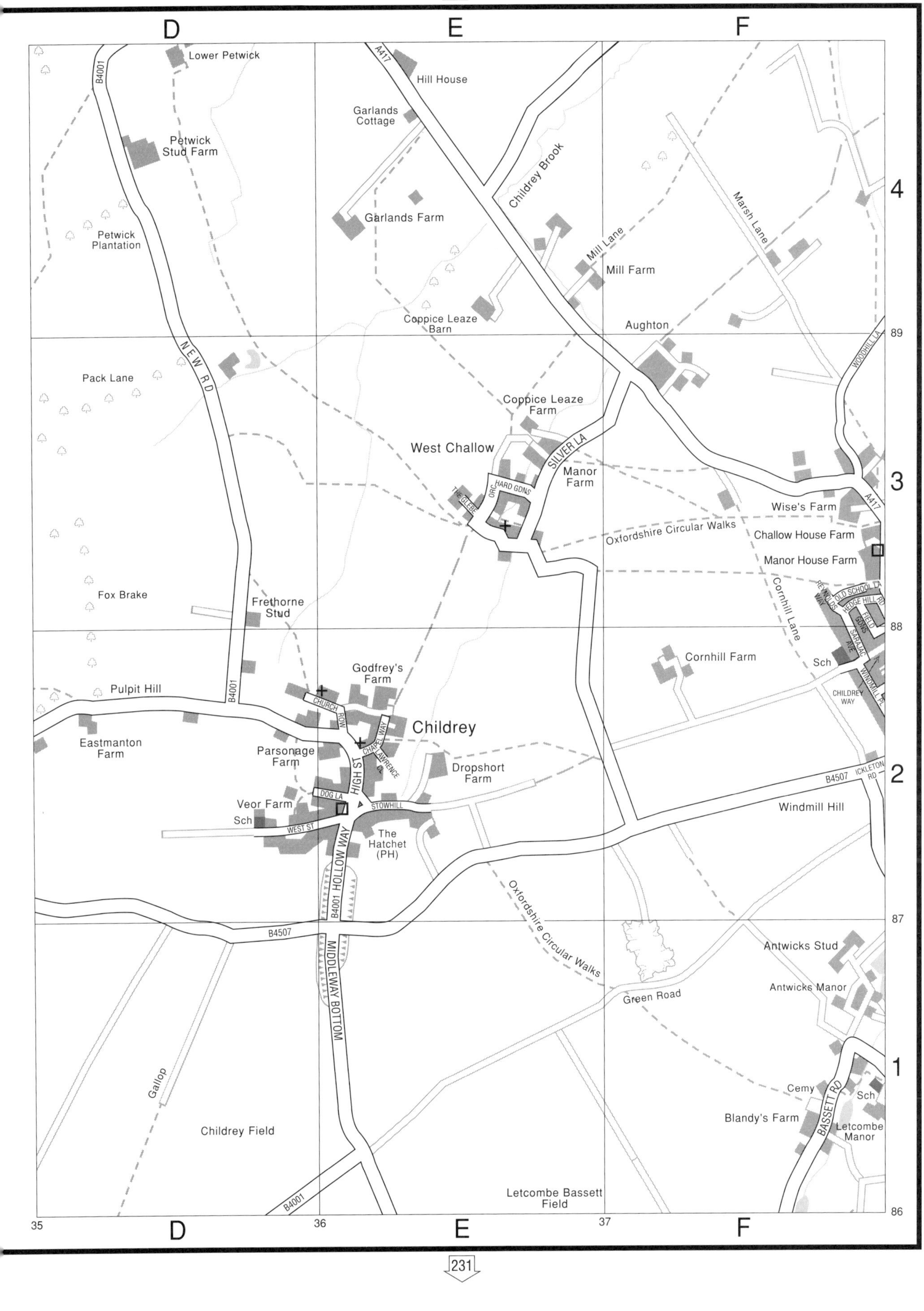
D
E
F
Lower Petwick
Hill House
Garlands Cottage
Petwick Stud Farm
Childrey Brook
Garlands Farm
Marsh Lane
Petwick Plantation
Mill Lane
Mill Farm
Coppice Leaze Barn
Aughton
NEW RD
Pack Lane
Coppice Leaze Farm
West Challow
SILVER LA
Manor Farm
HARD GDNS
THE GLEBE
Wise's Farm
Oxfordshire Circular Walks
Challow House Farm
Manor House Farm
Fox Brake
Frethorne Stud
Cornhill Lane
Cornhill Farm
Sch
Godfrey's Farm
Pulpit Hill
B4001
CHURCH ROW
Childrey
CHAPEL WAY
Eastmanton Farm
Parsonage Farm
Dropshort Farm
HIGH ST
LAWRENCE CL
B4507
Windmill Hill
DOG LA
Veor Farm
STOWHILL
Sch
WEST ST
The Hatchet (PH)
HOLLOW WAY
B4507
MIDDLEWAY BOTTOM
Oxfordshire Circular Walks
Antwicks Stud
Antwicks Manor
Green Road
Gallop
Cemy
BASSETT RD
Sch
Blandy's Farm
Letcombe Manor
Childrey Field
Letcombe Bassett Field
B4001
A417
OLD SCHOOL LA
HEDGE HILL RD
CHILDREY WAY
ICKLETON RD
WOODHILL LA
4
3
2
1
89
88
87
86
35
36
37
D
E
F

214

231

196

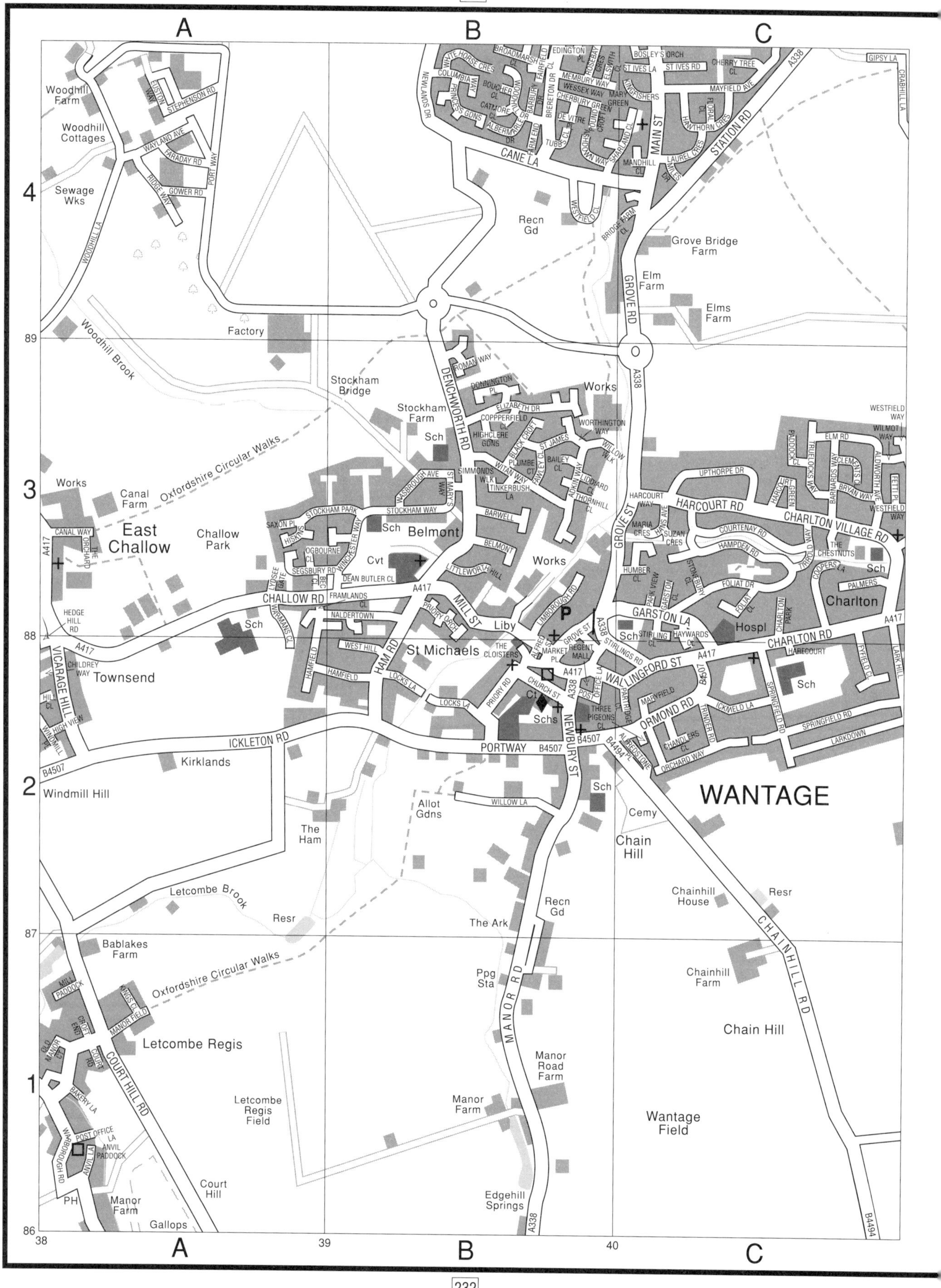
A
B
C
4
3
2
1
89
88
87
86
38
39
40
Woodhill Farm
Woodhill Cottages
Sewage Wks
WOODHILL LA
STEPHENSON RD
EUSTON WAY
WAYLAND AVE
FARADAY RD
PORT WAY
RIDGE WAY
GOWER RD
Factory
Woodhill Brook
Stockham Bridge
Stockham Farm
Sch
Works
Canal Farm
Oxfordshire Circular Walks
East Challow
Challow Park
CANAL WAY
THE ORCHARD
A417
HEDGE HILL RD
CHALLOW RD
Sch
Townsend
CHILDREY WAY
VICARAGE HILL
HIGH VIEW
WINDMILL
ICKLETON RD
B4507
Kirklands
Windmill Hill
Letcombe Brook
Resr
Bablakes Farm
MILL PADDOCK
KINGS CL
MANOR FIELD
CROFT END
OLD MANOR CT
COURT RD
COURT HILL RD
Letcombe Regis
BAKERY LA
POST OFFICE LA
ANVIL PADDOCK
ANVIL LA
WARBOROUGH RD
PH
Manor Farm
Gallops
Court Hill
Letcombe Regis Field
The Ham
Allot Gdns
WILLOW LA
The Ark
Recn Gd
Ppg Sta
MANOR RD
Manor Road Farm
Manor Farm
Edgehill Springs
A338
Wantage Field
Chain Hill
Chainhill Farm
Chainhill House
Resr
CHAINHILL RD
B4494
Cemy
Chain Hill
Sch
WANTAGE
BROADMARSH CL
EDINGTON PL
ROSEBAY CRES
ELSWITH CL
BOSLEY'S ORCH
ST IVES LA
ST IVES RD
CHERRY TREE CL
WHITE HORSE CRES
COLUMBIA WAY
NEWLANDS DR
PRINCESS GDNS
BOUCHER CL
CATMORE CL
ALBERMARLE DR
MEMBURY WAY
WESSEX WAY
CHERBURY GREEN
DE VITRE PL
TUBB CL
MARY GREEN
KINGFISHERS
MAIN ST
MAYFIELD AVE
FLORAL CL
HAWTHORN CRES
LAUREL CRES
STATION RD
A338
GIPSY LA
CRABHILL LA
CANE LA
MANDHILL CL
WESTFIELD CL
BRIDGE FARM CL
Recn Gd
Grove Bridge Farm
Elm Farm
GROVE RD
Elms Farm
DENCHWORTH RD
ROMAN WAY
DONNINGTON PL
ELIZABETH DR
COPPERFIELD CL
HIGHCLERE GDNS
BLACK CROFT
ST JAMES
WORTHINGTON WAY
WILLOW WLK
Works
SIMMONDS WLK
WITAN WAY
PLUMBE CT
BAILEY CL
ADKIN WAY
LIDDIARD CL
THORNHILL CL
TINKERBUSH LA
WASBROUGH AVE
ST MARY'S WAY
STOCKHAM PARK
STOCKHAM WAY
SAXON PL
HISKINS
OGBOURNE CL
WINCHESTER WAY
SEGSBURY RD
DEAN BUTLER CL
Sch
Belmont
Cvt
BARWELL
BELMONT
LITTLEWORTH HILL
Works
LYDSEE GATE
FRAMLANDS CL
NALDERTOWN
MILL ST
PRIORY ORCH
WARMANS CL
HAMFIELD
WEST HILL
HAM RD
St Michaels
LOCKS LA
THE CLOISTERS
PRIORY RD
CHURCH ST
Ct
Schs
Liby
P
LIMBOROUGH RD
GROVE ST
MARKET PL
REGENT MALL
STIRLINGS RD
POST OFFICE LA
WALLINGFORD ST
THREE PIGEONS CL
PARTRIDGE CL
NEWBURY ST
PORTWAY
B4507
GROVE ST
HARCOURT WAY
HAWS AVE
MARIA CRES
SUZAN CRES
HUMBER CL
PARK VIEW
GARSTON CL
STONEBURY CL
FOLIAT DR
FOLIAT CL
GARSTON LA
Sch
STIRLING CL
HAYWARDS CL
Hospl
CHARLTON RD
CHARLTON PARK
HARCOURT RD
CHARLTON VILLAGE RD
UPTHORPE DR
COURTENAY RD
HAMPDEN RD
THE CHESTNUTS
COOPERS LA
PALMERS
Charlton
Sch
WESTFIELD WAY
WILMOT WAY
ELM RD
PADDOCK CL
TRUELOCKS WAY
BARNARDS WAY
CLEMENTS CL
BRYAN WAY
ALDWORTH AVE
FETTIPLACE
WESTFIELD WAY
HARCOURT GREEN
THROLD WAY
ORMOND RD
MARYFIELD
ICKNIELD LA
SPRINGFIELD RD
TRINDER RD
CHANDLERS CL
ORCHARD WAY
ALFREDSTONE PL
HARECOURT
PYFIELD CL
LARK HILL
LARKDOWN
B4494

213

232

197

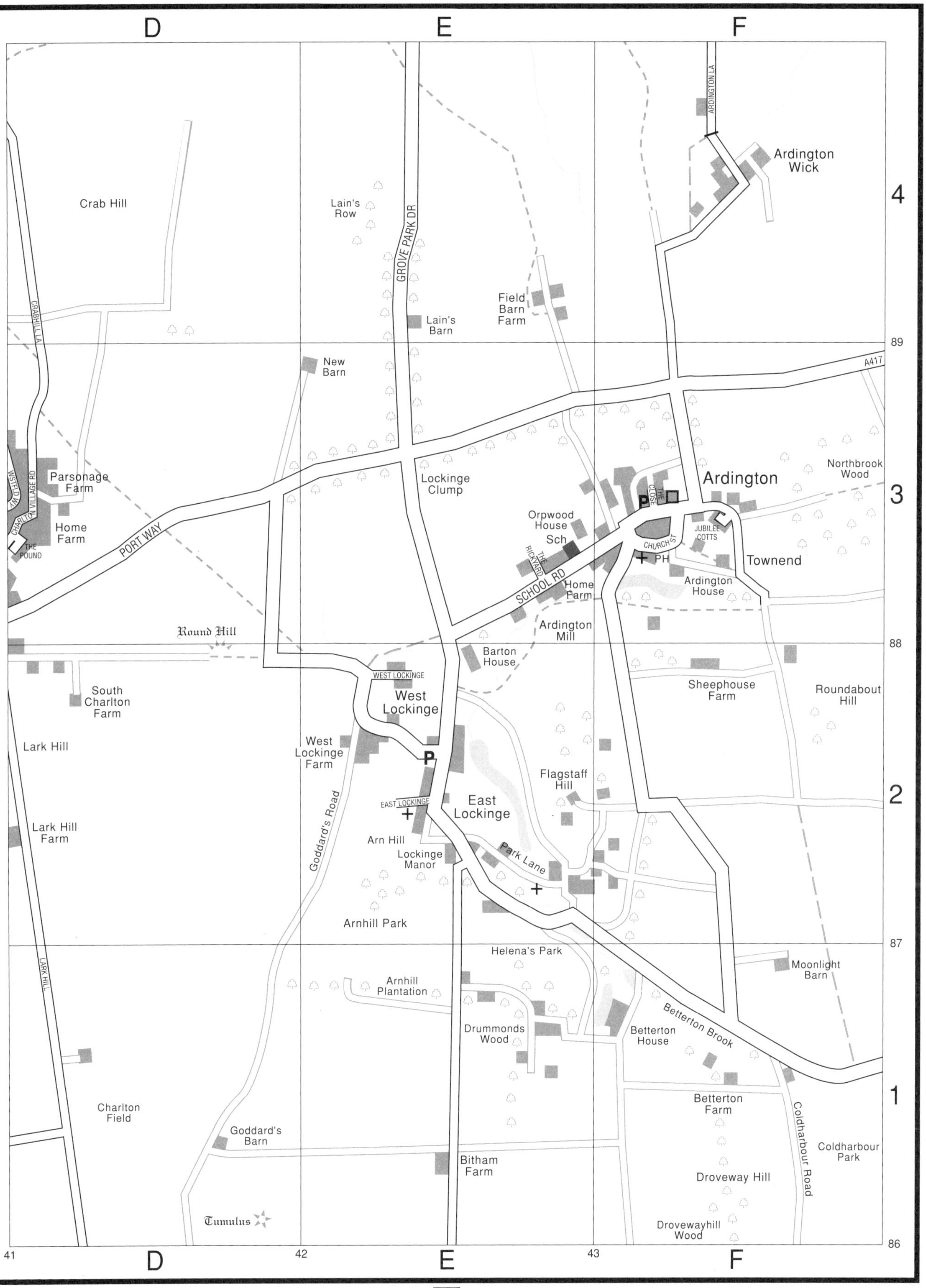

D
E
F
Crab Hill
Lain's Row
GROVE PARK DR
Lain's Barn
Field Barn Farm
ARDINGTON LA
Ardington Wick
CRABHILL LA
New Barn
A417
Parsonage Farm
CHARLTON VILLAGE RD
WSTFLD WY
Home Farm
THE POUND
PORT WAY
Lockinge Clump
Ardington
Northbrook Wood
THE CLOSE
Orpwood House
Sch
THE RICKYARD
SCHOOL RD
CHURCH ST
JUBILEE COTTS
PH
Townend
Home Farm
Ardington House
Ardington Mill
Round Hill
Barton House
South Charlton Farm
WEST LOCKINGE
West Lockinge
Sheephouse Farm
Roundabout Hill
Lark Hill
West Lockinge Farm
P
Flagstaff Hill
Goddard's Road
EAST LOCKINGE
East Lockinge
Lark Hill Farm
Arn Hill
Lockinge Manor
Park Lane
Arnhill Park
LARK HILL
Helena's Park
Moonlight Barn
Arnhill Plantation
Betterton Brook
Drummonds Wood
Betterton House
Charlton Field
Betterton Farm
Coldharbour Road
Goddard's Barn
Coldharbour Park
Bitham Farm
Droveway Hill
Tumulus
Drovewayhill Wood
4
3
2
1
89
88
87
86
41
42
43

216

233

198

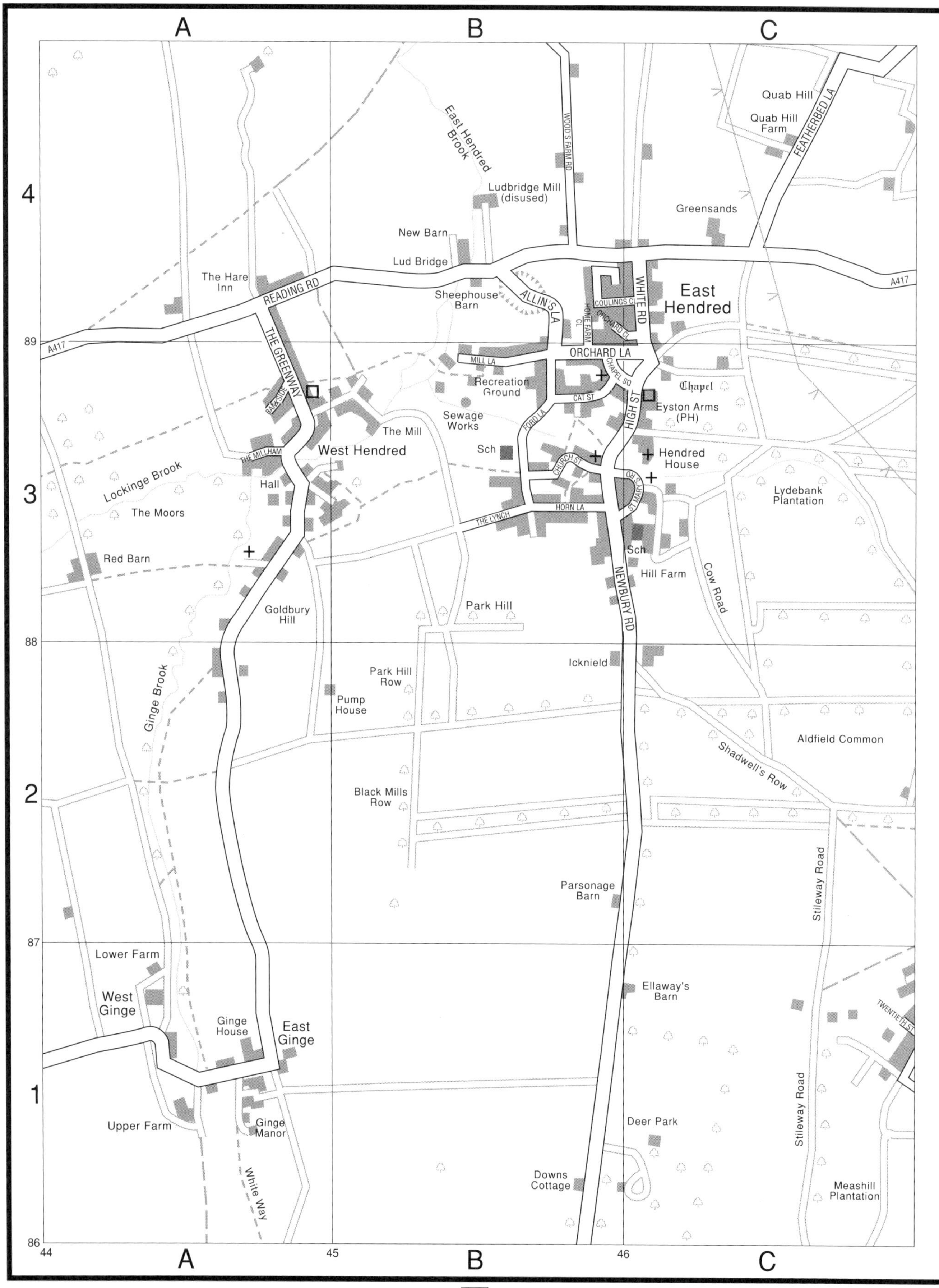
A
B
C
4
3
2
1
89
88
87
86
44
45
46
East Hendred Brook
Ludbridge Mill (disused)
New Barn
Lud Bridge
Quab Hill
Quab Hill Farm
FEATHERBED LA
WOOD'S FARM RD
Greensands
A417
The Hare Inn
READING RD
Sheephouse Barn
ALLIN'S LA
East Hendred
COULINGS CL
WHITE RD
HOME FARM CL
ORCHARD CL
ORCHARD LA
MILL LA
THE GREENWAY
Recreation Ground
CHAPEL SQ
Chapel
CAT ST
Eyston Arms (PH)
HIGH ST
Sewage Works
The Mill
FORD LA
West Hendred
Sch
Hendred House
THE MILLHAM
CHURCH ST
Lockinge Brook
Hall
ST MARY'S RD
Lydebank Plantation
The Moors
HORN LA
THE LYNCH
Red Barn
Sch
Hill Farm
Cow Road
NEWBURY RD
Goldbury Hill
Park Hill
Icknield
Park Hill Row
Ginge Brook
Pump House
Aldfield Common
Shadwell's Row
Black Mills Row
Stileway Road
Parsonage Barn
Lower Farm
Ellaway's Barn
West Ginge
TWENTIETH ST
Ginge House
East Ginge
Upper Farm
Ginge Manor
Deer Park
Stileway Road
White Way
Downs Cottage
Meashill Plantation

215

234

199

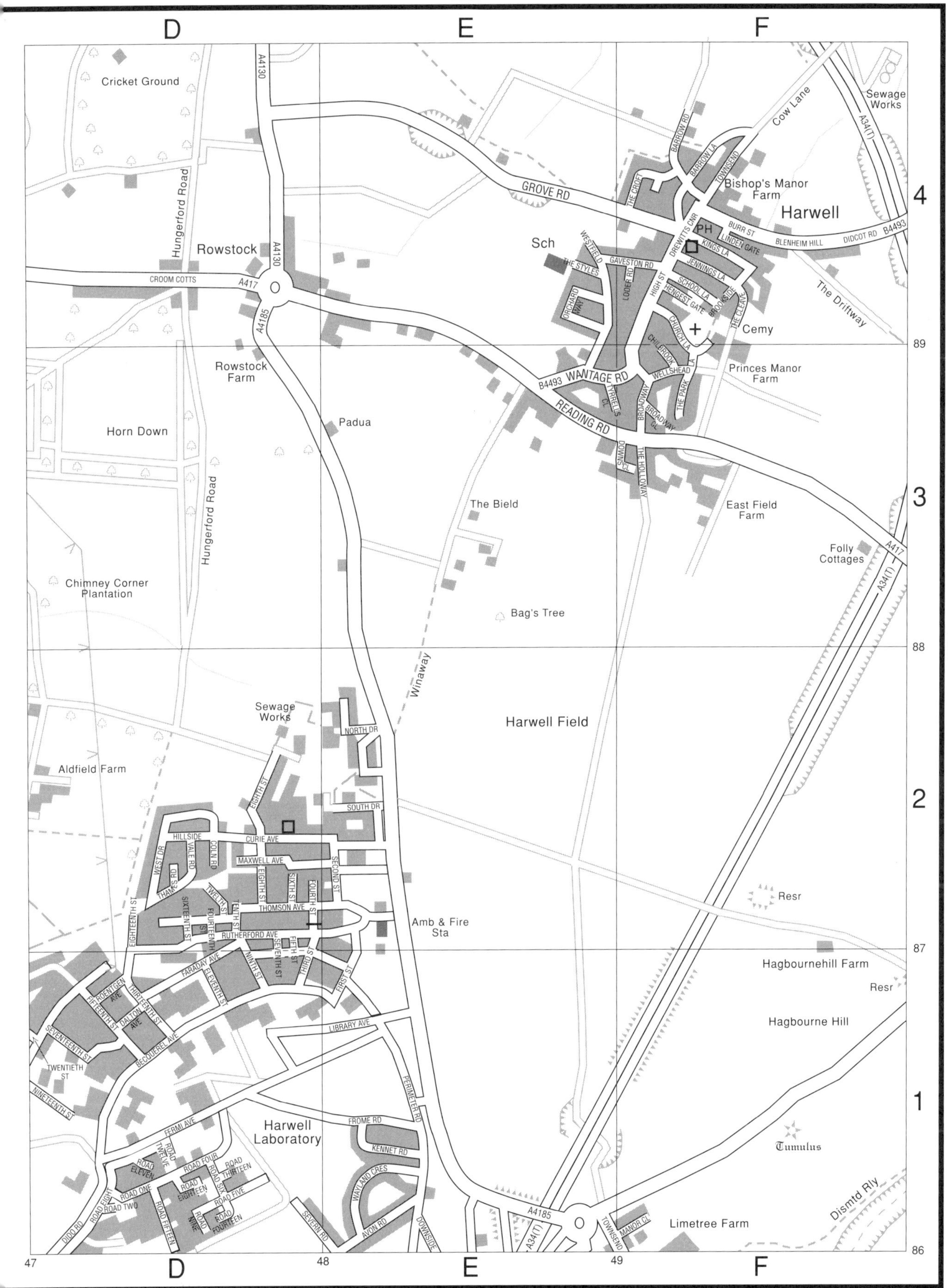
D
E
F
Cricket Ground
Hungerford Road
Rowstock
A4130
CROOM COTTS
A417
A4185
Rowstock Farm
Horn Down
Padua
Hungerford Road
Chimney Corner Plantation
GROVE RD
Sch
Harwell
Bishop's Manor Farm
Sewage Works
Cow Lane
A34(T)
BURR ST
LINDEN GATE
BLENHEIM HILL
DIDCOT RD
B4493
The Driftway
PH
Cemy
Princes Manor Farm
B4493
WANTAGE RD
READING RD
The Bield
East Field Farm
Folly Cottages
A417
Bag's Tree
Winaway
Harwell Field
Sewage Works
Aldfield Farm
NORTH DR
SOUTH DR
CURIE AVE
HILLSIDE
MAXWELL AVE
THOMSON AVE
RUTHERFORD AVE
Amb & Fire Sta
Resr
Hagbournehill Farm
Resr
Hagbourne Hill
LIBRARY AVE
Harwell Laboratory
FERMI AVE
FROME RD
KENNET RD
WAYLAND CRES
PERIMETER RD
Tumulus
A4185
A34(T)
Limetree Farm
Dismtd Rly
4
3
2
1
89
88
87
86
47
48
49

218

235

200

217

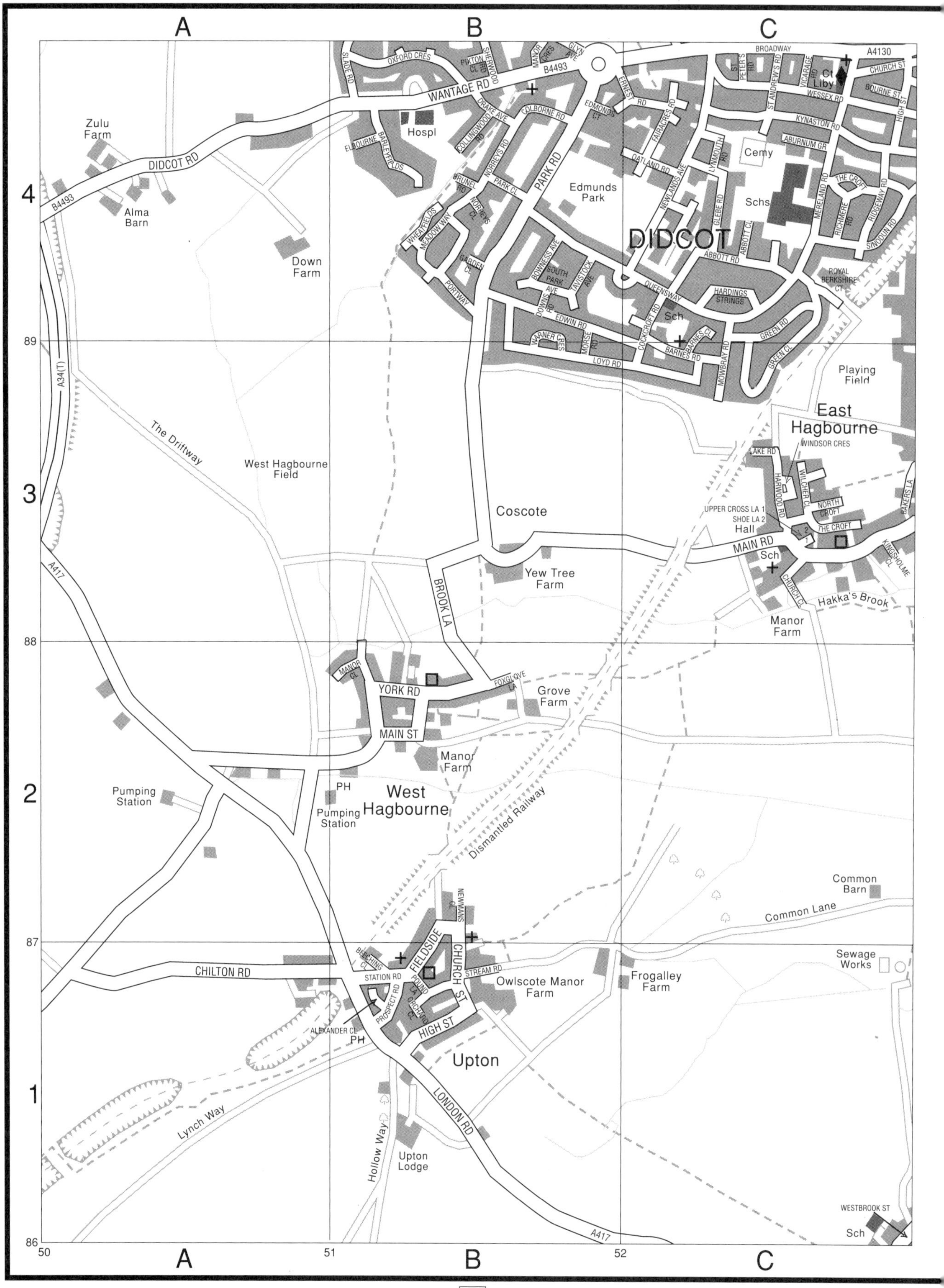

A
B
C
4
3
2
1
89
88
87
86
50
51
52
DIDCOT
Zulu Farm
Alma Barn
Down Farm
DIDCOT RD
B4493
WANTAGE RD
Hospl
Edmunds Park
Cemy
Schs
Sch
Ct Lby
BROADWAY
A4130
CHURCH ST
WESSEX RD
KYNASTON RD
ABURNUM GR
PARK RD
PARK CL
OXFORD CRES
SLADE RD
COLBORNE RD
EDMONDS CT
OATLAND RD
NEWLANDS AVE
GLEBE RD
ABBOTT RD
ABBOTT CL
QUEENSWAY
HARDINGS STRINGS
ROYAL BERKSHIRE CT
COCKCROFT RD
EDWIN RD
WARNER CRES
MORSE RD
LOYD RD
BARNES RD
MOWBRAY RD
GREEN RD
GREEN CL
SOUTH PARK AVE
BOWNESS AVE
TAVISTOCK AVE
PORTWAY
MEADOW WAY
WHEATFIELDS
GARDEN CL
BRUNEL RD
MERELAND RD
THE CROFT
RICHMERE RD
RIDGEWAY RD
SINODUN RD
HIGH ST
Playing Field
East Hagbourne
LAKE RD
WINDSOR CRES
HARWOOD RD
WILCHER CL
NORTH CROFT
UPPER CROSS LA
SHOE LA
Hall
THE CROFT
MAIN RD
BAKERS LA
KINGSHOLME CL
CHURCH CL
Hakka's Brook
Manor Farm
A34(T)
The Driftway
West Hagbourne Field
Coscote
Yew Tree Farm
BROOK LA
A417
MANOR CL
YORK RD
FOXGLOVE LA
Grove Farm
MAIN ST
Manor Farm
PH
West Hagbourne
Pumping Station
Pumping Station
Dismantled Railway
Common Barn
Common Lane
Sewage Works
CHILTON RD
BEECHING
STATION RD
FIELDSIDE
NEWMANS CL
CHURCH ST
STREAM RD
Owlscote Manor Farm
Frogalley Farm
PROSPECT RD
ALEXANDER CL
POUND LA
ORCHARD CL
HIGH ST
PH
Upton
Lynch Way
Hollow Way
LONDON RD
Upton Lodge
WESTBROOK ST
Sch

236

201

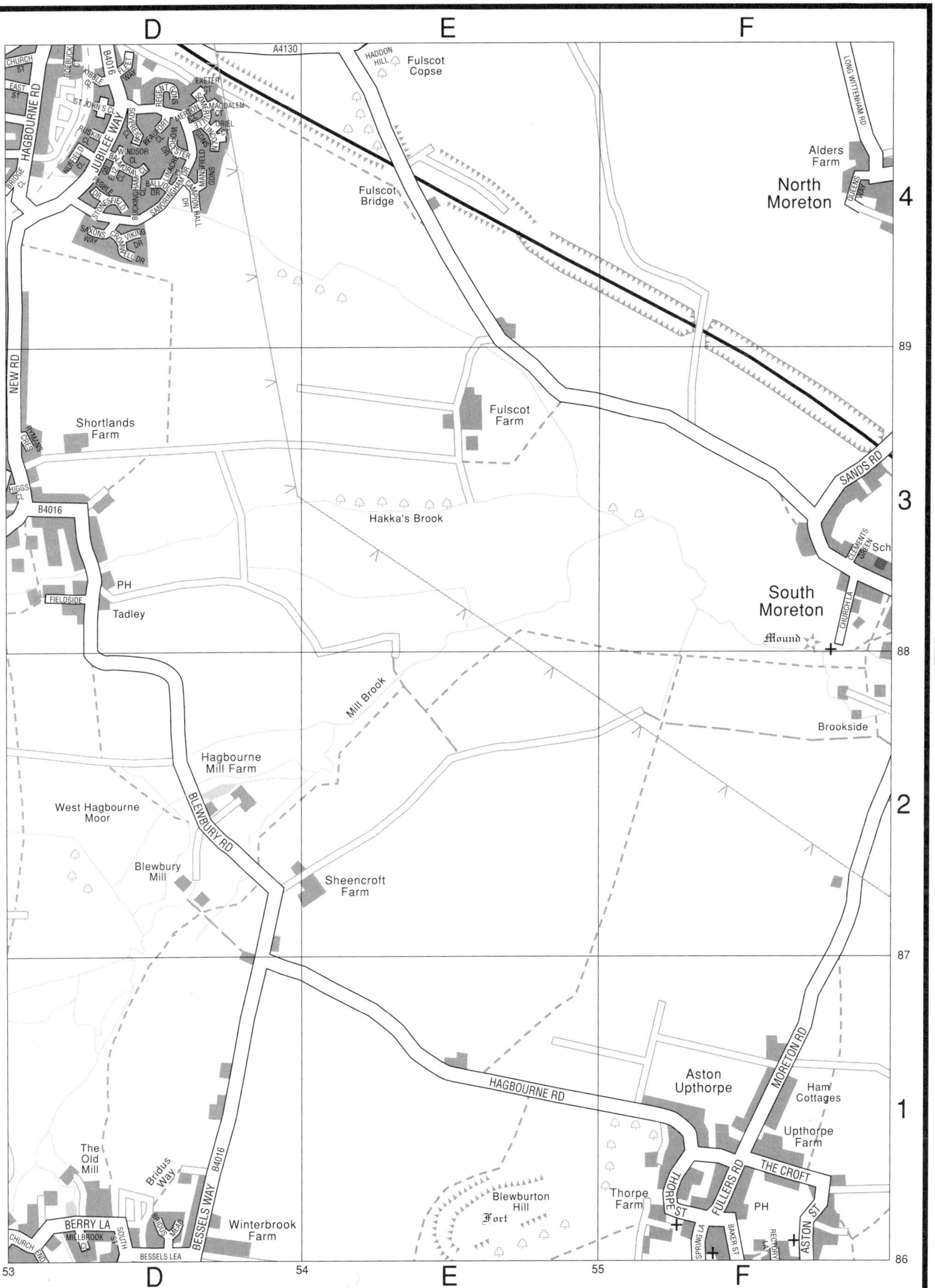
D
E
F
A4130
HADDON HILL
Fulscot Copse
LONG WITTENHAM RD
Alders Farm
North Moreton
QUEENS WAY
4
CHURCH ST
EAST ST
HAGBOURNE RD
ROEBUCK CT
KIBBLE CL
B4016
FLEET WAY
ST JOHN'S CL
JUBILEE WAY
REGENT GDNS
EXETER CT
MAGDALEN CT
ORIEL CT
MERTON CL
LINCOLN GDNS
SOMERVILLE
RUSKIN CL
NUFFIELD CL
WINDSOR CL
BALMORAL CL
BEAUFORT CL
WORCESTER DR
MANSFIELD GDNS
BUCKINGHAM CL
SANDRINGHAM DR
HAMPTON DR
STONESFIELD
PEBBLE DR
SAXONS WAY
CROMWELL DR
VIKING DR
BRIDGE CL
Fulscot Bridge
NEW RD
89
Shortlands Farm
RYMANS CRES
Fulscot Farm
SANDS RD
3
HIGGS CL
B4016
Hakka's Brook
CLEMENTS GREEN
Sch
PH
FIELDSIDE
Tadley
South Moreton
CHURCH LA
Mound
88
Mill Brook
Brookside
Hagbourne Mill Farm
BLEWBURY RD
2
West Hagbourne Moor
Blewbury Mill
Sheencroft Farm
87
MORETON RD
HAGBOURNE RD
Aston Upthorpe
Ham Cottages
1
Upthorpe Farm
The Old Mill
Bridus Way
B4016
THE CROFT
Blewburton Hill
Fort
Thorpe Farm
THORPE ST
FULLERS RD
PH
ASTON ST
BERRY LA
SOUTH MEAD
BRIDUS MEAD
BESSELS WAY
Winterbrook Farm
CHURCH END
MILLBROOK CL
BESSELS LEA
SPRING LA
BAKER ST
RECTORY LA
86
53
54
55
D
E
F

220

237

202

219

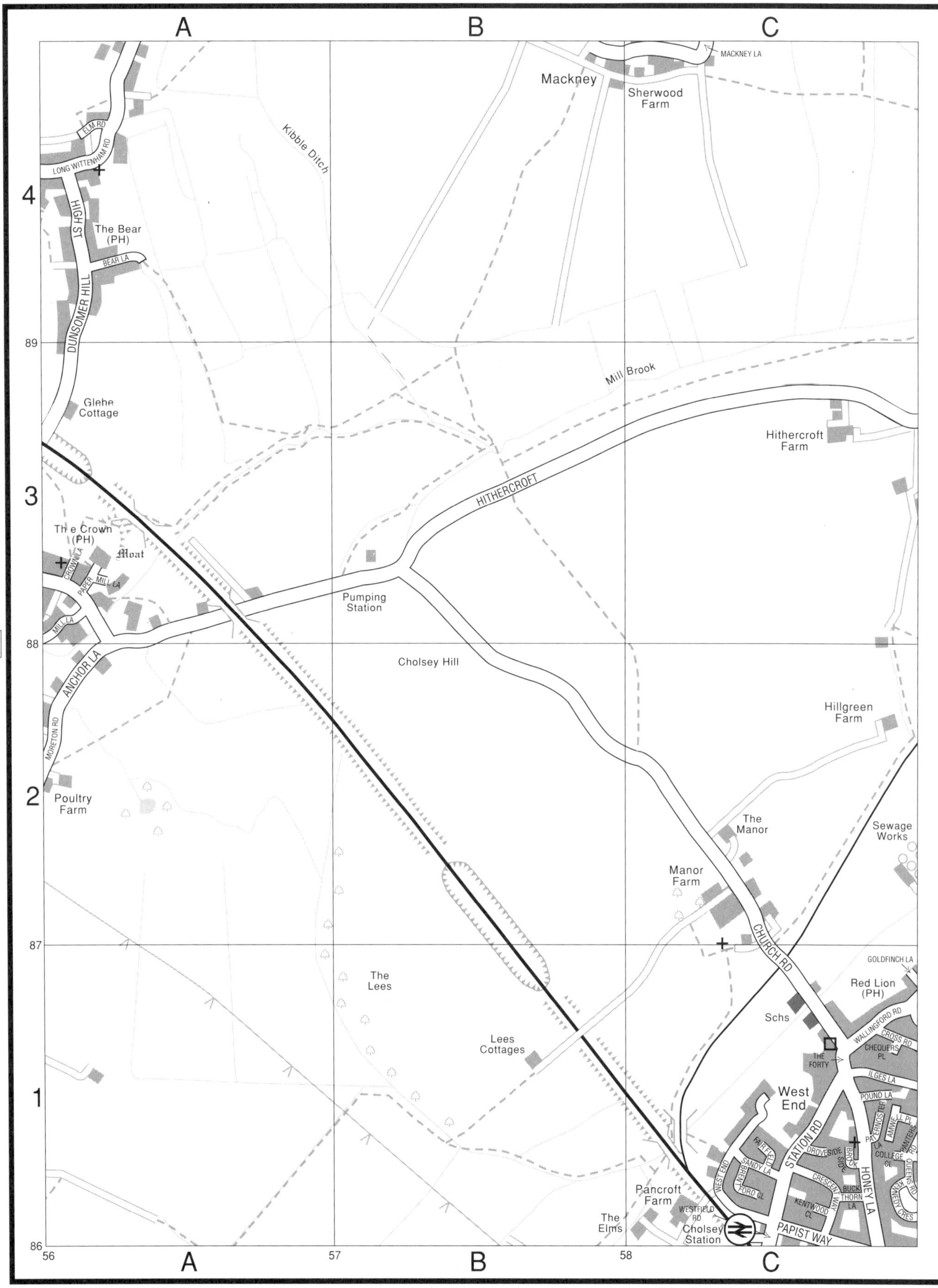
A
B
C
4
3
2
1
89
88
87
86
56
57
58
Mackney
MACKNEY LA
Sherwood Farm
Kibble Ditch
ELM RD
LONG WITTENHAM RD
HIGH ST
The Bear (PH)
BEAR LA
DUNSOMER HILL
Mill Brook
Glebe Cottage
Hithercroft Farm
HITHERCROFT
The Crown (PH)
CROWN LA
Moat
PAPER MILL LA
MILL LA
Pumping Station
ANCHOR LA
Cholsey Hill
MORETON RD
Hillgreen Farm
Poultry Farm
The Manor
Sewage Works
Manor Farm
CHURCH RD
GOLDFINCH LA
The Lees
Red Lion (PH)
Schs
Lees Cottages
WALLINGFORD RD
CROSS RD
CHEQUERS PL
THE FORTY
ILGES LA
West End
POUND LA
PATERNOSTER LA
AMWELL PL
STATION RD
DROVESIDE
BROOKSIDE
COLLEGE CL
PANTERS RD
QUEENS RD
KENNEDY CRES
FAIRFIELD
SANDY LA
WEST END
BRINDFORD CL
CRESCENT WAY
BUCKTHORN LA
HONEY LA
KENTWOOD CL
Pancroft Farm
WESTFIELD RD
The Elms
Cholsey Station
PAPIST WAY

238

203

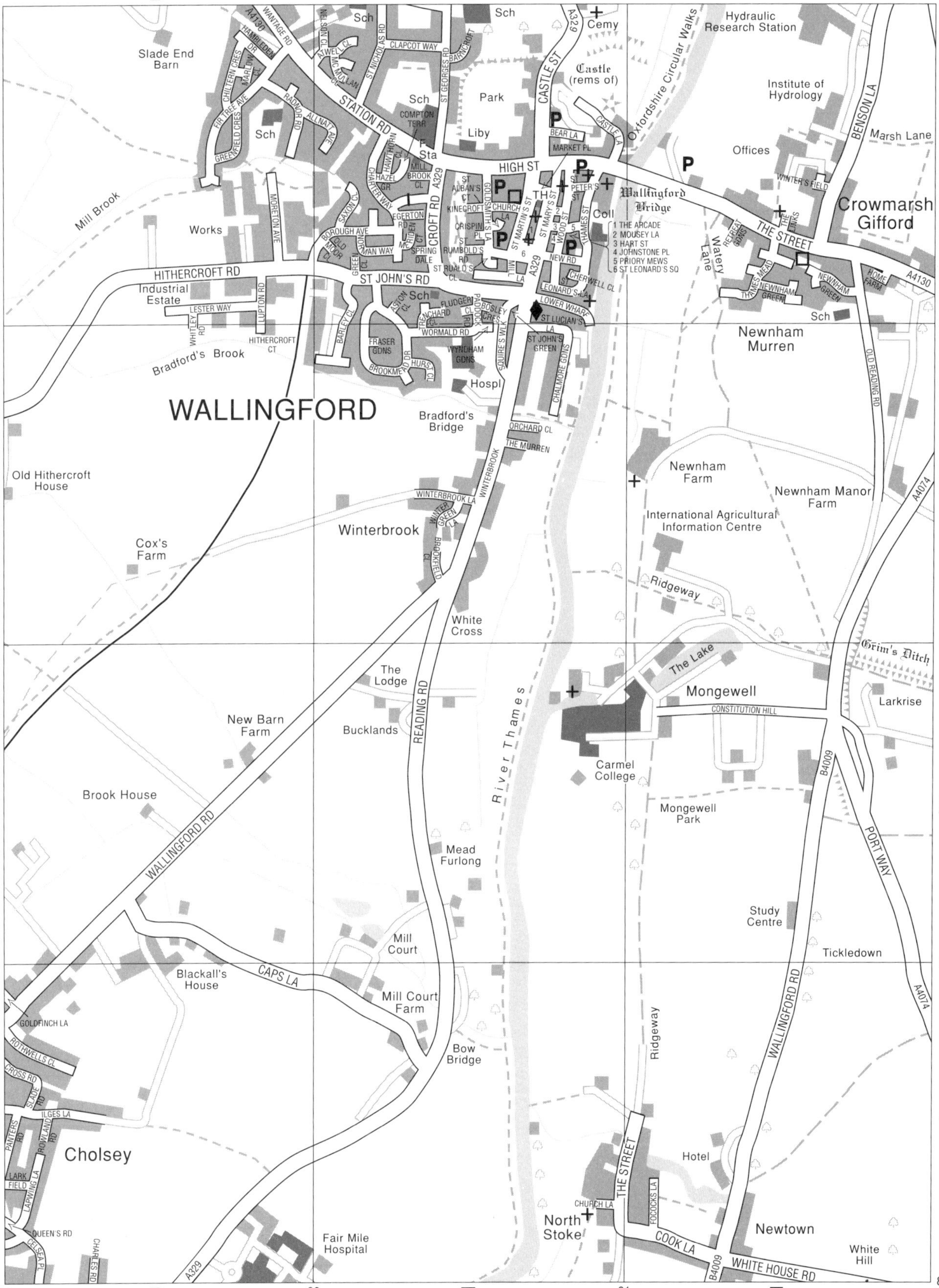
D
E
F
WALLINGFORD
Crowmarsh Gifford
Winterbrook
Cholsey
North Stoke
Newtown
Mongewell
Newnham Murren
Slade End Barn
Works
Industrial Estate
Old Hithercroft House
Cox's Farm
New Barn Farm
Brook House
Blackall's House
Fair Mile Hospital
Mill Court
Mill Court Farm
Bow Bridge
Mead Furlong
The Lodge
Bucklands
White Cross
Bradford's Bridge
Hospl
Castle (rems of)
Cemy
Park
Liby
Sch
Sta
Coll
Wallingford Bridge
Hydraulic Research Station
Institute of Hydrology
Offices
Marsh Lane
Newnham Farm
Newnham Manor Farm
International Agricultural Information Centre
The Lake
Carmel College
Mongewell Park
Larkrise
Study Centre
Tickledown
Hotel
White Hill
Grim's Ditch
River Thames
Ridgeway
Oxfordshire Circular Walks
Watery Lane
Mill Brook
Bradford's Brook
HITHERCROFT RD
ST JOHN'S RD
STATION RD
HIGH ST
CASTLE ST
THE STREET
WALLINGFORD RD
READING RD
CAPS LA
CONSTITUTION HILL
PORT WAY
BENSON LA
OLD READING RD
COOK LA
WHITE HOUSE RD
A4130
A329
A4074
B4009
1 THE ARCADE
2 MOUSEY LA
3 HART ST
4 JOHNSTONE PL
5 PRIORY MEWS
6 ST LEONARD'S SQ
89
88
87
86
59
60
61
4
3
2
1

222
239

204

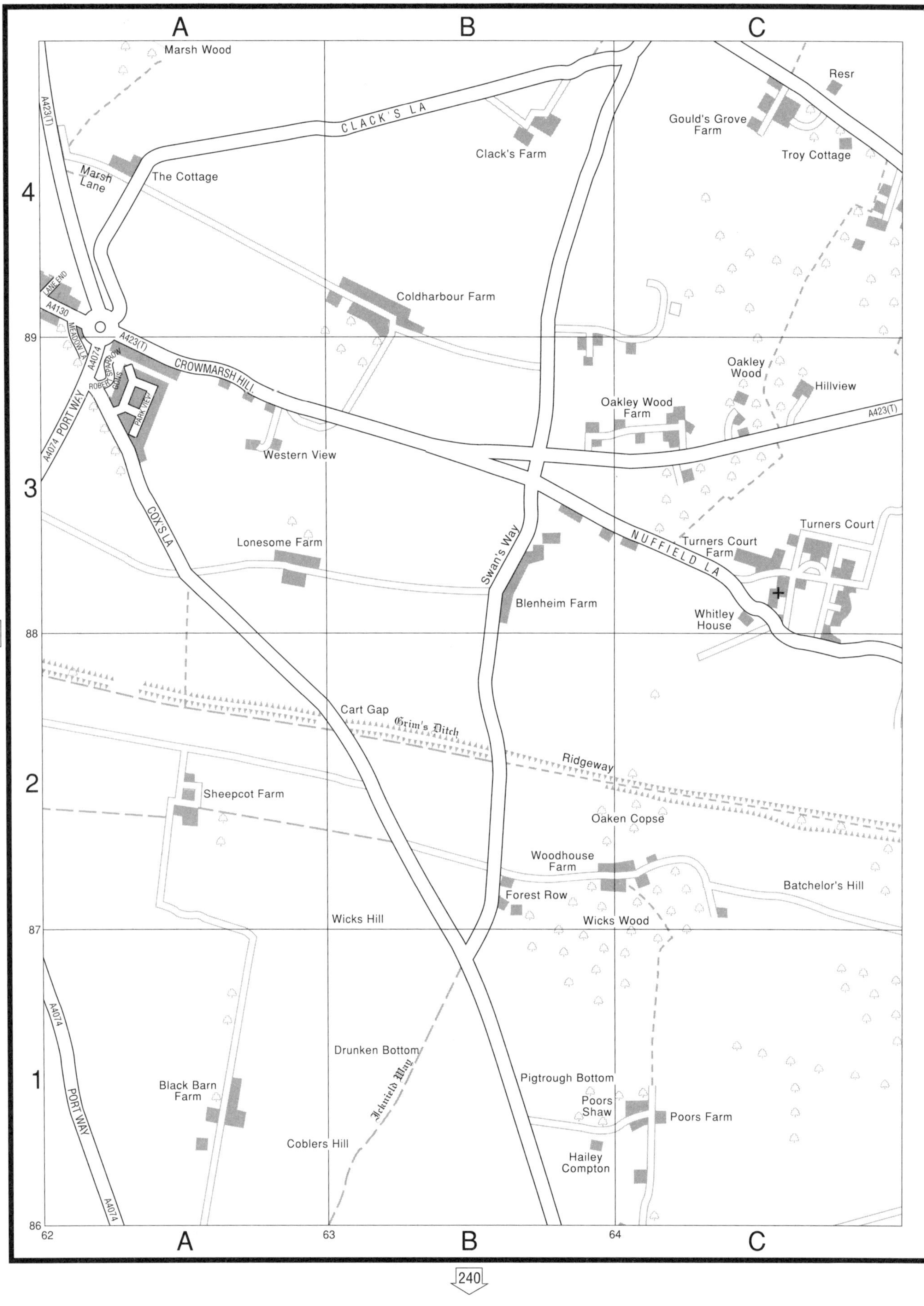
A
B
C
Marsh Wood
A423(T)
CLACK'S LA
Resr
Gould's Grove Farm
Clack's Farm
Troy Cottage
Marsh Lane
The Cottage
4
LANE END
A4130
Coldharbour Farm
MEADOW LA
89
A423(T)
A4074
ROBERT SPARROW GDNS
CROWMARSH HILL
PARK VIEW
Oakley Wood
Hillview
Oakley Wood Farm
A423(T)
A4074 PORT WAY
Western View
3
COX'S LA
Lonesome Farm
Swan's Way
NUFFIELD LA
Turners Court
Turners Court Farm
Blenheim Farm
Whitley House
88
Cart Gap
Grim's Ditch
Ridgeway
2
Sheepcot Farm
Oaken Copse
Woodhouse Farm
Batchelor's Hill
Forest Row
Wicks Hill
Wicks Wood
87
A4074
Drunken Bottom
Icknield Way
1
PORT WAY
Black Barn Farm
Pigtrough Bottom
Poors Shaw
Poors Farm
Coblers Hill
Hailey Compton
A4074
86
62
63
64

221

240

205

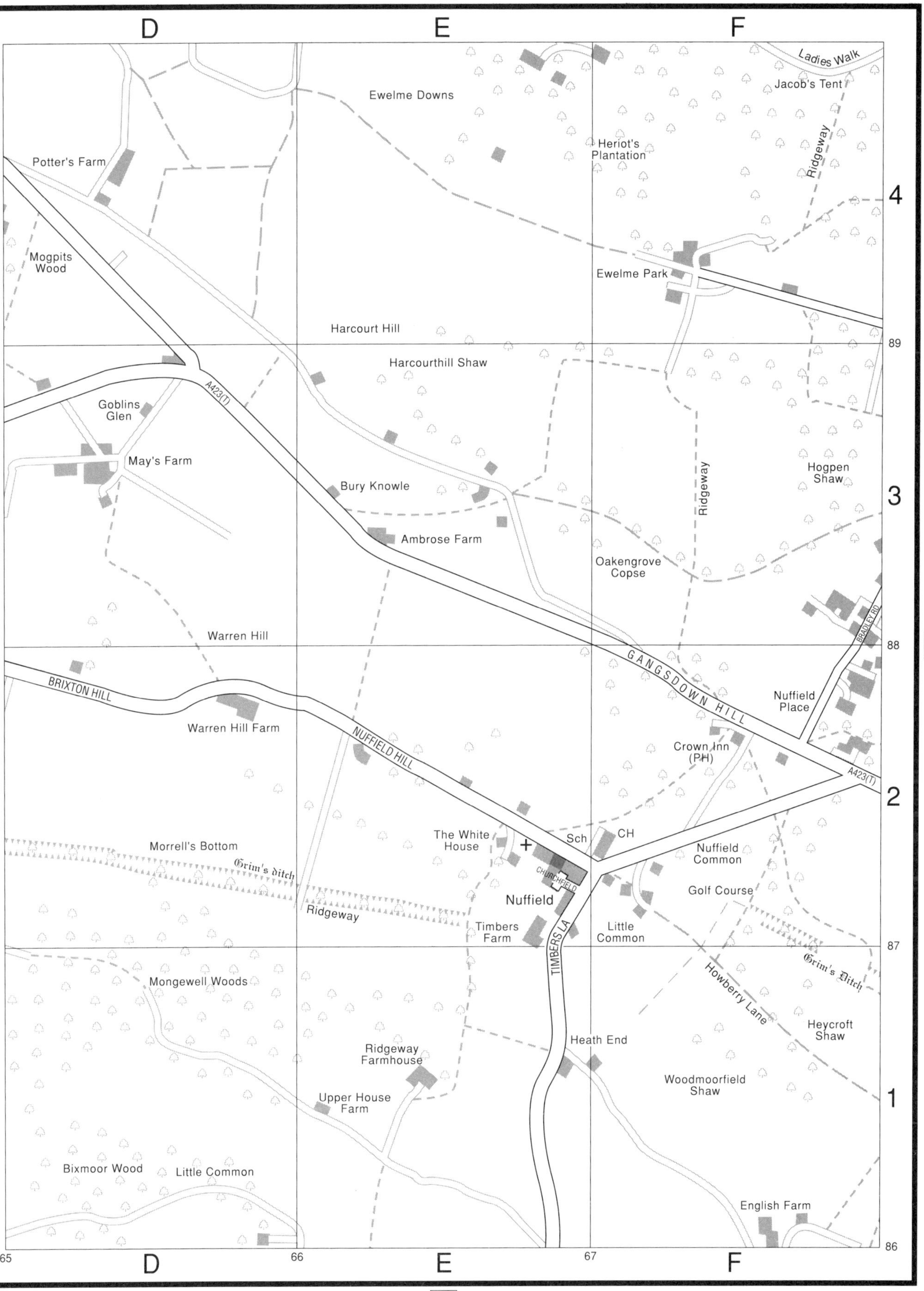
D
E
F
Ladies Walk
Jacob's Tent
Ewelme Downs
Heriot's Plantation
Ridgeway
Potter's Farm
Mogpits Wood
Ewelme Park
Harcourt Hill
Harcourthill Shaw
Goblins Glen
A423(T)
May's Farm
Bury Knowle
Ridgeway
Hogpen Shaw
Ambrose Farm
Oakengrove Copse
BRADLEY RD
Warren Hill
GANGSDOWN HILL
BRIXTON HILL
Nuffield Place
Warren Hill Farm
NUFFIELD HILL
Crown Inn (PH)
A423(T)
Morrell's Bottom
The White House
Sch
CH
Nuffield Common
Grim's ditch
CHURCHFIELD
Golf Course
Nuffield
Ridgeway
Timbers Farm
TIMBERS LA
Little Common
Grim's Ditch
Howberry Lane
Mongewell Woods
Heycroft Shaw
Heath End
Ridgeway Farmhouse
Woodmoorfield Shaw
Upper House Farm
Bixmoor Wood
Little Common
English Farm
4
89
3
88
2
87
1
86
65
66
67
D
E
F

224

241

206

223

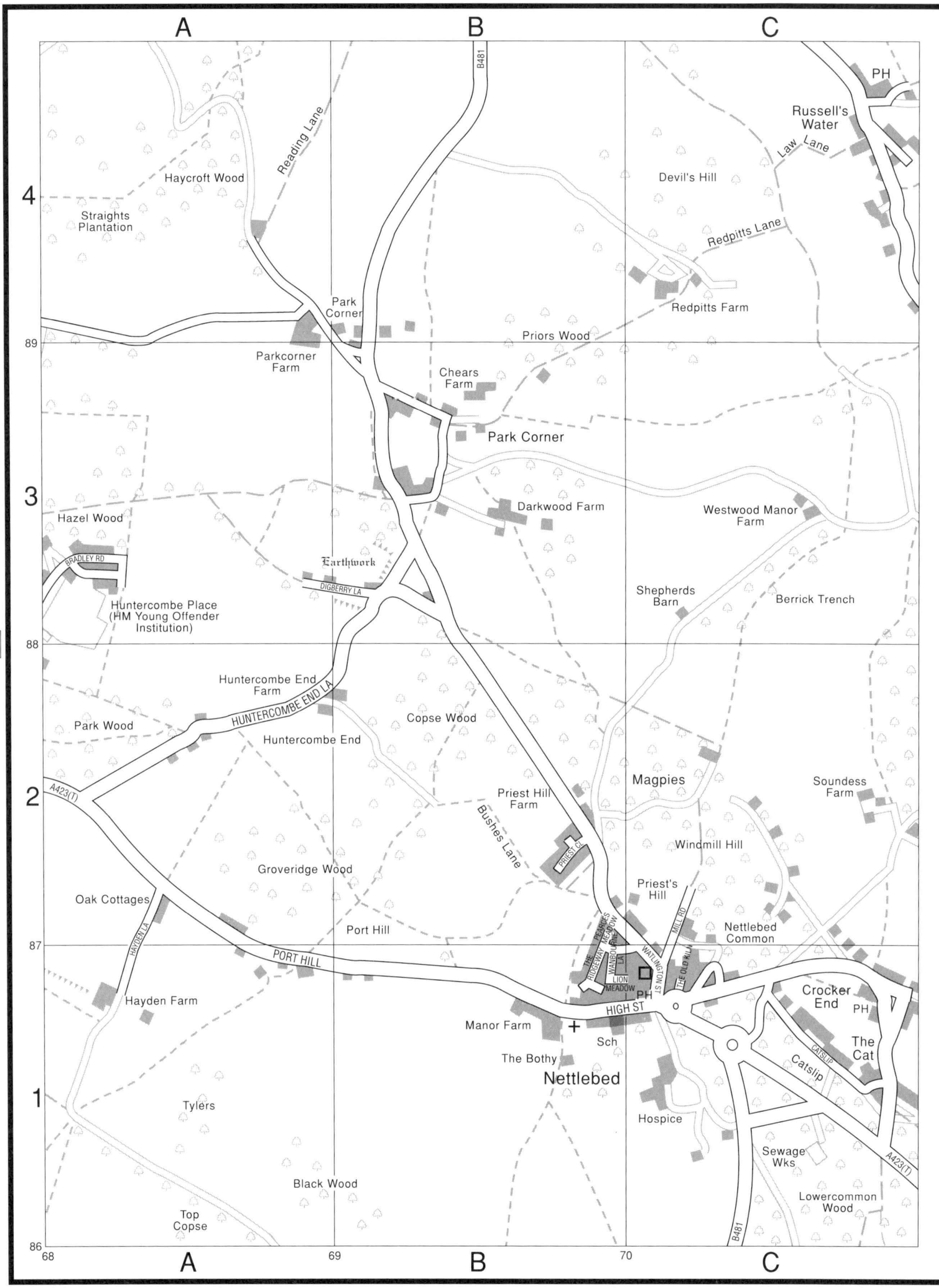

A
B
C
4
3
2
1
89
88
87
86
68
69
70
B481
PH
Russell's Water
Law Lane
Reading Lane
Haycroft Wood
Straights Plantation
Devil's Hill
Redpitts Lane
Redpitts Farm
Park Corner
Priors Wood
Parkcorner Farm
Chears Farm
Park Corner
Darkwood Farm
Westwood Manor Farm
Hazel Wood
BRADLEY RD
Earthwork
DIGBERRY LA
Shepherds Barn
Berrick Trench
Huntercombe Place (HM Young Offender Institution)
Huntercombe End Farm
HUNTERCOMBE END LA
Copse Wood
Park Wood
Huntercombe End
Magpies
Soundess Farm
A423(T)
Priest Hill Farm
Bushes Lane
PRIEST CL
Windmill Hill
Groveridge Wood
Oak Cottages
Priest's Hill
HAYDEN LA
Port Hill
Nettlebed Common
MILL RD
PEARCES MEADOW
THE RIDGEWAY
WANBOURNE LA
WATLINGTON ST
THE OLD KILN
LION MEADOW
PORT HILL
PH
Crocker End
PH
Hayden Farm
HIGH ST
Manor Farm
Sch
The Cat
CATSLIP
Catslip
The Bothy
Nettlebed
Tylers
Hospice
Sewage Wks
A423(T)
Black Wood
Lowercommon Wood
Top Copse
B481

242

207

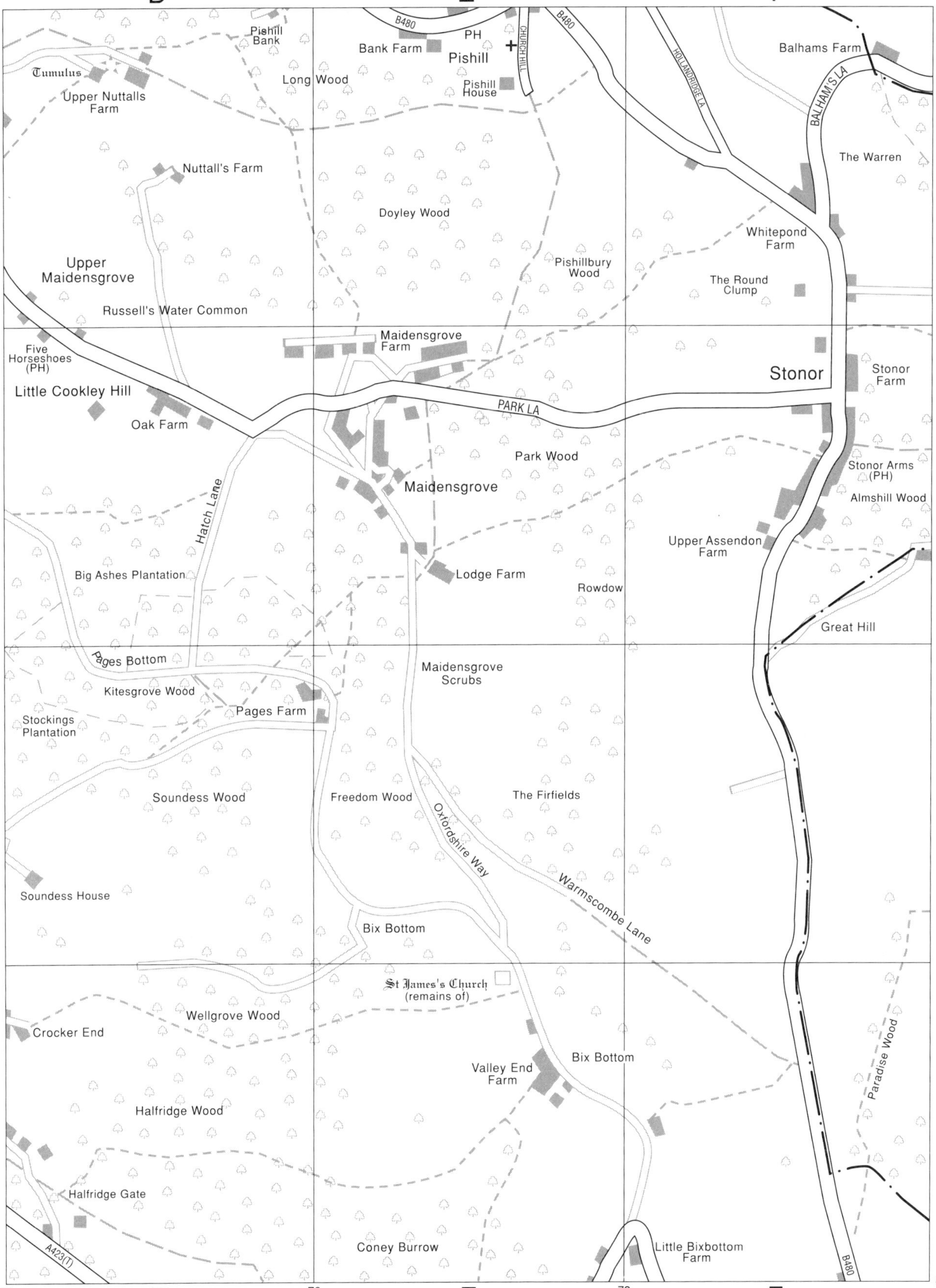
D
E
F
Pishill Bank
Tumulus
Upper Nuttalls Farm
Long Wood
Bank Farm
PH
Pishill
Pishill House
CHURCH HILL
B480
HOLLANDRIDGE LA
Balhams Farm
BALHAM'S LA
The Warren
4
Nuttall's Farm
Doyley Wood
Whitepond Farm
Upper Maidensgrove
Pishillbury Wood
The Round Clump
Russell's Water Common
89
Five Horseshoes (PH)
Maidensgrove Farm
Stonor
Stonor Farm
Little Cookley Hill
PARK LA
Oak Farm
Park Wood
Stonor Arms (PH)
Maidensgrove
3
Almshill Wood
Hatch Lane
Upper Assendon Farm
Big Ashes Plantation
Lodge Farm
Rowdow
Great Hill
Pages Bottom
88
Maidensgrove Scrubs
Kitesgrove Wood
Pages Farm
Stockings Plantation
Soundess Wood
Freedom Wood
The Firfields
2
Oxfordshire Way
Warmscombe Lane
Soundess House
Bix Bottom
87
St James's Church (remains of)
Wellgrove Wood
Crocker End
Paradise Wood
Valley End Farm
Bix Bottom
Halfridge Wood
1
Halfridge Gate
A423(T)
Coney Burrow
Little Bixbottom Farm
B480
86
71
72
73
D
E
F

226

243

not continued, see key diagram

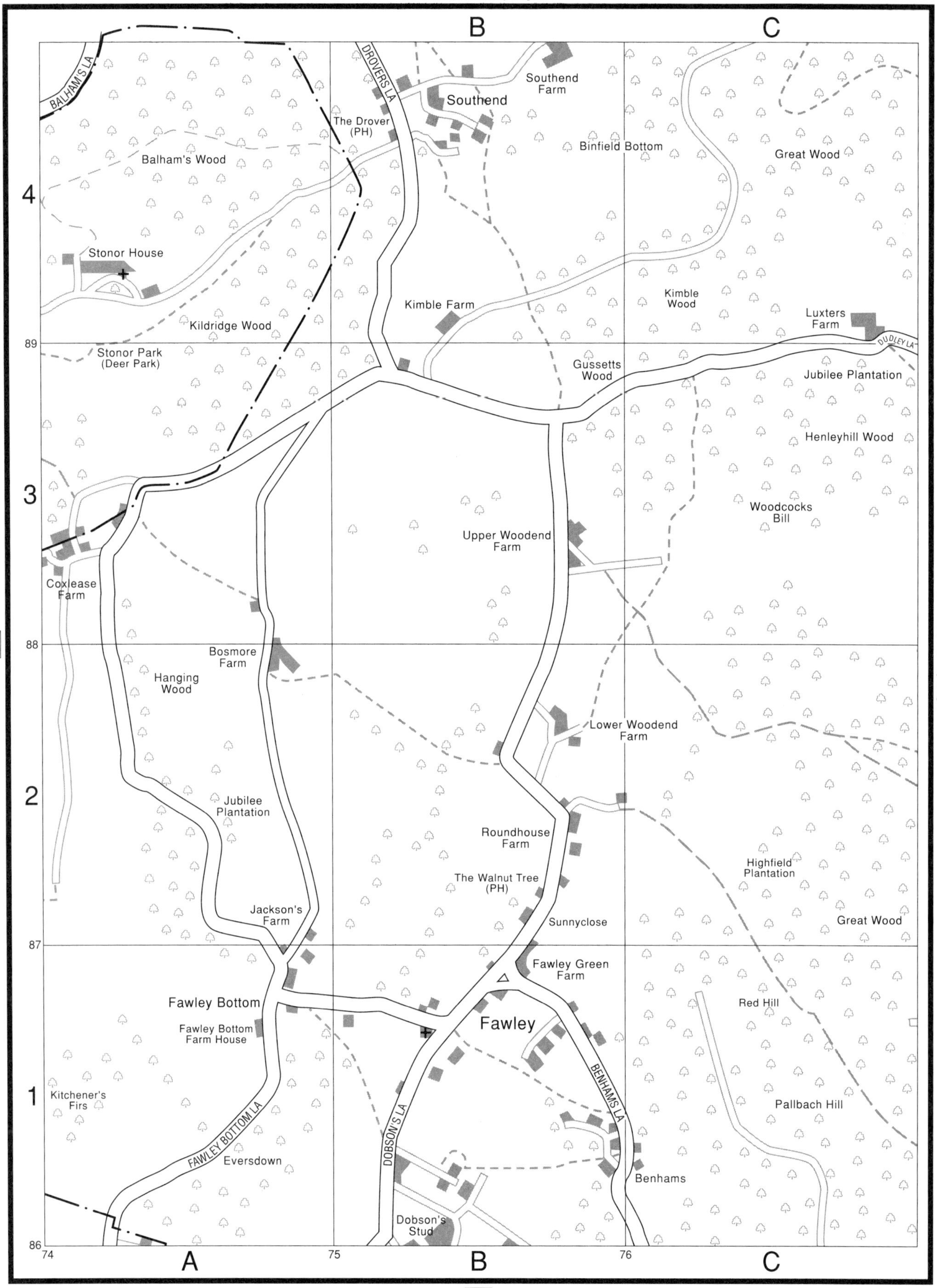

not continued, see key diagram

225

244

209

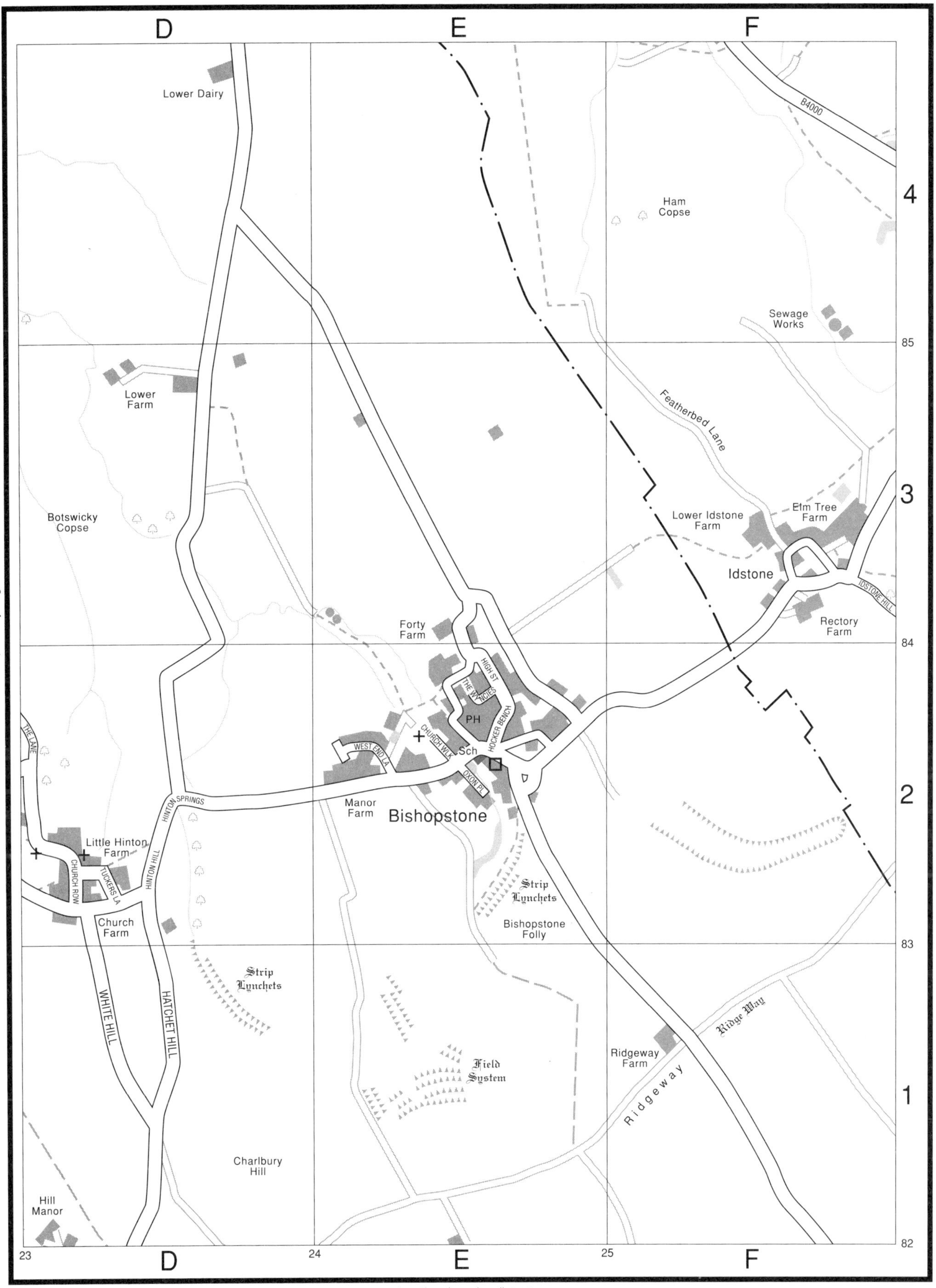

228

not continued, see key diagram

not continued, see key diagram

210

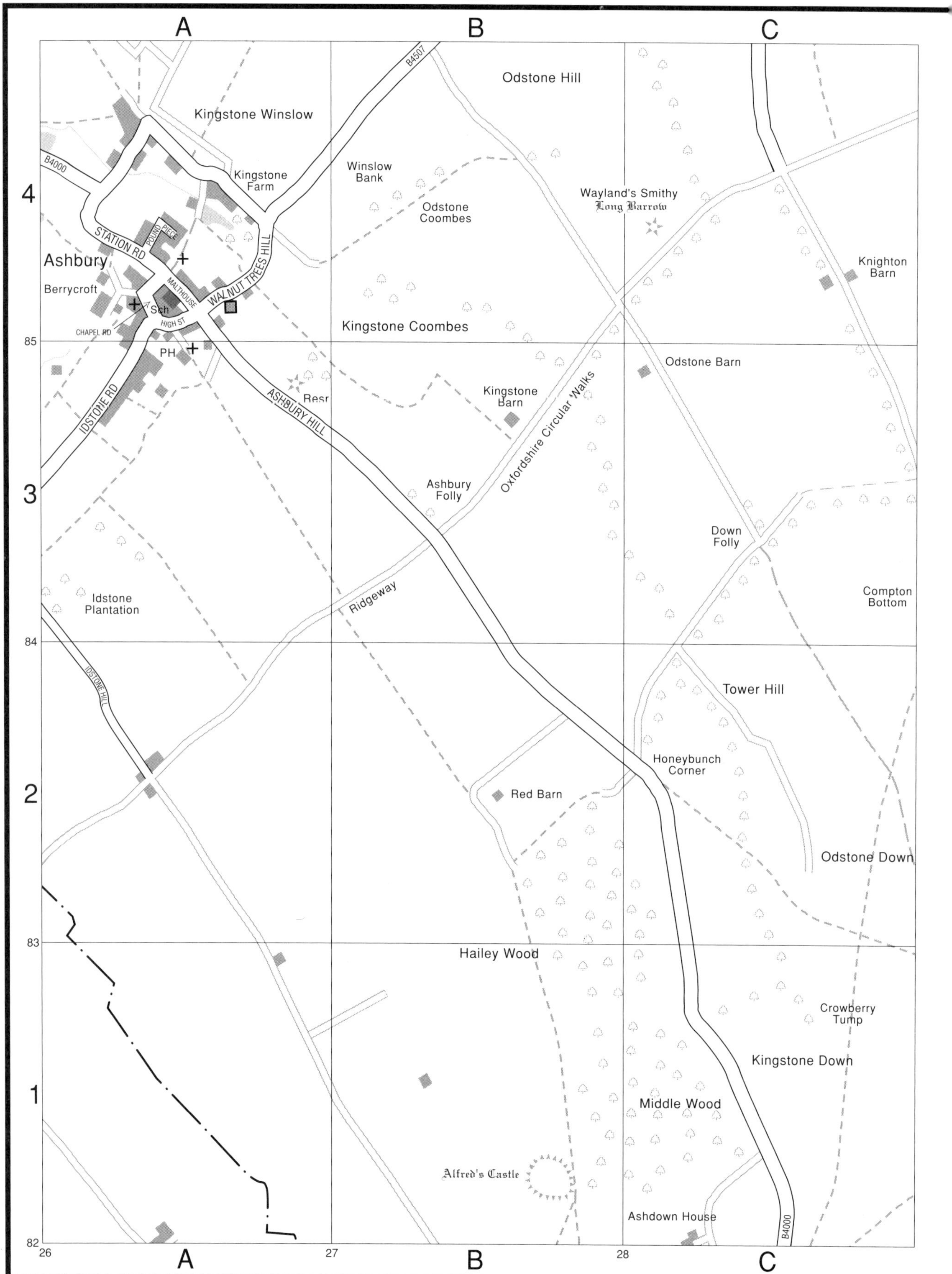
A
B
C
4
3
2
1
85
84
83
82
26
27
28
Odstone Hill
Kingstone Winslow
B4507
B4000
Kingstone Farm
Winslow Bank
Odstone Coombes
Wayland's Smithy
Long Barrow
Knighton Barn
STATION RD
POUND PIECE
WALNUT TREES HILL
MALTHOUSE
Ashbury
Berrycroft
Sch
CHAPEL RD
HIGH ST
PH
Kingstone Coombes
Odstone Barn
Resr
ASHBURY HILL
Kingstone Barn
Oxfordshire Circular Walks
IDSTONE RD
Ashbury Folly
Down Folly
Compton Bottom
Idstone Plantation
Ridgeway
IDSTONE HILL
Tower Hill
Honeybunch Corner
Red Barn
Odstone Down
Hailey Wood
Crowberry Tump
Kingstone Down
Middle Wood
Alfred's Castle
Ashdown House
B4000

227

245

211

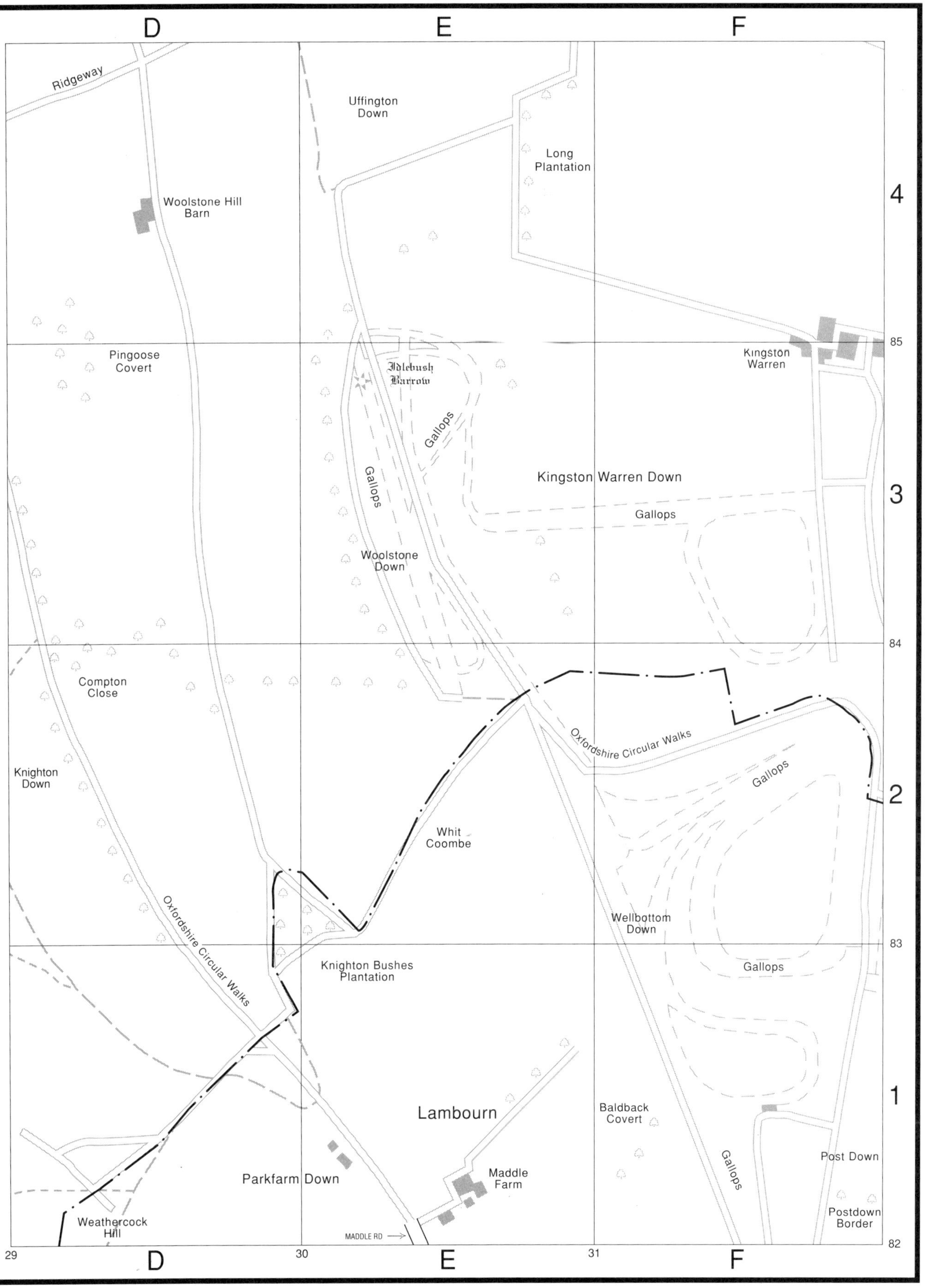

230

not continued, see key diagram

212

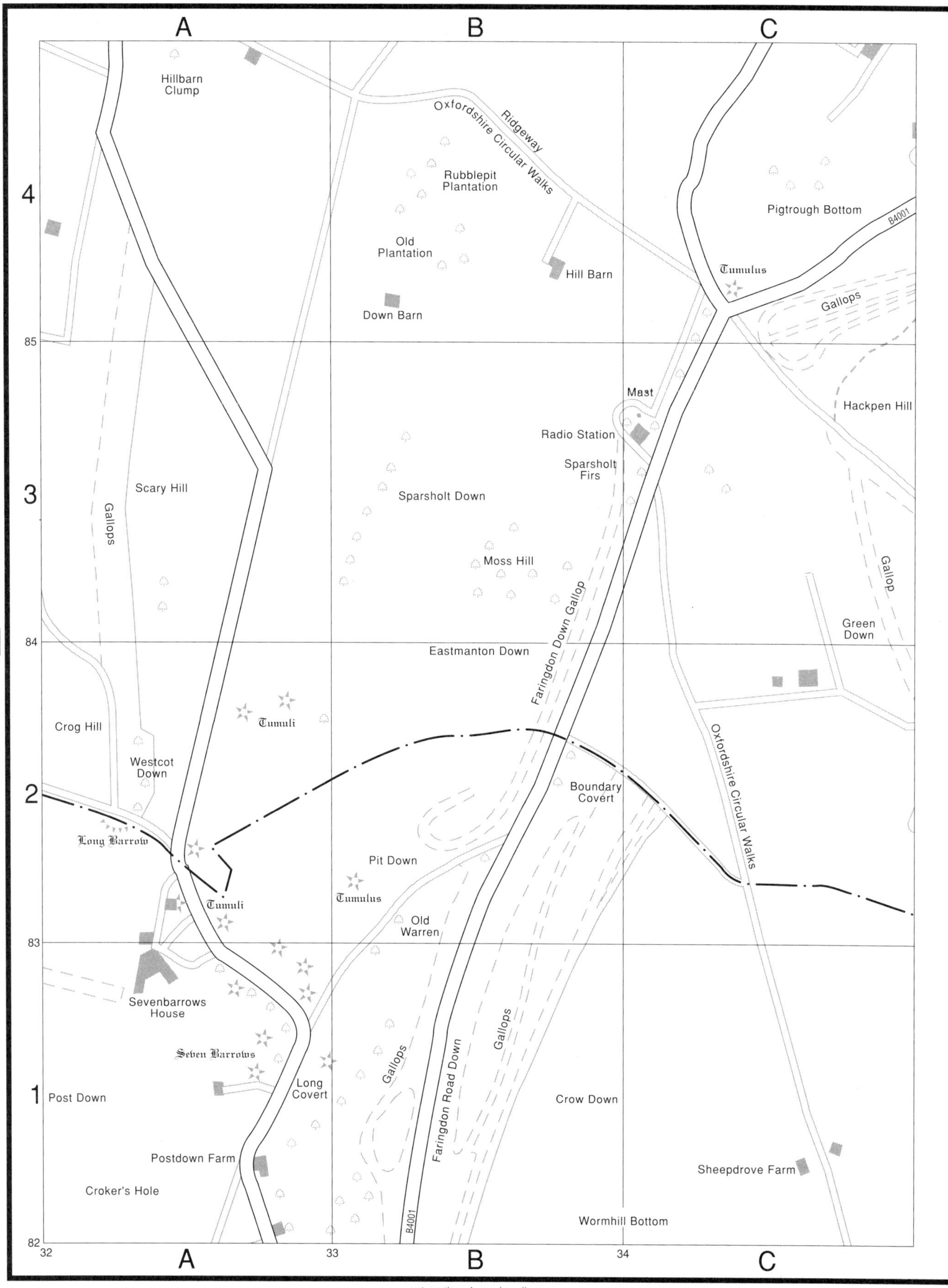

229

not continued, see key diagram

213

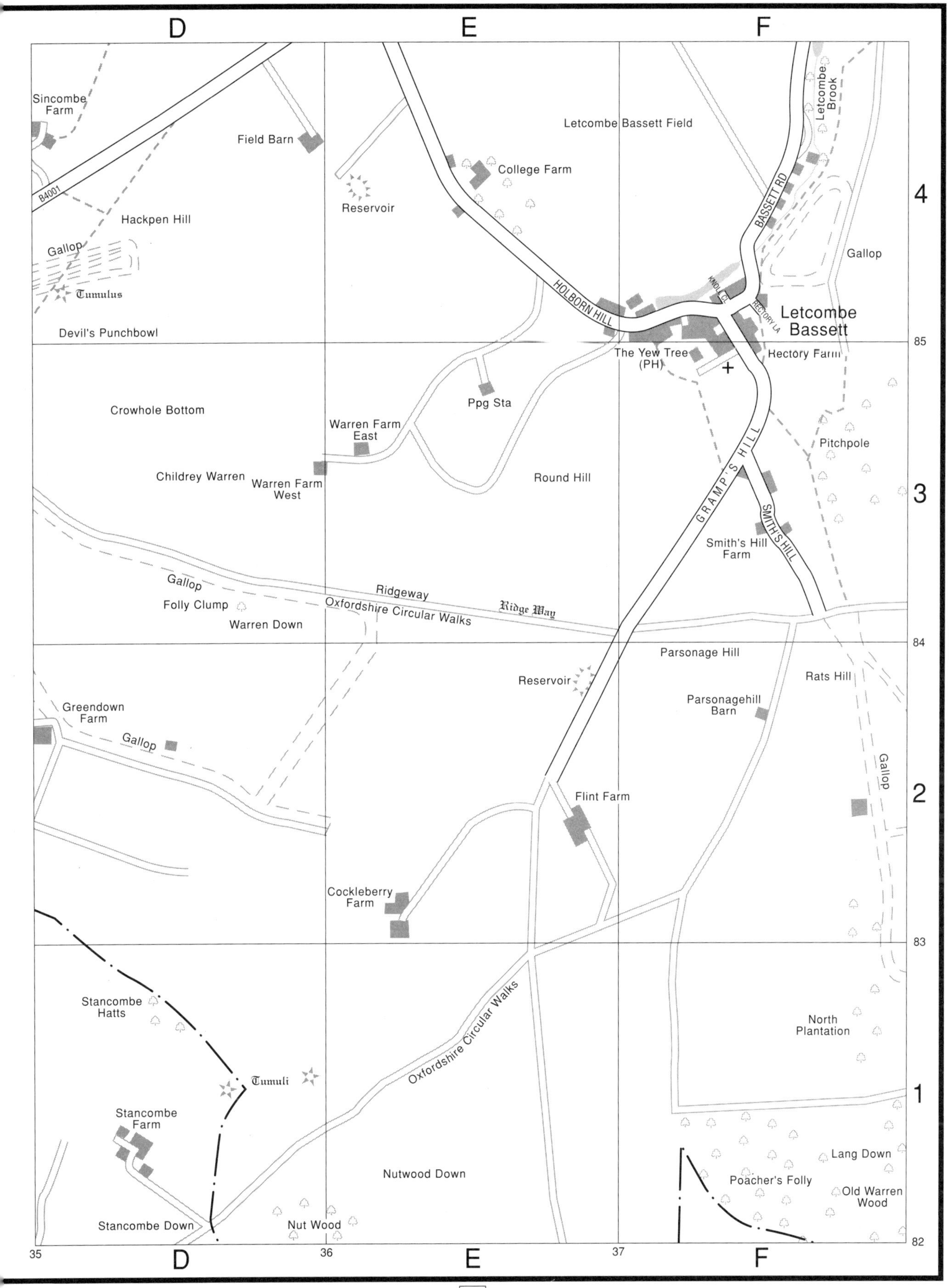
D
E
F
Sincombe Farm
Field Barn
B4001
Hackpen Hill
Gallop
Tumulus
Devil's Punchbowl
Reservoir
College Farm
Letcombe Bassett Field
Letcombe Brook
BASSETT RD
Gallop
HOLBORN HILL
KNOLL CL
RECTORY LA
Letcombe Bassett
The Yew Tree (PH)
Hectory Farm
Crowhole Bottom
Ppg Sta
Warren Farm East
Childrey Warren
Warren Farm West
Round Hill
Pitchpole
GRAMP'S HILL
SMITH'S HILL
Smith's Hill Farm
Gallop
Ridgeway
Oxfordshire Circular Walks
Ridge Way
Folly Clump
Warren Down
Parsonage Hill
Rats Hill
Reservoir
Parsonagehill Barn
Greendown Farm
Gallop
Gallop
Flint Farm
Cockleberry Farm
Stancombe Hatts
Oxfordshire Circular Walks
North Plantation
Tumuli
Stancombe Farm
Lang Down
Nutwood Down
Poacher's Folly
Old Warren Wood
Stancombe Down
Nut Wood
4
3
2
1
85
84
83
82
35
36
37
D
E
F

232

246

214

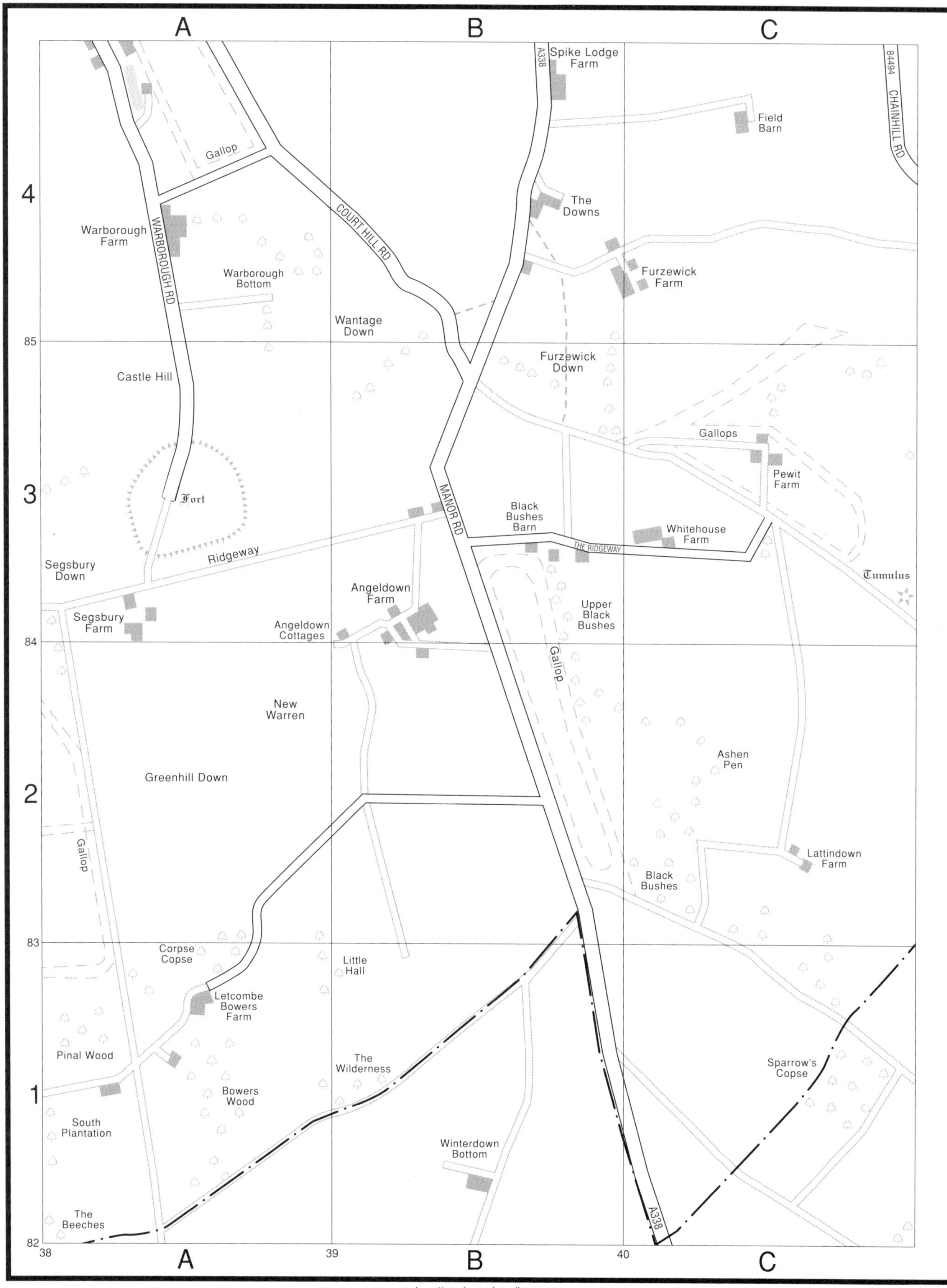

231

not continued, see key diagram

215

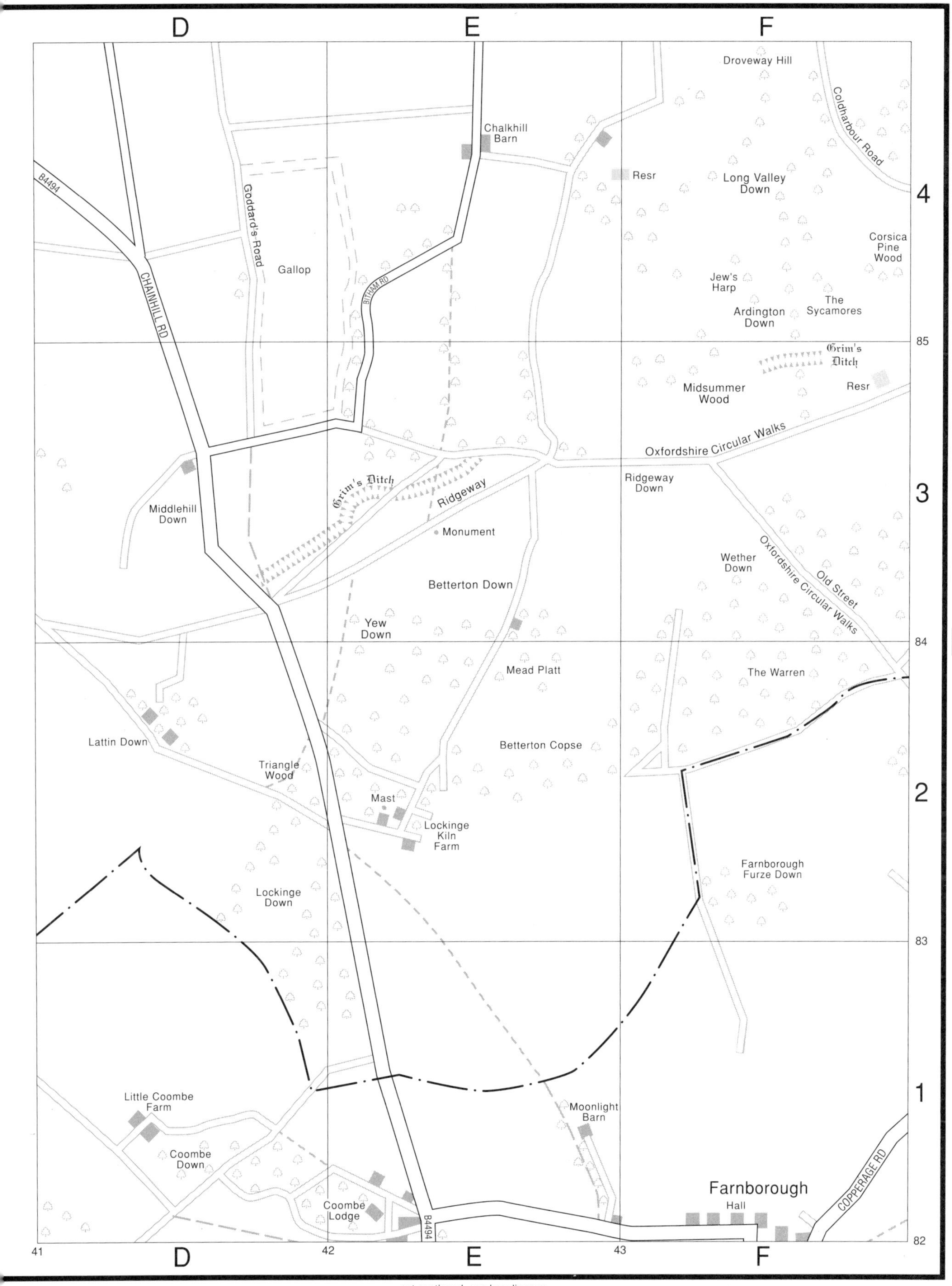

234

not continued, see key diagram

216

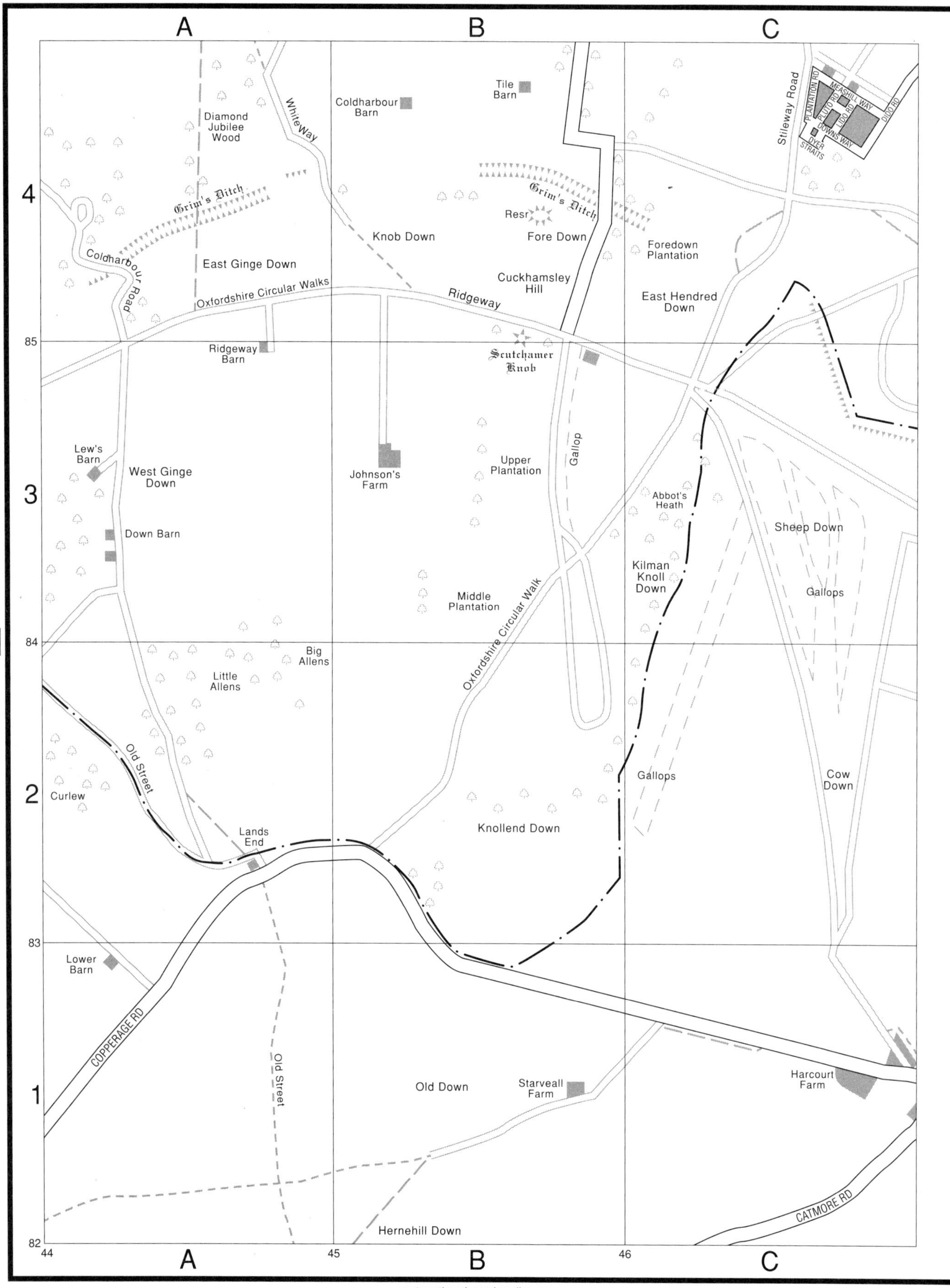

233

not continued, see key diagram

217

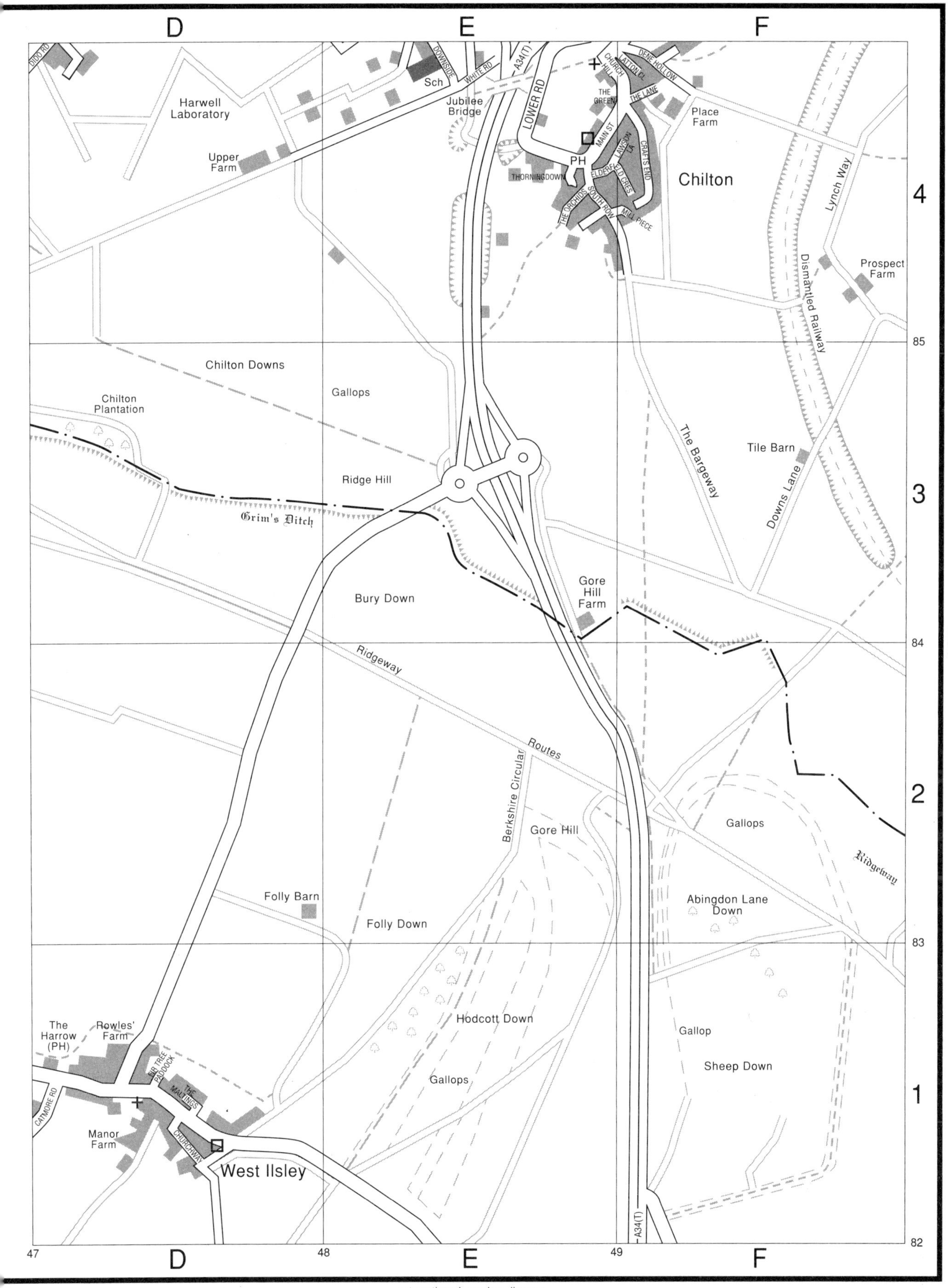

236

not continued, see key diagram

218

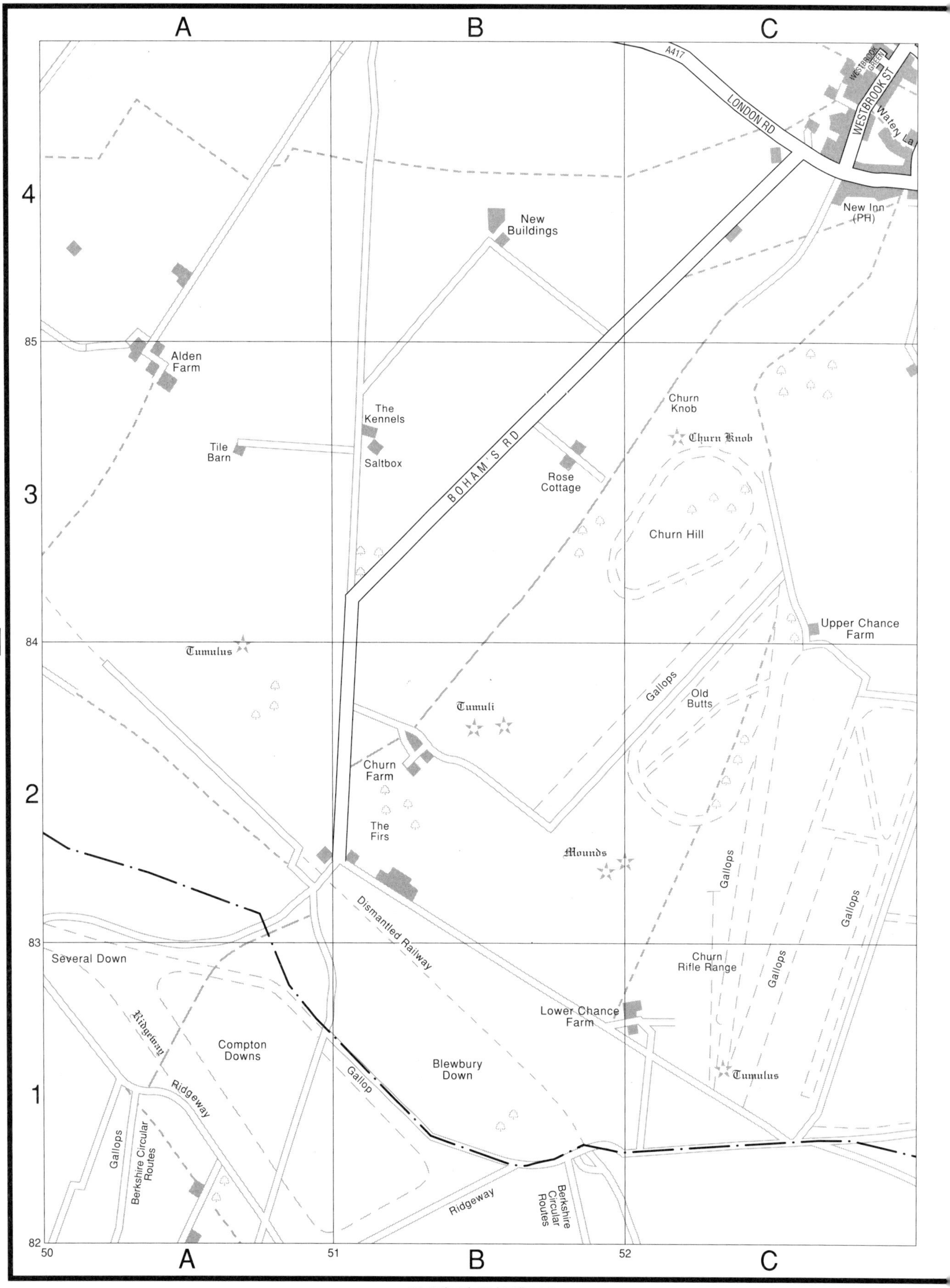

235

not continued, see key diagram

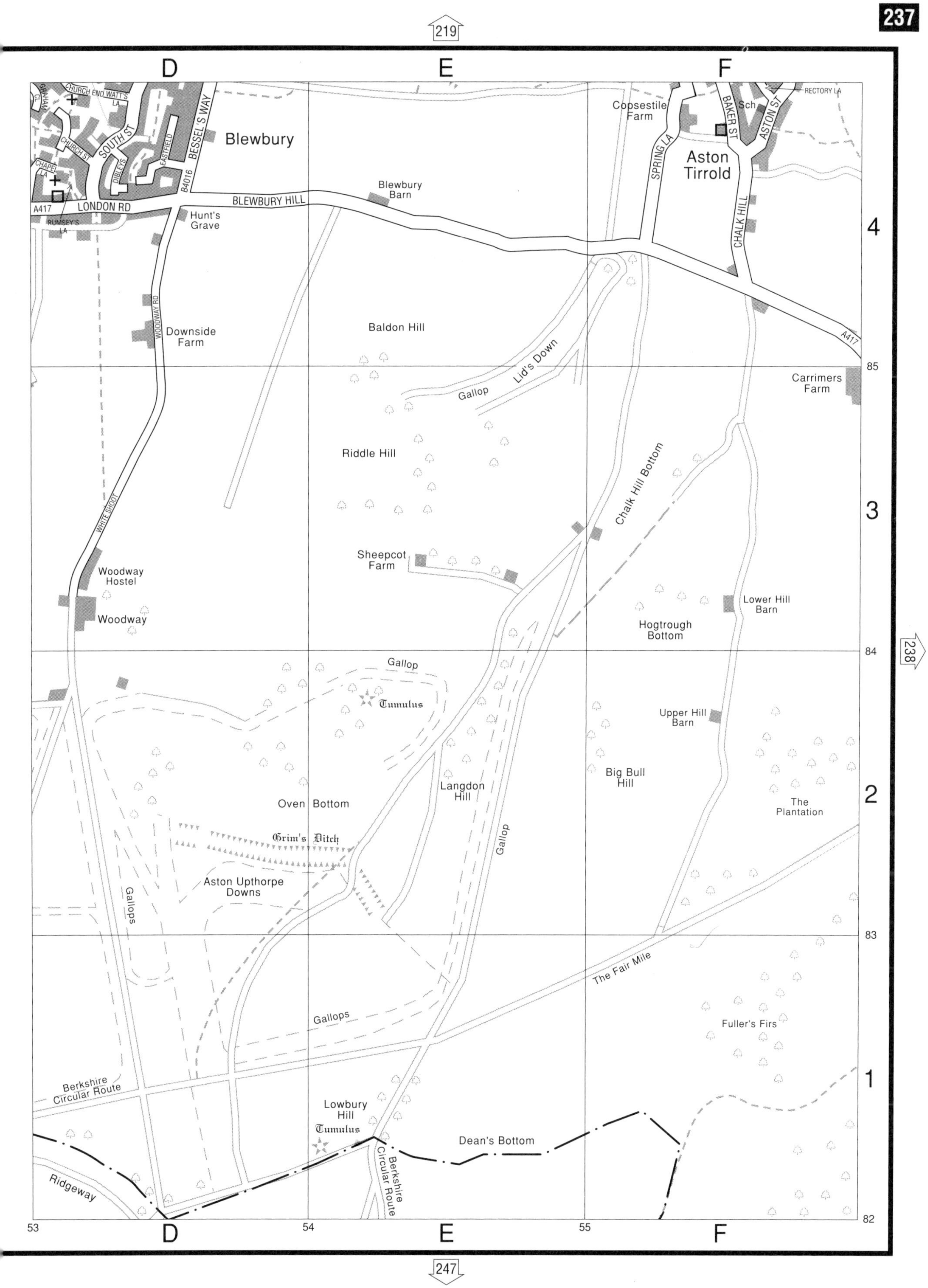
219
D
E
F
CHURCH END
WATT'S LA
CHURCH ST
SOUTH ST
CHAPEL LA
DIBLEYS
EASTFIELD
BESSEL'S WAY
B4016
Blewbury
A417
LONDON RD
RUMSEY'S LA
BLEWBURY HILL
Blewbury Barn
Hunt's Grave
Copsestile Farm
Sch
BAKER ST
ASTON ST
RECTORY LA
SPRING LA
Aston Tirrold
CHALK HILL
4
WOODWAY RD
Downside Farm
Baldon Hill
A417
85
Carrimers Farm
Lid's Down
Gallop
Riddle Hill
Chalk Hill Bottom
3
WHITE SHOOT
Sheepcot Farm
Woodway Hostel
Woodway
Lower Hill Barn
Hogtrough Bottom
84
238
Gallop
Tumulus
Upper Hill Barn
Langdon Hill
Big Bull Hill
2
Oven Bottom
The Plantation
Grim's Ditch
Gallop
Aston Upthorpe Downs
Gallops
83
The Fair Mile
Gallops
Fuller's Firs
1
Berkshire Circular Route
Lowbury Hill
Tumulus
Dean's Bottom
Ridgeway
Berkshire Circular Route
82
53
54
55
D
E
F
247

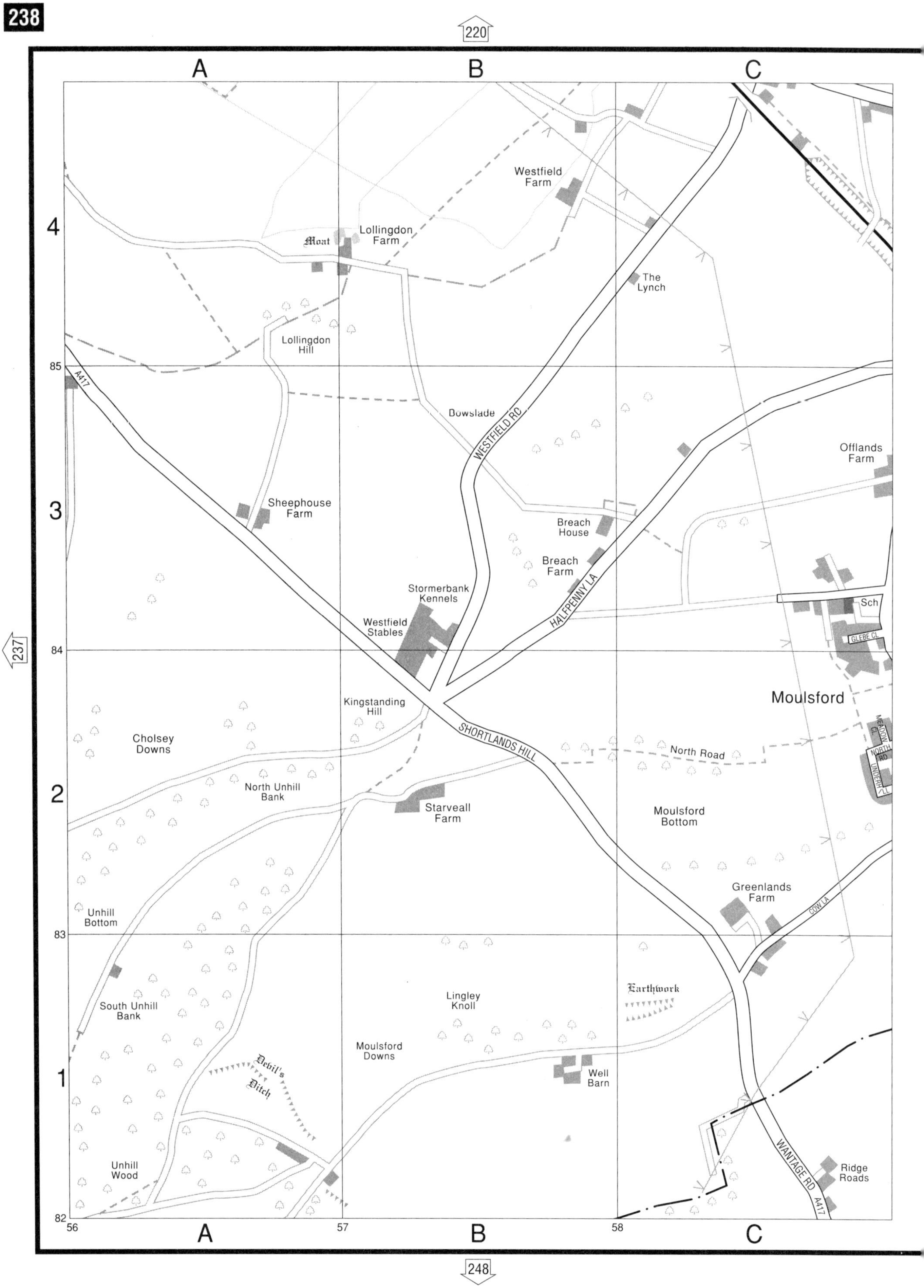
220
A
B
C
4
3
2
1
85
84
83
82
56
57
58
237
248
Westfield Farm
Moat
Lollingdon Farm
The Lynch
Lollingdon Hill
A417
Bowslade
WESTFIELD RD
Offlands Farm
Sheephouse Farm
Breach House
Breach Farm
HALFPENNY LA
Stormerbank Kennels
Westfield Stables
Sch
GLEBE CL
Kingstanding Hill
Moulsford
SHORTLANDS HILL
Cholsey Downs
North Road
MEADOW CL
NORTH RD
UNDERHILL
North Unhill Bank
Starveall Farm
Moulsford Bottom
Greenlands Farm
Unhill Bottom
COW LA
Lingley Knoll
Earthwork
South Unhill Bank
Moulsford Downs
Devil's Ditch
Well Barn
WANTAGE RD
A417
Ridge Roads
Unhill Wood

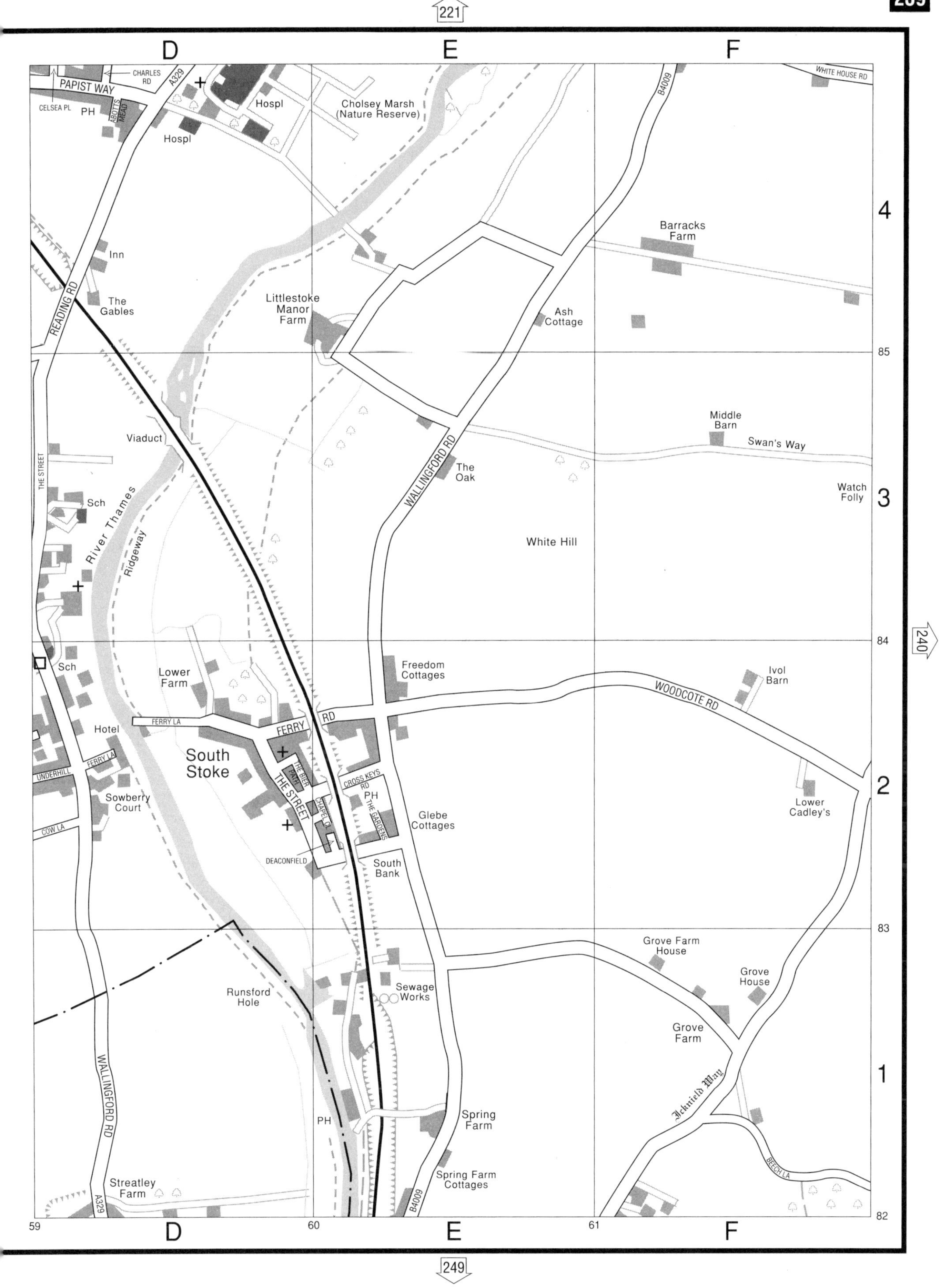
221
D
E
F
CHARLES RD
PAPIST WAY
A329
CELSEA PL
PH
ABOTTS MEAD
Hospl
Hospl
Cholsey Marsh (Nature Reserve)
B4009
WHITE HOUSE RD
4
Barracks Farm
Inn
The Gables
READING RD
Littlestoke Manor Farm
Ash Cottage
85
Viaduct
Middle Barn
Swan's Way
THE STREET
WALLINGFORD RD
The Oak
Sch
River Thames
Ridgeway
Watch Folly
3
White Hill
84
240
Sch
Lower Farm
Freedom Cottages
Ivol Barn
WOODCOTE RD
FERRY LA
FERRY RD
Hotel
South Stoke
FERRY LA
UNDERHILL
THE BIER PATH
CROSS KEYS RD
PH
THE STREET
THE GARDENS
CHAPEL CL
2
Lower Cadley's
Sowberry Court
Glebe Cottages
COW LA
DEACONFIELD
South Bank
83
Grove Farm House
Grove House
Runsford Hole
Sewage Works
Grove Farm
1
Icknield Way
WALLINGFORD RD
PH
Spring Farm
BEECH LA
Streatley Farm
A329
Spring Farm Cottages
B4009
82
59
60
61
249

222

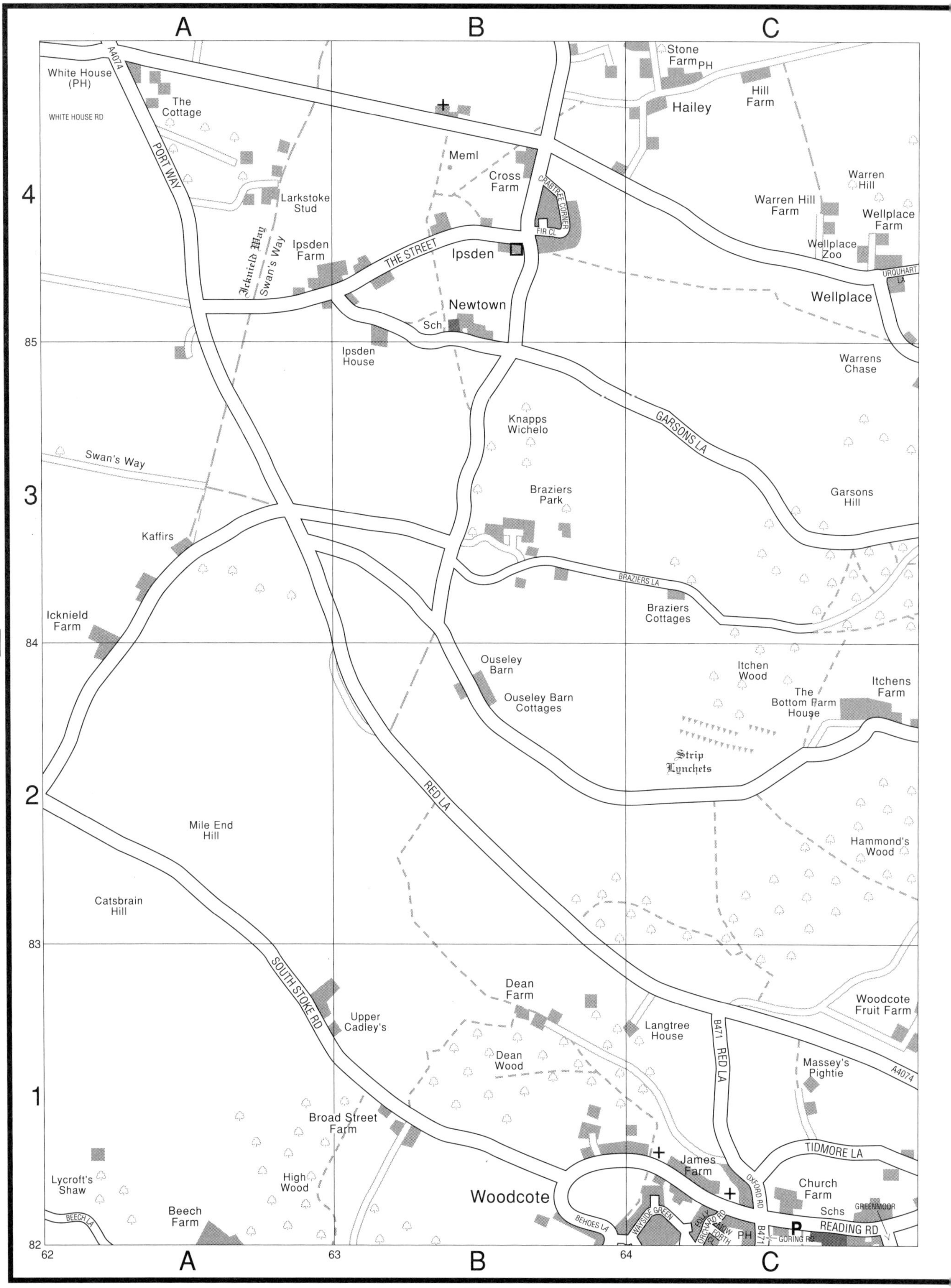
A
B
C
White House (PH)
WHITE HOUSE RD
A4074
The Cottage
PORT WAY
Larkstoke Stud
Icknield Way
Swan's Way
Ipsden Farm
THE STREET
Ipsden
Meml
Cross Farm
CRABTREE CORNER
FIR CL
Newtown
Sch
Ipsden House
Stone Farm
PH
Hailey
Hill Farm
Warren Hill
Warren Hill Farm
Wellplace Farm
Wellplace Zoo
URQUHART LA
Wellplace
Warrens Chase
GARSONS LA
Knapps Wichelo
Braziers Park
Garsons Hill
Swan's Way
Kaffirs
Icknield Farm
BRAZIERS LA
Braziers Cottages
Ouseley Barn
Ouseley Barn Cottages
Itchen Wood
The Bottom Farm House
Itchens Farm
Strip Lynchets
RED LA
Mile End Hill
Hammond's Wood
Catsbrain Hill
SOUTH STOKE RD
Upper Cadley's
Dean Farm
Langtree House
Woodcote Fruit Farm
B471 RED LA
Dean Wood
Massey's Pightie
A4074
Broad Street Farm
TIDMORE LA
James Farm
OXFORD RD
Church Farm
Lycroft's Shaw
High Wood
Woodcote
Schs
GREENMOOR
Beech Farm
BEECH LA
BEHOES LA
WAYSIDE GREEN
FOLLY ORCHARD RD
MEADOW CL
FORTH
PH
B471
GORING RD
P
READING RD
4
3
2
1
85
84
83
82
62
63
64
239

250

223

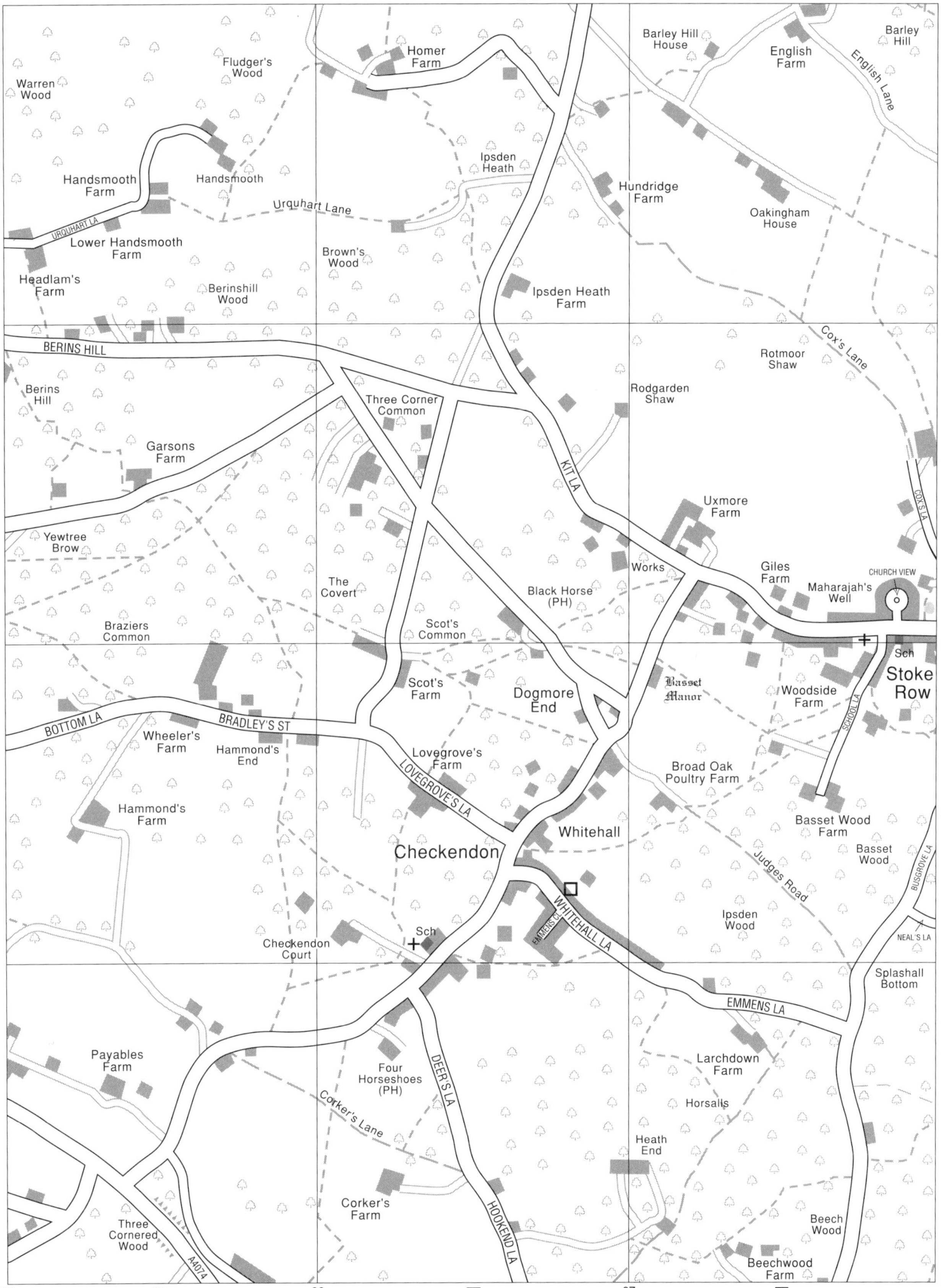
D
E
F
Barley Hill House
English Farm
Barley Hill
English Lane
Warren Wood
Fludger's Wood
Homer Farm
Handsmooth Farm
Handsmooth
Ipsden Heath
Hundridge Farm
Oakingham House
Urquhart Lane
URQUHART LA
Lower Handsmooth Farm
Brown's Wood
Headlam's Farm
Berinshill Wood
Ipsden Heath Farm
BERINS HILL
Rotmoor Shaw
Cox's Lane
Berins Hill
Three Corner Common
Rodgarden Shaw
Garsons Farm
KIT LA
COX'S LA
Uxmore Farm
Yewtree Brow
Works
Giles Farm
CHURCH VIEW
Maharajah's Well
The Covert
Black Horse (PH)
Braziers Common
Scot's Common
Sch
Stoke Row
Scot's Farm
Dogmore End
Basset Manor
Woodside Farm
BOTTOM LA
BRADLEY'S ST
SCHOOL LA
Wheeler's Farm
Hammond's End
Lovegrove's Farm
Broad Oak Poultry Farm
LOVEGROVE'S LA
Hammond's Farm
Basset Wood Farm
Whitehall
Basset Wood
Checkendon
Judges Road
BUSGROVE LA
EMMENS CL
WHITEHALL LA
Ipsden Wood
Sch
NEAL'S LA
Checkendon Court
Splashall Bottom
EMMENS LA
Payables Farm
Larchdown Farm
Four Horseshoes (PH)
DEER'S LA
Horsalls
Corker's Lane
Heath End
Corker's Farm
HOOKEND LA
Three Cornered Wood
A4074
Beech Wood
Beechwood Farm
65
66
67
82
83
84
85
1
2
3
4
242

251

224

241

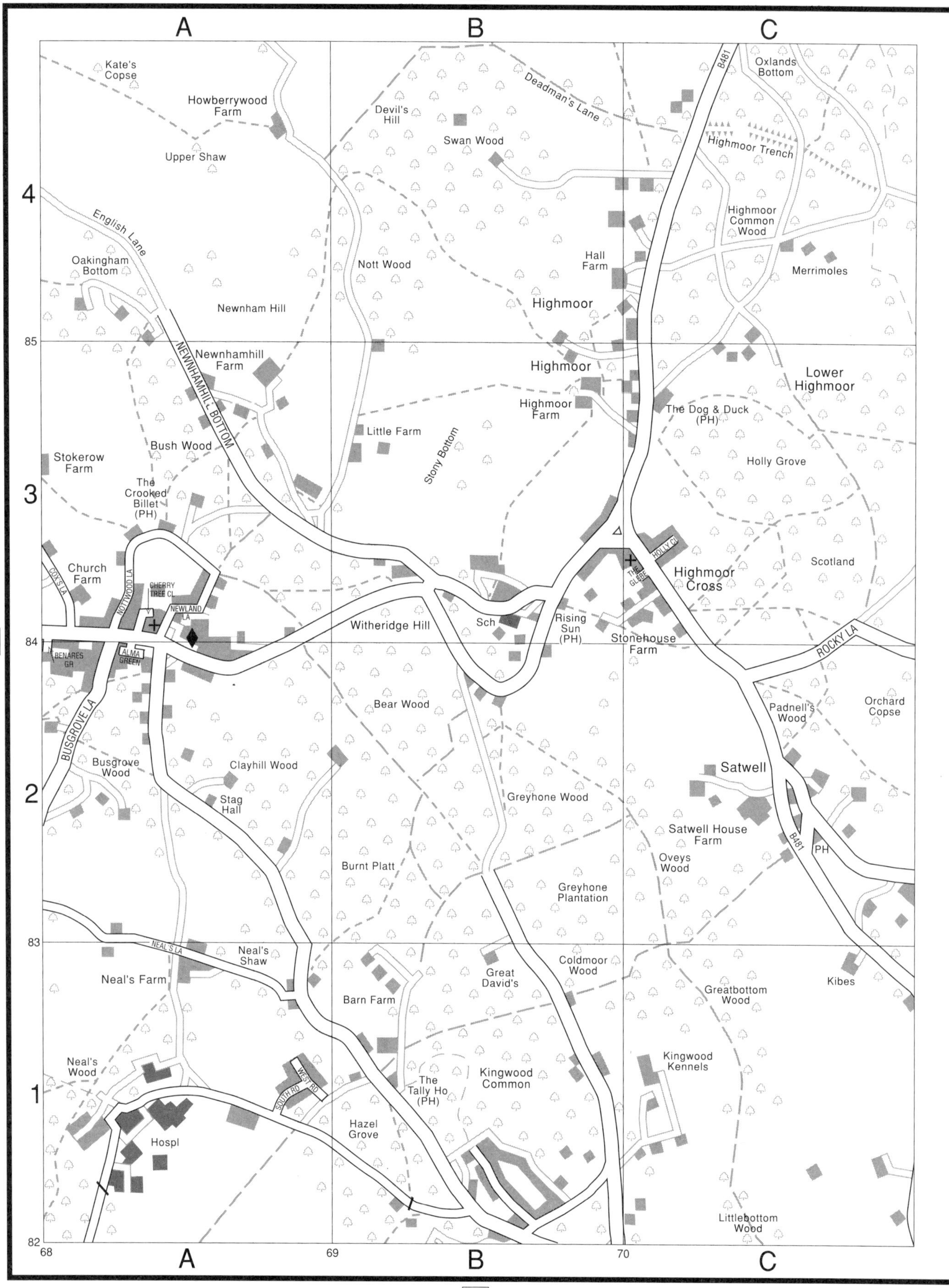
A
B
C
4
3
2
1
85
84
83
82
68
69
70
Kate's Copse
Howberrywood Farm
Upper Shaw
Devil's Hill
Swan Wood
Deadman's Lane
B481
Oxlands Bottom
Highmoor Trench
English Lane
Oakingham Bottom
Newnham Hill
Nott Wood
Hall Farm
Highmoor
Highmoor Common Wood
Merrimoles
Newnhamhill Farm
NEWNHAMHILL BOTTOM
Highmoor
Highmoor Farm
Lower Highmoor
The Dog & Duck (PH)
Little Farm
Stony Bottom
Stokerow Farm
Bush Wood
Holly Grove
The Crooked Billet (PH)
Church Farm
COX'S LA
NOTTWOOD LA
CHERRY TREE CL
NEWLAND LA
HOLLY CL
THE GLEBE
Highmoor Cross
Scotland
Witheridge Hill
Sch
Rising Sun (PH)
Stonehouse Farm
ROCKY LA
BENARES GR
ALMA GREEN
Bear Wood
Padnell's Wood
Orchard Copse
BUSGROVE LA
Busgrove Wood
Clayhill Wood
Stag Hall
Satwell
Greyhone Wood
Satwell House Farm
B481
PH
Burnt Platt
Oveys Wood
Greyhone Plantation
NEAL'S LA
Neal's Shaw
Neal's Farm
Great David's
Coldmoor Wood
Kibes
Greatbottom Wood
Barn Farm
Neal's Wood
WEST RD
SOUTH RD
The Tally Ho (PH)
Kingwood Common
Kingwood Kennels
Hazel Grove
Hospl
Littlebottom Wood

252

225

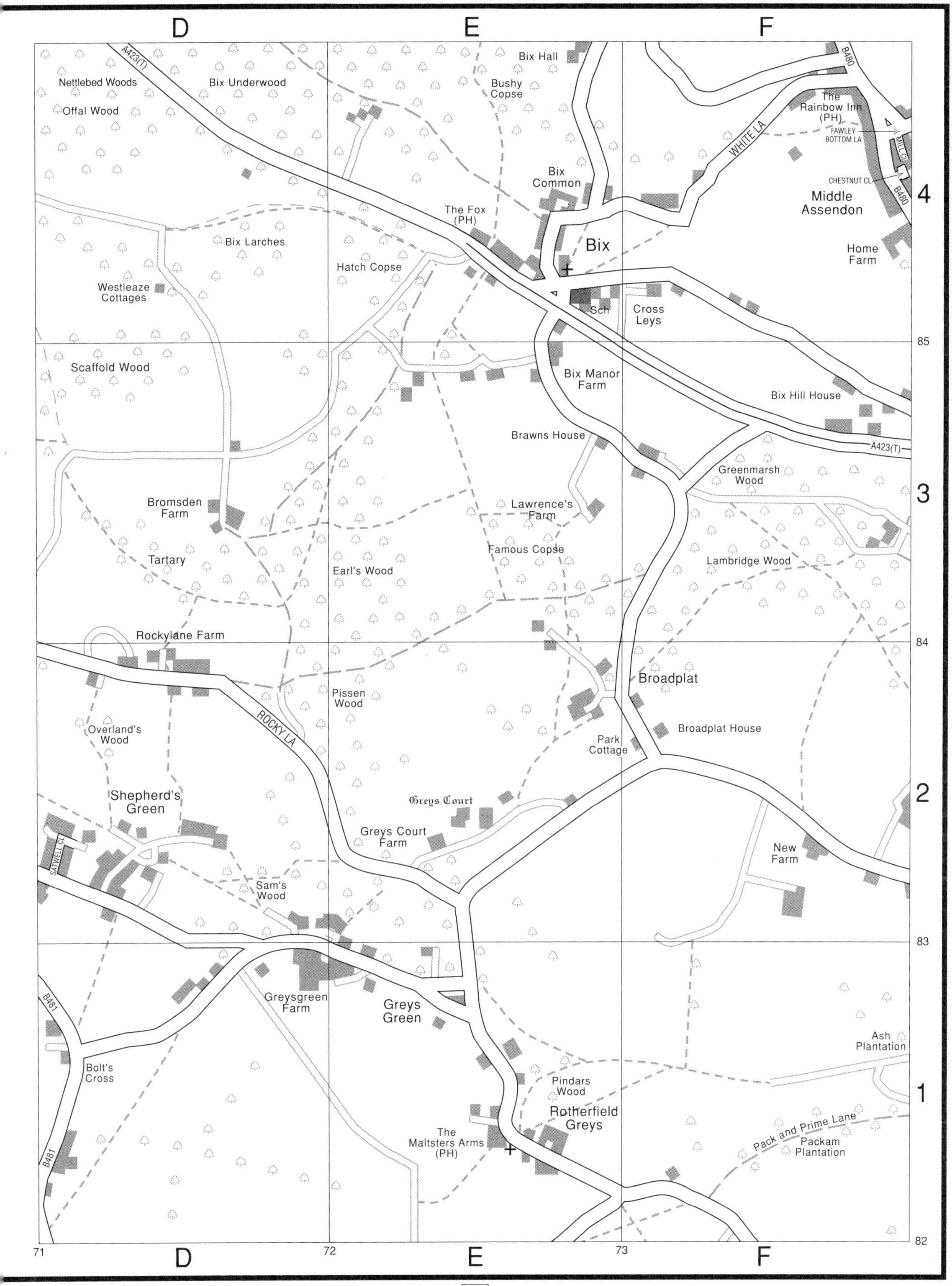

D
E
F
Nettlebed Woods
Offal Wood
Bix Underwood
A423(T)
Bix Hall
Bushy Copse
B480
The Rainbow Inn (PH)
WHITE LA
FAWLEY BOTTOM LA
MILL CL
CHESTNUT CL
B480
Middle Assendon
4
Bix Common
The Fox (PH)
Bix
Bix Larches
Hatch Copse
Home Farm
Westleaze Cottages
Sch
Cross Leys
85
Scaffold Wood
Bix Manor Farm
Bix Hill House
A423(T)
Brawns House
Greenmarsh Wood
3
Bromsden Farm
Lawrence's Farm
Tartary
Famous Copse
Earl's Wood
Lambridge Wood
Rockylane Farm
84
Broadplat
Pissen Wood
ROCKY LA
Overland's Wood
Broadplat House
Park Cottage
Shepherd's Green
Greys Court
2
SAIWELL CL
Greys Court Farm
New Farm
Sam's Wood
83
B481
Greysgreen Farm
Greys Green
Ash Plantation
Bolt's Cross
Pindars Wood
1
Rotherfield Greys
Pack and Prime Lane
The Maltsters Arms (PH)
Packam Plantation
B481
82
71
72
73
D
E
F

244

253

226

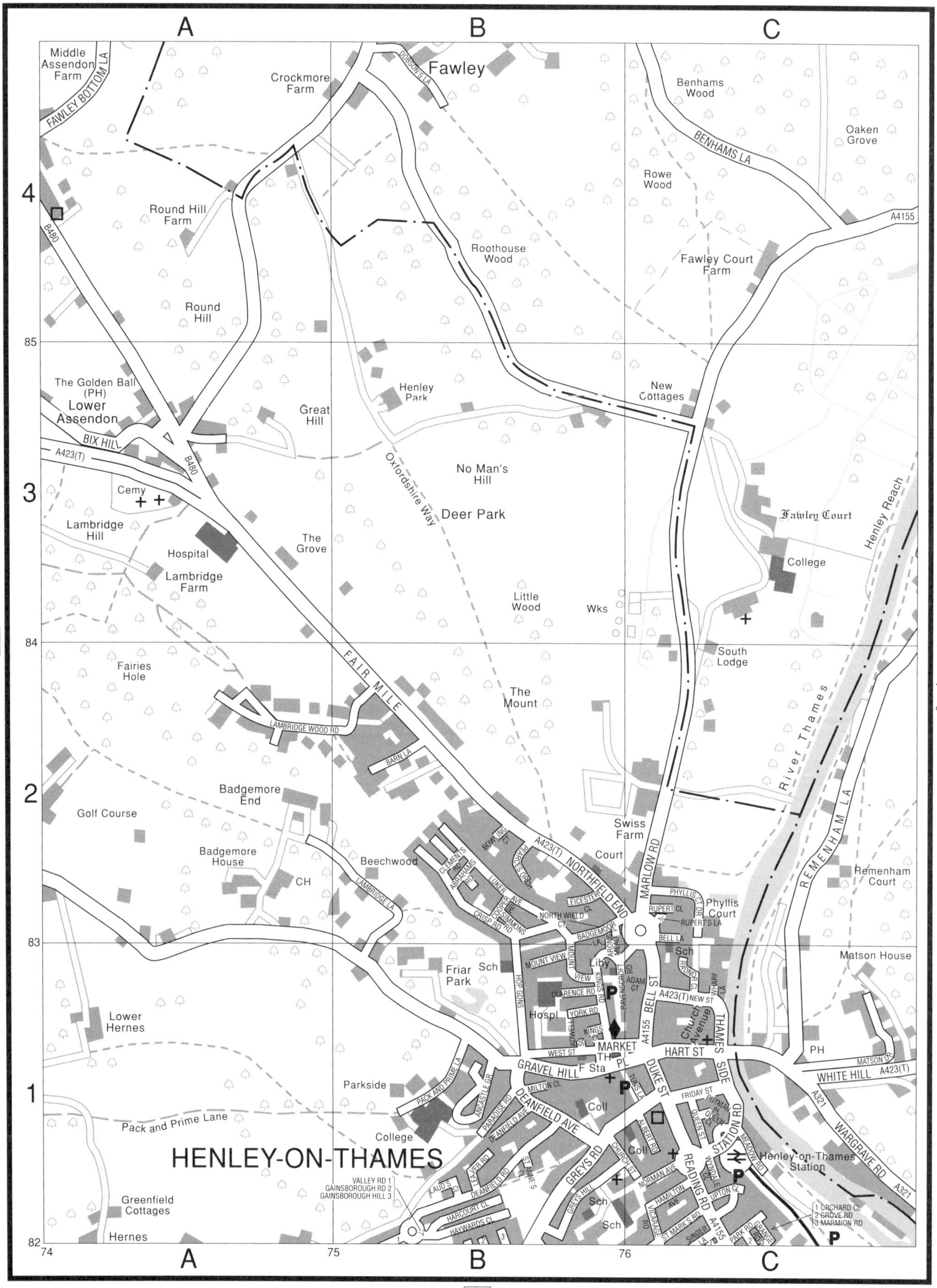

243

not continued, see key diagram

254

228

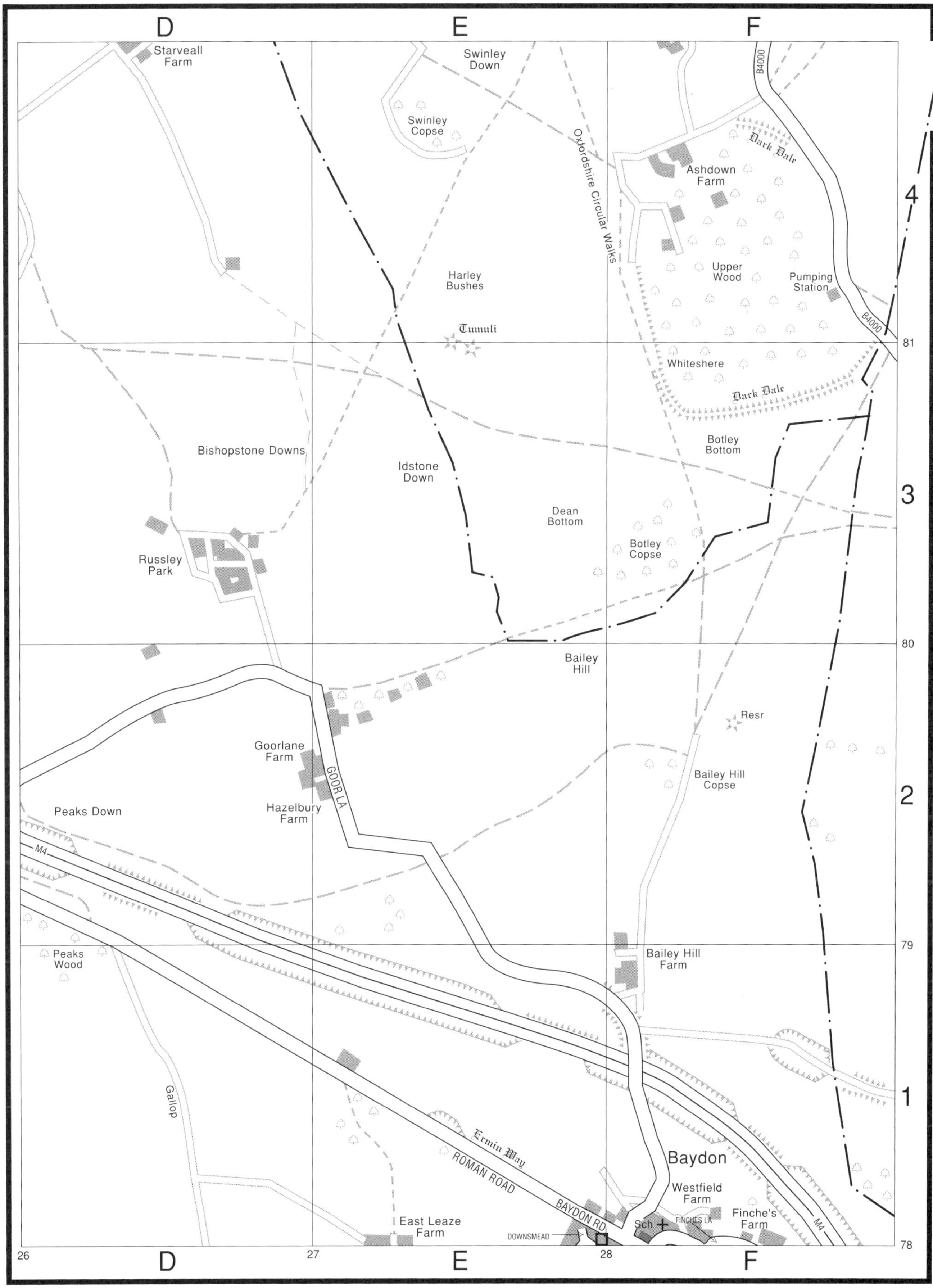

not continued, see key diagram

not continued, see key diagram

not continued, see key diagram

231

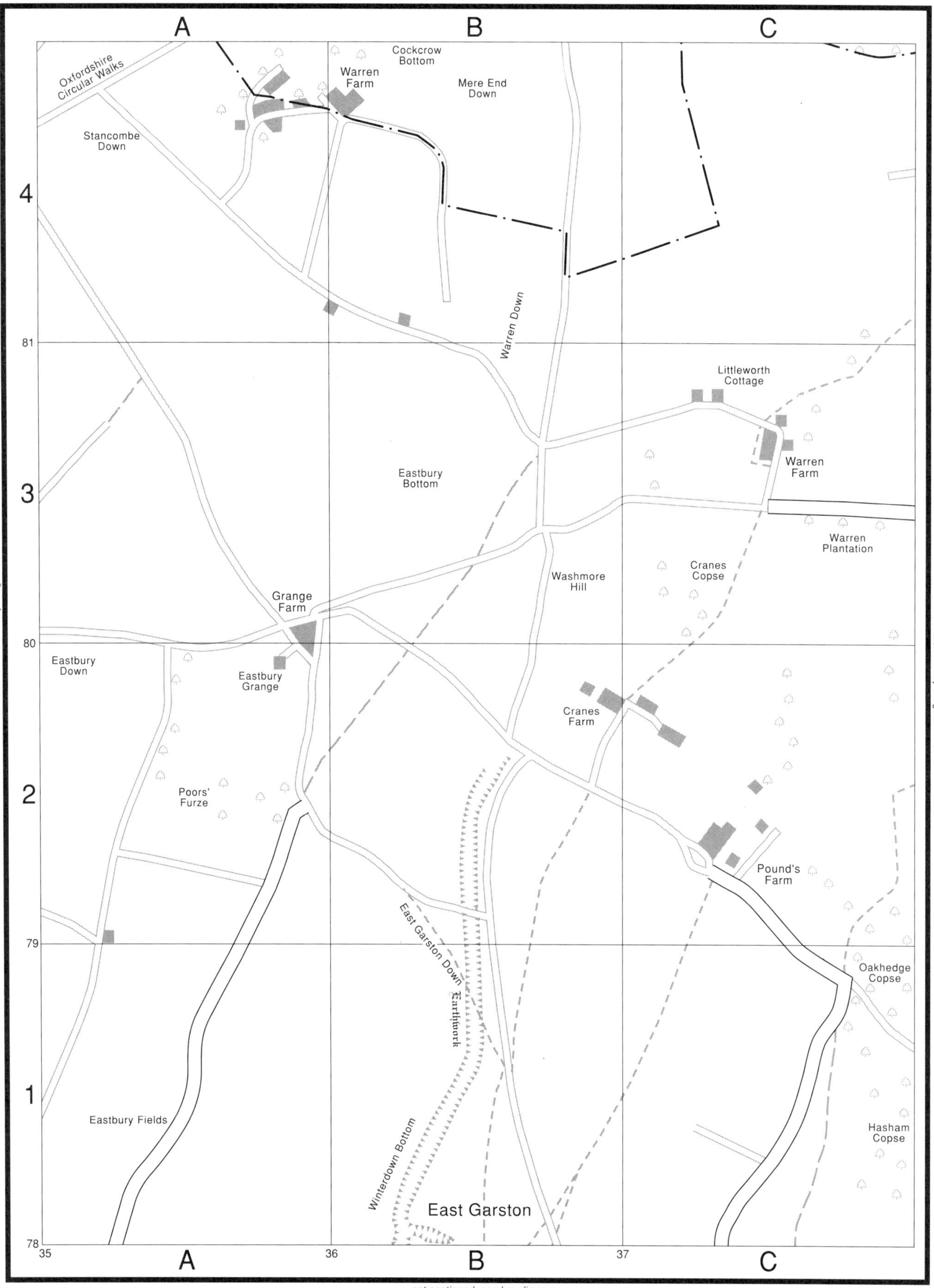

not continued, see key diagram

not continued, see key diagram

not continued, see key diagram

237

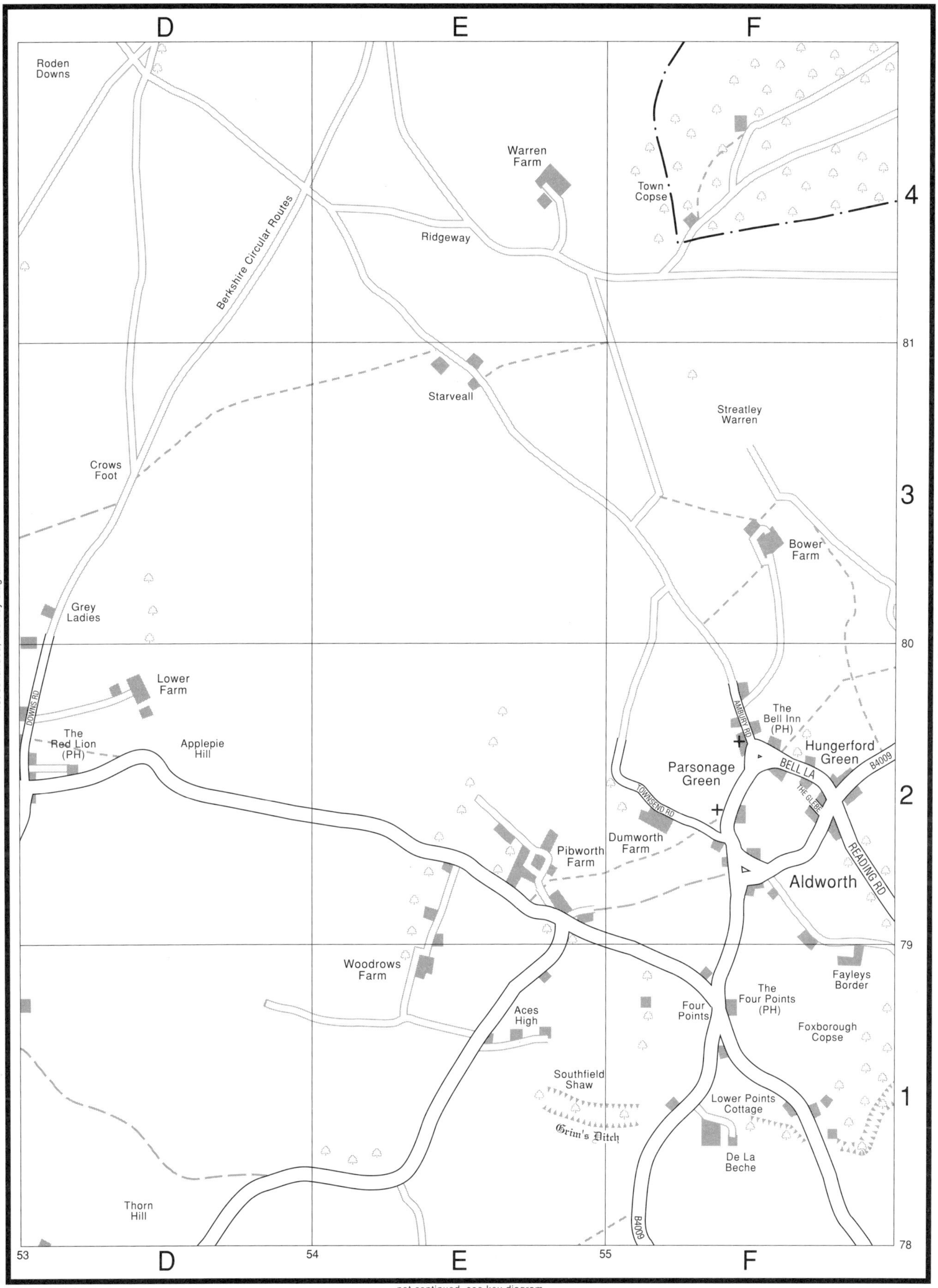

248

not continued, see key diagram

238

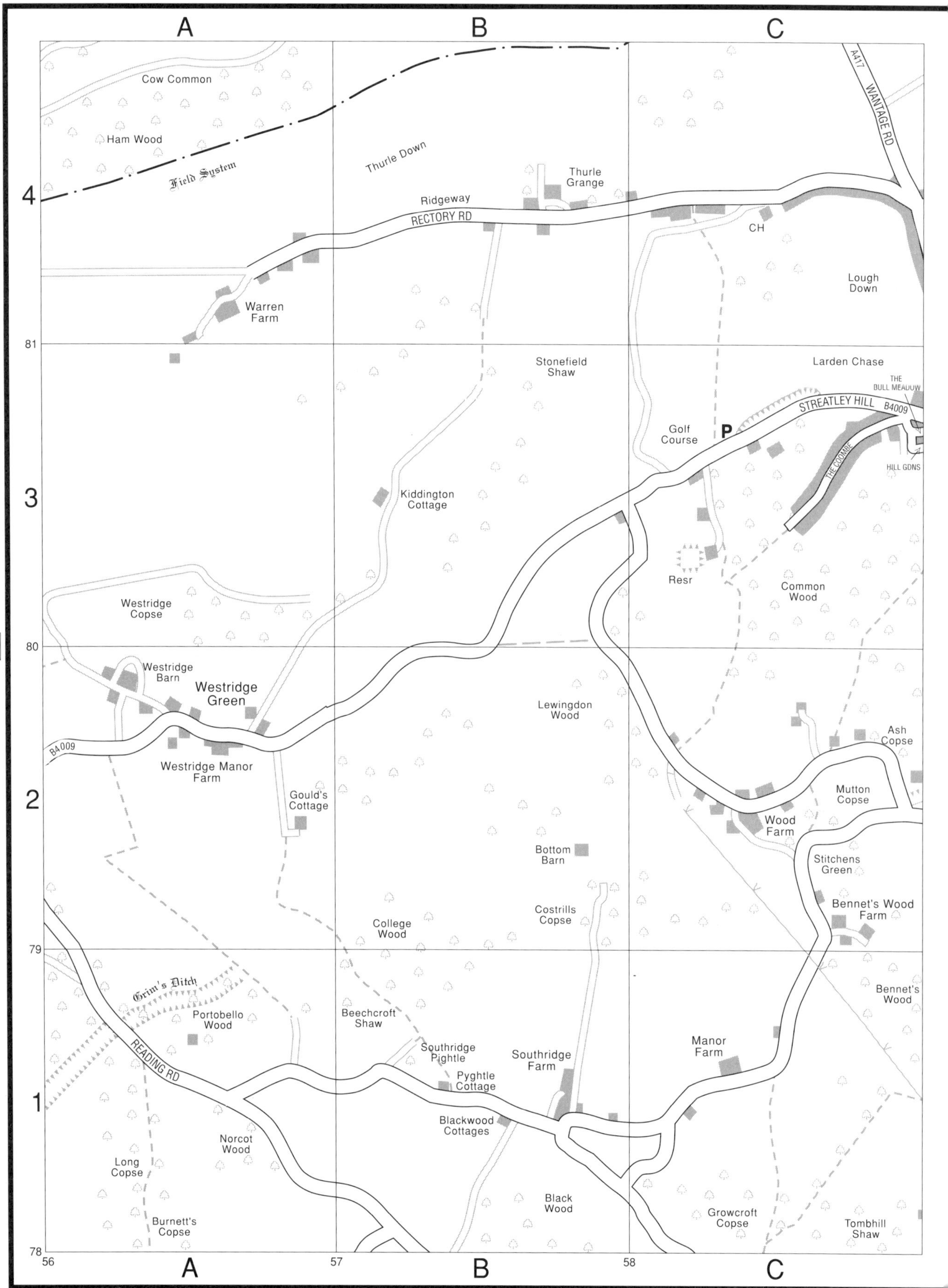

247

not continued, see key diagram

239

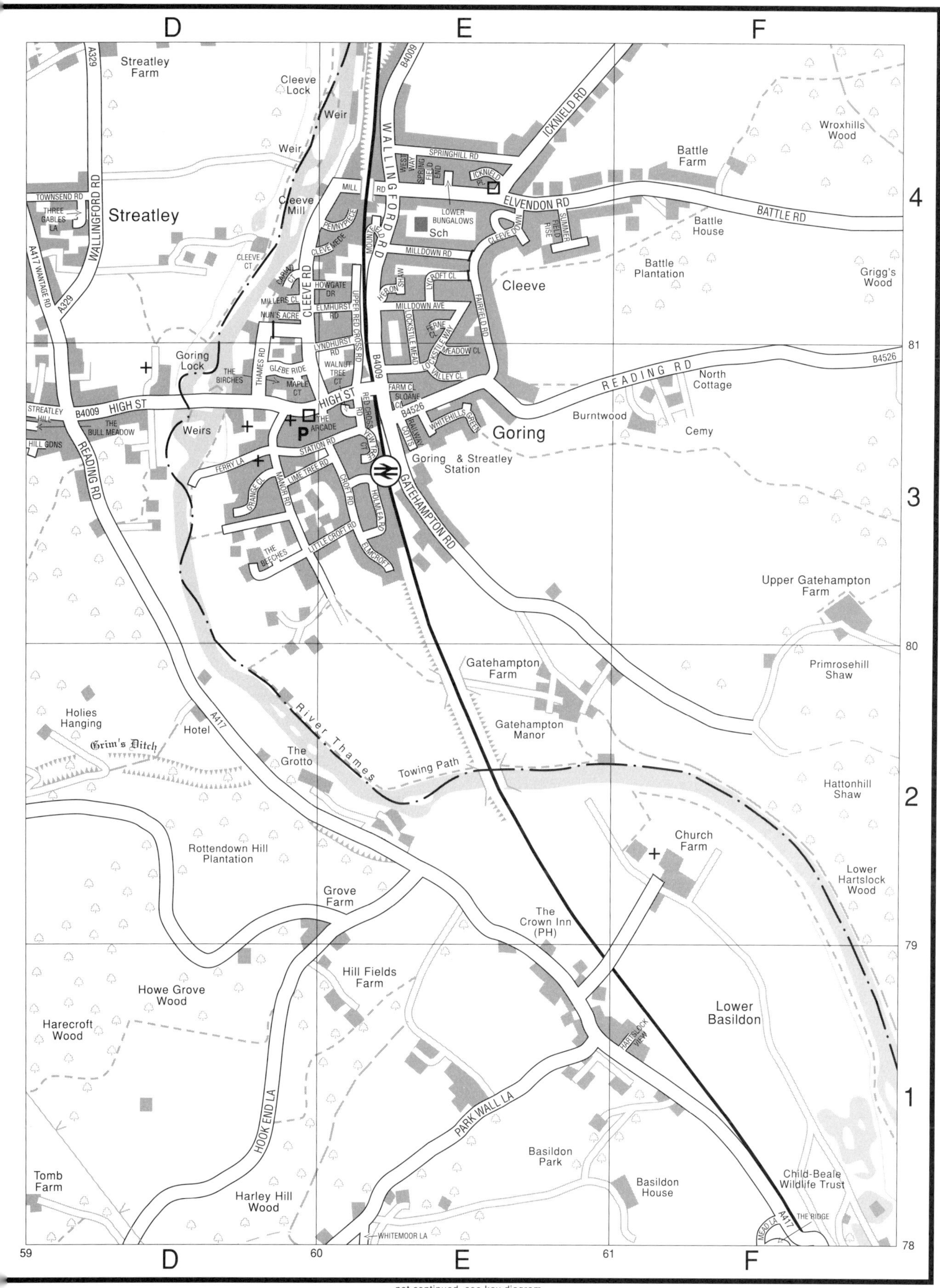

250

not continued, see key diagram

240

249

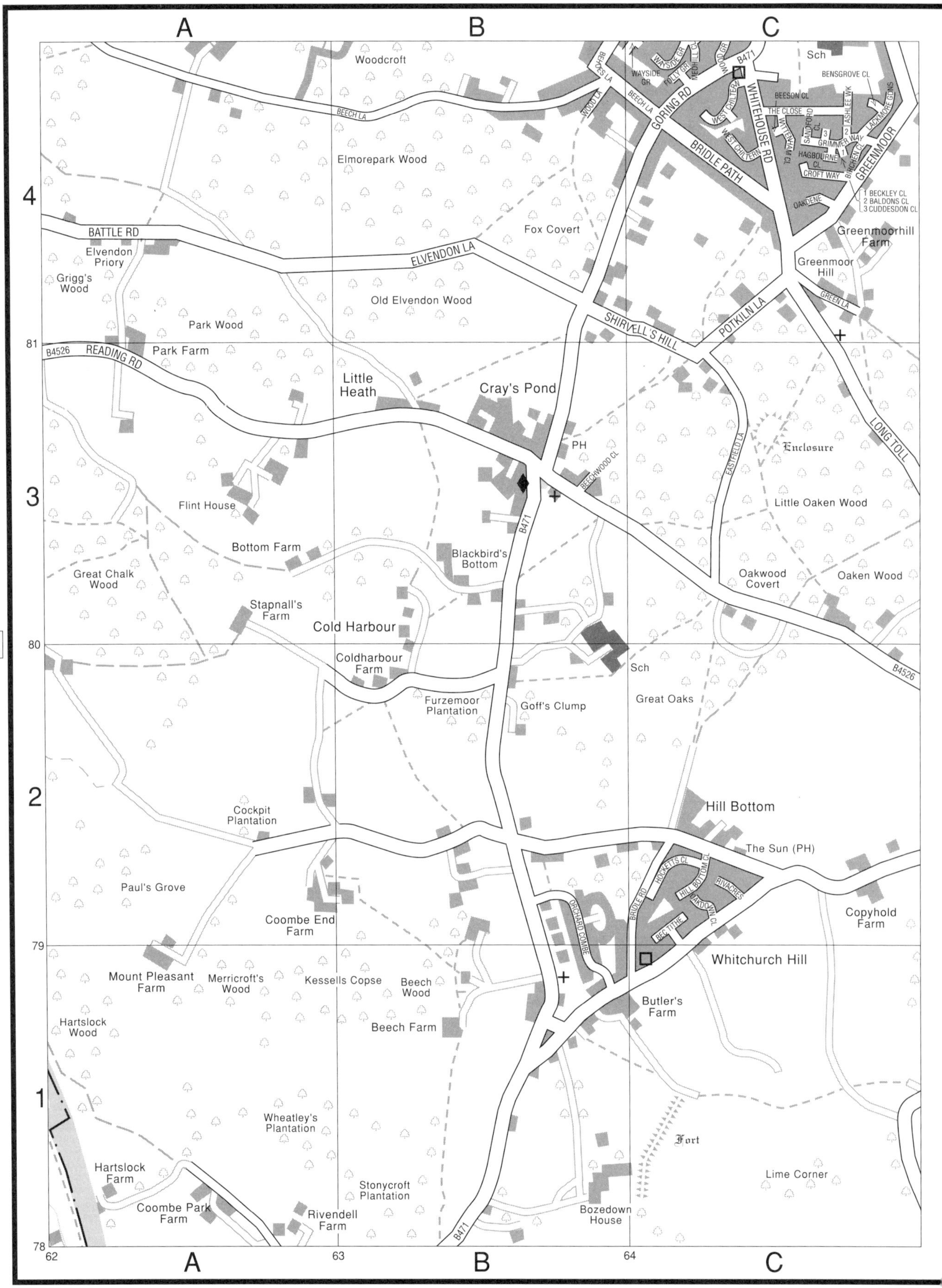
A
B
C
4
3
2
1
81
80
79
78
62
63
64
Sch
BENSGROVE CL
WAYSIDE GR
FOLLY GR
MEDHILL CL
WOOD GR
B471
BEECHES LA
WAYSIDE GR
BEECH LA
GORING RD
WHITEHOUSE RD
BEESON CL
THE CLOSE
SANDFORD CL
ASHLEE WK
LACKMORE GDNS
WEST CHILTERN
WYTENHAM CL
GRIMMER WAY
HAGBOURNE CL
CROFT WAY
BIRCHEN CL
GREENMOOR
OAKDENE
BRIDLE PATH
1 BECKLEY CL
2 BALDONS CL
3 CUDDESDON CL
Woodcroft
BEECH LA
WOOD LA
Elmorepark Wood
Fox Covert
Greenmoorhill Farm
Greenmoor Hill
GREEN LA
BATTLE RD
Elvendon Priory
ELVENDON LA
Grigg's Wood
Old Elvendon Wood
Park Wood
SHIRVELL'S HILL
POTKILN LA
B4526
READING RD
Park Farm
Little Heath
Cray's Pond
PH
BEECHWOOD CL
EASTFIELD LA
Enclosure
LONG TOLL
Flint House
B471
Little Oaken Wood
Bottom Farm
Blackbird's Bottom
Great Chalk Wood
Oakwood Covert
Oaken Wood
Stapnall's Farm
Cold Harbour
Coldharbour Farm
Sch
B4526
Furzemoor Plantation
Goff's Clump
Great Oaks
Hill Bottom
Cockpit Plantation
The Sun (PH)
HOCKETTS CL
HILL BOTTOM CL
RIVACRES
OAKDOWN CL
BEC TITHE
BRIDLE RD
ORCHARD COMBE
Paul's Grove
Coombe End Farm
Copyhold Farm
Whitchurch Hill
Mount Pleasant Farm
Merricroft's Wood
Kessells Copse
Beech Wood
Butler's Farm
Hartslock Wood
Beech Farm
Fort
Wheatley's Plantation
Hartslock Farm
Stonycroft Plantation
Lime Corner
Coombe Park Farm
Rivendell Farm
Bozedown House
B471

256

241

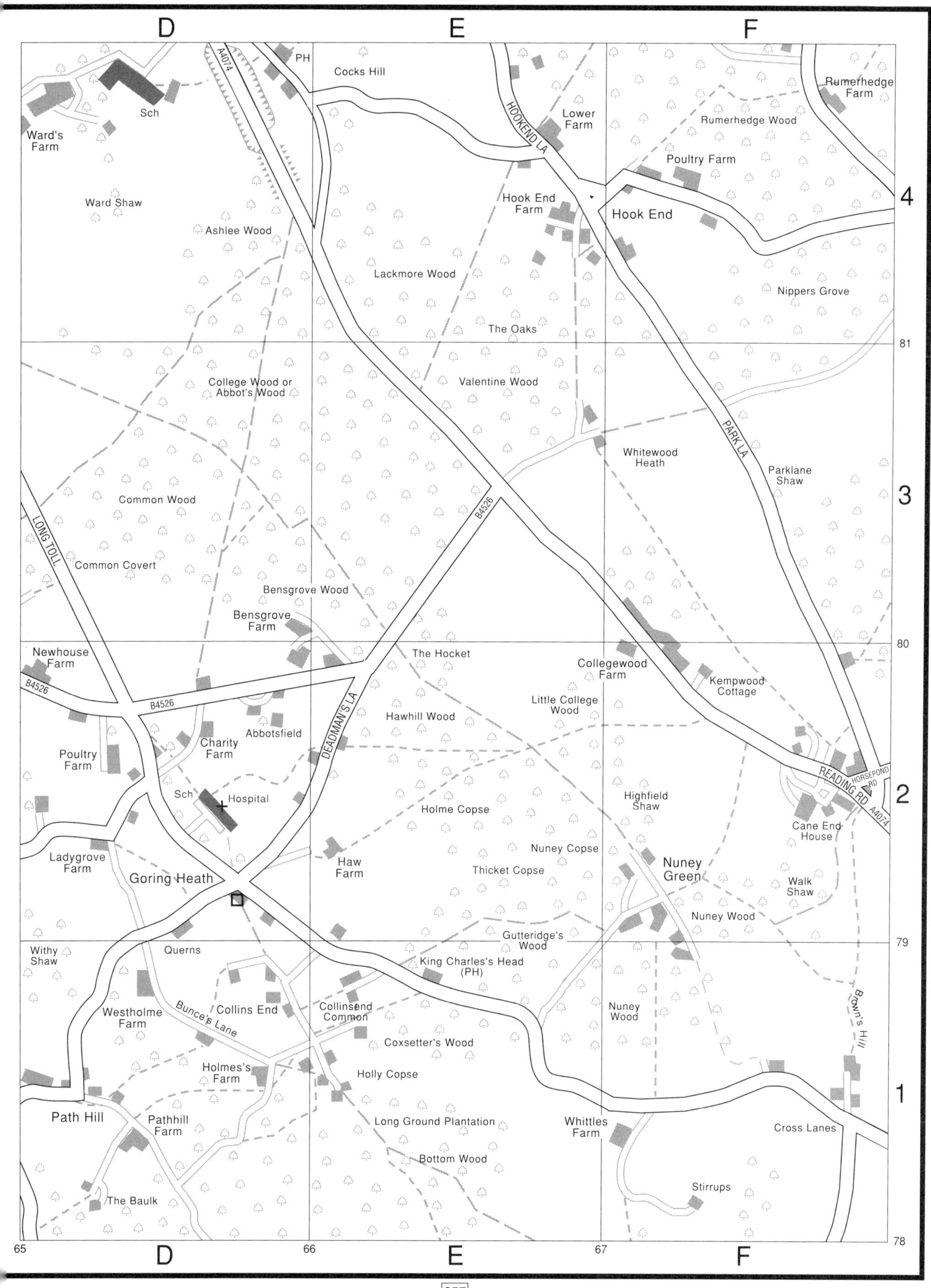
D
E
F
Sch
Ward's Farm
Ward Shaw
Ashlee Wood
PH
Cocks Hill
A4074
HOOKEND LA
Lower Farm
Rumerhedge Farm
Rumerhedge Wood
Poultry Farm
Hook End Farm
Hook End
Lackmore Wood
Nippers Grove
The Oaks
College Wood or Abbot's Wood
Valentine Wood
Whitewood Heath
PARK LA
Parklane Shaw
Common Wood
B4526
LONG TOLL
Common Covert
Bensgrove Wood
Bensgrove Farm
Newhouse Farm
The Hocket
Collegewood Farm
Kempwood Cottage
B4526
Little College Wood
Hawhill Wood
Abbotsfield
Charity Farm
Poultry Farm
DEADMAN'S LA
Highfield Shaw
READING RD
HORSEPOND RD
A4074
Cane End House
Sch
Hospital
Holme Copse
Nuney Copse
Ladygrove Farm
Haw Farm
Thicket Copse
Nuney Green
Walk Shaw
Goring Heath
Nuney Wood
Withy Shaw
Querns
Gutteridge's Wood
King Charles's Head (PH)
Brown's Hill
Westholme Farm
Bunce's Lane
Collins End
Collinsend Common
Nuney Wood
Coxsetter's Wood
Holmes's Farm
Holly Copse
Path Hill
Pathhill Farm
Long Ground Plantation
Whittles Farm
Cross Lanes
Bottom Wood
Stirrups
The Baulk
65
66
67
81
80
79
78
4
3
2
1
D
E
F

252

257

242

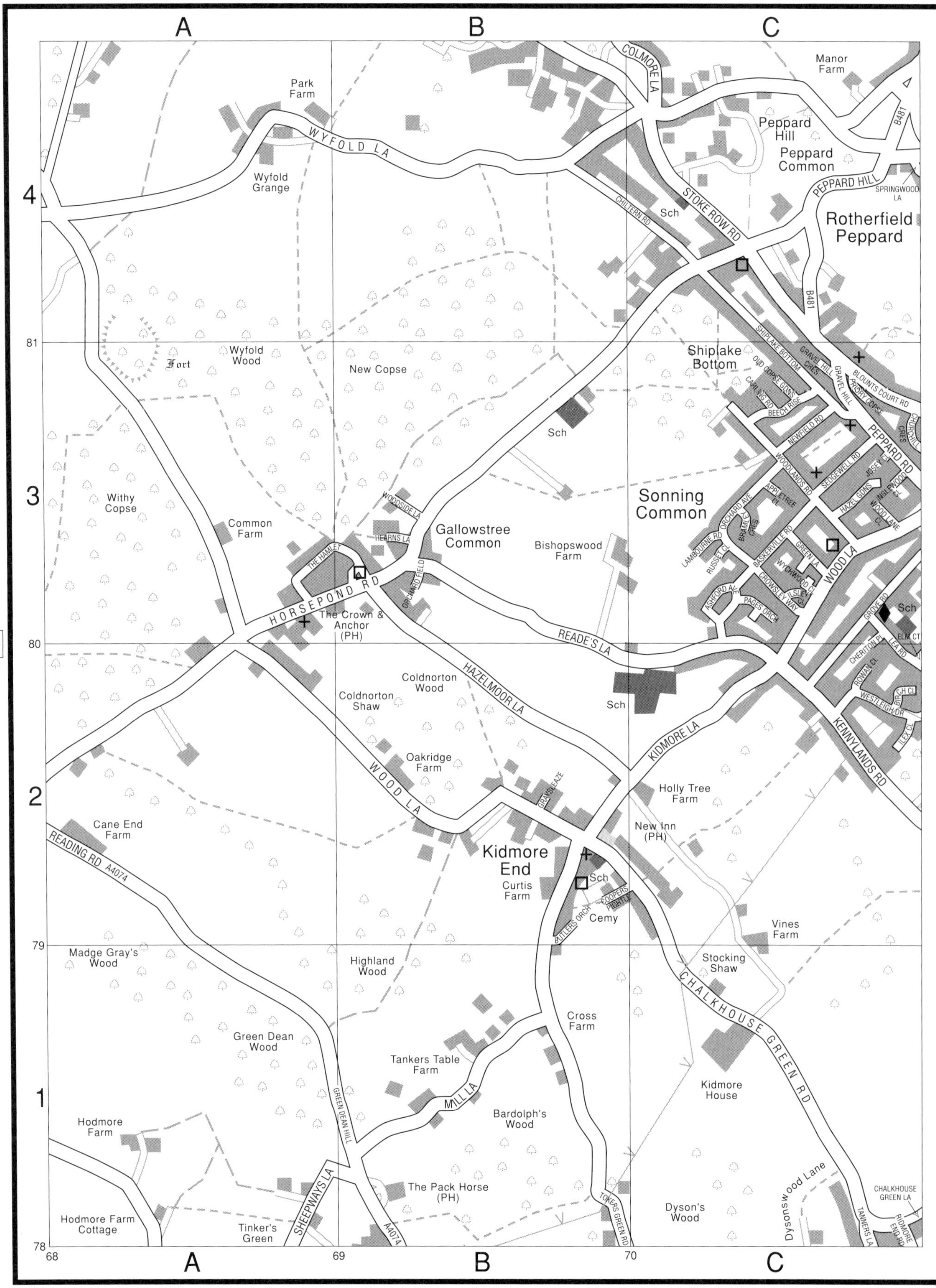
A
B
C
4
3
2
1
81
80
79
78
68
69
70
Park Farm
WYFOLD LA
Wyfold Grange
COLMORE LA
Manor Farm
Peppard Hill
Peppard Common
B481
PEPPARD HILL
SPRINGWOOD LA
Rotherfield Peppard
STOKE ROW RD
CHILTERN RD
Sch
Fort
Wyfold Wood
New Copse
Shiplake Bottom
SHIPLAKE BOTTOM
GRAVEL HILL
BLOUNTS COURT RD
PEPPARD RD
Withy Copse
Common Farm
WOODSIDE LA
HEARNS LA
Gallowstree Common
Bishopswood Farm
Sonning Common
WOOD LA
THE HAMLET
HORSEPOND RD
ORCHARD FIELD
The Crown & Anchor (PH)
READE'S LA
GROVE RD
KENNYLANDS RD
HAZELMOOR LA
Coldnorton Wood
Coldnorton Shaw
Oakridge Farm
KIDMORE LA
Holly Tree Farm
Cane End Farm
READING RD A4074
WOOD LA
GRAYS LEAZE
New Inn (PH)
Kidmore End
Curtis Farm
Cemy
BUTLERS ORCH
COOPERS PIGHTLE
Vines Farm
Madge Gray's Wood
Highland Wood
Stocking Shaw
CHALKHOUSE GREEN RD
Cross Farm
Green Dean Wood
Tankers Table Farm
Kidmore House
MILL LA
GREEN DEAN HILL
Hodmore Farm
Bardolph's Wood
SHEEPWAYS LA
The Pack Horse (PH)
Dysonswood Lane
CHALKHOUSE GREEN LA
Hodmore Farm Cottage
Tinker's Green
A4074
TOKERS GREEN RD
Dyson's Wood
TANNERS LA
RIDMORE END RD

251

258

243

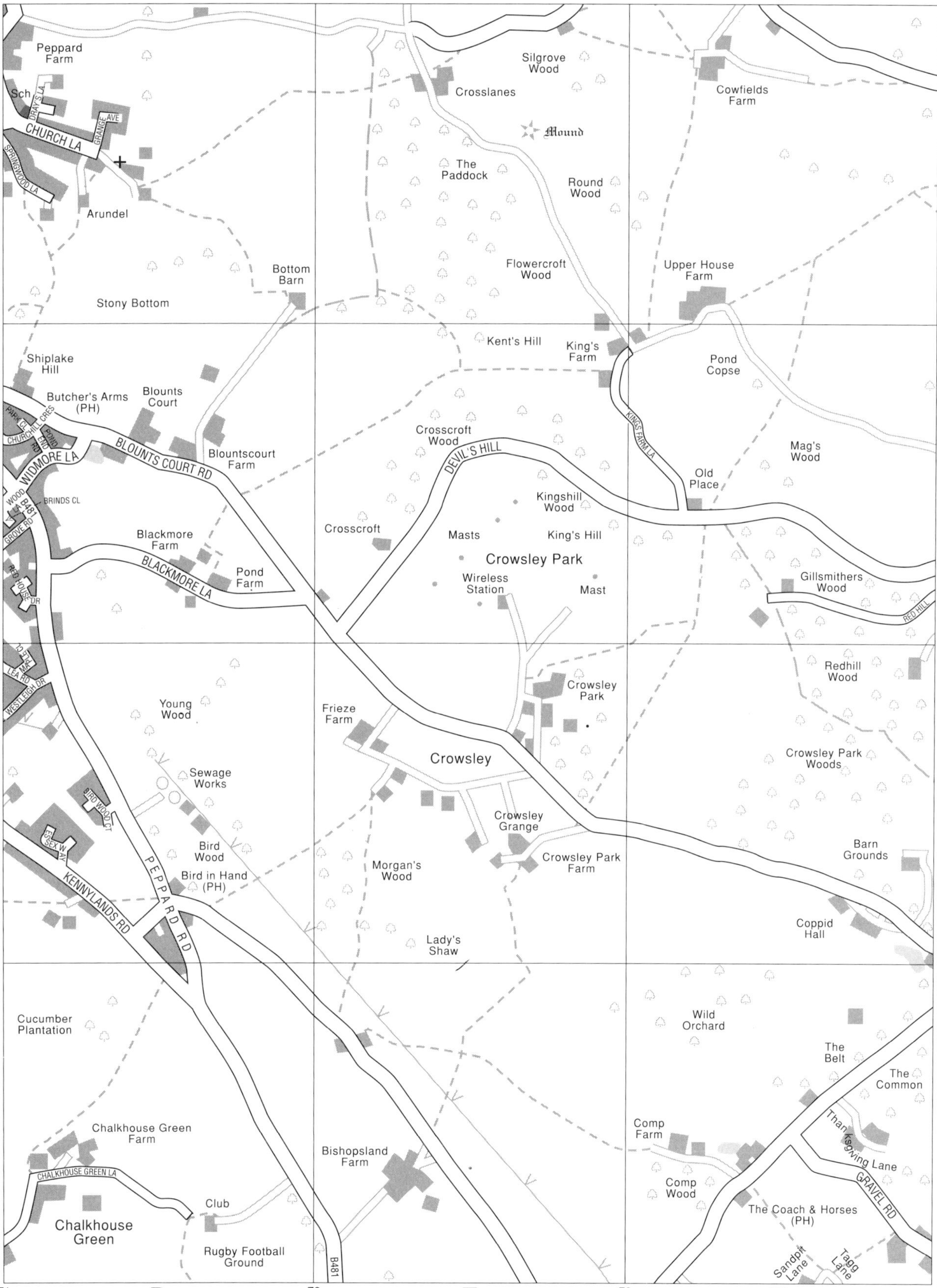
D
E
F
Peppard Farm
Sch
DRAY'S LA
CHURCH LA
GRANGE AVE
SPRINGWOOD LA
Arundel
Silgrove Wood
Crosslanes
Cowfields Farm
Mound
The Paddock
Round Wood
Flowercroft Wood
Upper House Farm
Bottom Barn
Stony Bottom
4
81
Shiplake Hill
Butcher's Arms (PH)
Blounts Court
Kent's Hill
King's Farm
Pond Copse
PARK LA
CHURCHILL CRES
POND END RD
WIDMORE LA
BLOUNTS COURT RD
Blountscourt Farm
Crosscroft Wood
DEVIL'S HILL
KINGS FARM LA
Mag's Wood
Old Place
Kingshill Wood
3
BRINDS CL
WOOD LA
B481
GROVE RD
Blackmore Farm
Crosscroft
Masts
King's Hill
Crowsley Park
BLACKMORE LA
Pond Farm
Wireless Station
Mast
Gillsmithers Wood
RED HILL
80
Redhill Wood
WESTLEIGH DR
LEA RD
Young Wood
Frieze Farm
Crowsley Park
Crowsley
Crowsley Park Woods
Sewage Works
2
BIRD WOOD CT
ESSEX WAY
Crowsley Grange
Bird Wood
Crowsley Park Farm
Barn Grounds
Morgan's Wood
Bird in Hand (PH)
PEPPARD RD
KENNYLANDS RD
Coppid Hall
Lady's Shaw
79
Wild Orchard
Cucumber Plantation
The Belt
The Common
Chalkhouse Green Farm
Comp Farm
1
Thanksgiving Lane
Bishopsland Farm
CHALKHOUSE GREEN LA
Comp Wood
GRAVEL RD
Club
The Coach & Horses (PH)
Chalkhouse Green
Rugby Football Ground
B481
Sandpit Lane
Tagg Lane
78
71
72
73

254

259

244

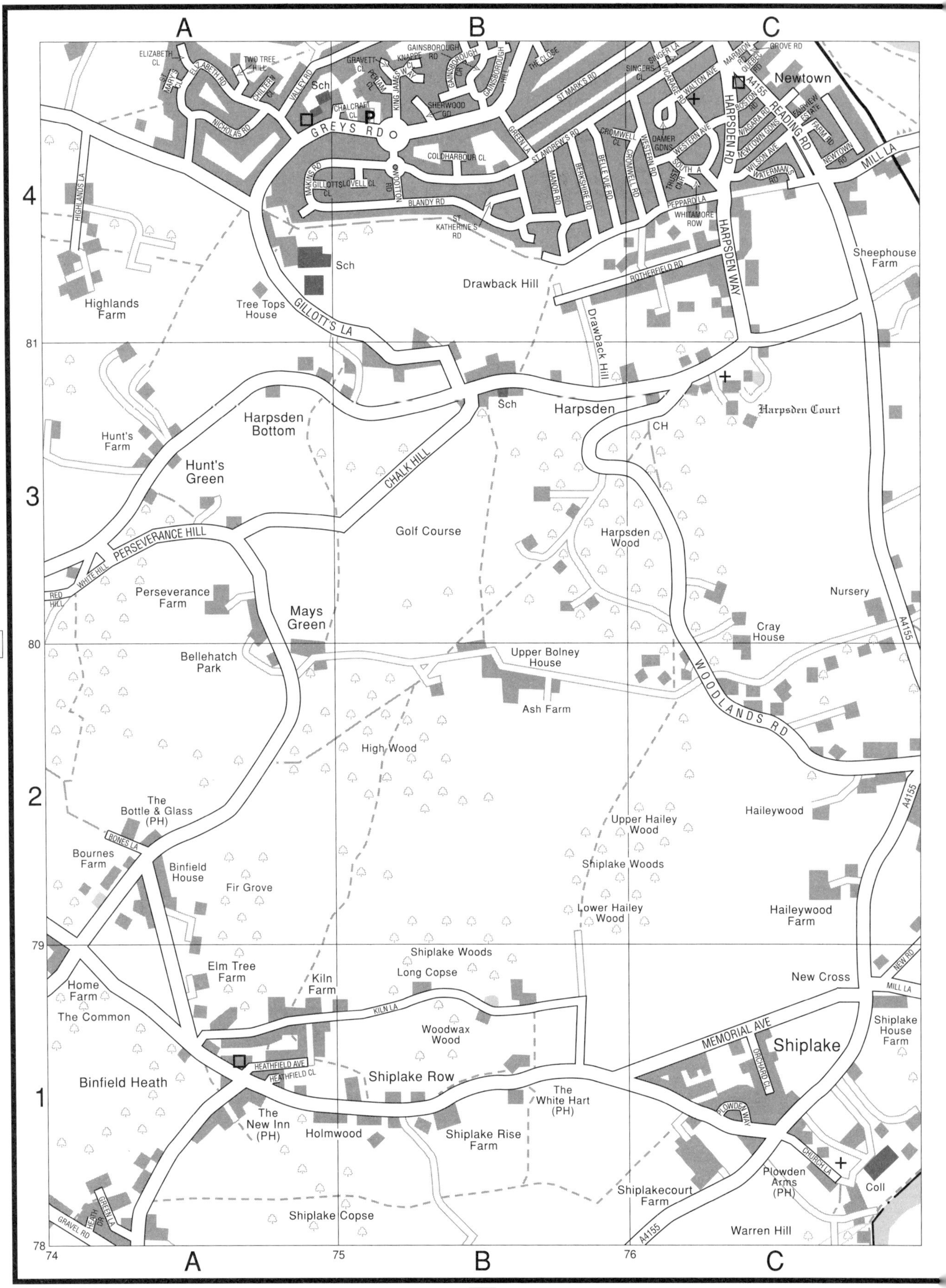
A
B
C
ELIZABETH CL
ST MARY'S CL
ELIZABETH RD
TWO TREE HILL
CHILTERN CL
VALLEY RD
NICHOLAS RD
Sch
GRAVETT CL
PERIAM CL
CHALCRAFT CL
P
GAINSBOROUGH RD
KNAPPE CL
KING JAMES WAY
GAINSBOROUGH CR
GAINSBOROUGH HILL
SHERWOOD GD
THE CLOSE
GREYS RD
MAKINS RD
GILLOTTS CL
LOVELL CL
WOOTTON RD
BLANDY RD
COLDHARBOUR CL
GREEN LA
ST MARK'S RD
ST ANDREW'S RD
ST KATHERINE'S RD
MANOR RD
BERKSHIRE RD
BELLE VUE RD
CROMWELL CL
CROMWELL RD
WESTERN RD
SINGERS CL
SINGER LA
VICARAGE RD
WALTON AVE
DAMER GDNS
WESTERN AVE
SOUTH AVE
TRUST COR
PEPPARD LA
WHITAMORE ROW
HARPSDEN RD
HARPSDEN WAY
MARMION RD
QUEBEC RD
GROVE RD
A4155
Newtown
BOSTON RD
NIAGARA RD
NEWTOWN GDNS
WILSON AVE
WATERMAN'S RD
READING RD
FAIRVIEW ESTATE
FARM RD
NEWTOWN RD
MILL LA
4
HIGHLANDS LA
Highlands Farm
Tree Tops House
Sch
GILLOTT'S LA
Drawback Hill
ROTHERFIELD RD
Drawback Hill
Sheephouse Farm
81
Sch
Harpsden
Harpsden Court
CH
Hunt's Farm
Harpsden Bottom
Hunt's Green
CHALK HILL
3
PERSEVERANCE HILL
WHITE HILL
RED HILL
Golf Course
Harpsden Wood
Perseverance Farm
Mays Green
Nursery
Cray House
A4155
80
Bellehatch Park
Upper Bolney House
Ash Farm
WOODLANDS RD
High Wood
2
The Bottle & Glass (PH)
Upper Hailey Wood
Haileywood
A4155
BONES LA
Bournes Farm
Binfield House
Fir Grove
Shiplake Woods
Lower Hailey Wood
Haileywood Farm
79
Shiplake Woods
Long Copse
Elm Tree Farm
Kiln Farm
Home Farm
New Cross
NEW RD
MILL LA
The Common
KILN LA
Woodwax Wood
MEMORIAL AVE
ORCHARD CL
Shiplake
Shiplake House Farm
HEATHFIELD AVE
HEATHFIELD CL
Binfield Heath
Shiplake Row
1
The White Hart (PH)
PLOWDEN WAY
The New Inn (PH)
Holmwood
Shiplake Rise Farm
CHURCH LA
Plowden Arms (PH)
Coll
Shiplakecourt Farm
GRAVEL RD
HEATH DR
GREEN LA
Shiplake Copse
A4155
Warren Hill
78
74
75
76
A
B
C

253

260

not continued, see key diagram

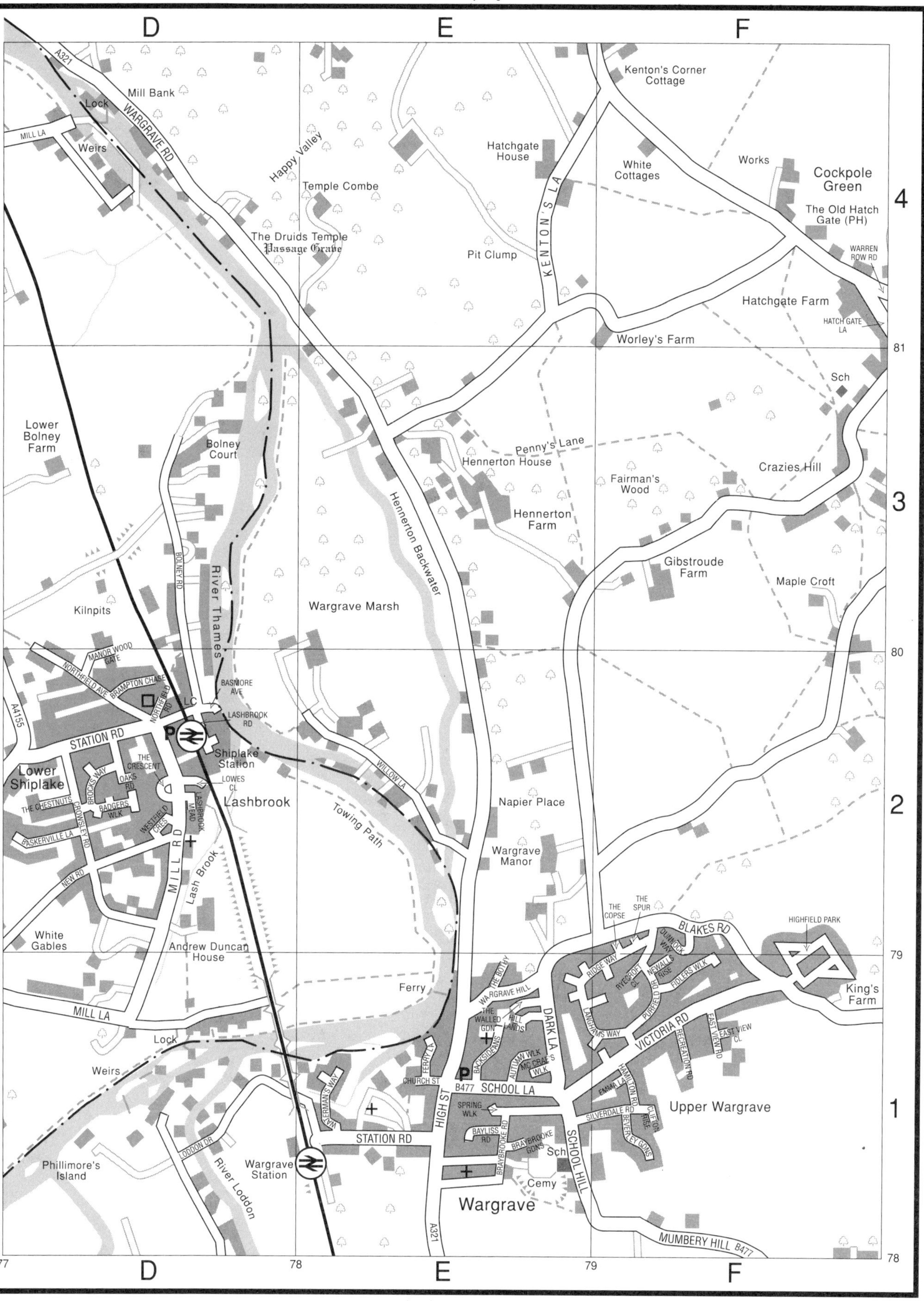

not continued, see key diagram

not continued, see key diagram

250

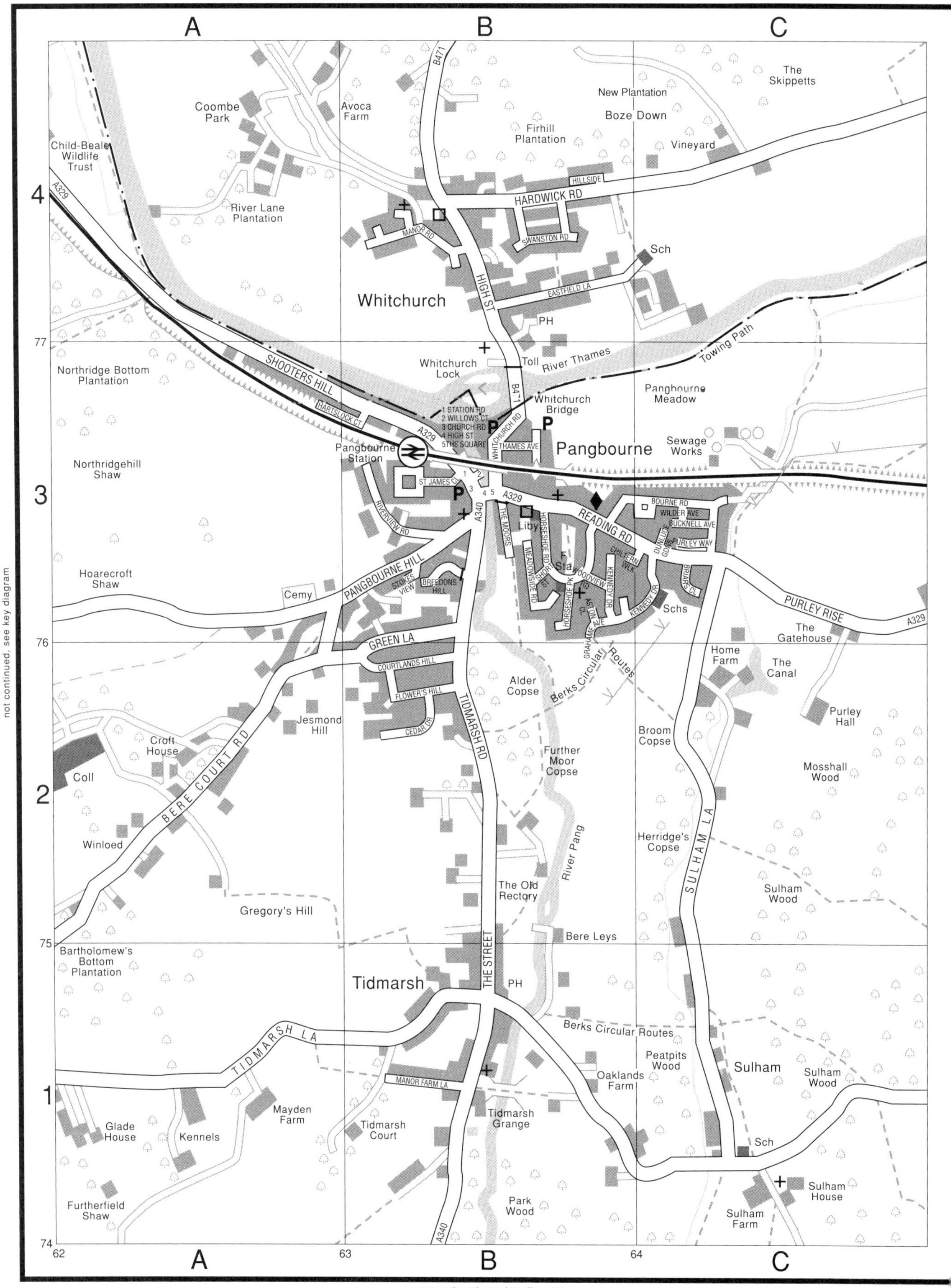

not continued, see key diagram

not continued, see key diagram

251

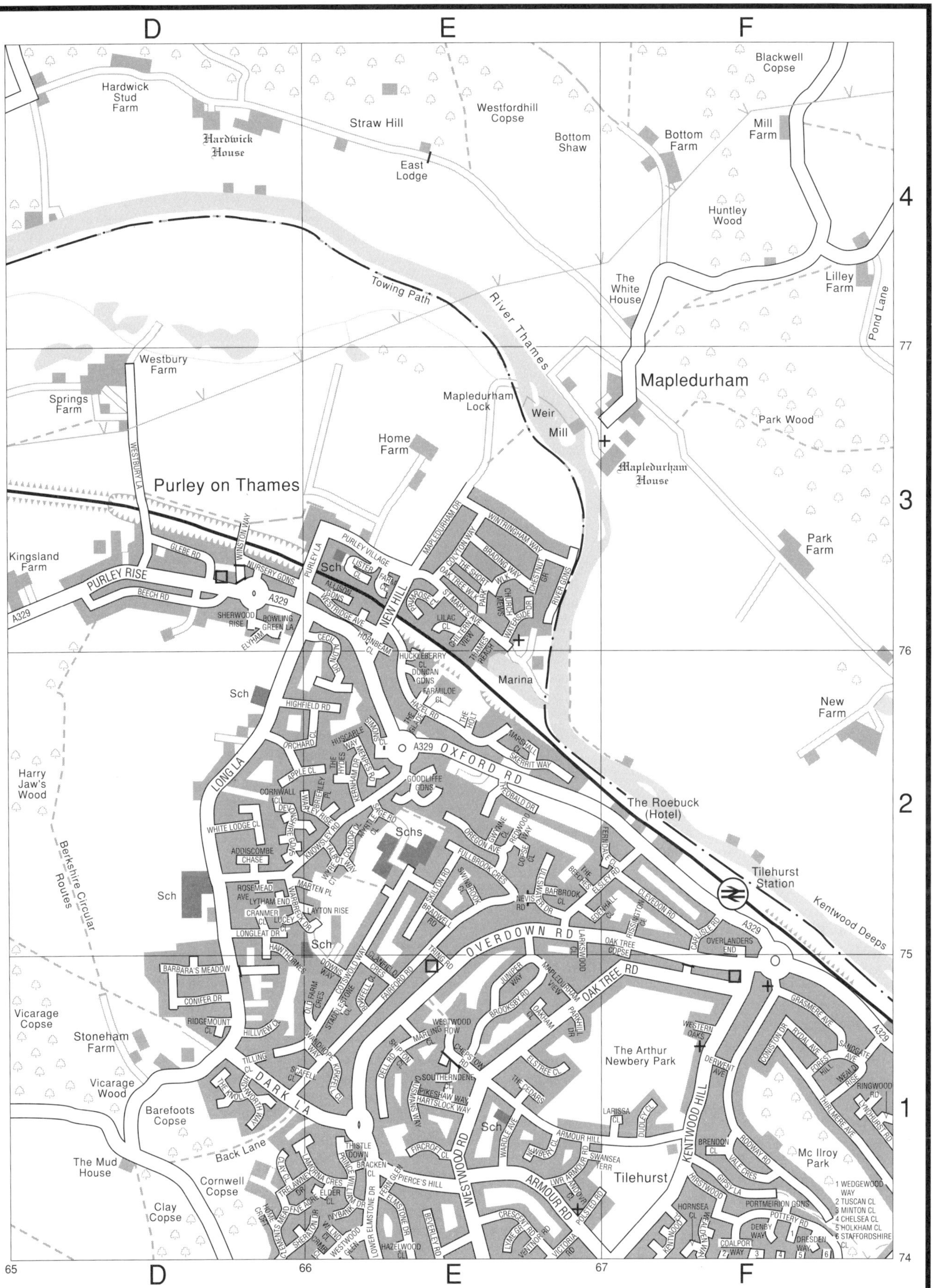

D
E
F
4
3
2
1
77
76
75
74
65
66
67
Hardwick Stud Farm
Hardwick House
Straw Hill
East Lodge
Westfordhill Copse
Bottom Shaw
Bottom Farm
Blackwell Copse
Mill Farm
Huntley Wood
The White House
Lilley Farm
Pond Lane
Towing Path
River Thames
Westbury Farm
Springs Farm
Mapledurham Lock
Weir
Mill
Mapledurham
Park Wood
Mapledurham House
Home Farm
Purley on Thames
Park Farm
Kingsland Farm
WESTBURY LA
PURLEY RISE
GLEBE RD
BEECH RD
A329
WINSTON WAY
NURSERY GDNS
SHERWOOD RISE
BOWLING GREEN LA
ELYHAM
PURLEY LA
PURLEY VILLAGE
Sch
LISTER CL
FARM CL
ALLISON GDNS
WESTRIDGE AVE
NEW HILL
MAPLEDURHAM DR
WINTRINGHAM WAY
COPTON WAY
BRADING WAY
THE SHORT
OAK TREE WLK
ST MARY'S AVE
PRIMROSE CL
PARK WLK
CHURCH MEWS
CHESTNUT GR
RIVER GDNS
LILAC CL
CHILTERN VIEW
THAMES REACH
WATERSIDE DR
HORNBEAM CL
Marina
CECIL ALDIN DR
HUCKLEBERRY CL
DUNCAN GDNS
FARMILOE CL
HAZEL RD
THE GLADE
THE HOLT
HIGHFIELD RD
HUSCARLE WAY
SIMONS CL
MARSHALL CL
SKERRIT WAY
New Farm
ORCHARD CL
APPLE CL
THE HYDES
MENNES RD
KERNHAM DR
GOODLIFFE GDNS
OXFORD RD
THEOBALD DR
Harry Jaw's Wood
LONG LA
CORNWALL CL
DEVONSHIRE GDNS
WHITE LODGE CL
BIRCHLEY PL
WAVERLEY RISE
KNOWSLEY RD
CONDOR CL
MYRTLE CL
SAGE RD
Schs
OREGON AVE
GWYNNE CL
REDWOOD WAY
The Roebuck (Hotel)
Berkshire Circular Routes
ADDISCOMBE CHASE
FULLBROOK CRES
COPSE WAY
ULLSWATER DR
FERNDALE CL
THE BEECHES
ELSLEY RD
Tilehurst Station
ROSEMEAD AVE
LYTHAM END
MARTEN PL
LAYTON RISE
CRANMER CL
LUCEY CL
LONGLEAT DR
SKILTON RD
SWINBROOK CL
BRADWELL RD
NEVIS RD
BARBROOK CL
EDENHALL CL
RISSINGTON CL
CLEVEDON RD
CARLISLE RD
Kentwood Deeps
HAWTHORNES
OVERDOWN RD
LARKSWOOD CL
OAK TREE COPSE
OVERLANDERS END
BARBARA'S MEADOW
DOWNS WAY
COTSWOLD WAY
CLANFIELD CRES
TRING RD
OAK TREE RD
JUNIPER WAY
MAPLEDURHAM VIEW
CONIFER DR
OLD FARM CRES
STADDLESTONE CL
BOWFELL CL
FAIRFORD RD
BROOKSBY RD
OAKHAM CL
PARKHILL DR
GRASMERE AVE
Vicarage Copse
RIDGEMOUNT CL
HILLVIEW CL
WESTWOOD ROW
MARLING CL
CHEPSTOW RD
WESTERN OAKS
The Arthur Newbery Park
DERWENT AVE
CONISTON DR
RYDAL AVE
SANDGATE AVE
FOREST HILL
WEALD RISE
Stoneham Farm
TILLING CL
DARK LA
WANDHOPE WAY
SCAFELL CL
KIRKFELL CL
DELL RD
SHIPTON CL
SOUTHERNDENE CL
ELSTREE CL
THE CEDARS
RINGWOOD RD
THIRLMERE AVE
LYNDHURST RD
Vicarage Wood
THE KNOLL
PIKESHAW WAY
HARTSLOCK WAY
CUSTANS WAY
KENTWOOD HILL
Barefoots Copse
Sch
WARDLE AVE
LARISSA CL
DUDLEY CL
ARMOUR HILL
BRENDON CL
RODWAY RD
Mc Ilroy Park
Back Lane
THISTLE DOWN
BRACKEN CL
FIRCROFT CL
NEWBERY CL
SWANSEA TERR
Tilehurst
VALE CRES
The Mud House
CLAY CL
TRELAWNEY DR
LAMORNA CRES
PRINCE WILLIAM DR
FERN GLEN
PIERCE'S HILL
WESTWOOD RD
ARMOUR RD
LWR ARMOUR RD
ANDOVER CL
HIRSTWOOD
GIPSY LA
1 WEDGEWOOD WAY
2 TUSCAN CL
3 MINTON CL
4 CHELSEA CL
5 HOLKHAM CL
6 STAFFORDSHIRE CL
Cornwell Copse
FIVE ACRE
ELDER CL
WYBANK CL
ELMSTONE DR
LOWER ELMSTONE DR
BEVERLEY RD
CRESCENT RD
POLSTED RD
HORNSEA CL
PORTMEIRION GDNS
POTTERY RD
Clay Copse
CLEMENTS MEAD
SHERATON DR
WESTWOOD GLEN
HAZELWOOD CL
LYME GR
VENTNOR RD
VICTORIA RD
KENTWOOD CL
WEALDEN WAY
DENBY WAY
COALPORT WAY
DRESDEN WAY

258

252

257

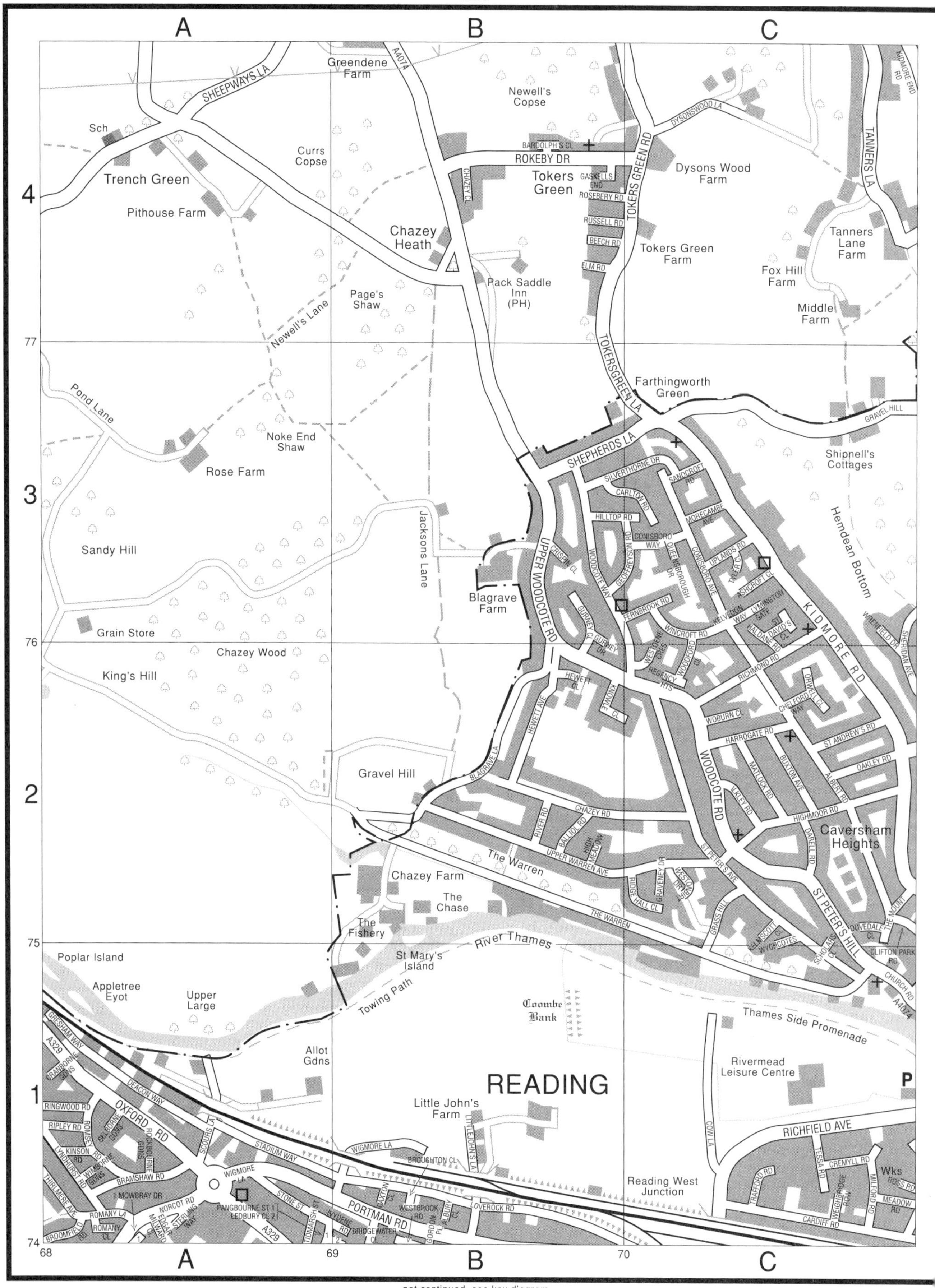

A
B
C
4
3
2
1
77
76
75
74
68
69
70
SHEEPWAYS LA
Greendene Farm
A4074
Newell's Copse
Sch
Trench Green
Pithouse Farm
Currs Copse
BARDOLPH'S CL
ROKEBY DR
CHAZEY CL
Tokers Green
GASKELLS END
ROSEBERY RD
RUSSELL RD
BEECH RD
ELM RD
TOKERS GREEN RD
DYSONSWOOD LA
Dysons Wood Farm
TANNERS LA
KIDMORE END RD
Tanners Lane Farm
Chazey Heath
Tokers Green Farm
Fox Hill Farm
Middle Farm
Pack Saddle Inn (PH)
Page's Shaw
Newell's Lane
TOKERSGREEN LA
Farthingworth Green
GRAVEL HILL
Pond Lane
Noke End Shaw
Rose Farm
SHEPHERDS LA
SILVERTHORNE DR
SANDCROFT RD
CARLTON RD
MORECAMBE AVE
HILLTOP RD
CONISBORO WAY
Shipnell's Cottages
Hemdean Bottom
Sandy Hill
Jacksons Lane
UPPER WOODCOTE RD
CRISPIN CL
WOODCOTE WAY
GEOFFREYSON RD
QUEENSBOROUGH DR
CONISBORO AVE
UPLANDS RD
TYLERS CL
ASHCROFT CL
Blagrave Farm
FERNBROOK RD
KELVEDON WAY
LYMINGTON GATE
ST DAVID'S CL
HALDANE RD
KIDMORE RD
WRENFIELD DR
SHERIDAN AVE
Grain Store
GURNEY CL
GURNEY DR
WESTDENE CRES
WINCROFT RD
WOODFORD CL
REGENCY HTS
RICHMOND RD
76
Chazey Wood
King's Hill
HEWETT CL
HEWETT AVE
KNOWLE CL
WOBURN CL
CHELFORD WAY
ORWELL CL
HARROGATE RD
ST ANDREW'S RD
BLAGRAVE LA
WOODCOTE RD
MATLOCK RD
BUXTON AVE
ALBERT RD
OAKLEY RD
Gravel Hill
CHAZEY RD
RIVER RD
BALLIOL RD
HIGH MEADOW
ILKLEY RD
HIGHMOOR RD
DARELL RD
Caversham Heights
UPPER WARREN AVE
The Warren
RIDGE HALL CL
GRAVENEY DR
WESTON DR
ST PETER'S AVE
Chazey Farm
The Chase
THE WARREN
GRASS HILL
KELMSCOTT CL
WYCHCOTES
SCHOLARS CL
ST PETER'S HILL
DOVEDALE CL
THE MOUNT
CLIFTON PARK RD
CHURCH RD
The Fishery
River Thames
Poplar Island
St Mary's Island
Appletree Eyot
Upper Large
Towing Path
Coombe Bank
Thames Side Promenade
GRESHAM WAY
A329
CRANBORNE GDNS
DEACON WAY
Allot Gdns
Rivermead Leisure Centre
P
READING
RINGWOOD RD
OXFORD RD
RIPLEY RD
ROMSEY RD
SELBORNE GDNS
ROCKBOURNE GDNS
Little John's Farm
RICHFIELD AVE
KINSON RD
LYNDHURST RD
WIMBORNE GDNS
BRAMSHAW RD
SCOURS LA
STADIUM WAY
WIGMORE LA
LITTLEJOHN'S LA
COW LA
BROUGHTON CL
TRAFFORD RD
TESSA RD
CREMYLL RD
WEIGHBRIDGE ROW
MILFORD RD
Wks
ROSS RD
THIRLMERE AVE
1 MOWBRAY DR
NORCOT RD
WIGMORE LA
STONE ST
ROMANY LA
ROMANY CL
STERLING WAY
EDGAR MILWARD CL
BROOMFIELD RD
PANGBOURNE ST 1
LEDBURY CL 2
TIDMARSH ST
IVYDENE RD
PORTMAN RD
BRIDGEWATER
COXTON CL
WESTBROOK RD
GORDON PL
ALBURY CL
LOVEROCK RD
Reading West Junction
CARDIFF RD
MEADOW RD

253

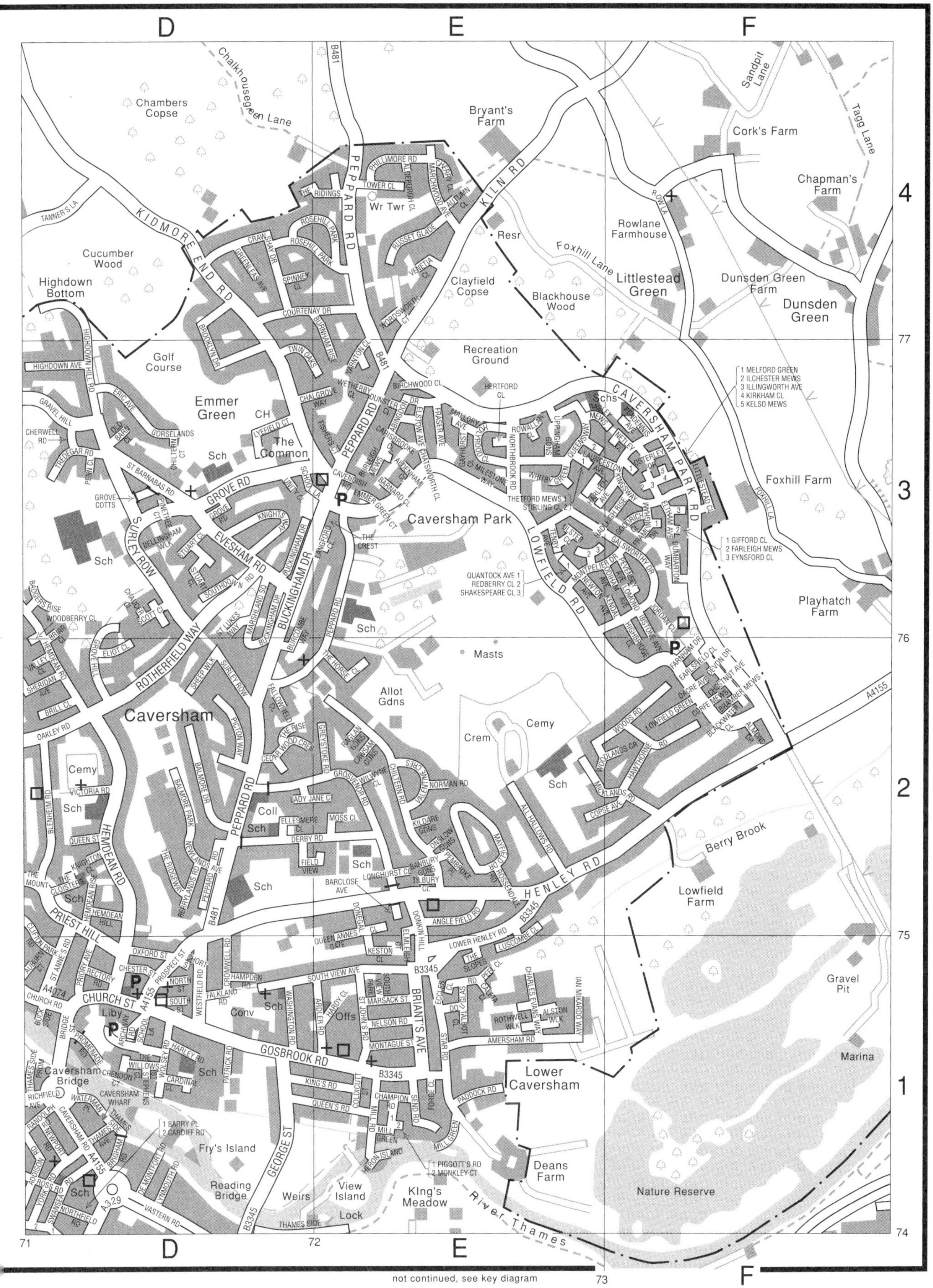

260

not continued, see key diagram

254

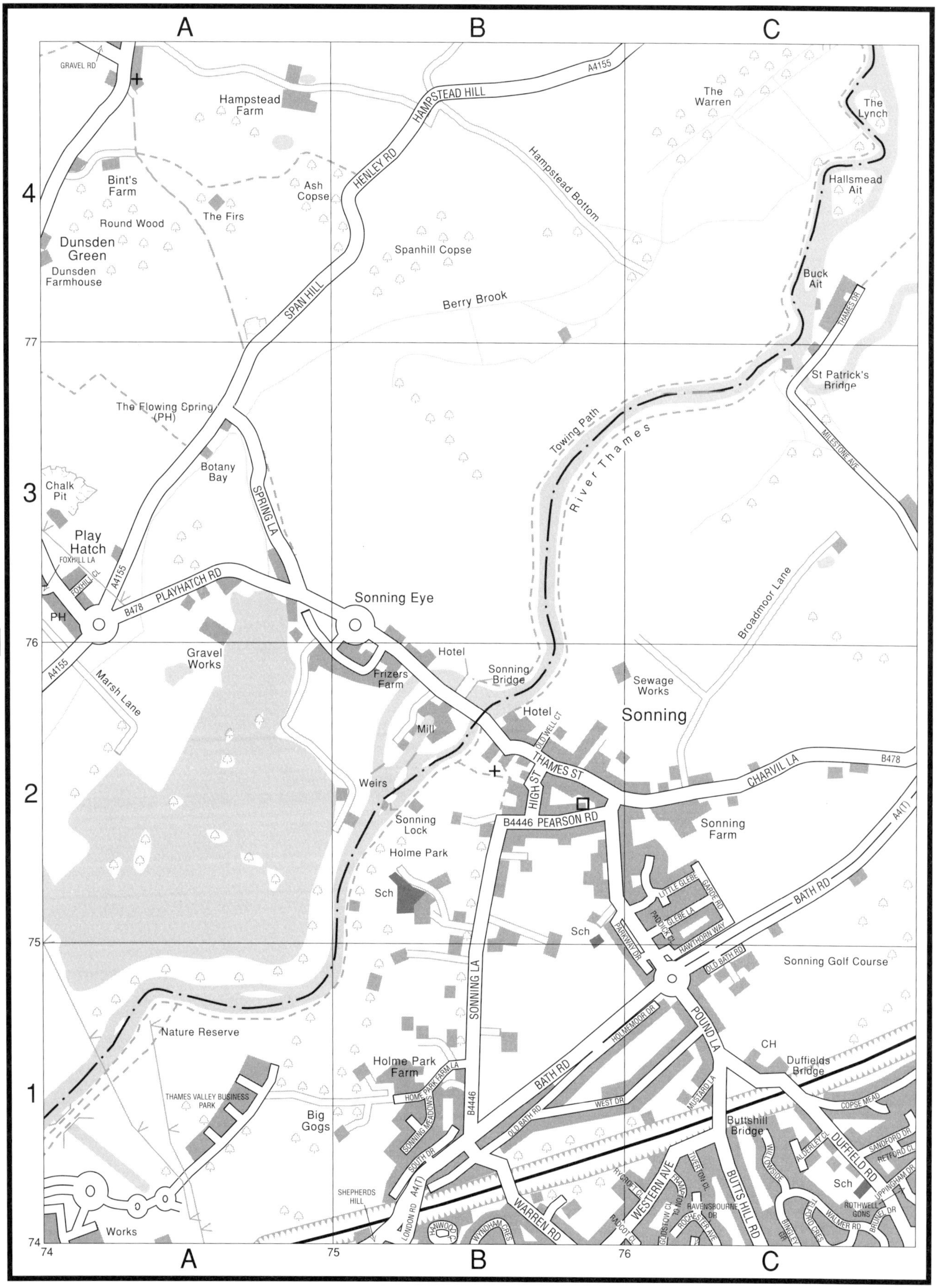

not continued, see key diagram

USER'S NOTES

EXPLANATION OF THE STREET INDEX REFERENCE SYSTEM

Street names are listed alphabetically and show the locality, the page number and a reference to the square in which the name falls on the map page.

Example:	Divinity Rd. Oxon..142 A4
Divinity Rd	This is the full street name, which may have been abbreviated on the map.
Oxon	This is the abbreviation for the town, village or locality in which the street falls.
142	This is the page number of the map on which the street name appears.
A4	The letter and figure indicate the square on the map in which the centre of the street falls. The square can be found at the junction of the vertical column carrying the appropriate letter and the horizontal row carrying the appropriate figure.

ABBREVIATIONS USED IN THE INDEX

Road Names

Approach	App	North	N
Avenue	Ave	Orchard	Orch
Broadway	Bwy	Parade	Par
By-Pass	By-Ps	Passage	Pas
Causeway	Cswy	Place	Pl
Common	Comm	Pleasant	Plea
Corner	Cnr	Precinct	Prec
Cottages	Cotts	Promenade	Prom
Court	Ct	Road	Rd
Crescent	Cres	South	S
Drive	Dri	Square	Sq
Drove	Dro	Street,Saint	St
East	E	Terrace	Terr
Gardens	Gdns	Walk	Wlk
Grove	Gr	West	W
Heights	Hts	Yard	Yd
Lane	La		

Towns, Villages and Rural Localities

Abingdon	Abing	180	B4
Adderbury	Adde	23	D2
Adlestrop	Adle	40	B1
Aldworth	Aldw	247	F2
Alvescot	Alve	133	E3
Ambrosden	Ambr	81	E2
Appleton	Apple	158	A4
Ardington	Ard	215	F3
Ascott-under-Wychwood	As u Wy	71	E1
Ashbury	Ashb	228	A4
Aston	Aston	135	F2
Aston Rowant	Ast R	167	E1
Aston Tirrold	Ast T	237	F4
Avon Dassett	Av Da	2	C4
Aynho	Ayn	35	E4
Bampton	Bamp	134	C2
Banbury	Banb	16	B4
Barford St Michael	B St M	32	C3
Barton-on-the-Heath	B on H	26	C3
Baydon	Bayd	245	F1
Beacon's Bottom	B Bot	189	E2
Beckley	Beck	111	D2
Begbroke	Begb	108	A4
Benson	Bens	204	A2
Berinsfield	Berin	182	B3
Berrick Salome	Ber S	184	A1
Bicester	Bice	65	F2
Bishopstone	Bish	227	E2
Bix	Bix	243	E4
Black Bourton	B Bou	133	F3
Blackthorn	Bktn	82	A2
Bladon	Blad	91	E1
Bledington	Bled	54	B1
Bledlow Ridge	Bled R	189	F4
Bletchingdon	Bletch	93	D4
Blewbury	Blew	237	D4
Bloxham	Blox	21	E3
Bodicote	Bod	22	B4
Bourton	Bourt	209	D2
Brackley	Brac	24	A4
Brightwell Baldwin	Br Ba	185	D1
Brightwell-cum-Sotwell	Br-c-S	202	B1
Brill	Bri	98	A1
Brize Norton	Br No	116	B2
Broughton	Brou	15	E1
Buckland	Buckl	154	C1
Bucknell	Buck	65	D4
Burford	Burf	100	C3
Buscot	Busc	171	D4
Carterton	Cart	115	F2
Cassington	Cass	107	E1
Caversham	Caver	259	D2
Chacombe	Chac	10	C2
Chadlington	Chadl	57	D1
Chalgrove	Chalg	184	C3
Charlbury	Charl	73	E2
Charlton-on-Otmoor	Ch-on-O	95	D2
Charney Bassett	Ch Ba	176	A1
Chastleton	Chas	40	B4
Checkendon	Check	241	E2
Chesterton	Chest	79	F4
Childrey	Child	213	E2
Chilson	Chils	71	F2
Chilton	Chil	235	F4
Chinnor	Chin	168	B4
Chipping Norton	Ch No	42	C1
Chipping Warden	Ch Wa	5	F3
Cholsey	Chol	221	D1
Church Westcote	Ch We	68	B3
Churchill	Churc	55	F3
Clanfield	Clan	152	C4
Claydon	Clay	1	B1
Clifton Hampden	Cl Ham	181	E2
Coleshill	Coles	191	D4
Combe	Combe	90	A3
Compton Wynyates	Co Wy	12	B4
Cornwell	Corn	41	E2
Cottisford	Cott	37	F2
Crawley	Crawl	103	F2
Cropredy	Cro	4	C1
Croughton	Crou	36	B4
Crowmarsh Gifford	Cr Gif	221	F4
Cuddesdon	Cudd	144	A2
Culham	Culh	180	A1
Cumnor	Cumn	139	E3
Curbridge	Curb	117	F3
Cutteslowe	Cutte	109	D1
Deddington	Dedd	33	F2
Denchworth	Dench	196	A2
Didcot	Didc	218	C4
Dorchester	Dorch	182	B1
Drayton	Dra	15	E4
Drayton	Dray	179	D1
Drayton St Leonard	D St L	183	D3
Ducklington	Duck	118	A2
Duns Tew	D Tew	47	E3
East Challow	E Cha	214	A3
East Garston	East G	246	B1
East Hagbourne	E Hag	218	C3
East Hanney	E Hann	197	D3
East Hendred	E Hen	216	C4
Eastleach Martin	Ea Mar	131	D4
Elsfield	Elsf	110	B1
Enstone	Enst	58	C3
Epwell	Epw	13	D3
Ewelme	Ewel	204	C2
Eynsham	Eyns	120	C4
Faringdon	Far	172	C2
Farnborough (Warks)	Farn	3	F4
Farnborough (Berks)	Farnb	233	F1
Fawley	Faw	226	B1
Fernham	Fern	193	D2
Fifield	Fif	69	E1
Filkins	Filk	132	B3
Finmere	Fin	39	E4
Finstock	Fins	88	B3
Forest Hill	For H	125	F2
Freeland	Free	106	A4
Fringford	Frin	52	B3
Fritwell	Frit	49	F4
Fulbrook	Fulb	100	C4
Fyfield	Fyf	157	E1
Garford	Garf	177	E3
Garsington	Gars	143	F1
Godington	Gdtn	53	F2
Goring	Gori	249	E3
Great Barrington	Gt Bar	99	E4
Great Bourton	Gt Bo	9	E4
Great Coxwell	Gt Cox	192	B4
Great Haseley	G Has	164	C4
Great Milton	G Mil	145	E1
Great Rollright	Gr Ro	29	D2
Great Tew	Gt Tew	45	E4
Grove	Grove	196	C1
Haddenham	Hadd	130	C3
Hailey	Hail	104	A3
Hampton Poyle	H Poy	93	D2
Hanwell	Hanw	8	C2
Hardwick	Hard	51	E4
Hardwick	Hardw	136	C4
Harwell	Harw	217	F4
Henley-on-Thames	Hen-on-T	244	B1
Hethe	Hethe	52	A4
Highworth	Highw	190	A3
Hinton Waldrist	H Wald	155	F2
Holton	Holt	126	B1
Hook Norton	Ho No	30	A4
Horley	Horl	8	A2
Hornton	Horn	7	E4
Horspath	Hors	143	E3
Horton-cum-Studley	Hor-c-S	111	F3
Ibstone	Ibst	207	F4
Ickford	Ick	128	A2
Idbury	Idb	69	D2
Ilmer	Ilm	149	F4
Islip	Islip	109	F4
Kelmscot	Kelms	151	E2
Kencot	Kenc	132	C3
Kennington	Kenn	141	F1
Kiddington	Kidd	60	A1
Kidlington	Kidl	92	C1
Kidmore End	K End	252	B2
Kingham	King	55	D2
Kings Sutton	K Sut	23	F3
Kingston Bagpuize	K Bag	156	C1
Kingston Lisle	K Lis	212	A2
Kirtlington	Kirt	77	F2
Lambourn	Lamb	229	E1
Langford	Lang	132	B1
Launton	Laun	66	B1
Leafield	Leaf	86	C2
Lechlade	Lech	150	B2
Letcombe Bassett	Let B	231	F4
Lewknor	Lewk	187	D4
Little Compton	Li Co	26	C1
Little Coxwell	Li Cox	192	C4
Little Faringdon	Li Far	150	C4
Little Milton	L Mil	164	A3
Little Tew	Li Tew	45	D3
Littleworth	Little	173	F4
Long Compton	Lo Co	27	F3
Long Crendon	L Cre	129	D3
Long Hanborough	Lo Han	90	B1
Long Wittenham	Lo Wit	201	E4
Longcot	Long	192	B1
Longworth	Longw	156	B2
Lower Heyford	Lo Hey	62	B3
Lower Odington	Lo Od	54	A4
Ludgershall	Lud	98	B4
Lyneham	Lyne	70	C3
Mapledurham	Maple	257	F3
Marcham	March	178	B3
Marsh Gibbon	M Gib	67	F2
Marston	Mars	123	F3
Merton	Mert	95	E4
Middle Barton	Mi Bar	46	C1
Middleton Cheney	Mid Ch	11	D1
Middleton Stoney	Mi Sto	64	A2
Milcombe	Milc	21	D1
Milton (Abingdon)	Mil	199	E3
Milton (Banbury)	Milt	22	B2
Milton under Wychwood	M u Wy	85	D4
Minster Lovell	M Lov	102	C1
Mixbury	Mix	38	B4
Mollington	Moll	4	A2
Moulsford	Moul	238	C2
Murcott	Mur	95	F2
Nettlebed	Nett	224	B1
Newton Purcell	Nwtn P	39	D1
Noke	Noke	110	B4
North Aston	N Ast	48	A3
North Hinksey Village	N Hink	140	C4
North Leigh	N Lei	105	D4
North Moreton	N Mor	219	F4
North Newington	N New	15	D2
Northmoor	Nrthm	138	B1
Nuneham Courtenay	Nu Cou	161	F2
Oddington	Odd	94	C1
Over Norton	O Nor	42	C3
Oxford	Oxon	123	F1
Pangbourne	Pangb	256	B3
Piddington	Pidd	97	F4
Poundon	Pndn	67	F4
Preston Bissett	Pres B	53	F4
Purley on Thames	Purl	257	D3
Radley	Radl	160	C2
Ramsden	Rams	88	A2
Ratley	Rat	2	A2
Reading	Read	258	B1
Rotherfield Peppard	R Pep	252	C4
Salford	Sal	41	F3
Sandford St Martin	S St M	46	B1
Sandford-on-Thames	Sa-on-T	161	D4
Shabbington	Shab	128	B2
Shalstone	Shal	25	F3
Shellingford	Shell	194	A4
Shenington	Shen	6	C1
Shilton	Shilt	115	D3
Shiplake	Shipl	254	C1
Shipton under Wychwood	S u Wy	85	F4
Shipton-on-Cherwell	Sh-on-C	92	A3
Shotteswell	Shot	8	B4
Shrivenham	Shrive	209	D4
Shutford	Shut	14	A3
Sibford Ferris	Si Fe	19	D4
Sibford Gower	Si Go	19	D4
Sonning	Sonn	260	C2
Sonning Common	S Com	252	C3
Souldern	Soul	35	F2
South Hinksey	S Hink	141	E3
South Leigh	S Lei	119	E3
South Moreton	S Mor	219	F3
South Newington	S New	31	F4
South Stoke	S Sto	239	D2
Southrop	Srop	131	D2
Sparsholt	Spars	212	C2
Spelsbury	Spel	72	C4
Stadhampton	Stadh	163	E1
Standlake	Stand	137	E2
Stanford in the Vale	S in V	194	C4
Stanton Harcourt	Sta Ha	137	F4
Stanton St John	St S J	125	F4
Steeple Aston	Ste As	62	A4
Steventon	Steve	198	C2
Stoke Lyne	S Lyn	51	D3
Stoke Row	St Row	241	F2
Stoke Talmage	Sto Ta	165	F2
Stokenchurch	Skch	188	C3
Stonesfield	Stone	89	E4
Stonor	Ston	225	F3
Stratton Audley	S Adly	52	B1
Streatley	Stre	249	D4
Sunningwell	Sunn	159	F3
Sutton Courtenay	Sut C	200	A4
Swalcliffe	Swal	19	F4
Swerford	Swer	30	C2
Swinbrook	Swin	101	F3
Sydenham	Syd	167	E4
Tackley	Tack	77	E3
Tadmarton	Tad	20	B4
Taynton	Tayn	100	A4
Tetsworth	Tet	166	A4
Thame	Tha	147	F4
Tiddington	Tidd	145	F4
Tidmarsh	Tidm	256	B1
Tingewick	Ting	39	F3
Towersey	Tow	148	C4
Turweston	Turw	24	B4
Uffington	Uff	211	E4
Upper Arncott	U Arn	96	C4
Upper Heyford	Up Hey	62	C4
Upton	Upt	218	B1
Wallingford	Wall	221	D3
Wantage	Want	214	C2
Warborough	Warb	203	D4
Wardington	Ward	5	F1
Wargrave	Warg	255	E1
Warkworth	Wark	17	E3
Warmington	Warm	3	D2
Watchfield	Watch	191	F1
Waterperry	Wtpy	127	D1
Watlington	Watl	186	B1
Wendlebury	Wend	80	A2
West Hagbourne	W Hag	218	B2
West Hanney	W Hann	196	C3
West Ilsley	West I	235	D1
Westbury	West	25	D2
Weston-on-the-Green	W-on-G	79	D1
Wheatley	Wheat	144	A4
Whichford	Whi	18	A1
Whitchurch	Whitc	256	B4
Wigginton	Wigg	31	D4
Witney	Witn	104	B1
Woodcote	Woodc	240	B1
Woodstock	Wood	91	D3
Woolstone	Wool	211	D2
Wootton (Kidlington)	Woott	75	F3
Wootton (Oxford)	Woot	159	D4
Worminghall	Worm	127	F3
Wormleighton	Wor	1	A4
Wroxton	Wrox	15	D4
Wytham	Wyth	122	A3
Yarnton	Yarn	108	A3

Abberbury Ave. Oxon 142 A2
Abberbury Rd. Oxon 141 F2
Abbey Cl. Abing 179 F4
Abbey Pl. Eyns 120 C4
Abbey Pl. Oxon 141 D4
Abbey Rd. Banb 16 A4
Abbey Rd. Oxon 123 D1
Abbey Rd. Witn 117 F4
Abbey St. Eyns 120 C4
Abbot Ridge. L Cre 129 E3
Abbot Wlk. L Cre 129 E3
Abbots Wlk. Lech 150 B2
Abbots Wood (E). Oxon 142 C4
Abbots Wood (W). Oxon 142 C4
Abbott Cl. Didc 218 C4
Abbott Rd. Abing 179 F4
Abbott Rd. Didc 218 C4
Abelwood Rd. Lo Han 90 A1
Abingdon Dr. Caver 259 E3
Abingdon Rd. Cart 115 F2
Abingdon Rd. Cl Ham 181 E2
Abingdon Rd. Culh 180 B2
Abingdon Rd. Cumn 139 F2
Abingdon Rd. Didc 201 D1
Abingdon Rd. Dorch 182 B2
Abingdon Rd. Dray 179 D1
Abingdon Rd. Kenn 141 E2
Abingdon Rd. Oxon 141 E3
Abingdon Rd. Stand 137 E2
Abingdon Rd. Steve 199 D3
Abingdon Rd. Sut C 180 A1
Abotts Mead. Chol 239 D4
Abrahams Rd. Hen-on-T 244 D2
Acacia Cl. Cart 115 F1
Acacia Gdns. K Bag 156 C1
Acacia Wlk. Banb 9 D1
Acorn Way. Banb 9 F1
Acre End St. Eyns 120 C4
Acremead Rd. Wheat 143 F4
Adderbury Ct. Adde 23 D2
Adderbury Park. Adde 22 C2
Addiscombe Chase. Purl 257 D2
Addison Cres. Oxon 141 F3
Addison Dr. Oxon 142 B2
Addison Rd. Banb 16 B2
Addison Rd. Read 259 D1
Adeane Rd. Chalg 184 B4
Adelaide St. Oxon 123 D2
Adkin Way. Want 214 B3
Adwell Sq. Hen-on-T 244 B1
Akeman Ave. Ambr 81 E2
Akeman Cl. Kirt 78 A3
Akeman St. Combe 90 A3
Akers La. Br-c-S 202 C1
Alan Bullock Cl. Oxon 123 F1
Albermarle Dr. Grove 214 B4
Albert Rd. Caver 258 C2
Albert Rd. Hen-on-T 244 C1
Albert St. Banb 16 B3
Albert St. Oxon 123 D1
Albion Pl. Ch No 42 C2
Albion Pl. Oxon 141 E4
Albion St. Ch No 42 C2
Albury Cl. Read 258 B1
Albury View. Tidd 146 A3
Alchester Rd. Chest 80 A4
Alchester Terr. Bice 65 F1
Aldbarton Dr. Oxon 124 C2
Aldbourne Cl. Bice 65 E1
Aldeburgh Cl. Caver 259 E4
Alden Cres. Oxon 124 C2
Aldenham Cl. Caver 259 E3
Alder Dr. Ambr 81 E2
Aldergate Rd. Bice 65 E1
Alderley Cl. Cart 115 E1
Alderley Cl. Sonn 260 C1
Aldrich Rd. Cutte 123 D4
Aldridge Cl. Bens 204 A2
Aldsworth Ct. Witn 117 F4
Aldworth Ave. Want 214 C3
Alesworth Gr. Oxon 124 A3
Alexander Cl. Abing 160 A2
Alexander Cl. Upt 218 B1
Alexandra Rd. Oxon 122 C1
Alexandra Sq. Ch No 42 B1
Alfred St. Oxon 123 E1
Alfred St. Want 214 B2
Alfred Terraces. Ch No 42 C1
Alfredstone Pl. Want 214 C2
Alfriston Pl. Banb 9 D1
Alice Smith Sq. Oxon 142 B1
Alister Taylor Ave. Bens 204 B1
All Hallows Rd. Caver 259 E2
All Saints Cl. March 178 B3
All Saints Ct. Didc 200 C1
All Saints La. Sut C 180 A1
All Saints Rd. Oxon 124 B1
Allam St. Oxon 123 D2
Allder Cl. Abing 159 F1
Allectus Ave. Ambr 81 E2
Allens La. Up Hey 48 C1
Allens Orch. Ch Wa 5 F3
Alley The. Charl 73 D2
Allin Cl. Oxon 142 C2
Allin's La. E Hen 216 B4
Allison Gdns. Purl 257 E3
Allnatt Ave. Wall 221 E4
Allnut Cl. Watl 186 A1
Alma Green. St Row 242 A2
Alma Pl. Oxon 141 F4
Almond Ave. Kidl 108 C3
Almond Dr. Caver 259 F2
Almond Rd. Bice 65 F2
Alpha Ave. Gars 143 E1
Alston Wlk. Caver 259 E1
Altus St. Up Hey 63 D4
Alvescot Rd. Cart 115 E1
Alvis Gate. Banb 15 F4
Amberley Ct. Banb 9 D1
Ambleside Dr. Oxon 124 A2
Ambrose Rise. Wheat 144 B4
Ambury Rd. Aldw 247 F2
Amersham Rd. Caver 259 E1
Amey Cres. Woot 159 D3
Amory Cl. Oxon 142 B2
Amos Ct. Banb 16 B3
Ampney Orch. Bamp 134 C2
Amwell Pl. Chol 220 C1
Amyoe Cl. Abing 160 A1
Ancastle Gr. Hen-on-T 244 B1
Anchor La. S Mor 220 A2
Ancil Ave. Laun 66 B1
Andersey Way. Abing 179 F2
Anderson Cl. Skch 188 C2
Andersons Cl. Kidl 108 B4
Andover Cl. Bice 66 A2
Andover Cl. Read 257 E1
Andover La. Cart 115 F1
Andover Rd. Bens 204 B2
Andrew Rd. Wall 203 D1
Andrews Ave. Crou 36 C3
Andromeda Cl. Oxon 142 C1
Angelica Cl. Oxon 142 C1
Angle Field Rd. Caver 259 E2
Angus Cl. Banb 16 A4
Annesley Cl. Bletch 93 D4
Annesley Rd. Oxon 142 A2
Ansell Way. Lyne 70 B3
Anson Ave. Cart 115 F1
Anson Cl. March 178 B3
Anson Cl. Wheat 144 B4
Anson Rd. Bens 204 B2
Anson Way. Bice 66 A2
Anthony Hill Rd. Bens 204 B1
Anvil La. Let B 214 A1
Anvil Paddock. Let B 214 A1
A P Ellis Rd. Ch We 68 A2
Apley Way. Witn 117 F4
Apple Cl. Purl 257 D2
Appleby Cl. Banb 15 F4
Appleford Dr. Abing 160 A1
Appleford Rd. Sut C 180 A1
Appleton Rd. Cumn 139 E2
Appleton Rd. K Bag 156 B2
Appleton Rd. Longw 156 B2
Appletree Cl. S Com 252 C3
Appletree Rd. Ch Wa 5 F3
Approach The. Bice 65 E2
Apsley Rd. Cutte 123 D4
Arbury Banks. Ch Wa 5 F3
Arbury Cl. Banb 16 C1
Arcade The. Gori 249 E3
Arcade The. Wall 221 E4
Archery Rd. Mid Ch 11 D1
Archway Rd. Caver 259 D1
Ardington La. Grove 197 F1
Ardler Rd. Caver 259 E1
Ardley Rd. Buck 64 A2
Ardley Rd. Mi Sto 50 B2
Argentan Cl. Abing 179 E2
Argosy Cl. Chalg 184 C3
Argosy Rd. Bens 204 B2
Argosy Rd. Cart 115 F1
Argyle St. Oxon 141 F3
Aristotle La. Oxon 123 D2
Arkell Ave. Cart 115 E1
Arkwright Rd. Bice 66 A2
Arlington Cl. Cart 115 F1
Arlington Dr. Mars 123 F3
Armour Hill. Read 257 E1
Armour Rd. Read 257 E1
Arncott Rd. Pidd 97 E4
Arncott Wood Rd. U Arn 96 C3
Arnold Way. Tha 147 F4
Arnold Rd. Oxon 141 F3
Arnold's Way. N Hink 140 B4
Arons Mead. Hen-on-T 244 B1
Arran Gr. Banb 16 B3
Arrow Cl. Mid Ch 11 D1
Arthray Rd. N Hink 140 B4
Arthur Evans Cl. Woot 159 D3
Arthur Garrard Cl. Oxon 123 D2
Arthur St. Oxon 123 D1
Arun Mews. Didc 201 D1
Arundel Cl. Cart 115 E1
Arundel Cl. K Sut 23 F3
Arundel Pl. Banb 15 F3
Ascott Rd. S u Wy 85 E4
Ash Cl. Far 172 C2
Ash Cl. Kidl 108 C4
Ash Cl. Watl 186 A1
Ash Gr. Chest 79 F4
Ash Gr. Oxon 124 B2
Ash La. Ambr 81 E2
Ashburton La. Ho No 30 A3
Ashbury Hill. Ashb 228 A3
Ashby Ct. Banb 16 B3
Ashby Rd. Bice 65 E1
Ashcombe Cl. Witn 118 A4
Ashcroft Cl. Caver 258 C3
Ashcroft Cl. N Hink 122 A1
Ashcroft Rd. Banb 16 B1
Ashdene Rd. Bice 65 E1
Ashdown Way. Grove 214 B4
Ashenden Cl. Abing 159 F1
Ashfield Rd. Cart 115 F1
Ashfields Cl. E Hann 197 E4
Ashfields La. E Hann 197 E4
Ashford Ave. S Com 252 C3
Ashgate. Abing 179 F2
Ashhurst Way. Oxon 142 A2
Ashlee Wk. Woodc 250 C4
Ashlong Rd. Mars 124 A3
Ashmole Pl. Oxon 142 C2
Ashmole Rd. Abing 179 F2
Ashridge Cl. Banb 16 B1
Ashridge. Chin 168 A3
Ashville Way. Oxon 142 C2
Asquith Rd. Oxon 142 A2
Astley Ave. Kidl 108 C3
Astley Rd. Tha 130 A1
Aston Cl. Abing 179 F4
Aston Cl. Banb 16 C1
Aston Cl. Pangb 256 B3
Aston Cl. Wall 221 E4
Aston Hill. Ast R 187 F4
Aston Park. Ast R 167 E1
Aston Rd. Duck 118 A1
Aston Rd. Stand 137 D2
Aston St. Ast T 237 F4
Aston St. Oxon 141 F4
Astrop Rd. K Sut 23 F3
Astrop Rd. Mid Ch 17 F3
Astrop Rd. Wark 17 F3
Atkinson Cl. Oxon 124 C3
Atkyns Rd. Oxon 142 C4
Atnho Rd. Adde 23 E2
Atwell Cl. Wall 221 E4
Atwell Pl. Oxon 124 B1
Aubrey Ct. Oxon 142 A2
Auburn Ct. Caver 259 D1
Audlett Dr. Abing 180 A4
Austen Wlk. Bice 65 E1
Austin Dr. Banb 15 F4
Austin Pl. Abing 159 F1
Austin Rd. Bod 22 C4
Austin's Way. Ho No 30 B4
Autumn Cl. Caver 259 E4
Autumn Wlk. Warg 255 E1
Avenue Four. Witn 118 A4
Avenue La. Oxon 141 F4
Avenue One. Witn 118 A3
Avenue Rd. Banb 16 C3
Avenue Rd. Bourt 209 D2
Avenue The. Blox 21 E2
Avenue The. Chin 168 B3
Avenue The. Gt Tew 45 E4
Avenue The. Kenn 160 C4
Avenue The. Wheat 144 B4
Avenue The. Worm 127 F3
Avenue Three. Witn 118 A3
Avenue Two. Witn 118 A3
Avocet Way. Banb 16 C2
Avon Carrow. Av Da 3 D4
Avon Cres. Bice 65 D2
Avon Rd. Abing 159 E1
Avon Rd. Harw 217 E1
Avonbury Ct. Brac 24 A3
Avro Rd. Ch We 68 A3
Axis Rd. Watch 191 F1
Axtell Cl. Kidl 92 B1
Aylesbury Rd. Hadd 130 B3
Aylesbury Rd. Tha 130 B3
Ayrshire Cl. Banb 9 D1
Aysgarth Rd. Yarn 108 A3
Azalea Ave. Kidl 108 C3
Azalea Wlk. Banb 9 D1
Azor's Ct. Oxon 142 A2

Bablock Hythe Rd. Apple 139 D2
Back La. Aston 135 E2
Back La. Duck 118 A2
Back La. Eyns 120 C4
Back La. Lo Co 28 A3
Back Row. Adle 40 B2
Back St. Skch 188 C3
Back St. Tet 166 A4
Backside La. Si Go 19 D4
Backsideans. Warg 255 E1
Bader Dr. Up Hey 63 E4
Badgemoor La. Hen-on-T 244 B2
Badger Cl. For H 125 F2
Badger La. S Hink 141 D1
Badger Way. Banb 16 C1
Badgers Copse. Abing 160 C1
Badgers Rise. Caver 259 D3
Badgers Wlk. Shipl 255 D2
Badswell La. Apple 158 A4
Bagley Cl. Kenn 141 F1
Bagley Wood Rd. Kenn 160 B4
Bailey Cl. Want 214 B3
Bailey Rd. Oxon 142 B2
Bailie Cl. Abing 179 F3
Bainton Rd. Buck 65 D4
Bainton Rd. Hethe 52 A4
Bainton Rd. Oxon 123 D3
Bakehouse La. Shot 8 B4
Baker Ave. Bens 204 B1
Baker Cl. Bens 204 B1
Baker Cl. Buck 65 F4
Baker Cl. Oxon 124 C1
Baker Rd. Abing 179 F3
Baker St. Ast T 237 F4
Baker's Piece. Ast R 167 F2
Bakers La. E Hag 218 C3
Bakers La. Let B 214 A1
Bakers La. Oxon 141 F2
Bakers La. S New 31 F4
Bakers La. Swal 19 F4
Bakers La. Tad 20 B4
Bakers Piece. Witn 104 A1
Bakery La. Let B 214 A1
Baldon La. Nu Cou 161 F2
Baldons Cl. Woodc 250 C4
Balfour Cotts. Cl Ham 182 A3
Balfour Rd. Oxon 142 C2
Balham's La. Ibst 225 F4
Balham's La. Ston 225 F4
Ball Lane. Tack 77 D3
Ballard Chase. Abing 160 A2
Ballard Cl. Mi Bar 46 C1
Ballards Cl. S u Wy 85 E4
Balliol Cl. Tack 77 E3
Balliol Dr. Didc 219 D4
Balliol Rd. Bice 65 F2
Balliol Rd. Caver 258 B2
Balmoral Ave. Banb 15 F2
Balmoral Ave. Banb 15 F3
Balmoral Cl. Didc 219 D4
Balmoral Way. K Sut 23 F3
Balmore Dr. Caver 259 D2
Balmore Park. Caver 259 D2
Bampton Cl. Oxon 142 B2
Bampton Rd. Aston 135 E1
Bampton Rd. Clan 133 F1
Bampton Rd. Curb 117 D2
Banbury Rd. Sh-on-C 92 A3
Banbury Gdns. Caver 259 E2
Banbury Hill. Charl 73 E3
Banbury La. K Sut 23 F3
Banbury La. Mid Ch 10 C1
Banbury Rd Crossing. Ch No 42 C2
Banbury Rd. Adde 23 D3
Banbury Rd. Ayn 35 E4
Banbury Rd. Bice 65 F2
Banbury Rd. Blox 21 F3
Banbury Rd. Ch No 42 C2
Banbury Rd. Ch Wa 5 F3
Banbury Rd. Chac 10 B2
Banbury Rd. Cutte 109 D1
Banbury Rd. Dedd 33 F3
Banbury Rd. Kidl 92 B1
Banbury Rd. N New 15 E2
Banbury Rd. O Nor 43 E3
Banbury Rd. Oxon 123 D3
Banbury Rd. Shut 14 A3
Banbury Rd. Swer 30 B1
Banbury Rd. Tack 76 C2
Banbury Rd. Warm 3 D1
Banbury Rd. Wood 91 E4
Bandet Way. Tha 148 A3
Banesberie Cl. Banb 9 D1
Banjo Rd. Oxon 142 B3
Banks Furlong. Chest 79 F4
Bankside. Banb 16 C2
Bankside. E Hen 216 A3
Bankside. Kidl 92 B1
Bankside. Oxon 124 C2
Bannister Rd. Tha 148 B4
Barbara's Meadow. Purl 257 D1
Barbrook Cl. Read 257 E2
Barbury Dr. Grove 214 B4
Barclose Ave. Caver 259 E2
Barcombe Cl. Banb 8 C1
Barcote La. Buckl 174 A3
Bardolph's Cl. Maple 258 B4
Bardwell Rd. Oxon 123 E2
Bardwell Terr. Bice 65 F1
Barfleur Cl. Abing 160 A2
Barford Rd. Blox 21 F1
Barford Rd. S New 32 A3
Barksdale Ave. Crou 36 C3
Barley Cl. Lewk 187 D4
Barley Cl. Si Go 19 D4
Barley Cl. Wall 221 E3
Barleycott La. S Hink 141 E2
Barleyfields. Didc 218 B4
Barlow Cl. Milc 21 D1
Barlow Cl. Wheat 143 F4
Barn Cl. Dench 196 A2
Barn Cl. Kidl 108 B4
Barn La. Burf 100 B3
Barn La. Hen-on-T 244 B2
Barn's Rd. Oxon 142 B2
Barnacre. Watl 186 A1
Barnard Cl. Caver 259 E3
Barnards Way. Want 214 C3
Barncroft. Wall 221 E4
Barnes Cl. Didc 218 C4
Barnes Rd. Didc 218 C3
Barnet St. Oxon 142 A4
Barnett Rd. Mid Ch 17 F4
Barnett Rd. Steve 198 C3
Barnett Way. Bens 204 B1
Barnfield Cl. Buck 65 F3
Barnfield. Ch Ba 175 F1
Barns Hay. Mars 123 F3
Barns La. Burf 100 C2
Barons Dr. Chalg 184 B3
Barracks La. Oxon 142 A4
Barracks La. Oxon 142 B3
Barrett St. Oxon 123 D1
Barrett's Way. Sut C 199 F3
Barretts Cl. Stone 89 E4
Barrington Ave. Watch 191 F1
Barrington Cl. Berin 182 B3
Barrington Cl. Oxon 124 B1
Barrington Cl. Witn 117 F4
Barrington Rd. Watch 209 E4
Barrow Hill Cl. Abing 160 B1
Barrow La. Harw 217 F4
Barrow Rd. Abing 179 D4
Barrow Rd. Harw 217 F4
Barry Ave. Bice 65 E2
Barry Pl. Read 259 D1
Bartholomew Ave. Yarn 108 A3
Bartholomew Rd. Oxon 142 B2
Bartlemas Cl. Oxon 142 A4
Bartlemas Rd. Oxon 142 A4
Barton Cl. K Sut 23 F3
Barton La. Abing 180 A4
Barton La. Oxon 124 B2
Barton Rd. Lo Co 27 E4
Barton Rd. Oxon 124 C2
Barton Village Rd. Oxon 124 B3
Barwell. Want 214 B3
Basil Hill Rd. Didc 200 B2
Baskerville La. Shipl 255 D2
Baskerville Rd. S Com 252 C3
Basmore Ave. Shipl 255 D2
Basset Way. Kidl 108 C4
Bassett Ave. Bice 65 F2
Bassett Rd. Let B 231 F4
Bassett Rd. Oxon 124 C2
Batchelors Row. Dedd 33 D2
Bateman St. Oxon 124 B1
Bates La. Soul 35 E2
Bath Pl. Oxon 123 E1
Bath Rd. Banb 16 B3
Bath Rd. Sonn 260 B1
Bath St. Abing 179 F4
Bath St. Oxon 123 F1
Battle Cl. Bice 66 A1
Battle Rd. Bens 204 B1
Battle Rd. Gori 249 F4
Baulking La. K Lis 194 B1
Baulking Rd. Uff 211 F4
Bay Rd. Bice 65 E1
Bay Tree Cl. Oxon 142 A2
Baydon Rd. Bayd 245 E1
Bayliss Rd. Warg 255 E1
Bayliss Yd. Charl 73 D2
Bayswater Farm Rd. Oxon 125 D2
Bayswater Rd. Oxon 124 C2
Bayswater Rd. St S J 125 D4
Beaconsfield Rd. Banb 16 B1
Beagle Cl. Abing 160 B1
Beagles Cl. Kidl 109 D4
Beanacre Rd. Ho No 30 A3
Beanfurlong. Chac 10 C2
Beanhill Rd. Duck 118 A3
Bear Cl. Wood 91 D3
Bear Ct. Burf 100 C3
Bear La. N Mor 220 A4
Bear La. Oxon 123 E1
Bear La. Stadh 163 E1
Bear La. Wall 221 E4
Beargarden Rd. Banb 16 B3
Bears Hedge. Oxon 142 A2
Beatrice Dr. Banb 16 A3
Beauchamp La. Oxon 142 B2
Beauchamp Pl. Oxon 142 A2
Beaufort Cl. Bice 66 A2
Beaufort Cl. Didc 219 D4
Beaulieu Cl. Banb 16 C3
Beaulieu Ct. Sunn 159 F3
Beaumaris Cl. Banb 15 F4
Beaumont Bldgs. Oxon 123 D1
Beaumont Cl. Banb 9 E1
Beaumont La. Oxon 123 E1
Beaumont Pl. Oxon 123 E1
Beaumont Rd. Banb 9 E1
Beaumont Rd. Oxon 124 C2
Beaumont St. Oxon 123 E1
Bec Cl. Want 214 A3
Bec Tithe. Whitc 250 C2
Beckdale Cl. Bice 65 D2
Becket St. Oxon 123 D1
Beckett Ave. Shriv 209 E4
Beckett Dr. Shriv 209 E4
Becketts Cl. Lo Han 90 A1
Beckley Cl. Woodc 250 C4
Beckley Ct. Beck 111 D1
Becquerel Ave. Harw 217 D1
Bedford Cl. Banb 15 F4
Bedford St. Oxon 141 F3
Bedwells Heath. Woot 140 B1
Beech Cl. Far 172 C2
Beech Cl. Skch 188 C2
Beech Cl. Watl 186 A1
Beech Cres. Kidl 108 C3
Beech Croft Rd. Cutte 123 D3
Beech Gr. Fulb 100 C3
Beech La. Woodc 250 B4
Beech Rd. Chin 168 B3
Beech Rd. Eyns 120 C4

Beech Rd. Maple 258 B4
Beech Rd. N Hink 140 B4
Beech Rd. Oxon 124 B2
Beech Rd. Purl 257 D3
Beech Rd. Tha 147 F4
Beech Rd. Wheat 144 A4
Beech Rd. Witn 117 F4
Beech Rise. S Com 252 C3
Beechcroft. Dorch 182 B1
Beeches The. Gori 249 D3
Beeches The. Read 257 E2
Beechey Ave. Mars 123 F2
Beechfield Cres. Banb 16 B2
Beeching Cl. Upt 218 B1
Beechwood Cl. Woodc 250 B3
Beesley Rd. Banb 16 A3
Beeson Cl. Woodc 250 C4
Begbroke Cres. Begb 92 A1
Begbroke La. Begb 92 A1
Beggar's La. Longw 156 B1
Beggarsbush Hill. Bens 204 B1
Behoes La. Woodc 240 B1
Belbroughton Rd. Oxon 123 E3
Belfast Rd. Bens 204 B2
Belgrove Cl. Kidl 108 B4
Bell Cl. Cass 107 F1
Bell Cl. Grove 196 C1
Bell Cl. Tha 129 F1
Bell Hill. Ho No 30 A4
Bell La. Aldw 247 F2
Bell La. Bamp 134 C2
Bell La. Bice 65 F1
Bell La. Br-c-S 202 C1
Bell La. Cass 107 E1
Bell La. Hen-on-T 244 C2
Bell La. Lech 150 B2
Bell La. Tha 129 E1
Bell La. Wheat 144 A4
Bell St. Hen-on-T 244 C1
Bell St. Horn 7 E3
Bell's La. Ho No 30 A4
Bellamy Cl. K Bag 156 C1
Belle Terr. Cart 115 E1
Belle Vue Rd. Hen-on-T 254 B4
Bellenger Way. Kidl 108 B4
Bellingham La. Highw 190 A1
Bellingham Wlk. Caver 259 D3
Belmont Mews. Tha 147 F4
Belmont. Want 214 B3
Belvedere Rd. Oxon 142 A4
Ben Cl. Kidl 92 C1
Benares Gr. St Row 242 A2
Benhams La. Faw 226 B1
Bennett Cl. Chac 10 C2
Bennett End Rd. Bled R 189 E4
Bennett Rd. Far 172 C2
Bensgrove Cl. Woodc 250 C4
Benson Cl. Bice 66 A2
Benson La. Bens 204 A1
Benson La. Cr Gif 221 F4
Benson Pl. Oxon 123 E2
Benson Rd. Abing 159 F1
Benson Rd. Oxon 142 B4
Bentley Cl. Banb 15 F4
Benton Dr. Chin 168 B4
Benwells. Chin 168 B3
Bere Court Rd. Pangb 256 A2
Berens Rd. Shriv 209 D3
Bergen Ave. Abing 179 E2
Berins Hill. Check 241 D3
Berkeley Cl. Banb 15 F4
Berkeley Rd. Sunn 140 C1
Berkeley Rd. Tha 130 A1
Berkshire Rd. Hen-on-T 254 B4
Bernard Cl. Yarn 108 B3
Berner's Way. Far 173 D2
Bernewood Cl. L Cre 129 E4
Bernwood Rd. Bice 65 F1
Bernwood Rd. Oxon 124 C2
Berrick Rd. Chalg 184 B3
Berry Cl. Oxon 142 C2
Berry Croft. Abing 159 F1
Berry Hill Rd. Adde 22 C1
Berry La. Blew 219 D1
Berry La. E Hann 197 D3
Berrylands Rd. Caver 259 D2
Berrymere Rd. Woot 159 D4
Berrymoor Rd. Banb 16 A3
Bertie Pl. Oxon 141 E3
Bertie Rd. Cumn 139 F3
Besbury La. Churc 55 F3
Bessel's Way. Blew 237 D4
Bessels Lea. Blew 219 D1
Besselsleigh Rd. Apple 158 C4
Besselsleigh Rd. Woot 159 D4
Bessemer Cl. Bice 66 A1
Bettina Cres. Banb 9 D1
Betty La. S Hink 141 E2
Between Towns Rd. Oxon 142 B3
Beverley Cl. Abing 159 F1
Beverley Cl. Bens 204 B2
Beverley Cl. Chalg 184 C3
Beverley Cres. Cart 115 F2
Beverley Gdns. Bice 66 A2
Beverley Gdns. Warg 255 F1
Beverley Rd. Read 257 E1
Bevington Rd. Oxon 123 E2
Bicester Rd. Buck 64 C4
Bicester Rd. Enst 58 C3
Bicester Rd. Kidl 109 D4
Bicester Rd. L Cre 129 E3
Bicester Rd. Laun 66 B1
Bicester Rd. Lud 98 B4
Bicester Rd. M Gib 67 F2
Bicester Rd. Mi Sto 64 A2
Bickerton Rd. Oxon 124 B1
Biddel Springs. Highw 190 A3
Biddlesden Rd. West 25 D3
Bier Path The. S Sto 239 D2
Bignell View. Chest 79 F4
Bignolds Cl. Clay 4 B4
Billwell. L Cre 129 E3
Bingley Gr. Sonn 260 C1
Binsey La. Oxon 122 C1
Binswood Ave. Oxon 124 C1
Birch Cl. S Com 252 C2
Birch Rd. Ambr 81 E2
Birch Rd. Gars 143 E1
Birchen Cl. Woodc 250 C4
Birches The. Gori 249 D3
Birchfield Cl. Oxon 142 C1
Birchwood Cl. Caver 259 E3
Birchwood. Banb 16 B2
Birchwood. Cart 115 F1
Bird Cl. Banb 16 A3
Bird Wood Ct. S Com 253 D2
Birds La. Epw 13 D3
Bishop's Wood. Cudd 144 B2
Bishops Cl. B St M 32 C3
Bisley Cl. Bice 66 A2
Bitham Rd. Farnb 233 E4
Bitterell. Eyns 120 C4
Bix Hill. Faw 244 A3
Black Bourton Rd. Cart 115 F1
Black Bourton Rd. Clan 133 F1
Black Croft. Want 214 B3
Black's La. Leaf 86 C1
Blackberry La. Sa-on-T 162 A4
Blackbird Assarts La. Rams 88 A1
Blackbird Leys Rd. Oxon 142 B1
Blackfriars Rd. Oxon 141 D4
Blackhall Rd. Oxon 123 E1
Blackhorse La. March 158 C2
Blacklands Rd. Bens 204 A3
Blacklands Way. Abing 179 E4
Blacklocks Hill. Mid Ch 17 D4
Blackmore La. S Com 253 D3
Blacknall Rd. Abing 179 F3
Blacksmith La. Ch-on-O 95 D2
Blacksmiths Hill. Ayn 35 E4
Blacksmiths La. Moll 4 A2
Blackstone Rd. Wall 203 E1
Blackthorn Cl. Bktn 82 A2
Blackthorn Cl. Oxon 124 C2
Blackthorn Rd. Laun 66 C1
Blackwater Cl. Caver 259 F2
Blackwood Pl. Bod 22 C4
Blackworth. Highw 190 A4
Bladon Cl. Cutte 122 C4
Bladon Rd. Kidl 91 E2
Blagrave Cl. Didc 200 C1
Blagrave La. Caver 258 B2
Blake Rd. Bice 65 F2
Blake Way. Tha 130 A1
Blake's Field. Didc 200 B1
Blakes Ave. Witn 118 B4
Blakes Rd. Warg 255 F2
Blandford Alley. Highw 190 A3
Blandford Ave. Cutte 109 D1
Blandy Ave. K Bag 156 C1
Blandy Rd. Hen-on-T 254 B4
Blay Cl. Oxon 142 C2
Bleache Pl. Oxon 142 B3
Bledlow Rd. Bled R 169 F4
Bledlow Ridge Rd. Bled 169 E4
Blencowe Cl. Buck 65 F3
Blenheim Cl. Didc 200 C1
Blenheim Dr. Bice 65 E2
Blenheim Dr. Cutte 123 D4
Blenheim Dr. Laun 66 C1
Blenheim Dr. Witn 117 F4
Blenheim Gdns. Grove 196 B1
Blenheim Hill. Harw 217 F4
Blenheim La. Free 106 A3
Blenheim Orch. E Hann 197 D3
Blenheim Pl. Bens 204 B1
Blenheim Rd. Banb 16 C1
Blenheim Rd. Caver 259 D2
Blenheim Rd. Kidl 108 C4
Blenheim Rd. L Mil 164 A3
Blenheim Rd. Lewk 186 B2
Blenheim Rise. K Sut 23 F3
Blenheim Way. Hors 143 E4
Blenheim. Crou 36 A4
Blenhiem La. Wheat 144 A4
Bleriot Rd. Ch We 68 A2
Bletchingdon Rd. Bletch 78 A2
Bletchingdon Rd. H Poy 93 D2
Bletchingdon Rd. Islip 93 F1
Blewbury Hill. Blew 237 D4
Blewbury Rd. E Hag 219 D2
Blomfield Pl. Oxon 123 D2
Blossoms Glade. Kenn 160 C3
Blounts Court Rd. S Com 253 D3
Blowings The. Free 106 A4
Blowingstone Hill. K Lis 212 A1
Bloxham Grove Rd. Blox 22 A3
Bloxham Rd. B St M 32 C4
Bloxham Rd. Banb 16 A2
Bloxham Rd. Blox 21 D1
Bloxham Rd. Milc 21 D1
Blue Boar St. Oxon 123 E1
Bluebell Ride. Kenn 160 C4
Blythe Pl. Bice 65 D2
Boddington La. N Lei 105 E4
Bodley Pl. Cutte 123 D4
Bodley Rd. Oxon 142 B2
Boham's Rd. Blew 236 B3
Bolney Rd. Shipl 255 D3
Bolton Rd. Banb 16 B3
Bolton's La. Combe 90 B2
Bonar Rd. Oxon 124 C1
Bones La. Shipl 254 A2
Bonnersfield. L Cre 129 E4
Boot St. Stone 89 E4
Boreford Rd. Abing 160 A1
Borough Ave. Wall 221 E4
Borough Rd. Brac 24 A3
Borough Wlk. Abing 159 F1
Borrowmead Rd. Oxon 124 A3
Bosley Cres. Wall 221 E4
Bosley's Orch. Didc 200 C1
Bosley's Orch. Grove 196 C1
Bostock Rd. Abing 179 F4
Boston Rd. Bice 66 A2
Boston Rd. Hen-on-T 254 C4
Boswell Rd. Oxon 142 B2
Bothy The. Ayn 35 E4
Bothy The. Warg 255 E1
Botley Rd. Oxon 122 C1
Bottle Square La. Bled R 189 E3
Bottom La. Check 241 D2
Boucher Cl. Grove 214 B4
Boulevard The. Kidl 92 A1
Boulter Dr. Abing 160 A2
Boulter St. Oxon 123 F1
Boults Cl. Mars 123 F3
Boults La. Mars 123 F3
Boundary Brook Rd. Oxon 142 A3
Boundary Cl. Wood 91 E3
Boundary Rd. Brac 24 A3
Bourne Cl. Bice 65 E1
Bourne Cl. Cutte 109 D1
Bourne La. Ho No 30 A4
Bourne Rd. Pangb 256 C3
Bourne St. Didc 218 C4
Bourne The. Ea Mar 131 D4
Bourne The. Ho No 30 A4
Bourton Cl. Clan 133 F1
Bourton Cl. Witn 117 F4
Bovewell. Soul 35 F2
Bovingdon Rd. Cart 115 F2
Bow Rd. S in V 174 C1
Bowbank Cl. Longw 156 B2
Bowbank. Longw 156 B2
Bower Green. Watch 191 F1
Bowerman Cl. Kidl 108 B4
Bowers La. Bled R 189 E4
Bowfell Cl. Read 257 E1
Bowgrave Copse. Abing 160 B1
Bowling Ct. Hen-on-T 244 B2
Bowling Gr. Skch 188 B3
Bowling Green Cl. Bamp 134 C2
Bowling Green La. Purl 257 D3
Bowmen's Lea. Ayn 35 E4
Bowmont Sq. Bice 65 D1
Bowness Ave. Didc 218 B4
Bowness Ave. Oxon 124 A2
Bowyer Rd. Abing 179 F4
Box Tree La. Ast R 166 C2
Boxhedge Rd W. Banb 16 A3
Boxhedge Rd. Banb 16 A3
Boxhedge Sq. Banb 16 A3
Boxhill Rd. Abing 179 F4
Boxhill Wlk. Abing 179 F4
Boxwell Cl. Abing 160 A1
Bracegirdle Rd. Oxon 124 C1
Bracken Cl. Cart 115 E2
Bracken Cl. Read 257 E1
Brackley Rd. Crou 36 B4
Brackley Rd. West 25 D3
Brading Way. Purl 257 E3
Bradlands. Mars 123 F4
Bradley Rd. Nett 224 A3
Bradley's St. Check 241 D2
Bradmore Rd. Oxon 123 E2
Bradshaw Cl. Ste As 62 A4
Bradstock's Way. Sut C 199 F3
Bradwell Rd. Read 257 E2
Braithwaite Cl. Banb 16 A3
Bramber Cl. Banb 15 F4
Bramber Mews. Caver 259 F2
Brambling Way. Oxon 142 B1
Bramley Cres. S Com 252 C3
Brampton Chase. Shipl 255 D2
Brampton Dr. Cart 115 F1
Brampton Rd. Oxon 124 C2
Bramshaw Rd. Read 258 A1
Brandon Cl. Kidl 108 B4
Brantwood Rise. Banb 16 A2
Brasenose Dr. Kidl 92 C1
Brasenose Driftway. Oxon 142 C3
Brasenose La. Oxon 123 E1
Brasenose Rd. Didc 200 B1
Brashfield Rd. Bice 65 F2
Braybrooke Gdns. Warg 255 E1
Braybrooke Rd. Warg 255 E1
Braze La. Bens 204 A3
Braziers La. Cr Gif 240 C3
Breedons Hill. Pangb 256 B3
Brenda Cl. Banb 16 A2
Brendon Cl. Read 257 F1
Brentford Cl. Chol 220 C1
Brereton Dr. Grove 196 B1
Bretch Hill. Banb 15 F3
Brett Cl. Tha 148 A4
Brewer St. Oxon 141 E4
Brewers Ct. Abing 179 F3
Brewery La. Ho No 29 F4
Brewery Row. Li Co 26 C1
Brewery St. Highw 190 A3
Briaily. B Bot 189 E1
Briant's Ave. Caver 259 E1
Briar Cl. Banb 16 B1
Briar Cl. Caver 259 D3
Briar Thicket. Wood 91 E3
Briar Way. Oxon 142 C2
Briars Cl. Pangb 256 C3
Briary Rd. Lech 150 B3
Brice Rd. Up Hey 63 E4
Brick Hill. Ho No 30 A3
Brickle La. Blox 21 F3
Bricks La. Bled R 189 E2
Bridens Way. Hadd 130 C3
Bridewell Cl. N Lei 105 D4
Bridge Cl. Didc 219 D4
Bridge End. Dorch 202 B4
Bridge Farm Cl. Grove 214 C4
Bridge Rd. Ick 127 F1
Bridge St. Abing 179 F4
Bridge St. Bamp 134 C2
Bridge St. Banb 16 B3
Bridge St. Caver 259 D1
Bridge St. Islip 109 F4
Bridge St. Oxon 123 D1
Bridge St. Witn 104 A1
Bridges Cl. Abing 179 E3
Bridgewater Cl. Read 258 B1
Bridle Cl. Banb 16 C2
Bridle Path. Woodc 250 C4
Bridle Rd. Whitc 250 C2
Bridus Mead. Blew 219 D1
Brierley Pl. Purl 257 E2
Briggs Cl. Banb 15 F2
Brigham Rd. Read 259 D1
Brill Cl. Caver 259 D2
Brill Rd. Lud 98 A4
Brinds Cl. S Com 253 D3
Brinkburn Gr. Banb 16 C4
Brinkinfield Rd. Chalg 184 B4
Bristol Rd. Bice 66 A2
Bristol Rd. Ch We 68 A3
Britannia Cl. Cart 115 F2
Britannia Rd. Banb 16 B3
Britwell Rd. Didc 200 C1
Britwell Rd. Ewel 204 C2
Britwell Rd. Watl 186 A1
Brixton Hill. Bens 223 D2
Brize Norton Rd. Cart 115 F1
Brize Norton Rd. M Lov 102 C1
Brizewood. Cart 115 E2
Broad Cl. B St M 32 C3
Broad Cl. Kidl 108 B4
Broad Cl. N Hink 122 A1
Broad Gap. Bod 16 C1
Broad Marsh La. Free 106 A3
Broad Oak. Oxon 142 C4
Broad St. Abing 179 F4
Broad St. Bamp 134 C2
Broad St. Banb 16 B3
Broad St. Lo Co 27 F3
Broad St. Oxon 123 E1
Broad St. Uff 211 E4
Broad Way. Uff 211 E3
Broadbrook La. Spars 212 C2
Broadfields. Oxon 142 B1
Broadhead Pl. Oxon 124 A3
Broadhurst Gdns. Oxon 142 A1
Broadmarsh Cl. Grove 214 B4
Broadwaters Ave. Tha 147 F4
Broadway Cl. Harw 217 F3
Broadway The. Ch-on-O 95 D2
Broadway. Didc 218 C4
Broadway. Harw 217 F3
Broadway. Kidl 108 C3
Broadwell Ct. Bice 65 E1
Broadwell Rd. Lang 132 B1
Brocklesby Rd. Oxon 142 A1
Brocks Way. Shipl 255 D2
Brode Cl. Abing 160 A1
Brogden Cl. N Hink 140 C4
Brome Pl. Oxon 124 C2
Bromeswell Cl. Lo Hey 62 C3
Bromsgrove. Far 172 C2
Brook Cl. Lud 98 B4
Brook Hill. Wood 91 D3
Brook La. Dench 196 A2
Brook La. Tha 129 F1
Brook La. Tha 147 F4
Brook La. W Hag 218 B3
Brook Rd. Bice 65 E2
Brook Rd. Gt Tew 45 E4
Brook St. Ast R 167 F2
Brook St. Bens 204 A2
Brook St. Oxon 141 E4
Brook St. Sut C 200 A4
Brook St. Watl 186 A1
Brook View. Gars 143 D1
Brook Way. Lo Han 90 A1
Brooke Rd. Banb 16 A2
Brookfield Cl. Chol 221 E3
Brookfield Cl. M u Wy 70 A1
Brookfield Cres. Oxon 124 A3
Brookhampton Cl. Stadh 163 E1
Brooklyn Dr. Caver 259 D3
Brookmead Dr. Wall 221 E3
Brooksby Rd. Read 257 E1
Brookside Cl. Tidd 145 F4
Brookside Estate. Chalg 184 B4
Brookside Way. Blox 21 E2
Brookside. Abing 159 F1
Brookside. Chol 220 C1
Brookside. E Hann 197 D3
Brookside. Gt Tew 45 E4
Brookside. Harw 217 F4
Brookside. Ho No 30 A4
Brookside. Oxon 124 B1
Brookside. Tha 129 F1
Brookside. Watl 186 A1
Broome Way. Banb 16 C4
Broomfield Rd. Read 258 A1
Broughton Cl. Read 258 B1
Broughton Rd. Banb 15 F2
Broughtons Cl. Mars 123 F3
Brown's La. Charl 73 D2
Brown's La. Wood 91 D3
Browning Dr. Bice 65 E2
Browning Rd. Banb 16 A2
Browns Cl. N Hink 140 A4
Bruern Rd. M u Wy 70 A2
Brumcombe La. Sunn 159 F4
Brunel Cres. Grove 196 B1
Brunel Dr. Sonn 260 C1
Brunel Rd. Didc 218 B4
Bryan Way. Want 214 C3
Bryony Cl. Gars 143 D1
Bryworth La. Lech 150 A3
Buchan Rd. Bice 65 E2
Buchanan Rd. U Arn 96 C4
Buck Side. Caver 259 D1
Buckingham Cl. Didc 219 D4
Buckingham Cres. Bice 65 F2
Buckingham Dr. Caver 259 D3
Buckingham Rd. Bice 65 F2
Buckingham Rd. Brac 24 A3
Buckingham St. Oxon 141 E4
Buckland Rd. Bamp 154 B4
Buckland Rd. Buckl 174 C4
Buckland Rd. Ch Ba 175 F1
Buckler Rd. Cutte 123 D4
Bucklers Bury Rd. Abing 160 A2
Bucknell Ave. Pangb 256 C3
Bucknell Rd. Bice 65 E2
Buckner's Cl. Bens 203 F2
Buckthorn La. Chol 220 C1
Bulan Rd. Oxon 142 C4
Bull Baulk. Mid Ch 11 D1
Bull Baulk. Mid Ch 17 F4
Bull Cl. Filk 132 A3
Bull Hill. Chadl 72 A4
Bull La. Aston 135 F1
Bull Meadow The. Stre 249 D3
Bull Ring. Dedd 33 F2
Bull St. Aston 135 F1
Bullingdon Ave. Berin 182 B3
Bullingdon Rd. Oxon 141 F4
Bullmarsh Cl. Mi Sto 64 A2
Bullockspits La. Longw 176 B4
Bulls La. Ick 128 A2
Bulls La. K Sut 23 F3
Bullsmead. Sunn 159 F3
Bullstake Cl. Oxon 122 C1
Bulrush Rd. Oxon 142 C1
Bulwarks La. Oxon 123 E1
Bunkers Hill. Sh-on-C 77 D1
Bunyan Rd. Bice 65 E2
Burbush Rd. Oxon 142 C3
Burchester Ave. Oxon 124 C2
Burcombe Way. Caver 259 D2
Burcot la. Berin 182 B2
Burcot Park. Cl Ham 181 F3
Burdell Ave. Oxon 125 D2
Burditch Bank. Woot 75 F3
Bure Pl. Bice 65 F1
Burford Rd. B Bou 133 F3
Burford Rd. Br No 115 F4
Burford Rd. Br No 116 A3
Burford Rd. Cart 115 E2
Burford Rd. Ch No 42 C1
Burford Rd. Curb 103 E1
Burford Rd. M Lov 102 B1
Burford Rd. Swin 102 B1
Burford Rd. Witn 103 E1
Burford St. Lech 150 B2
Burgan Cl. Oxon 142 B2
Burleigh Mews. Caver 259 E3
Burlington Cres. Oxon 125 D2
Burlington Gdns. Banb 16 A2
Burnham Rise. Caver 259 E4
Burnhams The. Shab 128 B2
Burns Cl. L Cre 129 E4
Burns Cres. Bice 65 E2
Burns Rd. Banb 16 A2
Burr Cl. Sta Har 120 A1
Burr La. Didc 201 D1

Burr St. Harw 217 F4
Burrows Cl. Oxon 124 B2
Bursill Cl. Oxon 125 D2
Burswin Rd. Cart 115 E3
Burt's La. L Cre 129 E3
Burton Cl. Abing 179 E3
Burton Pl. Oxon 142 C3
Burwell Cl. Witn 117 F4
Burwell Dr. Witn 117 F4
Burwell Meadow. Witn 117 F3
Bury Mead. Sta Har 138 A4
Bury St. Abing 179 F4
Burycroft Rd. Ho No 30 A3
Burycroft The. Culh 180 A2
Buryhook Cnr. Holt 126 B1
Buryway La. Lo Co 27 F4
Busby Cl. Stone 89 E4
Busby's Cl. Clan 152 C4
Buscot Dr. Abing 160 A1
Busgrove La. St Row 242 A2
Bush The. Hadd 130 C3
Bushey Cl. N Hink 122 A1
Bushey Leys Cl. Oxon 124 C3
Bushy Row. Bamp 134 C2
Butcher's Hill. Gt Tew 45 E4
Butcher's Row. Banb 16 B3
Butler Cl. Blox 21 F3
Butler Cl. Oxon 123 D2
Butler's Field. Lech 150 B3
Butlers Cl. Lo Co 28 A3
Butlers Dr. Cart 115 F1
Butlers Orch. K End 252 B2
Butlers Rd. Lo Co 28 B3
Butterfly Rd. Skch 188 C2
Buttermarket. Tha 147 F4
Buttermilk La. Leaf 86 C1
Butterworth Pl. Oxon 142 C1
Butterwyke Pl. Oxon 141 E4
Butts Cl. Ayn 35 E4
Butts Hill Rd. Sonn 260 C1
Butts La. Mars 123 F4
Butts Rd. Far 172 C1
Butts Rd. Hors 143 E3
Butts The. Ayn 35 E4
Butts The. Mert 95 E4
Butts Way. Ast R 167 E1
Buxton Ave. Caver 258 C2
Buzzards Cl. Gt Bo 9 E3
Byeway The. Banb 16 C4
Byfield Rd. Ch Wa 5 F4
Byres The. Hadd 130 C3
Byron Cl. Abing 179 E3
Byron Rd. Banb 16 A2
Byron Way. Bice 65 E2

Cadogan Park. Wood 91 D3
Caernarvon Way. Banb 15 F3
Caesars Gate. Brac 24 A3
Calais Dene. Bamp 134 C2
Calais La. Hardw 136 C3
Calais La. Stand 136 C3
Calcot Cl. Oxon 124 C1
Calcroft La. Clan 133 E1
Calcroft La. Kenc 132 C2
Caldecott Cl. Abing 179 E3
Calder Way. Didc 201 D1
Caldicott Cl. Warb 203 D3
Caleta Cl. Caver 259 E1
Calthorpe Rd. Banb 16 B3
Calthorpe St. Banb 16 B3
Calves Cl. Kidl 108 B4
Cambrai Cl. Sut C 200 C4
Cambridge Terr. Oxon 141 E4
Camden Cl. B on H 26 C3
Camellias The. Banb 9 D1
Cameron Ave. Abing 160 B1
Camp La. Warm 2 B2
Camp Rd. Rat 2 B2
Camp Rd. Up Hey 63 E4
Campbell Cl. Bice 65 F1
Campbell Rd. Oxon 142 A3
Campbells Cl. Wood 91 E3
Campion Cl. Cart 115 F1
Campion Hall Dr. Didc 219 D4
Campion Rd. Abing 180 A4
Canada La. Far 172 C2
Canal La. Bod 16 C1
Canal St. Banb 16 B3
Canal St. Oxon 123 D1
Canal Way. E Cha 214 A3
Cane La. Grove 214 B4
Canning Cres. Oxon 141 F3
Cannons Field. Mars 123 F3
Canon Hill's Gdns. Shriv 209 E3
Canterbury Cl. Banb 17 D4
Canterbury Rd. Oxon 123 D2
Capel Cl. Cutte 123 D4
Caps La. Chol 221 D1
Cardiff Rd. Read 258 C1
Cardigan St. Oxon 123 D1
Cardigan St. Oxon 123 D2
Cardinal Cl. Caver 259 D1
Cardinal Cl. Oxon 142 A2
Cardwell Cres. Oxon 124 A1
Carey Cl. Cutte 108 C1
Cariad Ct. Gori 249 D4
Carisbrooke Cl. Caver 259 E3
Carling Rd. S Com 252 C3
Carlisle Rd. Read 257 F2
Carlton Cl. Grove 196 B1
Carlton Rd. Caver 258 C3
Carlton Rd. Cutte 109 D1
Caroline St. Oxon 123 F1
Carpenter Cl. Oxon 142 B1
Carr Ave. Cart 115 E1
Carse Cl. Abing 160 A2
Carswell Cres. Up Hey 63 E4
Carswell La. Buckl 154 A1
Carter Cl. Oxon 124 C1
Carter Cres. Far 172 C1
Carters Cl. Cart 115 E1
Carters La. L Cre 129 D4
Carterton Rd. Br No 116 A2
Cartwright Gdns. Ayn 35 E4
Cassington Rd. Cass 121 D4
Cassington Rd. Eyns 121 D4
Cassington Rd. Yarn 108 A3
Castle Cl. Bens 203 F2
Castle Cl. Buck 65 F4
Castle Cres. Shell 193 F4
Castle Fields. Mi Sto 50 A2
Castle La. Wall 221 E4
Castle Rd. Lewk 186 B2
Castle Rd. Woot 75 F3
Castle Shopping Cen. Banb 16 B3
Castle Sq. Bens 203 F2
Castle St. Banb 16 B3
Castle St. Dedd 33 F2
Castle St. M Gib 67 F2
Castle St. Oxon 123 E1
Castle St. Steve 198 C2
Castle St. Wall 221 E4
Castle Wlk. Didc 200 C1
Caswell La. Curb 116 C3
Cat La. Ewel 204 C2
Cat La. Stadh 163 E1
Cat St. E Hen 216 B3
Catharine Cl. Radl 160 C2
Catherine Cl. Shriv 209 E3
Catherine St. Oxon 142 A3
Catmore Cl. Grove 214 B4
Catmore Rd. West I 234 C1
Catsham La. Chadl 72 B3
Catsham La. Chils 72 B3
Catslip. Nett 224 C1
Catte St. Oxon 123 E1
Cattle Mkt. Ch No 42 C2
Caudwell Cl. Dray 179 D1
Caudwell Cl. Grove 196 C1
Causeway The. E Hann 197 D3
Causeway The. Steve 198 C2
Causeway The. Wood 91 D3
Causeway. Banb 16 C3
Causeway. Bice 65 F1
Causeway. Bletch 93 D4
Causmans Way. Read 257 E1
Cavalier Rd. Tha 130 A1
Cavandish Wlk. Tha 130 A1
Cave St. Oxon 123 F1
Cavell Rd. Oxon 142 A3
Cavendish Dr. Mars 123 F3
Cavendish Pl. S Adley 52 B1
Cavendish Rd. Caver 259 E3
Cavendish Rd. Cutte 123 D4
Caversham Park Rd. Caver 259 F3
Caversham Rd. Read 259 D1
Caversham Wharf. Read 259 D1
Cawley Rd. Adde 23 D3
Cawsam Gdns. Caver 259 E2
Caxton Cl. Read 258 B1
Cecil Aldin Dr. Purl 257 E2
Cecil Sharpe Cl. Oxon 124 B1
Cedar Cl. Banb 16 B1
Cedar Cres. Tha 147 F4
Cedar Dr. Bice 65 F2
Cedar Dr. Pangb 256 B2
Cedar Rd. Far 172 C2
Cedar Rd. N Hink 140 B4
Cedar Villa. Banb 16 A3
Cedar Wood Cres. Caver 259 D2
Cedars The. Bens 204 A3
Cedars The. Read 257 E1
Celsea Pl. Chol 221 D1
Cemetery Rd. Abing 179 E4
Cemetery Rd. Bice 65 F1
Centre Rise. Hors 143 E3
Centre St. Banb 16 C4
Centremead. Oxon 141 D4
Chacombe Rd. Mid Ch 10 C1
Chadlington Rd. Oxon 123 E3
Chadlington Rd. Spel 72 C4
Chainhill Rd. Farnb 233 D4
Chainhill Rd. Want 214 C1
Chalcraft Cl. Hen-on-T 254 B4
Chalfont Rd. Oxon 123 D3
Chalford Cl. Ch No 42 C2
Chalford Rd. Ast R 167 D2
Chalgrove Rd. Tha 130 A1
Chalgrove Way. Caver 259 E3
Chalk Farm Rd. Skch 188 B3
Chalk Hill. Ast T 237 F4
Chalk Hill. Shipl 254 B3
Chalkhouse Green La. Maple 253 D1
Chalkhouse Green R. K End 252 C1
Challenor Cl. Abing 179 F2
Challow Rd. Want 214 A3
Chalmore Gdns. Wall 221 E3
Chalvey Cl. Bice 65 E1
Chalvey Rd. Bice 65 E1
Chamberlain Pl. Kidl 92 B1
Champion Rd. Caver 259 E1
Champion Way. Oxon 142 B2
Champs Cl. Abing 160 B1
Chancel Way. Lech 150 B2
Chancel Way. March 178 B4
Chandler Cl. Bamp 134 C2
Chandlers Cl. Abing 160 B1
Chandlers Cl. Want 214 C2
Chapel Cl. Leaf 86 C2
Chapel Cl. S Sto 239 E2
Chapel End. Crou 36 B4
Chapel Hill. Br No 116 A2
Chapel Hill. Swer 30 C2
Chapel Hill. Watch 191 E1
Chapel La. Adde 23 D2
Chapel La. Bens 203 F2
Chapel La. Ber S 204 A4
Chapel La. Bled 54 B1
Chapel La. Blew 237 D4
Chapel La. Bod 22 C4
Chapel La. Ch Ba 175 F1
Chapel La. Chalg 184 B3
Chapel La. Cro 4 C1
Chapel La. Enst 58 C3
Chapel La. Fern 193 D3
Chapel La. Gt Bo 9 E3
Chapel La. Hail 104 A3
Chapel La. King 55 D4
Chapel La. Li Tew 45 D3
Chapel La. Milt 22 B2
Chapel La. N Lei 105 D4
Chapel La. Nrthm 138 B2
Chapel La. Oxon 142 A1
Chapel La. Rat 2 A2
Chapel La. S u Wy 85 E4
Chapel La. Sal 41 F3
Chapel La. Stand 137 E2
Chapel La. Sut C 200 A4
Chapel La. Turw 24 A4
Chapel La. Uff 211 E4
Chapel Rd. Ashb 228 A4
Chapel Rd. S in V 194 C4
Chapel Sq. Dedd 33 F2
Chapel Sq. E Hen 216 C3
Chapel St. Bice 65 F1
Chapel St. Blox 21 F2
Chapel St. Dedd 34 C2
Chapel St. Ho No 30 A4
Chapel St. Oxon 141 F4
Chapel St. Warm 3 D2
Chapel St. Watl 186 A1
Chapel Way. Child 213 E2
Chapel Way. N Hink 122 B1
Chapelwick Cl. Shriv 209 D3
Chapmans La. Dedd 34 A2
Chapmans Piece. Burf 100 C3
Charbridge La. Bice 66 A1
Charlbury Cl. Kidl 92 B1
Charlbury Rd. Fins 88 B4
Charlbury Rd. Oxon 123 E3
Charlbury Rd. Shriv 209 D3
Charles Ct. Banb 16 B3
Charles Dr. Tha 130 A1
Charles Evans Way. Caver 259 E1
Charles Rd. Chol 221 D1
Charles St. Oxon 142 A3
Charlton Park. Want 214 C3
Charlton Rd. Ayn 35 E4
Charlton Rd. Want 214 C3
Charlton Village Rd. Want 214 C3
Charney Ave. Abing 160 B1
Charter Way. Wall 221 E4
Charterville Cl. M Lov 102 C1
Chartwell Dr. Charl 73 E2
Charvil La. Sonn 260 C2
Chatham Rd. Oxon 141 E3
Chatsworth Cl. Caver 259 E3
Chatsworth Dr. Banb 16 C2
Chatterpie La. Combe 89 F3
Chaucer Cl. Bice 65 E2
Chaucer Cl. Caver 259 D3
Chaucer Ct. Ewel 204 C2
Chaucer's La. Wood 91 D3
Chaundy Rd. Tack 77 E3
Chaunterell Way. Abing 179 E3
Chawley La. Cumn 140 A3
Chazey Cl. Maple 258 B4
Chazey Rd. Caver 258 B2
Chearsley Rd. L Cre 129 E4
Checker Wlk. Abing 179 F4
Chelford Way. Caver 258 C2
Chelmscot Row. Ward 10 C4
Chelsea Cl. Read 257 F1
Cheney La. Oxon 124 A1
Cheney Rd. Banb 16 C4
Cheney Wlk. Abing 159 F1
Chepstow Gdns. Banb 15 F3
Chepstow Rd. Read 257 E1
Chequers Pl. Chol 220 C1
Chequers Pl. Oxon 124 C2
Cherbury Green. Grove 214 B4
Cheriton Pl. S Com 252 C2
Cherry Cl. Caver 259 E4
Cherry Cl. Kidl 108 C4
Cherry Cl. Warb 203 D3
Cherry Orch. Highw 190 A3
Cherry Orchard La. Highw 190 A3
Cherry Rd. Banb 16 A4
Cherry Tree Cl. Grove 214 C4
Cherry Tree Cl. K Bag 176 B4
Cherry Tree Cl. St Row 242 A3
Cherry Tree Dr. Abing 159 E1
Cherry Tree Rd. Chin 168 B3
Cherrys Cl. Blox 21 E2
Cherwell Ave. Kidl 109 D4
Cherwell Bank. Lo Hey 62 C3
Cherwell Business Cen. Kidl 92 B1
Cherwell Cl. Abing 160 A1
Cherwell Cl. Bice 65 E1
Cherwell Cl. Wall 221 E4
Cherwell Dr. Mars 123 F3
Cherwell Rd. Berin 182 B3
Cherwell Rd. Caver 259 D3
Cherwell St. Banb 16 B3
Cherwell St. Oxon 123 F1
Cheshire Dr. Up Hey 63 E4
Cheshire Rd. Tha 148 B4
Chester St. Caver 259 D1
Chester St. Oxon 141 F4
Chester Way. Banb 15 F3
Chestnut Ave. Caver 259 F2
Chestnut Ave. Far 172 C2
Chestnut Ave. Oxon 124 B2
Chestnut Ave. Radl 160 C2
Chestnut Ave. Tha 147 E4
Chestnut Cl. Bix 243 F4
Chestnut Cl. Chest 80 A4
Chestnut Cl. Laun 66 B1
Chestnut Cl. Witn 104 A1
Chestnut Dr. S u Wy 71 D1
Chestnut End. Bice 65 F3
Chestnut Gr. Purl 257 E3
Chestnut Rd. Moll 4 A2
Chestnut Rd. N Hink 140 B4
Chestnut Tree Cl. Abing 159 E1
Chestnuts The. Abing 160 B1
Chestnuts The. Dedd 34 C2
Chestnuts The. Kirt 78 A2
Chestnuts The. Shab 128 B2
Chestnuts The. Shipl 255 D2
Chestnuts The. Want 214 C3
Chetwode. Banb 16 A4
Chetwyn Mead. Bamp 134 C2
Cheviot Way. Banb 8 C1
Cheyne La. Bamp 134 C2
Chibnall Cl. Chalg 184 B3
Chichester Cl. Bice 65 F1
Chichester Wlk. Banb 9 D1
Chiers Dr. Dray 179 E1
Chilbridge Rd. Eyns 120 B4
Chilbrook. Harw 217 F3
Childrey Way. Abing 160 A1
Childrey Way. E Cha 213 F2
Chilgrove Dr. Mi Sto 49 F1
Chillingworth Cres. Oxon 142 C4
Chilswell La. Sunn 141 D1
Chilswell La. Woot 140 C2
Chilswell Rd. Oxon 141 E4
Chiltern Cl. Bens 203 F3
Chiltern Cl. Berin 182 B3
Chiltern Cl. Chalg 184 C3
Chiltern Cl. Hen-on-T 254 A4
Chiltern Cres. Wall 221 D4
Chiltern Ct. Caver 259 D3
Chiltern Gdns. Watl 186 B1
Chiltern Gr. Tha 148 A4
Chiltern Rd. Caver 259 E2
Chiltern Rd. R Pep 252 C4
Chiltern Ridge. Skch 188 B2
Chiltern View. L Mil 164 A4
Chiltern View. Purl 257 E3
Chiltern View. Tet 166 A4
Chiltern Wlk. Pangb 256 B3
Chilton Cl. Abing 160 A1
Chilton Rd. L Cre 129 E4
Chilton Rd. Upt 218 A1
Chilworth Rd. G Mil 145 F3
Chinalls Cl. Fin 39 E3
Chinnor Hill. Chin 168 C2
Chinnor Rd. Ast R 167 E1
Chinnor Rd. Ast R 168 A2
Chinnor Rd. Bled R 169 E2
Chinnor Rd. Tha 148 B3
Chinnor Rd. Tow 148 C4
Chipmunk Rd. Bens 204 B2
Chipperfield Park Rd. Blox 21 F3
Chipping Norton Rd. Chadl 57 D2
Chipping Norton Rd. Ho No 30 A4
Choicehill Rd. O Nor 42 C3
Cholsey Cl. Oxon 142 B2
Cholswell Rd. Abing 159 E1
Chorefields. Kidl 92 B1
Chowns Cl. Tha 148 A4
Christchurch Ct. Banb 16 B3
Church Green. L Cre 129 E4
Church La. Bled 54 B1
Church Ave. K Sut 23 F3
Church Cl. Adde 23 D2
Church Cl. B Bou 133 F3
Church Cl. Bens 203 F2
Church Cl. Cudd 144 B2
Church Cl. Cumn 121 E1
Church Cl. E Hag 218 C3
Church Cl. Frin 52 B4
Church Cl. Gt Bo 9 E4
Church Cl. Islip 93 F1
Church Cl. Long 192 B1
Church Cl. Mert 95 E4
Church Cl. S u Wy 71 E1
Church Cl. W-on-G 79 D1
Church Cowley Rd. Oxon 142 A3
Church End. Blew 219 D1
Church End. Crou 36 B4
Church End. D St L 183 D3
Church End. Stand 137 E2
Church Fields. Stone 89 E4
Church Furlong. Tad 20 B4
Church Green. S in V 194 C4
Church Green. Witn 118 A4
Church Hill Rd. Oxon 142 A2
Church Hill. Chil 235 E4
Church Hill. G Has 164 C4
Church Hill. Stone 225 E4
Church Hill. Tack 77 D3
Church Hill. Warm 3 D2
Church La. Adde 23 D2
Church La. Ast R 167 E2
Church La. Banb 16 B3
Church La. Bice 65 F1
Church La. Bled R 189 E4
Church La. Bled R 189 F4
Church La. Br-c-S 202 C2
Church La. Burf 100 C3
Church La. Cass 107 E1
Church La. Ch No 42 C2
Church La. Ch-on-O 95 D2
Church La. Chac 10 C2
Church La. Chalg 184 B3
Church La. Charl 73 D2
Church La. Chin 168 B3
Church La. Coles 191 D4
Church La. Cr Gif 221 E1
Church La. Crou 36 B4
Church La. D St L 183 D3
Church La. Dray 179 E1
Church La. Ewel 206 A1
Church La. Fern 193 D2
Church La. Fulb 100 C3
Church La. H Poy 93 D2
Church La. Hail 104 A3
Church La. Hanw 8 C2
Church La. Harw 217 F4
Church La. Hor-c-S 112 A3
Church La. Horn 7 E3
Church La. Islip 93 F1
Church La. Kirt 78 A2
Church La. Lang 132 B1
Church La. Lo Hey 62 B3
Church La. Longw 156 A2
Church La. Lud 98 B4
Church La. Mars 123 F3
Church La. Mi Bar 61 D4
Church La. Mid Ch 10 C1
Church La. Milc 21 D1
Church La. Mix 38 C4
Church La. Moll 4 A2
Church La. R Pep 253 D4
Church La. S Mor 219 F3
Church La. Shilt 115 D3
Church La. Shipl 254 C1
Church La. Steve 198 C2
Church La. Tow 148 C4
Church La. W-on-G 79 D1
Church La. Wall 221 E4
Church La. Watl 186 A2
Church La. Wend 80 A2
Church La. Witn 118 B4
Church Meadow. M u Wy 70 A1
Church Mews. Purl 257 E3
Church Mill Cl. Stand 137 E2
Church Path. S in V 194 C4
Church Path. Skch 188 B3
Church Pl. Lo Od 54 A4
Church Rd. Apple 158 A4
Church Rd. Bens 203 F2
Church Rd. Bled 54 B1
Church Rd. Brac 24 A4
Church Rd. Caver 259 D1
Church Rd. Chadl 57 E1
Church Rd. Chin 168 B3
Church Rd. Chol 220 C2
Church Rd. G Mil 145 D1
Church Rd. H Wald 155 F1
Church Rd. Hors 143 E3
Church Rd. Ick 127 F2
Church Rd. Lewk 187 D4
Church Rd. Lo Han 106 B4
Church Rd. Lo Od 54 A4
Church Rd. M u Wy 70 A1
Church Rd. Mi Sto 50 B2
Church Rd. N Lei 105 D4
Church Rd. Pangb 256 B3
Church Rd. Radl 160 C2
Church Rd. Sa-on-T 161 D4
Church Rd. Skch 188 B3
Church Rd. Tha 129 F1
Church Rd. W-on-G 79 D1
Church Rd. Wheat 144 A4
Church Rise. Fins 88 B3
Church Row. Bish 227 D2
Church Row. Child 213 E2
Church Sq. Islip 93 F1
Church St. Ard 215 F3
Church St. B St M 32 C3
Church St. Bamp 134 C2

Church St. Beck 111 D2
Church St. Bice 65 F1
Church St. Blad 91 D1
Church St. Blew 237 D4
Church St. Blox 21 E2
Church St. Bod 22 C4
Church St. Caver 259 D1
Church St. Ch No 42 C2
Church St. Charl 73 D2
Church St. Dedd 33 F2
Church St. Didc 218 C4
Church St. Duck 118 A2
Church St. E Hen 216 B3
Church St. Far 172 C2
Church St. Fif 69 D1
Church St. Hen-on-T 244 B1
Church St. Idb 69 D2
Church St. Kidl 92 C1
Church St. King 55 D2
Church St. M Gib 67 F2
Church St. March 178 B3
Church St. S u Wy 85 E4
Church St. Shell 193 F4
Church St. Skch 188 C3
Church St. Stone 89 E4
Church St. Sut C 180 A1
Church St. Sut C 200 C4
Church St. Up Hey 48 C3
Church St. Upt 218 B1
Church St. W Hann 196 C3
Church St. Want 214 B2
Church St. Warg 255 E1
Church St. Watl 186 A1
Church St. Woot 75 F2
Church St. Wrox 15 D4
Church View Rd. Witn 117 F4
Church View. Bamp 134 C2
Church View. Banb 16 A2
Church View. Cart 115 F1
Church View. Ch-on-O 95 D3
Church View. Free 106 A3
Church View. S u Wy 71 E1
Church View. St Row 241 F3
Church Way. N Hink 122 B1
Church Way. Oxon 141 F2
Church Way. Spars 212 C2
Church Wlk. Banb 16 B3
Church Wlk. Bish 227 E2
Church Wlk. Oxon 123 D2
Church Wlk. S u Wy 70 B1
Church Wlk. Shriv 209 E4
Church Wlk. Up Hey 62 C4
Churchfield La. Bens 203 F2
Churchfield. Nett 223 E2
Churchill Cl. Didc 200 B1
Churchill Cl. Wood 91 D3
Churchill Cres. Tha 148 A4
Churchill Gate. Wood 91 E3
Churchill Pl. Cutte 122 C4
Churchill Rd. Bice 65 F2
Churchill Rd. Ch No 42 B1
Churchill Rd. Didc 200 B1
Churchill Rd. Kidl 108 C4
Churchill Rd. King 55 D4
Churchill Way. Lo Han 106 A4
Churchlea. Moll 4 A2
Churchmere Rd. Sut C 180 A1
Churchward Cl. Grove 196 B1
Churchward. Didc 200 C2
Churchway. West I 235 D1
Chure The. Ch-on-O 95 D2
Cinnaminta Rd. Oxon 142 C4
Cinnamon Cl. Chalg 184 B4
Circourt Rd. Dench 195 F2
Circular Rd. Ambr 81 D3
Circus St. Oxon 141 F4
City Rd. Bled R 189 E3
Clack's La. Bens 222 B4
Clack's La. Cr Gif 222 B4
Clanfield Cres. Read 257 E1
Clapcot Way. Wall 221 E4
Clare Terr. Cart 115 E1
Clarence Rd. Hen-on-T 244 B1
Clarendon Cl. Abing 180 A4
Clarendon Dr. Tha 130 A1
Clarks La. Lo Co 28 A3
Clarkston Rd. Cart 115 E1
Clay Bank. Ho No 30 A4
Clay Cl. Read 257 D1
Clay La. Bens 204 B1
Claydon Rd. Cro 4 C2
Clayfields. Bourt 209 D2
Claymond Rd. Oxon 124 C2
Claypit La. Wool 211 D4
Claypits La. Shriv 209 E4
Clays Cl. Mars 124 A3
Cleave The. Harw 217 F4
Cleavers. Chin 168 A3
Cleeve Ct. Stre 249 D4
Cleeve Down. Gori 249 E4
Cleeve Rd. Gori 249 D4
Cleeves Ave. Ch No 42 C3
Cleeves Cnr. O Nor 42 C3
Clematis Pl. Oxon 142 C1
Clements Cl. Want 214 C3
Clements Green. S Mor 219 F3
Clements La. M Gib 67 F1
Clements Mead. Read 257 D1
Clements Rd. Hen-on-T 244 B2
Clevedon Rd. Read 257 F2
Cleveland Cl. Kidl 109 D4
Cleveland Dr. Oxon 142 B3
Clevelands. Abing 160 A1
Cleveley Rd. Enst 58 C3
Clevemede. Gori 249 E4
Cleycourt Rd. Shriv 209 D3
Clifden Rd. Worm 127 E3
Clifford Pl. Cutte 122 B4
Clifton Dr. Abing 179 F4
Clifton Park Rd. Caver 259 D2
Clifton Rd. Dedd 34 B2
Clifton Rise. Warg 255 F1
Clinton Cl. Oxon 141 F2
Clive Rd. Oxon 142 B3
Clock Tower. Far 172 C1
Cloisters The. Caver 259 D2
Cloisters The. Want 214 B2
Close The. Ard 215 F3
Close The. Bens 203 F3
Close The. Ch Wa 5 F3
Close The. Epw 13 D3
Close The. Gt Bo 9 E4
Close The. Hen-on-T 254 B4
Close The. Lech 150 B3
Close The. Woodc 250 C4
Closes The. Kidl 92 C1
Clover Cl. Cumn 140 A3
Clover Pl. Eyns 120 B4
Clover Pl. Oxon 142 C1
Coach La. Far 173 D2
Coach Way. Bens 203 F2
Coalport Way. Read 257 F1
Coates La. Ewel 206 B1
Cobden Cres. Oxon 141 E4
Cochrane Rd. Bens 204 B1
Cockcroft Rd. Didc 218 C4
Cockington Green. Banb 16 C4
Cockpit Cl. Wood 91 D3
Cocks La. St S J 125 E4
Cockshoot Cl. Stone 89 E4
Cogges Hill Rd. Witn 118 B4
Coghill. Bletch 93 D4
Coker Cl. Bice 65 F1
Colborne Rd. Didc 218 B4
Coldharbour Cl. Hen-on-T 254 B4
Coldicutt St. Caver 259 E1
Colegrave Rd. Blox 21 F3
Colegrove Down. Cumn 140 A3
Colemans Hill. Oxon 124 C2
Coleridge Cl. Bice 65 D2
Coleridge Cl. Oxon 142 B3
Coleridge Dr. Abing 179 E3
Colerne Rd. Cart 115 F2
Coles La. Chalg 184 B4
Colesbourne Rd. Blox 21 E2
Collcutt Cl. Hors 143 E4
College Cl. Chol 220 C1
College Farm. Chadl 57 D1
College La. Oxon 123 E1
College La. Oxon 142 A1
College Way. Hors 143 D3
Collett Way. Grove 196 B1
Collett. Didc 200 C2
Colley Wood. Kenn 141 F1
Collice St. Islip 109 F4
Collier's La. Far 173 D2
Collingwood Cl. Abing 159 F1
Collingwood Rd. Didc 218 B4
Collins St. Oxon 141 F4
Collinsmith Dr. Grove 196 C1
Collinsons Row. Charl 73 D2
Collinwood Cl. Oxon 124 C2
Collinwood Rd. Oxon 124 C2
Collyer Rd. Skch 188 C2
Colmore La. R Pep 252 C4
Coln Rd. Harw 217 D2
Colne Cl. Bice 65 E1
Colne Cl. Grove 196 B1
Colne Dr. Berin 182 B3
Colterne Cl. Oxon 124 A3
Coltman Ave. L Cre 129 E3
Colton Rd. Shriv 209 D3
Columbia Way. Grove 214 B4
Colvile Cl. Bamp 134 C2
Colwell Dr. Abing 179 E4
Colwell Dr. Witn 117 F3
Colwell Rd. Berin 182 B3
Colyton Way. Purl 257 E3
Combe Gate. Combe 90 A2
Combe Rd. Oxon 123 D1
Combe Rd. Stone 89 E4
Combewell. Gars 143 E1
Comfrey Rd. Oxon 142 C2
Common Cl. N Lei 105 D3
Common Cl. Shriv 209 E4
Common La. Ch No 42 B1
Common Rd. Beck 110 C2
Common Rd. N Lei 105 D3
Compass Cl. Oxon 142 B2
Compton Ct. Lo Co 27 F4
Compton Dr. Abing 160 A1
Compton Rd. Banb 16 B3
Compton Terr. Wall 221 E4
Condor Cl. Purl 257 E2
Conduit Hill Rise. Tha 147 F4
Conduit Rd. Abing 179 F4
Conifer Cl. N Hink 140 B4
Conifer Dr. Purl 257 D1
Conifer Rise. Banb 9 D1
Conigre. Chin 168 A3
Conisboro Ave. Caver 258 C3
Conisboro Way. Caver 258 C3
Coniston Ave. Oxon 124 A2
Coniston Dr. Read 257 F1
Connolly Dr. Cart 115 E2
Constable's Croft. U Arn 96 C4
Constitution Hill. Cr Gif 221 F2
Conway Dr. Banb 15 F3
Conway Rd. Abing 159 E1
Cook La. Cr Gif 221 F1
Cook's Hill. Shut 14 A3
Cooks La. Sal 41 F3
Coolidge Cl. Oxon 124 B1
Coombe Hill Cres. Tha 147 F4
Coombe The. Stre 248 C3
Coombes Cl. S u Wy 85 E4
Cooper Cl. Ch No 42 C2
Cooper Pl. Oxon 124 C2
Cooper Rd. Hen-on-T 244 B2
Cooper's Court Rd. Skch 188 B3
Coopers La. Want 214 C3
Coopers Pightle. K End 252 B2
Cope Cl. N Hink 140 B4
Cope Rd. Banb 16 B3
Copenhagen Dr. Abing 159 E1
Copenhagen Dr. Abing 179 E4
Copperage Rd. Farnb 234 A1
Coppice Cl. Banb 16 C2
Coppock Cl. Oxon 124 C1
Coppperfield Cl. Want 214 B3
Copse Ave. Caver 259 F2
Copse Cl. Read 257 E2
Copse La. Oxon 124 A3
Copse Mead. Sonn 260 C1
Copse The. Abing 160 B1
Copse The. Warg 255 F2
Copson La. Stadh 163 E1
Copthorne Rd. Kidl 108 C4
Corbett Rd. Cart 115 E1
Cordrey Green. Oxon 141 F2
Corfe Mews. Caver 259 F2
Corn Avill Cl. Abing 160 B1
Corn St. Witn 118 A4
Corndell Gdns. Witn 118 A4
Corneville Rd. Dray 179 D1
Cornfield Cl. Witn 117 F4
Cornish Rd. Ch No 42 B1
Cornmarket St. Oxon 123 E1
Cornmarket. Far 172 C2
Cornmarket. Tha 147 F4
Cornwall Cl. Purl 257 D2
Cornwallis Cl. Oxon 142 A3
Cornwallis Rd. Oxon 142 A3
Coromandel. Abing 179 E2
Corunna Cres. Oxon 142 C3
Cote Rd. Aston 135 F2
Cothill Rd. March 158 C2
Cotman Cl. Abing 179 F3
Cotmore Cl. Tha 148 A4
Cotmore Gdns. Tha 148 A4
Cotswold Cl. M Lov 102 C1
Cotswold Cl. Si Fe 19 D4
Cotswold Cnr. Gr Ro 29 D2
Cotswold Cres Bungs. Ch No 42 C1
Cotswold Cres. Ch No 42 C1
Cotswold Cres. Mars 123 F3
Cotswold Meadow. Witn 117 E4
Cotswold Rd. Cumn 140 A3
Cotswold Terr. Ch No 42 C1
Cotswold View. Charl 73 D2
Cotswold Way. Cart 115 E2
Cotswold Way. Read 257 E1
Cottage Rd. S in V 194 B4
Cottages The. Filk 114 A3
Cottesmore La. Ewel 204 B3
Cottesmore Rd. Oxon 142 A2
Couching St. Watl 186 A1
Coulings Cl. E Hen 216 B4
Council Houses. Gt Tew 45 E4
County Rd. Brac 24 A3
County Trading Est. Oxon 142 C2
County View. Dedd 34 B2
Coupland Rd. Woot 159 D3
Court Cl. Kidl 108 B4
Court Cl. S u Wy 85 E4
Court Cl. Warm 3 D2
Court Close Rd. Tow 148 C4
Court Dr. Warb 203 D3
Court Farm Rd. Oxon 141 F2
Court Hill Rd. Farnb 232 B4
Court Hill Rd. Let B 214 A1
Court Place Gdns. Oxon 141 F2
Court Rd. Let B 214 A1
Court The. Abing 159 F1
Courtenay Cl. Sut C 200 A4
Courtenay Dr. Caver 259 D4
Courtenay Rd. Want 214 C3
Courtfield Rd. St S J 125 E4
Courtiers Green. Cl Ham 181 E2
Courtington La. Blox 21 E3
Courtland Rd. Oxon 142 A2
Courtlands Hill. Purl 256 A2
Courtlands Rd. S u Wy 85 E4
Courts Gdns. Witn 118 B4
Covent Cl. Abing 160 A2
Coverley Rd. Oxon 142 B4
Covert The. Wood 91 E3
Cow La. Dench 195 F2
Cow La. Didc 201 D1
Cow La. Grove 196 C2
Cow La. Kenn 141 F1
Cow La. Longw 156 B2
Cow La. Moul 238 C2
Cow La. Read 258 C1
Cow La. Ste As 62 A4
Cowell Pl. Witn 118 A4
Cowleaze Cl. Shriv 209 D3
Cowleaze. Chin 168 A3
Cowley Pl. Oxon 141 F4
Cowley Rd. Oxon 142 A2
Cowley Rd. Oxon 142 A4
Cowper Cl. Bice 65 D2
Cox La. Ch No 42 A1
Cox's Alley. Oxon 124 C2
Cox's La. Cr Gif 222 A3
Cox's La. St Row 241 F3
Cox's Rd. Shriv 209 D3
Coxwell Gdns. Far 172 C2
Coxwell Rd. Far 172 C1
Coxwell St. Far 172 C2
Cozens La. King 54 C2
Crabhill La. Grove 215 D4
Crabtree Cnr. Cr Gif 240 B4
Crabtree La. Dray 179 D1
Crabtree Rd. N Hink 140 B4
Crafts End. Chil 235 F4
Cranborne Gdns. Read 258 A1
Cranbrook Ct. Witn 118 A3
Cranbrook Dr. Kenn 160 C4
Crane Furlong. Highw 190 A4
Cranham St. Oxon 123 D2
Cranham Terr. Oxon 123 D2
Cranleigh Cl. Banb 16 A2
Cranley Rd. Oxon 124 C2
Cranmer Cl. Purl 257 D2
Cranmer Rd. Oxon 142 C3
Cranwell Ave. Cart 115 F1
Cratlands Cl. Stadh 163 E1
Craufurd Rd. Oxon 142 C3
Craven Comm. Uff 211 E4
Crawborough Rd. Charl 73 E2
Crawley Rd. Witn 104 A1
Crawshay Dr. Caver 259 D4
Creampot Cl. Cro 4 C1
Creampot Cres. Cro 4 C1
Creampot La. Cro 4 C1
Crecy Wlk. Wood 91 E3
Cremyll Rd. Read 258 C1
Crendon Ct. Caver 259 D1
Crescent Cl. Oxon 142 B3
Crescent Rd. Oxon 142 B3
Crescent Rd. Read 257 E1
Crescent The. Adde 23 D3
Crescent The. Bice 65 E2
Crescent The. Cart 133 E4
Crescent The. Sa-on-T 161 E4
Crescent The. Shipl 255 D2
Crescent The. Ste As 62 A4
Crescent The. Witn 104 B1
Crescent Way. Chol 220 C1
Cress Hill Pl. Oxon 124 C2
Crest The. Bled R 189 F4
Crest The. Caver 259 E3
Crick Rd. Oxon 123 E2
Cricket Ground. Skch 188 B3
Cricket Rd. Oxon 142 A3
Cricklade Rd. Highw 190 A3
Cripley Pl. Oxon 123 D1
Cripley Rd. Oxon 123 D1
Crisp Rd. Hen-on-T 244 B2
Crispin Cl. Caver 258 B3
Crispin Pl. Wall 221 E4
Croasdell Cl. Abing 179 F2
Crockwell Cl. Bice 65 F1
Crockwell St. Lo Co 27 F4
Croft Ave. Kidl 108 C4
Croft Cl. Tha 148 A4
Croft Courtyard. Hadd 130 C3
Croft End. Let B 214 A1
Croft La. Adde 23 D2
Croft Rd. Gori 249 E3
Croft Rd. Oxon 123 F2
Croft Rd. Tha 148 A4
Croft Rd. Wall 221 E4
Croft The. Ast T 219 F1
Croft The. Didc 218 C4
Croft The. E Hag 218 C3
Croft The. Hadd 130 C3
Croft The. Harw 217 F4
Croft The. Oxon 124 B2
Croft The. W Hann 196 C4
Croft Way. Woodc 250 C4
Croft's La. Ho No 30 A3
Crofts The. Witn 118 A4
Cromer Cl. Read 257 E1
Cromwell Ave. Tha 130 A1
Cromwell Cl. Chalg 184 C3
Cromwell Cl. Far 173 D2
Cromwell Cl. Hen-on-T 254 B4
Cromwell Cl. Mars 123 F2
Cromwell Dr. Didc 219 D4
Cromwell Park. Ch No 42 C2
Cromwell Rd. Banb 16 A3
Cromwell Rd. Caver 259 D1
Cromwell Rd. Hen-on-T 254 C4
Cromwell St. Oxon 141 E4
Cromwell Way. Kidl 109 D4
Cronshaw Cl. Didc 200 C1
Croom Cotts. Harw 217 D4
Cross Ave. Bens 204 B1
Cross Cl. Bens 204 C1
Cross Hill Rd. Adde 22 C2
Cross Keys Rd. S Sto 239 E2
Cross Leys. Ch No 42 C1
Cross Rd. Chol 220 C1
Cross St. Oxon 141 F4
Cross Tree La. Filk 132 A3
Cross's La. Chadl 56 C1
Crosslands Dr. Abing 159 F1
Crosslands. Frin 52 B3
Crossville Cres. Didc 200 B1
Crossway. Mi Bar 60 C4
Crotch Cres. Oxon 124 A2
Crouch Hill Rd. Banb 16 A2
Crouch St. Banb 16 B3
Croughton Rd. Ayn 35 E4
Crow La. Gt Bo 9 E4
Crowberry Rd. Oxon 142 C1
Crowell Rd. Oxon 142 B2
Crowmarsh Hill. Cr Gif 222 A3
Crowmarsh Rd. Buck 64 C3
Crown La. Bens 203 F2
Crown La. Dorch 182 B1
Crown La. S Mor 220 A3
Crown Rd. Kidl 108 B4
Crown Rd. Wheat 144 A4
Crown Sq. Bens 204 A2
Crown St. Oxon 141 F4
Crown Wlk. Bice 65 F1
Crowsley Rd. Shipl 255 D2
Crowsley Way. S Com 252 C3
Crozier Cl. N Hink 140 B4
Crutch Furlong. Berin 182 B3
Crutchmore Cres. Kirt 78 A2
Cuckamus La. N Lei 105 D3
Cuckoo Cl. Buck 65 F3
Cuckoo La. Eyns 106 A2
Cuckoo La. Free 106 A2
Cuddesdon Cl. Woodc 250 C4
Cuddesdon Rd. Hors 143 F3
Cuddesdon Way. Oxon 142 C1
Cullerne Cl. Abing 160 A2
Cullerns The. Highw 190 A3
Cullum Rd. Wheat 144 B4
Culworth Rd. Ch Wa 5 F3
Cumberford Cl. Blox 21 E2
Cumberford Hill. Blox 21 E2
Cumberford. Blox 21 E2
Cumberland Rd. Oxon 142 A4
Cumberlege Cl. Mars 123 F4
Cummings Cl. Oxon 124 C1
Cumnor Hill. Cumn 140 A4
Cumnor Hill. N Hink 140 A4
Cumnor Rd. Cumn 139 E4
Cumnor Rd. Woot 159 D4
Cumnor Rise Rd. N Hink 140 B4
Cunliffe Cl. Oxon 123 E3
Cup And Saucer. Cro 4 C1
Curbridge Rd. Duck 118 A2
Curbridge Rd. Witn 117 F4
Curie Ave. Harw 217 D2
Cursus The. Lech 150 B3
Curtis Ave. Abing 180 A4
Curtis Pl. Kidl 92 C1
Curtis Rd. Kidl 92 C1
Curtis Rd. Shriv 209 D3
Curtyn Cl. Abing 179 E4
Cuttlebrook Gdns. Tha 129 E1
Cuxham Rd. Watl 186 A1

Dacey Dr. Up Hey 63 D4
Dacre Ave. Caver 259 F2
Daedings The. Dedd 33 F2
Daimler Ave. Banb 15 F4
Dairyground The. Shut 14 A3
Daisy Bank. Abing 180 A4
Dale Cl. Brac 24 A4
Dale Cl. Oxon 141 D4
Dale Wlk. Duck 118 A3
Dalton Ave. Harw 217 D1
Damer Gdns. Hen-on-T 254 C4
Damson Trees. Shriv 209 D3
Dancers Hill. Charl 73 E2
Danes Rd. Bice 65 E1
Danesmoor. Banb 16 A4
Danvers Cl. Brou 15 E1
Danvers Rd. Brou 15 E1
Danvers Rd. Oxon 142 A2
Darell Rd. Caver 258 C2
Dark La. Read 257 E1
Dark La. Sunn 159 F3
Dark La. Warg 255 E1
Dark La. Witn 104 A1
Dark La. Wrox 15 D4
Darrell Way. Abing 159 F1
Dart Rd. Abing 159 E2
Dashwood Ave. Yarn 108 A3
Dashwood Mews. Kirt 77 F2
Dashwood Rd. Banb 16 B3
Dashwood Rd. Oxon 142 A2
Dashwood Rise. D Tew 47 E3
Datchet Green. Br-c-S 202 C1
Daubeny Rd. Oxon 141 F3
Daubigny Mead. Br No 116 B2
Davenant Rd. Cutte 123 D4

Davenport Pl. Watl 186 A1
Davenport Rd. Witn 103 F1
Daventry Rd. Banb 9 F1
Daventry Rd. Banb 16 C4
David Walter Cl. Cutte 109 D1
Davis Cl. Cart 115 F1
Davis Gdns. Buck 65 F4
Dawls Cl. S u Wy 71 D1
Dawson Pl. Oxon 123 D1
Dawson St. Oxon 141 F4
Day's La. Ewel 204 C1
Days Ground. Shriv 209 E4
De Havilland Rd. Ch We 68 A3
De Montfort Rd. Read 259 D1
De Vitre Pl. Grove 214 B4
Deacon Way. Banb 16 A3
Deacon Way. Read 258 A1
Deaconfield. S Sto 239 E2
Deadman's La. Woodc 251 E2
Deafort Cl. Kidl 92 C1
Dean Butler Cl. Want 214 B3
Dean Cl. Banb 16 C4
Dean Court Rd. N Hink 140 A4
Deanes Cl. Steve 198 C2
Deanfield Ave. Hen-on-T 244 B1
Deanfield Rd. Hen-on-T 244 B1
Deanfield Rd. N Hink 122 A1
Dearlove Cl. Abing 159 F1
Deddington Hill. Dedd 33 F3
Deene Cl. Adde 23 D2
Deer Park Rd. Witn 117 E4
Deer's Farm. Bod 22 C4
Deer's La. Check 241 E1
Deers Cl. Bod 22 C4
Defiant Cl. Bice 66 A2
Delamare Way. N Hink 140 A4
Delapre Dr. Banb 16 C4
Dell Rd. Read 257 E1
Delly Cl. Hail 104 A4
Denbigh Cl. Banb 15 F2
Denbigh Rd. Tha 130 A1
Denby Way. Read 257 F1
Denchfield Rd. Banb 16 B1
Denchworth Rd. Grove 196 B1
Denchworth Rd. Grove 214 B3
Denchworth Rd. Want 214 B3
Dene Hollow. Chil 235 F4
Dene Rd. Oxon 142 B4
Dene Rise. Witn 117 F4
Denman's La. Cumn 139 F3
Denmark St. Oxon 141 F4
Denton Cl. Abing 180 A4
Denton Cl. N Hink 140 A4
Denton Hill. Cudd 144 A1
Denton La. Cudd 144 A1
Denton La. Gars 143 F1
Dents Cl. Mars 124 A3
Derby Rd. Caver 259 D2
Derwent Ave. Didc 201 D1
Derwent Ave. Oxon 124 A2
Derwent Ave. Read 257 F1
Derwent Cl. Abing 159 E1
Derwent Rd. Bice 65 D2
Desborough Cres. Oxon 142 A2
Devereux Pl. Oxon 142 A2
Devil's Hill. Shipl 253 E3
Devon Cl. Bens 204 B2
Devon Dr. Caver 259 F2
Devon Pl. Cart 115 F1
Devon Way. Banb 16 A4
Devonshire Gdns. Purl 257 D2
Dexter Cl. Banb 16 B2
Diamond Pl. Cutte 123 D3
Dibleys. Blew 237 D4
Dickens Cl. Bice 65 E2
Dickredge The. Ste As 62 A4
Didcot Rd. Harw 218 A4
Didcot Rd. Lo Wit 201 E4
Dido Rd. Chil 234 C4
Dido Rd. Harw 217 D1
Digberry La. Nett 224 B3
Digging La. Fyf 157 E1
Diston's La. Ch No 42 C2
Ditchley Rd. Charl 73 F3
Divinity Rd. Oxon 142 A4
Dobson's La. Faw 244 B4
Dodd Dr. Ch We 68 A2
Dodgson Rd. Oxon 142 B2
Dodson Ct. Abing 179 F4
Dog Cl. Adde 22 C2
Dog Kennel La. S u Wy 85 E4
Dog La. Child 213 E2
Doily Cl. Ho No 30 A4
Dollicott. Hadd 130 C4
Dolphin La. Fulb 100 C3
Don Stuart Pl. Oxon 142 A4
Donegal Cl. Caver 259 E2
Donkin Hill. Caver 259 E2
Donnington Bridge Rd. Oxon 141 F3
Donnington Cl. Witn 117 E4
Donnington Pl. Want 214 B3
Dorchester Cres. Abing 160 A1
Dorchester Gr. Banb 15 F2
Dorchester Pl. Tha 147 F4
Dorchester Rd. Berin 182 C2
Dorchester Rd. D St L 183 D3
Dormer Rd. Tha 148 A3
Dormers The. Highw 190 A3
Dorn Cl. Mi Bar 60 C4
Dorn View. Woot 76 A2
Douglas Rd. Caver 259 E1
Dove Ct. Cart 115 F2
Dove Green. Bice 65 D2
Dove House Cl. Cutte 122 C4
Dovecote Cl. Hadd 130 C3
Dovecote. Hadd 130 C3
Dovedale Cl. Caver 258 C2
Dovehouse Cl. Eyns 120 C4
Doveleat. Chin 168 B4
Dover Ave. Banb 15 F3
Dovetrees. Cart 115 F2
Down End. Ho No 30 A4
Downhill La. Hail 104 A2
Downs Cl. Harw 217 F3
Downs Rd. Aldw 247 D2
Downs Rd. Curb 103 D1
Downs Rd. Didc 218 B4
Downs Rd. Stand 137 E3
Downs View. Highw 190 A3
Downs Way. Chil 234 C4
Downs Way. Read 257 E1
Downside End. Oxon 125 D2
Downside Rd. Oxon 125 D2
Downside. Chil 235 E4
Downside. Harw 217 E1
Downsmead. Bayd 245 E1
Doyley Rd. Oxon 141 D4
Doyley Rd. Wall 203 E1
Dragonhill Rd. Wool 211 D1
Drake Ave. Didc 218 B4
Dray's La. R Pep 253 D4
Draycott Rd. K Bag 156 B1
Draymans Croft. Bice 65 F1
Drayton Rd. Abing 179 E3
Drayton Rd. Dorch 182 B1
Drayton Rd. Dorch 182 C2
Drayton Rd. Mil 199 F4
Dresden Way. Read 257 F1
Drewitts Cnr. Harw 217 F4
Drive The. Enst 58 C3
Drove Acre Rd. Oxon 142 A4
Droveside. Chol 220 C1
Druce Way. Oxon 142 C2
Druids Wlk. Chin 168 B3
Druids Wlk. Didc 200 C1
Dry La. Crawl 103 E2
Dry La. Curb 103 E2
Dryden Ave. Bice 65 D2
Drylands Rd. M Lov 102 C1
Duck La. Lud 98 B4
Duck Sq. Chin 168 B3
Ducklington La. Witn 117 F4
Dudgeon Dr. Oxon 142 A1
Dudley Cl. Read 257 F1
Dudley Gdns. Oxon 123 F1
Duffield Cl. Abing 160 A1
Duffield Pl. March 178 B4
Duffield Rd. Sonn 260 C1
Duke Of York Ave. Mil 199 E2
Duke St. Banb 16 C3
Duke St. Hen-on-T 244 C1
Duke St. Oxon 122 C1
Dukes Cl. Shab 128 B1
Dukes Rd. Kidl 108 C4
Dumas Cl. Bice 65 E1
Dumbarton Way. Caver 259 F3
Dunbar Dr. Tha 130 A1
Duncan Cl. Eyns 120 B4
Duncan Gdns. Purl 257 E2
Dundas Cl. Abing 180 A4
Dunlin Ct. Banb 16 C2
Dunluce Gdns. Pangb 256 C3
Dunmore Rd. Abing 159 F1
Dunnock Way. Warg 255 F2
Dunsden Cl. Didc 200 B1
Dunsomer Hill. N Mor 220 A4
Dunstan Ave. Ch No 42 C1
Dunstan Rd. Oxon 124 B2
Dunster Cl. Caver 259 E3
Durham Mews. Banb 9 D1
Duxford Cl. Bice 66 A2
Duxford Cl. Cart 115 F2
Dyer Straits. Chil 234 C4
Dyer's Hill. Charl 73 D2
Dynham Pl. Oxon 124 B1
Dysonswood La. Maple 258 C4

Eady Rd. Up Hey 63 D4
Eagle Ind Est. Witn 118 A4
Eagle La. Watch 191 E1
Eagle Sq. Li Cox 192 C4
Eagles. Far 172 C2
Earl St. Oxon 122 C1
Earl's La. Dedd 33 F2
Earlsfield Cl. Caver 259 F2
Early Rd. Witn 104 B1
Easington Gdns. Banb 16 B2
Easington Rd. Banb 16 B2
Eason Dr. Abing 160 B1
East Ave. Oxon 142 A4
East Cl. Banb 16 C4
East End. Ho No 30 A4
East Hawthorn Rd. Ambr 81 E2
East Lockinge. Ard 215 E2
East St Helen St. Abing 179 F3
East St. Banb 16 C4
East St. Bice 65 E2
East St. Bod 22 C4
East St. Didc 219 D4
East St. Frit 49 F4
East St. Lo Co 27 F3
East St. Oxon 123 D1
East St. Tha 148 A4
East View Cl. Warg 255 F1
East View Rd. Warg 255 F1
East Way. Dray 199 D4
Eastbrook Cl. Pidd 97 F4
Eastchurch. Oxon 141 F2
Easterfield. Grove 196 C1
Eastern Ave. Oxon 142 A2
Eastern By-pass Rd. Oxon 142 C3
Eastfield La. Whitc 256 B4
Eastfield La. Woodc 250 C3
Eastfield Rd. Witn 104 A2
Eastfield. Blew 237 D4
Eastgate. Horn 7 E4
Eastmanton La. Spars 212 C2
Eastrop. Highw 190 A3
Eastwood Rd. Curb 103 E1
Eastwood Rd. Skch 188 C2
Eaton Rd. Apple 139 D1
Ebbes La. E Hann 197 D4
Eccles Cl. Caver 259 E1
Eden Croft. Abing 160 A1
Eden Ct. Didc 201 D1
Eden Dr. Oxon 124 A2
Eden Way. Bice 65 D1
Edencroft. Highw 190 A4
Edenhall Cl. Read 257 E2
Edgar Milward Cl. Read 258 A1
Edgecombe Rd. Oxon 124 C2
Edgehill. Tha 129 F1
Edgeway Rd. Oxon 123 F2
Edgeworth Dr. Cart 115 E1
Edinburgh Cl. Banb 15 F4
Edinburgh Dr. Didc 200 C1
Edinburgh Dr. Kidl 109 D4
Edinburgh Way. Banb 15 F3
Edington Pl. Grove 196 B1
Edington Rd. Witn 117 E4
Edith Rd. Oxon 141 E4
Edmonds Ct. Didc 218 B4
Edmund Rd. Oxon 142 B3
Edmunds Rd. Banb 15 F3
Edward Rd. Kenn 141 F1
Edward St. Abing 179 E4
Edward St. Banb 16 C3
Edwin Rd. Didc 218 B4
Egerton Cl. Brac 24 A4
Egerton Rd. Oxon 142 A2
Egerton Rd. Wall 221 E4
Eglin St. Up Hey 63 D4
Eighteenth St. Harw 217 D2
Eighth Ave. Oxon 142 C4
Eighth St. Harw 217 D2
Elbourne. Didc 218 B4
Elder Cl. Read 257 E1
Elderdene. Chin 168 B4
Elderfield Cres. Chil 235 E4
Elderfield Rd. Buck 65 F4
Eldridge Cl. Abing 159 F1
Eleanor Cl. Oxon 142 A2
Electric Ave. Oxon 141 D4
Eleventh St. Harw 217 D1
Eliot Cl. Caver 259 D2
Elizabeth Ave. Abing 160 B1
Elizabeth Cl. Hen-on-T 254 A4
Elizabeth Dr. Want 214 B3
Elizabeth Rd. Hen-on-T 254 A4
Elizabeth Rd. Skch 188 C3
Elizabeth Rise. Banb 16 A2
Ell's La. Blox 21 E4
Ellesmere Cl. Caver 259 D2
Ellesmere Rd. Oxon 142 A2
Elm Cl. Ambr 81 E2
Elm Cl. Bice 65 F2
Elm Cl. Chin 168 B3
Elm Cl. Tet 166 A4
Elm Cl. Wheat 144 B4
Elm Cl. Witn 117 F4
Elm Cres. Charl 73 E2
Elm Ct. S Com 252 C2
Elm Dr. Chin 168 B3
Elm Dr. Gars 143 E1
Elm Gr. Kidl 108 C3
Elm La. Ambr 81 E2
Elm Rd. Far 172 C2
Elm Rd. Maple 258 B4
Elm Rd. N Mor 220 A4
Elm Rd. Want 214 C3
Elm Tree Cl. Oxon 142 A2
Elm Tree Wlk. Abing 159 E1
Elm Trees. L Cre 129 D4
Elmcroft. Gori 249 E3
Elmhurst Rd. Gori 249 E4
Elmleigh Ct. Caver 259 E2
Elms Dr. Mars 124 A3
Elms Par. N Hink 122 B1
Elms Rd. Cass 107 E1
Elms Rd. N Hink 122 B1
Elms Rd. Tha 147 F4
Elms The. Highw 190 A3
Elms The. Lang 132 B1
Elmscote Rd. Banb 16 B1
Elmstone Dr. Read 257 E1
Elmthorpe Rd. Cutte 122 C4
Elsfield Rd. Mars 123 F3
Elsfield Way. Cutte 109 D1
Elsley Rd. Read 257 F2
Elstow Ave. Caver 259 E3
Elstree Cl. Read 257 E1
Elswith Cl. Grove 214 B4
Eltham Ave. Caver 259 F3
Elton Cres. Wheat 144 B4
Elton Rd. Banb 16 C1
Elvendon La. Woodc 250 B4
Elvendon Rd. Gori 249 E4
Elwes Cl. Abing 180 A4
Elwes Rd. March 178 B3
Ely Cl. Abing 179 E3
Ely Cl. Cart 115 F2
Elyham. Purl 257 D3
Emma La. Warg 255 F1
Emmens Cl. Check 241 E2
Emmer Green Ct. Caver 259 E3
Eney Cl. Abing 160 B1
Enstone Rd. Charl 73 D2
Enstone Rd. Li Tew 45 D3
Enstone Rd. Mi Bar 60 C4
Epwell Rd. Shut 13 F3
Eric Ave. Caver 259 D3
Erica Cl. Banb 9 D1
Erica Cl. Oxon 142 C2
Ermont Way. Banb 16 C4
Ernest Rd. Didc 218 C4
Ernicote Cl. Ambr 81 F2
Essex Rd. Tha 148 A4
Essex St. Oxon 142 A4
Essex Way. S Com 253 D2
Estover Way. Chin 168 A3
Ethelhelm Cl. Abing 160 B2
Ethelred Ct. Oxon 124 B2
Eton Cl. Witn 118 B4
Euston Way. E Cha 214 A4
Evans Cl. Eyns 120 C4
Evans Ct. Kidl 108 C4
Evans La. Kidl 108 C4
Evans Rd. Eyns 120 C4
Evelin Rd. Abing 159 F1
Evelyn Cl. N Hink 140 A4
Evenlode Cl. Bice 65 E1
Evenlode Cl. Charl 73 D2
Evenlode Cl. Grove 196 B1
Evenlode Cl. N Lei 105 D3
Evenlode Cres. Kidl 92 A1
Evenlode Dr. Berin 182 B3
Evenlode Dr. Lo Han 90 A1
Evenlode Park. Abing 160 A1
Evenlode. Banb 16 A4
Everard Cl. Oxon 124 B1
Eversley Cl. Chadl 57 D1
Evesham Rd. Caver 259 D3
Evesham Rd. N Hink 140 A4
Ewart Cl. Bice 65 E2
Ewert Pl. Cutte 123 D3
Ewin Cl. Mars 123 F3
Exbourne Rd. Abing 179 E4
Exeter Ct. Didc 219 D4
Eynsford Cl. Caver 259 F3
Eynsham Rd. Cass 107 E1
Eynsham Rd. Cumn 121 F1
Eyre's La. Ewel 204 C3
Eyston Way. Abing 179 E4

Faber Cl. Oxon 142 B1
Fair Cl. Bice 65 F2
Fair Mile. Hen-on-T 244 B2
Fair View. Oxon 142 B4
Fairacres Rd. Didc 218 C4
Fairacres Rd. Oxon 141 F3
Fairacres. Abing 179 E4
Fairfax Ave. Mars 123 F2
Fairfax Cl. Banb 16 A3
Fairfax Cl. Tha 148 A4
Fairfax Rd. Chalg 184 B3
Fairfax Rd. Kidl 108 C3
Fairfax Rd. Oxon 142 C3
Fairfield Cl. Grove 214 B4
Fairfield Dr. Witn 117 F4
Fairfield Pl. Abing 179 F4
Fairfield Rd. Gori 249 E4
Fairfield. Chol 220 C1
Fairford Rd. Read 257 E1
Fairford Way. Bice 66 A2
Fairhaven Rd. Buck 65 F4
Fairlawn End. Cutte 122 C4
Fairlie Rd. Oxon 142 A2
Fairspear Rd. Leaf 86 C2
Fairthorne Way. Shriv 209 D3
Fairview Estate. Hen-on-T 254 C4
Fairview Rd. Banb 16 B2
Fairway The. Banb 16 A3
Falcon Cl. Banb 16 A2
Falcon Cl. Cart 115 E2
Falkland Rd. Caver 259 D1
Falkner's Cl. Adde 23 D2
Fallow Way. Banb 16 C1
Fallowfield Cl. Caver 259 D2
Fallowfields. Bice 65 F1
Falstaff Cl. Eyns 120 C4
Fane Cl. Bice 65 E2
Fane Dr. Berin 182 B3
Fane Rd. Mars 123 F3
Fanshawe Pl. Oxon 142 C3
Fanshawe Rd. Tha 148 A4
Faraday Ave. Harw 217 D1
Faraday Rd. E Cha 214 A4
Faringdon Rd. Apple 139 F1
Faringdon Rd. K Bag 156 C1
Faringdon Rd. S in V 194 B4
Faringdon Rd. Shriv 209 E4
Faringdon Rd. Watch 191 F1
Farleigh Mews. Caver 259 F3
Farleigh Rd. Shriv 209 D3
Farley Cl. Stone 89 E4
Farm Cl. Aston 135 F1
Farm Cl. Chalg 184 C3
Farm Cl. Gori 249 E3
Farm Cl. Kidl 92 C1
Farm Cl. Purl 257 E3
Farm Close La. Wheat 144 A4
Farm Close Rd. Wheat 144 A4
Farm End. Grove 214 B4
Farm End. Wood 91 D4
Farm La. Crawl 103 E3
Farm Mill La. Witn 118 A4
Farm Rd. Abing 159 F1
Farm Rd. Brac 24 A3
Farm Rd. Hen-on-T 254 C4
Farm Way. Banb 16 C2
Farman Cres. Ch We 68 A2
Farmer Pl. Oxon 123 F2
Farmers Cl. Witn 104 A1
Farmfield Rd. Banb 16 B2
Farmhouse Mews. Watl 186 A1
Farmiloe Cl. Purl 257 E2
Farmstead Cl. Grove 196 B1
Farndon Rd. Oxon 123 D2
Farnham Dr. Caver 259 F2
Farrier's Mead. Wend 80 A2
Farriers Rd. Mi Bar 60 C4
Farringdon Rd. Abing 159 D1
Farthings The. March 178 B4
Faulder Ave. Cart 115 E2
Faulkner St. Oxon 141 E4
Fawler La. Fins 88 B4
Fawler Rd. K Lis 211 F3
Fawler Rd. Uff 211 F3
Fawley Bottom La. Faw 226 A1
Fawley Cl. Want 214 B3
Featherbed La. E Hen 216 C4
Featherbed La. Mil 199 D1
Featherbed La. Mix 38 B3
Feilden Cl. Duck 118 A2
Feilden Gr. Oxon 124 A2
Fells Cl. L Cre 129 E3
Feltwell Cl. Cart 115 F2
Fencott Rd. Ch-on-O 95 D2
Fennel Way. Abing 180 B4
Fenny Compton Rd. Clay 1 B1
Fenway. Ste As 48 A1
Ferguson Pl. Abing 180 B4
Fergusson Rd. Banb 16 C4
Fermi Ave. Harw 217 D1
Fern Glen. Read 257 E1
Fern Hill Rd. Oxon 142 B3
Fernbrook Rd. Caver 258 C3
Ferndale Cl. Read 257 F2
Ferndale Cl. Skch 188 C2
Ferndale Rd. Banb 15 F4
Ferndale St. Far 173 D2
Ferne Cl. Gori 249 E4
Fernham Rd. Far 172 C1
Fernham Rd. Fern 193 E3
Fernham Rd. Li Cox 192 C4
Fernham Rd. Long 192 B1
Fernham Rd. Shell 193 E3
Fernhill Cl. Kidl 108 B4
Fernhill Cl. Milc 21 D1
Fernhill Cl. Tidd 146 A4
Fernhill Rd. Begb 108 A4
Ferny Cl. Radl 160 C2
Ferriston. Banb 9 D1
Ferry Hinksey Rd. Oxon 123 D1
Ferry La. Gori 249 D3
Ferry La. S Sto 239 D2
Ferry La. Warg 255 E1
Ferry Mills. Oxon 141 D4
Ferry Pool Rd. Cutte 123 D3
Ferry Rd. Oxon 123 F2
Ferry Rd. S Sto 239 E2
Ferry Wlk. Abing 179 F3
Fetti Pl. Want 214 C3
Fettiplace Cl. Apple 158 A4
Fettiplace Rd. March 178 B3
Fettiplace Rd. Oxon 124 C3
Fettiplace Rd. Witn 117 F4
Fettiplace. Lyne 70 B3
Fewcott Rd. Frit 49 F4
Fidlers Wlk. Warg 255 F1
Field Rd. Mur 96 A3
Field Ave. Oxon 142 C1
Field Cl. Ick 128 A2
Field Cl. Kidl 108 C4
Field Cl. Stone 89 E4
Field Cl. Yarn 108 A3
Field End. L Cre 129 F3
Field Gdns. E Cha 213 F3
Field Gdns. Steve 199 D3
Field House Dr. Cutte 123 D4
Field Rd. King 54 C2
Field St. Bice 65 F1
Field The. Woot 158 C3
Field View. Caver 259 D2
Fielden Cl. Bens 204 B1

Fielden Rd. Bens 204 B1
Fieldmere Cl. Witn 117 F4
Fieldside. Abing 159 E1
Fieldside. E Hag 219 D3
Fieldside. Lo Wit 201 E4
Fieldside. Upt 218 B1
Fiennes Rd. Banb 16 A3
Fiennes Rd. Oxon 142 A2
Fifteenth St. Harw 217 D1
Fifth Ave. Crou 36 C4
Fifth St E. Crou 36 C4
Fifth St. Crou 36 C4
Fifth St. Harw 217 D2
Filkins Rd. Lang 132 B1
Finch Cl. Oxon 124 B1
Finchdale Cl. Cart 115 E2
Finches La. Bayd 245 F1
Finchley La. Bice 65 E1
Finmore Cl. Abing 179 F4
Finmore Rd. N Hink 140 B4
Finsbury Pl. Ch No 42 C2
Fir Cl. Cr Gif 240 B4
Fir La. Ste As 48 A1
Fir Tree Ave. Wall 221 D4
Fir Tree Cl. K Bag 156 C1
Fir Tree Paddock. West I 235 D1
Fircroft Cl. Read 257 E1
Firebrass Hill. Ewel 204 C3
Firs The. Wrox 15 D4
First Ave. Didc 200 B1
First Ave. Hors 142 C4
First St. Crou 36 C3
First St. Harw 217 E1
First Turn. Cutte 122 C4
Fish Ponds La. Tha 129 E1
Fisher Cl. Dray 179 D1
Fisher Row. Oxon 123 D1
Fisher's La. Charl 73 D2
Fishermans Wharf. Abing 179 F2
Fishers Ct. Caver 259 E3
Fitzcount Way. Wall 203 E1
Fitzharris Ind Est. Abing 179 F4
Fitzharry's Rd. Abing 179 F4
Fitzherbert Cl. Oxon 141 F2
Five Acre. Read 257 D1
Five Mile Dr. Cutte 109 D1
Flatford Pl. Kidl 92 B1
Flavius Gate. Brac 24 A4
Flaxfield Rd. Oxon 142 C1
Fleet Way. Didc 219 D4
Fleetwood Way. Tha 129 F1
Fleming Cl. Bice 65 E2
Fleming Dr. Mi Bar 60 C4
Flemings Rd. Wood 91 E3
Flemming Ave. Chalg 184 B4
Fletcher Cl. Yarn 108 A3
Fletcher Rd. Oxon 142 C3
Flexney Pl. Oxon 124 B1
Flexneys Paddock. Sta Har 138 A4
Flint Hollow. Chin 168 A3
Floral Cl. Grove 214 C4
Florence Cl. Kidl 108 C4
Florence Park Rd. Oxon 142 A3
Florey's Cl. Hail 104 A3
Flower's Hill. Pangb 256 A2
Floyd's Row. Oxon 141 E4
Fludger Cl. Wall 221 E4
Fococks La. Cr Gif 221 F1
Fogwell Rd. N Hink 122 A1
Foliat Cl. Want 214 C3
Foliat Dr. Want 214 C3
Folland Dr. Ch We 68 A3
Follets Cl. Yarn 108 A3
Folly Cl. Highw 190 A4
Folly Cres. Highw 190 A4
Folly Cres. Watch 191 F1
Folly Dr. Highw 190 A4
Folly Gr. Woodc 250 C4
Folly Orchard Rd. Woodc 240 C1
Folly View Cres. Far 172 C1
Folly View Rd. Far 172 C1
Folly Way. Highw 190 A4
Ford La. D St L 183 D3
Ford La. E Hen 216 B3
Ford La. Garf 178 A4
Ford's Cl. Bled R 189 F4
Fords Cl. Hors 143 E3
Forest Cl. Lyne 70 B3
Forest Hill. Read 257 F1
Forest Rd. Charl 73 D2
Forest Rd. Oxon 124 C2
Forest Side. Kenn 141 F1
Foresters. B Bot 189 E3
Foresters. Chin 168 A3
Forge Cl. Caver 259 E1
Forge Cl. Hor-c-S 112 A3
Forge Cl. M Gib 67 F2
Forge Cl. Mert 95 E4
Forge Pl. Frit 49 F4
Forgeway. Banb 9 D1
Forster La. Cumn 139 F2
Forsythia Wlk. Banb 9 D1
Fortescue Dr. Chest 80 A4
Forties The. G Mil 145 D1
Fortnam Cl. Oxon 124 A2
Forty Green. Bled 149 F2
Forty The. Chol 220 C1
Foscote Rise. Banb 16 C2
Fosseway The. Br No 116 B2
Foster Rd. Abing 159 F2
Foundry St. Banb 16 B3
Fourteenth St. Harw 217 D2
Fourth Ave. Crou 36 C3
Fourth Ave. Hors 142 C4
Fourth St. Crou 36 C3
Fourth St. Harw 217 D2
Fowler Rd. Banb 16 C4
Fowler's Rd. King 55 D2
Fowlers Farm Rd. Skch 188 C2
Fox Cl. Bamp 134 C2
Fox Cl. Ch No 42 C1
Fox Cl. Gars 143 E1
Fox Cl. Hail 104 A2
Fox Cover. Chin 168 B3
Fox Cres. Oxon 141 F3
Fox La. Bice 65 E1
Fox La. Mi Bar 60 C4
Fox La. Soul 35 F2
Fox La. Woot 159 E4
Foxborough Rd. Radl 160 C1
Foxburrow Cl. Sta Har 120 A1
Foxburrow La. Crawl 103 F2
Foxburrow La. Hail 103 F2
Foxcombe Ct. Abing 179 E4
Foxcombe La. Sunn 141 D1
Foxcombe Rd. Sunn 140 C1
Foxcroft Dr. Cart 115 E1
Foxfield. Ch No 42 C1
Foxglove La. W Hag 218 B2
Foxglove Rd. Begb 108 A4
Foxhall Rd. Didc 200 B1
Foxhill Cl. Shipl 260 A3
Foxhill La. Shipl 259 F3
Foxton Cl. Cutte 108 C1
Foxwell Dr. Oxon 124 A3
Foxwood Cl. Aston 135 F2
Foxwood Cl. Banb 16 B1
Foxwood. Aston 135 F2
Framlands Cl. Want 214 B3
Framlingham Dr. Caver 259 F3
Frampton Cl. Sonn 260 C1
Frances Rd. Mi Bar 60 C4
Francis Little Dr. Abing 179 E3
Franklin Cl. Chalg 184 B3
Franklin Rd. Oxon 124 A2
Franklyn Cl. Abing 159 F1
Fraser Ave. Caver 259 E3
Fraser Gdns. Wall 221 E3
Frax Cl. K Bag 156 C1
Frederick Rd. Oxon 142 B2
Freeborn Cl. Kidl 92 C1
Freehold St. Lo Hey 62 B3
Freelands Rd. Oxon 141 F3
Freeman Rd. Didc 200 B1
Freemans Rd. Bod 22 C4
French Cl. Witn 117 F4
French Laurence Way. Chalg 184 B3
Frenchay Rd. Oxon 123 D3
Frensham Cl. Banb 9 D1
Frethern Cl. Burf 100 C2
Friars Cl. Shriv 209 D3
Friars Furlong. L Cre 129 E4
Friars Wharf. Oxon 141 E4
Friars' Entry. Oxon 123 E1
Friday La. Wheat 144 A4
Friday St. Hen-on-T 244 C1
Friends Cl. Stone 89 E4
Frilford Rd. March 178 B3
Frilsham St. Sut C 200 A4
Fritwell Rd. Mi Sto 50 A2
Frog La. Lyne 70 B3
Frogmore La. S in V 194 C4
Frome Rd. Harw 217 E1
Fruitlands. Eyns 120 B4
Fuchsia Wlk. Banb 9 D1
Fullbrook Cres. Read 257 E2
Fullers Field. G Mil 145 E1
Fullers Rd. Ast T 219 F1
Fullwell Cl. Abing 159 F1
Fulmar Ct. Bice 66 A2
Fulmar Pl. Grove 196 B1
Fulton Rd. Ch We 68 A2
Fulwell Rd. West 25 D2
Furlong Cl. Oxon 142 B2
Furlong Row. Clan 152 C4
Furlongs The. Tha 147 E3
Fyfield Cl. Want 214 C2
Fyfield Rd. Oxon 123 E2
Gadge Cl. Tha 129 F1
Gainsborough C. Hen-on-T 254 B4
Gainsborough Green. Abing 179 F3
Gainsborough Hill. Hen-on-T 254 B4
Gainsborough Rd. Hen-on-T 254 B4
Gaisford Rd. Oxon 142 B2
Gall Cl. Abing 180 B4
Galley Field. Abing 180 A4
Gallowstree Rd. R Pep 252 C4
Galsworthy Dr. Caver 259 F3
Gangsdown Hill. Nett 223 F2
Gap The. March 178 B3
Garde Rd. Sonn 260 C2
Garden Cl. Banb 16 B4
Garden Cl. Didc 218 B4
Gardens The. Radl 160 C2
Gardens The. S Sto 239 E2
Gardiner Cl. Abing 180 B4
Gardiner St. Oxon 124 B1
Garford Cl. Abing 160 A1
Garford Rd. Oxon 123 E3
Garne's La. Fulb 100 C3
Garner Cl. Cart 115 E3
Garsington Rd. Oxon 142 C2
Garsons La. Cr Gif 240 C3
Garston Cl. Want 214 C3
Garston La. Want 214 C3
Garth Rd. Didc 200 C1
Garth The. N Hink 140 B4
Garth The. Yarn 108 A3
Gas La. S u Wy 85 E4
Gascoigne Way. Blox 21 F1
Gaskells End. Maple 258 B4
Gassons Rd. Lech 150 B3
Gassons Way. Lech 150 B2
Gatehampton Rd. Gori 249 E3
Gathorne Rd. Oxon 124 B1
Gatteridge St. Banb 16 B3
Gauntlets Cl. Blox 21 F3
Gaveston Rd. Harw 217 F4
Gaydon Cl. Cart 115 F2
Gaydon Wlk. Bice 66 A2
Gayhurst Cl. Caver 259 E3
Gentian Rd. Oxon 142 C1
Geoffrey Barbour Rd. Abing 179 F4
Geoffrey Tuttle Dr. Bens 204 B1
Geoffreyson Rd. Caver 258 C3
George Moore Cl. Oxon 142 A3
George Rd. Skch 188 C3
George St. Banb 16 B3
George St. Bice 65 E2
George St. Caver 259 D1
George St. Oxon 123 E1
George Street Mews. Oxon 123 D1
Gerard Pl. Oxon 142 B3
Gerrard Rd. Ch We 68 A2
Gibbs Cres. Oxon 141 D4
Gibbs Rd. Banb 16 C4
Gibson Cl. Abing 160 A2
Gibson Dr. Up Hey 63 E4
Gidley Way. Hors 143 E4
Giernalls La. Hail 104 A3
Giffard Way. L Cre 129 E4
Gifford Cl. Caver 259 F3
Giles Cl. Oxon 142 A1
Giles Rd. Oxon 142 B1
Gillett Cl. Banb 16 A3
Gillett Rd. Banb 16 A3
Gillians Way. Oxon 142 A3
Gillott's La. Shipl 254 A4
Gillotts Cl. Hen-on-T 254 A4
Ginge Cl. Abing 160 A1
Gipsy La. Grove 214 C4
Gipsy La. Oxon 124 A1
Gipsy La. Read 257 F1
Girdlestone Cl. Oxon 124 B1
Girdlestone Rd. Oxon 124 B1
Glade The. Purl 257 E2
Glades The. Laun 66 B1
Gladstone Rd. Oxon 124 C2
Glamis Pl. Banb 15 F3
Glanville Gdns. Banb 16 A3
Glanville Rd. Oxon 142 A4
Glebe Cl. Ambr 81 E2
Glebe Cl. Chol 238 C3
Glebe Cotts. Ast R 166 C2
Glebe Ct. D Tew 47 E3
Glebe Dr. Brac 24 A4
Glebe Gdns. Grove 196 C1
Glebe La. Sonn 260 C2
Glebe Rd. Cumn 139 F3
Glebe Rd. Didc 218 C4
Glebe Rd. Purl 257 D3
Glebe Rd. S in V 194 B4
Glebe Ride. Gori 249 D3
Glebe St. Oxon 123 F1
Glebe The. Aldw 247 F2
Glebe The. Ayn 35 E4
Glebe The. Culh 180 A2
Glebe The. Cumn 139 F3
Glebe The. E Cha 213 E3
Glebe The. Ho No 30 A4
Glebe The. R Pep 242 C3
Glebe The. Stand 137 E2
Glebe The. Wheat 144 A4
Glebelands. Bamp 134 C2
Glebelands. Oxon 142 B4
Glen Cl. S Adley 52 B1
Glenham Rd. Tha 130 A1
Glenmore Rd. Cart 115 E2
Glimbers Gr. Chin 168 B3
Gloucester La. Oxon 123 D1
Gloucester Mews. Far 172 C2
Gloucester Pl. Oxon 123 E1
Gloucester Pl. Witn 104 A1
Gloucester St. Far 172 C2
Gloucester St. Oxon 123 E1
Glovers Cl. Wood 91 E3
Glovers La. Mid Ch 10 C1
Glyme Cl. Abing 160 A1
Glyme Cl. Wood 91 D4
Glyme Dr. Berin 182 B3
Glyme Way. Lo Han 106 A4
Glympton Rd. Woot 75 F3
Glyn Ave. Didc 218 B4
Glyn Rd. Wall 203 E1
Glyndebourne Gdns. Banb 9 D1
Glynswood. Chin 168 B3
Godfrey Cl. Abing 179 F3
Godfreys Cl. Grove 196 C1
Godstow Cl. Sonn 260 C1
Godstow Rd. Cutte 122 C4
Godwyn Cl. Abing 179 F4
Goffe Cl. Tha 148 A4
Goggs The. Watl 186 A1
Golafre Rd. Abing 179 F3
Golden Cross. Oxon 123 E1
Golden Hill. Chin 168 B3
Golden Rd. Oxon 142 A4
Golden Villa Cl. Banb 16 A3
Golder's Cl. Ick 127 F2
Goldfinch La. Chol 221 D1
Goldsmith Cl. Bice 65 D2
Goldsmith's La. Wall 221 E4
Goodlake Ave. Far 173 D2
Goodliffe Gdns. Read 257 E2
Goodrich Cl. Caver 259 F3
Goodrington Cl. Banb 16 A3
Goodson Wlk. Oxon 123 F2
Goodsons Ind Mews. Tha 147 F4
Goor La. Bayd 245 D2
Goose Green Cl. Cutte 122 C4
Goose Green. Dedd 33 F2
Goose La. Bod 22 B4
Gooseacre. Radl 160 C1
Goosey La. Dench 195 D2
Gordon Cl. Mars 123 F3
Gordon Dr. Abing 160 B1
Gordon Pl. Read 258 B1
Gordon St. Oxon 141 E3
Goring Rd. Woodc 250 C4
Gorse Leas. Oxon 124 A3
Gorselands. Caver 259 D3
Gorton Playne. S u Wy 70 B1
Gorwell. Watl 186 A1
Gosbrook Rd. Caver 259 D1
Gosford Cl. Kidl 108 C3
Goslyn Cl. Oxon 124 B1
Gott Cl. Buck 66 A3
Gouldland Gdns. Oxon 124 A3
Goulds Villas. Banb 16 A3
Gower Rd. E Cha 214 A4
Grafton Orch. Chin 168 B4
Graham Cl. Blew 237 D4
Graham Rd. Bice 65 E2
Grahame Ave. Pangb 256 B3
Grammar School Hill. Charl 73 D2
Gramp's Hill. Let B 231 F3
Grange Ave. R Pep 253 D4
Grange Cl. Gori 249 D3
Grange Cl. Highw 190 A3
Grange Ct. N Hink 140 A4
Grange Farm Rd. Bled R 189 D4
Grange La. Si Fe 19 E4
Grange Park Rd. Ste As 48 A1
Grange Rd. Banb 16 B2
Grange Rd. Hen-on-T 244 C1
Grange Rd. Oxon 142 A1
Granville Way. Bice 66 A1
Grasmere Ave. Read 257 F1
Grass Hill. Caver 258 C2
Grates The. Oxon 142 B2
Gravel Hill Cres. S Com 252 C3
Gravel Hill. Caver 259 D3
Gravel Hill. Hen-on-T 244 B1
Gravel Hill. S Com 252 C3
Gravel La. Dray 179 D1
Gravel La. Warb 203 D4
Gravel Pits La. Yarn 108 A3
Gravel Rd. Shipl 253 F1
Gravel Wlk. D St L 183 D3
Gravel Wlk. Far 172 C2
Graveney Dr. Caver 258 C2
Gravenhill Rd N. Ambr 81 D4
Gravett Cl. Hen-on-T 254 B4
Grays Cl. Chalg 184 B4
Grays Rd. Oxon 124 A1
Graysleaze. K End 252 B2
Great Clarendon St. Oxon 123 D1
Great Close Rd. Yarn 108 B3
Great Western Dr. Didc 200 C1
Grebe Rd. Banb 16 C2
Grebe Sq. Ch We 68 A2
Green Cl. Bens 204 A3
Green Cl. Bice 65 F1
Green Cl. Didc 218 C3
Green Cl. Wall 221 E4
Green Dean Hill. K End 252 B1
Green End Rd. Bled R 189 F3
Green Farm. Adde 23 D2
Green Furlong. Berin 182 B3
Green Heart Way. K Bag 156 C1
Green Hill. Gars 143 D1
Green Hitchings. G Mil 145 E1
Green La. Abing 159 D3
Green La. Banb 16 B2
Green La. Bled R 189 E3
Green La. Chest 79 F4
Green La. Ewel 204 B2
Green La. Hen-on-T 254 B4
Green La. Li Tew 44 B3
Green La. Longw 156 B1
Green La. Lyne 70 B3
Green La. N Lei 105 D4
Green La. Pangb 256 A2
Green La. S Com 252 C3
Green La. S New 31 F4
Green La. Shipl 254 A1
Green La. Skch 188 B3
Green La. Sunn 160 A3
Green La. U Arn 96 C4
Green La. Warb 203 D4
Green La. Wood 91 D4
Green La. Woodc 250 C4
Green N The. Warb 203 E4
Green Pl. Oxon 141 E3
Green Rd. Didc 218 C4
Green Rd. Kidl 108 C4
Green Rd. Oxon 124 C2
Green Ridges. Oxon 125 D2
Green S The. Warb 203 E4
Green St. Oxon 142 A4
Green The. Adde 23 D2
Green The. Alve 133 E3
Green The. Ast R 167 E2
Green The. B St M 32 C3
Green The. Blad 91 D1
Green The. Cass 107 E1
Green The. Ch Ba 176 A1
Green The. Ch No 42 C1
Green The. Chalg 184 B3
Green The. Charl 73 E2
Green The. Chest 79 F4
Green The. Chil 235 F4
Green The. Dray 179 D1
Green The. E Hann 197 D4
Green The. Fern 193 D2
Green The. Fif 69 E1
Green The. Frin 52 B3
Green The. Gr Ro 29 D2
Green The. Gt Bo 9 E4
Green The. Highw 190 A3
Green The. Ho No 30 A4
Green The. Hor-c-S 112 A3
Green The. Horn 7 E3
Green The. Hors 143 E3
Green The. Laun 66 C1
Green The. Milc 20 C1
Green The. S u Wy 71 E1
Green The. Sta Har 138 A4
Green The. Stand 137 E2
Green The. Steve 199 D3
Green The. Swal 19 F4
Green The. Tack 77 D3
Green The. W Hann 176 B1
Green The. W Hann 196 C3
Green's Rd. Eyns 120 C4
Greenacres La. Aston 135 E2
Greenacres. Dray 179 D1
Greenfield Cres. Stone 89 E4
Greenfield Cres. Wall 221 D4
Greenfield Rd. Stone 89 E4
Greenfields. U Arn 96 B4
Greenhills Park. Blox 21 E2
Greenleas Ave. Caver 259 D4
Greenmere. Br-c-S 202 C2
Greenmoor. Woodc 250 C4
Greens Garth. Blox 21 F3
Greensward The. Ward 5 F1
Greenway The. E Hen 216 A3
Greenway. Hadd 130 C3
Greenway. Lo Hey 63 D2
Greenwich La. Leaf 87 D2
Greenwood Ave. Chin 168 B3
Greenwood Dr. Bice 65 D2
Greenwood Meadow. Chin 168 B3
Gregory Estate. Br Ba 185 E2
Grenoble Rd. Gars 143 D1
Grenoble Rd. Sa-on-T 142 B1
Grenville Way. Tha 130 A1
Gresham Way. Read 258 A1
Greygoose La. Chas 41 D3
Greys Cl. Banb 15 F3
Greys Hill. Hen-on-T 244 B1
Greys Rd. Hen-on-T 254 B4
Greystoke Rd. Caver 259 E2
Griffin Rd. Tha 148 B4
Griffiths Cl. Nrthm 138 B2
Griffiths Gdns. Buck 66 A4
Grimmer Way. Woodc 250 C4
Grimsbury Dr. Banb 16 C4
Grimsbury Green. Banb 16 C4
Grimsbury Sq. Banb 16 C4
Grosvenor Rd. Banb 16 B3
Grosvenor Rd. Caver 259 E2
Grosvenor Rd. N Hink 140 C3
Grove Cotts. Caver 259 D3
Grove Hill. Caver 259 D2
Grove Hill. Highw 190 A4
Grove La. Ewel 205 D3
Grove Park Dr. Ard 215 E4
Grove Park Dr. Grove 197 D1
Grove Rd. Blad 91 E2
Grove Rd. Caver 259 D3
Grove Rd. Grove 214 C4
Grove Rd. Harw 217 E4
Grove Rd. Hen-on-T 244 C1
Grove Rd. S Com 252 C3
Grove St. Banb 16 B3
Grove St. Cutte 123 D4
Grove St. Want 214 C3
Grove The. Abing 160 A1
Grove The. Bourt 209 D2
Grove The. Dedd 33 F2
Grovelands Centre. Grove 196 B1
Grovelands Rd. Oxon 125 D1

Grovelands. Kidl 108 B4
Grundy Cres. Kenn 141 F1
Grunsell Cl. Oxon 124 B3
Guildenford. Burf 100 C3
Gullicote La. Hanw 8 C2
Gulliver's Cl. Horl 8 A2
Gurden Pl. Oxon 124 C2
Gurl Cl. Oxon 124 C2
Gurney Cl. Caver 258 B3
Gurney Dr. Caver 258 B3
Gwyneth Rd. Oxon 142 A1
Gwynne Cl. Read 257 E2

Hackers La. Churc 55 F2
Hadden Hill. S Mor 201 E1
Hadland Rd. Abing 180 B4
Hadleigh Rise. Caver 259 F3
Hadow Rd. Oxon 124 A2
Hadrians Gate. Brac 24 A4
Hagbourne Cl. Woodc 250 C4
Hagbourne Rd. Ast T 219 E1
Hagbourne Rd. Didc 219 D4
Hagbourne Rd. E Hag 219 E1
Hailey Ave. Ch No 42 C1
Hailey Cres. Ch No 42 C1
Hailey Croft. Chin 168 A3
Hailey Rd. Ch No 42 B1
Hailey Rd. Witn 104 A2
Haines Ct. March 178 B4
Haldane Rd. Caver 258 C3
Haldane Rd. Oxon 142 C1
Hale Rd. Bens 203 F3
Halfpenny La. Chol 238 B3
Halifax Rd. Bice 66 A2
Hall Cl The. N Ast 48 A3
Hall Cl. Watl 186 A2
Halliday Hill. Oxon 124 A3
Halls Cl. Dray 179 E1
Halls Cl. N Hink 140 A4
Halls La. E Hann 197 D4
Halton Rd. Cart 115 F1
Ham La. Aston 135 F1
Ham Rd. Want 214 B2
Hamble Dr. Abing 160 A1
Hamble Rd. Didc 201 D1
Hambleden Dr. Wall 221 D4
Hambleside. Bice 65 D1
Hambridge La. Lech 150 B3
Hamel The. Oxon 123 D1
Hamels La. Sunn 140 C1
Hamfield. Want 214 A2
Hamilton Ave. Hen-on-T 244 C1
Hamilton Rd. Cutte 123 D4
Hamilton Rd. Tha 130 A1
Hamilton Rd. Warg 255 F1
Hamlet The. K End 252 A3
Hammer La. Warb 183 D1
Hampden Ave. Tha 147 F4
Hampden Cl. Banb 15 F3
Hampden Cl. Bice 66 A2
Hampden Cl. Chalg 184 B3
Hampden Cl. Far 173 D2
Hampden Dr. Kidl 108 C3
Hampden Rd. Caver 259 D1
Hampden Rd. Oxon 142 B2
Hampden Rd. Want 214 C3
Hampden Way. Ewel 204 C2
Hampstead Hill. Shipl 260 B4
Hampton Dr. K Sut 23 F3
Hanborough Cl. Eyns 120 C4
Hanborough Rd. Eyns 120 C4
Handlo Pl. Oxon 124 C2
Hanney Rd. K Bag 176 B4
Hanney Rd. Steve 198 B3
Hannis Rd. Ch No 42 B1
Hanover Cl. Charl 73 E2
Hanover Gdns. Bice 65 F1
Hans Ave. Want 214 C3
Hanson Rd. Abing 159 F2
Hanwell Ct. Hanw 8 C2
Hanwood Cl. Sonn 260 B1
Harberton Mead. Oxon 123 F2
Harbord Rd. Cutte 109 D1
Harborne Rd. Tack 77 E3
Harcourt Cl. Hen-on-T 244 B1
Harcourt Green. Want 214 C3
Harcourt Hill. N Hink 140 C3
Harcourt Rd. Skch 188 C2
Harcourt Rd. Want 214 C3
Harcourt Terr. Oxon 124 A1
Harcourt Way. Abing 159 F1
Harcourt Way. Want 214 C3
Harding Rd. Abing 179 E4
Hardings Cl. Oxon 142 A2
Hardings Strings. Didc 218 C4
Hardings. Chalg 184 B3
Hardwell Cl. Grove 196 B1
Hardwick Ave. Kidl 108 C4
Hardwick Park. Banb 8 C1
Hardwick Rd. Hethe 52 A4
Hardwick Rd. Whitc 256 B4
Hardy Cl. Caver 259 E1
Harebell Rd. Oxon 142 C1
Harecourt. Want 214 C2
Harefields. Cutte 109 D1
Harewood Rd. Banb 16 C1
Harlech Ave. Caver 259 E3
Harlech Cl. Banb 15 F3
Harlequin Way. Banb 9 D1
Harley Rd. Caver 259 D1
Harley Rd. Oxon 122 C1
Harlington Ave. Grove 196 C1
Harlow Way. Mars 123 F4
Harmon Cl. Buck 66 A3
Harold White Cl. Oxon 124 C1
Harolde Cl. Oxon 124 B2
Harolds Cl. Leaf 87 D2
Harpes Rd. Cutte 123 D4
Harpsden Rd. Hen-on-T 254 C4
Harpsden Way. Hen-on-T 254 C4
Harpsichord Pl. Oxon 123 F1
Harrier Park. Didc 200 B2
Harrier Way. Bice 66 A2
Harriers View. Banb 16 B2
Harris Rd. Up Hey 63 E4
Harris's La. Longw 156 B1
Harrison Pl. Tha 129 F1
Harrison's La. Wood 91 D3
Harrisville. Ste As 62 A4
Harroell. L Cre 129 E3
Harrogate Rd. Caver 258 C2
Harrow Rd. Oxon 142 C2
Harrowby Rd. Banb 16 B1
Hart Ave. Far 172 C2
Hart Cl. Abing 180 B4
Hart Pl. Bice 66 A2
Hart St. Hen-on-T 244 C1
Hart St. Oxon 123 D1
Hart St. Wall 221 E4
Harthmoor Cl. Skch 188 C2
Harts Cl. Kidl 108 B4
Hartslock Ct. Pangb 256 A3
Hartslock View. Stre 249 F1
Hartslock Way. Read 257 E1
Harwell Rd. Sut C 199 F3
Harwood Rd. E Hag 218 C3
Haslemere Gdns. Cutte 109 D1
Haslemere Way. Banb 16 C3
Hastings Cl. Banb 15 F3
Hastings Dr. Cart 115 F1
Hastings Hill. Churc 55 F3
Hastings Rd. Banb 15 F4
Hatch Cl. Kirt 77 F2
Hatch End. Kirt 77 F2
Hatch Gate La. Warg 255 F4
Hatch Way. Kirt 77 F2
Hatchet Hill. Bish 227 D1
Hatching La. Leaf 87 D2
Hatfield Pits La. Hail 104 B4
Hathaways. Wheat 144 A4
Havelock Rd. Oxon 142 B3
Haven Cl. Dorch 202 B4
Havers Ave. Mil 199 E1
Hawk's La. Si Go 19 E4
Hawke La. Blox 21 E2
Hawker Sq. Ch We 68 A2
Hawkins St. Oxon 141 F4
Hawkins Way. Woot 159 D3
Hawksmoor Rd. Cutte 109 D1
Hawkswell Gdns. Cutte 123 E4
Hawksworth Cl. Grove 196 B1
Hawksworth. Didc 200 B2
Hawthorn Ave. Oxon 124 B2
Hawthorn Ave. Tha 147 E4
Hawthorn Cl. N Hink 140 B4
Hawthorn Cl. Wall 221 E4
Hawthorn Cres. Grove 214 C4
Hawthorn Gr. Cart 115 E1
Hawthorn Rd. Eyns 120 C4
Hawthorn Rd. Far 172 C2
Hawthorn Way. Kidl 108 C4
Hawthorn Way. Sonn 260 C2
Hawthorne Ave. Abing 159 E1
Hawthorne Rd. Caver 259 F2
Hawthornes. Purl 257 D2
Hayden La. Nett 224 A2
Haydon Rd. Didc 200 C1
Hayes Ave. K Bag 176 B4
Hayes Cl. Oxon 123 F2
Hayfield Rd. Oxon 123 D3
Haynes Rd. Mars 123 F3
Hayward Dr. Cart 115 E1
Hayward Rd. Cutte 109 D1
Haywards Cl. Hen-on-T 244 B1
Haywards Cl. Want 214 C3
Haywards Rd. Dray 199 D4
Hazel Ave. Tha 147 F4
Hazel Cres. Kidl 108 C3
Hazel End. Gars 143 E1
Hazel Gdns. S Com 252 C3
Hazel Gr. Bice 65 F2
Hazel Gr. Wall 221 E4
Hazel Rd. N Hink 122 B1
Hazel Rd. Purl 257 E2
Hazel Wlk. Kidl 108 C3
Hazeldene Gdns. Banb 16 B2
Hazell's La. Shriv 209 E3
Hazells La. Filk 132 A3
Hazelmoor La. K End 252 B2
Hazelnut Path. Kenn 160 C4
Hazelrig Cl. Tha 148 A4
Hazelton Cl. Tha 147 F4
Hazelwood Cl. Read 257 E1
Headington Rd. Oxon 124 A1
Headley Way. Oxon 124 A2
Healey Cl. Abing 179 F3
Hean Cl. Abing 160 A1
Hearns La. K End 252 B3
Hearthway. Banb 9 D1
Heath Cl. Milc 20 C1
Heath Cl. Oxon 142 B4
Heath Dr. Shipl 254 A1
Heath La. Blad 91 D1
Heathcote Ave. Banb 16 C1
Heathcote Pl. Abing 160 B1
Heather Cl. Cart 115 E3
Heather Pl. Oxon 123 F2
Heather Rd. Mil 199 E3
Heathfield Ave. Shipl 254 A1
Heathfield Cl. Shipl 254 A1
Hedge End. Wood 91 E3
Hedge Hill Rd. E Cha 213 F3
Hedgemead Ave. Abing 160 B1
Hedgerley. Chin 168 A3
Helen Rd. Oxon 122 C1
Helwys Pl. Kidl 92 B1
Hemdean Hill. Caver 259 D2
Hemdean Rd. Caver 259 D2
Hemdean Rise. Caver 259 D2
Hemingway Dr. Bice 65 E1
Hempton Rd. Dedd 33 F2
Hendon Pl. Bice 66 A2
Hendred St. Oxon 142 A3
Hendred Way. Abing 160 A1
Henfield View. Warb 203 D4
Hengest Gate. Harw 217 F4
Hengrove Cl. Oxon 124 B2
Henley Ave. Oxon 142 A3
Henley Dr. Highw 190 A4
Henley Rd. Caver 259 E2
Henley Rd. Dorch 202 C4
Henley Rd. Sa-on-T 161 D4
Henley Rd. Shipl 260 B4
Henley St. Oxon 141 F4
Henleys La. Dray 179 D1
Hennef Way. Banb 16 C4
Henor Mill Cl. Abing 160 A1
Henrietta Rd. Tha 130 A1
Henry Rd. Oxon 122 C1
Henry Taunt Cl. Oxon 124 C3
Hensington Cl. Wood 91 E3
Hensington Rd. Wood 91 D3
Henwood Dr. Woot 140 A1
Herald Way. Bice 66 A2
Herbert Cl. Oxon 142 A4
Hereford Way. Banb 9 D1
Heritage La. S u Wy 71 D1
Herman Cl. Abing 180 A4
Hermitage Rd. Abing 179 F3
Hernes Cl. Cutte 123 D4
Hernes Cres. Cutte 123 D4
Hernes Rd. Cutte 123 D4
Heron Cl. Cart 115 E2
Heron Island. Caver 259 E1
Heron Rd. Bens 204 B2
Heron Shaw. Gori 249 E4
Heron Way. Banb 16 A2
Heron's Wlk. Abing 159 F1
Herons Pl. Cutte 123 D4
Herringcote. Dorch 182 B1
Herschel Cres. Oxon 142 B2
Hertford Cl. Bice 65 F2
Hertford Cl. Caver 259 E3
Hertford St. Oxon 142 A4
Hethe Rd. Cott 38 A2
Hethe Rd. Hard 51 E4
Hewett Ave. Caver 258 B2
Hewett Cl. Caver 258 B2
Hewetts Cl. Leaf 87 D2
Heycroft. Eyns 120 C4
Heydons Terr. Farn 3 F4
Heyford Cl. Stand 137 E3
Heyford Hill La. Oxon 141 F1
Heyford Mead. Kidl 92 B1
Heyford Rd. Kirt 77 F2
Heyford Rd. Mi Sto 64 A2
Heyford Rd. Ste As 62 A4
Hid's Copse Rd. Cumn 140 A4
Higgs Cl. E Hag 219 D3
High Acres. Banb 16 C2
High Cross Way. Oxon 124 C3
High Furlong. Banb 16 A4
High Land Cl. Bri 98 A1
High Meadow. Caver 258 B2
High Meadow. Si Go 13 D1
High Rd. Beck 111 D2
High Rd. Br-c-S 202 C2
High Rd. Br-c-S 203 D1
High St. Abing 179 F4
High St. Adde 23 D2
High St. Ashb 228 A4
High St. Ast R 167 F2
High St. Aston 135 E2
High St. B St M 32 C3
High St. Bamp 134 C2
High St. Banb 16 B3
High St. Bens 203 F2
High St. Bish 227 E2
High St. Blox 21 F3
High St. Bod 22 B4
High St. Burf 100 C3
High St. Ch Ba 175 F1
High St. Ch No 42 C2
High St. Ch-on-O 95 D2
High St. Chalg 184 B4
High St. Child 213 E2
High St. Chin 168 B4
High St. Cl Ham 181 E2
High St. Cro 4 C1
High St. Crou 36 B4
High St. Cudd 144 A1
High St. Culh 180 A2
High St. Cumn 139 E3
High St. D St L 183 D3
High St. Dedd 33 F2
High St. Didc 218 C4
High St. Dorch 182 B1
High St. Dray 179 D1
High St. E Hen 216 C3
High St. Ewel 204 C2
High St. Eyns 120 C4
High St. Fern 193 D2
High St. Fif 69 D1
High St. Fins 88 A3
High St. G Mil 145 D1
High St. Gori 249 E3
High St. H Wald 155 F1
High St. Hadd 130 C3
High St. Harw 217 F4
High St. Highw 190 A3
High St. Ho No 30 A4
High St. Islip 93 F1
High St. L Cre 129 E3
High St. Lech 150 B2
High St. Lewk 187 D4
High St. Lo Wit 201 E4
High St. Lud 98 A4
High St. Lyne 70 B3
High St. M u Wy 70 A1
High St. Mid Ch 17 F4
High St. Mil 199 E3
High St. N Mor 220 A4
High St. Nett 224 B1
High St. Oxon 123 E1
High St. Pangb 256 B3
High St. Rams 88 A2
High St. Rat 2 A2
High St. S in V 194 C4
High St. S New 31 F4
High St. S u Wy 71 E1
High St. S u Wy 85 E4
High St. Shriv 209 E3
High St. Shut 14 A3
High St. Sonn 260 B2
High St. Soul 35 F2
High St. Stand 137 E2
High St. Steve 199 D2
High St. Stone 89 E4
High St. Stre 249 D3
High St. Sut C 200 A4
High St. Tet 166 A4
High St. Tha 129 F1
High St. Uff 211 E4
High St. Up Hey 48 C1
High St. Upt 218 B1
High St. Wall 221 E4
High St. Warg 255 E1
High St. Watch 191 E1
High St. Watl 186 A1
High St. Wheat 144 A4
High St. Whitc 256 B4
High St. Witn 118 A4
High St. Wood 91 D3
High St. Woot 75 F2
High View. E Cha 214 A2
Highbridge Cl. Caver 259 F2
Highclere Gdns. Want 214 B3
Highdown Ave. Caver 259 D3
Highdown Hill Rd. Caver 259 D3
Highfield Ave. Oxon 124 B1
Highfield Park. Warg 255 F2
Highfield Rd. Purl 257 E2
Highfield. L Cre 129 E4
Highlands La. Shipl 254 A4
Highlands. Banb 9 D1
Highmoor Rd. Caver 258 C2
Hightown Gdns. Banb 16 B2
Hightown Rd. Banb 16 B2
Highworth Pl. Witn 118 A4
Highworth Rd. Far 172 C1
Highworth Rd. Shriv 209 D4
Highworth Way. Read 257 D1
Hill Bottom Cl. Whitc 250 C2
Hill Cl. Ch No 42 C1
Hill Cl. Charl 73 E2
Hill Cl. E Cha 214 A2
Hill Cres. Fins 88 B3
Hill End. Kidl 93 D1
Hill Farm La. D Tew 47 E3
Hill Gdns. Stre 249 D3
Hill La. Clan 152 B4
Hill Lands. Warg 255 E1
Hill Rd. Chin 168 B3
Hill Rd. Lewk 187 D4
Hill Rd. Lewk 187 E3
Hill Rd. Watch 191 E1
Hill Rd. Watl 206 C4
Hill Rise. Gr Ro 29 D2
Hill Rise. Hors 143 E3
Hill Rise. Wood 91 D4
Hill The. Bourt 209 D2
Hill The. Gars 143 F1
Hill Top La. Chin 168 C2
Hill Top Rd. Oxon 142 A4
Hill View Cres. Banb 16 A4
Hill View La. Woot 159 D4
Hill View. Cart 115 E2
Hill View. K Lis 212 A2
Hill View. Oxon 125 D2
Hill View. Uff 211 E4
Hillary Way. Wheat 144 B4
Hillcraft Rd. St S J 125 E4
Hilliat Fields. Dray 179 D1
Hilliers Cl. Sut C 200 A4
Hillsborough Cl. Oxon 142 A2
Hillsborough Rd. Oxon 142 A2
Hillside Cl. Banb 16 C2
Hillside Cl. U Arn 96 C4
Hillside Rd. Mi Bar 46 C1
Hillside. Harw 217 D2
Hillside. Whitc 256 B4
Hilltop Gdns. Islip 93 F1
Hilltop Rd. Caver 258 B3
Hilltop. L Cre 129 E3
Hillview Cl. Purl 257 D1
Hillview Rd. Abing 159 F1
Hillview Rd. Oxon 123 D1
Hillwerke. Chin 168 B3
Hilly Lawn Ct. Ch No 42 C2
Hillyard Barns. Sut C 200 A4
Hilton Rd. Banb 16 A3
Hinksey Hill. S Hink 141 D2
Hinton Hill. Bish 227 D2
Hinton Rd. H Wald 156 A2
Hinton Rd. Longw 156 A2
Hinton Springs. Bish 227 D2
Hirstwood. Read 257 F1
Hiskins. Want 214 A3
Hitchman Dr. Ch No 42 C2
Hithercroft Ct. Wall 221 D3
Hithercroft Rd. Wall 221 D4
Hithercroft. Chol 220 B3
Hithercroft. S Mor 220 B3
Hive Mews. Abing 179 F3
Hixet Wood. Charl 73 D2
Hobbs Cl. Abing 180 A4
Hobson Rd. Cutte 123 D4
Hocker Bench. Bish 227 E2
Hocketts Cl. Whitc 250 C2
Hockmore St. Oxon 142 B2
Hogarth Pl. Abing 179 F3
Hogg End. Blox 21 F2
Hogg End. Ch Wa 5 F3
Holborn Hill. Let B 231 E4
Holcombe La. Ber S 183 E3
Holford Rd. Witn 117 F4
Holis Cl. Witn 118 B4
Holkam Cl. Read 257 F1
Holland Cl. Chin 168 B4
Holland Pl. Oxon 142 C4
Holland Rd. Abing 160 A1
Hollandridge La. Ston 207 E2
Hollandridge La. Ston 225 F4
Hollands Rise. K Sut 23 F2
Holley Cres. Oxon 124 C2
Holliers Cl. Syd 167 E4
Holliers Cl. Tha 147 F4
Holliers Cres. Mi Bar 60 C4
Hollington. L Cre 129 D1
Hollow Furlong. Cass 107 E1
Hollow Way. Ayn 35 E4
Hollow Way. Child 213 E2
Hollow Way. Oxon 142 B3
Holloway Hill. Co Wy 12 A1
Holloway La. Co Wy 12 A1
Holloway Rd The. Gt Cox 192 A4
Holloway Rd. Wheat 144 A4
Holloway The. Harw 217 F3
Holloway The. Moll 4 A2
Holly Cl. Bice 65 F3
Holly Cl. Kidl 108 C4
Holly Cl. R Pep 242 C3
Hollybush Rd. Cart 115 E1
Hollybush Rd. Ho No 30 A4
Hollybush Row. Oxon 123 D1
Holmemoor Dr. Sonn 260 C1
Holmlea Rd. Gori 249 E3
Holoway Rd. Witn 118 A4
Holt The. Abing 179 F4
Holt The. Moll 3 F2
Holt The. Purl 257 E2
Holt Weer Cl. Cutte 109 D1
Holyoake Rd. Oxon 124 B2
Holyrood Cl. Caver 259 E3
Holywell Cl. Abing 160 B1
Holywell St. Oxon 123 E1
Home Cl. Cart 115 E1
Home Cl. Cutte 122 B4
Home Cl. Kidl 92 C1
Home Cl. Woot 159 D3
Home Croft. Read 257 D1
Home Farm Cl. Ambr 81 E2
Home Farm Cl. E Hen 216 B4
Home Farm Cl. Adde 23 D2
Home Farm. Cr Gif 221 F4
Home Park Farm La. Sonn 260 B1
Homefield Cl. Skch 188 C2
Homeleaze Rd. Watch 209 F4
Homestall Cl. N Hink 122 A1
Homestead Cres. Up Hey 63 D4
Homestead Rd. Banb 16 C1
Homestead The. Blad 91 E2
Homestead The. Kidl 108 B4
Honey La. Chol 220 C1
Honeybottom La. Abing 159 D3

Honeyham Cl. Br No 116 B2
Honeysuckle Gr. Gars 143 D1
Honor Cl. Kidl 108 C4
Hook End La. Stre 249 D1
Hook Norton Rd. Si Fe 19 D4
Hookend La. Check 251 E4
Hop Gdns. Hen-on-T 244 B1
Hopcraft Cl. U Arn 96 C4
Hopcraft La. Dedd 33 F2
Hopton Rd. Tha 130 A1
Horley Path Rd. Wrox 8 A1
Horley Path Rd. Wrox 15 D4
Horn Hill Rd. Adde 22 C2
Horn Hill. B St M 32 C3
Horn La. Adle 40 A3
Horn La. E Hen 216 B3
Hornbeam Cl. Banb 16 A3
Hornbeam Cl. Purl 257 E3
Hornbeam Dr. Gars 143 D1
Hornsea Cl. Read 257 F1
Hornton Hollow. Blox 21 E2
Horse Cl The. Caver 259 E2
Horse Close Cotts. G Has 164 B4
Horse Fair. Banb 16 B3
Horse Fair. Ch No 42 C2
Horse Fair. Dedd 33 F2
Horse Shoe La. Chadl 72 A4
Horsecroft. S in V 194 C4
Horseman Cl. Mars 124 A3
Horsemere La. Cass 107 E1
Horsepond Rd. K End 252 A3
Horseshoe La. Woot 75 F2
Horseshoe Pk. Pangb 256 B3
Horseshoe Rd. Bled R 189 E4
Horseshoe Rd. Pangb 256 B3
Horseshoes La. Bens 203 F2
Horsham Cl. Banb 8 C1
Horsham Cl. Banb 15 F4
Horspath Driftway. Oxon 142 C4
Horspath Rd. Oxon 142 C3
Horton Ave. Tha 148 A4
Horton Cl. Tha 148 A4
Horton La. Milc 21 D1
Horton View. Banb 16 B2
Horwood Cl. Oxon 124 B2
Hosker Cl. Oxon 125 D2
Hound Cl. Abing 160 B1
Howard Ave. Grove 196 C1
Howard Cornish Rd. March 178 B4
Howard Rd. Banb 16 C3
Howard St. Oxon 142 A3
Howe Cl. Wheat 144 A4
Howe Rd. Watl 206 B4
Howgate Dr. Gori 249 E4
Howland Rd. Tha 148 A3
Hoyle Cl. Witn 104 A2
Huckleberry Cl. Purl 257 E2
Hudleston Ave. Bens 204 B1
Hudson St. Bice 65 E2
Hudson St. Dedd 33 F2
Hugh Allen Cres. Oxon 123 F2
Hughes Cl. Charl 73 E1
Hughes Cres. Long 192 B2
Humber Cl. Want 214 C3
Humber St. Blox 21 F2
Humber Wlk. Banb 15 F4
Humfrey Rd. Oxon 124 C2
Humphries Cl. Cart 115 F2
Hunsdon Rd. Oxon 142 A2
Hunt Cl. Bice 65 F1
Hunt Rd. Tha 148 A4
Hunt's Cl. Stone 89 E4
Hunter Cl. Abing 160 A2
Hunter Cl. Oxon 142 C3
Huntercombe End La. Nett 224 A2
Hunters Cl. Grove 196 B1
Hunters Field. S in V 194 C4
Hunters Piece. Bourt 209 D1
Hunters Point. Chin 168 B3
Hurdeswell. Lo Han 90 A1
Hurdlers Green. Watl 186 A1
Hurst Cl. Wall 221 E3
Hurst La. Cumn 140 A3
Hurst Rise Rd. N Hink 140 B4
Hurst St. Oxon 141 F4
Huscarle Way. Purl 257 E2
Hutchcomb Rd. N Hink 140 B4
Huxley Cl. Bice 65 E2
Huxley Cl. Woot 159 D3
Hyde Copse. March 178 B4
Hyde Gr. Blox 21 E2
Hyde Pl. Abing 179 E3
Hyde Rd. Dench 196 A3
Hyde The. Abing 179 E3
Hydes The. Purl 257 E2
Hydrangea Wlk. Banb 9 D1
Hythe Bridge St. Oxon 123 D1

Ian Mikardo Way. Caver 259 E1
Ibstone Ave. Caver 259 F3
Ibstone Rd. Skch 188 B2
Ickford Rd. Shab 128 B1
Ickford Rd. Tidd 145 F4
Ickford Rd. Worm 127 F3
Ickleton Rd. E Cha 214 A2
Ickleton Rd. Want 214 A2
Icknield Cl. Ast R 168 A2
Icknield Cl. Didc 200 B1
Icknield La. Want 214 C2
Icknield Pl. Gori 249 E4
Icknield Rd. Gori 249 E4
Idbury Cl. Witn 117 E4
Idstone Hill. Ashb 228 A2
Idstone Rd. Ashb 228 A3
Iffley Rd. Oxon 141 F4
Iffley Turn. Oxon 142 A3
Ilchester Mews. Caver 259 F3
Ilex Cl. S Com 252 C2
Ilges La. Chol 221 D1
Ilkley Rd. Caver 258 C2
Illingworth Ave. Caver 259 F3
Ilsley Cl. S Com 252 C3
Ingham La. Watl 186 A1
Ingle Cl. Oxon 124 A2
Inglewood Cl. S Com 252 C3
Inkerman Cl. Abing 159 E1
Innsworth Rd. Cart 115 F2
Inott Furze. Oxon 142 B4
Ireton Cl. Chalg 184 B3
Ireton Ct. Tha 129 F1
Iron Down Hill. B St M 32 B2
Iron Down Hill. S New 31 F2
Ironstones. Banb 16 A4
Isis Ave. Bice 65 D1
Isis Cl. Abing 160 B1
Isis Cl. Lo Han 106 A4
Islip Rd. Bletch 93 D4
Islip Rd. Cutte 123 D4
Islsley Rd. Oxon 124 C2
Ivatt Wlk. Banb 16 C4
Ivy La. Moll 4 A2
Ivy La. Oxon 124 B2
Ivybank. Read 257 E1
Ivydene Rd. Read 258 B1

Jack Straw's La. Oxon 124 A2
Jackdaw La. Oxon 141 F4
Jackies La. Wheat 144 B4
Jackman Cl. Abing 180 A4
Jackson Cl. Cart 115 E1
Jackson Dr. Kenn 141 F1
Jackson Rd. Bled 54 B1
Jackson Rd. Cutte 109 D1
Jacobs Cl. Witn 104 A1
Jacobs Yd. Mi Bar 60 C4
James Ct. Clan 152 C4
James St. Oxon 141 F4
James Wolfe Rd. Oxon 142 C4
Japonica Wlk. Banb 9 D1
Jarn Way. Woot 140 B1
Jarvis La. Bice 66 A1
Jasmine Cl. Oxon 142 C2
Javelin Way. Bens 204 B2
Jaynes Cl. Banb 16 B1
Jefferson Way. Tha 148 A4
Jeffersons Piece. Charl 73 E3
Jemmetts Cl. Dorch 182 B1
Jennings La. Harw 217 F4
Jericho St. Oxon 123 D2
Jerome Way. Sh-on-C 92 B3
Jersey Dr. Banb 9 D1
Jersey Rd. Oxon 142 A2
Jervis Cl. Mi Bar 60 C4
Jespers Hill. Far 173 D2
Jesse's La. L Cre 129 E3
Jessops Cl. Mars 123 F3
Jeune St. Oxon 123 F1
Jeune St. Oxon 141 F4
John Buchan Rd. Oxon 124 A3
John Garne Way. Oxon 124 A1
John Lopes Rd. Eyns 120 C4
John Mason Rd. Abing 180 A4
John Morris Rd. Abing 179 F3
John Piers La. S Hink 141 E3
John Snow Pl. Oxon 124 C2
Johnston's Way. Ch No 42 C1
Johnstone Pl. Wall 221 E4
Jordan Cl. Caver 259 F3
Jordan Hill. Cutte 109 D1
Josey Cl. S Com 252 C3
Jourdain Rd. Oxon 142 C2
Jowett Wlk. Oxon 123 E1
Joyce's Rd. S in V 194 B4
Jubilee Cl. Ste As 62 A4
Jubilee Cotts. Ard 215 F3
Jubilee Ct. Banb 16 B3
Jubilee La. M u Wy 85 D4
Jubilee Rd. Skch 188 C2
Jubilee Way. Didc 219 D4
Judd's Cl. Witn 118 B4
Judges Cl. Kidl 108 C4
Junction Rd. Banb 16 C3
Junction Rd. Churc 55 F2
Junction Rd. Oxon 142 B3
Juniper Cl. Banb 9 D1
Juniper Dr. Oxon 142 C1
Juniper Way. Read 257 E1
Juxon St. Oxon 123 D2

Kames Cl. Oxon 142 A3
Katchside. Sut C 199 F3
Katherine's Wlk. Lech 150 B2
Keats Cl. Bice 65 D2
Keats Rd. Banb 16 A2
Keble Cl. Lech 150 B3
Keble Rd. Bice 65 F2
Keble Rd. Oxon 123 E2
Kedleston Rise. Banb 16 C1
Keens La. Chin 168 B3
Keeys Cl. Mi Sto 50 B2
Kelburne Rd. Oxon 142 A2
Kelly's Rd. Wheat 143 F4
Kelmscott Cl. Caver 258 C2
Kelso Mews. Caver 259 F3
Kelvedon Way. Caver 258 C3
Kemps Rd. Adde 23 D3
Kempson Cres. Oxon 142 A1
Kempster Cl. Abing 180 A4
Kendal Ave. Caver 259 F3
Kendal Cres. Cutte 109 D1
Kendal Piece. Charl 73 E2
Kenhill Rd. Shen 6 B1
Kenilworth Ave. Oxon 142 A4
Kenilworth Rd. Cumn 139 F2
Kenilworth Way. Banb 15 F3
Kenley Ave. Cart 115 F2
Kennedy Cl. Oxon 142 C4
Kennedy Cres. Chol 220 C1
Kennedy Dr. Pangb 256 B3
Kennedy Rd. Bice 65 E1
Kennel La. Ch No 42 A1
Kennel La. Steve 199 D3
Kennet Cl. Berin 182 B2
Kennet Cl. Bice 65 E1
Kennet Cl. Grovo 196 B1
Kennet Rd. Abing 160 A1
Kennet Rd. Harw 217 E1
Kennett Rd. Oxon 124 B1
Kennington Rd. Kenn 141 F1
Kennington Rd. Kenn 160 C3
Kennington Rd. Radl 160 C3
Kennylands Rd. S Com 253 D2
Kensington Cl. Abing 179 F2
Kensington Cl. K Sut 23 F3
Kent Cl. Abing 180 A4
Kent Cl. Oxon 142 C2
Kenton's La. Warg 255 E4
Kentwood Cl. Chol 220 C1
Kentwood Cl. Read 257 F1
Kentwood Hill. Read 257 F1
Kenville Rd. Kenn 141 F1
Kernham Dr. Purl 257 E2
Kerry Cl. Banb 9 D1
Kersington Cres. Oxon 142 B2
Kerwood Cl. Wood 91 D4
Keston Cl. Caver 259 E1
Kestrel Cl. Cart 115 E2
Kestrel Cres. Oxon 142 B1
Kestrel Pl. Oxon 142 B1
Kestrel Way. Bice 81 D4
Kestrels The. Grove 196 B1
Ketchmere Cl. L Cre 129 E3
Keydale Rd. Wheat 143 F4
Keyser Rd. Bod 22 C4
Keyte's Cl. Adde 23 D2
Kibble Cl. Didc 219 D4
Kiddington Rd. Mi Bar 60 C4
Kidlington Business Pk. Kidl 92 B1
Kidlington Rd. Islip 93 F1
Kidmore End Rd. Caver 259 D4
Kidmore End Rd. Maple 259 D4
Kidmore La. K End 252 C2
Kidmore Rd. Caver 258 C3
Kilbale Cres. Banb 16 B2
Kildare Gdns. Caver 259 E2
Kilkenny La. Br No 115 F3
Kiln Cl. Sa-on-T 161 E4
Kiln La. Gars 143 E1
Kiln La. Oxon 124 C1
Kiln La. Shipl 254 B1
Kiln La. Wheat 144 A4
Kiln Rd. Caver 259 E4
Kiln Rd. Shipl 259 E4
Kimbells Cl. Shab 128 B1
Kimber Rd. Abing 179 E4
Kimbers Cl. Dench 196 A2
Kinecroft. Wall 221 E4
Kineton Rd. Oxon 141 E4
King Alfred Dr. Didc 200 C1
King Edward St. Oxon 123 E1
King James Way. Hen-on-T 254 B4
King St. Oxon 123 D2
King Wlk. Didc 200 C1
King's Ave. Bice 65 E1
King's Cl. Tha 147 F4
King's Cross Rd. Cutte 123 D4
King's End. Bice 65 E1
King's Head La. Islip 93 F1
King's Head Mews. Ch No 42 C2
King's La. Long 192 A2
King's Mill La. Oxon 123 F1
King's Rd. Banb 16 A3
King's Rd. Caver 259 E1
King's Rd. Tha 148 A4
Kingfisher Cl. Abing 179 F2
Kingfisher Dr. Banb 16 C2
Kingfisher Way. Bice 81 D4
Kingfishers. Grove 214 C4
Kingham Dr. Cart 115 E1
Kingham Rd. Churc 55 F3
Kings Ave. Highw 190 A3
Kings Ave. March 178 B4
Kings Cl. Br-c-S 202 C2
Kings Cl. Hen-on-T 244 B1
Kings Cl. Let B 214 A1
Kings Cl. Worm 127 E3
Kings Farm La. Shipl 253 F3
Kings La. Harw 217 F4
Kings La. Kenc 132 B2
Kings Rd. Blox 21 E2
Kings Rd. Hen-on-T 244 B1
Kings Stile. Mid Ch 10 C1
Kings Way Dr. Kidl 109 D4
Kingsclere Rd. Bice 65 E1
Kingsey Rd. Tha 148 A4
Kingsholme Cl. E Hag 218 C3
Kingsley Rd. Bice 65 D2
Kingsmead. Lech 150 B3
Kingston Cl. Abing 179 F4
Kingston Hts. N Lei 105 D4
Kingston Rd. Oxon 123 D2
Kingstone Hill. Ast R 188 A4
Kingsway. Banb 16 A3
Kingsway. Caver 259 F3
Kingswood La. W Und 98 C3
Kinson Rd. Read 258 A1
Kipling Cl. Bice 65 E2
Kirby Cl. Mi Bar 60 C4
Kirby Rd. Ch We 68 A2
Kirk Cl. Cutte 109 D1
Kirk Cl. Kenn 160 C4
Kirkfell Cl. Read 257 E1
Kirkham Cl. Caver 259 F3
Kirtlington Rd. Up Hey 63 D4
Kit La. St Row 241 E3
Knapp Cl. Abing 179 E4
Knappe Cl. Hen-on-T 254 B4
Knapton's Croft. Lo Hey 62 B3
Knighton Cl. Caver 259 D2
Knighton Hill. Wool 210 C1
Knights Rd. Oxon 142 B1
Knights Way. Caver 259 D3
Knightsbridge La. Sto Ta 186 A3
Knoll Cl. Let B 231 F4
Knoll The. Read 257 D1
Knolles Rd. Oxon 142 B2
Knollys Cl. Abing 160 A2
Knowlands. Highw 190 A4
Knowle Cl. Caver 258 B2
Knowle La. W-on-G 79 D1
Knowsley Rd. Purl 257 E2
Kybald St. Oxon 123 E1
Kynaston Rd. Didc 218 C4
Kysbie Cl. Abing 159 F2

Laburnum Ave. Abing 159 E1
Laburnum Cl. Ambr 81 E2
Laburnum Cres. Kidl 108 C3
Laburnum Gr. Banb 16 B1
Laburnum Gr. Didc 218 C4
Laburnum Rd. N Hink 140 B4
Lacemakers. Chin 168 B3
Lacemakers. L Cre 129 E4
Lacey Dr. Tha 148 A4
Lackmore Gdns. Woodc 250 C4
Ladburn La. Shilt 115 D3
Ladder Hill. Wheat 144 A4
Ladenham Rd. Oxon 142 C2
Lady Gr. Lo Wit 201 D2
Lady Jane Ct. Caver 259 D2
Lady Wlk. Uff 211 E4
Ladygrove Paddock. Abing 179 E3
Ladywell Cl. N Lei 105 E3
Lake Rd. E Hag 218 C3
Lake Rd. Shriv 209 E4
Lake St. Oxon 141 E3
Lake View. Cott 38 A2
Lakeside Ind Est. Stand 137 F4
Lakeside. Cutte 108 C1
Lamarsh Rd. Oxon 122 C1
Lamb La. Blad 91 D1
Lamb's Cres. Banb 16 C3
Lambe Ave. Mil 199 E2
Lambert Wlk. Tha 129 F1
Lamborough Hill. Woot 159 D3
Lambourn Rd. Oxon 142 A2
Lambourne Cres. Bice 65 F1
Lambourne Rd. S Com 252 C3
Lambrick Way. Abing 179 F2
Lambridge La. Hen-on-T 244 B2
Lambridge La. Hen-on-T 244 B2
Lambridge Wd R. Hen-on-T 244 A2
Lambs Cl. Kidl 92 C1
Lambton Cl. Oxon 142 C3
Lammas Cl. Abing 159 F1
Lamorna Cres. Read 257 E1
Lampitts Green. Wrox 15 D4
Lancaster Ave. Bens 204 B2
Lancaster Cl. Bice 66 A2
Lanchester Dr. Banb 15 F4
Lancott La. Stand 137 D2
Lancut Rd. Witn 103 F1
Landells. Bamp 134 C2
Landseer Wlk. Abing 179 F3
Lane Cl. Horl 8 A2
Lane Cl. Kidl 108 B4
Lane End. Cr Gif 222 A4
Lane The. Bish 227 D2
Lane The. Chas 40 B4
Lane The. Chil 235 F4
Lane The. Cudd 144 A1
Lane The. Dedd 33 D2
Lane The. Frit 49 F4
Lane The. Gt Tew 45 E4
Lane The. Lo Hey 62 B3
Lanes The. Bamp 134 C2
Langdale Gate. Witn 118 A4
Langdale Rd. Tha 148 A4
Langford Cl. Caver 259 E3
Langford Gdns. Bice 65 E1
Langford La. Kidl 92 A1
Langford La. Wend 80 B3
Langhams Way. Warg 255 F1
Langley Cl. Oxon 124 B1
Langley La. Clan 152 B3
Langley Rd. Abing 159 F1
Langley Rd. Chalg 184 B3
Langley's La. Stand 137 E1
Langton Ave. Ambr 81 E2
Lanham Way. Oxon 142 A1
Lansdown Cl. Banb 16 A2
Lansdown Rd. Far 173 D2
Lansdowne Rd. Woot 159 D3
Lapwing La. Chol 221 D1
Larch Cl. Bice 65 F3
Larch Cl. K Bag 156 C1
Larch End. Gars 143 E1
Larches The. Cart 115 E1
Larches The. Oxon 125 D2
Larissa Cl. Read 257 F1
Lark Hill. Ard 215 D1
Larkdown. Want 214 C2
Larkfield. Chol 221 D1
Larkfields. Oxon 124 C1
Larkhill Pl. Abing 179 E4
Larkhill Rd. Abing 179 F4
Larkins La. Oxon 124 B2
Larksfield Cl. Cart 133 E4
Larksfield Rd. Banb 16 B1
Larkswood Cl. Read 257 E2
Larsen Rd. Up Hey 63 E4
Lashbrook Mead. Shipl 255 D2
Lashbrook Rd. Shipl 255 D2
Lashford La. Woot 158 C4
Lashford Rd. Woot 158 C4
Lashlake Rd. Tha 129 F1
Latchford La. G Has 164 C4
Lathbury Rd. Oxon 123 D3
Latimer Rd. Cart 115 F1
Latimer Rd. Oxon 124 B1
Latton Cl. Chil 235 F4
Latton Cl. K Bag 156 B1
Laud's Cl. Hen-on-T 244 B1
Laughton Hill. Stone 89 E4
Launceston Ave. Caver 259 F3
Laundry La. Aston 135 E2
Launton Rd. Bice 66 A1
Laurel Cl. Banb 16 B1
Laurel Cl. Chalg 184 B4
Laurel Cres. Grove 214 C4
Laurel Dr. K Bag 156 C1
Laurel Farm Cl. Oxon 124 B2
Laurels The. Frin 52 B3
Laurels The. Gt Cox 192 B4
Laurels The. Tet 166 A4
Lavender Cl. Banb 9 D1
Lavender Pl. Cart 115 E1
Lavender Sq. Bamp 134 C2
Lawns The. Bri 98 A1
Lawrence Cl. Child 213 E2
Lawrence La. Burf 100 C3
Lawrence Leys. Blox 21 F3
Lawrence Rd. Oxon 142 B3
Lawrence Way. Bice 65 E1
Lawson La. Chil 235 F4
Lawton Ave. Cart 115 E1
Lay Ave. Berin 182 B3
Layton Rise. Purl 257 E2
Lea Rd. S Com 252 C2
Leabrook Cl. Banb 16 B1
Leach Rd. Berin 182 B3
Leach Rd. Bice 65 E1
Leafield Rd. Crawl 103 F3
Leafield Rd. Oxon 142 B3
Leafield Rd. S u Wy 86 A3
Leamington Dr. Far 172 C1
Leaver Rd. Hen-on-T 244 B1
Lechlade Rd. Busc 171 E4
Lechlade Rd. Far 172 B3
Lechlade Rd. Highw 190 A4
Lechlade Rd. Lang 132 B1
Leckford Pl. Oxon 123 D2
Leckford Rd. Oxon 123 D2
Ledbury Cl. Read 258 B1
Ledgers Cl. Oxon 142 B1
Lee Ave. Abing 180 A4
Lee Cl. Charl 73 E2
Lee Cl. Kidl 92 B1
Lee Ct. Tha 147 F4
Lee Rd. Bled R 169 F3
Lees Hts. Charl 73 E2
Lees The. Far 172 C2
Leicester Cl. Hen-on-T 244 B2
Leiden Rd. Oxon 142 C4
Leigh Cl. N Lei 105 D3
Leigh Gr. Banb 16 B3
Lely Ct. Abing 179 F3
Lennox Gdns. Banb 16 A2
Lenthal. Bletch 93 D4
Lenthall Rd. Abing 179 F4
Lenthall Rd. Oxon 141 F2
Lenton Rd. Banb 16 B1
Leopold St. Oxon 142 A4
Lerwick Croft. Bice 66 A2
Lester Way. Wall 221 D4

Letcombe Ave. Abing 179 F4
Letcombe Wlk. Grove 196 B1
Levenot Cl. Banb 16 C3
Levery Cl. Abing 180 B4
Lewell Ave. Mars 123 F2
Lewin Cl. Oxon 142 B2
Lewington Cl. G Has 164 B4
Lewis Cl. Oxon 125 D1
Lewis Rd. Ch No 42 B1
Ley The. Wood 91 E3
Leybourne Gdns. Chin 168 B4
Leys App. Ch No 42 C1
Leys Cl. Wrox 15 D4
Leys Pl. Oxon 142 A4
Leys Rd. Cumn 139 E3
Leys The. Adde 22 C2
Leys The. Ch No 42 B1
Leys The. Sal 41 F3
Leys Villas. Witn 118 A4
Leyshon Rd. Wheat 144 B4
Library Ave. Harw 217 E1
Liddell Rd. Oxon 142 B2
Lidderdale Rd. Ch We 68 A2
Liddiard Cl. Kenn 160 C4
Liddiard Cl. Want 214 B3
Liddon Rd. Chalg 184 B3
Lido Rd. Chil 234 C4
Lidsey Rd. Banb 16 A3
Lilac Cl. Purl 257 E3
Limborough Rd. Want 214 B3
Lime Ave. Banb 16 C2
Lime Cres. Bice 65 F3
Lime Gr. Chin 168 B3
Lime Gr. K Bag 156 B1
Lime Kiln Rd. Tack 77 E3
Lime Rd. N Hink 140 B4
Lime Tree Rd. Gori 249 D3
Lime Wlk. Oxon 124 B1
Limes The. Dorch 182 B1
Limes The. S Adley 52 B1
Limetree Cl. Grove 196 B1
Linacre Cl. Didc 219 D4
Lince La. Kirt 77 F1
Lincoln Cl. Banb 16 A3
Lincoln Cl. Bice 66 A2
Lincoln Cl. Stand 137 E2
Lincoln Gdns. Didc 219 D4
Lincoln Pl. Tha 147 F4
Lincoln Rd. Oxon 141 E3
Lincombe La. Sunn 159 F4
Lincraft Cl. Kidl 108 C4
Linden Cres. Grove 196 C1
Linden Gate. Harw 217 F4
Linden Rd. Bice 65 F1
Lindsay Dr. Abing 160 A1
Link The. Banb 16 A3
Link The. Mars 123 F2
Link The. Oxon 124 C2
Links Rd. Kenn 160 C4
Links The. Cr Gif 221 F4
Linkside Ave. Cutte 108 C1
Linkwood Rd. Curb 103 E1
Linnet Cl. Oxon 142 B1
Linton Rd. Oxon 123 E3
Lion Meadow. Nett 224 B1
Lipscombe Pl. Cart 115 E2
Lister Cl. Purl 257 E3
Litchfield Cl. Enst 58 C3
Lithgow Rd. Ch We 68 A2
Little Acreage. Mars 123 F3
Little Brewery St. Oxon 123 F1
Little Bridge Rd. Blox 21 E2
Little Bury. Gars 143 D1
Little Clarendon St. Oxon 123 E1
Little Croft Rd. Gori 249 E3
Little Glebe. Sonn 260 C2
Little Green. Blox 21 E2
Little Howe Cl. Radl 160 C2
Little La. Ayn 35 E4
Little La. Mil 199 E3
Little Lees. Charl 73 E2
Littlegate St. Oxon 141 E4
Littlehay Rd. Oxon 142 A3
Littlejohn's La. Read 258 B1
Littlemore Rd. Oxon 142 B2
Littlestead Cl. Caver 259 F3
Littlewood. Skch 188 C3
Littleworth Hill. Want 214 B3
Littleworth Rd. Bens 203 F2
Littleworth Rd. Wheat 144 A4
Lobelia Rd. Oxon 142 C1
Lock Cres. Kidl 108 C3
Lockheart Cres. Oxon 142 B2
Locks La. Want 214 B2
Lockstile Mead. Gori 249 E4
Lockstile Way. Gori 249 E3
Lockway. Dray 199 D4
Locombe Hill. Ea Mar 131 D4
Lodden Ave. Berin 182 B3
Loddon Cl. Abing 160 A1
Loddon Cl. Bice 65 E1
Loddon Dr. Didc 201 D1
Loddon Dr. Warg 255 D1
Loder Rd. Harw 217 F4
Loder's Field. Lech 150 B2
Loders The. Lech 150 B2
Lodge Cl. Banb 16 B2
Lodge Cl. Mars 123 F4
Lodge Rd. Lo Han 90 C1
Logic La. Oxon 123 E1
Lombard St. Abing 179 F4
Lombard St. Eyns 120 C4
Lomond Ave. Caver 259 F3
London La. S u Wy 71 E1
London Pl. Oxon 123 F1
London Rd. Bice 80 C4
London Rd. Blew 236 C4
London Rd. Ch No 43 D2
London Rd. G Has 146 A2
London Rd. Holt 126 A1
London Rd. Oxon 124 B2
London Rd. Sonn 260 B1
London Rd. Upt 218 B1
London Rd. Wheat 144 B4
London St. Far 173 D2
Long Cl. N Hink 122 A1
Long Cl. Oxon 142 C4
Long Crendon Rd. Shab 128 B2
Long Ford Cl. Oxon 141 E4
Long Furlong Rd. Sunn 159 E2
Long Furlong. Hadd 130 C3
Long La. Oxon 142 B2
Long La. Purl 257 D2
Long Toll. Woodc 251 D3
Long Tow. Abing 159 E1
Long Wall. Hadd 130 C3
Long Wittenham Rd. N Mor 220 A4
Longcot Rd. Long 192 A1
Longcot Rd. Shriv 209 E3
Longelandes Way. Banb 16 A4
Longfellow Cl. Bice 65 E2
Longfellow Dr. Abing 179 E3
Longfellow Rd. Banb 16 A2
Longfields. Bice 65 F1
Longhurst Cl. Caver 259 E2
Longlands Rd. Oxon 142 C2
Longleat Cl. Banb 16 C1
Longleat Dr. Purl 257 D2
Longmead. Abing 159 F1
Longmore Ave. Ch We 68 A2
Longore. Stone 89 E4
Longwall St. Oxon 123 E1
Longwall. Oxon 142 A2
Longworth Rd. Ch Ba 176 A2
Longworth Rd. Oxon 123 D2
Lonsdale Rd. Cutte 123 D4
Lord Cl. Cart 115 E2
Lords Piece Rd. Ch No 42 B1
Lovatt Cl. Cart 115 E3
Love La. Watl 186 A1
Lovegrove's La. Check 241 E2
Lovelace Cl. Abing 160 A2
Lovelace Dr. Kidl 109 D4
Lovelace Rd. Cutte 109 D1
Lovell Cl. Duck 118 A2
Lovell Cl. Hen-on-T 254 B4
Lovell Cl. Swin 102 A2
Loverock Rd. Read 258 B1
Lower Armour Rd. Read 257 E1
Lower Bungalows. Gori 249 E4
Lower Cherwell St. Banb 16 B3
Lower Church St. Skch 188 C3
Lower Cl. Bod 22 C4
Lower Cres. M Lov 102 C2
Lower Elmstone Dr. Read 257 E1
Lower End. G Mil 145 D1
Lower End. Pidd 97 F4
Lower End. Sal 41 F2
Lower End. Shut 14 A3
Lower Farm Cl. Shab 128 B2
Lower Farm La. Moll 3 F2
Lower Hades Rd. Tack 77 D3
Lower Henley Rd. Caver 259 E2
Lower Heyford Rd. Lo Hey 63 D3
Lower Icknield Way. Chin 168 B4
Lower Rd. Ast R 166 C2
Lower Rd. Bktn 82 A2
Lower Rd. Chil 235 E4
Lower Rd. Chin 168 B4
Lower Rd. Lo Han 90 C1
Lower St. B St M 32 C3
Lower St. Islip 93 F1
Lower Wharf. Wall 221 E4
Lower Whitley Rd. Cumn 139 E4
Lowes Cl. Shipl 255 D2
Lowes Cl. Skch 188 B3
Lowfield Green. Caver 259 F2
Lowfield Rd. Caver 259 E3
Loyd Cl. Abing 160 A2
Loyd Rd. Didc 218 B3
Lucca Dr. Abing 179 E3
Lucerne Rd. Cutte 123 E4
Lucey Cl. Purl 257 D2
Lucky La. Banb 16 B3
Ludgershall Rd. Pidd 97 F4
Ludlow Dr. Tha 148 A4
Ludsden Gr. Tha 148 A4
Luker Ave. Hen-on-T 244 B2
Lumberd Rd. Abing 160 A1
Lune Cl. Didc 201 D1
Lupton Rd. Tha 148 A4
Lupton Rd. Wall 221 D4
Luscombe Cl. Caver 259 E1
Luther Ct. Oxon 141 E4
Lych Gate La. G Mil 145 D1
Lycroft Cl. Gori 249 E4
Lydalls Cl. Didc 200 C1
Lydalls Rd. Didc 200 C1
Lydia Cl. Oxon 124 C2
Lydsee Gate. Want 214 A3
Lye Valley. Oxon 142 B4
Lyefield Ct. Caver 259 D3
Lyford Cl. Dray 179 D1
Lyford Way. Abing 160 A1
Lymbrook Cl. S Lei 119 E3
Lyme Gr. Read 257 E1
Lymington Gate. Caver 258 C3
Lynch The. E Hen 216 B3
Lyndene Rd. Didc 200 B2
Lyndhurst Rd. Gori 249 E3
Lyndhurst Rd. Read 258 A1
Lyndworth Cl. Oxon 124 C2
Lyndworth Mews. Oxon 124 C2
Lyneham Cl. Cart 115 F2
Lyneham Rd. Bice 66 A2
Lyneham Rd. M u Wy 70 A1
Lynges Cl. Abing 160 A1
Lynmouth Rd. Didc 218 C4
Lynmouth Rd. Read 259 D1
Lynn Cl. Oxon 123 F2
Lynt Rd. Highw 170 A3
Lynton La. Cass 107 E1
Lyon Cl. Abing 160 A1
Lysander Cl. Bice 66 A2
Lytham End. Purl 257 D2
Lytton Rd. Oxon 142 A3

Maberley Cl. Abing 179 E3
Macaulay Cl. Bice 65 E2
Macdonald Cl. Didc 200 B1
Mackenzie Cl. Bice 65 E2
Mackley Cl. Dedd 33 F2
Macray Rd. Duck 118 A2
Maddle Rd. Lamb 229 E1
Mafeking Row. Lewk 186 C2
Magdalen Cl. Bice 65 F2
Magdalen Ct. Didc 219 D4
Magdalen Rd. Oxon 142 A4
Magdalen St. Oxon 123 E1
Magnolia Cl. Kidl 108 C4
Magnolias The. Banb 9 D1
Magpie La. Oxon 123 E1
Maidcroft Rd. Oxon 142 B3
Maiden's Cl. Watch 191 E1
Maidley Cl. Witn 104 B1
Main Ave. Sa-on-T 161 E4
Main Rd. Brou 15 E1
Main Rd. E Hag 218 C3
Main Rd. Fyf 157 E1
Main Rd. Lo Han 90 B1
Main Rd. Mid Ch 17 F4
Main Rd. Sut C 200 C4
Main Rd. W Hann 196 C3
Main St. Adle 40 B2
Main St. Bled 54 B1
Main St. Chil 235 E4
Main St. E Hann 197 D3
Main St. Fins 88 C4
Main St. Frin 52 B3
Main St. Grove 196 C1
Main St. Hanw 8 C2
Main St. Hethe 52 A4
Main St. Moll 4 A2
Main St. N New 15 D2
Main St. O Nor 42 C3
Main St. Shal 25 F3
Main St. Tad 20 B4
Main St. Turw 24 B4
Main St. W Hag 218 B2
Main St. West 25 D2
Main St. Wrox 15 D4
Majors Rd. Watch 191 F1
Makins Rd. Hen-on-T 254 A4
Malford Rd. Oxon 124 C2
Mall The. Shriv 209 F4
Mallard Cl. Oxon 142 B1
Mallard Way. Grove 196 B1
Mallins La. Long 192 B2
Mallory Ave. Caver 259 E3
Maltfield Rd. Oxon 124 A3
Malthouse La. Bod 22 B4
Malthouse La. Dorch 182 B1
Malthouse La. Lo Co 27 F3
Malthouse La. Shut 14 A3
Malthouse Paddock. Buckl 174 C4
Malthouse. Ashb 228 A4
Maltings Ct. Blox 21 E2
Maltings The. West I 235 D1
Maltsters. Stone 89 E4
Malvern Cl. Banb 16 B1
Malyns Cl. Chin 168 B4
Mandarin Pl. Grove 196 B1
Mandeville Cl. Abing 160 A1
Mandhill Cl. Grove 214 C4
Manning Cl. Blox 21 F1
Manor Cl. Aston 135 F1
Manor Cl. Cass 107 E1
Manor Cl. Dray 179 D1
Manor Cl. Gt Bo 9 E4
Manor Cl. Shriv 209 D4
Manor Cl. Sut C 200 C4
Manor Cl. W Hag 218 B2
Manor Cres. Didc 200 B1
Manor Cres. S in V 194 C4
Manor Cres. Stand 137 E2
Manor Ct. Abing 179 F3
Manor Ct. Banb 16 C4
Manor Ct. Chadl 57 E1
Manor Dr. Hors 143 E3
Manor Farm Cl. King 54 C3
Manor Farm Cl. Mert 95 E4
Manor Farm Ct. Woot 75 F2
Manor Farm La. Tidm 256 B1
Manor Farm Rd. Dorch 182 B1
Manor Farm Rd. Hors 143 E3
Manor Field. Let B 214 A1
Manor Gr. Kenn 160 C4
Manor La. Shriv 209 D3
Manor Park. Clay 1 B1
Manor Pl. Oxon 123 F1
Manor Rd. Adde 22 C2
Manor Rd. Banb 16 C4
Manor Rd. Blad 91 D1
Manor Rd. Br No 116 A2
Manor Rd. Cart 115 E3
Manor Rd. Didc 200 B1
Manor Rd. Duck 118 A2
Manor Rd. Farnb 232 B3
Manor Rd. Frin 52 B4
Manor Rd. Gori 249 D3
Manor Rd. Gt Bo 9 E4
Manor Rd. Hen-on-T 254 B4
Manor Rd. Oxon 123 F1
Manor Rd. S Hink 141 D3
Manor Rd. Tow 149 D3
Manor Rd. Want 214 B1
Manor Rd. Whitc 256 B4
Manor Rd. Witn 118 B4
Manor Rd. Wood 91 D4
Manor Way. Kidl 92 C1
Manor Wood Gate. Shipl 255 D2
Manorsfield Rd. Bice 65 F1
Mansell Cl. Lo Han 106 B3
Mansfield Gdns. Didc 219 D4
Mansfield Rd. Oxon 123 E1
Mansion Hill. Mid Ch 17 F4
Mansmoor Rd. Ch-on-O 94 C4
Manston Cl. Bice 66 A2
Manzel Rd. Buck 66 A3
Maple Ave. Kidl 108 C4
Maple Cl. Banb 16 C1
Maple Cl. N Hink 140 B4
Maple Cl. S Com 253 D2
Maple Ct. Gori 249 D3
Maple Ct. Kidl 108 C4
Maple Rd. Bice 65 F1
Maple Rd. Far 172 C2
Maple Way. S u Wy 71 D1
Maple Well. Stone 89 E4
Mapledurham Dr. Purl 257 E3
Mapledurham View. Read 257 E1
Maples The. Cart 115 E1
Maples The. Grove 196 B1
March Rd. Moll 3 E2
Marcham Rd. Abing 179 D4
Marcham Rd. Dray 179 D1
Marcham Rd. March 179 D4
Marchwood Ave. Caver 259 E4
Margaret Cl. Banb 16 A3
Margaret Cl. Bice 65 E2
Margaret Rd. Adde 23 D3
Margaret Rd. Oxon 124 C1
Maria Cres. Want 214 C3
Marines Dr. Far 172 C1
Marjoram Cl. Oxon 143 D1
Mark Rd. Oxon 124 C1
Market End Way. Bice 65 E2
Market Pl. Abing 179 F4
Market Pl. Banb 16 B3
Market Pl. Dedd 33 F2
Market Pl. Far 172 C2
Market Pl. Hen-on-T 244 B1
Market Pl. Lech 150 B2
Market Pl. Wall 221 E4
Market Pl. Want 214 B2
Market Pl. Wood 91 D3
Market Sq. Bice 65 F1
Market Sq. Witn 118 A4
Market St. Ch No 42 C2
Market St. Charl 73 D2
Market St. Oxon 123 E1
Market St. Wood 91 D3
Marlborough Ave. Kidl 92 B1
Marlborough Cl. Cart 115 F1
Marlborough Cl. Eyns 120 C4
Marlborough Cl. Far 172 C2
Marlborough Cl. K Sut 23 F3
Marlborough Cl. Kidl 92 B1
Marlborough Cl. Oxon 142 A1
Marlborough Cr. Lo Han 106 A4
Marlborough Cr. Wood 91 D4
Marlborough Ct. Oxon 122 C1
Marlborough Dr. Cass 107 E1
Marlborough Gdns. Far 172 C1
Marlborough La. S in V 194 C4
Marlborough La. Witn 118 A4
Marlborough Pl. Banb 16 B3
Marlborough Pl. Charl 73 D2
Marlborough Pl. Eyns 120 C4
Marlborough Pl. Far 172 C1
Marlborough Rd. Banb 16 B3
Marlborough Rd. Ch No 42 C2
Marlborough Rd. Oxon 141 E4
Marlborough St. Far 172 C2
Marley Ind Est. Banb 16 B4
Marley La. Chalg 184 B4
Marling Cl. Read 257 E1
Marlow Cl. Wall 221 D4
Marlow Rd. Hen-on-T 244 C2
Marlowe Cl. Banb 15 F3
Marmion Rd. Hen-on-T 254 C4
Marriott Cl. Cutte 109 D1
Marriott's Cl. Hadd 130 C3
Marriott's La. Hadd 130 C3
Marriott's Way. Hadd 130 C3
Marsack St. Caver 259 E1
Marsh Cl. Yarn 108 B3
Marsh End. Tet 147 D1
Marsh La. Clan 152 C4
Marsh La. Fyf 157 D2
Marsh La. Mars 124 A3
Marsh Rd. Oxon 142 B3
Marsh Rd. Shab 128 B2
Marsh Way. Wool 211 D3
Marshall Cl. Ch No 42 C1
Marshall Cl. Purl 257 E2
Marshall Cres. Mi Bar 46 C1
Marshall Rd. Oxon 142 B3
Marshalls Cl. Shen 6 B1
Marshland Sq. Caver 259 D3
Marston Ferry Rd. Cutte 123 E3
Marston Ferry Rd. Mars 123 E3
Marston Rd. Oxon 123 F2
Marston Rd. Tha 130 A1
Marston St. Oxon 141 F4
Marten Gate. Banb 16 B2
Marten Pl. Purl 257 D2
Martens Cl. Shriv 209 D3
Martens Rd. Shriv 209 D3
Martin's La. Dorch 182 B1
Martyn's Way. Ewel 204 C2
Maryfield. Want 214 C2
Marygreen. Grove 214 B4
Marylands Green. Nu Cou 162 B1
Mascall Ave. Oxon 142 C4
Mascord Cl. Banb 16 A3
Mascord Rd. Banb 16 A3
Masefield Cl. Bice 65 E2
Masefield Cres. Abing 179 E3
Masefield Rd. Banb 16 A2
Masons' Rd. Oxon 124 C1
Massey Cl. Oxon 124 B1
Mather Rd. Oxon 124 C2
Mathews Way. Woot 159 D3
Matlock Rd. Caver 258 C2
Matson Dr. Hen-on-T 244 C1
Mattock Way. Abing 160 A2
Mattock's Cl. Oxon 124 B1
Maud Cl. Bice 65 E2
Maule Cl. Blox 21 F1
Maunds The. Dedd 33 F2
Mavor Cl. Wood 91 D4
Mawles La. S u Wy 85 E4
Maxwell Ave. Harw 217 D2
May's Cl. Frit 49 F4
Mayfair Rd. Oxon 142 A2
Mayfield Ave. Grove 196 C1
Mayfield Cl. Cart 115 E1
Mayfield Cl. Chalg 184 B3
Mayfield Dr. Caver 259 E2
Mayfield Rd. Banb 16 B1
Mayfield Rd. Cumn 121 D1
Mayfield Rd. Cutte 123 D4
Mayott's Rd. Abing 179 F4
Mc Crae's Wlk. Warg 255 E1
Mc Kee Sq. Bens 204 B1
Mc Mullan Cl. Wall 221 E4
Mead La. Stre 249 F1
Mead Platt. Skch 188 B3
Mead Rd. B St M 32 C4
Mead The. Moll 3 F2
Mead Way. Kidl 92 C1
Mead Wlk. Didc 200 C1
Meaden Hill. Oxon 124 A3
Meadow Bank. Far 172 C2
Meadow Cl. Cumn 121 D2
Meadow Cl. Gori 249 E3
Meadow Cl. Grove 196 C1
Meadow Cl. Moul 238 C2
Meadow Cl. S u Wy 70 B1
Meadow La. Cr Gif 222 A3
Meadow La. Fulb 100 C3
Meadow La. Oxon 141 F3
Meadow La. S u Wy 70 B1
Meadow Prospect. Cutte 122 B4
Meadow Rd. Chin 168 B3
Meadow Rd. Hen-on-T 244 C1
Meadow Rd. Read 258 C1
Meadow Rd. Watch 191 F1
Meadow View Rd. Kenn 160 C4
Meadow View. Adde 23 D2
Meadow View. Banb 16 C2
Meadow View. Kidl 92 C1
Meadow View. L Cre 129 F2
Meadow View. Wend 79 F2
Meadow View. Witn 118 B4
Meadow Way. Didc 218 B4
Meadow Way. Far 172 C1
Meadow Way. Tha 129 F1
Meadow Way. Yarn 108 B3
Meadow Wlk. Wood 91 E3
Meadowbank Cl. L Cre 129 E4
Meadowbank Cl. S u Wy 71 D1
Meadows The. Watl 186 A1
Meadowside Rd. Pangb 256 B3

Meadowside. Abing 179 F3
Meads Cl. Dray 179 D1
Meads The. W Hann 196 C4
Meadside. Dorch 202 C4
Meashill Way. Chil 234 C4
Medcroft Rd. Tack 77 F2
Medhill Cl. Woodc 250 C4
Medina Cl. Didc 201 D1
Medina Gdns. Bice 65 D1
Medlar Rd. Shriv 209 E4
Medlicott Dr. Abing 179 E3
Medway Cl. Abing 159 E2
Medway Rd. Abing 159 E2
Medway. E Hann 197 D3
Melbourne Cl. Banb 16 C2
Melford Green. Caver 259 F3
Melton Dr. Didc 200 C1
Melville Cl. Bice 65 D1
Membury Way. Grove 214 B4
Memorial Ave. Shipl 254 C1
Menmarsh Rd. Worm 127 F3
Menpes Rd. Purl 257 E2
Mercury Cl. Bamp 134 C2
Mercury Rd. Oxon 143 D1
Mere Dyke Rd. Steve 198 C3
Mere Rd. Cutte 122 C4
Meredith Cl. Bice 65 E2
Mereland Rd. Didc 218 C4
Merewood Ave. Oxon 125 D2
Meriden Ct. Wall 221 E4
Merlin Cl. Cart 115 E2
Merlin Rd. Abing 159 D1
Merlin Rd. Oxon 142 C1
Merlin Way. Bice 81 D4
Merritt Rd. Didc 200 B1
Merrivale's La. Blox 21 F2
Merrymouth Rd. Fif 69 D1
Merton Cl. Didc 219 D4
Merton Cl. Eyns 120 B4
Merton Rd. Ambr 81 E2
Merton St. Banb 16 C3
Merton St. Oxon 123 E1
Merton Way. Yarn 108 A3
Merton Wlk. Bice 65 F2
Metcalf Cl. Abing 179 F2
Metcalfe Cl. Dray 15 E4
Meteor Cl. Bice 66 A2
Mewburn Rd. Banb 16 A3
Mews The. Highw 190 A3
Micklands Rd. Caver 259 F2
Mickle Way. For H 125 F2
Middle Aston La. N Ast 48 A3
Middle Aston La. Ste As 48 A3
Middle Hill. Ho No 30 A4
Middle La. Shot 8 B4
Middle La. Wrox 14 B4
Middle Rd. Gt Bar 99 D3
Middle St. Islip 93 F1
Middle Way. Chin 168 A3
Middle Way. Cutte 123 D4
Middle Way. Islip 93 F1
Middleton Rd. Banb 16 C4
Middleton Rd. Buck 64 C4
Middleton Rd. Chac 10 C2
Middleton Stoney Rd. Bice 65 E1
Middleway Bottom. Child 213 E1
Middleway Rd. Child 213 E1
Midget Cl. Abing 179 E3
Midway. Mid Ch 11 D1
Miles Dr. Grove 214 C4
Milestone Ave. Sonn 260 C3
Milestone Rd. Cart 115 E1
Milestone Way. Caver 259 E3
Milford Rd. Read 258 C1
Milford Rd. Woot 76 A2
Milking La. Witn 104 A2
Mill Cl. Bix 243 F4
Mill Cl. Ch-on-O 95 D3
Mill Cl. Chadl 57 D1
Mill Cl. Dedd 33 F2
Mill Green Cl. Bamp 134 C1
Mill Green. Bamp 134 C1
Mill Green. Caver 259 E1
Mill La. Adde 23 D2
Mill La. Alve 133 E3
Mill La. Banb 16 B3
Mill La. Bens 203 F2
Mill La. Brac 24 A3
Mill La. Ch Wa 5 F3
Mill La. Chalg 184 B3
Mill La. Chin 168 A4
Mill La. Crou 36 B4
Mill La. Dra 15 E4
Mill La. E Hen 216 B3
Mill La. G Has 164 B4
Mill La. Hadd 130 A2
Mill La. Hen-on-T 254 C4
Mill La. Hor-c-S 112 A3
Mill La. K End 252 B1
Mill La. K Sut 23 F2
Mill La. Kirt 77 F2
Mill La. Lech 150 C2
Mill La. Lo Hey 62 B3
Mill La. Mars 123 F4
Mill La. Mi Bar 60 C4
Mill La. Mil 199 E3
Mill La. Oxon 141 F2
Mill La. S Mor 220 A3
Mill La. Shipl 255 D1
Mill La. Skch 188 B3
Mill La. Sut C 199 F4
Mill La. U Arn 96 C4
Mill La. Up Hey 48 C1
Mill La. Wall 221 E4
Mill La. West 25 D2
Mill La. Woot 75 F2
Mill Orch. E Hann 197 D3
Mill Paddock. Abing 179 F3
Mill Paddock. Let B 214 A1
Mill Piece. Chil 235 F4
Mill Rd. Abing 179 E3
Mill Rd. Caver 259 E1
Mill Rd. Cutte 122 B4
Mill Rd. Gori 249 E4
Mill Rd. March 178 B3
Mill Rd. Nett 224 C2
Mill Rd. Shipl 255 D2
Mill Rd. Skch 188 B3
Mill St. Eyns 120 C4
Mill St. Islip 109 F4
Mill St. Kidl 92 C1
Mill St. Oxon 123 D1
Mill St. St S J 125 F4
Mill St. Steve 198 C2
Mill St. Want 214 B3
Mill St. Witn 104 A1
Millaway La. Dench 195 E3
Millbrook Cl. Blew 219 D1
Millbrook Cl. Wall 221 E4
Milldown Ave. Gori 249 E4
Milldown Rd. Gori 249 E4
Miller Rd. Banb 16 A3
Miller Rd. Wheat 144 B4
Miller's Acre. Cutte 109 D1
Millers Cl. Chalg 184 B4
Millers Cl. Gori 249 D4
Millers La. Horn 7 E4
Millers Turn. Chin 168 A3
Millfield Ave. M Gib 67 F2
Millfield Cl. M Gib 67 F2
Millham The. E Hen 216 A3
Millmoor Cres. Eyns 120 C4
Mills La. Wrox 15 D4
Millstream Ct. Cutte 122 B4
Millview. Ch No 42 C1
Millway Cl. Cutte 122 C4
Millway La. Apple 157 F3
Millwood End. Lo Han 90 A1
Millwood Vale. Lo Han 90 A1
Milne Pl. Oxon 124 A3
Milton Cl. Bice 65 E2
Milton Cl. Hen-on-T 244 B1
Milton Cres. For H 125 F2
Milton La. Steve 199 D3
Milton Manor Dr. L Mil 163 F3
Milton Park. Mil 199 E2
Milton Rd. Blox 21 F2
Milton Rd. Milt 22 B1
Milton Rd. Oxon 142 A3
Milton Rd. S u Wy 70 B1
Milton Rd. Sut C 199 F3
Milton Rd. Sut C 200 A2
Milton St. Banb 16 B3
Milvery Way. Oxon 142 A2
Minchery Farm Cotts. Oxon .. 142 B1
Minchery Rd. Oxon 142 B1
Minchins Cl. Abing 180 B4
Minnow La. Gt Bar 99 E3
Minns Ind Est. N Hink 122 B1
Minns Rd. Grove 196 C1
Minster Rd. Br No 116 A3
Minster Rd. Oxon 142 A4
Minster Riding. M Lov 102 C2
Minton Cl. Read 257 F1
Minty Cl. Cart 115 E1
Mirfield Rd. Witn 117 F4
Mitchell Cl. Tha 147 F4
Mitchell Cl. Woot 159 D4
Moat Cl. Br No 116 A2
Moat La. M Gib 67 F1
Moat The. King 54 C3
Moat's Cres. Tha 148 A4
Mobbs La. Ho No 30 A4
Moberly Cl. Oxon 141 F4
Mold Cres. Banb 16 A3
Mollington La. Warm 3 D2
Molyneux Dr. Bod 22 C4
Monarchs Ct. Bens 203 F2
Monique Ct. Banb 9 D1
Monkley Ct. Caver 259 E1
Monks Cl. Dorch 182 C1
Monks Cl. Oxon 142 B1
Monks Mead. Br-c-S 202 C1
Monmouth Rd. Oxon 141 E3
Mons Way. Abing 159 E1
Montabaur Rd. Brac 24 A4
Montagu Rd. N Hink 140 B4
Montague St. Caver 259 E1
Montgomery Rd. Buck 66 A4
Montpelier Dr. Caver 259 E3
Montrose Way. Tha 148 A4
Monument Ind Park. Chalg 184 C4
Monument Rd. Chalg 184 C3
Monument St. Banb 16 B3
Moody Rd. Oxon 123 F2
Moor Ave. Witn 104 A1
Moor La. S New 31 F4
Moor Pond Cl. Bice 65 F1
Moorbank. Oxon 142 C2
Moorbrook. Didc 200 B2
Moorend La. Tha 129 F1
Moorend La. Tha 130 A1
Moorgate. Lech 150 A2
Moorland Rd. Witn 117 F4
Moorlands Cl. Witn 103 F1
Moorlands The. Bens 204 A2
Moorlands The. Kidl 92 C1
Moors Cl. Duck 118 A3
Moors Drive The. Mid Ch 17 F4
Moors The. Kidl 92 B1
Moors The. Pangb 256 B3
Morecambe Ave. Caver 258 C3
Moreton Ave. Wall 221 D4
Moreton La. Nrthm 156 C4
Moreton La. Tha 147 F4
Moreton Rd. Ast T 219 F1
Moreton Rd. Cutte 123 D3
Morgan Cl. Banb 15 F4
Morland Rd. March 178 B3
Morlands. E Hann 197 D4
Morrell Ave. Oxon 142 A4
Morrell Cl. Kidl 108 B4
Morrell Cres. Oxon 142 A1
Morrells Cl. Didc 200 B1
Morris Cres. Oxon 142 A3
Morris Dr. Banb 15 F4
Morse Rd. Didc 218 B3
Mortimer Dr. Mars 123 F2
Mortimer Rd. Oxon 141 F2
Morton Ave. Kidl 108 C4
Morton Cl. Abing 180 B4
Morton Cl. Kidl 108 C4
Mosquito La. Bens 204 B1
Moss Cl. Caver 259 E2
Motte The. Abing 179 F4
Mount Owen Rd. Bamp 135 D2
Mount Pl. Oxon 123 D1
Mount Pleasant. Lech 150 B2
Mount St. Oxon 123 D1
Mount The. Caver 258 C2
Mount The. Tet 166 A4
Mount View. Hen-on-T 244 B1
Mountfield Rd. Witn 117 F4
Mountfield. Gori 249 E4
Mousey La. Wall 221 E4
Mowbray Dr. Read 258 A1
Mowbray Rd. Didc 218 C3
Mowforth Cl. Woodc 240 C1
Mulberry Dr. Wheat 144 A4
Mulcaster Ave. Kidl 108 C4
Mullard Way. Abing 179 F4
Mumbery Hill. Warg 255 F1
Murcott Rd. U Arn 96 B3
Murdock Cl. Dedd 33 F2
Murdock Rd. Bice 66 A1
Murren The. Chol 221 E3
Museum Rd. Oxon 123 E1
Musgrave Rd. Chin 168 B1
Mustard La. Sonn 260 C1
Myrtle Cl. Lo Han 90 A1
Myrtle Cl. Read 257 E2

Naldertown. Want 214 B3
Napier Ct. Abing 180 A4
Napier Rd. Oxon 142 B3
Nappins Cl. L Cre 129 E3
Naseby Cl. Tha 130 A1
Nash Dr. Abing 179 E3
Nash La. Free 106 A4
Neal's La. St Row 242 A1
Needlemakers. L Cre 129 E4
Neithrop Ave. Banb 16 A4
Neithrop Cl. Banb 16 A4
Nelson Cl. Wall 221 E4
Nelson Rd. Caver 259 E1
Nelson St. Oxon 123 D1
Nelson St. Tha 147 F4
Nene Gr. Didc 201 D1
Nene Rd. Abing 159 E1
Nether Cl. Brac 24 A4
Netheravon Cl. Cart 115 F1
Nethercote La. Lewk 167 D1
Nethercote Rd. Tack 77 E3
Netherton La. Fyf 157 E2
Netherton Rd. Apple 157 F3
Netherwoods Rd. Oxon 124 C1
Netherworton Rd. B St M 32 C3
Netley Cl. Caver 259 F3
Netting St. Ho No 30 A4
Nettleton Dr. Up Hey 63 E4
Neville Way. S in V 194 C4
Nevis Rd. Read 257 E2
New Cross Rd. Oxon 124 C2
New High St. Oxon 124 B1
New Hill. Purl 257 E3
New Inn Hall St. Oxon 123 E1
New Inn Rd. Beck 111 D1
New Pond La. Ch-on-O 95 D3
New Rd. Adde 22 C2
New Rd. Bamp 134 C2
New Rd. Banb 16 B3
New Rd. Bled 54 B1
New Rd. Bletch 93 D4
New Rd. Ch Ba 175 F1
New Rd. Child 213 D3
New Rd. E Hag 219 D3
New Rd. Gt Tew 45 E3
New Rd. Hail 104 A3
New Rd. Kidd 75 E4
New Rd. King 54 C2
New Rd. Lo Han 90 A1
New Rd. March 178 B3
New Rd. Oxon 123 D1
New Rd. Radl 160 C1
New Rd. Rat 2 A2
New Rd. Shipl 255 D2
New Rd. Shot 8 B4
New Rd. Skch 188 C2
New Rd. Wall 221 E4
New Rd. Warb 203 D3
New Rd. Watl 186 A1
New Rd. Wood 91 D3
New Row. Buck 64 C4
New St. Abing 179 F4
New St. Bice 65 F2
New St. Ch No 42 C2
New St. Dedd 33 F2
New St. Hen-on-T 244 C1
New Yatt La. Hail 104 C4
New Yatt Rd. Hail 104 B2
New Yatt Rd. Witn 104 B2
Newalls Rise. Warg 255 F1
Newbery Cl. Read 257 E1
Newbold Cl. Banb 16 C2
Newbury Rd. E Hen 216 C3
Newbury St. Want 214 B2
Newcombe Cl. Milc 21 D1
Newells Cl. Stadh 163 E1
Newfield Rd. S Com 252 C3
Newgate Rd. Mur 95 F3
Newington Rd. Stadh 163 E1
Newland Cl. Eyns 120 C4
Newland La. St Row 242 A3
Newland Pl. Banb 16 B3
Newland Rd. Banb 16 B3
Newland St. Eyns 120 C4
Newland. Witn 104 B1
Newlands Ave. Caver 259 D2
Newlands Ave. Didc 218 C4
Newlands Dr. Grove 196 B1
Newlands Mill. Witn 104 B1
Newlin Cl. Oxon 141 F2
Newman Ct. Curb 103 E1
Newman Ct. Oxon 123 F1
Newman Rd. Oxon 142 A2
Newmans Cl. W Hag 218 B2
Newmill La. Witn 103 F1
Newnham Green. Cr Gif 221 F4
Newnhamhill Bottom. St Row 242 A3
Newport Cl. Kidl 108 B4
Newport Rd. Read 259 D1
Newton Ave. Caver 259 E3
Newton Rd. Oxon 141 E4
Newton Way. Bens 204 A3
Newtown Gdns. Hen-on-T 254 C4
Newtown Rd. Hen-on-T 254 C4
Niagara Rd. Hen-on-T 254 C4
Nicholas Ave. Mars 123 F2
Nicholas Rd. Hen-on-T 254 A4
Nicholson Rd. Oxon 123 F2
Nightingale La. Highw 208 A3
Nine Acres Cl. Charl 73 D2
Nine Acres La. Charl 73 D2
Nineteenth St. Harw 217 D1
Ninety Cut Hill. Swin 102 A2
Ninth Ave. Oxon 142 C4
Ninth St. Harw 217 D1
Nixon Rd. Oxon 141 F3
Nizewell Head. Ste As 62 A4
Nobles Cl. Grove 196 B1
Nobles Cl. N Hink 140 A4
Nor Brook Cl. Abing 160 B1
Norcot Rd. Read 258 A1
Norfolk Cl. Abing 160 C1
Norfolk St. Oxon 141 E4
Norham Gdns. Oxon 123 E2
Norham Rd. Oxon 123 E2
Norman Ave. Abing 160 A1
Norman Ave. Hen-on-T 244 C1
Norman Rd. Caver 259 E2
Norman Way. Wall 221 E4
Normandy Cres. Oxon 142 C3
Norreys Ave. Oxon 141 E3
Norreys Cl. Didc 218 B4
Norreys Rd. Cumn 139 F3
Norreys Rd. Didc 218 B4
Norries Dr. Wall 203 E1
Norris Cl. Abing 160 B1
Norris Cl. Adde 22 C1
Norris Rd. U Arn 96 C4
North Ave. Abing 160 A1
North Bar Pl. Banb 16 B3
North Bar St. Banb 16 B3
North Cl. Tidd 145 F4
North Croft. E Hag 218 C3
North Dr. Grove 196 C1
North Dr. Harw 217 E2
North Green. W Hann 196 C4
North Hinksey La. N Hink 140 C4
North La. W-on-G 79 D1
North Manor Est The. Gars 143 F1
North Parade Ave. Oxon 123 E2
North Pl. Oxon 124 B2
North Quay. Abing 179 F2
North Rd. Didc 200 B1
North Rd. Moul 238 C2
North Side. Ste As 48 A1
North St. Aston 135 F2
North St. Banb 16 C4
North St. Bice 65 F1
North St. Caver 259 D1
North St. Frit 49 F4
North St. Islip 93 F1
North St. March 178 B3
North St. Mi Bar 60 C4
North St. Oxon 123 D1
North St. Tha 129 E1
North St. Watch 191 E1
North Way. Cutte 109 D1
North Way. Oxon 124 C2
North Way. Steve 198 C2
North Wield Ct. Hen-on-T 244 B2
Northampton Rd. Oxon 141 E3
Northbrook Rd. Caver 259 E3
Northcourt La. Abing 160 A1
Northcourt Rd. Abing 159 F1
Northcourt Wlk. Abing 180 A4
Northern By - Pass Rd. Cutte 108 C1
Northern By-pass Rd. Mars 124 B3
Northern By-pass Rd. Oxon 124 B3
Northfield Ave. Shipl 255 D2
Northfield Cl. Oxon 142 B1
Northfield End. Hen-on-T 244 B2
Northfield Rd. Abing 160 A2
Northfield Rd. Oxon 124 C2
Northfield Rd. Read 259 D1
Northfield Rd. Shipl 255 D2
Northford Hill. Watch 209 E4
Northmead La. Dench 196 A4
Northmoor Rd. Oxon 123 E3
Northolt Rd. Cart 115 F2
Northwood Cres. Cart 115 F2
Northwood Rd. Curb 103 E1
Norton Cl. Oxon 124 B1
Norwood Ave. K Bag 156 C1
Nottwood La. St Row 242 A3
Nowell Rd. Oxon 141 F2
Nuffield Cl. Bice 65 F2
Nuffield Cl. Didc 219 D4
Nuffield Dr. Banb 16 A4
Nuffield Hill. Nett 223 E2
Nuffield La. Bens 222 C3
Nuffield Rd. Oxon 124 C1
Nuffield Way. Abing 179 E4
Nun's Acre. Gori 249 D4
Nuneham Sq. Abing 179 F4
Nunnery Cl. Oxon 142 B1
Nurseries Rd. Kidl 108 B4
Nursery Cl. Oxon 124 B1
Nursery Dr. Banb 16 B4
Nursery Gdns. Purl 257 D3
Nursery La. Banb 16 B4
Nursery The. Sut C 200 A4
Nyatt Rd. Abing 180 B4

Oak Ave. Kenn 160 C3
Oak Cl. Bice 65 F2
Oak Dr. Kidl 92 C1
Oak End Way. Chin 168 B3
Oak La. Ambr 81 E2
Oak La. S in V 194 C3
Oak Rd. Watch 191 E1
Oak St. Lech 150 B2
Oak Tree Copse. Read 257 F2
Oak Tree Rd. Read 257 F1
Oak Tree Wlk. Purl 257 E3
Oakdene. Woodc 250 C4
Oakdown Cl. Whitc 250 C2
Oakfield Rd. Cart 115 E1
Oakfields Ind Est. Eyns 120 B3
Oakham Cl. Read 257 E1
Oakham Rd. Li Co 27 D1
Oakland Cl. Free 105 F4
Oakland Rd. Banb 16 B1
Oakley La. Chin 168 A3
Oakley Rd. Caver 258 C2
Oakley Rd. Chin 168 B3
Oaks Rd. Shipl 255 D2
Oaksmere. Apple 158 A3
Oakthorpe Pl. Cutte 123 D3
Oakthorpe Rd. Cutte 123 D3
Oasis Park. Eyns 120 B3
Oatland Rd. Didc 218 C4
Oatlands Rd. Oxon 122 C1
Observatory Cl. Bens 204 A2
Observatory St. Oxon 123 D2
Ock Dr. Berin 182 B3
Ock Mill Cl. Abing 179 E3
Ock St. Abing 179 F3
O'connors Rd. M Lov 102 C1
Octavian Way. Brac 24 A4
Odiham Ave. Caver 259 F3
Odiham Cl. Cart 115 F2
Offas Cl. Bens 204 A3
Ogbourne Cl. Want 214 A3
Old Arncott Rd. Ambr 81 E2
Old Barn Cl. Bens 204 A2
Old Barn Cl. Caver 259 D3
Old Bath Rd. Sonn 260 B1
Old Bridge Rd. Blox 21 F2
Old Burford Rd. Bled 54 B1
Old Chapel Cl. Kidl 92 C1
Old Coachyard The. Witn 104 A1
Old Copse Gdns. S Com 252 C3
Old Croft Cl. Ast R 167 F2

Old Dashwood Hill. La En 189 F1
Old Farm Cl. Abing 180 B4
Old Farm Cl. Worm 127 E3
Old Farm Cres. Read 257 E1
Old Field. L Mil 164 A4
Old Forge Cl. Bled 54 B1
Old George Yd. Burf 100 C3
Old Glebe. Tad 20 B4
Old Greyfriars St. Oxon 141 E4
Old Grimsbury Rd. Banb 16 C4
Old High St. Oxon 124 B2
Old Kiln The. Nett 224 C1
Old London Rd. Bens 204 A2
Old London Rd. Tidd 145 F2
Old London Rd. Wheat 144 B4
Old Manor Ct. Let B 214 A1
Old Marston Rd. Oxon 123 F2
Old Mill Cl. Grove 196 C1
Old Moor Cl. Wall 221 E4
Old Moor. Mil 199 E3
Old Orch. Chin 149 F1
Old Parr Cl. Banb 16 B3
Old Parr Rd. Banb 16 B3
Old Place Yd. Bice 65 F1
Old Pound The. Woot 159 D3
Old Rd. Gt Tew 45 E4
Old Rd. Oxon 124 C1
Old Rd. Rat 2 A2
Old Rd. Wheat 143 F4
Old Reading Rd. Cr Gif 221 F3
Old Sawmills Rd. Far 172 C1
Old School Cl. Buck 65 F4
Old School Cl. Skch 188 C2
Old School La. E Cha 213 F3
Old Stables The. Oxon 124 B2
Old Town. Brac 24 A4
Old Well Ct. Sonn 260 B2
Old Wharf Rd. Long 210 B4
Old Windmill Way. L Cre 129 E4
Old Witney Rd. Eyns 120 B4
Oliver Rd. Oxon 142 C3
One End La. Bens 203 F2
Onslow Dr. Tha 130 A1
Onslow Gdns. Caver 259 E2
Orange Cl. Highw 190 A3
Orchard Ave. S Com 252 C3
Orchard Cl. Abing 160 A1
Orchard Cl. Banb 16 A3
Orchard Cl. Buckl 174 C4
Orchard Cl. Cass 107 E1
Orchard Cl. Ch Ba 175 F1
Orchard Cl. Chalg 184 B4
Orchard Cl. Chol 221 E3
Orchard Cl. Combe 90 A2
Orchard Cl. Didc 200 C1
Orchard Cl. E Hann 197 D3
Orchard Cl. E Hen 216 C4
Orchard Cl. Hen-on-T 244 C1
Orchard Cl. Lech 150 B2
Orchard Cl. Purl 257 E2
Orchard Cl. Sal 41 F2
Orchard Cl. Shipl 254 C1
Orchard Cl. Tha 148 A4
Orchard Cl. Upt 218 B1
Orchard Cl. Warb 203 D4
Orchard Cl. Wheat 144 A4
Orchard Combe. Whitc 250 B2
Orchard Field La. Blad 91 E2
Orchard Field. K End 252 B3
Orchard Gdns. E Cha 213 E3
Orchard Gr. Blox 21 E2
Orchard Haven. Dorch 202 B4
Orchard Hill. Far 172 C2
Orchard La. Cro 4 C1
Orchard La. E Hen 216 B3
Orchard La. Up Hey 62 C4
Orchard La. Woot 140 B1
Orchard Piece. Moll 4 A2
Orchard Pl. West 25 D2
Orchard Rd. Buckl 174 C4
Orchard Rd. Ho No 30 A4
Orchard Rd. Mi Sto 50 A2
Orchard Rd. N Hink 140 A4
Orchard Rise. Chest 79 F4
Orchard Row. Fulb 100 C3
Orchard The. Apple 158 A4
Orchard The. E Cha 214 A3
Orchard The. Eyns 120 C4
Orchard The. Mert 95 E4
Orchard View. Cro 4 C1
Orchard Way. Banb 16 A3
Orchard Way. Bice 65 E2
Orchard Way. Chin 168 B3
Orchard Way. Harw 217 E4
Orchard Way. Kidl 108 C4
Orchard Way. King 54 C2
Orchard Way. March 178 B3
Orchard Way. Mi Bar 46 C1
Orchard Way. Oxon 142 B2
Orchard Way. Want 214 C2
Orchard Way. Witn 118 A4
Orchard Wlk. Watl 186 B1
Orchids The. Chil 235 E4
Ordnance Rd. Didc 200 B1
Oregon Ave. Read 257 E2
Oriel Ct. Didc 219 D4
Oriel Sq. Oxon 123 E1
Oriel St. Oxon 123 E1
Oriel Way. Bice 65 F2
Orkney Pl. Witn 117 F4
Ormond Rd. Tha 130 A1
Ormond Rd. Want 214 C2
Orpwood Way. Abing 179 E3
Orwell Cl. Caver 258 C2
Osberton Rd. Cutte 123 D4
Osborne Cl. Bice 65 E1
Osborne Cl. Cutte 122 C4
Osborne Cl. Kidl 108 B4
Osiers The. D St L 183 D3
Osler Rd. Oxon 124 B2
Osney Cl. Ho No 30 A4
Osney La. Oxon 123 D1
Osney Mead. Oxon 141 D4
Osterley Dr. Caver 259 F3
Osterley Gr. Banb 16 A2
Oswestry Rd. Oxon 141 E3
Otmoor La. Beck 111 D2
Otmoor La. Ch-on-O 95 D2
Otters Reach. Kenn 141 F1
Otwell Cl. Abing 160 A1
Ouseley Cl. Oxon 123 F2
Outram Rd. Oxon 142 A3
Oval The. Bice 65 E2
Oval The. Didc 200 B1
Oval The. Oxon 142 A2
Over Norton Rd. Ch No 42 C2
Overbrooke Gdns. Gars 143 D1
Overdale Cl. Oxon 124 C2
Overdown Rd. Read 257 E2
Overlanders End. Read 257 F2
Overmead Green. Oxon 142 C1
Overmead. Abing 179 F2
Overstrand Cl. Bice 66 A2
Overthorpe Rd. Banb 16 C3
Overton Dr. Tha 130 A1
Owlington Cl. N Hink 122 B1
Ox Cl. Abing 180 A4
Oxford Cl. Kirt 77 F2
Oxford Cres. Didc 218 B4
Oxford Hill. Witn 118 B4
Oxford La. Grove 196 C1
Oxford Rd. Abing 160 A3
Oxford Rd. Adde 23 D2
Oxford Rd. Banb 16 B2
Oxford Rd. Bens 203 F2
Oxford Rd. Bice 80 B4
Oxford Rd. Bletch 93 D4
Oxford Rd. Burf 100 C2
Oxford Rd. Cl Ham 181 F3
Oxford Rd. Cumn 121 D2
Oxford Rd. Cumn 139 F3
Oxford Rd. Cutte 109 D2
Oxford Rd. Dedd 33 F1
Oxford Rd. Dorch 182 B1
Oxford Rd. Enst 58 C3
Oxford Rd. Eyns 120 C4
Oxford Rd. Gars 143 E1
Oxford Rd. H Poy 93 D2
Oxford Rd. Hors 143 D3
Oxford Rd. Kenn 160 A3
Oxford Rd. Kidl 108 C4
Oxford Rd. Kirt 77 F2
Oxford Rd. Mars 123 F3
Oxford Rd. Mi Sto 64 A2
Oxford Rd. N Ast 47 F3
Oxford Rd. Oxon 142 A2
Oxford Rd. Oxon 142 B3
Oxford Rd. Oxon 142 C2
Oxford Rd. Purl 257 E2
Oxford Rd. Radl 160 A3
Oxford Rd. Read 257 E2
Oxford Rd. Skch 188 B3
Oxford Rd. Ste Ast 47 F3
Oxford Rd. Tha 147 F4
Oxford Rd. Tidd 145 F3
Oxford Rd. Wood 91 E3
Oxford Rd. Woodc 240 C1
Oxford Sq. Watch 191 E1
Oxford St. Caver 259 D1
Oxford St. Wood 91 D3
Oxhey Hill. Cro 4 B2
Oxhey Rise. Wigg 31 D4
Oxlease. Witn 118 B4
Oxon Pl. Bish 227 E2
Oxpens Rd. Oxon 141 D4
Pack & Prime L. Hen-on-T 244 B1
Packhorse La. March 178 B3
Paddick Cl. Sonn 260 C2
Paddock Cl. Bens 204 A2
Paddock Cl. Chalg 184 B4
Paddock Cl. Want 214 C3
Paddock Farm La. Bod 22 B4
Paddock Rd. Caver 259 E1
Paddock Rd. Mi Sto 50 A2
Paddock Rd. Wall 221 E4
Paddock The. Highw 190 A3
Paddock The. Up Hey 48 C3
Paddocks The. Dedd 33 F2
Paddocks The. Moll 3 F2
Paddocks The. Soul 35 F2
Paddocks The. Yarn 108 A3
Paddox Cl. Cutte 123 D4
Paddox The. Cutte 123 D4
Page Furlong. Dorch 182 B1
Pages La. Horn 7 E3
Pages Orch. S Com 252 C3
Paget Rd. Oxon 142 C3
Pagisters Rd. Abing 160 B1
Paines Hill. Ste As 62 A4
Painters Cl. Blox 21 E2
Palmer Ave. U Arn 96 C4
Palmer Pl. Abing 179 F3
Palmer Rd. Oxon 124 C1
Palmers. Want 214 C3
Pampas Cl. Cart 115 F1
Pangbourne Hill. Pangb 256 B3
Pangbourne St. Read 258 A1
Panters Rd. Chol 221 D1
Paper Mill La. S Mor 220 A3
Papist Way. Chol 239 D4
Parade The. Kidl 108 C3
Paradise La. Milc 21 D1
Paradise Rd. Hen-on-T 244 B1
Paradise Sq. Oxon 123 D1
Paradise St. Oxon 123 D1
Paradise Terr. Ch No 42 B1
Park Ave. Highw 190 A3
Park Ave. Kidl 92 B1
Park Ave. Shriv 209 E4
Park Cl. Av Da 2 C4
Park Cl. Banb 16 B3
Park Cl. Blad 91 D2
Park Cl. Cutte 109 D1
Park Cl. Didc 218 B4
Park Cl. Hanw 8 C2
Park Cl. Ho No 30 A3
Park Cl. Kirt 77 F3
Park Cl. Mi Sto 64 A2
Park Cl. N Lei 105 E3
Park Cl. S Com 253 D3
Park Cl. Yarn 108 A2
Park Cres. Abing 179 F4
Park End Pl. Oxon 123 D1
Park End St. Oxon 123 D1
Park End. Bod 16 C1
Park End. Crou 36 B4
Park Hill. Ho No 30 A4
Park Hill. Holt 126 A1
Park La. Apple 158 A4
Park La. Ast R 167 F2
Park La. Check 251 F3
Park La. Lo Han 90 B1
Park La. N New 15 E2
Park La. S in V 195 D3
Park La. Skch 188 C3
Park La. Ston 225 E3
Park La. Swal 19 F4
Park La. Wood 91 D3
Park Rd. Abing 179 F4
Park Rd. Banb 16 A3
Park Rd. Ch No 42 C2
Park Rd. Combe 90 A3
Park Rd. Didc 218 B4
Park Rd. Duck 118 A2
Park Rd. Far 172 C2
Park Rd. Hen-on-T 244 C1
Park Rd. Ho No 30 A4
Park Rd. N Lei 105 D3
Park Rd. Witn 103 F1
Park Rise. Ambr 81 E2
Park Side. March 178 B3
Park Side. Wood 91 E3
Park St. Blad 91 D1
Park St. Charl 73 D2
Park St. Tha 148 A4
Park St. Wood 91 D3
Park Terr. Tha 148 A4
Park The. Cumn 139 F2
Park The. Harw 217 F3
Park Town. Oxon 123 E2
Park View. Cr Gif 222 A3
Park View. Syd 148 C1
Park View. Want 214 C3
Park Wall La. Stre 249 E1
Park Way. Mars 123 F4
Park Wlk. Purl 257 E3
Parker St. Oxon 141 F3
Parkers Cl. Far 173 D2
Parkers Hill. Tet 166 A4
Parkhill Dr. Read 257 E1
Parklands. Free 105 F4
Parks Rd. Oxon 123 E1
Parkside. Cudd 144 B2
Parkside. N Lei 105 E3
Parkway Dr. Sonn 260 C2
Parliament Rd. Tha 129 F1
Parrs Rd. Skch 188 C2
Parry Cl. Oxon 123 F2
Parson's La. Ewel 204 C2
Parson's St. Banb 16 B3
Parsons Mead. Abing 159 F1
Parsons Pl. Oxon 142 A4
Parsons St. Adde 23 D2
Partridge Cl. Want 214 C2
Partridge Pl. Kidl 92 B1
Pascali Pl. Banb 9 D1
Patemore La. Watl 206 C1
Paternoster La. Chol 220 C1
Patrick Haugh Rd. U Arn 96 C4
Patrick Rd. Caver 259 D1
Patricks Orch. Uff 211 E4
Pattison Pl. Oxon 142 A2
Pauling Rd. Oxon 124 C1
Pauls Way. Watl 186 A1
Paynes End. Buck 65 F3
Peachcroft Centre. Abing 160 A1
Peachcroft Rd. Abing 160 A1
Peacock Rd. Oxon 123 F2
Peaks La. Stone 89 E4
Pear Tree Cl. Lyne 70 B3
Pearce Ct. Tha 147 F4
Pearce Dr. Ch No 42 C1
Pearce Way. Tha 148 A4
Pearces Meadow. Nett 224 B2
Pearces Orch. Hen-on-T 244 B2
Pearson Rd. Sonn 260 B2
Peascroft. L Cre 129 E3
Peat Moors. Oxon 142 B4
Pebble Ct. Swin 101 E3
Pebble Dr. Didc 219 D4
Pebble La. Bruc 24 A4
Peel Cl. Caver 259 E1
Peel Cl. Duck 118 A2
Peel Pl. Cart 115 F1
Peel Pl. Oxon 141 E3
Peep-o-day La. Abing 179 F2
Pegasus Ct. Oxon 142 C2
Pegasus Rd. Oxon 142 C1
Pegswell La. G Mil 145 D1
Pelham Rd. Tha 130 A1
Pelican Pl. Eyns 120 C4
Pembroke Ct. Oxon 141 F4
Pembroke La. Mil 199 E3
Pembroke Pl. Caver 259 E2
Pembroke Sq. Oxon 141 E4
Pembroke St. Oxon 123 E1
Pembroke Way. Bice 65 F2
Pemscott Cl. Alve 133 E3
Pen Way. Banb 9 E1
Pendennis Ave. Caver 259 F3
Penly Cl. Chin 168 A3
Penn Cl. Abing 160 B1
Penn Cl. Caver 259 D3
Pennington Pl. Tha 130 A1
Pennycress Rd. Oxon 143 D1
Pennyfarthing Pl. Oxon 123 E1
Pennygreen La. Br-c-S 202 C1
Pennypiece. Gori 249 E4
Pennywell Dr. Cutte 109 D1
Penrhyn Cl. Banb 15 F4
Penrose Cl. Banb 16 A3
Penrose Dr. Banb 16 A3
Pensclose. Witn 104 B1
Pensfield. Bens 203 F2
Penson's Gdns. Oxon 123 F1
Peppard Hill. R Pep 252 C4
Peppard La. Hen-on-T 254 C4
Peppard Rd. Caver 259 E3
Peppard Rd. S Com 253 D2
Peppard Rd. Shipl 259 E4
Pepper Alley. Dedd 34 C2
Peppercorn Ave. Oxon 142 C4
Percy St. Oxon 141 F3
Peregrine Rd. Oxon 142 B1
Peregrine Way. Bice 81 D4
Peregrine Way. Grove 196 B1
Periam Cl. Hen-on-T 254 B4
Perimeter Rd. Harw 217 E1
Periwinkle Pl. Oxon 143 D1
Perkins Cl. Horn 7 E4
Perrin St. Oxon 124 B1
Perrinsfield. Lech 150 B3
Perrott Cl. N Lei 105 D4
Perry's Rd. S in V 194 B4
Perseverance Hill. Shipl 254 A3
Peter's Way. Oxon 142 B2
Peterley Rd. Oxon 142 C3
Pether Rd. Oxon 124 C1
Pethers Piece. Burf 100 B3
Petre Pl. Kidl 92 C1
Pettiwell. Gars 162 B4
Pevensey Ave. Caver 259 F3
Pheasant Wlk. Oxon 142 A1
Phelps The. Kidl 108 B4
Philcote St. Dedd 33 F2
Phillimore Rd. Caver 259 E4
Phipps Rd. Oxon 142 B2
Phyllis Ct Dr. Hen-on-T 244 C2
Pickett Ave. Oxon 142 C4
Picklers Hill. Abing 160 A1
Picton Way. Caver 259 D2
Piddington Rd. Lud 98 A4
Pieces The. Bamp 134 C2
Pierce's Hill. Read 257 E1
Pigeon Farm Rd. Skch 188 C3
Pigeon House La. Lo Han 106 B3
Pigeonhouse La. Mur 95 F2
Piggott's Rd. Caver 259 E1
Piggy La. Bice 65 F1
Pike Terr. Oxon 141 E4
Pikeshaw Way. Read 257 E1
Pill La. Li Co 26 C1
Pimpernel Cl. Oxon 143 D1
Pine Cl. Gars 143 E1
Pine Cl. Oxon 142 C2
Pine Woods Rd. Longw 156 A1
Pinecroft. Cart 115 E1
Pines The. Far 172 C2
Pinetree Ct. Caver 259 D3
Pinhill Rd. Banb 16 A4
Pinkhill La. Eyns 120 C3
Pinnocks Way. N Hink 140 A4
Pinsley Rd. Lo Han 106 A4
Pioneer Rd. Ambr 81 D3
Pioneer Rd. Far 172 C1
Piper St. Oxon 124 B1
Pipers Croft. Banb 16 A2
Pipkin Way. Oxon 142 A3
Pitch The. B Bot 189 E2
Pitreavie Ave. Cart 115 F2
Pitts Rd. Oxon 124 C2
Pixey Pl. Cutte 122 C4
Pixton Cl. Didc 218 B4
Plain Rd The. Shut 14 A3
Plain The. Oxon 141 F4
Plane Tree Way. Wood 91 E3
Plantation Rd. Chil 234 C4
Plantation Rd. Oxon 123 D2
Playfield Rd. Kenn 160 C4
Playford Ct. Tha 147 F4
Playhatch Rd. Shipl 260 A3
Pleck La. Ast R 167 F2
Plot Rd. Shut 14 A3
Plough Cl. Warb 203 D3
Plough Cnr. Syd 148 C1
Ploughley Cl. Kidl 108 B4
Ploughley Cl. Mi Sto 50 B2
Ploughley Rd. Ambr 81 E2
Ploughley Rd. U Arn 96 C4
Plowden Park. Ast R 167 F2
Plowden Way. Shipl 254 C1
Plum La. S u Wy 85 E4
Plumbe Ct. Want 214 B3
Pluto Rd. Chil 234 C4
Pococks Cl. Bamp 134 C2
Puffley End La. Hail 104 A3
Polecat End La. For H 125 F2
Polstead Rd. Oxon 123 D2
Polsted Rd. Read 257 E1
Pond End Rd. S Com 253 D3
Pond Hill. Stone 89 E4
Ponds La. Mars 123 F3
Pony Rd. Oxon 142 C3
Pool Close Cotts. Li Co 26 C1
Pooles La. Charl 73 D2
Popes Acre. Hadd 130 C3
Poplar Cl. Banb 16 C1
Poplar Cl. Gars 143 E1
Poplar Cl. Kidl 108 C4
Poplar Farm Cl. M u Wy 70 A1
Poplar Farm Rd. Chalg 184 B4
Poplar Gr. Kenn 160 C4
Poplar Rd. N Hink 122 B1
Poplars Rd. Chac 10 C2
Poplars The. Laun 66 B1
Port Hill Rd. Bens 203 F3
Port Hill. Nett 224 A1
Port Way. Cr Gif 221 F2
Port Way. E Cha 214 A4
Port Way. Kirt 78 A4
Port Way. Lo Hey 62 C3
Port Way. Want 215 D3
Portal Dr N. Up Hey 63 E4
Portal Dr S. Up Hey 63 E4
Portal Dr. Up Hey 63 E4
Portland Pl. Ch No 42 C2
Portland Rd. Cutte 123 D4
Portland Rd. Milc 21 D1
Portman Rd. Read 258 B1
Portmeirion Gdns. Read 257 F1
Portway Cres. Crou 36 C4
Portway Dr. Crou 36 B4
Portway Gdns. Ayn 35 E4
Portway. Ayn 35 E4
Portway. Banb 16 A4
Portway. Crou 36 C4
Portway. Didc 218 B4
Portway. Far 172 C2
Portway. Want 214 B2
Post Office La. Let B 214 A1
Post Office La. Want 214 B2
Potenger Way. Abing 179 E3
Potkiln La. Woodc 250 C4
Pott's Cl. G Mil 145 D2
Pottery Rd. Read 257 F1
Pottle Cl. N Hink 122 A1
Poultney Pl. Cart 115 E2
Poulton Pl. Oxon 142 C2
Pound Cl. Kirt 77 F2
Pound Cl. Yarn 108 A3
Pound Croft. Grove 214 B4
Pound Field Cl. Oxon 124 C3
Pound Hill. Charl 73 D2
Pound La. Cass 107 E1
Pound La. Chol 220 C1
Pound La. Clan 133 F1
Pound La. Si Go 13 D1
Pound La. Sonn 260 C1
Pound La. St S J 125 E4
Pound La. Upt 218 B1
Pound Piece. Ashb 228 A4
Pound The. Blox 21 F3
Pound The. N New 15 D2
Pound The. Want 215 D3
Pound Way. Oxon 142 B3
Powell Cl. For H 125 F2
Powys Gr. Banb 15 F4
Preachers La. Oxon 141 E4
Prescott Ave. Banb 15 F3
Prescott Cl. Banb 16 A3
Preston Rd. Abing 179 F2
Prichard Rd. Oxon 124 A2
Priest Cl. Nett 224 B2
Priest Hill La. Hail 103 F3

Priest Hill. Caver 259 D2
Primrose Cl. Purl 257 E3
Prince Gr. Abing 160 A2
Prince William Dr. Read 257 E1
Princes Ride. Wood 91 E3
Princes St. Oxon 141 F4
Princess Gdns. Grove 214 B4
Prior's Forge. Cutte 109 D1
Prior's La. H Wald 155 F2
Priory Ave. Caver 259 D1
Priory Cl. Bice 65 F1
Priory Cl. Hor-c-S 112 A3
Priory Copse. S Com 252 C3
Priory Ct. Bice 65 F1
Priory Green. Highw 190 A3
Priory La. Bice 65 F1
Priory La. Burf 100 C3
Priory La. Lyne 70 B3
Priory La. March 178 B3
Priory Mead. Long 192 B1
Priory Mews. Wall 221 E4
Priory Orch. Want 214 B3
Priory Rd. Bice 65 F1
Priory Rd. Lyne 70 B3
Priory Rd. Oxon 142 B1
Priory Rd. Want 214 B2
Pritchard Cl. Berin 182 B3
Promenade Rd. Caver 259 D1
Prospect Cl. Stone 89 E4
Prospect Pl. Watl 186 A1
Prospect Rd. Banb 16 B3
Prospect Rd. Upt 218 B1
Prospect St. Caver 259 D1
Prunus Cl. Oxon 142 C2
Puck La. Witn 104 A1
Puddleduck La. Gt Cox 192 A4
Pudlicote La. Chils 71 F3
Pudsey Cl. Abing 179 F2
Pugsden La. Steve 199 D2
Pulker Cl. Oxon 142 B2
Pullens Field. Oxon 124 A1
Pullens La. Oxon 124 A1
Pulling Cl. Far 172 C2
Pumbro. Stone 89 E4
Purcell Rd. Oxon 123 F2
Purfield Dr. Warg 255 F1
Purland Cl. Oxon 142 B3
Purley La. Purl 257 E3
Purley Rise. Purl 256 C3
Purley Village. Purl 257 E3
Purley Way. Pangb 256 C3
Purslane. Abing 180 A4
Pusey La. Oxon 123 E1
Pusey St. Oxon 123 E1
Putman Cl. Tha 148 A4
Putman Pl. Hen-on-T 244 C1
Pye St. Far 173 D2
Pykes Cl. Abing 160 A1
Pym Wlk. Tha 129 F1
Pyrton La. Watl 186 A1
Pytenry Cl. Abing 160 A2
Pytt's La. Burf 100 C3

Quadrangle The. Bice 65 F1
Quadrangle The. Wood 91 E4
Quadrant The. Abing 180 A4
Quaker La. Warb 203 D4
Quantock Ave. Caver 259 E3
Quarhill Cl. O Nor 42 C3
Quarry Cl. Enst 59 D3
Quarry Cl. L Cre 129 E4
Quarry End. Begb 108 A4
Quarry High St. Oxon 124 C2
Quarry Hollow. Oxon 124 C1
Quarry Rd. Chadl 57 D1
Quarry Rd. Oxon 124 C1
Quarry Rd. Sunn 159 F4
Quarry Rd. Witn 104 A2
Quarry School Pl. Oxon 124 C1
Quartermain Cl. Oxon 142 A3
Quartermain Rd. Chalg 184 B3
Quebec Rd. Hen-on-T 254 C4
Queen Annes Gate. Caver 259 E2
Queen Cl. Hen-on-T 244 C1
Queen Elizabeth Cl. Didc 219 D4
Queen Emmas Dyke. Witn 117 F4
Queen St. Abing 179 F4
Queen St. Bamp 134 C2
Queen St. Caver 259 D2
Queen St. Dorch 182 B1
Queen St. Eyns 120 C4
Queen St. Hen-on-T 244 C1
Queen St. Mid Ch 17 F4
Queen St. Oxon 123 E1
Queen's Cl. Eyns 120 C4
Queen's Cres. Clan 152 C4
Queen's Cres. Dray 15 E4
Queen's La. Oxon 123 E1
Queen's Rd. Banb 16 A3
Queen's Rd. Cart 115 F1
Queen's Rd. Caver 259 E1
Queen's Rd. Tha 148 A4
Queen's St. Ho No 30 A4
Queens Ave. Bice 65 F1
Queens Ave. Highw 190 A3
Queens Ave. Kidl 109 D4
Queens Ave. Wall 203 D1
Queens Cl. Dorch 182 B1
Queens Cl. N Hink 140 A4
Queens Cl. Tha 129 F1
Queens La. Eyns 120 C4
Queens Rd. Chol 220 C1
Queens St. Blox 21 E2
Queens Way. N Mor 219 F4
Queensborough Dr. Caver 258 C3
Queensway. Banb 16 A2
Queensway. Caver 259 E3
Queensway. Didc 218 C4
Quickset Cl. Spel 72 C4
Quintan Ave. Ambr 81 E2

Rack End. Stand 137 E2
Radbone Hill. O Nor 42 C3
Radcliffe Rd. Oxon 141 F3
Radcliffe Sq. Oxon 123 E1
Radcot Cl. Sonn 260 C1
Radcot Rd. Far 172 C3
Radford Cl. Oxon 141 F2
Radley Rd. Abing 160 B1
Radnage Com R. Bled R 189 E3
Radnor Cl. Hen-on-T 244 C1
Radnor Rd. Wall 221 D4
Raghouse La. Frit 49 F3
Raglan Gdns. Caver 259 E2
Raglegh Cres. Curb 117 E4
Ragley Mews. Caver 259 E3
Ragnall's La. Hor-c-S 112 A3
Rahere Rd. Oxon 142 B2
Railway Cotts. Gori 249 E3
Railway La. Oxon 142 A1
Rainbow Way. Abing 160 A2
Raleigh Park Rd. N Hink 140 C4
Rampion Cl. Oxon 143 D1
Ramsay Rd. Oxon 124 C2
Ramsons Way. Abing 180 B4
Randall Rd. Ch We 68 A2
Randolph Rd. Read 259 D1
Randolph St. Oxon 141 F4
Range Rd. Curb 103 E1
Rannal Dr. Chin 168 B3
Rattlecombe Rd. Shen 6 B1
Rau Ct. Buck 66 A4
Raven Rd. Skch 188 C2
Ravensbourne Dr. Sonn 260 C1
Ravenscroft Rd. Hen-on-T 244 B1
Ravensmead. Banb 16 A2
Ravensmead. Chin 168 B3
Rawlings Gr. Abing 179 E4
Rawlinson Cl. Chadl 57 D1
Rawlinson Rd. Oxon 123 D3
Rawson Cl. Cutte 108 C1
Raymond Rd. Bice 65 E2
Raymund Rd. Mars 123 F3
Raynham Cl. Cart 115 F2
Reade Ave. Abing 180 A4
Reade Cl. Lyne 70 B3
Reade's La. S Com 252 B2
Reading Rd. Aldw 247 F2
Reading Rd. Chol 221 E2
Reading Rd. E Hen 216 A4
Reading Rd. Gori 249 F3
Reading Rd. Harw 217 E3
Reading Rd. Hen-on-T 254 C4
Reading Rd. K End 252 A2
Reading Rd. Moul 239 D3
Reading Rd. Pangb 256 B3
Reading Rd. Stre 249 D3
Reading Rd. Wall 221 E2
Reading Rd. Woodc 240 C1
Recreation Rd. Warg 255 F1
Recreation Rd. Wood 91 E3
Rectory Cl. M Gib 67 F2
Rectory Cl. Up Hey 48 C1
Rectory Cl. Warm 3 D2
Rectory Cl. Wend 80 A2
Rectory Cres. Mi Bar 60 C4
Rectory Ct. Lewk 187 D4
Rectory Farm Cl. W Hann 196 C4
Rectory Gdns. Dra 15 E4
Rectory Hill. Ewel 206 A1
Rectory La. Ast T 237 F4
Rectory La. Frin 52 B3
Rectory La. K Bag 176 C4
Rectory La. Let B 231 F4
Rectory La. Lewk 166 C1
Rectory La. Longw 156 A2
Rectory La. Mid Ch 10 C1
Rectory La. Wood 91 D3
Rectory Meadow. Chin 168 B1
Rectory Rd. Caver 259 D1
Rectory Rd. G Has 164 C4
Rectory Rd. Ho No 30 A4
Rectory Rd. Oxon 141 F4
Rectory Rd. Stre 248 B4
Red Copse Rd. Sunn 140 C1
Red Cross Rd. Gori 249 E3
Red Hill. Shipl 253 F3
Red House Dr. S Com 253 D3
Red House Rd. Bod 22 C4
Red La. Ewel 206 B1
Red La. Watl 206 B1
Red La. Woodc 240 B2
Red Lion Dr. Skch 188 B3
Red Lion Sq. Oxon 123 E1
Red Lion St. Cro 4 C1
Red Lion St. K Sut 23 F3
Red Poll Cl. Banb 16 A4
Redberry Cl. Caver 259 E3
Rede Cl. Oxon 124 C1
Redland Rd. Oxon 124 A3
Redmoor Cl. Oxon 142 B1
Redmoor Ct. Bice 65 E2
Redwood Cl. Gars 143 D1
Redwood Cl. K Bag 156 C1
Redwood Way. Read 257 E2
Regal Way. Far 172 C2
Regency Hts. Caver 258 C2
Regent Gdns. Didc 219 D4
Regent Mall. Want 214 B2
Regent Mews. Far 172 C2
Regent St. Oxon 141 F4
Reid Cl. Banb 16 A3
Reid Pl. Up Hey 63 D4
Remenham La. Rem H 244 C2
Remus Gate. Brac 24 A3
Rest Harrow. Oxon 142 C1
Retford Cl. Sonn 260 C1
Retreat Gdns. Cr Gif 221 F4
Rewley Rd. Oxon 123 D1
Reynolds Way. Abing 179 F3
Reynolds Way. E Cha 213 F3
Richards La. Cutte 123 D4
Richards Way. Oxon 124 C1
Richens Dr. Cart 115 E1
Richfield Ave. Read 258 C1
Richman Gdns. Banb 15 F4
Richmere Rd. Didc 218 C4
Richmond Rd. Caver 258 C2
Richmond Rd. Oxon 123 D1
Richmond St. K Sut 23 F3
Rickyard The. Ard 215 E3
Rickyard The. Fulb 100 C3
Riddell Pl. Cutte 109 D1
Ride The. Fyf 158 A3
Riders Way. Chin 168 B3
Ridge Cl. Banb 16 B2
Ridge Hall Cl. Caver 258 C2
Ridge The. Stre 249 F1
Ridge Way. E Cha 214 A4
Ridge Way. Warg 255 F1
Ridgefield Rd. Oxon 142 A4
Ridgemont Cl. Cutte 123 D4
Ridgemount Cl. Purl 257 D1
Ridgeway Rd. Didc 218 C4
Ridgeway Rd. Oxon 124 C2
Ridgeway The. Bloxh 21 F2
Ridgeway The. Caver 259 D2
Ridgeway The. Farnb 232 B3
Ridgeway The. Nett 224 B1
Ridgeway. Woot 140 B1
Riding La. Crawl 103 E4
Riding The. Leaf 86 C1
Ridings The. Caver 259 E4
Ridings The. For H 142 C4
Ridings The. Kidl 92 B1
Ridings The. Oxon 142 C4
Ridley Rd. Oxon 142 C3
Riely Cl. Lo Han 90 B1
Riley Cl. Abing 179 E3
Riley Dr. Banb 15 F4
Rimes Cl. K Bag 156 C1
Ringwood Rd. Oxon 125 D2
Ringwood Rd. Read 258 A1
Ripley Rd. Read 258 A1
Rippington Ct. Dray 179 D1
Rippington Dr. Mars 123 F2
Rise The. Adde 23 D3
Rise The. Ast R 167 F2
Rise The. Caver 259 D2
Rise The. Islip 93 F1
Rissington Cl. Read 257 F2
Rissington Dr. Witn 117 F4
Rivacres. Whitc 250 C2
River Cl. Abing 179 F3
River Gdns. Purl 257 E3
River Rd. Caver 258 B2
River View. Kenn 141 F1
River View. Sa-on-T 161 D4
Rivermead Rd. Oxon 141 F2
Riverside Gdns. Witn 104 A1
Riverside Rd. Oxon 122 C1
Riverside. Banb 16 C3
Riverview Rd. Pangb 256 B3
Rivy Cl. Abing 180 B4
Road Eight. Harw 217 D1
Road Eighteen. Harw 217 D1
Road Eleven. Harw 217 D1
Road Fifteen. Harw 217 D1
Road Five. Harw 217 D1
Road Four. Harw 217 D1
Road Fourteen. Harw 217 D1
Road Nine. Harw 217 D1
Road One. Harw 217 D1
Road Six. Harw 217 D1
Road Thirteen. Harw 217 D1
Road Twelve. Harw 217 D1
Road Two. Harw 217 D1
Robert Sparrow Gdns. Cr Gif 222 A3
Roberts Cl. Oxon 125 D2
Robin Hill. Combe 90 A2
Robins Cl. B St M 32 C3
Robins Cl. Gr Ro 29 D2
Robins Platt. Chin 168 A3
Robinson Cl. Cart 115 E2
Robsart Pl. Cumn 139 F2
Rochester Ave. Sonn 260 C1
Rochester Pl. Charl 73 E2
Rochester Way. Adde 23 D3
Rochford Gdns. Bice 66 A2
Rock Cl. Cart 115 E2
Rock Edge. Oxon 124 B1
Rock Farm La. Sa-on-T 161 D4
Rock Hill. Ch No 42 C2
Rock Rd. Cart 115 E2
Rock The. B St M 32 C3
Rockbourne Gdns. Read 258 A1
Rocky La. R Pep 243 D2
Roding Way. Didc 201 D1
Rodway Rd. Read 257 F1
Roebuck Ct. Didc 219 D4
Roentgen Ave. Harw 217 D1
Rofford La. Chalg 164 A2
Rogers St. Cutte 123 D4
Rokeby Dr. Maple 258 B4
Rolfe Pl. Oxon 124 A2
Roman Pl. Didc 200 B1
Roman Rd. Wheat 144 B4
Roman Way. Beck 111 D2
Roman Way. Bice 65 F1
Roman Way. Brac 24 A4
Roman Way. Lech 150 B3
Roman Way. Oxon 142 C3
Roman Way. Want 214 B3
Romany Cl. Read 258 A1
Romany La. Read 258 A1
Romney Rd. Banb 8 C1
Romsey Rd. Read 258 A1
Romulus Way. Brac 24 A3
Rookery Cl. Abing 159 D1
Rookery Cl. Bod 22 C4
Rookery The. Kidl 92 B1
Rookery Way. Bice 65 E2
Rooks La. Tha 147 F4
Roosevelt Rd. Lo Han 106 A4
Rope Way. Ho No 30 A3
Rope Wlk. Banb 16 B3
Roper Rd. Up Hey 63 E4
Rosamund Dr. Wood 91 D4
Rosamund Rd. Cutte 122 C4
Rose Ave. Abing 159 F2
Rose Cl. Cart 115 E1
Rose Cnr. Skch 188 C3
Rose Ct. Oxon 142 A2
Rose Gdns. N Hink 140 B4
Rose Hill. Oxon 142 A2
Rose La. Oxon 123 E1
Rose Pl. Oxon 141 E4
Rosebay Cres. Grove 214 B4
Rosebery Rd. Maple 258 B4
Rosedale Ave. Banb 9 D1
Rosehill Park. Caver 259 E4
Rosemary La. Bamp 134 C2
Rosemead Ave. Purl 257 D2
Roses La. Sal 41 F3
Rosina Wlk. Banb 9 D1
Ross Rd. Read 258 C1
Ross Rd. Read 259 D1
Rossendale Rd. Caver 259 E2
Rotha Field Rd. Cutte 109 D1
Rotherfield Rd. Hen-on-T 254 C4
Rotherfield Way. Caver 259 D2
Rothwell Gdns. Sonn 260 C1
Rothwell Wlk. Caver 259 E1
Rothwells Cl. Chol 221 D1
Rotten Row. Dorch 182 B1
Round Close Rd. Adde 22 C2
Round Close Rd. Ho No 30 A4
Roundham Cl. Kidl 92 B1
Roundhead Dr. Tha 129 F1
Roundhill Rd. Moll 4 A2
Roundhills Mead. Highw 190 A4
Roundtown. Ayn 35 E4
Roundway The. Oxon 124 C2
Rouses La. Filk 132 A3
Rousham Rd. Tack 77 E4
Routh Rd. Oxon 124 C2
Roves La. Highw 208 A4
Row La. Shipl 259 F4
Row The. H Wald 155 F1
Rowallan Cl. Caver 259 E3
Rowan Cl. Kidl 108 C4
Rowan Cl. S Com 252 C2
Rowan Rd. Bice 65 F2
Rowel Dr. Begb 92 A1
Rowell Way. Ch No 42 C2
Rowland Cl. Cutte 122 C4
Rowland Cl. Wall 203 E1
Rowland Rd. Chol 221 D1
Rowles Cl. Kenn 141 F1
Rowney Pl. Oxon 142 A2
Roxburgh Dr. Didc 200 B2
Royal Berkshire Ct. Didc 218 C4
Ruck Keene Cl. Bice 65 E1
Rumbolds Cl. Bens 203 F3
Rumsey's La. Blew 237 D4
Rupert Cl. Hen-on-T 244 C2
Rupert Rd. Chalg 184 B3
Rupert Rd. Oxon 142 C3
Rupert Way. Tha 130 A1
Rupert's La. Hen-on-T 244 C2
Ruscote Ave. Banb 16 A4
Ruscote Sq. Banb 16 A4
Rushall Rd. Tha 130 A1
Rushmead Copse. Abing 160 B1
Ruskin Ave. Abing 179 F3
Ruskin Cl. Didc 219 D4
Ruskin Rd. Banb 16 B2
Ruskin Wlk. Bice 65 F2
Russell Jackson Cl. Berin 182 B3
Russell Rd. Maple 258 B4
Russell St. Oxon 123 D1
Russet Cl. S Com 252 C3
Russet Glade. Caver 259 E4
Russet Rd. Mi Sto 50 B2
Rutherford Ave. Harw 217 D2
Rutten La. Yarn 108 A3
Rutters Cl. Kidl 108 B4
Rycote La. G Has 146 B3
Rycroft Cl. Sonn 260 C1
Rydal Ave. Read 257 F1
Rydes The. Bod 22 C4
Rye Cl. Banb 8 C1
Rye Grass. Wood 91 E3
Ryecroft Cl. Warg 255 F1
Rymans Cres. E Hag 219 D3
Rymers La. Oxon 142 A3

Sackville Cl. Hanw 8 C2
Sadler Wlk. Oxon 141 D4
Sadlers Croft. Gars 143 F1
Sadlers Ct. Abing 160 A2
Saffron Ct. Abing 180 A4
Sage Rd. Read 257 E2
St Alban's Ct. Wall 221 E4
St Aldgates. Oxon 141 E4
St Amand Dr. Abing 179 F3
St Andrew Ct. Tha 147 F4
St Andrew's La. Oxon 124 B2
St Andrew's Rd. Caver 258 C2
St Andrew's Rd. Chin 168 B3
St Andrew's Rd. Didc 218 C4
St Andrew's Rd. Hen-on-T 254 B4
St Andrew's Rd. Oxon 124 B2
St Andrews Cl. Abing 160 B1
St Anne's Cl. Hen-on-T 244 B1
St Anne's Rd. Banb 16 B2
St Anne's Rd. Caver 259 D1
St Anne's Rd. Oxon 124 B1
St Annes Cl. Bice 65 F2
St Barnabas Rd. Caver 259 D3
St Barnabas St. Oxon 123 D1
St Bernard's Rd. Oxon 123 D2
St Birinus Ct. Lech 150 B3
St Clement's St. Oxon 123 F1
St Cross Rd. Oxon 123 E1
St David's Cl. Caver 258 C3
St Denys Cl. S in V 194 C4
St Ebbes St. Oxon 141 E4
St Edburg's Cl. Bice 65 E1
St Edith's Way. Bice 65 E1
St Edmund's La. Abing 179 F3
St Edward's Ave. Cutte 123 D4
St Francis Rd. B Bot 189 E2
St George's Cres. Banb 16 B2
St George's Pl. Oxon 123 E1
St George's Rd. Buckl 154 B1
St Georges Green. Wall 203 E1
St Georges Rd. Wall 221 E4
St Giles Cl. Wend 80 A2
St Giles'. Oxon 123 E1
St Giles. Bletch 93 D4
St Helen's Ave. Bens 203 F2
St Helen's Cres. Bens 204 A2
St Helen's Ct. Abing 179 F3
St Helen's Mews. Abing 179 F3
St Helen's Pas. Oxon 123 E1
St Helen's Way. Bens 203 F2
St Helen's Wharf. Abing 179 F3
St Hilda's Cl. Bice 65 F2
St Hugh's Cl. Bice 65 F2
St Hugh's Pl. Skch 188 C2
St Hughs Cl. Banb 16 B2
St Ives La. Grove 214 C4
St Ives Rd. Grove 214 C4
St James Cl. Pangb 256 B3
St James Rd. Radl 160 C2
St James View. E Hann 197 D4
St James. Want 214 B3
St John St. Oxon 123 E1
St John's Cl. Didc 219 D4
St John's Cl. Fyf 157 D1
St John's Green. Wall 221 E3
St John's Rd. Abing 180 A4
St John's Rd. Banb 16 B3
St John's Rd. Caver 259 E1
St John's Rd. Grove 196 C1
St John's Rd. Wall 221 E4
St John's Row. Lo Wit 201 E4
St John's St. Bice 65 F1
St John's St. Lech 150 B2
St John's Way. Dedd 33 D2
St Johns Dr. Cart 115 F2
St Johns Dr. Kidl 92 C1
St Johns Rd. Tack 77 E3
St Katherine's Rd. Hen-on-T 254 B4
St Kenelm's Cl. M Lov 102 C1
St Lawrence Cl. Warb 203 D4
St Lawrence Rd. Lech 150 B2
St Lawrence Rd. S Hink 141 D3
St Leonard's Cl. Banb 16 C3
St Leonard's La. Wall 221 E4
St Leonard's Rd. Oxon 124 B2
St Leonard's Sq. Wall 221 E4
St Leonards Cl. Watl 186 A1
St Lucian's La. Wall 221 E3

St Luke's Rd. Oxon 142 B3
St Lukes Way. Caver 259 D3
St Margaret's Rd. Oxon 123 D2
St Mark's Rd. Hen-on-T 254 B4
St Martin's Rd. Oxon 142 A2
St Martin's St. Wall 221 E4
St Mary's Ave. Purl 257 E3
St Mary's Cl. Bice 65 E1
St Mary's Cl. Hen-on-T 254 A4
St Mary's Cl. Kidl 92 C1
St Mary's Cl. Oxon 142 A1
St Mary's Ct. Witn 118 A4
St Mary's Green. Abing 159 F1
St Mary's La. Swer 30 C2
St Mary's Mead. Witn 118 A4
St Mary's Rd. Adde 22 C1
St Mary's Rd. E Hen 216 C3
St Mary's Rd. Oxon 141 F4
St Mary's St. Wall 221 E4
St Mary's Way. Want 214 B3
St Marys Cl. Wheat 144 A4
St Michael's Ave. Abing 179 F4
St Michael's Ave. Highw 190 A3
St Michael's Cl. Frin 52 B3
St Michael's La. Begb 107 F4
St Michael's St. Oxon 123 E1
St Michael's Way. Steve 198 C2
St Michaels Cl. S u Wy 85 E4
St Nicholas Rd. Oxon 142 B1
St Nicholas Rd. Tack 77 E3
St Nicholas Rd. Wall 221 E4
St Nicholas' Green. Abing 159 F1
St Omer Rd. Oxon 142 B3
St Paul's Cres. N Hink 140 B4
St Peter's Ave. Caver 258 C2
St Peter's Cl. Cass 107 E1
St Peter's Cl. Woot 159 D3
St Peter's Cres. Bice 65 F2
St Peter's Hill. Caver 258 C2
St Peter's Rd. Abing 160 B1
St Peter's Rd. Brac 24 A4
St Peter's Rd. Cutte 122 C4
St Peter's Rd. Didc 218 C4
St Peter's St. Wall 221 E4
St Peters Gate. Brac 24 A4
St Ruald's Cl. Wall 221 E4
St Rumbold's Rd. Wall 221 E4
St Stephens Ct. Caver 259 D1
St Swithun's Rd. Kenn 160 C4
St Thomas St. Dedd 33 F2
St Thomas' St. Oxon 123 D1
St Thomas's Cl. H Wald 155 F1
Salegate La. Oxon 142 B3
Salford Rd. Mars 123 F2
Salisbury Cres. Cutte 123 D4
Salmon Cl. Blox 21 F3
Salop Cl. Shriv 209 D3
Salt La. Lewk 166 C1
Salter Cl. Oxon 141 E4
Salters La. Lud 98 B4
Salvia Cl. Banb 9 D1
Samian Way. Dorch 202 B4
Samphire Rd. Oxon 142 C1
Sand Hill. Shriv 209 D4
Sand View. Far 172 C1
Sandcroft Rd. Caver 258 C3
Sandell Cl. Banb 16 B3
Sanderling Wlk. Banb 16 C2
Sandfield Rd. Oxon 124 A2
Sandfine Rd. Brou 15 D1
Sandford Cl. Abing 160 A1
Sandford Cl. Woodc 250 C4
Sandford Dr. Sonn 260 C1
Sandford Green. Banb 15 F4
Sandford La. Kenn 160 C4
Sandford Park. Charl 73 E2
Sandford Rd. Oxon 142 A1
Sandford Rise. Charl 73 E2
Sandgate Ave. Read 257 F1
Sandhill Rd. Begb 108 A4
Sandleigh Rd. Woot 159 D4
Sandpit Hill. Ting 39 F3
Sandringham Dr. Didc 219 D4
Sandringham Rd. K Sut 23 F3
Sands Cl. Cumn 139 F3
Sands La. S New 31 F4
Sands Rd. S Mor 219 F3
Sands The. Bens 204 B3
Sands The. Ewel 204 B3
Sands The. Lyne 70 B3
Sands Way. Bens 203 F3
Sandy La W. Oxon 142 B2
Sandy La. Beck 111 D1
Sandy La. Ch We 68 A2
Sandy La. Chol 220 C1
Sandy La. K Bag 156 C1
Sandy La. L Cre 129 D3
Sandy La. Oxon 142 C2
Sandy La. S in V 174 B2
Sandy La. Shriv 209 D3
Sandy La. Tidd 145 F3
Sandy La. Woot 140 B1
Sandy La. Yarn 108 B4
Sandy Lane Ct. Ch We 68 A2
Sarajac Ave. E Cha 213 F2
Sarsden Cl. Chadl 57 D1
Sarum Cl. Cart 115 F2
Satwell Cl. R Pep 243 D2
Saunders Cl. Watl 186 A1
Saunders Rd. Oxon 142 A3
Saunders Wd Cps. Skch 188 C2
Savile Rd. Oxon 123 E1
Savile Way. Grove 196 B1
Saw Cl. Chalg 184 B4
Sawpit Rd. Oxon 142 C2
Sawpits La. Lo Od 40 A1
Saxel Cl. Aston 135 F2
Saxon Cl. Wall 221 E4
Saxon Pl. Want 214 A3
Saxon Way. Oxon 124 A2
Saxon Way. Witn 118 A4
Saxons Heath. Lo Wit 201 E4
Saxons Way. Didc 219 D4
Saxton Rd. Abing 179 F3
Sayers Orch. Didc 200 B1
Scafell Cl. Read 257 E1
Scampton Cl. Bice 66 A2
Schilling St. Up Hey 63 D4
Schofield Ave. Witn 104 A2
Schofield Gdns. Witn 104 A2
Schofields Way. Blox 21 F3
Scholars Cl. Caver 258 C1
Schongau Cl. Abing 179 E2
School Cl. Ick 128 A2
School Cl. Lo Co 27 F3
School Cl. Longw 156 B2
School Cl. Steve 198 C2
School End. Ayn 35 E4
School Hill. M Lov 102 C2
School Hill. Moll 3 F2
School Hill. Warg 255 E1
School La. Ast R 167 F2
School La. B Bou 133 F3
School La. Caver 259 D1
School La. Caver 259 D3
School La. Chils 71 F3
School La. Coles 191 D4
School La. Gt Bo 9 E4
School La. Harw 217 F4
School La. K Bag 156 C1
School La. M Lov 102 C2
School La. Mi Sto 64 A2
School La. Mil 199 E2
School La. Mil 199 E3
School La. N New 15 E2
School La. St Row 241 F2
School La. Stadh 163 E1
School La. Sut C 200 C4
School La. Up Hey 62 C4
School La. Warg 255 E1
School La. Warm 3 D2
School Paddock. Buck 64 C4
School Pl. Oxon 141 E3
School Rd. Ard 215 E3
School Rd. Fins 88 B3
School Rd. Kidl 92 C1
School Rd. W Hann 196 C3
School View. Banb 16 C3
School Yd. Stadh 163 E1
Schooler's La. Adle 40 B2
Scotland End. Ho No 30 A4
Scotsgrove Hill. Hadd 130 A2
Scott Cl. Bice 65 E2
Scott Cl. Caver 259 D3
Scott Cl. Kidl 108 B4
Scott Rd. Cutte 123 D4
Scotts La. M Gib 67 F1
Scours La. Read 258 A1
Scruton Cl. Oxon 124 C2
Seacourt Rd. N Hink 122 B1
Sealham Rd. Duck 118 A2
Second Ave. Didc 200 B1
Second St. Crou 36 C3
Second St. Harw 217 E2
Sedgemoor Dr. Tha 130 A1
Sedgewell Rd. S Com 252 C3
Sefton Pl. Bod 22 C4
Sefton Rd. Oxon 124 C2
Segsbury Rd. Want 214 A3
Selborne Gdns. Read 258 A1
Sellwood Dr. Cart 115 F2
Sellwood Rd. Abing 159 F1
Selwyn Cres. Radl 160 C1
Send Rd. Caver 259 E1
Sermon Cl. Oxon 124 C1
Seven Acres. L Cre 129 D4
Seven Acres. Tha 148 A4
Sevenfields. Highw 190 A4
Seventeenth St. Harw 217 D1
Seventh Ave. Hors 142 C4
Seventh St. Harw 217 D2
Severalls Cl. Wall 203 E1
Severn Cl. Bice 65 D2
Severn Rd. Abing 159 E1
Severn Rd. Harw 217 D1
Sewell Cl. Abing 160 B1
Shackleton Cl. Bice 66 A2
Shades The. Banb 16 B3
Shadwell Rd. Berin 182 B3
Shaftesbury Rd. Oxon 124 C3
Shakespeare Cl. Caver 259 E3
Shakespeare Dr. Bice 65 E2
Shakespeare Rd. Eyns 120 B4
Shannon Cl. Grove 196 C1
Shannon Rd. Bice 65 D1
Sharland Cl. Grove 214 C4
Sharman Beer Ct. Tha 147 F4
Shaw Cl. Bice 65 E2
Sheards La. S in V 194 C4
Sheen Cl. Buck 65 F3
Sheep St. Bice 65 F1
Sheep St. Burf 100 C3
Sheep St. Charl 73 D2
Sheep St. Highw 190 A3
Sheep Wlk. Caver 259 D2
Sheepwash La. Steve 199 D3
Sheepway Ct. Oxon 142 A2
Sheepways La. Maple 258 A4
Sheerstock. Hadd 130 C3
Sheldon Rd. Ick 128 A2
Sheldon Way. Oxon 142 B2
Shelford Pl. Oxon 124 B1
Shelley Cl. Abing 160 A1
Shelley Cl. Banb 16 A2
Shelley Cl. Bice 65 E2
Shelley Cl. Oxon 124 C1
Shelley Rd. Oxon 142 A3
Shepard Way. Ch No 42 C2
Shepherd Gdns. Abing 179 E3
Shepherds Cl. Grove 196 B1
Shepherds Cl. W-on-G 79 D1
Shepherds Hill. Sonn 260 B1
Shepherds La. Caver 258 B3
Sheraton Dr. Read 257 E1
Sherborne St. Lech 150 B2
Sherbourne Rd. Witn 117 E4
Sheridan Ave. Caver 258 C2
Sheriff's Dr. Cutte 122 C4
Sherwood Ave. Abing 180 A4
Sherwood Cl. Laun 66 B1
Sherwood Gdns. Hen-on-T 254 B4
Sherwood Rd. Didc 218 B4
Sherwood Rise. Purl 257 D3
Shilbrook Manor. B Bou 133 F2
Shillbrook Ave. Cart 115 E3
Shilldeane Dr. Cart 115 E2
Shilton Rd. Burf 100 C2
Shilton Rd. Cart 115 E2
Ship St. Oxon 123 E1
Shiplake Bottom. S Com 252 C3
Shipston Rd. Lo Co 27 F4
Shipton Cl. Read 257 E1
Shipton Rd. Lyne 70 B3
Shipton Rd. S u Wy 71 D1
Shipton Rd. Wood 91 E3
Shirburn Rd. Watl 186 B1
Shirburn St. Watl 186 B1
Shirelake Cl. Oxon 141 E4
Shires Rd. Brac 24 A3
Shirvell's Hill. Woodc 250 C4
Shoe La. E Hag 218 C3
Shoe La. Oxon 123 E1
Shooters Hill. Pangb 256 A3
Short St. Caver 259 D1
Short St. Pangb 256 B3
Short St. Watch 191 E1
Short The. Purl 257 E3
Shortlands Hill. Moul 238 B2
Shrieves Cl. Abing 160 A1
Shrivenham Hundred. Watch 191 E1
Shrivenham Rd. Highw 190 A2
Shrivenham Rd. Long 192 B1
Shute Ave. Watch 209 E4
Shutford Rd. N New 15 D2
Shutford Rd. Tad 20 C4
Sibford Rd. Ho No 30 A4
Sibford Rd. Shut 13 F2
Sideleigh Rd. Bod 22 C4
Sidings Rd. Churc 55 F3
Sidney St. Oxon 141 F4
Signet End. Burf 100 C2
Silkdale Cl. Oxon 142 B3
Silver Birches. St S J 125 F4
Silver La. E Cha 213 E3
Silver Rd. Oxon 142 A4
Silver St. Bourt 209 D1
Silver St. Chac 10 C2
Silver St. Fern 193 D2
Silver St. Tet 166 A4
Silver St. Wrox 15 D4
Silverdale Rd. Warg 255 F1
Silvermead. Worm 127 E3
Silverthorne Dr. Caver 258 C3
Simmonds Wlk. Want 214 B3
Simmons Rd. Hen-on-T 244 B2
Simmons Way. Tha 129 F1
Simon's Cl. Wheat 144 A4
Simons Cl. Purl 257 E2
Simons La. S u Wy 85 E4
Simpsons Way. Kenn 160 C4
Sinclair Ave. Banb 16 A4
Sinclair Dr. Banb 16 A4
Singer La. Hen-on-T 244 C1
Singers Cl. Hen-on-T 254 C4
Sinnels Field. S u Wy 85 F4
Sinodun Cl. Lo Wit 201 E4
Sinodun Rd. Didc 218 C4
Sinodun Rd. Wall 203 E1
Sinodun View. Warb 203 D4
Sint Niklaas Cl. Abing 179 E2
Sir Georges La. Adde 23 D2
Siskin Rd. Ch We 68 A3
Sixpenny La. Chalg 184 C3
Sixteenth St. Harw 217 D2
Sixth St. Crou 36 C4
Sixth St. Harw 217 D2
Skerrit Way. Purl 257 E2
Skilton Rd. Read 257 E2
Skimmingdish La. Buck 65 F3
Skimmingdish Rd. Laun 66 A2
Skinner Rd. Laun 66 B1
Skippett La. Rams 88 A2
Skippon Way. Tha 129 F1
Skittle Alley. Ayn 35 E4
Slade Cl. Oxon 124 B1
Slade Rd. Chol 221 D1
Slade Rd. Didc 200 B1
Slade Rd. Skch 188 C2
Slade The. Charl 73 E2
Slade The. Oxon 142 C4
Slave Hill. Hadd 130 C3
Slaymaker Cl. Oxon 124 C1
Sloane Cl. Gori 249 E3
Slopes The. Caver 259 E1
Smith Barry Cres. Ch We 68 A2
Smith Barry Rd. Ch We 68 A2
Smith's Cl. Aston 135 F1
Smith's Hill. Let B 231 F3
Smith's La. Wtpy 126 C4
Snakehill La. Dedd 33 D2
Snipe Rd. Ch We 68 A2
Snowdon Mede. Oxon 124 A2
Snowswick La. Busc 170 C3
Snuff La. Shot 8 B4
Snuggs La. E Hann 197 D4
Soden Rd. Up Hey 63 E4
Solters Cl. Lud 98 B4
Somerton Rd. Mi Sto 50 A2
Somerton Rd. N Ast 48 A4
Somerton Rd. Up Hey 48 C1
Somerville Dr. Bice 65 F2
Somerville. Didc 219 D4
Songers Cl. N Hink 140 A4
Sonning La. Sonn 260 B1
Sonning Meadows. Sonn 260 B1
Sopwith Rd. Ch We 68 A3
Sorrel Rd. Oxon 143 D1
South Ave. Abing 159 F1
South Ave. Hen-on-T 254 C4
South Ave. Kidl 108 C3
South Bar St. Banb 16 B3
South Cl. Kidl 108 C3
South Dr. Harw 217 E2
South Dr. Sonn 260 B1
South End. Gr Ro 29 D2
South End. Hadd 130 C3
South Gate Ct. Ch We 68 A2
South Mere. Br No 116 B2
South Newington Rd. B St M 32 B3
South Newington Rd. Blox 21 D1
South Par. Cutte 123 D4
South Park Ave. Didc 218 B4
South Parks Rd. Oxon 123 E1
South Rd. St Row 242 A1
South Row. Chil 235 E4
South Side. Ste As 62 A4
South St. Banb 16 C4
South St. Blew 237 D4
South St. Caver 259 D1
South St. Lo Hey 63 D3
South St. Mi Bar 60 C4
South St. Oxon 141 D4
South St. Watch 191 E1
South Stoke Rd. Woodc 240 A1
South View Ave. Caver 259 E1
South View Park. Caver 259 E1
South View. Gt Bo 9 E4
Southam Rd. Banb 9 E2
Southam Rd. Cro 4 A2
Southam Rd. Gt Bo 9 E2
Southam Rd. Moll 4 A2
Southampton St. Far 172 C2
Southby Cl. Apple 158 A4
Southcroft. Mars 123 F3
Southdale Rd. Cutte 123 D4
Southdown Ct. S in V 194 C4
Southdown Rd. Caver 259 D3
Southend. Gars 162 C4
Southern By-pass Rd. Kenn 141 E2
Southern By-pass Rd. N Hink 140 C4
Southern By-pass Rd. Oxon 141 F2
Southern By-pass Rd. S Hink 141 D2
Southern Rd. Tha 147 F4
Southerndene Cl. Read 257 E1
Southfield Dr. Sut C 199 F4
Southfield La. Frit 49 F4
Southfield Park. Oxon 142 A4
Southfield Rd. Oxon 142 A4
Southlands. Aston 135 F1
Southlawn. Witn 117 F4
Southmoor Pl. Oxon 123 D2
Southmoor Rd. Oxon 123 D2
Southmoor Way. Abing 179 F4
Southrop Rd. Ho No 30 A3
Southwold. Bice 65 F3
Southwood Rd. Curb 103 E1
Sovereign Cl. Didc 219 D4
Spa Cl. Highw 190 A4
Span Hill. Shipl 260 A4
Spareacre La. Eyns 120 C4
Sparsey Pl. Cutte 109 D1
Sparsholt St. Spars 212 C2
Spears The. Yarn 108 A3
Speedwell St. Oxon 141 E4
Spencer Cl. Bice 65 E2
Spencer Cres. Oxon 142 A2
Spencers Cl. S in V 194 B4
Spenlove Cl. Abing 159 F1
Spenser Ave. Yarn 108 A3
Spey Rd. Abing 159 E2
Spier's La. M Gib 67 F1
Spindleberry Cl. Oxon 142 C1
Spindlers. Kidl 92 C1
Spindleside. Bice 65 F3
Spinney Cl. Caver 259 D4
Spinney Dr. Banb 16 C2
Spinney The. Laun 66 B1
Spinney The. Lech 150 B2
Spinneys Cl. Radl 160 C2
Spinneys The. Enst 58 C3
Spitfire Cl. Bice 66 A2
Sprigs Holly La. Bled R 189 D4
Spring Cl. Witn 118 A4
Spring Copse. S Hink 141 E2
Spring Farm. D Tew 47 E3
Spring Gdns. Abing 179 E4
Spring Hill Rd. Begb 107 F4
Spring Hill. Longw 176 B4
Spring La. Ast T 237 F4
Spring La. Gt Bo 9 E3
Spring La. Hors 143 E4
Spring La. Idb 69 D2
Spring La. Oxon 124 C1
Spring La. Oxon 142 B1
Spring La. Shipl 260 A3
Spring La. Watl 186 B1
Spring Path. Tha 147 F4
Spring Rd. Abing 179 E4
Spring St. Ch No 42 C2
Spring Wlk. Warg 255 E1
Springdale. Wall 221 E4
Springfield Ave. Banb 16 B2
Springfield Cl. Shriv 209 D3
Springfield Cl. Watl 186 B1
Springfield Dr. Abing 179 F4
Springfield End. Gori 249 E4
Springfield Gdns. Chin 168 B4
Springfield Oval. Witn 103 F1
Springfield Park. Witn 103 F1
Springfield Rd. Buck 65 F4
Springfield Rd. Kidl 108 C4
Springfield Rd. N Hink 140 B4
Springfield Rd. Skch 188 C2
Springfield Rd. Want 214 C2
Springhill Rd. Gori 249 E4
Springs The. Witn 118 A4
Springwell Hill. Bletch 78 A1
Springwood La. R Pep 253 D4
Spruce Rd. Kidl 108 C4
Spur The. Warg 255 F2
Square Firs. Combe 90 A3
Square The. Abing 179 F4
Square The. Aston 135 F2
Square The. Ayn 35 E4
Square The. Duck 118 A2
Square The. Eyns 120 C4
Square The. K Sut 23 F3
Square The. L Cre 129 E3
Square The. Longw 156 A2
Square The. N Hink 122 B1
Square The. Oxon 142 B2
Square The. Pangb 256 B3
Square The. Swal 19 F4
Squire's Wlk. Wall 221 E3
Squires Cl. Br No 116 B2
Squires Rd. Watch 191 E1
Squitchey La. Cutte 123 D4
Stable Rd. Bice 65 F2
Staddlestone Cl. Read 257 E1
Stadhampton Rd. D St L 183 D3
Stadium Way. Read 258 A1
Staffordshire Cl. Read 257 F1
Stainer Pl. Oxon 123 F2
Stainfield Rd. Oxon 124 A3
Stainswick La. Shriv 209 E2
Stallpits Rd. Shriv 209 D4
Stanbridge Cl. Banb 16 A3
Standlake Rd. Duck 118 B2
Standlake Rd. Hardw 118 B2
Stanford Dr. Abing 179 F4
Stanford Rd. Far 173 D2
Stanier Pl. Banb 16 C4
Stanley Cl. N Hink 140 B4
Stanley Rd. Oxon 141 F4
Stanmore Cres. Cart 115 F2
Stansfeld Pl. Oxon 124 C1
Stansfield Cl. Oxon 124 C1
Stanton Harcourt Rd. Witn 118 B4
Stanton Rd. For H 125 F2
Stanton Rd. N Hink 140 C3
Stanville Rd. N Hink 140 A4
Stanway Rd. Oxon 125 D2
Stanwell Cl. Mid Ch 11 D1
Stanwell Dr. Mid Ch 11 D1
Stanwell Lea. Mid Ch 11 D1
Stanwell Rd. Gt Bo 9 E4
Stapleton Rd. Oxon 124 B1
Star La. Watch 191 E1
Star Rd. Caver 259 E1
Starina Croft. Banb 9 D1
Starnham Rd. Duck 118 A2
Starwort Path. Oxon 142 C1
Station App. Bice 65 F1
Station App. Kidl 92 B1
Station Field Ind Est. Kidl 92 B1

Station La. Witn 118 A3
Station Rd. Ashb 228 A4
Station Rd. Ayn 35 D3
Station Rd. B Bou 133 F3
Station Rd. Bamp 134 C3
Station Rd. Bktn 82 A2
Station Rd. Bletch 93 D4
Station Rd. Br No 116 B2
Station Rd. Ch No 42 B1
Station Rd. Chin 168 B3
Station Rd. Chol 220 C1
Station Rd. Churc 54 C2
Station Rd. Cro 4 C1
Station Rd. Culh 180 C2
Station Rd. Didc 200 C1
Station Rd. Eyns 120 C4
Station Rd. Far 172 C2
Station Rd. Gori 249 D3
Station Rd. Grove 214 C4
Station Rd. Hadd 130 C3
Station Rd. Hen-on-T 244 C1
Station Rd. Highw 190 A3
Station Rd. Ho No 30 B4
Station Rd. King 54 C2
Station Rd. Laun 66 C2
Station Rd. Lech 150 B3
Station Rd. Lo Hey 62 B3
Station Rd. M Gib 67 F2
Station Rd. Mi Sto 50 B2
Station Rd. Pangb 256 B3
Station Rd. S Lei 119 E3
Station Rd. S u Wy 70 C1
Station Rd. Shipl 255 D2
Station Rd. Shriv 209 D3
Station Rd. Upt 218 B1
Station Rd. Wall 221 E4
Station Rd. Warg 255 E1
Station Rd. Wheat 144 A4
Station Rd. Wool 211 D4
Station Yard Ind Est. Adde 23 D1
Station Yd. Tha 148 A4
Staunton Rd. Oxon 124 A2
Staverton Rd. Oxon 123 D3
Steady's La. Sta Har 138 A4
Steep Rise. Oxon 124 B3
Steeple Cl. Blox 21 F2
Steepness Hill. B St M 32 C2
Stenton Cl. Abing 179 F3
Stephen Rd. Oxon 124 B2
Stephenson Rd. E Cha 214 A4
Steptoe Cl. Grove 196 B1
Sterling Cl. Bice 66 A2
Sterling Cl. Kidl 108 C4
Sterling Rd. Kidl 108 C4
Sterling Road App. Kidl 92 C1
Sterling Way. Read 258 A1
Stert Rd. Ast R 167 F2
Stert St. Abing 179 F4
Stevenson Cl. Bice 65 E2
Stevenson Dr. Abing 179 E4
Steventon Rd. Dray 199 D4
Steventon Rd. E Hann 197 F4
Stewart St. Oxon 141 E3
Stile Rd. Oxon 124 B2
Stimpsons Cl. N Hink 122 A1
Stirling Cl. Cart 115 E2
Stirling Cl. Caver 259 E3
Stirling Cl. Want 214 C3
Stirling Ct. Banb 15 F3
Stirlings Rd. Want 214 C2
Stockey End. Abing 160 B1
Stockham Park. Want 214 B3
Stockham Way. Want 214 B3
Stocking La. Shen 6 B1
Stockleys Rd. Mars 124 A3
Stockmore St. Oxon 141 F4
Stocks La. Steve 198 C2
Stocks Tree Cl. Yarn 108 A3
Stoke Pl. Oxon 124 B2
Stoke Row Rd. R Pep 252 C4
Stokes View. Pangb 256 B3
Stone Cl. N Hink 122 A1
Stone Croft. Chadl 57 E1
Stone Ct. Gr Ro 29 D2
Stone Hill. Blox 21 E2
Stone House Cl. K Bag 156 C1
Stone Quarry La. Oxon 142 A2
Stone St. Oxon 142 A4
Stone St. Read 258 A1
Stonebridge Rd. Steve 198 C3
Stoneburge Cres. Bice 65 F2
Stonebury Cl. Want 214 C3
Stonefield Dr. Highw 190 A2
Stonefield Way. Shriv 209 E3
Stonefields Riding. Stone 89 E4
Stonehill La. K Bag 176 B4
Stonehill Wlk. Abing 179 F2
Stonehill. Dray 179 E2
Stoneleigh Dr. Cart 115 E3
Stonesfield La. Charl 73 E1
Stonesfield Rd. Combe 90 A3
Stonesfield Riding. Spel 74 B1
Stonesfield. Didc 219 D4
Stoney La. Sto Ta 185 F4
Stonhouse Cres. Abing 160 C1
Stonor Cl. Didc 200 C1
Stonor Pl. Oxon 124 A1
Stour Cl. Didc 201 D1
Stow Rd. Bled 54 B1
Stow Rd. Fif 69 D1
Stowford Rd. Oxon 124 C2
Stowhill. Child 213 E2
Stowood Cl. Oxon 124 C2
Strafford Way. Tha 148 A4
Stratfield Rd. Cutte 123 D3
Stratfield Rd. Kidl 108 C3
Stratford Dr. Eyns 120 B4
Stratford La. Woot 76 A1
Stratford Rd. Dra 15 F4
Stratford Rd. Shen 6 C3
Stratford Rd. Wrox 14 C4
Stratford St. Oxon 141 F4
Strathmore Cl. Cart 115 F3
Stratton Audley Rd. Frin 52 B3
Stratton Audley Rd. S Lyn 51 D3
Stratton Way. Abing 179 F4
Strawberry Hill. Blox 21 F3
Strawberry Path. Oxon 142 C1
Strawberry Terr. Blox 21 F3
Stream Rd. Upt 218 B1
Streatley Hill. Stre 249 D3
Street The. Br-c-S 202 C1
Street The. Cr Gif 221 E1
Street The. Cr Gif 221 F4
Street The. Cr Gif 240 B4
Street The. Moul 239 D3
Street The. S Lyn 51 D3
Street The. S Sto 239 D2
Street The. Tidm 256 B1
Stuart Cl. Caver 259 D3
Stuart Way. Tha 130 A1
Stubble Cl. N Hink 140 A4
Stubbs Ave. Oxon 142 C4
Studdridge Ct. Skch 188 B2
Sturges Cl. Oxon 124 C2
Sturt Cl. Charl 73 E1
Sturt Rd. Charl 73 E2
Styles Cl. M Gib 67 F1
Styles The. Harw 217 E4
Sudbury Ct. Far 173 D2
Sudbury La. Longw 156 B2
Suffolk Ct. M Gib 67 F2
Suffolk Way. Abing 179 E3
Sugarswell La. Ratl 6 A3
Sugarswell La. Shen 6 A3
Sugworth Cres. Radl 160 C3
Sugworth La. Radl 160 B3
Sulham La. Pangb 256 C2
Summer Fields. Abing 160 A2
Summer Ley. B St M 32 C3
Summerfield Rd. Cutte 123 D4
Summerfield Rise. Gori 249 E4
Summerfield. Oxon 141 E3
Summerhill Rd. Cutte 123 D4
Summerside Rd. Buckl 174 C4
Summerton Pl. Ch No 42 C2
Summertown. E Hann 197 D3
Sunderland Ave. Cutte 109 D1
Sunderland Dr. Bice 66 A2
Sundew Cl. Oxon 143 D1
Sunningwell Rd. Oxon 141 E3
Sunningwell Rd. Sunn 159 F2
Sunny Rise. Hors 143 E3
Sunnyside. Bens 203 F3
Sunnyside. Oxon 142 B3
Sunnyside. Wheat 144 B4
Surley Row. Caver 259 D2
Surley Row. Caver 259 D3
Sussex Dr. Banb 9 D1
Sutton Cl. Abing 179 F4
Sutton Courtenay Rd. Sut C 199 F3
Sutton La. Sta Har 120 A1
Sutton Rd. Mil 199 F3
Sutton Rd. Oxon 124 A3
Sutton Wick La. Dray 179 E1
Suzan Cres. Want 214 C3
Swalcliffe Lea. Swal 14 A1
Swalcliffe Rd. Swal 20 A4
Swalcliffe Rd. Tad 20 A4
Swallow Cl. Bice 81 D4
Swan Cl. Grove 196 B1
Swan Cl. Lech 150 B2
Swan Cl. Mid Ch 17 F4
Swan Close Rd. Banb 16 B3
Swan Ind Est. Banb 16 B3
Swan La. Burf 100 C3
Swan La. Far 172 C2
Swan La. Gt Bo 9 E4
Swan Lane Cl. Burf 100 C3
Swan St. Eyns 120 C4
Swan St. Oxon 123 D1
Swan Wlk. Tha 147 F4
Swanhall La. Hail 104 A3
Swansea Rd. Read 259 D1
Swansea Terr. Read 257 E1
Swanston Rd. Whitc 256 B4
Sweeps La. Burf 100 C3
Sweet Briar. March 178 B3
Sweetmans Rd. N Hink 140 B4
Swerford Rd. Ho No 30 A3
Swift Cl. Bice 65 E2
Swift Cl. Didc 81 D4
Swift Way. Bens 204 B2
Swinbourne Rd. Oxon 142 A1
Swinbrook Cl. Read 257 E2
Swinbrook Rd. Cart 115 E3
Swinbrook Rd. S u Wy 85 F3
Swinburne Rd. Abing 180 A4
Swinburne Rd. Oxon 141 F3
Swindon Rd. Highw 190 A3
Swindon St. Highw 190 A3
Swingburn Pl. Witn 118 A4
Swinstead Ct. Chalg 184 B3
Sworford La. G Mil 144 C3
Sycamore Cl. Abing 159 E1
Sycamore Cl. L Cre 129 E3
Sycamore Cl. Si Go 19 D4
Sycamore Cl. Watl 186 A1
Sycamore Cl. Witn 104 B1
Sycamore Cres. Kenn 160 C4
Sycamore Dr. Banb 16 B1
Sycamore Dr. Cart 115 E2
Sycamore Dr. Tha 147 F4
Sycamore Gdns. Bice 65 F2
Sycamore Rd. Ambr 81 E2
Sycamore Rd. Laun 66 B1
Sycamore Rd. N Hink 140 B4
Sycamore Wlk. Grove 196 B1
Sydenham Gr. Syd 167 F4
Sylvester Cl. Burf 100 C3
Sympson Cl. Abing 179 F3
Syringa Wlk. Banb 9 D1

Tackley Pl. Oxon 123 D2
Tadmarton Rd. Blox 21 D3
Tadmarton Rd. Tad 21 D3
Taggs Gate. Oxon 124 C3
Tait Dr. Up Hey 63 D4
Talbot Cl. Banb 15 F4
Talbot Cl. Caver 259 E1
Talbot Fields. Bamp 135 D2
Talbot Rd. Cutte 109 D1
Talbot Way. Purl 257 E2
Tamar Cres. Bice 65 D2
Tamar Way. Didc 201 D1
Tangmere Ave. Cart 115 F2
Tangmere Cl. Bice 66 A2
Tanner's La. Burf 100 B3
Tanners Ct. Charl 73 D2
Tanners La. Adde 22 C2
Tanners La. Eyns 120 C4
Tanners La. Maple 258 C4
Tannery Cl. Burf 100 C3
Taphouse Ave. Witn 104 A1
Tarrant Ave. Witn 104 B1
Taston Rd. Spel 73 D4
Tatham Rd. Abing 159 F1
Tatlings Rd. Steve 198 C3
Taverner Pl. Oxon 123 F2
Tavistock Ave. Didc 218 B4
Tawney St. Oxon 142 A4
Taylor Cl. Bice 65 F2
Tchure The. Dedd 33 F2
Teal Cl. Banb 16 C2
Teal Cl. Grove 196 B1
Teale Cl. U Arn 96 C4
Telford Cres. Sonn 260 C1
Telford Rd. Bice 66 A2
Templar Rd. Cutte 109 D1
Templars Cl. Wheat 144 A4
Temple Rd. Oxon 142 B3
Temple St. Bri 98 A1
Temple St. Oxon 141 F4
Tenby Ave. Caver 259 E3
Tenlands. Mid Ch 17 F4
Tennis The. Cass 107 E1
Tennyson Cl. Banb 16 A2
Tennyson Dr. Abing 179 E3
Tenpenny. Dorch 202 B4
Tenth St. Harw 217 D2
Terrington Cl. Abing 160 A1
Tessa Rd. Read 258 C1
Tew La. Woot 75 F3
Tewer The. Stone 89 E4
Thackley End. Oxon 123 D3
Thame La. Cl Ham 181 D3
Thame La. Culh 180 B2
Thame Park Rd. Tha 148 A3
Thame Rd. Bktn 82 A2
Thame Rd. Chin 168 A4
Thame Rd. G Has 164 C4
Thame Rd. G Mil 145 E1
Thame Rd. Hadd 130 B3
Thame Rd. L Cre 129 E2
Thame Rd. L Mil 164 A4
Thame Rd. Pidd 97 E3
Thame Rd. Tow 148 C4
Thame Rd. Warb 203 D4
Thames Ave. Bice 65 D2
Thames Ave. Pangb 256 B3
Thames Ave. Read 259 D1
Thames Dr. Sonn 260 C4
Thames Gdns. Charl 73 D2
Thames Mead. Cr Gif 221 F4
Thames Rd. Gori 249 D3
Thames Rd. Harw 217 D2
Thames Reach. Purl 257 E3
Thames Side Prom. Read 259 D1
Thames Side. Hen-on-T 244 C1
Thames Side. Read 259 D1
Thames St. Abing 179 F3
Thames St. Charl 73 D2
Thames St. Eyns 120 C4
Thames St. Lech 150 B2
Thames St. Oxon 141 E4
Thames St. Sonn 260 B2
Thames St. Wall 221 E4
Thames Valley Bsns P. Sonn 260 A1
Thames View Ind Park. Abing 180 A4
Thames View Rd. Oxon 141 F2
Thames View. Abing 180 A4
Thatchers Cl. Epw 13 D3
Thenford Rd. Mid Ch 11 E1
Theobald Dr. Read 257 E2
Thesiger Rd. Abing 179 F4
Thetford Mews. Caver 259 E3
Third Acre Rise. N Hink 140 A4
Third St. Crou 36 C3
Third St. Harw 217 D1
Thirlmere Ave. Read 257 F1
Thirteenth St. Harw 217 D1
Thistle Dr. Gars 143 D1
Thistlecroft Cl. Abing 160 A1
Thistledown. Read 257 E1
Thompson Dr. Buck 65 F4
Thomson Ave. Harw 217 D2
Thomson Terr. Oxon 142 A1
Thornbury Rd. Eyns 120 B4
Thorncliffe Rd. Cutte 123 D3
Thorne Cl. Kidl 92 B1
Thorney Leys. Witn 117 F4
Thornhill Cl. Want 214 B3
Thornhill Wlk. Abing 159 F1
Thornhill. Chac 10 C2
Thorningdown. Chil 235 E4
Thorpe Cl. Banb 16 C3
Thorpe Dr. Banb 16 C3
Thorpe La. Banb 16 C3
Thorpe Pl. Banb 16 C3
Thorpe Rd. Chac 10 C2
Thorpe Rd. Ward 10 C4
Thorpe St. Ast T 219 F1
Thorpe Way. Banb 16 C3
Three Corners Rd. Gars 143 D1
Three Fields Rd. Oxon 142 C4
Three Gables La. Stre 249 D4
Three Pigeons Cl. Want 214 B2
Thrift Pl. Oxon 142 C1
Thrupp La. Radl 160 B1
Thurne View. Didc 201 D1
Thurston Cl. Abing 179 F3
Tichborne. Tha 148 A4
Tidmarsh La. Oxon 123 D1
Tidmarsh La. Tidm 256 A1
Tidmarsh Rd. Pangb 256 B2
Tidmarsh St. Read 258 A1
Tidmore La. Woodc 240 C1
Tilbury Cl. Caver 259 E2
Tilbury La. N Hink 122 B1
Tilehouse Cl. Oxon 124 C2
Tilgarsley Rd. Eyns 120 B4
Tilling Cl. Read 257 D1
Tilsley Rd. Ch No 42 B1
Timbers La. Nett 223 E1
Timms Rd. Banb 16 B1
Timothy Way. Oxon 142 C1
Tinker's La. Bice 65 F1
Tinkerbush La. Want 214 B3
Tinkers La. Moll 3 F2
Tippings. Skch 188 C3
Tirrold Way. Want 214 C3
Titchener Cl. Bice 65 E2
Tite La. Ho No 30 A4
Tithe Ct. Banb 16 A3
Tithe La. Dedd 34 B3
Titup Hall La. Oxon 124 C1
Tiverton Cl. Sonn 260 C1
Tokers Green Rd. Maple 258 C4
Tokersgreen La. Maple 258 B3
Tollgate Rd. Culh 180 A2
Tompkins La. M Gib 67 F1
Toot Hill Butts. Oxon 124 C2
Torridge Dr. Didc 201 D1
Tothill. S u Wy 70 B1
Tower Cl. Caver 259 E4
Tower Cl. March 178 B3
Tower Cres. Oxon 123 E1
Tower Dr. Abing 179 E3
Tower Hill. Witn 117 F4
Tower Rd. Berin 182 B3
Tower View. Far 172 C1
Towersey Dr. Tha 148 A4
Towersey Rd. Tha 148 B4
Town Cl. Fin 39 E3
Town Cl. Sut C 200 A4
Town End Rd. Bled R 189 E4
Town End Rd. Far 172 C1
Town Furlong. Apple 158 A4
Town Furlong. Bod 22 B4
Town Furze. Oxon 142 B4
Town Green The. Kidl 92 C1
Townhill. Rat 2 A2
Townsend La. Mid Ch 11 F3
Townsend Rd. Aldw 247 F2
Townsend Rd. Shriv 209 D3
Townsend Rd. Stre 249 D4
Townsend Sq. Oxon 141 F3
Townsend. Abing 179 F3
Townsend. B St M 32 C3
Townsend. Banb 16 A3
Townsend. Harw 217 E1
Townsend. Harw 217 F4
Townsend. M Gib 67 F1
Townside. Hadd 130 C3
Toy La. Ch No 42 B1
Toynbee Cl. N Hink 140 B4
Trafford Rd. Oxon 124 C2
Trafford Rd. Read 258 C1
Traitor's Ford La. Ho No 18 B2
Traitor's Ford La. Whi 29 D4
Tramhill. Bri 98 A1
Tramway Rd. Banb 16 C3
Treadwells. S in V 194 C4
Tredegar Rd. Caver 259 D3
Tree La. Oxon 142 A2
Treeground Pl. Kidl 108 C4
Trefoil Pl. Gars 143 D1
Trelawney Dr. Read 257 D1
Trenchard Ave. Mil 199 E2
Trenchard Cl. Wall 221 E4
Trenchard Cres. Up Hey 49 E1
Trendell Pl. Abing 159 F1
Trent Cres. Bice 65 D2
Trent Rd. Didc 201 D1
Trevor Pl. Oxon 142 A3
Trill Mill Ct. Oxon 141 E4
Trinder Rd. Want 214 C2
Tring Rd. Read 257 E2
Trinity Cl. Abing 160 A1
Trinity Cl. Banb 15 F4
Trinity Cl. Bice 65 F2
Trinity Rd. Oxon 124 C1
Trinity St. Oxon 141 E4
Tristram Rd. Duck 118 A2
Troika Cl. Banb 9 D1
Trot La. Kirt 77 F2
Trot's La. S u Wy 85 E4
Truelocks Way. Want 214 C3
Truemper Gr. Buck 65 F4
Trust Cnr. Hen-on-T 254 C4
Tubb Cl. Bice 65 E1
Tubbs Cl. Grove 214 B4
Tuck's La. Longw 156 A2
Tucker Rd. Oxon 142 C2
Tuckers La. Bish 227 D2
Tudor Cl. Banb 16 B1
Tudor Cl. Oxon 141 F2
Tullis Cl. Sut C 199 F4
Tulwick La. Grove 197 D1
Tumbledown Hill. Cumn 139 E3
Tuns La. Hen-on-T 244 C1
Turberville Cl. Abing 179 F3
Turl St. Oxon 123 E1
Turley La. Hail 104 A4
Turn Again La. Oxon 141 E4
Turnagain La. Abing 179 F3
Turnberry Cl. Bice 66 A2
Turner Cl. Oxon 142 B3
Turner Rd. Abing 179 E3
Turnfields. Ick 128 A2
Turnpike Rd. Buck 66 A3
Turnpike Rd. Cumn 140 A3
Turnpike Rd. Highw 190 A3
Tuscan Cl. Read 257 F1
Tweed Cres. Bice 65 D2
Twelth St. Harw 217 D2
Twelve Acre Dr. Abing 160 B2
Twentieth St. Harw 216 C1
Twin Oaks. Caver 259 D3
Two Rivers Ind Est. Witn 118 A3
Two Tree Hill. Hen-on-T 254 A4
Twyford Ave. Adde 23 D3
Twyford Gr. Adde 23 D3
Twyford Rd. Adde 23 E4
Twynhams Rd. Tack 77 E3
Tyler Cl. Caver 258 C3
Tyndale Pl. Wheat 144 B4
Tyndale Rd. Oxon 141 F4
Tyne Rd. Abing 159 E1
Tyrell Cl. S in V 194 B4
Tyrrell's Way. Sut C 199 F3
Tyrrells Cl. Harw 217 E3

Ulfgar Rd. Cutte 122 C4
Ullswater Dr. Read 257 E2
Ulster Cl. Caver 259 E3
Underhill Circus. Oxon 124 C2
Unicorn St. Blox 21 E2
Union St. Banb 16 A3
Union St. Oxon 141 F4
Union St. Wood 91 D4
Union Way. Witn 117 F4
Unity Cl. Caver 259 D3
Untons Pl. Far 173 D2
Upavon Way. Cart 115 E2
Upland Park Rd. Cutte 123 D4
Upland Rise. Gt Bo 9 E3
Uplands Rd. Caver 258 C3
Upper Barr. Oxon 142 B2
Upper Brook Hill. Wood 91 D3
Upper Campsfield Rd. Sh-on-C 91 F3
Upper Comm. Uff 211 E4
Upper Crale. S in V 194 B4
Upper Cres. M Lov 102 C1
Upper Cross La. E Hag 218 C3
Upper Fisher Row. Oxon 123 D1
Upper High St. Tha 147 F4
Upper Rd. Kenn 141 F1
Upper Red Cross Rd. Gori 249 E4
Upper Warren Ave. Caver 258 B2
Upper Windsor St. Banb 16 B3
Upper Woodcote Rd. Caver 258 B3
Uppingham Dr. Sonn 260 C1
Uppingham Gdns. Caver 259 E3
Upthorpe Dr. Want 214 C3

Upton Cl. Abing 160 A1
Upton Cl. Hen-on-T 244 C1
Upton Cl. Oxon 142 B1
Upway Rd. Oxon 124 A3
Upwood Dr. Cart 115 F2
Urquhart La. Check 241 D4

Vale Ave. Grove 196 C1
Vale Cres. Read 257 F1
Vale Rd. Harw 217 D2
Vale Rd. Witn 117 F4
Valence Cres. Curb 103 F1
Valentia Cl. Bletch 92 C4
Valentia Rd. Oxon 124 B1
Valentine Cres. Caver 259 E2
Valetta Way. Bens 204 B2
Valley Cl. Brac 24 A4
Valley Cl. Caver 259 D2
Valley Cl. Gori 249 E3
Valley Cres. Brac 24 A4
Valley Rd. Banb 16 B2
Valley Rd. Brac 24 A4
Valley Rd. Fin 39 E3
Valley Rd. Hen-on-T 254 A4
Valley Rd. Hors 143 F3
Valley Rise. Brac 24 A4
Valley View. Gt Bo 9 E4
Valley View. Lo Hey 62 C3
Van Dieman's Rd. Tha 147 F4
Van Dieman's. S in V 194 B4
Van Diemens Cl. Chin 168 B4
Van-Dieman's La. Oxon 142 B2
Vanbrugh Cl. Wood 91 D4
Vane Rd. Tha 130 A1
Vanner Rd. Witn 104 B2
Vastern Rd. Read 259 D1
Vauxhall Way. Didc 200 B1
Venables Cl. Oxon 123 D2
Venetia Cl. Caver 259 E4
Ventfield Cl. Hor-c-S 112 A3
Ventnor Rd. Read 257 E1
Venvell Cl. Enst 58 C3
Vermont Dr. Wood 91 D4
Vernon Ave. N Hink 140 C3
Vetch Pl. Oxon 142 C1
Vicarage Cl. Aston 135 E2
Vicarage Cl. Chalg 184 B4
Vicarage Cl. Grove 196 C1
Vicarage Cl. Oxon 142 A1
Vicarage Gdns. Cro 4 C1
Vicarage Hill. E Cha 214 A2
Vicarage La. Highw 190 A3
Vicarage La. Lo Co 27 F3
Vicarage La. Oxon 141 E3
Vicarage La. Pidd 97 F3
Vicarage La. Shriv 209 E3
Vicarage Rd. Didc 218 C4
Vicarage Rd. Hen-on-T 254 C4
Vicarage Rd. Kidl 92 C1
Vicarage Rd. Oxon 141 E3
Vicarage Rd. Steve 198 C2
Vickers Rd. Ch We 68 A3
Victor St. Oxon 123 D1
Victoria Ct. Oxon 123 E1
Victoria Mead. Tha 148 A4
Victoria Pl. Banb 16 C3
Victoria Pl. Ch No 42 C2
Victoria Rd. Abing 179 E4
Victoria Rd. Bice 65 F1
Victoria Rd. Caver 259 D2
Victoria Rd. Cutte 123 D4
Victoria Rd. Read 257 E1
Victoria Rd. Warg 255 F1
Viking Dr. Didc 219 D4
Viking Terr. Bens 204 B2
Villeboys Cl. Abing 180 B4
Villiers La. Oxon 142 A2
Villiers Rd. Bice 65 E1
Vine The. Shab 128 B2
Viner Cl. Witn 104 B1
Vineyard Cl. Banb 16 B4
Vineyard. Abing 179 F4
Virginia Gdns. Bled R 189 F4
Virginia Way. Abing 179 E2
Vorda Rd. Highw 190 A4

Wadard's Meadow. Witn 118 B4
Wadham Cl. Bice 65 F2
Wainwrights. L Cre 129 E3
Wales St. K Sut 23 F3
Walk The. Islip 93 F1
Walker Dr. Tha 148 A4
Walker's Cl. Burf 101 F2
Walker's Ht. Fins 88 B3
Walkers Cl. Free 106 A3
Wallace Cl. Abing 179 F3
Walled Gdn The. Warg 255 E1
Wallingford Rd. Chol 221 D2
Wallingford Rd. Cr Gif 221 F1
Wallingford Rd. Gori 249 E4
Wallingford Rd. S Sto 239 E3
Wallingford Rd. Stre 249 D4
Wallingford Rd. Warb 203 D3
Wallingford St. Want 214 C2
Walls The. S in V 194 C4
Walmer Rd. Sonn 260 C1
Walnut Cl. Bice 65 F3
Walnut Ct. Far 172 C2
Walnut Rise. Up Hey 48 C3
Walnut Tree Ct. Gori 249 E3
Walnut Trees Hill. Ashb 228 A4
Walpole Cl. Bice 65 D2
Walterbush Rd. Ch No 42 C1
Waltham Gdns. Banb 17 D3
Walton Ave. Adde 23 D3
Walton Ave. Hen-on-T 254 C4
Walton Cl. Bod 22 C4
Walton Cres. Oxon 123 D1
Walton La. Oxon 123 D1
Walton St. Oxon 123 D1
Walton Well Rd. Oxon 123 D2
Wanbourne La. Nett 224 B1
Wandhope Way. Read 257 E1
Wansbeck Dr. Bice 65 D1
Wantage Rd. Didc 218 B4
Wantage Rd. Harw 217 E3
Wantage Rd. Stre 238 C1
Wantage Rd. Stre 249 D4
Wantage Rd. Wall 203 D1
Wapping. L Cre 129 E3
Warborough Rd. Let B 232 A4
Warborough Rd. Warb 203 D3
Warbreck Dr. Purl 257 D2
Warburg Cres. Oxon 142 C2
Ward Rd. Brac 24 A3
Wardington Rd. Ward 10 B3
Wardle Ave. Read 257 E1
Wards Cres. Bod 22 C4
Wards Rd. Ch No 42 C2
Ware Leys Cl. M Gib 67 F2
Wargrave Hill. Warg 255 F1
Wargrave Rd. Rem H 244 C1
Wargrave Rd. Warg 255 D4
Warkworth Rd. Mid Ch 17 F4
Warley Rise. Purl 257 E2
Warmans Cl. Want 214 A3
Warnborough Rd. Oxon 123 D2
Warneford La. Oxon 124 A1
Warneford Rd. Oxon 142 A4
Warner Cres. Didc 218 B4
Warren Cres. Oxon 142 B4
Warren Hill. Stadh 163 E1
Warren Rd. Sonn 260 B1
Warren Row Rd. Warg 255 F4
Warren The. Abing 180 A4
Warren The. Caver 258 B2
Warwick Cl. Abing 180 A4
Warwick Cl. Cart 115 E2
Warwick Cl. S in V 194 C4
Warwick Ct. Bice 66 A2
Warwick Rd. Banb 8 C2
Warwick Rd. Hanw 8 C2
Warwick St. Oxon 141 F3
Wasbrough Ave. Want 214 B3
Washington Rd. Caver 259 D1
Wastie's Orch. Lo Han 90 A1
Watcombe Rd. Watl 186 A1
Water Eaton La. Kidl 109 D4
Water Eaton Rd. Cutte 123 E4
Water End Rd. Bled R 189 E2
Water La. Adde 23 D2
Water La. Blox 21 F3
Water La. Brac 24 A4
Water La. D St L 183 D3
Water La. Li Tew 45 D3
Water La. Mi Sto 50 A2
Water La. Ste As 62 A4
Waterman Pl. Read 259 D1
Waterman's Rd. Hen-on-T 254 C4
Waterman's Way. Warg 255 E1
Watermead. Kidl 109 D4
Waterperry Rd. Worm 127 E3
Waters La. Mid Ch 11 D1
Waterside Dr. Purl 257 E3
Waterslade Pens. Hadd 130 C3
Watery La. Brac 24 A4
Watery La. Cl Ham 181 E2
Watery La. Ho No 30 A4
Watery La. Spars 212 C2
Watling La. Dorch 182 B1
Watlington Ind Est. Watl 186 A1
Watlington Rd. Bens 203 F2
Watlington Rd. Gars 162 B4
Watlington Rd. Lewk 186 C3
Watlington Rd. Oxon 142 C2
Watlington St. Nett 224 C1
Watson Cres. Woot 159 D4
Watsons Cl. Cart 115 F1
Watt's La. Blew 237 D4
Watts Way. Kidl 92 C1
Waveney Cl. Bice 65 D1
Waveney Cl. Didc 201 D1
Waverley Ave. Kidl 109 D4
Waxes Cl. Abing 160 B1
Wayland Ave. E Cha 214 A4
Wayland Cres. Harw 217 E1
Wayland Rd. Grove 196 B1
Waynflete Rd. Oxon 125 D2
Wayside Green. Woodc 240 C1
Weald Rise. Read 257 F1
Weald St. Bamp 134 C1
Wealden Way. Read 257 F1
Wear Rd. Bice 65 D1
Weavers Cl. Witn 118 A4
Weavers Row. Shut 14 A3
Webb Cl. Banb 16 C4
Webb Cres. Ch No 42 B1
Webb's Cl. Cutte 122 B4
Webb's Way. Kidl 92 C1
Webster Cl. Tha 129 F1
Webster's Cl. Free 106 A3
Wedgewood Way. Read 257 F1
Wedgwood Rd. Bice 66 A2
Weeping Cross. Bod 22 C4
Weighbridge Row. Read 258 C1
Weir La. Bktn 82 A2
Weirs La. Oxon 141 E3
Welch Way. Witn 118 A4
Weldon Rd. Oxon 123 F2
Weldon Way. Tha 148 A4
Welford Gdns. Abing 160 A1
Well Bank. Ho No 30 A4
Well Hill. Fins 88 B3
Well La. Curb 117 E3
Well La. Stone 89 E4
Welland Ave. Didc 201 D1
Welland Cl. Abing 159 E1
Welland Cl. Read 257 E1
Welland Croft. Bice 65 D2
Weller Cl. Ber S 204 A4
Wellesbourne Cl. Abing 180 A4
Wellington Cl. Bice 66 A2
Wellington Pl. Oxon 123 E1
Wellington Sq. Oxon 123 E1
Wellington Sq. Watch 191 E1
Wellington St. Oxon 123 D1
Wellington St. Tha 148 A4
Wellshead La. Harw 217 F3
Wellsprings. Br-c-S 202 C1
Wenham Rd. Witn 117 F4
Wenman Rd. Tha 148 A3
Wenrisc Dr. M Lov 102 C1
Wensum Cres. Bice 65 D2
Wentworth Rd. Cutte 123 D4
Wentworth Rd. Tha 148 A4
Wesley Cl. Bice 65 E2
Wesley Cl. Oxon 142 C2
Wesley Dr. Banb 16 A2
Wesley La. Bice 65 F1
Wesley Pl. Chac 10 C2
Wessex Cl. Far 173 D2
Wessex Rd. Didc 218 C4
Wessex Way. Grove 214 B4
Wessex Way. Highw 190 A4
West Ave. Abing 160 A1
West Bar St. Banb 16 B3
West Chiltern. Woodc 250 C4
West Cotts. S Adley 52 B1
West Croft. Berin 182 B3
West Dr. Harw 217 D2
West Dr. Sonn 260 B1
West Edge. M Gib 67 F1
West End Cl. Laun 66 B1
West End Ind Est. Witn 104 A1
West End La. Bish 227 E2
West End. Ch No 42 C1
West End. Chol 220 C1
West End. Combe 90 A2
West End. Horn 7 E3
West End. King 54 C2
West End. Laun 66 B1
West End. Witn 104 A1
West End. Woot 75 F2
West Hawthorn Rd. Ambr 81 E2
West Hill. Want 214 B2
West Lockinge. Ard 215 E2
West Oxon Ind Park. Br No 115 F2
West Rd. St Row 242 A1
West St Helen St. Abing 179 F3
West St. Banb 16 C4
West St. Bice 65 E2
West St. Ch No 42 C1
West St. Child 213 D2
West St. Hen-on-T 244 B1
West St. King 54 C3
West St. Oxon 123 D1
West St. Shut 14 A3
West St. Spars 212 C2
West View. Oxon 142 A2
West View. Up Hey 49 D3
West Way. Lech 150 B3
West Way. N Hink 122 B1
Westacott Rd. Ambr 81 D3
Westbeech Ct. Banb 16 B3
Westbourne Ct. Blox 21 F2
Westbrook Green. Blew 236 C4
Westbrook Rd. Read 258 B1
Westbrook St. Blew 236 C4
Westbrook. Far 172 C2
Westbrook. Grove 196 C1
Westbury Cres. Oxon 142 A2
Westbury La. Purl 257 D3
Westcot La. Spars 212 C3
Westcote Cl. Witn 117 E4
Westdene Cres. Caver 258 C2
Western Ave. Hen-on-T 254 C4
Western Ave. Sonn 260 C1
Western By - Pass Rd. Cutte 108 C1
Western By-pass Rd. Wyth 122 B3
Western Cres. Banb 16 C2
Western Oaks. Read 257 F1
Western Rd. Hen-on-T 254 C4
Western Rd. Oxon 141 E4
Westfield Cl. Bens 204 A2
Westfield Cl. Grove 214 B4
Westfield Cl. Oxon 142 A3
Westfield Cres. Shipl 255 D2
Westfield Rd. Bens 204 A2
Westfield Rd. Caver 259 D1
Westfield Rd. Chol 238 B3
Westfield Rd. Lo Wit 201 E4
Westfield Rd. Wheat 144 A4
Westfield Rd. Witn 104 A1
Westfield Way. Want 215 D3
Westfield. Harw 217 E4
Westfields. Abing 179 E4
Westgate Shop Cen. Oxon 123 E1
Westholm Ct. Bice 65 F1
Westland Rd. Far 172 C1
Westland Way. Wood 91 D4
Westlands Ave. W-on-G 79 D1
Westlands Dr. Oxon 124 A3
Westleigh Dr. S Com 252 C2
Westminster Cl. Brac 24 A4
Westminster Cres. Brac 24 A4
Westminster Way. Banb 16 C3
Westminster Way. N Hink 140 C4
Weston Ct. Lo Co 28 A3
Weston La. G Has 146 C4
Weston Rd. Lewk 186 C4
Westonbirt Dr. Caver 258 C2
Westridge Ave. Purl 257 E3
Westrop. Highw 190 A3
Westrup Cl. Oxon 123 F2
Westway. Gori 249 E4
Westwood Glen. Read 257 E1
Westwood Rd. Curb 103 E1
Westwood Rd. Read 257 E1
Westwood Row. Read 257 E1
Wetherby Cl. Caver 259 E3
Wey Rd. Berin 182 B3
Weyland Rd. Oxon 124 C1
Whales La. M Gib 67 F1
Wharf Cl. Abing 179 F3
Wharf La. Hen-on-T 244 C1
Wharf La. Lech 150 B2
Wharf La. Soul 35 D2
Wharf Rd. Warb 203 D3
Wharton Rd. Oxon 124 B2
Wheatcroft Cl. Abing 160 A1
Wheatfields. Didc 218 B4
Wheatley Cl. Banb 16 C1
Wheatley Rd. Gars 143 F2
Wheatley Rd. Islip 109 F4
Wheatley Rd. St S J 125 F2
Wheeler Rd. Chin 168 B3
Wheeler's Rise. Crou 36 B4
Whimbrel Way. Banb 16 C2
Whirlwind Way. Bens 204 B2
Whitamore Row. Hen-on-T 254 C4
Whitby Green. Caver 259 E3
Whitchurch Rd. Pangb 256 B3
White Cross. Woot 159 E2
White Hart. Lud 98 A4
White Hill La. Woot 140 A1
White Hill. Bish 227 D1
White Hill. Burf 101 D2
White Hill. Shipl 254 A3
White Horse Cres. Grove 214 B4
White House Rd. Cr Gif 239 F4
White La. Bix 243 F4
White Lodge Cl. Purl 257 D2
White Mews. Burf 100 C2
White Post Rd. Bod 16 C1
White Rd. Chil 235 E4
White Rd. E Hen 216 C4
White Rd. Oxon 142 C3
White Shoot. Blew 237 D3
White Way. Kidl 108 C4
White's La. Radl 160 B2
Whitecross Rd. Hadd 130 C3
Whitehall Cl. M Lov 102 B1
Whitehall La. Check 241 E2
Whitehills Green. Gori 249 E3
Whitehorn Way. Oxon 142 C1
Whitehorns Way. Dray 179 D1
Whitehouse Cl. Abing 159 E1
Whitehouse La. Ch No 42 C2
Whitehouse Rd. Oxon 141 E4
Whitehouse Rd. Woodc 250 C4
Whitelock Rd. Abing 159 F1
Whitemoor La. Stre 249 D1
Whites Forge. Apple 158 A4
Whiteway. Moll 3 F2
Whitings La. Hail 104 A4
Whitley Cres. Bice 66 A2
Whitley Dr. Up Hey 63 E4
Whitley Rd. Wall 221 D3
Whitson Pl. Oxon 142 A4
Whittall St. K Sut 23 F3
Whittington Pl. Cart 115 E1
Whittle Rd. Tha 148 A4
Whittons Cl. Ho No 30 A4
Wick Cl. Abing 160 B1
Wick Cl. Oxon 124 C2
Wick Green. Grove 196 B1
Wicks Cl. Clan 152 C4
Widmore La. S Com 253 D3
Widnell La. Pidd 97 E4
Wigginton Rd. S New 31 E4
Wigmore La. Read 258 A1
Wigmore La. Read 258 B1
Wigod Way. Wall 203 E1
Wilberforce St. Oxon 124 B1
Wilcher Cl. E Hag 218 C3
Wilcote La. Rams 88 A2
Wilcote Rd. Oxon 124 C2
Wilcote Riding. Fins 88 B3
Wilcote View. N Lei 105 E3
Wilder Ave. Pangb 256 C3
Wilding Rd. Wall 203 E1
Wildmere Cl. Banb 16 C4
Wildmere Rd. Banb 9 F1
Wildmoor Gate. Abing 159 F1
Wilkins Rd. Oxon 142 B3
Willes Cl. Far 172 C2
William Bliss Ave. Ch No 42 C1
William Cl. Banb 15 F4
William Kimber Cres. Oxon 124 C2
William Orchard Cl. Oxon 124 B2
William St. Oxon 123 F2
Williamscot Hill. Ward 10 A3
Williamson Way. Oxon 142 A2
Willoughby Rd. Banb 16 B1
Willow Cl. Gars 143 E1
Willow Cl. Watl 186 A1
Willow Cl. Yarn 108 A3
Willow La. Want 214 B2
Willow La. Warg 255 E2
Willow Mead. Chalg 184 B3
Willow Rd. Ambr 81 E2
Willow Rd. Banb 16 B1
Willow Rd. Brac 24 A3
Willow Rd. Chin 168 B3
Willow Rd. Tha 129 F1
Willow Tree Cl. Abing 159 E1
Willow Way. Begb 92 A1
Willow Way. Kenn 160 C4
Willow Way. Oxon 142 C1
Willow Wlk. Want 214 B3
Willowbrook. Stand 137 F4
Willows Ct. Pangb 256 B3
Willows The. Caver 259 D1
Willows The. Highw 190 A3
Willows The. Witn 104 B1
Willows The. Woot 159 D4
Willowside. Sonn 260 C1
Wills Rd. Didc 200 B1
Wilmot Way. Want 214 C3
Wilmots. Nu Cou 162 A3
Wilsdon Way. Kidl 92 B1
Wilsham Rd. Abing 179 F3
Wilson Ave. Hen-on-T 254 C4
Wilson Cl. Witn 117 F3
Wilson Way. Buck 65 F4
Wilsons Cl. Lo Wit 201 E4
Wilwyne Cl. Caver 259 E2
Wimblestraw Rd. Berin 182 B3
Wimborne Ave. Banb 16 A3
Wimborne Gdns. Read 258 A1
Winchelsea Cl. Banb 8 C1
Winchester Cl. Banb 16 C4
Winchester Rd. Oxon 123 D2
Winchester Way. Want 214 B3
Wincroft Rd. Caver 258 C3
Windale Ave. Oxon 142 C1
Windle Gdns. Bice 65 E1
Windmill Ave. Bice 65 F2
Windmill Cl. Banb 16 B2
Windmill Cl. Dedd 33 F2
Windmill Cl. N Lei 105 D3
Windmill Cl. Tow 148 C4
Windmill La. Wheat 144 A4
Windmill Pl. E Cha 213 F2
Windmill Rd. Hadd 130 C3
Windmill Rd. N Lei 105 D3
Windmill Rd. Oxon 124 B1
Windmill Rd. Tha 130 C1
Windmill Rd. Tha 147 F4
Windmill Rd. Tow 148 C4
Windmill St. Bri 98 A1
Windmill St. Dedd 33 F2
Windrush Cl. Bice 65 E1
Windrush Cl. Burf 100 C2
Windrush Cl. Grove 196 B1
Windrush Cl. Witn 103 F1
Windrush Ct. Abing 179 E4
Windrush Park Rd. Curb 103 E1
Windrush Rd. Berin 182 B2
Windrush Valley Rd. Witn 103 F1
Windrush Way. Abing 160 A1
Windrush Way. Stand 137 E3
Windrush. Banb 16 A4
Windsor Cl. Cart 115 E1
Windsor Cl. Didc 219 D4
Windsor Cl. K Sut 23 F3
Windsor Cres. E Hag 218 C3
Windsor Cres. Mars 123 F3
Windsor St. Banb 16 B3
Windsor St. Oxon 124 B1
Windsor Terr. Banb 16 B3
Windy Ridge. Far 173 D2
Wingate Cl. Oxon 142 C2
Winnyards The. Cumn 139 F2
Winsmore La. Abing 179 F3
Winston Cl. Kidl 108 C4
Winston Way. Purl 257 D3
Winter La. W Hann 196 C4
Winter's Field. Cr Gif 221 F4
Winterborne Rd. Abing 179 E4
Winterbourne Cl. Bice 65 E1
Winterbrook La. Chol 221 E3
Winterbrook. Chol 221 E3
Wintergreen La. Chol 221 E3
Winters Way. Blox 21 E2

intringham Way. Purl 257 E3
ise Ave. Kidl 92 B1
ise Cl. Bod 22 C4
ise Cres. Frin 52 B3
isteria The. Banb 9 D1
itan Way. Wan't 214 B3
itan Way. Witn 118 A4
ithers Way. Ch No 42 C1
ithington Ct. Abing 179 F4
ithington Rd. Bice 65 F1
ithycombe Dr. Banb 15 F3
itney La. Leaf 86 C2
itney Rd. Br No 116 B3
itney Rd. Crawl 103 F2
itney Rd. Duck 118 A3
itney Rd. Eyns 120 B4
itney Rd. Fins 88 A3
itney Rd. Leaf 87 D1
itney Rd. Lo Han 90 A1
itney Rd. Stand 137 D2
itney St. Burf 100 C3
ittenham Cl. Wall 203 E1
ittenham Cl. Woodc 250 C4
ittenham La. Dorch 202 B4
oburn Cl. Caver 258 C2
olseley Cl. Banb 16 A4
olsey Rd. Caver 259 D1
olsey Rd. Cutte 109 D1
olvercote Green. Cutte 122 C4
ood End. Banb 16 C2
ood Farm Rd. Oxon 124 C1
ood Gr. Woodc 250 C4
ood La. K End 252 B2
ood La. Leaf 87 F1
ood La. S Com 252 C3
ood La. Woodc 250 B4
ood Lane Cl. S Com 252 C3
ood St. Wall 221 E4
ood's Farm Rd. E Hen 216 B4
Woodberry Cl. Caver 259 D3
Woodbine Pl. Oxon 123 D1
Woodbridge Cl. Aston 135 F1
Woodcote Rd. Buck 66 A4
Woodcote Rd. Caver 258 C2
Woodcote Rd. S Sto 239 F2
Woodcote Way. Abing 179 F2
Woodcote Way. Caver 258 B3
Woodcroft. Kenn 141 F1
Woodfield Dr. Charl 73 E2
Woodfield Rd. Bice 65 F2
Woodfield. Banb 16 A4
Woodford Cl. Caver 258 C2
Woodford Cl. Enst 58 C3
Woodgate Cl. Grove 196 B1
Woodgreen Ave. Banb 16 A3
Woodgreen Hill. Witn 104 B1
Woodhall Dr. Banb 16 C2
Woodhill Dr. Grove 214 B4
Woodhill La. E Cha 214 A4
Woodhouse Way. Oxon 142 A2
Woodland Rise. Stone 89 E4
Woodlands Rd. Witn 104 B1
Woodlands Cl. Lyne 70 B3
Woodlands Cl. Oxon 124 A2
Woodlands Dr. Ho No 30 A3
Woodlands Gr. Caver 259 F2
Woodlands Rd. Oxon 124 A2
Woodlands Rd. S Com 252 C3
Woodlands Rd. Shipl 254 C2
Woodlands. Free 106 A4
Woodlands. Kidl 109 D4
Woodlands. Stand 137 E2
Woodley Cl. Abing 159 F2
Woodperry Rd. Beck 111 D1
Woodpiece Rd. U Arn 96 C4
Woodruff Cl. Oxon 142 C1
Woods Rd. Caver 259 F2
Woodside La. K End 252 B3
Woodside. N Lei 105 E3
Woodstock Cl. Cutte 123 D4
Woodstock Rd. Begb 108 B2
Woodstock Rd. Charl 73 E1
Woodstock Rd. Cutte 108 B2
Woodstock Rd. Kidl 91 F2
Woodstock Rd. Oxon 123 D3
Woodstock Rd. Stone 89 E4
Woodstock Rd. Witn 104 B1
Woodstock Rd. Yarn 108 B2
Woodview Rd. Pangb 256 B3
Woodview. Far 172 C2
Woodville. Chin 168 B3
Woodway Rd. Blew 237 D4
Woodway Rd. Mi Bar 60 C4
Woolgate. Witn 118 A4
Woolstone Rd. Uff 211 D3
Woolstone Rd. Wool 211 D3
Wootten Dr. Oxon 142 A2
Wootten End. Stone 89 E4
Wootton Rd. Abing 159 F1
Wootton Rd. Hen-on-T 254 B4
Worcester Dr. Didc 219 D4
Worcester Pl. Oxon 123 D1
Worcester Rd. Ch No 42 B1
Worcester St. Oxon 123 D1
Wordsworth Cl. Bice 65 D2
Wordsworth Cl. S in V 194 B4
Wordsworth Ct. Caver 259 E4
Wordsworth Rd. Abing 179 E3
Workhouse La. Blox 21 E3
Wormald Rd. Wall 221 E3
Worminghall Rd. Ick 127 F2
Wormsley Cres. Skch 188 B2
Wortham Rd. Didc 200 B1
Worthington Way. Want 214 B3
Worton Rd. Mi Bar 46 C1
Wotton End. Lud 98 B4
Wren Rd. Cutte 109 E1
Wrenfield Dr. Caver 258 C3
Wright Cl. Ch We 68 A3
Wright Rd. Ch We 68 A3
Wrightson Cl. Hors 143 E3
Wroslyn Rd. Free 106 A4
Wroxton Ct. Wrox 15 D4
Wyatt Rd. Cutte 109 D1
Wychcotes. Caver 258 C2
Wychwood Cl. Bens 204 A2
Wychwood Cl. Cart 115 E3
Wychwood Cl. Charl 73 E2
Wychwood Cl. M u Wy 85 D4
Wychwood Cl. S Com 252 C3
Wychwood Cl. Witn 117 F4
Wychwood Dr. Lyne 70 B3
Wychwood Gdns. Banb 16 A2
Wychwood La. Oxon 125 D1
Wychwood Paddocks. Charl 73 D2
Wychwood View. M Lov 102 C1
Wycombe Rd. B Bot 189 E2
Wycombe Rd. Skch 188 C2
Wycombe Way. Cart 115 F1
Wye Cl. Bice 65 D2
Wyfold La. R Pep 252 B4
Wykeham Cres. Oxon 142 A2
Wykeham Gate. Hadd 130 C3
Wykeham Park. Tha 148 A4
Wykeham Rise. Chin 168 B3
Wykeham Way. Hadd 130 C3
Wykham Gdns. Banb 16 A2
Wykham La. Banb 16 A1
Wykham La. Brou 15 F1
Wykham Pl. Banb 16 A2
Wylie Cl. Oxon 124 B1
Wynbush Rd. Oxon 142 A2
Wyncies The. Bish 227 E2
Wyndale Cl. Hen-on-T 244 C1
Wyndham Cres. Sonn 260 B1
Wyndham Gdns. Wall 221 E3
Wyndham Way. Cutte 123 D4
Wyndyke Furlong. Abing 179 E4
Wyre Ct. Purl 257 E2
Wysdom Way. Burf 100 C2
Wytham Cl. Eyns 120 C4
Wytham St. Oxon 141 E3
Wytham View. Eyns 120 C4

Yare Cl. Didc 201 D1
Yarnell's Hill. N Hink 140 B4
Yarnell's Rd. N Hink 140 B4
Yarnton Cl. Caver 259 E3
Yarnton Ct. Kidl 108 C4
Yarnton La. Yarn 108 B3
Yarnton Rd. Cass 107 E2
Yarnton Rd. Kidl 108 C4
Yatesbury Rd. Cart 115 F2
Yeates Cl. Tha 129 F1
Yeats Cl. Oxon 142 C3
Yeftly Dr. Oxon 142 A1
Yeld Hall Rd. Abing 160 A1
Yew Cl. Gars 143 D1
Yew Tree Ct. Gori 249 E3
Yew Tree Mews. Abing 179 F4
Yew Tree Rise. Crou 36 B4
Yolsum Cl. Hadd 130 C3
York Ave. Oxon 124 C1
York Cl. Bice 66 A2
York Pl. Oxon 123 F1
York Rd. Cart 115 F2
York Rd. Hen-on-T 244 B1
York Rd. Oxon 124 C1
York Rd. Read 259 D1
York Rd. W Hag 218 B2
Youghal Cl. Shriv 209 D3
Ypres Way. Abing 159 E1